THE LETTERS OF

Mary W. Shelley

COLLECTED AND EDITED BY

FREDERICK L. JONES

VOLUME II

UNIVERSITY OF OKLAHOMA PRESS

NORMAN MCMXLIV

THE PUBLICATION OF THIS VOLUME
HAS BEEN AIDED BY A GRANT FROM
THE AMERICAN COUNCIL OF LEARNED SOCIETIES
FROM A FUND PROVIDED BY
THE CARNEGIE CORPORATION OF NEW YORK

Contents of Volume II

List of Letters   *ix*

The Letters   3

Appendices

  I. *Other Mary Shelley Letters*   343

  II. *Mary Shelley, John Howard Payne, and Washington Irving*   347

  III. *Mary Shelley's Second Defense of Velluti*   354

  IV. *Mary Shelley's Last Illness and Death*   357

  V. *Owners of the Original Letters*   361

  VI. *Table of Correspondents*   363

Index   367

Illustrations in Volume II

Mary Shelley's pencil sketch of Shelley   *facing page* 12

Mary W. Shelley   76

Edward John Trelawny   108

Jane Williams   172

Leigh Hunt   204

Letter 617   268

24 Chester Square   300

The Grave of Mary W. Shelley   332

The Letters in Volume II

*Letters Hitherto Unpublished   †Letters Not Available for Publication

All street addresses are London addresses

1828

Number		Place	To	Page
312.	[June 28]	Hastings	Jane Williams Hogg	3
313.	August 20	Park Cottage, Paddington	John Murray	5
314.*	September 1	Park Cottage	William Whitton	6
315.*	September 4	Park Cottage	William Whitton	6
316.*	September 5	Park Cottage	William Whitton	7
317.†	September 10	Park Cottage	John Murray	7
318.*	[October 28]	Park Cottage	J. H. Payne	7
319.*	December 1	Park Cottage	William Whitton	8
320.*	December 1	Park Cottage	William Whitton	8
321.*	December 9	Park Cottage	William Whitton	9
322.*	[December 10]	Park Cottage	J. H. Payne	9

1829

Number		Place	To	Page
323.*	[? January, 1829]	Somerset St.	[Cyrus Redding]	10
324.	January 8	33 Somerset St.	W. Galignani	10
325.*	January 15	4 Oxford Terrace	William Whitton	11
326.*	February 3	4 Oxford Terrace	John Bowring	11
327.†	[1829–32]	Somerset St., Portman Square	James Kenney	12
328.*	[April 6]	[London]	J. H. Payne	12
329.	April	London	E. J. Trelawny	12
330.*	[May 22]	33 Somerset St.,	John Bowring	14
331.	May 25	33 Somerset St.,	Sir Walter Scott	15
332.*	[June 1]	Somerset St.	John Bowring	16
333.*	[June 4]	Somerset St.	John Bowring	16
334.*	[June 16]	Somerset St.	F. M. Reynolds	16

Number		Place	To	Page
335.*	[July 1]	33 Somerset St.	John Bowring	17
336.*	July 27	33 Somerset St.	E. J. Trelawny	17
337.*	August 29	Somerset St.	John Bowring	19
338.*	September 1	33 Somerset St.	William Whitton	20
339.	November 12	33 Somerset St.	John Murray	20
340.	December 2	33 Somerset St.	William Whitton	21
341.*	[? December 7]	33 Somerset St.	John Murray	21
342.	[1829–33]	33 Somerset St.	[Addressee Unknown]	21
343.	[? 1827–33]	[London]	T. J. Hogg	22
344.*	December 12	33 Somerset St.	Henry Colburn	22
345.*	[? December 12]	[London]	[Charles Ollier]	22
346.	December 15	33 Somerset St.	E. J. Trelawny	23
347.*	[December]	33 Somerset St.	John Murray	25
348.*	[? December 31]	Somerset St.	Charles Ollier	26

1830

Number		Place	To	Page
349.†	[? 1830]	Somerset St.	John Murray	26
350.*	January 5	33 Somerset St.	[Charles Ollier]	26
351.*	[January 7]	33 Somerset St.	John Bowring	27
352.	January 14	33 Somerset St.	Charles Ollier	27
353.	January 15	33 Somerset St.	W. Galignani	28
354.	January 19	33 Somerset St.	John Murray	28
355.†	[January 20]	33 Somerset St.	John Murray	29
356.*	January 25	33 Somerset St.	John Murray	29
357.*	[January 25]	Somerset St.	John Murray	30
358.†	[January 26]	Somerset St.	John Murray	30
359.*	March 1	33 Somerset St.	William Whitton	30
360.†	March 5	33 Somerset St.	John Murray	31
361.*	May 24	33 Somerset St.	William Whitton	31
362.*	May 24	33 Somerset St.	Sir T. Shelley	31
363.†	May 25	33 Somerset St.	John Murray	32
364.*	June 2	33 Somerset St.	William Whitton	32
365.*	June 14	33 Somerset St.	William Whitton	32
366.*	June 16	33 Somerset St.	Maria J. Jewsbury	33
367.†	August 9	Park Cottage	John Murray	33
368.*	September 1	Park Cottage	William Whitton	34
369.†	September 8	Park Cottage	John Murray	34
370.†	October 20	Park Cottage	John Murray	35
371.*	December 2	33 Somerset St.	William Whitton	35
372.	December 27	33 Somerset St.	E. J. Trelawny	36
373.†	December 29	33 Somerset St.	John Murray	37
374.*	December 30	33 Somerset St.	R. D. Owen	37

1831

Number		Place	To	Page
375.	[February 1]	Somerset St.	J. H. Payne	38
376.*	February 1	33 Somerset St.	William Whitton	38
377.*	[? March 15]	[ ]	[Charles Ollier]	38
378.*	March 16	33 Somerset St.	[Charles Ollier]	39
379.	March 22	Somerset St.	E. J. Trelawny	39
380.*	May 5	33 Somerset St.	William Whitton	42
381.*	May 6	33 Somerset St.	William Whitton	43
382.*	May 10	Somerset St.	Charles Ollier	43
383.	[May 18]	33 Somerset St.	J. H. Payne	43
384.*	June 3	33 Somerset St.	William Whitton	44
385.*	[June 6]	33 Somerset St.	William Whitton	44
386.*	June 6	33 Somerset St.	William Whitton	45
387.	June 14	Somerset St.	E. J. Trelawny	45
388.*	June 22	33 Somerset St.	William Whitton	47
389.	July 26	Somerset St.	E. J. Trelawny	49
390.*	September 7	33 Somerset St.	John Murray	50
391.	October 2	33 Somerset St.	E. J. Trelawny	50
392.*	[December]	[London]	E. J. Trelawny	51

1832

Number		Place	To	Page
393.*	[? January, 1832]	[London]	Charles Ollier	52
394.*	January 24	33 Somerset St.	William Whitton	53
395.*	January 27	33 Somerset St.	John Gregson	54
396.*	February 10	33 Somerset St.	John Gregson	55
397.*	March 2	33 Somerset St.	John Gregson	55
398.*	[March 2]	33 Somerset St.	John Gregson	56
399.*	[March 4–10]	[London]	John Gregson	56
400.*	March 14	33 Somerset St.	John Gregson	56
401.*	[March (? 15)]	33 Somerset St.	John Gregson	57
402.*	[April 21]	[London]	Mrs. Manners–Sutton	57
403.†	April 30	33 Somerset St.	John Murray	57
404.	May 4	33 Somerset St.	John Murray	58
405.	May 14	33 Somerset St.	[Alaric A. Watts]	59
406.*	June 6	33 Somerset St.	John Gregson	59
407.	[? June 8]	Somerset St.	John Murray	60
408.*	[June (? 9)]	33 Somerset St.	John Gregson	62
409.	[August 2]	Sandgate	F. M. Reynolds	62
410.*	August 24	Sandgate	Maria Gisborne	63
411.*	September 1	Sandgate	John Gregson	65
412.*	September 5	Sandgate	John Gregson	65

Number		Place	To	Page
413.	[October 8]	Somerset St.	E. J. Trelawny	66
414.*	October 8	33 Somerset St.	John Gregson	66
415.*	October 25	33 Somerset St.	John Murray	67
416.*	[? 1831–32]	[London]	Jane Williams Hogg	67
417.*	December 1	33 Somerset St.	John Gregson	68
418.*	[December 2]	[London]	John Gregson	68
419.*	[December 3]	[London]	John Gregson	69
420.*	December 16	33 Somerset St.	John Gregson	69

1833

421.*	January 2	33 Somerset St.	John Gregson	70
422.*	January 3	33 Somerset St.	John Gregson	71
423.*	January 13	33 Somerset St.	John Gregson	71
424.	January 16	33 Somerset St.	Maria Gisborne	71
425.*	January	33 Somerset St.	E. J. Trelawny	73
426.†	January 31	33 Somerset St.	[Charles Ollier]	75
427.*	February 11	33 Somerset St.	[Charles Ollier]	75
428.*	March 2	33 Somerset St.	John Gregson	75
429.	March 18	33 Somerset St.	Charles Ollier	76
430.*	April 15	33 Somerset St.	John Murray	76
431.*	June 1	Harrow on the Hill	John Gregson	77
432.*	September 2	2 Melbury Terrace, Dorset Square	John Gregson	77
433.*	[November 10]	Harrow	Charles Ollier	78
434.*	December 2	Harrow	John Gregson	78

1834

435.*	[March 15]	Harrow	Charles Ollier	78
436.	May 7	Harrow	E. J. Trelawny	79
437.	July 17	Harrow	Maria Gisborne	81
438*	August 9	13 New Palace Yard	Douglas Jerrold	85
439.*	August 19	7 Upper Eaton St.	Maria Gisborne	85
440.	October 30	Harrow	Maria Gisborne	87

1835

441.	February 3	Harrow	Leigh Hunt	89
442.	February 9	Harrow	Maria Gisborne	91
443.†	February 10	Harrow	John Murray	92
444.	[February]	Harrow	John Murray	92
445.	April 3	Harrow	Gabriele Rossetti	93
446.	April 20	Harrow	Gabriele Rossetti	94
447.*	May 1 [? 1835]	[?]	Mr. Mignot	96

Number		Place	To	Page
448.	June 11	Harrow	Maria Gisborne	96
449.*	[July]	Harrow	E. J. Trelawny	100
450.*	August 6	Dover	Charles Ollier	101
451.*	[? September]	[London]	Charles Ollier	101
452.*	[? September]	[? Harrow]	E. J. Trelawny	102
453.†	[September]	[?]	E. J. Trelawny	103
454.†	[September]	[Harrow]	E. J. Trelawny	103
455.*	October 3	Harrow	John Bowring	103
456.	October 12	[?]	E. J. Trelawny	104
457.	October 13	Harrow	Maria Gisborne	105
458.*	November	Harrow	Maria Gisborne	107

1836

Number		Place	To	Page
459.*	[February 5]	Harrow	Maria Gisborne	109
460.	March 1	Harrow	John Gregson	110
461.*	March 4	Harrow	Maria Gisborne	111
462.*	April 8	14 North Bank, Regent's Park	John Gregson	112
463.†	[April 10]	[London]	E. J. Trelawny	113
464.*	[April 12]	[London]	J. C. Hudson	113
465.	April 20	14 North Bank	Mary Hays	113
466.*	May 27	14 North Bank	H. C. Robinson	114
467.*	June 1	14 North Bank	John Gregson	115
468.*	June 6	14 North Bank	John Gregson	115
469.*	June 8	14 North Bank	[Henry Colburn]	116
470.*	October 10	4 Lower Belgrave St.	William Hazlitt, Jr.	116

1837

Number		Place	To	Page
471.	January 3	Brighton	E. J. Trelawny	117
472.	January 27	Brighton	E. J. Trelawny	119
473.*	[? February–March]	41 d Park St.	Leigh Hunt	121
474.*	[? May]	[London]	E. J. Trelawny	122
475.*	June 1	24 South Audley St.	John Bowring	122
476.†	June 20	Brighton	Leigh Hunt	123
477.*	July 3	17 South Audley St.	John Bowring	123
478.*	July 13	24 South Audley St.	John Bowring	123

1838

Number		Place	To	Page
479.	[? March]	41 d Park St.	Edward Bulwer	124
480.*	April 26 [? 1838]	84 Park St.	[G. H.] Lewes	125
481.*	[October 5]	41 d Park St.	Richard Rothwell	125

Number		Place	To	Page
482.†	[1838–39]	41 d Park St.	Lady Morgan	126
483.	December 11	41 d Park St.	T. J. Hogg	126
484.*	December 12	41 d Park St.	[? Charles Ollier]	126
485.	December 12	41 d Park St.	Leigh Hunt	127
486.	[December 14]	41 d Park St.	Leigh Hunt	127
487.*	December 14	41 d Park St.	A. Hayward	128

1839

488.†	January 12	41 d Park St.	T. J. Hogg	128
489.†	[? January 14]	[41 d Park St.]	T. J. Hogg	128
490.*	[? January 15]	41 d Park St.	Charles Sumner	128
491.*	[? January 19]	41 d Park St.	[? Charles Ollier]	129
492.	[January]	[41 d Park St.]	Thomas Moore	130
493.*	[January 22]	41 d Park St.	Mary Peacock	130
494.*	March 4	41 d Park St.	Edward Moxon	131
495.*	March 5	41 d Park St.	Edward Moxon	131
496.*	March 30	Layton House, Putney	Mary Peacock	132
497.*	April 4	Putney	Edward Moxon	132
498.*	[April 5]	Putney	Mrs. Stanhope	133
499.*	May 2	Putney	Edward Moxon	133
500.*	May 12 [? 1839]	Putney	Mrs. Jones	134
501.*	August 3	Putney	Mrs. A. Berry	135
502.	[August]	Putney	Leigh Hunt	136
503.*	August 29	[London]	Mary Peacock	137
504.*	September 5	Putney	[? G. A. Mantell]	137
505.*	September 18	Putney	[? G. A. Mantell]	138
506*	September 30	Putney	Edward Moxon	138
507.	[October 6]	Putney	Leigh Hunt	139
508.*	[? October]	[Putney]	Leigh Hunt	139
509.*	[? October, 1839]	[Putney]	Leigh Hunt	140
510.	[? October]	Putney	Leigh Hunt	140
511.	November 14	Putney	Leigh Hunt	141
512.*	[? November]	[Putney]	Leigh Hunt	141
513.*	[1839–46]	Putney	Leigh Hunt	142
514.	December 19	[Putney]	Edward Moxon	143
515.	December 22 [? 1839]	Putney	A. Hayward	143
516.*	[? December, 1839]	[?]	Charles Ollier	144

1840

517.*	[January 30]	[Putney]	Leigh Hunt	144
518.*	[February 27]	Putney	Leigh Hunt	145

Number	Place	To	Page
519.* March 1	Putney	Everina Wollstonecraft	145
520.* March 3	Putney	A. Hayward	146
521.* [April 6]	Richmond	Leigh Hunt	146
522.* June 6	Brighton	Marianne Hunt	146
523. October 26	Paris	A. Hayward	147

1841

524.* June 28	Dolgelly, North Wales	Edward Moxon	149
525. July 14	Dolgelly, N. W.	Edward Moxon	150

1842

526.* March 4	[?]	C. Clairmont	151
527.* May 11	Cowes [Isle of Wight]	C. Clairmont	152
528.* June 2	Exberry	C. Clairmont	153
529.* June 5	34 Half Moon St.	[? Monsieur Galloni]	155
530. [June 6]	34 Half Moon St.	Leigh Hunt	156
531.* June 28	Kissingen, Bavaria	C. Clairmont	156
532.* July 17	Kissingen	C. Clairmont	159
533.* [August 16]	[Dresden]	C. Clairmont	161
534.* August 17	Dresden	Leigh Hunt	163
535.* October 1	Venice	C. Clairmont	165
536.* November 4	Florence	C. Clairmont	169
537.* November 5	Florence	C. Clairmont	170
538.* November 24	Florence	Everina Wollstonecraft	171
539.* November 25	Florence	C. Clairmont	172
540.* November 29	[Florence]	C. Clairmont	174
541.* December 3	Florence	C. Clairmont	176
542.* December 15	Florence	Leigh Hunt	178

1843

543.* February 20	Florence	C. Clairmont	179
544.* March 23	Rome	C. Clairmont	179
545.* April 15	Rome	C. Clairmont	181
546.* May 17	Sorrento	C. Clairmont	183
547.* June 5	Sorrento	C. Clairmont	184
548.* June 17	Sorrento	C. Clairmont	186
549.* [June 20]	[Sorrento]	Marianna Hammond	187
550.* June 30	Sorrento	C. Clairmont	188
551.* July 9	Sorrento	Jane Williams Hogg	189
552.* July 19	Marseilles	C. Clairmont	191
553.* [September 11, 1844][1]	[Putney]	C. Clairmont	192

[1] This letter has, unfortunately, been misplaced. It should follow Letter 590, to which it is probably a postscript.

Number		Place	To	Page
554.*	August 30	London	C. Clairmont	192
555.*	August 30	11 Portugal St.	Edward Moxon	195
556.*	September 2	Putney	Edward Moxon	195
557.*	September 3	11 Portugal St., May Fair	Leigh Hunt	196
558.*	September 10	London	C. Clairmont	196
559.*	September 11	Putney	C. Clairmont	199
560.*	September 20	White Cottage, Putney	Edward Moxon	200
561.*	September 20	White Cottage, Putney	C. Clairmont	201
562.*	October 7	Putney	C. Clairmont	204
563.*	[October 9]	[Putney]	C. Clairmont	205
564.*	October 13	[Putney]	C. Clairmont	205
565.*	October 28	[Putney]	C. Clairmont	207
566.*	[? November]	Putney	C. Clairmont	208
567.*	November 10	[Putney]	C. Clairmont	209
568.	November 21	Putney	Marianne Hunt	210
569.*	December 5	[Putney]	C. Clairmont	210
570.	December 15	Paris	Joseph Severn	211

1844

571.*	[February]	[Putney]	C. Clairmont	212
572.†	February 16	Putney	A. Hayward	214
572A.	[March]	Putney	Thomas Moore	214
573.*	March 11	Putney	C. Clairmont	214
574.*	[April 12]	[Putney]	C. Clairmont	216
575.*	April 19	[Putney]	C. Clairmont	216
576.	April 20	Putney	Leigh Hunt	217
577.†	April 24	Putney	T. J. Hogg	219
578.*	April 24	Putney	C. Clairmont	219
579.*	April 27	Putney	C. Clairmont	219
580.*	[? May, 1844]	Putney	[Marianna Hammond]	220
581.*	June 4	Putney	C. Clairmont	221
582.*	June 25	Putney	Marianne Hunt	222
583.*	July 1	Putney	C. Clairmont	223
584.*	[July]	[?]	C. Clairmont	225
585.†	[? July]	Putney	Edward Moxon	227
586.*	[? August]	[?]	[Leigh Hunt]	227
587.*	[?]	Putney	Leigh Hunt	228
588.*	[?]	[Putney]	Leigh Hunt	228
589.†	September 5	Putney	Joseph Severn	229
590.*	[September 11]	[Putney]	C. Clairmont	229
591.*	[September 27]	Sandgate	C. Clairmont	230

Number		Place	To	Page
592.*	October 27	Putney	C. Clairmont	231
593.*	December 6	Putney	C. Clairmont	233
594.	December 23	Putney	Leigh Hunt	233

1845

595.*	[January]	[Putney]	[? Nerina Mason Cini]	234
596.	[January 9]	Putney	L. & M. Hunt	235
597.*	January 15	[Putney]	C. Clairmont	235
598.*	May 14	Putney	C. Clairmont	236
599.*	May 17	[Putney]	C. Clairmont	237
600.*	May 23	[Putney]	C. Clairmont	238
601.*	[May 23]	[Putney]	C. Clairmont	239
602.*	May 27	[?]	C. Clairmont	239
603.*	[June]	[Putney]	C. Clairmont	240
604.*	[June]	[Putney]	C. Clairmont	241
605.*	July 5	[Putney]	C. Clairmont	243
606.*	[July] 7	[Putney]	C. Clairmont	244
607.*	[July 17]	[Putney]	C. Clairmont	246
608.*	August 5	Putney	C. Clairmont	247
609.*	[August 12]	Putney	C. Clairmont	249
610.*	[? September]	[Putney]	A. A. Knox	251
611.*	[September 15]	[Putney]	C. Clairmont	252
612.*	[October 1]	Broadstairs	C. Clairmont	253
613.*	[October 8]	[Brighton]	C. Clairmont	254
614.*	[October 9]	Brighton	C. Clairmont	255
615.*	[October 12]	Brighton	C. Clairmont	257
616.*	[October 13]	Brighton	C. Clairmont	258
617.*	[October 14]	Brighton	C. Clairmont	259
618.*	[October 18 or 25]	Putney	C. Clairmont	260
619.*	October 24	Putney	Alex. Berry	261
620.*	October 24 [? 1845]	Putney	[Addressee Unknown]	263
621.*	October 28	Putney	[Thos. Hookham]	263
622.*	October 30	Putney	[Thos. Hookham]	265
623.*	[October 31]	Putney	[Thos. Hookham]	266
624.*	[October 31]	[Putney]	[Thos. Hookham]	267
625.*	[November 1 (?)]	[Putney]	[Thos. Hookham]	268
626.*	[November 3(?)]	[Putney]	[Thos. Hookham]	268
627.*	[November 3 (?)]	[Putney]	[Thos. Hookham]	269
628.*	[November]	[Putney]	[Thos. Hookham]	269
629.*	[November 5]	[Putney]	C. Clairmont	270
630.*	[November 10]	[Putney]	C. Clairmont	271
631.*	[November 14]	[Putney]	C. Clairmont	273

Number		Place	To	Page
632.*	[December 1]	Putney	C. Clairmont	273
633.*	[December 11]	Putney	C. Clairmont	276
634.*	[December 12]	[Putney]	C. Clairmont	279
635.*	[December 22]	Putney	C. Clairmont	280
636.*	December 29	[Putney]	C. Clairmont	281

1846

637.*	[?]	[Putney]	Leigh Hunt	283
638.*	[January 30]	Putney	Edward Moxon	284
639.*	[January 30]	Putney	C. Clairmont	284
640.*	[February]	[Putney]	C. Clairmont	286
641.*	February 9	Putney	C. Clairmont	286
642.*	February 9	Putney	[Addressee Unknown]	287
643.	[May]	[?]	Thomas Medwin	287
644.	[May or June]	[London]	Jane Williams Hogg	289
645.	[May or June]	[?]	Leigh Hunt	290
646.*	[?]	[?]	W. S. Landor	290
647.*	[August 26]	Baden [Baden]	C. Clairmont	291
648.*	[? August]	[?]	Leigh Hunt	291
649.*	August 30	Baden Baden	C. Clairmont	292
650.*	September 5	Baden Baden	C. Clairmont	293
651.*	September 12	[Baden Baden]	[Thos. Hookham]	294
652.*	September 12	Baden Baden	Thos. Hookham	295
653.*	[?October-November]	24 Chester Square	[Thos. Hookham]	296
654.*	November 12	24 Chester Square	Alex. Berry	296
655.*	November 17	Brighton	Marianne Hunt	297
656.*	[1846–48]	24 Chester Sq.	Mrs. Milner–Gibson	298

1847

657.*	January 3 [1847–48]	24 Chester Sq.	[Addressee Unknown]	298
658.*	March 29	24 Chester Sq.	Alex. Berry	299
659.*	[? April, 1847]	[?]	C. Clairmont	300
660.*	[c. April]	24 Chester Sq.	Leigh Hunt	300
661.*	April 18 [? 1847]	24 Chester Sq.	Mr. Halford	301
662.*	April 20 [? 1847]	24 Chester Sq.	R. M. Milnes	301
663.*	[? April 27]	[?]	C. Clairmont	302
664.	June 10	Chester Sq.	Leigh Hunt	302
665.*	June 29	Brighton	Leigh Hunt	303
666.*	[July 28]	[Brighton]	C. Clairmont	303
667.*	[August 1]	Brighton	C. Clairmont	304
668.*	August 17	Brighton	Alex. Berry	305

Number		Place	To	Page
669.	[August 27]	[?]	Leigh Hunt	307
670.*	[August 31]	24 Chester Sq.	C. Clairmont	309
671.*	[? September 2]	Brighton	Leigh Hunt	309
672.†	December 4	[?]	[Addressee Unknown]	310
672A.*	December 4 [? 1847]	Elcott House, Hungerford	Mr. Blewitt	310
672B.*	December 13 [? 1847]	24 Chester Sq.	[? Mr. Blewitt]	311
673.†	December 23 [? 1847]	[?]	[Addressee Unknown]	311
674.*	[December 26]	[?]	C. Clairmont	311

1848

675.*	[February 10]	24 Chester Sq.	C. Clairmont	311
676.*	March 15	24 Chester Sq.	Mary [Peacock Nicolls]	312
677.*	[March]	[?]	Charles [Robinson]	313
678.	March 28	24 Chester Sq.	Alex. Berry	313
679.*	[April 8]	[?]	C. Clairmont	315
680.*	May 4	24 Chester Sq.	[Addressee Unknown]	315
681.*	June 10	24 Chester Sq.	Mrs. E. J. Trelawny	316
682.*	June 30	24 Chester Sq.	Alex. Berry	317
683.*	July 7	24 Chester Sq.	John Gregson	319
684.*	[July 24]	Sandgate	C. Clairmont	319
685.*	[July 28]	Sandgate	C. Clairmont	320
686.*	[August 14]	Field Place	C. Clairmont	321
687.*	[August 30]	Field Place	C. Clairmont	322
688.*	[October 19]	Brighton	C. Clairmont	323
689.*	[November 23]	[Brighton]	C. Clairmont	323
690.*	[November 24]	[Brighton]	C. Clairmont	324
691.*	November 30	77 Warwick Sq.	C. Clairmont	324
692.*	[December 10]	77 Warwick Sq.	C. Clairmont	325

1849

693.*	January	[London]	C. Clairmont	326
694.*	[February 11]	[Field Place]	C. Clairmont	327
695.*	[? March 16]	Field Place	Mr. Touchet	328
696.*	[March 19]	Field Place	C. Clairmont	329
697.*	[April 15]	Field Place	C. Clairmont	330
698.*	[April 26]	Field Place	C. Clairmont	331
699.*	September 6	Field Place	T. L. Peacock	332
700.*	September 24	Field Place	Mrs. E. J. Trelawny	333

1850

Number		Place	To	Page
701.	February 24	Nice	Mrs. E. J. Trelawny	335
702.*	August 2	Field Place	Mr. Touchet	337
703.*	[? August 9]	Field Place	Mr. Touchet	337
704.*	August 12	Field Place	Mrs. E. J. Trelawny	338
705.*	September 8	Field Place	Mr. Touchet	339

The Letters of Mary W. Shelley

PART II : AFTER SHELLEY'S DEATH
(CONTINUED)

The Letters of Mary W. Shelley

PART II : AFTER SHELLEY'S DEATH

(CONTINUED)

312. *To Jane Williams Hogg* 6 Meadow Cottages, Priory,
Hastings,
Saturday [June 28, 1828]

I am delighted, my dear Jane, to hear of your brother's arrival,[1] and the comfort that he promises to be to you. This is a good turn of fortune—God send you many such! I am very sorry that I hurt you, yet glad I confess, that I awakened your pride— I cannot tell why, but we seem to stand more equally now. It is painful to go over old grounds—I go only on what you have allowed; long you gave ear to every idle & evil tale against me—& repeated them —not glossed over—nor can I—tho' I allow myself changed, admit as just the sweeping sentence you pass over my early years—the past is too dear to me—& I feel that tho' now more just to myself I was then as just to others as now   What can I say? My devotion to you was too entire; the discovery caused so deep a wound, that my health sank under it—from the hour it was disclosed till my recovery from this odious illness I never knew health— You ask what good has been done— I must feel the truth a good— You speak of beings to whom I link myself—speak, I pray you, in the singular number— if Isabel[2] has not answered your letter, she will—but the misery to which she is a victim is so dreadful and merciless, that she shrinks like a wounded person from every pang—and you must excuse her on the score of her matchless sufferings. What D. now is, I will not describe in a letter—one only trusts that the diseased body acts on the diseased mind, & that both may be at rest ere long. For the rest I look forward without hope or pleasure—it is summer weather, and so I am not often in ill spirits— I shut my eyes and enjoy—but a restless spirit stirring in my heart whispers to me that this is not life, & youth flies the while— I know the occasion and opportunity is only wanted, for me to feel some return of good—but it is vain to court these—they must come —& they will not while I am as I am now—so at least I have lost one year of

---

[1] John Wheeler Cleveland, who had been in India. For the first part of this letter, see Letter 295, note 1.
[2] Either Isabel Robinson (Mrs. Sholto Douglas) or Isabel Booth.

my life—but I have gained so much in health—& even in good looks, when these marks disappear, that I will not too much repine,—and in a few weeks I hope not to be a fright, tho' it will take months to lose every trace.—My poor hair! it is a wonder I did not lose it all—but it has greatly suffered, and I am forced to keep it clipped still. How you would have pitied me!

I like this place very much—the air is so pure and the sea bathing is so advantageous to Percy and myself that I earnestly desire to remain here another month— Trelawny has written to me to return to town— I have replied by asking him to come here, and anxiously await his reply—town would be odious—for I *will not* see people as I am. I had enough of that in Paris— we are as quiet as mice here— Papa is now down with us, & returns to town on Monday—on which day we expect Mr. [Joshua] Robinson— I do not find Percy altered—he is the same boy—without evil—& without sentiment— docile and querelous—self willed and yielding—unsocial yet frank—without one ill fold—and the open space apparently well fitted for culture but greatly requiring it.—

Poor Medwin!—from first to last—poor Medwin! I am glad he will not see me, or the Guiccioli would no longer be the ugliest woman he *ever saw in his life*— I cannot say that I believe the scandal about Pierino[3]—that of the old Pope may be—but too much has been said & believed of me, for me to give ear to tales about others— I wrote to her from Paris, but have had no answer—

The Hunts! how completely à la Marianne is the last [procèdeur]—I suppose I should have had a visit—after her cutting me on Mary's account— I can hardly pity her for she has her *consolation*[4]—but Hunt—what a fate— what a bitter & dread fate is his—& if we say it is partly his own fault, must one not accuse the Gods who formed him to his own ruin— It is the only comfort one has (& that a sorry one) in one's total inability to serve them, that it is impossible to render them service— I shall write to Statia—

Sontag & the opera! I ought to be in London now—but that I should be as far from these delights there as here— I saw very little of these things in Paris for they were too expensive— I hope your brother will understand that happiness does not consist merely in a good dinner going to sleep after it—& going to bed at night,[5] but will forge amusement for his sweet sister— a brother! what a dear name if linked to affection! How I envy you—a dear man person—on whom—the first best link not existing—one can repose as one's support in life, is a vain dream too generally. Friendships lead to love— or, quite certainly, to such scandal, as—as was my case, tarnishes the reputation and hurts the guiltless in the eyes of those with whom they would stand well— Fraternal love is too often linked to fraternal tyranny—where it is not,

---

3 Count Pietro Gamba.

4 Apparently a reference to Mrs. Hunt's drinking.

5 As Hogg did.

it is the second blessing of life—for however devotedly one may love a woman, she can never support, defend, & protect as a man.

Tomorrow I hope to know my fate from Trelawny—& I shall then finish this letter— God bless you, my pretty pet!—

(Sunday) No letter from our friend— I am sufficiently annoyed; the prospect of returning to town before the end of July is odious, but any thing is better than this suspense.

Dear Girl, I cannot tell you how sincerely and excessively I rejoice in the gain you have made this year. Has fortune done its worst and will it now be kind to you? To know that you are happy to see you surrounded by those who love—who worship you—to feel that your affectionate heart has a resource in this well you call it queer world is so true so real a pleasure to me that I thank *one person* for it as [for] good to myself—the greatest I have had this many a day.

You perceive I cannot say when we meet—probably next week—certainly in a month.

Affectionately Yours

M S.

ADDRESS: Mrs. Jefferson Hogg/ 22 Devonshire Place/ Edgware Road/ London. POSTMARKS: (1) HASTINGS/ JU.29/ 1828   (2) E/ 30 JU 30/ 1828. ORIGINAL: British Museum (T. J. Wise Collection); A.L.S., 4 pp. 4to. PRINTED: *A Shelley Library*, edited by Wise, 19–20 (quot., 15 lines). TEXT: From original letter.

313. *To John Murray**

Park Cottage, Paddington

20 August [1828]

My dear Sir

You were good enough to say that you would supply me with any book I might want for my novel. Will you let me have Leland's history of Ireland— Les Memoires de Philipe de Comines[1]— I want also some description of Cork which I suppose may be found in almost any minute travels in Ireland, but if you happened to know of one that treated more of the antiquities than as it now is, it would best suit my purpose.

I was sorry to hear from Mr. Marshall that you decided against the Promessi Sposi.[2]

I am dear Sir

Your Obt. Servant

Mary Shelley

ORIGINAL: Sir John Murray; A.L.S., 2 pp. 8vo. PRINTED: S. Smiles, *A Publisher and His Friends* (1891), II, 310 (quot., 2 lines). TEXT: From original letter.

[1] Some of the scenes of *Perkin Warbeck* are in Ireland. Thomas Leland, *The History of Ireland, from the Invasion of Henry II, with a Preliminary Discourse on the Antient State of that Kingdom.* (London, 1773, 3 vols.); *Les Memoires*, first published in 1524, went through many editions before 1828.

[2] Mary had probably suggested that she be engaged to translate Alessandro **Manzoni's** *I Promessi Sposi; Storia Milanese del Secolo XVII* (Milano, 1825, 3 tom.).

314. *To William Whitton*

Park Cottage, Paddington.
1 September, 1828.

Dear Sir,

I attend with anxiety the result of any communication you may have had with Sir Tim. Shelley on the increase of my allowance. As I remember you said, when first Sir Tim was kind enough to appoint a settled income for me, that you proposed £300, and Sir Tim desired to delay this till Percy was older, I think you will have been good enough to represent my request aided by your influence. Now that Percy is at school the bills become heavy, and as I had hoped to have received the encreased allowance at Midsummer, I shall be embarrassed from its having been refused. The school bills are above £60 p. an. —and his dress now is very expensive; I have not been able to pay the last quarter, and shall be seriously disappointed if Sir Tim is not good enough to consider these things and to make the advance I have been led to expect.

I had hoped to see you to explain this better in an interview, and to request your kind interference—but I was disappointed and did not find you. Percy spent his holidays with me by the seaside, and went back to school in excellent health and spirits— I have seen him since he appears very happy, and Mr. Slater is perfectly satisfied with him.

Pray thank Sir Tim for me for the kind interest he has shewn in him. It would give me great pleasure when he comes to town again if he permitted me personally to thank him.

I am, dear Sir,
Your Obt. Servt.
Mary W. Shelley

ADDRESS: William Whitton Esq./ Stone House,/ Tunbridge, Kent. ORIGINAL: Sir John Shelley-Rolls. UNPRINTED and UNPUBLISHED. TEXT: From copy made by Sir John Shelley-Rolls.

315. *To William Whitton**

Park Cottage, Paddington.
4 September, 1828.

Dear Sir,

I wrote to you last Monday concerning my allowance from Sir Tim. Shelley, as this is the time when I receive a quarterly payment— I should not trouble you again but that I am fearful that I mistook your address— I directed it to you at Stone House, Tunbridge, Kent— As you will get this letter from the Post Office at Tunbridge if it has not been delivered, I will not repeat here what I said concerning the encrease of my allowance—become now through the expence, Percy puts me to, absolutely necessary.

I am,
Yr. Obt. Sert.
Mary Shelley

ADDRESS: William Whitton Esq./ 18 Bedford Row. ORIGINAL: Sir John Shelley-Rolls. UNPRINTED and UNPUBLISHED. TEXT: From copy made by Sir John Shelley-Rolls.

316. *To William Whitton*

Park Cottage, Paddington.
5 September, 1828.

Dear Sir,

You will oblige me by sending me a cheque for £62.10. my quarterly allowance.

I am indeed disappointed by Sir Timy.'s refusal to encrease the payment—Percy's expences encrease—and mine were already on the most economical footing I can devise— I have hitherto kept myself carefully free from embarrassment, though with a difficulty of which you, who have never felt the extreme difficulty of living on so small an income, cannot be aware. The addition of the heavy school bills I shall be wholly unable to meet— What I am to do I cannot tell— I should like to see you first, for I think you would kindly advise me for the best; is it possible that if I wrote Sir Tim. stating the impossibility of living now that my son's expences are at least £100, on the same sum that barely sufficed when he did not cost me more than half that sum, that he would consent to make that addition which I cannot think it unreasonable in me to ask, and always trusted he would concede?

I am, dear Sir,
Yr. Obt. Sert.
Mary Shelley

ADDRESS: W. Whitton Esq./ Stone Wall, Tunbridge, Kent. ORIGINAL: Sir John Shelley-Rolls. UNPRINTED and UNPUBLISHED. TEXT: From copy made by Sir John Shelley-Rolls.

317. *To John Murray*

Park Cottage, Paddington,
Sept. 10, 1828.

[*Summary*] Mary is obliged for the loan of books; "Mr. Croker's volume was quite to my purpose." She wants some travels in Andalusia, with descriptions of the scenery, & plates too; wishes descriptions would dwell on "the antique Moorish mansions."[1]

ORIGINAL: Sir John Murray; A.L.S., 1 p. 8vo, addressed, with seal. POSTMARK: 12 NOON/ 10.SP/ 1828. UNPRINTED and UNPUBLISHED. SUMMARY: From the original letter.

318. *To John Howard Payne*

Tuesday [October 28, 1828]
Park Cottage

I have written to you at Arundel St—but as I fear the note may miss you

[1] Mary was seeking a background for the Spanish scenes of *Perkin Warbeck*.

(remember the other note is a *pretty* one this is in haste—) I write also to your other habitation to ask you to obtain 4 orders for Thursday for Covent Garden— Kean does not draw to the boxes—pray let us know soon—& come with us if you can

ADDRESS: J. Howard Payne Esq/ 17 Speldhurst St./ Burton Crescent. POST-MARKS: (1) T.P./ Crawford St.   (2) 10.F.NOON.10/ 28.OC/ 1828. ORIG-INAL: Huntington Library (HM 10794); A.L., 1 p. 16mo. UNPRINTED and UN-PUBLISHED. TEXT: From original letter.

319. *To William Whitton*

Park Cottage, Paddington.
1st December, 1828.

Dear Sir,

Now that the period of the payment of my allowance is come, I become anxious to know whether Sir Timothy will attend to my request of aug-menting it. I feel quite sure that if Sir Timothy were fully aware of the neces-sity he would not refuse. I cannot charge myself with any extravagance and yet I find the present sum quite inadequate. I do not know whether it is understood that my visit to France occasioned no additional expence to my usual mode of living— I went with a friend, I staid with a friend during the very few weeks I remained there—it seems almost needless to assert this, as with the extreme economy I practice, I had nothing to spare for a journey of any sort. I have told you that nothing could prevent my attending to Percy's bills in the first place—a half year, which with extras cannot be less than £30, will be due this Christmas, besides his taylor's bill— How I can pay these and live for three months—six weeks of which he will be at home with me for the holydays on the payment I have hitherto received, I am at a loss to conjecture.

Will you lay this statement before Sir Timothy. Perhaps when he again comes to town he will permit me a pleasure I have long desired, namely—of seeing him; at any rate I beg you to assure him of my respect and thanks.

I am,
Yr. Obt. Sert.,
Mary W. Shelley

ADDRESS: William Whitton Esq./ 18 Bedford Row. ORIGINAL: Sir John Shelley-Rolls. UNPRINTED and UNPUBLISHED. TEXT: From copy made by Sir John Shel-ley-Rolls.

320. *To William Whitton*

Park Cottage, Paddington.
1 Decr., 1828.

Dear Sir,

I am disappointed to find that Sir Timothy has not apparently been in town and that no opportunity has been afforded me for seeing him. I do not know how far you will judge it right to lay the accompanying letter before him, and I beg you to use your own judgment upon it—the simple facts I state will shew you how necessary it is for me to receive an augmentation of income without which I cannot keep from the embarrassment I have hitherto so sedulously avoided. You will be so good as to let me hear from you on the subject soon.

I am,

Yrs. Obly.

Mary W. Shelley

ADDRESS: W. Whitton Esq. ORIGINAL: Sir John Shelley-Rolls. UNPRINTED and UNPUBLISHED. TEXT: From copy made by Sir John Shelley-Rolls.

321. *To William Whitton**   Park Cottage, [Paddington] 9 December [1828]

My dear Sir,

I trust that on Sir Timothy's visit to town I shall have the honor of seeing him—in which case I should not wish my letter to be given him. Otherwise I must rely on his kindness, on which I found my application, that he will not be displeased by a request forced from me by necessity only—and which he at one time seemed to justify by the prospect held out to me that my allowance would be encreased on Percy's going to school. If therefore I should be prevented from seeing Sir. Timy. will you present my letter with such explanation from you as may efface any idea of my pressing too much upon him.

I forward the rec[eip]t—could you have the goodness to send me cash instead of a cheque in the city—but if this is inconvenient give the cheque uninclosed to the bearer who will go on for the money.

I am,

Yr. Obly.

Mary Shelley

ENDORSED. 9th Decr. 1828. Mrs. Shelley. ORIGINAL: Sir John Shelley-Rolls. UNPRINTED and UNPUBLISHED. TEXT: From copy made by Sir John Shelley-Rolls.

322. *To John Howard Payne*

Wednesday [December 10, 1828]

Park Cottage

I hope you are alive though I begin to be a little fearful on that point—if you are, my dear Friend, have the goodness, if you can contrive it—to send me 2 admissions to Drury Lane for Saturday—& add to the favor by being in the theatre at ¼ to seven to attend us to our places

Yours Ever

M S.

ADDRESS: John Howard Payne Esq/ 29 Arundel St./ Strand. POSTMARK: 12. NOON.12/ 12.DE/ 1828. ORIGINAL: Huntington Library (HM 10795); A.L.S., 1 p. 16mo. UNPRINTED and UNPUBLISHED. TEXT: From original letter.

323. *To [Cyrus Redding]**

Somerset St.
Thursday [? January, 1829].

My dear Sir

I send you the Errata of the Prometheus—Some changes Mr. Shelley wished made in the Adonais—and a suppressed stanza of Hellas. I am tempted to offer to write a brief outline of Mr. Shelleys life if Galignani[1] chose—but then my secret must be kept religiously—& no alterations made—it would [be] very short & its chief merit the *absence* of incorrectness— I have some hopes of the portrait—the Lady who painted it is in town & will meet Mr. Pavis & offer her suggestions tomorrow—but I would give the world to have it engraved here—where any defect in the drawing might be corrected & we superintend the whole—at any rate it will be better than a likeness after the imagination of a Frenchman—that is the drollest & stupidest idea—ever man intent on selling an edition hit upon.

I am, dear Sir
Yours truly
Mary Shelley

[P.S.] The drawing is getting better & better— Pray keep them to their promise of letting me have it— I shall feel highly gratified

As it is now finished and at my house perhaps you will call Come as soon after 12 as you can

ORIGINAL: Huntington Library (HM 13413); A.L.S., 3 pp. 8vo. UNPRINTED and UNPUBLISHED. (Referred to by Forman, who then owned the MS, in *The Shelley Library*, 1886, 103.) TEXT: From original letter.

324. *To W. Galignani**

33 Somerset St.
London
8 Jan. 1829[2]

My dear Sir

I should have been glad to lend you a portrait of Shelley for the Paris edition of the Poems had I one to spare—but that which alone I possess—although imperfect—is far too precious to me to let it out of my hands—

Were your engraver in London I should not be disinclined to let him copy it here—but as you say this is not possible I have made a little pencil sketch

[1] In 1829 Galignani published Shelley's Poetical Works along with those of Coleridge and Keats. Cyrus Redding (1785–1870) wrote the Life of Shelley and apparently was mainly instrumental, with Mary's help, in assembling the MS and negotiating with Galignani. In his *Yesterday and Today* (London, T. C. Newby, 1863), III, 108, he wrote: "I wrote Shelley's memoir for Galignani's Edition of the English poets, I . . . was indebted to Mrs. Shelley for nearly all the matter I obtained." Redding, a journalist, was in France from 1814 to 1819, and in 1815–18 was editor of Galignani's English newspaper, the *Messenger*. From 1821 to 1830 he was the working editor of the *New Monthly Magazine*. Besides the life of Shelley, he also wrote for Galignani's Complete Edition of the Poets (Paris, 1829–30) the lives of Keats, Coleridge, Wilson, Rogers, and Campbell.
[2] Only the date is at the end of the MS.

which I enclose in the hope that it will serve your purpose—especially as
you mention that the likeness is to be very small.[3]

I am

Yours truly

M W Shelley

ADDRESS:Mr. W. Galignani/ No. 18. Rue Vivienne/ Paris. ORIGINAL: Stark Collection, University of Texas; A.L.S., 2 pp. 8vo. PRINTED: W. E. Peck, *Shelley:
His Life and Work* (1927), II, 441–42. TEXT: From original letter.

325. *To William Whitton**

4 Oxford Terrace,
Edgware Road.
15th Janry., 1829.

Dear Sir,

I inform you as you ask that the death of Mr. Shelley took place on the
8th July 1822.

I do not know whether you have thought it advisable to mention the encrease of my income to Sir Timothy— I enclose you Percy's half year's bill,
not as a thing to be presented to Sir Timothy—but merely to shew you that
my statements are not exagerated, and that with the addition of his taylor's
account, Percy costs me a sum that makes my income less than when I had
only £200 p. ann— I hope this will be considered before next quarter as
otherwise I shall be considerably embarrassed.

I am,

Yr. Obt. Servant,

Mary W. Shelley

ORIGINAL: Sir John Shelley-Rolls. UNPRINTED and UNPUBLISHED. TEXT: From
copy made by Sir John Shelley-Rolls.

326. *To Sir John Bowring**

4 Oxford Terrace
3 Feby. [1829]

I have received the cheque for £5-5[1] I was unaware that the article was
of such instant necessity—or that the W[estminster] R[eview] would appear
so soon— The subject is not France but Italy— Do you intend that I
should not complete it?—At present I am too much occupied by my novel to
be able to give you much time—but if you wish for my assistance & can think
of some work which would only require a short easy notice I will accomplish
it—& do better still for the number after[2]—

[3] The engraved portrait, by J. T. Wedgwood, was very small. Mary was not pleased with it.
See Letter 353.

[1] For the article on Mérimée in the January *Westminster Review*. See Letter 308 and note.

[2] Mary's article on "Modern Italy" appeared in the *Westminster Review*, No. XXI (July, 1829),
127–40, as a review of *Italy As It Is* (Anon.) and J. Simond's *A Tour in Italy and Sicily*. Though
certainly by Mary, the article makes no references to persons, places, or events that would lead us
to identify Mary as the author without the help of these hints in her letters. Mary gives an enthusiastic description of Italy as one sees it after he crosses the Alps and approaches Bologna and
Florence; describes Rome with feeling and knowledge; and expresses contempt for the degenerate
modern Italians. The article is well written and has the air of authority. For further references to
this article, see Letters 332 and 335.

I am very glad to hear of your child's convalescence— You are better off
than poor Moore—whose only little girl will I fear hardly recover & whose
long protracted suffering is a sad misfortune[1]—

I am very truly ys
Mary Shelley

ADDRESSED: John Bowring Esq/ 7 North Place/ Gray's Inn Lane. POSTMARKS:
(1) T.P/ Crawford St (2) 7.NIGHT.7/ 4.FE/ 1829. ENDORSED: Feby. 3,
1829/ Mary Shelley. ORIGINAL: Huntington Library (HM 2760); A.L.S.,
2 pp. 8vo, with seal. UNPRINTED and UNPUBLISHED. TEXT: From original
letter.

327. *To James Kenney*

Somerset Street, Portman Square,
Friday [1829–32]

Will you be so amiable as to indulge me with a night [? sight] of your
new piece.[2]

ORIGINAL: Owned by Walter T. Spencer, London, in 1937; A.L.S., 2 pp. 8vo.
UNPRINTED and UNPUBLISHED. TEXT: Quotation sent me by Spencer, who
would not permit me to copy the letter.

328. *To John Howard Payne*

[London] Monday [April 6, 1829]

May I ask you to use your influence for an opera box for next Thursday—
or an early succeeding night— You would highly oblige & please me—&
also if you would accompany us— I shall be at the Cottage[3] for the next
week—where I hope to see or hear from you

I was very sorry to find you called the other day when I was from home—
Will you try me again

Your
M S.

ADDRESS: John Howard Payne Esq/ 29 Arundel St./ Strand. POSTMARK: (1)
[C]rawford (2) 8.Morn/ 7.AP/ 1829. ORIGINAL: Huntington Library (HM
10796); A.L.S., 1 p. 8vo. UNPRINTED and UNPUBLISHED. TEXT: From original
letter.

329. *To Edward John Trelawny*[4]

London—April—1829

My dear Trelawny

Your letter reminded me of my deeds of omission and of not writing to

[1] Thomas Moore's child, Anastasia Mary, was born on March 16, 1813, and died on March 8,
1829. See Lord John Russell (ed.), *Memoirs, Journal, and Correspondence of Thomas Moore,*
Abridged Edition (London, Longman, Brown, Green, & Longmans, 1860), I, 337; VI, 18–22.
[2] Of the several plays by Kenney during Mary's residence in Somerset Street, it is impossible
to identify the one referred to here.
[3] Park Cottage, Paddington, the home of the Robinsons.
[4] Trelawny left England in January, 1829 (he was in Calais on January 8), and settled in
Florence, where Landor and Charles Armitage Brown were already. On March 11 he wrote to
Mary: "I am actually writing my own life [published as *The Adventures of a Younger Son*]. Brown

From the pencil sketch by Mary W. Shelley

you as I ought—and it assured me of your kind thoughts in that happy land, where, as Angels in heaven you can afford pity to us Arctic islanders— It is too bad, is it not? that when such a Paradise does exist as fair Italy—one should be chained here?— Without the infliction of much absolutely cold weather —I have never suffered a more ungenial winter—winter it is still—a cold east wind has prevailed for the last six weeks, making exercise in the open air a positive punishment— This is truly English! half a page about the weather —but here this subject has every importance—is it fine—you guess I am happy and enjoying myself—is it—as it always is—you know that one is fighting against a domestic enemy—which saps [at *crossed out*] the very foundation of pleasure.

I am glad that you are occupying yourself—and I hope that your two friends will not cease urging you till you really put to paper the strange wild adventures you recount so well. With regard to the other subject—you may guess, my dear Friend, that I have often thought—often done more than think on the subject There is nothing I shrink from more fearfully than publicity—I have too much of it—& what is worse I am forced by my hard situation to meet it in a thousand ways— Could you write my husband's life, without naming me it were something—but even then I should be terrified at the rousing the slumbering voice of the public—each critique, each mention of your work, might drag me forward— Nor indeed is it possible to write Shelley's life in that way. Many men have his opinions—none fearlessly and conscientiously act on them, as he did—it is his act that marks him—and that—You know me—or you do not, in which case I will tell you what I am—a silly goose—who far from wishing to stand forward to assert myself in any way, now that I am alone in the world, have but the desire to wrap night and the obscurity of insignificance around me. This is weakness—but I cannot help it—to be in print—the subject of *men's* observations—of the bitter hard world's commentaries, to be attacked or defended!—this ill becomes one who knows how little she possesses worthy to attract attention—and whose chief merit—if it be one —is a love of that privacy which no woman can emerge from without regret— Shelley's life must be written—I hope one day to do it myself, but it must not be published now— There are too many concerned to speak against him—

and Landor are spurring me on . . . moreover, I am commencing as a tribute of my great love for the memory of Shelley his life and moral character. . . . Do you approve of this? Will you aid in it? . . . Will you give documents? Will you write anecdotes? . . . if you in the least dislike it, say so, and there is an end of it."—Marshall, II, 192.

Upon Mary's refusal in the letter below, Trelawny made no immediate comment. But on [October 20, 1829] he wrote: "I am anything but satisfied with your reply to my request—regarding Shelley—and I must say your reasons for not doing so—are most unsatisfactory—mere evasion —had Shelley's *detractor* and your very good *friend* Tom Moore—made the request, I feel confident he would not have been so fobbed off—as is proved by your having aided him in Byron's memoirs— of which I shall speak in my Life, what I think I say and shall not hesitate to write."—Grylls, *Mary Shelley*, 217. (See Letter 346.)

Trelawny's plans to write Shelley's life, though suspended, resulted many years later in his *Recollections of Byron and Shelley* (1858), in the second edition of which (*Records*, 1878) he allowed himself to do irreparable wrong to the Mary Shelley he had once loved.

it is still too sore a subject— Your tribute of praise, in a way that cannot do harm, can be introduced into your own life— But remember, I pray for omission—for it is not that you will not be too kind too eager to do me more than justice— But I only seek to be forgotten—

Claire has written to you— She is about to return to Germany— She will I suppose explain to you the circumstances that make her return to the lady she was before with, desirable— She will go to Carlsbad and the baths will be of great service to her. Her health is improved—though very far from restored. For myself I am as usual, well in health—occupied—and longing for summer when I may enjoy the peace that alone is left [for] me— I am another person under the genial influence of the sun—I can live unrepining with no other enjoyment but the country made bright and cheerful by its beams— till then I languish. Percy is quite well—he grows very fast and looks very healthy—

It gives me great pleasure to hear from you, dear Friend—do write often— I have now answered your letter though I can hardly call this one—so you may very soon expect another— Take care of yourself— How are your dogs? & where is Roberts—have you given up all idea of shooting. I hear Medwin is a great man at Florence—so Pisa and economy are at an end— Adieu

Yours
M S.

[P.S., *above address on p. 1*] Direct to me at my Father's 44 Gower Place— Gower St. and to Claire at 5 Carmarthen St—Tottenham C^t Road

> ADDRESS: Edward Trelawny/ Ferma in Posta/ Firenze/ La Toscane, Italia
> [*In another hand, on back:*] Via Fonache/ 2578. POSTMARKS: (1) PONT/
> B[EA]UVOISIN (2) 12/ JUIN/ 1829 (3) GENOVA (4) 28/
> GI[UGN]O/ 1829. ORIGINAL: Keats-Shelley Memorial, Rome; A.L.S., 4 pp.
> 4to, with seal. PRINTED: Marshall, II, 192–94; *The Letters of Edward J.
> Trelawny,* edited by Forman, 118–19n (from Marshall, but less complete).
> TEXT: From original letter.

330. *To Sir John Bowring*

Friday [May 22, 1829]
33 Somerset St.
Portman Sq

My dear Sir

Can you tell me how I can obtain a German work called "Das Bild" by *Houwald*[1]—we have in vain tried to get it at the foreign booksellers—if we could only have the loan of it for a short time *immediately,* you would greatly oblige me by procuring it—

I trust you & your family are well

Yours truly
Mary Shelley

[1] Christoph Ernst Houwald (1778–1845), German dramatist and author. His *Das Bild* is described as one of several "Fate tragedies."

ADDRESSED: John Bowring Esq/ 7 North Place/ Gray's In[n Lane]. POST-MARKS: (1) T.P./ Duke St M.S (2) 10.F.NOON.10/ 23.MY/ 1829. EN-DORED: May 22 1829/ Mrs. Shelly. ORIGINAL: Huntington Library (HM 2761); A.L.S., 1 p. 8vo. UNPRINTED and UNPUBLISHED. TEXT: From original letter.

331. *To Sir Walter Scott**

London,
33 Somerset St., Portman Sq.,
25 May, 1829.

Sir

I have been encouraged by the kind politeness you have afforded to others, and by the indulgence with which I have been informed you have regarded some of my poor productions, to ask you if you could assist me in my present task.

I am far advanced in a romance whose subject is Perkin Warbeck. Of course you know that he visited the court of James IV and married the daughter of the Earl of Huntly. In consulting our historians as to his story, I have found the earlier ones replete with interesting anecdotes and documents entirely passed over by Hume &c and in the forgotten or neglected pages of English and Irish writers of a distant date I discover a glimmering of the truth about him, even more distinct than that afforded in the dissertations of the modern writers in favor of his pretentions. You are completely versed in the Antiquities of your country, and you would confer a high favor on me if you could point out any writer of its history—any document, anecdote or queer ballad connected with him generally unknown, which may have come to your knowledge. I have consulted as yet only Buchanan & Lyndsay—(the latter does not even allude to him in his history of the James's)—and among later writers Pinkerton.[1]

I hope you will forgive my troubling you—it is almost impertinent to say how foolish it appears to me that I should intrude on your ground, or to compliment one all the world so highly appretiates—but as every traveller when they visit the Alps, endeavours however imperfectly, to express their admiration in the Inn's Album, so it is impossible to address the Author of Waverly without thanking him for the delight and instruction derived from the inexhaustible source of his genius, and trying to express a part of the enthusiastic admiration his works inspire

I am, Sir
Your obt. Servant
Mary Shelley

ADDRESS: Sir Walter Scott, Bart.,/ Edinburgh. POSTMARK: May 27 1829. ORIGINAL: Sir Hugh Walpole, in the great Letter-Books of Sir Walter Scott (No. 18, ff.284–85), which will ultimately go to the National Library of

[1] George Buchanan (1506–82), *History of Scotland,* 1582 (written in Latin and translated several times before 1800). Robert Lindsay (?1500–?65), *The History of Scotland* (1436–1565), first published in 1728. John Pinkerton, *The History of Scotland from the Accession of the House of Stuart to that of Mary* (London, 1797, 2 vols.).

Scotland; A.L.S., 4 pp. 4to. PRINTED: Wilfred Partington, *Sir Walter's Post-Bag* 1932), 271 (omissions). TEXT: From copy made for me from the original letter by W. M. Parker.

332. *To Sir John Bowring**

Somerset St.
Monday [June 1, 1829]

My dear Sir

I am certainly a very wrong person to have delayed answering you so long — One reason is that I was out of town for a day or two— I now send the proof[1]— Thank you for your offer to breakfast with me— May I expect you next Saturday?—It will afford me great pleasure

I am truly yours
Mary Shelley

ENDORSED: June 1 1829/ Mary Shelly. ORIGINAL: Huntington Library (HM 2762); A.L.S., 1 p. 8vo. UNPRINTED and UNPUBLISHED. TEXT: From original letter.

333. *To Sir John Bowring**

Thursday [June 4, 1829]
Somerset St.—

My dear Sir

I am so very much indisposed that with great regret I am obliged to ask you to defer your promised visit till next week— May I expect you on Wednesday?—by that time surely I shall be quite well

It is too bad to be ill in summer and so to be deprived of my best pleasure— the enjoyment of warm weather—

Yours truly
Mary Shelley

ADDRESS: For/ John Bowring Esq/ 7 North Place —Gray's Inn Lane. POST-MARKS: (1) T.P/ [   ] (2) 7.NIGHT.7/ 4.JU/ 182[9]. ENDORSED: June 4 1829/ Mrs. Shelly. ORIGINAL: Huntington Library (HM 2763); A.L.S., 1 p. 8vo. UNPRINTED and UNPUBLISHED. TEXT: From original letter.

334. *To Frederic M. Reynolds**

Somerset St.
Tuesday [June 16, 1829]

Dear Fred—

It shall be as you please— I continue your debtor therefore until next year— I am a great deal better than when you called—tho' not yet quite strong

Yours ever
Mary Shelley

ADDRESS: For F. Mansel Reynolds, Esq/ 48 Warren St., Fitzroy Sq. POSTMARK: 17.JU/ 1829. ORIGINAL: British Museum (Add. MSS 27,925, ff.123–24); A.L.S., 1 p. 8vo. UNPRINTED and UNPUBLISHED. TEXT: From original letter.

[1] Of the article on "Modern Italy." See Letter 326, note 2.

335. *To Sir John Bowring**

33 Somerset St.
Wednesday [July 1, 1829]

My dear Sir

Ever since I last wrote I have been indisposed but I am now getting better — Will you let me avail myself of my convalescence by breakfasting with me on Saturday—or some morning next week which is convenient to you—

I am Yours truly
Mary Shelley

[P.S.] Do you know where I could get (in French) The History of the Court of Burgundy by M. de Barante[1]

[P.P.S.] I had written the enclosed when your note & cheque[2] came—so I must delay seeing you till you return—when both the weather and my health will be I hope better

I have L[ord] B[yron]'s letters safe. I meant & mean to give them you when I see you here[3]

What an excellent portrait there is of you in the Exhibition
Adieu

ADDRESSED: John Bowring Esq/ 7 North Place — Grays Inn Road. POSTMARKS: (1) T.P/ Duke St. M.S   (2) 2 A.NOON.2/ 2.JY/ 1829. ENDORSED: July 1, 1829/ Mrs. Shelley. ORIGINAL: Huntington Library (HM 2764); A.L.S., 2 pp. 8vo. UNPRINTED and UNPUBLISHED. TEXT: From original letter.

336. *To Edward John Trelawny*

33 Somerset St., Portman Sq.,
27 July [1829].

I gave your letter, my dear Trelawny, to Jane who will answer it—you have been so zealous, so kind, so dear a friend that you must not wonder that she should feel hurt at being (as she was) much passed over by you; the affectionate tone of your letters from Greece made her readily believe that you loved her as well as Edward— I confess I did not wonder at your not going there oftener; but the fact you had so often insisted upon to me, of your slight affection for her, was not for me to report—however the eagerness of your defence is complimentary and I suppose she is satisfied. I once almost deified Jane; and she poor girl suffers for my folly, for finding her very human, and having reason to complain of her failure in the most obvious duties of a friend, it is with reluctance I contemplate in her the destruction of my last [? desire] of happiness— I should love her better now, had I not loved her too well formerly.

Claire has written to you— I need say little about her— She returns to Dresden to an agreable situation and I envy any one who quits this sad land

1 Amable G. P. Brugière, Baron de Barante (1782–1866), *Histoire des ducs de Bourgogne de la Maison de Valois.*
2 For the article on "Modern Italy." (See Letter 326, note 2.)
3 See Letter 308.

too much not to congratulate her on her departure: for herself, surrounded by needy and in some cases unamiable relatives—she finds here not one of the necessary comforts of life—she began to vegetate, and to be content with vegetation—she is torn from this, and in society of persons agreable to her in Germany, will arrange a mode of life very far to be preferred to the one she is doomed to here.

For myself—I find little in life to please me—without exercising my affections I cannot be happy—and on every side I am disappointed— My boy grows and improves, and thus I have a consolation. But I am very weary— Thus scattered about the world, useless to others, a burthen to themselves, are human beings destined to be—who might be happy, did not a thousand circumstances—tyrannical passions, and want of sympathy prevent their ever uniting to any purpose.

You are unhappy, my dear Trelawny? How legibly was the existence of untold suffering written on your brow—and the coldness, and want of that zeal we all fondly hoped would shed forgotten sunshine over us, more from reserve on your part—this was not well— In a mere selfish point of view I wish you had been more confiding—and now in Italy in a land where my memory and fancy place Paradise, you are wretched— What is to be done? Once you loved me sufficiently to confide in me—that time I know and feel to be gone—at least such was the case in the winter. You distorted my motives —did not understand my position, and altogether I lost in your eyes during your last visit— You were quite in the wrong—I never was more worthy of your love and esteem—but blind miserable beings thus we grope in the dark we depend on each other yet we are each a mystery to the other—and the heart which should be in the hand of a friend, either shuns the contact, or is disdainfully rejected. I neither like life—nor the mechanism of society—nor the modes in which human beings present themselves—but I cannot mould them to my will, and in making up my mind merely to take them as they are, enthusiasm fades, and cold reality makes me each day more willing to quit a scene in which I am an alien.

Can nothing be done, my friend, to diminish the causes of your unhappiness? You are occupied by writing— I know too well that that excitement is the parent of pain rather than pleasure.

Did you not receive a letter from me in answer to yours concerning Shelley's life.[1] I sent one. I do not wish at present to renew the recollection of the past— Your recollections of our lost one will be precious as a record of his merit—but I am averse to having those mingled with a history which will be the subject of cavill. I hope one day to write his life myself—not to be published in my lifetime or even my child's. Meanwhile we neither desire the

---

[1] Trelawny did receive the letter. On July 3 he wrote to Claire: "Mary has written me a letter which I have just received, —with a good deal of mawkish cant —as to her love of retirement —opinion of the world —and a deal of namby-pamby stuff—as different from her real character and sentiments as Hell is from Helicon."—*The Letters of Edward J. Trelawny*, 126.

pity nor justice of the few attended as they would be by the barking and railing of his enemies, and the misjudgment of the multitude. With regard to letters it seems that an unfortunate mistake caused those I had preserved previous to our visiting Italy to be destroyed. The others are almost entirely descriptions and I mean to publish them together with the rest of his prose works at a future day. I am eager to hear of the progress of your "Life."

My very dear Friend, I wish some kind spirit would visit you with happiness— I wish that I could influence your life sufficiently to render it less painful. All this is vain. Write to me, I entreat you

Yours,
M. S.

[P.S.] The Cottage girls congratulate themselves that the kindness they were eager to shew to a friend of mine was not thrown away on an ingrate— they desire to live in your remembrance— You can partly repay their attentions to you by showing some [?kindness] to their brother George who will shortly visit Florence—the sons of this family are people with whom I have little intercourse notwithstanding my affection for their sisters still on the present occasion I should be glad that George met with civilties from you.

ADDRESS: Edward J. Trelawny Esq/ Ferma in Posta/ Firenze/ Florence. POSTMARK: 10 AGOSTO. ORIGINAL: Sir John Shelley-Rolls. UNPRINTED and UNPUBLISHED. TEXT: From copy made by Sir John Shelley-Rolls.

337. *To Sir John Bowring**

Somerset St—
29 August [1829]

My dear Sir

It will give me great pleasure to prove to you that I am well visible & at home— Will you breakfast with me on Saturday— Should you welcome an Article on the "Loves of the Poets"?[1]

I am truly ys
M Shelley

ADDRESS: For/ John Bowring Esq/ 5 Millman St. POSTMARKS: (1) T.P./ Duke St M.S (2) [ ].A.NOON.2/ 1.SP/ 1829. ENDORSED: Sep 1 1829/ Mary Shelley.

[1] Evidently Bowring did, for in the *Westminster Review,* No. XXII (October, 1829) 472–77, is a review of *The Loves of the Poets,* By the Author of the "Diary of an Ennuyée (2 vols., Colburn), which is unmistakably by Mary Shelley. The subject was one that naturally aroused Mary's deepest emotions. Mary quotes from Shelley's translation of the *Symposium* (eleven lines) and his "Essay on Love" (fifteen lines). The following paragraph is worth preserving:

"What is a Poet? Is he not that which wakens melody in the silent chords of the human heart? A light which arrays in splendor things and thoughts which else were dim in the shadow of their own insignificance? His soul is like one of the pools in the Ilex woods of the Maremma, it reflects the surrounding universe, but it beautifies, groupes, and mellows their tints, making a little world within itself, the copy of the outer one; but more entire, more faultless. But above all, a poet's soul is Love; the desire of sympathy is the breath that inspires his lay, while he lavishes on the sentiment and its object, his whole treasure-house of resplendant imagery, burning emotion, and ardent enthusiasm. He is the mirror of nature, reflecting her back ten thousand times more lovely; what then must not his power be, when he adds beauty to the most perfect thing in nature —even Love."

ORIGINAL: Huntington Library (HM 2765); A.L.S., 1 p. 8vo. UNPRINTED and UNPUBLISHED. TEXT: From original letter.

338. *To William Whitton**

33 Somerset St.
1 September, 1829.

My dear Sir,

May I send the receipt for £75 to have the cheque in return?[1]

I was very much pleased these holydays to find Percy in every respect improved—his disposition appears to me so tractable that I think that at no time will he occasion us any trouble—but on the contrary be every thing his family could wish. I was half in hopes that Sir Timothy might have taken more notice of him during these holydays—for he grows a big boy now— He was never in better health.

I am, Sir,
Yr. Obly.
Mary W. Shelley

ADDRESS: William Whitton Esq./ 18 Bedford Row. ORIGINAL: Sir John Shelley-Rolls. UNPRINTED and UNPUBLISHED. TEXT: From copy made by Sir John Shelley-Rolls.

339. *To John Murray**

12 November, 1829
33 Somerset St.
Portman Sq.

My dear Sir

I am sorry to hear from Mr. Moore that you decline my Romance—because I would rather that you published it, than any other person.

I can assure you I feel all the kindness of your message to me through Mr. Moore. Do you remember speaking to me about a Life of the Empress Josephine, Mme de Stael, &c.? When I have got free from my present occupation, I will communicate with you on the subject, and I hope that by some plan, either of my writing for your Family Library, or in some other way, to liquidate my debt—or I must do it even in a more usual manner— I am aware of your kindness concerning it, but I could not consent that an act of civility on my part to Mr. Moore should be brought forward as cancelling my debt to you—besides it would make me break a vow I made never to make money of my acquaintance with Lord Byron—his ghost would certainly come and taunt me if I did. This does not decrease but rather enhance the value I have for your kind intention.

I am, dear Sir
Yours obliged
Mary Shelley

ORIGINAL: Sir John Murray; A.L.S., 4 pp. 12mo (4½ x 3½ inches). PRINTED: S. Smiles, *A Publisher and His Friends* (1891), II, 311. TEXT: From original letter.

[1] With the June quarter Mary's allowance had been increased to £300 per annum.

340. *To William Whitton*

33 Somerset St., Portman Sq.
2 December, 1829.

My dear Sir,

I shall send on Friday with your permission my receipt for £75—in exchange for your cheque.

I have the pleasure to tell you that Percy is quite well— I have directed that he shall attend the lessons in drilling which are given at his school—the Dancing Master was not enough to cure a stoop he was getting—but the sergeant has done him already a great deal of good— I think Sir Timothy would find him improved—he is really very good and above all tractable—which is not quite the virtue of his father's family.

I am, dear Sir,
Yours Obliged,
Mary Shelley

[P.S.] I hope Sir Timothy is well—it would be very kind if he permitted me to see him when he next comes to town.

> ADDRESS: William Whitton Esq./ 18 Bedford Row. ORIGINAL: Sir John Shelley-Rolls. PRINTED: Ingpen, *Shelley in England,* 603 (quot., 3 lines). TEXT: From copy made by Sir John Shelley-Rolls.

341. *To John Murray*

Monday, [? December 7, 1829][1]
33 Somerset St.

My dear Sir

Permit me to ask you to lend me for a few days Washington Irving's last exquisitely written and interesting work—the Conquest of Granada—I want to consult it, and have been disappointed in having it from Hookham— No book has delighted me so much for a very long time— Your kind offer with regard to books has made me take this liberty— I hope I do not do wrong

Yours obliged
Mary Shelley

> ADDRESS: John Murray/ 50 Albemarle St. ORIGINAL: Sir John Murray; A.L.S., 1 p. 8vo. (Letter bears the date Dec. 7, 1827, in another hand; but this is certainly wrong.) UNPRINTED and UNPUBLISHED. TEXT: From original letter.

342. *To [Addressee Unknown]**

33 Somerset St.
Wednesday [1829–33]

My dear Sir

I am only now recovering from the indisposition which prevented me from seeing you when you did me the favor to call—but I am well enough to

---

[1] The MS has the date "Dec. 7, 1827" in another hand. The year at least is certainly wrong. *The Conquest of Granada* was published by Murray in April, 1829.

see you, and shall be very glad whenever you are good enough to spend an hour here

Yours truly

Mary Shelley

ORIGINAL: Not traced. In 1865 it was in the Collection of John Watkins, Esq; A.L.S., 1 p. 8vo. PRINTED: In facsimile as No. 117 in the *Autographic Mirror,* August 26, 1865. (A biographical sketch of Mary is on 37; no page number for the facsimile.) TEXT: From facsimile of original letter in the *Autographic Mirror.*

343. *To Thomas Jefferson Hogg*

[London, ? November 1827–April 1833]

[Original letter owned by Captain R. J. J. Hogg. See Letters 6–16.]

344. *To Henry Colburn**

33 Somerset St.

Portman Sq.

Saturday, 12 Dec. 1829.

My dear Sir

You were so good as to say when you sent for my MS. that I might count upon an *immediate arrangement*—this was several weeks ago—the work is still in progress—that is—copying—it was *written* when I first communicated with you— I hope no circumstances have made you hesitate about becoming my publisher—I trust there is no reason for that— One is an bad judge oneself—but I should guess that for a thousand reasons, there is a better chance for "Perkin Warbeck"—than for the "Last Man"— I am less anxious about the terms & time of payment, than to be made secure that I may depend upon you as my publisher— If you have made up your mind on that subject—and I believe that you must—& in the *affirmative*—only have the goodness to send me a line to say so—and, as such may be your wish, we will defer all consideration of price &c till the MS. is perfectly finished—which will be before long—it has been somewhat interrupted by a severe cold

I am   Ys. Obly

Mary Shelley

ADDRESS: Henry Colburn Esq/ 8 New Burlington St. ORIGINAL: Owned by Maggs Brothers in July, 1937; A.L.S., 2 pp. 4to. UNPRINTED and UNPUBLISHED. TEXT: From original letter.

345. *To [Charles Ollier]**

[London] Saturday Evening [? December 12, 1829]

My dear Sir

After all *this* was forgotten—I am not sorry as it affords me an opportunity to say a few words—as perhaps I was misunderstood— I should certainly like to come to an *immediate agreement*—indeed without that I should not have spirits to proceed but I should not desire any payment until *all* is written—nor the whole payment even then—it might be arranged as Colburn liked—

This would make the first payment to be made I should imagine at the end of this month—

I must add a few words to thank you for your consideration & kindness— I am the opposite of a business person and your interesting yourself in this matter is tenfold more valuable to me— I commit it to you in the full assurance that you will do your best—*your* best being *the* best—

Do I pay a compliment? O no! I only give trouble— But you will excuse me

Yours obliged
M Shelley

ORIGINAL: Sylva Norman, Oxford; A.L.S., 3 pp. 3¾ x 6 inches). UNPRINTED and UNPUBLISHED. TEXT: From original letter.

346. *To Edward John Trelawny**

33 Somerset St.
15 Decr., 1829.

My very dear Trelawny,

Your letter would have occasioned me a great deal of pain had it not relieved me from my painful suspense about yourself— Is it true that I have been remiss? I thought I had been better than you by two letters—but I write a good deal and get as weary of the sight of a pen that I know I do neglect writing when I ought—besides—however a page of excuses would be ridiculous— I however loved—I do love you—write or not this is one of the warmest sentiments of my heart—and is it not better to feel this than to write twenty letters— Ah have pity on my miserable clouded faculties—free and engaging beneath an Italian sky you cannot participate our northern island miseries—not to talk of a climate which has outdone itself this year in rain and fogs. The peculiar situation of my relations is heavy on me—my spirits are depressed by care and I have no resource save in what sunshine my friends afford me—afford me you a little, Dearest friend—seal up words sweeter than vernal breezes—flatteries if you will—warm tokens of kindliness—I need them — I have been so long accustomed to turn to you as the spot whence distant, but certain good must emanate that a chill from you is indeed painful— I will be a good girl in return and write often.

Your last letter[1] was not at all kind—you are angry with me   you speak of evasions— What do you ask, what do I refuse? Let me write to you as to my own heart and do not shew this letter to any one. You talk of writing Shelley's life and ask me for materials.—Shelley's life as far as the public had to do with it consisted of very few events and these are publickly known— The private

[1] Dated October 20, 1829. See Letter 329, note 4.

events were sad and tragical. How would you relate them? as Hunt has,[2] slurring over the real truth—Wherefore write fiction? and the truth—any part of it is hardly for the rude cold world to handle— His merits are acknowledged—his virtues—to bring forward actions which right or wrong, and that would be a matter of dispute, were in their results tremendous, would be to awaken calumnies and give his enemies a voice— For myself—am I to be left out in this life?—if so half my objections, more than half, would disappear —for with me would depart that portion which is most painful— I do not see what you could make of his life without me—but if that is your intention tell me—and we will see what can be done— I have made it my earnest request to all who have meddled with our Shelley to leave me out—they have assented and I consider myself fortunate— I fear publicity—as to my giving those materials for L[ord] B[yron]'s life I thought I think I did right— I think I have achieved a great good by it— I wish it not to be kept secret— Decidedly I am averse to its being published, for it would destroy me to be brought forward in print. I commit myself on this point to your generosity—I confided this fact to you—as I would any thing I did—being my dearest friend and had no idea that I was to find in you a harsh censor and public denouncer— There was something false in our mutual position when you were in England— God knows I do not accuse you of being a worldling—but—alas! of course I know any, every fault must be mine—but are we not shall we not ever be friends?

Did I uphold and dared [*sic*] Medwin?[3]—I thought that I had always disliked him— I am sure I thought him a great annoyance and he was always borrowing crowns which he never meant to pay and we could ill spare— He was Jane's friend more than any ones—to be sure, we did not desire a duel nor an horsewhipping—and Lord Byron and Mrs. Beauclerk worked hard to promote peace[4]— Can any thing be as frightful as the account you give? Poor Mrs. Medwin—I shall be very glad to hear that you have done any thing for her—you [can] if any body can— Claire is at Dresden as of course you know —she says they have had fine weather ever since her arrival—we have nothing but bad since her departure—she complains that she has not heard from you— Charles Clairmont her brother after an unsuccessful struggle here has returned to Vienna— The Hunts are at Brompton she has just had another child— Jane went to see them the other day—and he called at my father's—he is out of spirits— Your love Caroline Beauclerk married the other day—well I believe— The pretty Cottagers are charmed by your remembrance— The little Invisibility preserves the little red arrangements among her bijouterie— Jane

---

2 In *Lord Byron and Some of His Contemporaries*, 1828. (See Letter 225, note 1.)

3 Trelawny had written (October 20, 1829): "You used to like him [Medwin] and thought me rash and violent in asserting him to be a coward, a liar, and a scoundrel—nevertheless he has proved himself all these." He goes on to say that Medwin had dissipated his wife's fortune of £10,000 and that she had called upon him for help and advice. (Grylls, *Mary Shelley*, 217–18.)

4 This is very mysterious.

is well— Nothing can be more stupid than London. Miss Fanny Kemble's success[5] is our only event—twelve guineas have been offered vainly for a private box on her nights— But while fog and ennui possesses London, despair and convulsion reign over the country—some change some terrible event is expected—rents falling—money not to be got—every one poor and fearful— Will any thing come of it— Was not the panic and poverty of past years as great— Yet if parliament meet as they say it will in January—something is feared—something about to be done—besides fishing in Virginia Water and driving about in a pony phaeton.

I should be very glad to hear more of your child[6]— I had thoughts—I desired to make an offer—but I dread a denial—and besides Italy is better than England for a child of the south—is she not lovely, delightful, full of sensibility.

Adieu, my dear friend—have we quarrelled are we reconciled?— What is it— I know little more than that I have never ceased being warmly attached to you and that I am always

Affectionately Yours,
M. W. Shelley

ADDRESS: Edward Trelawny Esq./ Ferma in Posta/ Firenze/ Florence—L'Italie. ORIGINAL: Sir John Shelley-Rolls. PRINTED: Marshall, II, 195 (extracts); *The Letters of Edward J. Trelawny,* edited by Forman, 119n (from Marshall). TEXT: From copy made by Sir John Shelley-Rolls.

347. *To John Murray**

33 Somerset St.
Sunday Evening [December, 1829]

My dear Sir

Will you forward this to Mr. Moore.[1] I do not know his exact address—and you will have opportunities of sending it or getting it franked—if a member be to be found during Christmas— I am rather in haste as it is an answer to a question concerning THE "Life"—which I am delighted to hear is on the point of appearing—

I am sorry that I am at your Antipodes—especially as I do not gain in climate— I am sure that I am at the North Pole—but the South pole is also very cold— I would make an appointment to prevent the chance of your finding me not at home—but it might be inconvenient—as I sometimes wander into your Antarctic region I will call and ask if you are at leisure— After all—as I am not idle yet, except that I should be glad to see you—nothing is lost by the "line" between us being yet uncrossed

A thousand thanks for "Granada"—the world is a common place—a buying

[5] Fanny Kemble's first appearance as an actress (Covent Garden, October 5, 1829, as Juliet) created a sensation. She was a tremendous success throughout the season.

[6] Zella, who arrived in Italy from Corfu about July 27, 1829.

[1] Moore left London on November 28, returned on December 20, left again on the twenty-fourth, and apparently did not return again until about February 1.

and selling—& not even a well dressed world—not to take interest in the romantic silken-suited Cavaliers of Andalusia—

I am yours obliged
Mary Shelley

[P.S.] Do you expect Mr. Moore in town *very* soon again—

> ORIGINAL: Sir John Murray; A.L.S., 3 pp. 8vo. PRINTED: S. Smiles, *A Publisher and His Friends* (1891), II, 310 (quot., 2 lines). TEXT: From original letter.

348. *To Charles Ollier*

Thursday [? December 31, 1829]
Somerset St.

My dear Sir

Do you imagine that I have heard from Mr. Colburn or Mr. Bentley? O,
no! I hear nothing from any body—& am annoyed to death— So much to
excite your good nature—to which I trust

Yours obliged
M S.

[P.S.] Is the Exclusives[1] come out

> ADDRESS: Charles Ollier Esq/ 5 Maida Hill. ORIGINAL: Owned by B. F. Stevens & Brown, Ltd., London, in 1936; A.L.S., 1 p. 8vo. UNPRINTED and UNPUB-LISHED. TEXT: From original letter

349. *To John Murray*

Somerset St.,
Saturday [? 1830]

[*Summary*] Mary is very sorry she was prevented from calling this morning as she intended. She wants to see Murray for three minutes, though she
is not in a hurry to do so. She will take a chance on finding him in some morning early next week.

> ORIGINAL: Sir John Murray; A.L.S., 1 p. 8vo, addressed. UNPRINTED and UN-PUBLISHED. SUMMARY: From original letter.

350. *To [Charles Ollier]**

33 Somerset St.
5 Jan. 1830

My dear Sir

You brought me two propositions from Mr. Colburn concerning my book
—one concerned the dividing of profits— I confess that this does not please
me, for I am no woman of business—

The other proposal was to purchase my manuscript for £150— I accept
this proposal—and wish to know how soon Mr. Colburn will go to the press—

---

1 *The Exclusives,* a novel by Lady Charlotte Maria Bury (1830, 3 vols.).

You had better call on me to make the agreement— I should be glad that as
little delay as possible should occur—

With many excuses for the trouble I give you—

I am Yours obliged

Mary Shelley

[P.S.] My father has seen Mr. Colburn on the subject—and he received
a letter from him about it yesterday— But the modifications occasioned by
this interview none of them please me so well as the one made through you
which I accept—

Nevertheless this one is sufficiently unfavorable—but I believe I know **Mr.**
Colburn enough to be satisfied that if the book succeed far beyond his expectation he will take his mistake into consideration

This will make however no part of the agreement which will simply be
for the sale of Poor Perkin Warbeck for £150—

ORIGINAL: Owned by Myers & Co., London, in January 1939; A.L.S., 4 pp. 8vo.
UNPRINTED and UNPUBLISHED. TEXT: From original letter.

351. *To Sir John Bowring**

33 Somerset St [January 7, 1830]

My dear Sir

I have a great horror of my name being in public—even the select public
of an Album—but I could not refuse you—& to imitate your other contributors
I have added some nonsense (the addition is an imitation not the nonsense)
to my *sign manual*

I half wished to have offered an article on Irving's Granada but thought
you would accomplish this—for the next number *che dice?* I admire it excessively[1]

I have lost your note after having glanced at it once only—but I think
there was no other subject mentioned Welcome home—from the north[2]
one may say this—from any other part of the world what horror to return to
this region affreux

Yours Ever

M S.

ADDRESSED: For/ Doctor Bowring/ &c &c/ 2 Wellington St. POSTMARKS: (1)
T.P/ Duke St M.S (2) 10.F.NOON.10/ 8.J[A]/ 183[0]. ENDORSED: Jany 7
1830/ Mary Shelley. ORIGINAL: Huntington Library (HM 2766); A.L.S., 1 p.
8vo. UNPRINTED and UNPUBLISHED. TEXT: From original letter.

352. *To Charles Ollier*

33 Somerset St.

14 Janry., 1830.

My dear Sir

I do not hear from you I suppose because you deem all things settled—

[1] No article on Irving appeared in the *Westminster Review* for 1830.
[2] Bowring had been in Denmark.

Things have been delayed so long that I now want money— I have promised
to pay a Christmas bill at the end of this week and it breaks my heart not to
keep such a promise— Will you get £50 from Colburn—the Manuscript
[of *Perkin Warbeck*] is ready for the printer—

Yours obliged
M Shelley

ADDRESS: For Charles Ollier Esq/ 5 Maida Hill/ Paddington. ORIGINAL:
Bodleian Library (MS Shelley Adds. d.5 ff.87–88); A.L.S., 1 p. 8vo.
PRINTED: *Bodleian Quarterly Record*, VIII, No. 95 (1937), 416. TEXT: From
original letter.

353. *To W. Galignani**

33 Somerset St.
London
15 Jan. 1830[1]

Mrs. Shelley is sorry she troubled Mr. Galignani about the little engraved
likeness of Shelley[2] for the Paris edition of the Poems—but she could not help
thinking it would have been better to have sent her a proof of Mr. Wedgwood's engraving—when she could have pointed out its defects as a likeness
of her husband—

It may be that the small pencil sketch was deficient in artistic merit—but
at least it bore—in her opinion a likeness to the original—

If the engraver will refer again to it he will perceive that in his copy he
has *closed* the lips and so given them a thick appearance entirely out of character—

Mrs. S[helley] mentions this detail particularly in order to prevent its possible repetition on a larger scale—

ORIGINAL: Stark Collection, University of Texas; A.L. (in 3rd person), 3 pp.
8vo. PRINTED: W. E. Peck, *Shelley: His Life and Work* (1927), II, 442. TEXT:
From original letter.

354. *To John Murray*

33 Somerset St.
Portman Sq.
19 Jan., [1830]

My dear Sir

Except the occupation of one or two annoyances, I have done nothing but
read since I got Lord Byron's Life[3]—

I have no pretensions to being a critic—yet I know infinitely well what
pleases me— Not to mention the judicious arrangement and happy *tact* displayed by Mr. Moore, which distinguish this book—I must say a word concerning the style, which is elegant and forcible. I was particularly struck by

1 Only the date is at the end of the letter.
2 See Letter 324.
3 Volume I was published on January 15, 1830.

the observations on Lord Byron's character before his departure to Greece—
and on his return. There is strength and richness as well as sweetness—

The great charm of the work to me, and it will have the same for you, is
that the Lord Byron I find there is our Lord Byron—the fascinating—faulty—
childish—philosophical being—daring the world—docile to a private circle—
impetuous and indolent—gloomy and yet more gay than any other. I live with
him again in these pages—getting reconciled (as I used in his lifetime) to those
waywardnesses which annoyed me when he was away, through the delightful & buoyant tone of his conversation and manners—

His own letters and journals mirror himself as he was, and are invaluable.
There is something cruelly kind in this single volume. When will the next
come? impatient before how tenfold now am I so.

Among its many other virtues this book is *accurate* to a miracle. I have
not stumbled on one mistake with regard either to time place or feeling.

> I am dear Sir,
> Your obt. & obliged Servant
> Mary Shelley

ORIGINAL: Sir John Murray; A.L.S., 4 pp. 12 mo. PRINTED: S. Smiles, *A Publisher and His Friends* (1891), II, 318–19. TEXT: From original letter.

355. *To John Murray*

> 33 Somerset St.
> Wednesday [January 20, 1830]

[*Summary*] Mary asks Murray if he would advance money on a bill Colburn had given her in payment [for *Perkin Warbeck*]. It is the first she ever
got, and she does not know a thing about bills. "As if I could do anything
with a Bill! . . . Before he paid me in a gentlemanly way with a cheque—I
mean as a gentleman should pay a *woman*. I dare say gentlemen have Bills
among one another." She meant to send this note with the former, but has
just received the bill.

ORIGINAL: Sir John Murray; A.L.S., 4 pp. 12 mo. (The date on the letter,
January 23, is in another hand and is certainly wrong, as the letter of Monday,
January 25, shows.) PRINTED: A 3-line quot. in Grylls, *Mary Shelley*, 212.
SUMMARY: From original letter. Quotation from Grylls, *Mary Shelley*.

356. *To John Murray**

> Monday 25 Jan. [1830]
> 33 Somerset St.

My dear Sir

A thousand thanks—   I return the bill—it is ridiculous that I should be so
ignorant of the forms of their affairs.

My book is called "Perkin Warbeck"—I believe it will go to the press immediately—& I believe it is to appear on the first of March—at least I have
[been] promised this—

I have written one or two observations on his book which I should be glad if you would forward to Mr. Moore by the first occasion

I am dear Sir

Yours truly

Mary Shelley

ORIGINAL: Sir John Murray; A.L.S., 2 pp. 12 mo. UNPRINTED and UNPUBLISHED. TEXT: From original letter.

357. *To John Murray**   Somerset St.
Monday [January 25, 1830]

My dear Sir

    I am sorry to trouble you but will you send me back my letter to Mr. Moore — I have heard from him—and do not wish it to go—send it by the 2d post—

I am dear Sir

Yours obliged

M Shelley

ADDRESS: John Murray Esq/ 50 Albermarle St. POSTMARK: 4.EVEN/ 26.JA/ 1830. ORIGINAL: Sir John Murray; A.L.S., 1 p. 8vo. UNPRINTED and UNPUBLISHED. TEXT: From original letter.

358. *To John Murray*

Somerset St.

Tuesday Evening [January 26, 1830]

[*Summary*] Mary asks Murray to send back her letter to Moore[1] enclosed in her letter of the day before and which she had asked Murray to forward. Now she does not wish it sent. Her father is delighted with Moore's book [*Life of Byron*], as "indeed who is not." He likes particularly the beautiful account of "the first acquaintance between Lord Byron & Mr. Moore."

ORIGINAL: Sir John Murray; A.L.S., 3 pp. 12mo. UNPRINTED and UNPUBLISHED. SUMMARY: From original letter.

359. *To William Whitton**   33 Somerset St.
1 March 1830

My dear Sir,

    I will send a receipt tomorrow in exchange for the cheque.

    Percy is quite well— I hope this spring he will see Sir Timothy perhaps more of him [*sic*]—and if Sir Timothy comes to town, I trust to your kindness, if possible, to obtain an interview for me with him.

I am, Sir,

Yr. Obliged

Mary Shelley

ORIGINAL: Sir John Shelley-Rolls. UNPRINTED and UNPUBLISHED. TEXT: From copy made by Sir John Shelley-Rolls.

[1] Mary evidently forgot that she had already written Murray on the subject.

360. *To John Murray*
33 Somerset St.
March 5 [1830].

[*Summary*] Mary had written to a friend in Paris about the possibilities of getting materials there on Madame de Stäel. The friend replied that M. Benjamin Constant will gladly supply her with what materials he can, in the little time he can snatch from his pressing political engagements. He will, moreover, give her an introduction to the duc de Broglie, Mme. de Stäel's son-in-law. Materials for a life of Empress Josephine are so abundant that all she will need to do is cull them.

"This is written under the idea that I shall visit Paris—but I trust the best part of the information will be attainable without that journey." Murray had said that Sir James MacIntosh had letters that he might let her use.

"At present after neglecting my book—Colburn is in a great hurry to get it out—so I shall be very busy for two or three weeks after which time I will see you."

Mary is impatient for the second volume of Moore's *Life of Byron*.

ORIGINAL: Sir John Murray; A.L.S., 4 pp. 12 mo. UNPRINTED and UNPUB-
LISHED. SUMMARY: From original letter.

361. *To William Whitton**
33 Somerset St., Portman Sq.,
24 May, 1830.

Dear Sir,

Hearing that Sir Timothy is in town, I cannot help requesting to see him — I send you my note which will you be so good as to let him have—it contains simply this request— I am sorry that Lady Shelley has not seen my son either this year or last— As Percy grows up, it would be of great benefit to him, surely, to be in more frequent communication with his father's family. He is getting a big boy now—and as it is more than probable that there will be no change in his situation for years—I feel anxious that he should not be always a stranger with those who have in reality the direction of his education.

Permit me to ask you to interfere in my favor—and if you do not find Sir Timothy wholly unwilling, to do the kind office of inducing him to receive me.

I am, dear Sir,
Yr. Obly.
M. W. Shelley

ORIGINAL: Sir John Shelley-Rolls. UNPRINTED and UNPUBLISHED. TEXT: From
copy made by Sir John Shelley-Rolls.

362. *To Sir Timothy Shelley*
33 Somerset St.
24 May, 1830.

Sir,

Permit me very sincerely to thank you for your kindness to my son. Hearing that you are in town I feel as if I should fail in a duty, if I did not solicit permission to wait on you. I cannot express the pleasure it would give me to see you. It appeared to me, at one time, from something Mr. Peacock said, that you were not averse to it, and indeed it is this that encourages me to make the request—for I should be very sorry to press any gratification of my own that would annoy you. It appears to me that as Percy grows older, much good would result to him from my having a more frequent communication with you about him—and I trust that since my return to England, I have proved in every way that his interests and welfare are the only objects of my life.

> I am, Sir,
> Your obedient Servant and daughter-in-law,
> M. W. Shelley

ADDRESS: For/ Sir Tim^thy Shelley Bart. ORIGINAL: Sir John Shelley-Rolls. UN-PRINTED and UNPUBLISHED. TEXT: From copy made by Sir John Shelley-Rolls.

363. *To John Murray*

33 Somerset St., Portman Sq.,
May 25 [1830]

[*Summary*] Mary asks Murray to return by the bearer her father's MS,[1] which Murray had had for a good while. She had hoped that his delay in answering indicated his intention to publish.

"Mr. Moore told me that you would soon communicate with me on the subject of the proposed life of Mme. de Staël. To make it at all *perfect,* I should fear that a visit to Paris is almost necessary—   At all events I should be very glad to hear from you about it."

ORIGINAL: Sir John Murray; A.L.S., 3 pp. 12mo. UNPRINTED and UNPUBLISHED. SUMMARY: From original letter.

364. *To William Whitton**

33 Somerset St.
2 June, 1830.

My dear Sir,

I will send my receipt tomorrow in exchange for the Cheque for my quarter.

> Yours Obly.
> M. W. Shelley

ADDRESS: William Whitton Esq./ 18 Bedford Row. ENDORSED: Sent Check for 75 in Letter left by Mr. Pater 15th. ORIGINAL: Sir John Shelley-Rolls. UN-PRINTED and UNPUBLISHED. TEXT: From copy made by Sir John Shelley-Rolls.

365. *To William Whitton**

33 Somerset St.
14 June 1830.

My dear Sir,

I am afraid by some mistake you have not received my note—   My re-

---

[1] Of *Thoughts on Man* (published in 1831). See Godwin's letter to Mary, April 15, 1830, in Marshall, II, 233–34.

ceipt has been for some time in the hands of your Clerk— As I understand that you return to town tomorrow—may I ask you to send me the cheque.

My son's holydays commence on Wednesday— Mr. Lawrence strongly advised me to take him to the sea side this summer, and as my time is up in my present abode, I mean next week to go to a sea port[1] for the six weeks he will pass with me— Your absence from town perhaps prevented your receiving my previous note.

I am, dear Sir,

Yrs. Obly.

M. W. Shelley

ORIGINAL: Sir John Shelley-Rolls. UNPRINTED and UNPUBLISHED. TEXT: From copy made by Sir John Shelley-Rolls.

366. *To Miss Maria Jane Jewsbury**[2]

33 Somerset St.

Portman Square

16 June—1830

I have been very much flattered, My dear Madam, by Mr. Rothwell,[3] who assures me that you are good enough to desire my acquaintance. As your stay in town is so short, I have been induced to believe that you would waive ceremony, and do me the pleasure of drinking tea with me either this evening or tomorrow. May I expect you?—I enclose the autograph of Mr. Shelley's handwriting which Mr. Rothwell tells me your sister wishes to have. I hope your sister will do me the favor of accompanying you.

I am dear Madam

Your Obt. Servant

Mary W. Shelley

ENDORSED: This interview was brought on by R[othwell] having overestimated the force of an expression—but it is only just to say the [*illegible*] note to Mrs. Jameson conveyed my real impression of Mrs. S———. The evening was divided between them—the most interesting of my [*word illegible*]. ORIGINAL: Historical Society of Pennsylvania, Philadelphia; A.L.S., 2 pp. 8vo. UNPRINTED and UNPUBLISHED. TEXT: From original letter.

367. *To John Murray*

Park Cottage, Paddington,

Aug. 9, 1830.

[*Summary*] Mary had now returned to town and would like to discuss with Murray some work she might write for his Family Library in order to repay his £100 loan to her and to earn additional money. The work, as Murray said, must be *amusing* as well as instructive. Murray had mentioned a life of

[1] Mary's journal for June 30: "I go to Southend for a month with Percy." She went before the thirtieth, as the next sentence tells us she had been back to London once.

[2] Miss Jewsbury (1800–33) was a writer. Her younger sister, Geraldine, was (later) a novelist.

[3] Richard Rothwell (1800–68), R. H. A., painted a portrait of Mary in 1841. It is now in the National Portrait Gallery.

Madam de Staël, which appealed to Mary very much. She could go to Paris and get new material from M. B. Constant & others. Other possibilities were a life of Mahomet, Conquests of Mexico & Peru. The work most attractive to her is a history of manners and literature of England from Queen Anne to the French Revolution, from Pope to H. Walpole. Later she might write a similar book on Continental manners and literature. Someone had suggested The Lives of the English Philosophers, "but this would hardly be so amusing."

She is relatively unoccupied now, and would like to get busy at something & make some money.

[P.S.] Have any copies of Moore's 2nd vol. of Byron been made up? She is "not a little anxious to see it."

> POSTMARK: 7 Night/ 10.AU/ 1830. ENDORSED: The last suggestion capital, if Mrs. S. be capable of undertaking it. ORIGINAL: Sir John Murray; A.L.S., 3 pp. 4to, addressed. UNPRINTED and UNPUBLISHED. SUMMARY: From original letter.

368. *To William Whitton*

> Park Cottage, Paddington.
> 1 September, 1830.

My dear Sir,

I shall send tomorrow, the receipt for the cheque, which you will oblige me by giving sealed up to the bearer.

I hope you are well. Percy has come back in the best possible health from our excursion to the Sea Side. You would very much oblige me by letting me know when it is probable that Sir Timothy will visit town.

> I am,
> Yr. Obly.
> M. W. Shelley

> ORIGINAL: Sir John Shelley-Rolls. UNPRINTED and UNPUBLISHED. TEXT: From copy made by Sir John Shelley-Rolls.

369. *To John Murray*

> Park Cottage, Paddington,
> Sept. 8, 1830.

[*Summary*] Mary had received no answer to her letter to Murray in which she had mentioned several subjects she might write upon for Murray's Family Library. The delay is inconvenient, especially if Murray already knows he does not wish to employ her. Mr. Murray being out of town and not expected back for a month, Mary wishes whoever reads the letter at the office[1] to communicate with him and get some kind of answer as soon as possible.

She had forgotten exactly which subjects she mentioned in her letter; she would like to mention some others. One, a history of the Earth, in its earlier state. This would deal with antideluvian remains, changes in the surface of

---

[1] Though this and the next letter are addressed by Mary to John Murray, it is evident that she expected someone else to read them.

the earth, and relics of states and kingdoms before the period of regular history. She had long been interested in the subject.

Another, Lives of Celebrated Women, or a History of Woman;—also, a History of Chivalry.

Marshall had suggested she might write for the *Quarterly.* She would be glad to do so.

"I wrote once a Review for the Westminster[2]—it appeared in one of the earlier numbers I forget which—it was upon 'The English in Italy'—and as I received a good many compliments about it—I suppose in some degree it may be received as a specimen—if the Editor wished to have one on the subject."

> ORIGINAL: Sir John Murray; A.L.S., 3 pp. 4to. UNPRINTED and UNPUBLISHED.
> SUMMARY: From original letter.

370. *To John Murray*

Park Cottage, Paddington,
Thursday, October 20 [1830]

[*Summary*] Mr. Murray had said in a note to Mary that on her return to town he would call on her. It would be better if Mary called in Albermarle St. instead.

"I shall remove to Somerset St. on Monday next [October 24].

"I write under the idea that some one of my propositions for the Family Library may be acceptable & because I am very unwilling to lose more time."

She wishes to see Moore's second volume of *Lord Byron.* Will it not come out before January? "that is a very long time to wait."

> ORIGINAL: Sir John Murray; A.L.S., 2 pp. 8vo. UNPRINTED and UNPUBLISHED.
> SUMMARY: From original letter.

371. *To William Whitton**

Mrs. Shelley
Robinson Esq.
Park Cottages
Paddington.
33 Somerset St., Portman Sq.[1]
2nd Decr., 1830.

My dear Sir,

If my messinger finds you at home, you will perhaps be so good as to give him (sealed up) the usual cheque in exchange for the receipt which I enclose. Otherwise will you have the kindness to send it to me—or I will send again for it in a day or two.

Percy, thank God, is quite well and Mr. Slater informs me, improves very

---

2 "The English in Italy," *Westminster Review* (October, 1826), 325–41. See Letter 265.
1 Only the date and the place are at the end of the MS.

much. I hope you are quite well—and that Percy's family are well, and not
disturbed by the frightful state of the country.

I am, dear Sir,

Yours Obly. and Obliged

M. W. Shelley

ORIGINAL: Sir John Shelley-Rolls. UNPRINTED and UNPUBLISHED. TEXT: From
copy made by Sir John Shelley-Rolls.

372. *To Edward John Trelawny*[1]

33 Somerset Street,
27th December, 1830.

My dear Trelawny—

At present I can only satisfy your impatience with the information that I
have received your MS. and read the greater part of it. Soon I hope to say more.
George Baring did not come to England, but after considerable delay forwarded it to me from Cologne.

I am delighted with your work; it is full of passion, energy, and novelty;
it concerns the sea, and that is a subject of the greatest interest to me. I should
imagine that it must command success.

But, my dear friend, allow me to persuade you to permit certain omissions.
In one of your letters to me you say that "there is nothing in it that a woman
could not read." You are correct for the most part, and yet without the omission
of a few words here and there—the scene before you go to school with the
mate of your ship—and above all the scene of the burning the house, following your scene with your Scotch enemy—I am sure that yours will be a book
interdicted to women. Certain words and phrases, pardoned in the days of
Fielding, are now justly interdicted, and any gross piece of ill taste will make
your booksellers draw back.

I have named all the objectionable passages, and I beseech you to let me
deal with them as I would with Lord Byron's *Don Juan,* when I omitted all
that hurt my taste. Without this yielding on your part I shall experience great
difficulty in disposing of your work; besides that I, your partial friend, strongly
object to coarseness, now wholly out of date, and beg you for my sake to
make the omissions necessary for your obtaining female readers. Amidst so
much that it beautiful and imaginative and exalting, why leave spots which,
believe me, are blemishes? I hope soon to write to you again on the subject.

The burnings, the alarms, the absorbing politics of the day render booksellers almost averse to publishing at all. God knows how it will all end, but
it looks as if the autocrats would have the good sense to make the necessary
sacrifices to a starving people.

I heard from Clare[2] today; she is well and still at Nice. I suppose there is

[1] This letter relates to Trelawny's letters of August 16 and October 28, 1830 (Marshall, II,
205–207). The MS was, of course, *The Adventures of a Younger Son.*
[2] Claire's letter, one of the best she ever wrote, is dated Nice, December 11, 1830, and is
printed in *Shelley and Mary,* IV, 1133-37.

no hope of seeing you here. As for me, I of course still continue a prisoner. Percy is quite well, and is growing more and more like Shelley. Since it is necessary to live, it is a great good to have this tie to life, but it is a wearisome affair. I hope you are happy.

Yours, my dearest friend, ever,
Mary Shelley.

ORIGINAL: Not traced. PRINTED: Marshall, II, 207–209; *The Letters of Edward J. Trelawny,* edited by Forman, 136–37n (from Marshall). TEXT: From Marshall, II, 207–209.

373. *To John Murray*

33 Somerset St., Portman Sq.,
Dec. 29, 1830.

[*Summary*] Mary is very anxious to see Moore's second volume of Byron's life, which has just been published. She hopes Murray will send her "my copy soon."

She is "so sorry that I have not been able to arrange writing for your Library—or for any other publication of yours." If she felt sure Murray would like a subject, she would venture writing and hoping that the result would be accepted by him. "As it is I fear that my debt must stand over till better times—but be assured that I *shall never forget* it."

ORIGINAL: Sir John Murray; A.L.S., 3 pp. 8vo, addressed. UNPRINTED and UNPUBLISHED. SUMMARY: From original letter.

374. *To Robert Dale Owen**

33 Somerset St.
Portman Sq
30 Dec. 1830

My dear Dale—

I am tardy in thanking you for your letter—yet I have thanked you a thousand times only you do not know it—for Procrastination has stolen my expression of them. Your letter gave me the greatest pleasure—first it proved to me that I was not forgotten by Fanny nor yourself and then it gave me tidings of the former, of her success and happiness, which delighted me.

My enclosed letter to her speaks of the subject that must interest us all so highly.—the triumph of the *Cause* in Europe—I wonder if nations have *bumps* as well as individuals— *Progressiveness* is certainly finely developed just now in Europe—together with a degree of *tyrant quellingtiveness* which is highly laudable—it is a pity that in our country this should be mingled with an *sick destructiveness;* yet the last gives action to the former—and without, would our Landholders be brought to reason? Yet it is very sad—the punishment of the poor men being not the least disaster attendant on it.

If you are good you will write to me again. When shall you again visit

England? Will Fanny never come over? Talk to her of me sometimes Remember me yourself—

I am Yours ever
M W Shelley

ORIGINAL: Historical Society of Pennsylvania, Philadelphia; A.L.S., 3 pp. 8vo. UNPRINTED and UNPUBLISHED. TEXT: From original letter.

375. *To John Howard Payne**

Somerset St. Tuesday [February 1, 1831]

My dear Payne

Parties and this weather so little suit me that I have declined Mrs. Wood's invitation— Besides I am not fond of going into crowded rooms where I shall not know a soul scarcely. I am grown old—shy—& lazy—& moreover am giving up parties as too expensive—I being desperately poor—

Marshall having stated that he arranged the *grand affair* on the strength of my note, I cannot help going shares with him— God send we all laugh at such *magnificences* this time twelvemonths—it is too much to be dwelling for ever on the minutia of trash

Yours ever
M W S

ADDRESS: J. Howard Payne Esq/ 77 Margaret St./ Cavendish Sq. POSTMARK: 10.F.NOON.10/ 2.FE/ 1831. ORIGINAL: Huntington Library (HM 6829); A.L.S., 2 pp. 8vo. PRINTED: *Romance*, 98–99. TEXT: From original letter.

376. *To William Whitton*

33 Somerset St.
1 Febry., 1831.

My dear Sir,

I am so stupid that I am by no means sure that I have worded my receipt properly. I shall do myself the pleasure of calling on you with Percy on Saturday next—when it can be set right. And then (unless it is convenient to you to forward it to me before) I can receive in exchange your cheque.

I am, dear Sir,
Yours Obt. & Obld.
M. W. Shelley

ORIGINAL: Sir John Shelley-Rolls. UNPRINTED and UNPUBLISHED. TEXT: From copy made by Sir John Shelley-Rolls.

377. *To [Charles Ollier]**

Teusday [? March 15, 1831]

My dear Sir

I wish much to see you to make the final arrangements about Mr. Trelawny's MS. Can you call tomorrow at about twelve—or will you tell me when that I may not miss you—

Yours &c
M W Shelley

ORIGINAL: Dr. Herman T. Radin, New York; A.L.S., 1 p. 12mo. UNPRINTED and UNPUBLISHED. TEXT: From original letter.

378. *To [Charles Ollier]**
33 Somerset St.
[Wednesday] 16 March 1831

My dear Sir

I have received the cheque of £5-5 for the Memoir.[3] I am annoyed beyond measure at this delay about Mr. Trelawny— I hope to see you tomorrow *before 4* as I go out at that hour—& I shall not be at home all Friday—so there will be another delay unless I can write on Friday

Remember to learn from Colburn the fate of the two articles—if accepted and it is not *hors de regle*—it would convenience me if they were paid for *now* —and besides I should like to understand the terms I should write for in future —and whether, if they satisfied me, Mr. Colburn wished me to continue to contribute

I hope to see you tomorrow

Yours obliged,
M W Shelley

ORIGINAL: Sylva Norman, Oxford; A.L.S., 3 pp. 8vo. UNPRINTED and UNPUBLISHED. TEXT: From original letter.

379. *To Edward John Trelawny*
Somerset Street,
22nd March, 1831.

My dear Trelawny—

What can you think of me and of my silence? I can guess by the contents of your letters and your not having yet received answers. Believe me that if I am at all to blame in this it arises from an error in judgment, not from want of zeal. Every post-day I have waited for the next, expecting to be able to communicate something definitive, and now still I am waiting; however, I trust that this letter will contain some certain intelligence before I send it. After all, I have done no more than send your manuscripts to Colburn, and I am still in expectation of his answer. In the first place, they insist on certain parts being expunged,—parts of which I alone had the courage to speak to you, but which had before been remarked upon as inadmissible. These, however (with trifling exceptions), occur only in the first volume. The task of deciding upon them may very properly be left to Horace Smith, if he will undertake it—we shall see.[1] Meanwhile, Colburn has not made up his mind as to the price. He will

[3] In the 1831 numbers of the *New Monthly Magazine* is a series of "Living Literary Characters." Of these there are only two which Mary could have written: the life of Mrs. Norton (February), or that of James Fenimore Cooper (April). It is by no means certain that she wrote either of them. The life of Cooper shows a considerable grasp of the subject, and understanding of Cooper's novels and their relationship with European and American literature.

[1] From the first Trelawny had stated positively that no changes were to be made. But on January 19, 1831, he wrote: "Let Hogg or Horace Smith read it, and, without your *giving any* opinion, hear theirs; then let the booksellers, Colburn or others, see it, and then if it is their general opinion that there are *words* which are better omitted, why I must submit to their being omitted. . . . My life . . . is not written for the amusement of women; it is not a novel."—Marshall, II, 209–10.

not give £500. The terms he will offer I shall hope to send before I close this letter, so I will say no more except to excuse my having conceded so much time to his dilatoriness. In all I have done I may be wrong; I commonly act from my own judgment; but alas!I have great experience. I *believe* that, if I sent your work to Murray, he would return it in two months unread; simply saying that he does not print novels. Your end part would be a temptation, did not your intention to be severe on Moore make it improbable that he would like to engage in it; and he would keep me as long as Colburn in uncertainty; still this may be right to do, and I shall expect your further instructions by return of post. However, in one way you may help yourself. You know Lockhart. He reads and judges for Murray; write to him; your letter shall accompany the MS. to him. Still, this thing must not be done hastily, for if I take the MS. out of Colburn's hands, and, failing to dispose of it elsewhere, I come back to him, he will doubtless retreat from his original proposal. There are other booksellers in the world, doubtless, than these two, but, occupied as England is by political questions, and impoverished miserably, there are few who have enterprise at this juncture to offer a price. I quote examples. My father and myself would find it impossible to make any tolerable arrangement with any one except Colburn. He at least may be some guide as to what you may expect. Mr. Brown remembers the golden days of authors. When I first returned to England I found no difficulty in making agreements with publishers; they came to seek me; now money is scarce, and readers fewer than ever. I leave the rest of this page blank. I shall fill it up before it goes on Friday.

Friday, 25th March.

At length, my dear friend, I have received the ultimatum of these great people. They offer you £300, and another £100 on a second edition; as this was sent me in writing, and there is no time for further communication before post-hour, I cannot *officially* state the number of the edition. I should think 1000. I think that perhaps they may be brought to say £400 at once, or £300 at once and £200 on the second edition. There can be no time for parleying, and therefore you must make up your mind whether after doing good battle, if necessary, I shall accept their terms. Believe *my experience* and that of those about me; you will not get a better offer from others, because money is not to be had, and Bulwer and other fashionable and selling authors are now obliged to content themselves with half of what they got before. If you decline this offer, I will if you please, try Murray; he will keep me two months at least, and the worst is, if he won't do anything, Colburn will diminish his bargain, and we shall be in a greater mess than ever. I know that, as a woman, I am timid, and therefore a bad negotiator, except that I have perseverance and zeal, and, I repeat, experience of things as they are. Mr. Brown knows what they were, but they are sadly changed. The omissions mentioned must be made, but I will watch over them, and the mottoes and all that shall be most carefully attended to, depend on me.

Do not be displeased, my dear friend, that I take advantage of this enormous sheet of paper to save postage, and ask you to tear off one half sheet, and to send it to Mrs. Hare.[2] You talk of my visiting Italy. It is impossible for me to tell you how much I repine at my imprisonment here, but I dare not anticipate a change to take me there for a long time. England, its ungenial clime, its difficult society, and the annoyances to which I am subjected in it weigh on my spirits more than ever, for every step I take only shows me how impossible [it is], situated as I am, that I should be otherwise than wretched. My sanguine disposition and capacity to endure have borne me up hitherto, but I am sinking at last; but to quit so stupid a topic and to tell you news, did you hear that Medwin contrived to get himself gazetted for full pay in the Guards? I fancy that he employed his connection with the Shelleys, who are connected with the King through the Fitz Clarences. However, a week after he was gazetted as retiring. I suppose the officers cut him at mess; his poor wife and children! how I pity them![3] Jane is quite well, living in tranquillity. Hogg continues all that she can desire. . . .

She lives where she did; her children are well, and so is my Percy, who grows more like Shelley. I hear that your old favourite, Margaret Shelley, is prettier than ever; your Miss Burdett is married. I have been having lithographed your letter to me about Caroline. I wish to disperse about 100 copies among the many hapless fair who imagine themselves to have been the sole object of your tenderness. Clare is to have a first copy. Have you heard from poor dear Clare? She announced a little time ago that she was to visit Italy with the Kaisaroff to see you. I envied her, but I hear from her brother Charles that she has now quarreled with Madame K. and that she will go to Vienna.[4] God grant that her sufferings end soon. I begin to anticipate it, for I hear that Sir Tim is in a bad way. I shall hear more certain intelligence after Easter. Mrs. P. spends her Easter with Caroline, who lives in the neighbourhood, and will dine at Field Place. I have not seen Mrs. Aldridge since her marriage; she has scarcely been in town, but I shall see her this spring, when she comes up as she intends. You know, of course, that Elizabeth St. Aubyn is married, so you know that your ladies desert you sadly. If Clare and I were either to die or marry you would be left without a Dulcinea at all, with the exception of the sixscore new objects for idolatry you may have found among the pretty

---

[2] Trelawny replied on April 8: "I received your Titanic letter, and sent Mrs. Hare her fathom of it."—Marshall, II, 216.

[3] In the *London Gazette*, February 1, 1831, Medwin was gazetted as lieutenant in the First Regiment of Life Guards. On February 15 (in the *Gazette*) his retirement was announced. (Medwin's *Life of Shelley*, xxvii.)

[4] Claire was governess in the Kaiseroff family, whom she had known in Moscow in 1825–26. Natalie was her particular charge. Her connection with this family continued for many years, as a friend at least. On April 13, 1831, Claire wrote from Nice: "In two hours we set out for Genoa and Florence . . . nor can I imagine how Charles could say for a certainty that I was going to Vienna, when I wrote to him the very great uncertainty of it."—*Shelley and Mary*, IV, 1144.

girls in Florence. Take courage, however; I am scarcely a Dulcinea, being your friend and not the Lady of your love, but such as I am, I do not think that I shall either die or marry this year, whatever may happen the next; as it is only spring you have some time before you.

We are all here on the *qui vive* about the Reform Bill; if it pass, and Tories and all expect it, well,—if not, Parliament is dissolved immediately, and they say that the new writs are in preparation. The Whigs triumphed gloriously in the boldness of their measure. England will be free if it is carried. I have had very bad accounts from Rome, but you are quiet as usual in Florence. I am scarcely wicked enough to desire that you should be driven home, nor do I expect it, and yet how glad I should be to see you. You never mention Zella. Adieu, my dear Trelawny. I am always

Affectionately yours,
Mary W. Shelley.

[P.S.] Hunt has set up a little 2d. paper, the *Tatler*,[5] which is succeeding; this keeps him above water. I have not seen him very lately. He lives a long way off. He is the same as ever, a person whom all must love and regret.

> ORIGINAL: Not traced. PRINTED: Marshall, II, 212–16; *The Letters of Edward J. Trelawny,* edited by Forman, 158–60n (from Marshall). TEXT: From Marshall.

380. *To William Whitton**

33 Somerset St.
5 May, 1831.

My dear Sir,

I am very much obliged to you for your attention and interest concerning the question of my son's school. If I still encline to Eton or another public school, it arises from Percy's peculiar situation and disposition. Not noticed by his own family—and my own circumstances being so restricted as to preclude my entering much into society, the forming of friends at school is of importance to him—at the same time that I think that the bustle of a school would develop his chances the better than the seclusion of a private tutor— However I am not obstinate, if Sir Timothy positively wishes the one rather than the other.

I suppose that Sir Timothy will be in town soon, when not only this question may be settled, but I shall indulge a hope of at last being permitted to see him.

I am, dear Sir,
Yr. Obly.
Mary W. Shelley

> ORIGINAL: Sir John Shelley-Rolls. UNPRINTED and UNPUBLISHED. TEXT: From copy made by Sir John Shelley-Rolls.

[5] *The Tatler,* A Daily Journal of Literature and the Stage, 1830–32.

381. *To William Whitton**
33 Somerset St.
6 May, 1831.

My dear Sir,

It seems my fate to be unlucky in my written communications with you—so much so, that I would not venture on another letter, but call myself in Bedford Row, to make my excuses and explanations, had you not intimated that you should be out of town.

It pains me very much to imagine that my letter insinuates that you have taken any part to prevent Sir Timothy from seeing you. Permit me to assure you, that I have always felt and feel, exceedingly obliged to you for your mediation, and perfectly satisfied with it. If, as a Mother, I regretted that Percy was not permitted to visit Field Place, and expressed this regret, it arose from over anxiety for him, and certainly not under any idea of appearing ungrateful to you. Do not then, be offended with me, my dear Sir, for be assured that I disavow any expression that fell from my pen that could at all offend you. I thank you sincerely for your kind offices and should be exceedingly glad of the continuation of them.

Being always
Yr. Obliged Sert.
M. W. Shelley

ADDRESS: W. Whitton Esq./ 18 Bedford Row. ORIGINAL: Sir John Shelley-Rolls. UNPRINTED and UNPUBLISHED. TEXT: From copy made by Sir John Shelley-Rolls.

382. *To Charles Ollier*
Somerset St. 10 May [1831]

My dear Sir

I hear nothing from you.—I receive no MS. is this your haste—pray do let some thing be *done* without more delay—

Will you send me the Tuilleries—the Young Duke & the No. of the N[ew] M[onthly Magazine] containing Mr. Bulwer's portrait[1]—& will you let me see you—

Y[s]

M Shelley

ADDRESS: Chas Ollier Esq/ 8 New Burlington St. ORIGINAL: New York Public Library; A.L.S., 1 p. 8vo. UNPRINTED and UNPUBLISHED. TEXT: From original letter.

383. *To John Howard Payne**
33 Somerset St.
Wednesday [May 18, 1831]

My dear Payne

Is it in your power to do me a pleasure? if it is I am sure you will—and it

---

[1] *The Tuileries;* a tale, By the author of *Hungarian Tales* [Mrs. Catherine Frances Gore] (1831, 3 vols.). It was reviewed in the *New Monthly* for March, 1831. *The Young Duke,* by Benjamin Disraeli (1831, 3 vols.). Bulwer's portrait was in the May number of the *New Monthly.*

will be a VERY great one to me if you can— I am an enthusiastic admirer of Paganini[1]—& wish excessively to go to hear him but the *tariffe* they put on the boxes renders this impossible— This tariffe is arbitrary, because not half the boxes are filled—& still fewer at the stated price. Could you through your acquaintance with Laporte arrange that I should have a box at a moderate price—such as I have given at the beginning of the opera season—a good box on the pit tier or the ground tier or the one above it—not higher—on taking 3 tickets at half a guinea each— If you can manage this I cant tell you how obliged I should be to you—let me know speedily yes or no —

Will you not let me see the Frisandeau?

Yours truly
M W Shelley

ORIGINAL: Huntington Library (HM 6830); A.L.S., 3 pp. 8vo. PRINTED: *Romance*, 99–100. TEXT: From original letter.

384. *To William Whitton**

33 Somerset St.
3 June, 1831.

My dear Sir,

I enclose a receipt in the form you sent me for the last—and I will send for the usual cheque in a day or two.

I called as you desired in Bedford Row—and they promised me there to let you know that I had been. But I have not heard from you since— I shall be very glad to hear that you are better—and hope for some communication about Percy who is perfectly well.

I am, dear Sir,
Yrs. Obd.,
M. W. Shelley

ORIGINAL: Sir John Shelley-Rolls. UNPRINTED and UNPUBLISHED. TEXT: From copy made by Sir John Shelley-Rolls.

385. *To William Whitton**

33 Somerset St.
Monday [June 6, 1831]

My dear Sir,

I hope the accompanying note is properly worded—and I write another not to mix two distinct subjects. The result of Sir Timothy['s] determination is of course that Percy should remain at his present school. This I confess much disappoints me; as for many reasons it would be more eligible that he went to an establishment more suited to his future station. At the age of twelve—at which he will soon arrive, manners and habits are formed, and at Mr. Slater's

[1] Nicolo Paganini (1784–1840), the great Italian violin virtuoso, made his first appearance in London at the King's Theatre on June 3, 1831. He had been scheduled to appear on May 21, but the public outcry at the high prices of tickets made it advisable to postpone the concert. Paganini finally consented to allow the regular prices to be charged. (H. C. Colles [ed.], *Grove's Dictionary of Music and Musicians*, Third Edition [New York, The Macmillan Co., 1935, 5 vols.].)

he will not acquire such as are suitable. As Sir Timothy is averse to a public school, a private tutor, where other boys of his own situation were placed, is exceedingly desirable. And I must hope that Sir Timothy has not relinquished this idea but only defers it for a short period of time.

I am very sorry to hear of your indisposition—and should be very glad to see you when you can afford me an opportunity.

I am, my dear Sir,

Yr. Obliged,

M. W. Shelley

ADDRESS: William Whitton Esq./ (To be forwarded). ENDORSED: Mrs. Shelley, recd. with note of 6 June/31. ORIGINAL: Sir John Shelley-Rolls. UNPRINTED and UNPUBLISHED. TEXT: From copy made by Sir John Shelley-Rolls.

386. *To William Whitton**

33 Somerset St.

6 June, 1831.

Dear Sir,

In answer to your communication I reply that I agree to the liquidation of the balance stated in the account you sent me; and that I agree to [? secure] the amount now due on the property I possess under my husband's will.

I am, dear Sir,

Yours Obly.

Mary Shelley

ADDRESS: William Whitton Esq. ORIGINAL: Sir John Shelley-Rolls. UNPRINTED and UNPUBLISHED. TEXT: From copy made by Sir John Shelley-Rolls.

387. *To Edward John Trelawny*

Somerset Street,

14th June, 1831.

My dear Trelawny[1]—

Your work is in progress at last, and is being printed with great rapidity. Horace Smith undertook the revision, and sent a very favourable report of it to the publishers; to me he says: "Having written to you a few days ago, I have only to annex a copy of my letter to Colburn and Bentley, whence you will gather my opinion of the MS.; it is a most powerful, but rather perilous work, which will be much praised and much abused by the liberal and bigoted. I have read it with great pleasure and think it admirable, in everything but the conclusion"; by this he means, as he says to Colburn and Bentley, "The conclusion is abrupt and disappointing, especially as previous allusions have been made to his later life which is not given. Probably it is meant to be continued, and if so it would be better to state it, for I have no doubt that his first part will create a sufficient sensation to ensure the sale of a second."

[1] Trelawny's reply, dated June 29, is in Marshall, II, 220–23.

In his former letter to me H. S. says: "Any one who has proved himself the friend of yourself and of him whom we all deplore I consider to have strong claims on my regard, and I therefore willingly undertake the revision of the MS. Pray assure the author that I feel flattered by this little mark of his confidence in my judgment, and that it will always give me pleasure to render him these or any other services." And now, my dear Trelawny, I hope you will not be angry at the title given to your book; the responsibility of doing anything for any one so far away as you is painful, and I have had many qualms, but what could I do? The publishers strongly objected to the *History of a Man* as being no title at all, or rather one to lead astray.[2] The one adopted is taken from the first words of your MS., where you declare yourself a younger son—words pregnant of meaning in this country, where to be the younger son of a man of property is to be virtually discarded,—and they will speak volumes to the English reader; it is called, therefore, *The Adventures of a Younger Son*. If you are angry with me for this I shall be sorry, but I knew not what to do. Your MS. will be preserved for you; and remember, also, that it is pretty well known whom it is by. I suppose the persons who read the MS. in Italy have talked, and, as I told you, your mother speaks openly about it. Still it will not appear in print, in no newspaper accounts over which I have any control as emanating from the publisher. Let me know immediately how I am to dispose of the dozen copies I shall receive on your account. One must go to H. Smith, another to me, and to whom else? The rest I will send to you in Italy.

There is another thing that annoys me especially. You will be paid in bills dating from the day of publication, now not far distant; three of various dates. To what man of business of yours can I consign these? the first I should think I could get discounted at once, and send you the cash; but tell me what I am to do. I know that all these hitches and drawbacks will make you vituperate womankind, and had I ever set myself up for a woman of business, or known how to manage my own affairs, I might be hurt; but you know my irremediable deficiencies on these subjects, and I represented them strongly to you before I undertook my task; and all I can say in addition is, that as far as I have seen, both have been obliged to make the same concessions, so be as forgiving and indulgent as you can.

We are full here of reform or revolution, whichever it is to be; I should think something approaching the latter, though the first may be included in the last. Will you come over and sit for the new parliament? what are you doing? Have you seen Clare? how is she? She never writes except on special occasions, when she wants anything. Tell her that Percy is quite well.

You tell me not to marry,—but I will,—any one who will take me out of my present desolate and uncomfortable position. Any one,—and with all this

---

[2] Trelawny replied: "I did not mean to call my book *The History of a Man,* but simply thus, *A Man's Life.*"—Marshall, II, 221. Earlier, Trelawny had considered other titles: *The Life of a Man* and *Treleon* (a family name).

46

do you think that I shall marry? Never,—neither you nor anybody else. Mary Shelley shall be written on my tomb,—and why? I cannot tell, except that it is so pretty a name that though I were to preach to myself for years, I never should have the heart to get rid of it.[3]

Adieu, my dear friend. I shall be very anxious to hear from you; to hear that you are not angry about all the *contretemps* attendant on your publication, and to receive your further directions.

> Yours very truly,
> M. W. Shelley.

ORIGINAL: Not traced. PRINTED: Marshall, II, 218–20; *The Letters of Edward J. Trelawny,* edited by Forman, 162–63n (like and from Marshall). TEXT: From Marshall, II, 218–20.

388. *To William Whitton*

33 Somerset St.
22 June, 1831.

My dear Sir,

I have deferred several days writing that I might the more carefully consider the subject before me. One word I must premise. It is my desire to restrict any demand for addition to my income strictly to the question of the greater expenditure to be made for my son, without reference whatever to my own means. At the same time I must mention that Percy's encreased age requires a very great encrease of expence, so that even in the present state of things, I feel very sensibly and with no small inconvenience, the encreased demands which his bills, &c. make upon my income— For my own maintenance I have considered £200 a year necessary, including in that the expences occasioned by Percy's residence with me during the holydays. But the latter event now so materially adds to my expences, that I find it quite impossible to keep within that compass. To prove that my consideration is wholly turned to Percy's expences, without reference to encrease of income to myself personally, I may add that when he is settled with a tutor in the country, it is my intention to take up my residence out of town, so as much as possible to restrict my mode of life.

The Tutors and private schools in question appear invariably to make the

---

[3] The history of Trelawny's proposal of marriage to Mary seems clearly to be no more than the following. In her letter of March 22, Mary, after mentioning the marriage of several of Trelawny's women friends, indulged in a little badinage, including: "If Clare and I were either to die or marry you would be left without a Dulcinea at all . . . however, I am scarcely a Dulcinea, being your friend and not the Lady of your love."

Trelawny replied on April 8: "Do not you, dear Mary, abandon me by following the evil examples of my other ladies. I should not wonder if fate, without our choice, united us; and who can control his fate. I blindly follow his decrees, dear Mary."—Marshall, II, 217–18.

Mary's reply to this is that above (June 14): ". . . do you think that I shall marry? Never— neither you nor anybody else," etc. Trelawny's comment on this was (June 29): "I was more delighted with your resolve not to change your name than with any other portion of your letter. Trelawny, too, is a good name, and sounds as well as Shelley; it fills the mouth as well and will as soon raise a spirit."—Marshall, II, 222. Mary had the last word. On July 26 she wrote: "My name will *never* be Trelawny."

charge of £150 for board and education—more than £100 more than his present school—to this must be added various extras for books, &c.—His dress at such a place would be attended with greater expence—and it is already very considerable. I have come therefore to the conclusion that to meet the encreased demands, without spending one additional shilling on myself personally, £150 p. ann. must be added to my income. If this appear much to Sir Timothy, perhaps on his side he will make enquiries—and if any Gentleman who has a son at a similar school can estimate his son's whole yearly expenses taken collectively at less than £250 p. annum, I shall suppose that my calculation is a false one.

With regard to the Tutor with whom he is to be placed many things are to be considered. In talking on the subject with men conversant with it, I am told that while at most of these private schools great attention is payed to the physical and moral education of the pupils, very great difference exists in the more severe branches of education—their learning being well attended to by some and much neglected by others. I wish my son to be a good classic scholar —and above all to be educated in habits of great industry—and real attention to the acquirement of knowledge.

That I may do my best to make a good selection, it is my intention to apply to a Gentleman of my acquaintance, Mr. Julius Stone, a man of great literary reputation, a Clergyman, and a Professor of Trinity College, Cambridge. He is in the habit of examining and attending to young men on their first entrance in College, and has the means therefore of judging accurately as to who sends the best educated, and the most moral pupils out of his hands.

I hope Sir Timothy will permit me to lay Mr. Stone's answer before him— and that he will favor me with his opinion, or at least his advice as to the choice I should make.

With many thanks for the trouble you give yourself,

I am, my dear Sir,

Yours Obdly.

Mary W. Shelley

[P.S.] I arranged for Mr. Amory to see the deed in question. I have received no communication whatever from him on the subject. Of course I expect one daily.

Percy is now at home for the holydays— He is very well—and I should be glad that Sir Timothy saw him. Percy writes to make this request—will you be so good as to give his Grandfather his letter.[1]

ADDRESS: W. Whitton Esq./ 18 Bedford Row. ORIGINAL: Sir John Shelley-Rolls. UNPRINTED and UNPUBLISHED. TEXT: From copy made by Sir John Shelley-Rolls.

[1] Percy's letter is printed by Ingpen (*Shelley in England*, 605), with Sir Timothy's remark, "dictated artfully."

389. *To Edward John Trelawny*

Somerset Street, .
26th July, 1831.

My dear Trelawny—

Your third volume is now printing, so I should imagine that it will very soon be published; everything shall be attended to as you wish. The letter to which I alluded in my former one was a tiny one enclosed to Clare, which perhaps you have received by this time. It mentioned the time of the agreement; £300 in bills of three, six, and eight months, dated from the day of publication, and £100 more on a second edition. The mention I made of your mother was, that she speaks openly in society of your forthcoming memoirs, so that I should imagine very little real secrecy will attend them. However, you will but gain reputation and admiration through them.

I hope you are going on, for your continuation will, I am sure, be ardently looked for. I am so sorry for the delay of all last winter, yet I did my best to conclude the affair; but the state of the nation has so paralysed bookselling that publishers were very backward, though Colburn was in his heart eager to get at your book. As to the price, I have taken pains to ascertain; and you receive as much as is given to the best novelists at this juncture, which may console your vanity if it does not fill your pocket.

The Reform Bill will pass, and a considerable revolution in the government of the country will, I imagine, be the consequence.

You have talents of a high order. You have powers; these, with industry and discretion, would advance you in any career. You ought not, indeed you ought not to throw away yourself as you do. Still, I would not advise your return on the speculation, because England is so sad a place that the mere absence from it I consider a peculiar blessing.

My name will *never* be Trelawny.[1] I am not so young as I was when you first knew me, but I am as proud. I must have the entire affection, devotion, and, above all, the solicitous protection of any one who would win me. You belong to womenkind in general, and Mary Shelley will *never* be yours.

I write in haste, but I will write soon again, more at length. You shall have your copies the moment I receive them. Believe me, with all gratitude and affection,

Yours,
M. W. Shelley.

[P.S.] Jane thanks you for the book promised. I am infinitely chagrined at what you tell me concerning Clare. If the B[eauclerc]s spoke against her, that means Mrs. B[eauclerc] and her stories were gathered from Lord Byron, who feared Clare and did not spare her; and the stories he told were such as to excuse the prejudice of any one.[2]

---

1 See Letter 387, note 3.
2 On June 29 Trelawny had written: "Clare only remained in Florence about ten days; some sudden death of a relative of the family she resides with recalled them to Russia. I saw her three

ORIGINAL: Not traced. PRINTED: Marshall, II, 224–25; Lucy M. Rossetti, *Mrs. Shelley* 183 (quot., 5 lines); *The Letters of Edward J. Trelawny,* edited by Forman, 171–72n (like and from Marshall). TEXT: From Marshall.

390. *To John Murray**

33 Somerset St.
7 Sep. 1831

My dear Sir

Not having had the pleasure of hearing from you—I pray forgive my troubling you by sending to know whether you can conveniently discount the bill I inclosed to you on Monday last— I am ashamed to trouble you—but an immediate answer would gratify me very much

Ys. truly & obliged
M W Shelley

ORIGINAL: Sir John Murray; A.L.S., 2 pp. 8vo, addressed. UNPRINTED and UNPUBLISHED. TEXT: From original letter.

391. *To Edward John Trelawny*

33 Somerset St.
2 Oct., 1831.

My dear Trelawny,

I suppose that I have now some certain intelligence to send you though I fear that it will both disappoint and annoy you. I am indeed ashamed that I have not been able to keep these people in better order—but I trusted to honesty when I ought to have ensured it. However, thus it stands   your book is to be published in the course of the month of November, and then your bills are to be dated— As soon as I get them I will dispose of them as you direct—and you shall receive notice on the subject without delay. I cannot procure for you a copy until then— They pretend that it is not all printed— if I can get an opportunity I will send you one by a private hand—at any rate I shall send them by sea without delay. I will write to [Horace] Smith about negociating your bills—and I have no doubt that I shall be able somehow or other to get you money on them. I will go myself to the city to pay Barff's correspondant as soon as I get the cash. This your pretty dear (how fascinating is flattery) will do her best as soon as those tiresome people fulfil their engagements. In some degree they have the right on their side—as the day of publication is a usual time from which to date the bills and that was the time which I acceded to—but they talked of such hurry and speed that I expected that that day was nearer at hand than it now appears to be   November *is* the publishing month and no new things are coming out now. In fact the Reform Bill swallows up every other thought.

---

or four times. She was very miserable, and looked so pale, thin and haggard. . . . Mrs. Hare once saw her, but she was so prejudiced against her, from stories she had heard against her from the Beauclercs, that she could hardly be induced to notice her."—Marshall, II, 222.

You have heard of the Lords majority against it—much larger than was expected because it was not imagined that so many bishops would vote against Government— Lord Brougham [*MS defective*] the birth of her little boy— Do whenever you write send me news of Claire— She never writes herself and we are excessively anxious about her. I hope she is better— God knows when fate will do anything for us—I despair— Percy is very well—I fancy that he will go to Harrow in the spring—it is not finally arranged but this is what *I wish*—and therefore I suppose it will be—as they have promised to encrease my allowance for him, and leave me pretty nearly free—only with Eton prohibited—but Harrow is now in high reputation under a new head Master. I am delighted to hear that Zella is in such good hands[1]—it is so necessary in this world of woe that children should learn by times to yield to necessity—and a girl allowed to run wild makes an unhappy woman.

Hunt has set up a penny daily paper [*The Tatler*]—literary and theatrical —it is succeeding very well—but his health is wretched, and when you consider that his sons, now young men—do not contribute a penny towards their own support you may guess that the burthen on him is very heavy— I see them very seldom for they live a good way off—and when I go—he is out—she busy—so I am entertained by the children who do not edify me. Jane has just moved into a house about half a mile further from town, on the same road— they have furnished it themselves. Dina improves—or rather she always was and continues to be a very nice child.

I think, my dear Trelawny, that I have told you all the news— If you write to Claire tell her that Mr. and Mrs. Godwin are well—my father [*the remainder of the letter is missing*]

ORIGINAL: Sir John Shelley-Rolls (MS incomplete). PRINTED: Marshall, II, 225–27; *The Letters of Edward J. Trelawny*, edited by Forman, 172–73n (like and from Marshall). TEXT: From copy made by Sir John Shelley-Rolls.

392. *To Edward John Trelawny*

[London, December, 1831]

. . . me news of Claire. She has not written for more than 2 months—she was then at Naples, having left the Kaisaroffs—and I am beyond measure anxious to learn how she is and what doing. When will her trials be over? When will independence be her lot? Time alone can answer. I am assured that my father-in-law cannot last long—and his stinginess concerning the education of my son makes me indeed wish that he was no longer the Master of our Destiny. Shelley's eldest sister, Elizabeth, has just died[2]—of a decline— but this will not soften their hearts. A few lines concerning dear Claire will

[1] On September 1, 1831, Trelawny had written: ". . . an English lady now married to a Lucchese, the Marquis Boschella, has adopted my little child Zella; she has a considerable fortune, which is settled on herself, and has yet no children of her own."—*Shelley and Mary*, IV, 1151. For more details of Zella and Jane Boccella (the usual spelling) see Massingham, *The Friend of Shelley*, 278–82.

[2] On December 17, 1831; she was buried at Warnham Church.

relieve her friends here from infinite inquietude, so pray add them to your letter. And if you write to her tell her that I and her Mother and Jane have all written, and long for answers. Jane is not well—she has had an attack of liver —but is recovering. Her children are well—and my boy bright and gay—and the consolation of my life. How lucky you are for your Zella to be under such kind protection—you were very wise to place her under a woman. When you see Mrs. Hare will you tell her that I have not heard from her for a long time— and that I beg she will write. I wrote not long ago.

(Friday). Paul promised to send me word the exact sum he has of yours in his hands—but he has omitted to do so—however calculating discount and the full sum of £100 paid to Mr. Lister I suppose it is about £190—for which you can draw— I will write to you again next week on the subject but I do not wish to lose this post.

We have heard of Claire thro' her brother Charles—and learn that she is at present at Pisa—this has tranquillized us— Pray let her know that her Mother—Jane and I have written lately Ferma in Posta, Napoli.

I will write speedily again and in haste.

Ever yrs.
M. W. S.

ADDRESS: John Edward Trelawny Esq./ Ferma in Posta/ Firenze. ORIGINAL: Sir John Shelley-Rolls (MS incomplete). UNPRINTED and UNPUBLISHED. TEXT: From copy made by Sir John Shelley-Rolls.

393. *To Charles Ollier**

[London] Saturday [? January, 1832]

Dear Sir

You were kind enough to promise to lend me Eugene Aram[1]— You would very greatly oblige me by giving it to my servant—or leaving it out so that she could have it on calling again. If you would lend me this week's C[our]t Journal & the New Monthly for Jany. I should be exceedingly glad.

Yours truly
M W Shelley

[P.S.] I hope you got the last note I sent you, which had been forgotten for some days—to thank you for all the trouble you took in Mr. Trelawny's affair.[2]

I will return Cavendish[3] in a few days.—It is very clever—but the beginning is best—& it is immoral—why write about certain things; it is bad enough that they are.

ADDRESS: Chas. Ollier Esq/ 8 New Burlington St. ORIGINAL: Pierpont Morgan Library; A.L.S., 1 p. 8vo. UNPRINTED and UNPUBLISHED. TEXT: From original letter.

[1] Bulwer-Lytton, *Eugene Aram,* 1832. The preface is dated December 22, 1831.
[2] "Trelawny's affair" was, of course, the publication of *The Adventures of a Younger Son.* Ollier had conducted most of the negotiations with Colburn and Bentley.
[3] *Cavendish* was a novel by William Johnson Neale, barrister (1831, 3 vols.).

394. *To William Whitton*

33 Somerset St., Portman Sq.
24 Janry., 1832.

My dear Sir,

I am exceedingly sorry to find myself obliged to trouble you with a request, which I assure you, were it possible, I would refrain from making. After your last letter perhaps it would be your wish that I should apply to Mr. Gregson[1]—but as it was to you that I mentioned the circumstance—and you gave me hopes that you would kindly mediate with Sir Timothy for me—and as I believe you have hitherto done all you can for my advantage with my father-in-law—I prefer, I confess, applying to you.

You will guess after all this preface my purpose is that you would have the goodness to forward to Sir Timothy a request that he would advance me some money, without which I shall be placed in a most difficult situation. When you asked me to write down what I required for Percy, I mentioned that I had been involved ever since he first went to school—from the circumstance of my income being then limited to £250, which could not cover his encreasing expences. Now at the complete age of twelve, his expences are so very much greater than they were—and encrease so much, that these [   ] are continually added to. The only mode by which I can meet them is by retrenching my own expences—to do this I must leave my present habitation—and it is my purpose to reside in some spot in the country, where I shall be able to spend less on my own wants than in London it is possible for me to do.—But I cannot quit my present abode without a sum of money to pay off a few debts. Under these circumstances, if you will add your influence I trust Sir Timothy would not refuse me £50—without which I see no hope of extricating myself from my present situation. Excuse my troubling you—this £50 will not add very greatly to my debt to my father-in-law[2]—and if he were to see what a fine boy his grandson has become, I scarcely think he would have the heart to refuse me a favor necessary for his comfort as well as my own.

I hope your health is better—and that it will continue to improve with the advancing season.

I am, dear Sir,
Yours Obliged,
M. W. Shelley

ADDRESS: William Whitton Esq./ Stone Wall,/ Tunbridge. ORIGINAL: Sir John Shelley-Rolls. UNPRINTED and UNPUBLISHED. TEXT: From copy made by Sir John Shelley-Rolls.

[1] Whitton had been in bad health for some time. At this time he turned over Sir Timothy's affairs to John Gregson. Whitton died in July, 1832.

[2] All money received by Mary from Sir Timothy was to be paid back by her to his estate with interest.

395. *To John Gregson*

33 Somerset St., Portman Sq.
27 Jany., 1832.

Dear Sir,

Mr. Whitton has informed me that you will have the goodness to further any application of mine to Sir Timothy Shelley, and being at the moment in an embarrassment that obliges me to trouble him, I shall be much obliged to you if you will communicate and second my request.

You may remember that when I signed the deed last year in Bedford Row —I applied for an encrease of income that I might send my son to a school of higher qualifications than Mr. Slater's— Mr. Whitton gave me hopes that this request would be complied with— I mentioned then that I had been embarrassed for money ever since Percy went to school, when my income had not been encreased as I had expected. Afterwards Sir Timothy declined making any addition to my allowance, saying that he hoped that I should be able to give my son a good education on the sum I at present receive.

Percy is now turned twelve years old; you may imagine that his school and taylors bills encrease every year—that his incidental expences are very great, and that to defray them consumes a great part of my income. To meet these calls I have but one resource which is to diminish my own personal expences as much as possible—for which purpose I have long contemplated going to a quiet spot in the country, where I could spend far less than I do now. I have been prevented, because it always demands some small command of money to make any change. I had hoped that at Xmas I might have been enabled, but found it impossible— I am forced to continue in my present abode (where I have lived nearly 3 years) my debts encreasing—and perfectly unable to change and retrench from want of such a sum as permitting me to get rid of my embarrassments—would enable me to execute my economical plan. Under these circumstances I can only apply to Sir Timothy—and ask for the sum of £50, upon which I shall immediately remove—and establishing myself on the cheapest plan, continue to defray the encreasing expenses of Percy's education. If I am refused this, I am at a loss to imagine what I can do—as without an entire alteration of abode and leaving London, it is impossible for me to extricate myself from my present position.

Percy desires his duty and love to Sir Timothy and Lady Shelley—he is a very fine boy and did his grandfather see him I am sure he would not have the heart to deny me a request which has for its ultimate object his well bringing up. I would have called on you with him, but the weather prevents my going out, and I am unwilling to delay a solicitation on which my present hopes of doing my duty by him depend. May I ask you therefore to forward my wishes at your earliest convenience—and I trust with success.

I am, dr. Sir,
Your Obt. Servant,
M. W. Shelley

[P.S.] I ought to mention perhaps that as Percy will continue with Mr. Slater, my new abode will not be at *too great* a distance from town—sufficiently far only to ensure economy.

Percy was very much obliged to his Grandfather for some pocket money he was kind enough to send him last Easter thro' Mrs. Paul. I hope this family are well after their affliction.[1]

ADDRESS: John Gregson Esq./ 18 Bedford Row. ORIGINAL: Sir John Shelley-Rolls. UNPRINTED and UNPUBLISHED. TEXT: From copy made by Sir John Shelley-Rolls.

396. *To John Gregson**

33 Somerset St.
10 Feb. 1832.

Dear Sir,

I have called to ask if you have made the communication I requested to Sir Timothy Shelley—and if you have received any answer. My comfort and respectability so entirely depend on having a favorable one—and on being enabled to quit town—that I am most anxious on the subject. If any explanation would facilitate my wish, I will call on you at any hour you may appoint.

I am,
Yr. Obt. Servant,
Mary Shelley

ADDRESS: John Gregson, Esq./ 18 Bedford Row. ORIGINAL: Sir John Shelley-Rolls. UNPRINTED and UNPUBLISHED. TEXT: From copy made by Sir John Shelley-Rolls.

397. *To John Gregson*

33 Somerset St.
2nd March, 1832.

Dear Sir,

I enclose the usual receipt—and shall be glad if you will have the goodness to give the cheque in exchange to the bearer.

The entire neglect with which my request has been met, arises, I suppose, from its being refused. I was in hopes, I confess, that Sir Timothy Shelley would have viewed my motives with greater kindness—and that desirous as I am to limit my expences so as to meet the encreasing ones of my son, he would have been good enough to have assisted me— Is there no hope that Sir Tim. may yet be induced to make me an advance which need not be considered as a precedent.

Percy is quite well, and I have very good accounts of him.

I am, dr. Sir,
Yr. Obt. Servant,
M. W. Shelley

ORIGINAL: Sir John Shelley-Rolls. UNPRINTED and UNPUBLISHED. TEXT: From copy made by Sir John Shelley-Rolls.

[1] The death of Elizabeth Shelley on December 17, 1831.

398. *To John Gregson**

33 Somerset St.
Friday [March 2, 1832].

Dear Sir,

I shall do myself the pleasure of calling on you at 12 tomorrow morning.

Yrs. Obdly.

M. W. Shelley

ADDRESS: John Gregson Esq./ 18 Bedford Row. ENDORSED: 2nd March 1832. Mrs. Shelley. ORIGINAL: Sir John Shelley-Rolls. UNPRINTED and UNPUBLISHED. TEXT: From copy made by Sir John Shelley-Rolls.

399. *To John Gregson*

[London, March 4–10, 1832]

Dear Sir,

I am sorry to trouble you again, but I am truly uneasy at not hearing from you— When I saw you last you asked me if the promise of an encrease of income would meet my wants. I said that it would if I received the additional £25 this quarter but that was essential to me— You appeared to think that Sir Timothy would kindly make no difficulty as to that— I would not press the point, were it not one of absolute necessity—and I should be glad to hear that Sir Timothy had given you a favorable answer.

If you could let me see you on this point soon I should be glad— I would call—but you would probably be too engaged to see me. I shall be at home at five today or any day you will please to name as convenient to yourself.

I am, dr. Sir,

Yrs. Obtly.

M. W. Shelley

ENDORSED: March 1832. Mrs. Shelley. ORIGINAL: Sir John Shelley-Rolls. UNPRINTED and UNPUBLISHED. TEXT: From copy made by Sir John Shelley-Rolls.

400. *To John Gregson**

33 Somerset St.,
14 March, 1832.

Dear Sir,

Your continued silence frightens me—as the £25 I was in hopes to receive through you is beyond every thing essential—and the very delay occasions the continuance of expence of which I could otherwise get rid. Will you let me know what hopes I have.

Percy came to see me on Sunday—he is quite well—and Mr. Slater gives a very good account of him. I have given notice that he will quit his present school—and am taking steps for placing him with Dr. Longley (the Head Master) at Harrow.

I am, dear Sir,

Yours Obly.,

M. W. Shelley

ORIGINAL: Sir John Shelley-Rolls. UNPRINTED and UNPUBLISHED. TEXT: From copy made by Sir John Shelley-Rolls.

401. *To John Gregson*

33 S[omerset] St.
Thursday Morn[in]g, [March (? 15), 1832]

Dear Sir,

I enclose a receipt which I hope is right. Pray when you write, tell Sir Timothy that I am very sensible of his goodness in complying with my request[2]— And if when he comes to town he will permit me to thank him in person he will add greatly to the obligation. Will you tell him also that I saw Mr. Slater the other day, who praises Percy for his improvement and docility— With many thanks for the trouble you have taken,

I am, dr. Sir,
Yr. Obetly.,
M. W. Shelley

ENDORSED: March 1832. Mrs. Shelley. ORIGINAL: Sir John Shelley-Rolls. UNPRINTED and UNPUBLISHED. TEXT: From copy made by Sir John Shelley-Rolls.

402. *To Mrs. Manners-Sutton (a fragment)*

[London, April 21, 1832]

... for you may be sure that you do quite right in following the injunctions of the very wise & very kind Speaker.[3]

I am quite sure your Party will be a success—for numbers except at a Ball, are by no means necessary—I write though I see you so soon under the idea of your going to [? Mistley] on Monday—if I am wrong in this supposition, I shall hope to attain a little chat with you next week, notwithstanding this note—

Believe me, dear Mrs. Manners Sutton,
Ever truly yrs.
M W Shelley

ADDRESS: Mrs. Manners Sutton/ Palace Y[ar]d/ Westminster. POSTMARK: 21.AP/ 1832. ORIGINAL: Pierpont Morgan Library; A.L.S., 1 p. 4to (a fragment). UNPRINTED and UNPUBLISHED. TEXT: From original letter.

403. *To John Murray*

33 Somerset St.,
Monday, April 30 [1832].

[*Summary*] Mary has not heard from Murray since he called on her. "You spoke concerning notes for Lord Byron's Poems—& said you would send the

---

[2] Apparently, Mary's allowance had been increased to £400 per annum, according to Gregson's suggestion.
[3] This lady's husband, Charles Manners-Sutton (1780–1845), first Viscount Canterbury, was for some years Speaker of the House of Commons.

volumes—not having received them, I have done nothing, but it has occurred to me that you may imagine that I have been forgetful— I write therefore merely to say that I have not seen Mr. Finden."—Murray had also said something about a picture. Mary wishes to know if Murray still wishes the notes on Byron, and whatever was said about the picture.

Is it true that the Countess Guiccioli has arrived?[4] Can Murray give Mary her address?

ORIGINAL: Sir John Murray; A.L.S., 3 pp. 8vo. UNPRINTED and UNPUBLISHED.
SUMMARY: From original letter.

404. *To John Murray*＊

33 Somerset St.
4 May—1832

My dear Sir

I do not know how to thank you sufficiently for the very agreeable presents you have made me and my friend. You are quite magnificent in your generosity—and nothing can be more welcome than your books.

I am afraid I shall scarcely meet all your wishes in the intended notes.[1] The subject of Lord Byron's adventures is greatly exhausted—and besides the names of ladies are scarcely fair subjects for publication. However, I will do what I can—of course you will take care that I am not brought forward or named, as you are aware how sedulously I try to keep in the background. By the bye I must mention that early next month I leave town for some little time—so that I should be glad that Mr. Finden[2] should see me during the course of this present one.

May I without intruding on you, mention another subject? You apparently consider the closing of your family library as conclusive on the subject of my father's writing for you. Is this necessary? You are but too well aware of the evil days on which literature is fallen—and how difficult it is for a man however gifted, whose existence depends on his pen, to make one engagement succeed another with sufficient speed to answer the calls of his situation. Nearly all our literati have found but one resource in this—which is in the ample scope afforded by periodicals. A kind of literary pride has prevented my father from mingling in these—and never having published any thing anonimously, he feels disenclined to enter on a to him new career.

I feel persuaded that he would render his proposed Lives of the Necromancers[3] a deeply interesting and valuable work. There is a life and energy

[4] The Countess Guiccioli remained in England until January, 1833. (See Letter 424.)
[1] Notes for *The Works of Lord Byron*: With his Letters and Journals and his Life, by Thomas Moore, in 17 volumes. Volumes 1 and 12 were published in 1835; volumes 2–11 in 1832; volumes 13–17 in 1833.
[2] The engraver William Finden (1787–1852) and his younger brother, Edward F. Finden, engraved and published on their own account and at their own cost the *Illustrations to Lord Byron's Works*, 1833. William Finden engraved the portrait of Shelley.
[3] Godwin wrote this book (published in 1834).

in his writings which always exalts them above those of his contemporaries. If this subject, which seems to me a fortunate one, does not please you—there are many others which would offer themselves, were he certain that you would accede to them, and give him that encouragement which he has been accustomed hitherto to find. He had thought of the Lives of the English philosophers— I should certainly be glad that the Publisher of Byron and Moore, and all the best writers, added the name of Godwin to the list—and if upon consideration you find that your views do not oppose an engagement with him, you will perhaps invite him to further communication on the subject.

Excuse my pressing this point—which after all must be decided by the laws of expediency, and believe me,

Yours truly & obliged,
M W Shelley.

ADDRESS: John Murray Esq./ 50 Albemarle St. POSTMARK: 4.EVEN/ 4.MY/ 1832. ORIGINAL: Sir John Murray; A.L.S., 3 pp. 4to. PRINTED: S. Smiles, *A Publisher and His Friends* (1891) II, 328–29. TEXT: From original letter.

405. To [*Alaric A. Watts*]

33 Somerset St.
Portman Sq
14 May, 1832.

Sir

I do not know whether the enclosed drama will suit your Annual or whether it may be considered as more befitting the beautiful Juvenile one, edited by Mrs. Watts— If it should please you, I shall be glad that it appeared in either publication—& I refer to your usual terms, to arrange the question of remuneration.[1]

I am, Sir,

Ys. Obg.
M W Shelley

[P.S.] I may mention that this drama has been seen & liked by two or three good judges whose opinion emboldens me to send it you

ORIGINAL: The John Rylands Library, Manchester (Rylands, Eng. MSS 383 (1814); A.L.S., 1 p. 8vo. PRINTED: Frederick L. Jones, "Mary Shelley and Midas," London *Times Literary Supplement,* June 25, 1938, 434. TEXT: From copy sent me by Dr. Henry Guppy, Librarian of the John Rylands Library.

406. To John Gregson

33 Somerset St.
6th June [18]32.

Dear Sir,

Will you be so good as to let me know when I may send for the cheque— If you wish to communicate with me—I shall be very glad if you will appoint

[1] *Proserpine* having been published in *The Winter's Wreath* for 1832 (printed in 1831), the drama must be *Midas*. It was not published either in Watts's *Literary Souvenir* or in Mrs. Zillah Watts's *New Year's Gift and Juvenile Souvenir* (1829–35, 7 vols.). It remained unpublished until 1922. (See Letter 268.)

a time when I can see you either in Bedford Row or Cumberland St. and I will call— I have made every arrangement to leave town for Sandgate in Kent which I hear is an healthy and cheap place— After the Summer holydays Percy goes to Harrow[1]— He is to board with Mr. Kennedy the Under Master —Dr. Longley the Head Master, not having a vacancy— I am very anxious that he should get as strong as possible by the seaside, before entering on a Public School.

May I request an answer this evening.

Yours Obly.,
M. W. Shelley

ADDRESS: John Gregson Esq./ 1 Cumberland St. ORIGINAL: Sir John Shelley-Rolls. UNPRINTED and UNPUBLISHED. TEXT: From copy made by Sir John Shelley-Rolls.

407. *To John Murray*   Sunday Morning [? June 8, 1832]
                                    Somerset St.

Dear Sir

The more I look over Lord Byron, the less do I see what I can say in illustration—historical, since the Life so copiously treats of them—for instance in Don Juan, the only things I can discover is in Canto IV cxi—

I knew one woman of that purple school which the Lady C. alluded to in the life—Vol. II, 268— But as Lady Charlemont would recognize herself in such an assertion, it would not be right to put it in—and in Canto XIV, c. where the dangerous passion arising from a game of billiards alludes to Lady F. W. W. the Heroine of the Bride—and the Ginevra of the sonnets—of the Poems to tell you that Florence is Mrs. Spencer Smith—is to tell you what you know already

"When all around was dark & drear"

was to Mrs. Leigh

Thou art not false but thou art fickle

to Lady Oxford—

"Though the day of my destinys over

to Mrs. Leigh

Well thou art happy & I feel

to Mary Charworth

All this you know already— The feelings which gave rise to each poem, are so dwelt on in the Letters in Mr. Moore's Life—that there seems nothing left to say on that subject.—and by printing the poems in a chronological order, you force on the readers apprehension his state of mind when he wrote them. The difficulty of clothing well his ideas resulting from youth—though they forced expression—which made the Hours of Idleness a failure. The depth of

[1] Sir Timothy had forbidden Mary to send Percy to Eton, to which at first she was inclined. Percy entered Harrow at Michaelmas. (See Letter 411.)

passion, nursed in solitude—and wild romantic scenery which breathes in his poem to Thirza—who she was I do not know—I believe a cousin—at any rate she was a real person *decidedly*—and his feelings of misery on her death most real— I have heard him express the sensations of acute despair that produced those poems—and those [lines] "on a Cornelian heart that was broken"— Alone in Greece—his imagination imparted its fire to his feelings—and encreased their impression on his own heart, as well as bestowing greater power of language and poetry— Returned to England & mingling with the world, a certain elegance mingled itself with his with his [*sic*] inspiration, and was diffused over his productions—remarkable especially in the "Bride"— Attached one after the other to women of fashion his heroines displayed the delicacy & refinement of civilization.

When he quitted England, feeling himself wronged—an outcast & a mourner—his mind took a higher flight— It fed upon his regrets—& on his injuries—& Manfred & the 3d Canto of C[hilde] H[arold] bear marks of solitary ruminations in wild scenery—detached from the spirit of fashion & the world— The gaieties and incorrectness of his Venetian Life breathed their Influence in Beppo & D[on] Juan—while solitary Lido—the moonlit palaces—and the deserted ruined grandeurs of that city awakened the vein that displayed itself in the 4th Canto of C[hilde] H[arold] in Mazeppa—in the Ode on Venice.

As his mind became more subdued—he became more critical—but his school of criticism being of the narrow order, it confined his faculties in his tragedies & Lord Byron became sententious & dull—except where character still shone forth—or where his critical ideas did not *intrude* to mar— Sarcasm, before confined to his speech—now acquiring a sting from his susceptibility to the attacks made on him induced him to write the Vision—& the solitude in which he lived at Ravenna gave birth to deep thoughts—to Cain— and Heaven & Earth—

At Pisa he again belonged more to the English world— It did him little good— Werner he wrote chiefly because he had for many years thought it a good subject. He was very anxious to go on with D. Juan—and verging on the time when people revert to past feelings, instead of dwelling on the present —he amused himself by descanting on English fashionable life— The last Cantos of D. J. were written with great speed— I copied them. There were scarcely any erasures and his chief delight was in sending them to me, to date the beginning & end with the name of the same month to prove how quickly they were composed— The opposition he met concerning the Liberal made him defy the world in D. Juan— Then it made him despise the Liberal itself so that when he wrote expressly for it, he wrote tamely—as is the case with The Island— But, in the end, this war gave him a disgust to Authorship— and he hurried to Greece to get a new name as a man of action—having arrived at the highest praise as a poet.

I have thus run through his works, to shew you what I think and know of the periods of their composition and the moods of mind in which they were written. If you think that a few lines of their history appended to each (which you could alter & frame as you like) would be of use you can judge by this sketch, what my view would be, & I should be happy to furnish them—but still I think, the life supplies the place of any such observations.

I write in haste. Next week I leave town for 3 months— Would it not be better that I saw Mr. Finden before I went? I have been reading Contarini Fleming—Who is the Author?[1] I like parts of it excessively—especially the 1st volume— Thanks for the 6th of the Life— Permit me to remind you that the copy you gave Mrs. Williams needs also a 6th vol.—

I am dr. Sir

Ys. truly
M W. Shelley

ADDRESS: John Murray Esp/ 50 Albermarle St. POSTMARK: [? 8.JU]/ 1832. ORIGINAL: British Museum (Add. MSS 38,510, ff.56–60); A.L.S., 9 pp. 8vo. PRINTED: Grylls, *Mary Shelley*, 282–84. TEXT: From original letter.

408. *To John Gregson**

33 Somerset St.
Saturday [June (? 9), 1832]

Dear Sir,

I enclose the receipt and will you be so good as to give the cheque to the Bearer. I leave town with Percy in less than a fortnight, as soon as his holydays begin— I shall go to Sandgate in Kent—that being a quiet and healthy place. Percy has lately been taking riding lessons at the Knightsbridge Barracks— It is arranged that he goes to Harrow after the Summer holyday—he will board with Mr. Kennedy, the Under Master—Dr. Longley, the Head Master, not having a vacancy— I called with him twice at your house, on our return from Church, but was not so fortunate as to find you.

I am, dear Sir,
Yours Obly.,
M. W. Shelley

ORIGINAL: Sir John Shelley-Rolls. UNPRINTED and UNPUBLISHED. TEXT: From copy made by Sir John Shelley-Rolls.

409. *To Frederic M. Reynolds*

Sandgate—Thursday [August 2, 1832]

Dear Fred

Many thanks for the cash—and tell Mr. Heath that I am much obliged to him for sending it me so soon. There wanted a page of my story in the proof—

[1] Benjamin Disraeli (1832, 4 vols.).

I should like to have corrected that also—as it was the *last* & the most likely to be incorrect in the manuscript[1]—

I have taken your advice and Miss Trelawny is paying me a visit—to make assurance doubly sure her father has accompanied her—to be sure he stays only a few days[2]—

As to the question you ask me, after reminding you that friendship is but a name, I add also with the Poet

And love is still an emptier sound[3]

if it makes you thin, you find it worse than I doo—for I am not thin—

Adieu I write in haste

Yours truly
M S.

ADDRESS: F. M. Reynolds Esqre. ORIGINAL: British Museum (Add. MSS 27,925, ff.125–26); A.L.S., 3 pp. (3½ x 4½ inches). PRINTED: Grylls, *Mary Shelley*, 216. TEXT: From original letter.

410. *To Maria Gisborne*

Sandgate,
24 August [1832].

Our letters, dearest Friend, it would seem crossed on the road—the stupidity of the people of Somerset St.—so arranged it that I did [not] get yours till last Friday.—Not being in town and unable to hunt out and see people—the best thing I could do, as it appeared to me, was to enclose your *interesting* and *well written* letter to Dr. Bowring, with whom I am acquainted. I have this moment got his answer—he is at Exeter—and he tells me that in a few days he will be at Plymouth, and he adds—"I will then call on Mrs. Gisborne, whom I have heard Bentham mention with tenderness—and whose visit to him was a great delight." "I think Bentham mentioned the letter more than once." If you have not already seen Bowring, you will now expect him—and I write and send this letter immediately, that you may have previous intimation— How could you imagine that I should not be delighted to do any commission for you and this one was most easily executed.[4]

Here I am still. Trelawny and his daughter are still with me— Thank God he remains—for I do not know how I should be able to support her frivolity, but for the aid of his more amusing company—she is amiable, lively

[1] Two of Mary's stories appeared in *The Keepsake* (edited by Reynolds) for 1833: "The Invisible Girl" and "The Brother and Sister."

[2] Trelawny returned to England in May, 1832. His daughter Julia ("my first-born daughter") arrived at Mary's house at Sandgate on Wednesday, August 1, Trelawny with her. For Trelawny's letters arranging for the visit, see Marshall, II, 244–45. Julia had been living with Trelawny's mother, but was soon to be sent to the Continent and put in the care of some lady. Trelawny asked Mary to take Julia to Dover.

[3] Goldsmith, "The Hermit, A Ballad," line 77 (*The Vicar of Wakefield*, chapter 8).

[4] Mrs. Gisborne had been writing with the hope of publishing. Sir John Bowring was editor of the *Westminster Review*. Mr. Gisborne later wrote a story and (in 1835) tried, with Mary's help, to get it published (see Letter 448).

and polite, but so unidea'd   so silly in her gaiety—so childish yet overgrown in her merriment, that it is hard to bear—never was there such an opposite to her father—   He talks of visiting Plymouth, and I shall make him call on you—   You must please him—for he loves good sense, liberality and enthusiasm, beyond all things—he is too violent in his politics for me—he is radical à l'outrance—and altogether unprejudiced—to use the common phrase—and yet as full of prejudices as he can hold—which contradiction you will have no difficulty in understanding—   If you have any *very* pretty girl among your acquaintance, enchant him by shewing her to him—he is sadly off here—I never found so great a dearth of female beauty as at Sandgate.

My Percy is gone back to school—   I love the dear fellow more and more every day—he is my sole delight and comfort—   On going away he insisted on having his supper alone in his own room—telling me, to persuade me, that Sancho liked an onion behind a door, and why might he not enjoy the pleasures of solitary fare? I cannot tell you how much cleverer—and more companionable he was than my present companion—   We have had a good deal of rain and eternal wind; this one day has risen cloudless and breezeless on us— There is a want of wood here—but the sea is open—and the hills the most singular in the world—   They are so precipitous, that they look mountains— yet three steps leads you to their summits—and when you get up one rather higher than the rest—you see them sprinkled about, in conical shapes each distinct, with ravines between, but so low that you could almost step from one to the other—   They are verdant, and covered with sheep and cattle. I am reading a little Greek—and amusing myself as well as I can—but I am very stupid—and not at all in an energetic mood—though not quite so languid as when I was in town—   I am here, wishing for nothing but an exemption from pecuniary annoyances, both for myself and my father—unwilling to return to town, yet I must next month tho' but for a short time only—   I shall settle myself not far from Richmond. Jane, Jeff and her children are at [? Jolito]—   Will any change ever come there? None, I imagine, but what grim necessity may bring—and I hope that will keep afar.

You do not mention the cholera[1]—as with us in London, I suppose you hear less of it on the spot, than we do at a distance from you—   Is it not strange that it should have got to New York? And reign there so violently— fear is its great auxillary—and as that seems very great among the Yankees, that will explain it. By the bye, Trelawny is *America-mad*—a feeling with which I have no sympathy—if you have, cela vous fera fortune—   Have you

[1] The cholera appeared in many places in 1832—London, Paris, Vienna, New York. Claire became very apprehensive about her relatives in England. On March 24, 1832, she wrote from Pisa urging Mary to flee from London with Percy: "I am nearly mad with fear about the cholera. . . . I have taken it into my head you will surely have it."—*Shelley and Mary*, IV, 1157. Her fears were partly realized, for her half-brother, William Godwin, died of cholera on September 8, 1832. On February 1, 1833, Claire wrote to Jane Williams Hogg from Pisa: "I have at length insured Percy's life for a thousand pounds, and now all my end must be to keep up the payment of it." —*Shelley and Mary*, IV, 1176.

read his book? Pray do— After all his going to Plymouth is very uncertain. Let me hear from you as often as you can. You write very good letters. As is often the case with those who possessing great talents, yet find difficulty in writing—for then they do not pay us with words merely—but with ideas, concisely and energetically clothed. If you had not been in the midst of a great town like Plymouth—when I wanted the open country so much, I should have visited Devonshire, instead of coming here— Remember me with all kindness to Signor Giovanni, who I hope is quite recovered—take care of your precious self—Maria Carissima and love ever

Your true friend

M. W. Shelley

ADDRESS: Mrs. Gisborne/ 17 Union St./ Plymouth,/ Devon. ENDORSED: Sandgate 24th Aug. 1832. 27th. ORIGINAL: Sir John Shelley-Rolls. UNPRINTED and UNPUBLISHED. TEXT: From copy made by Sir John Shelley-Rolls.

411. *To John Gregson*

Sandgate, Kent.
1 September, 1832.

Dear Sir,

I send the receipt, will you have the goodness to send me the cheque in return to this place.

I have been spending the Midsummer holydays with Percy in this quiet watering place— He is now returned to Mr. Slaters, and enters at Harrow at Michaelmas—by which time I shall be in town for the purpose of placing him there and I shall call on you with him, hoping to be more fortunate than hitherto in finding you.

I was sorry to see poor Mr. Whitton's death[1] in the papers, I hope you are quite well.

I am, Sir,

Yours obtly.

Mary W. Shelley

ADDRESS: J. Gregson Esq.,/ Bedford Row,/ London. ORIGINAL: Sir John Shelley-Rolls. UNPRINTED and UNPUBLISHED. TEXT: From copy made by Sir John Shelley-Rolls.

412. *To John Gregson**

Sandgate,
5 Sep. 1832.

Dear Sir,

I have safely received the check for £100 and am much obliged to you— I think this place the healthiest in the world (though a little windy and cold)

[1] He died in July. See Letter 394, note 1.

Percy learnt to swim, and I sent him up to town robust and stout. He is a good boy and the greatest possible comfort to me.

    I am, dr. Sir,

      Yrs. Obly.,

        M. W. Shelley

> ADDRESS: John Gregson Esq./ Bedford Row,/ London. ORIGINAL: Sir John Shelley-Rolls. UNPRINTED and UNPUBLISHED. TEXT: From copy made by Sir John Shelley-Rolls.

413. *To Edward John Trelawny*

Somerset St.

Monday [October 8, 1832]

Dear Trelawny,

    I came home this morning and am impatient to see you. I enjoyed myself at Harrow as much as the vile weather would permit. Percy is very happy—he likes his school and is delighted with the freedom and comfort he enjoys. There are 30 boys in the same House with him—only two of whom have the power of fagging—so that he does not in the least suffer by the only evil of a Public School.

    I send you Claire's Article with Mr. Bulwer's note. Her Article is excellent and perfectly adapted, I should think for a Magazine. I have an idea that Lady Blessington is the person who is furnishing them with articles on Italy—and compared to Claire's they must be poor. Do let Marryatt[1] see them—and make him be pleased with them—print them in the No. for November—and desire more. Take great care it is not lost and if he rejects it, let me have it back immediately—as I must get it in somewhere with as little delay as possible.

    I return to all my cares—which are sufficiently weighty—but when you call I will forget them—and for a short time enjoy a respite.

Yours ever,

M. S.

[P.S.] Perhaps if Mr. M[arryatt] knew that the New Monthly were bringing out a series of Articles on Italy—he may be eager for rival ones for the Metropolitan.

> ORIGINAL: Sir John Shelley-Rolls. PRINTED: Grylls, *Mary Shelley,* 212n, 228n (quots., 7 and 5 lines). TEXT: From copy made by Sir John Shelley-Rolls.

414. *To John Gregson**

33 Somerset St.

8 October, 1832.

Dear Sir,

    I should be glad if you will let Sir Timothy know that Percy has now been

---

[1] Frederick Marryat (1792–1848), editor of the *Metropolitan Magazine.* Claire's article did not appear in this periodical. On September 1 Trelawny had written: "If Bulwer makes any difficulty regarding the article written by Clare, I shall readily, if you like, try the 'Metropolitan,' which seems as good, if not better."—*Shelley and Mary,* IV, 1167. Claire wrote from Pisa on October 26: "Thank Trelawny for me for his kindness about the article."—*Ibid.,* IV, 1172.

a fortnight at Harrow—   I have been spending a week there on a visit to Lady
Paul, and found my Son perfectly contented and happy. He is at the house of
Mr. Kennedy, the Under Master, who expresses himself pleased with his
progress and his docility. Percy has been disappointed in not seeing his Grandfather this year and desires his duty and love to him. He is in the 2nd Remove
of the 4th Form—and will go higher before Xmas. As he went immediately
from Kensington[1] to Harrow I was unable to bring him to you as I wished.

I am, dear Sir,

Yours Obdly.

M. W. Shelley

ADDRESS: John Gregson Esq./ Bedford Row. ORIGINAL: Sir John Shelley-Rolls.
UNPRINTED and UNPUBLISHED. TEXT: From copy made by Sir John Shelley-
Rolls.

415. *To John Murray*

33 Somerset St.
Portman Sq
25 Oct. 1832

My dear Sir

I am very tardy in returning the volumes of Ld Byron's works[2]—because I
felt that after all, I had little to say to any purpose. I send them now,—but I am
afraid you will be disappointed. May I ask for the volumes of the New Edition,
which I have not received. The 6th was the last sent to me I think—the last
of the "Life" it was. I have not yet seen Mr. Finden to see how he proceeds
with the Engraving[3]—for I have not long returned to town—and have been
much occupied since I came back. I have placed my Son at Harrow—& spent
a week with some friends of mine, who have a house there—   The school is
in excellent repute now—and Percy is very happy there—   I hope that you
& your Family are quite well—   I am, dear Sir

truly Ys. obliged

M W Shelley

ORIGINAL: Keats Museum, Hampstead (given by Colonel [Sir John] Murray);
A.L.S., 1 p. 4to. UNPRINTED and UNPUBLISHED. TEXT: From original letter.

416. *To Jane Williams Hogg*[4]

[London, ? 1831–32]

Dearest Jane—

I send the fly for you—   Come to me immediately as you love me. I may
say that I send for you on a matter of *life & death*—   Yet be not alarmed—

---

[1] That is, from Mr. Slater's school.
[2] Which Mary had been annotating for the "New Edition" in 17 vols. See Letters 404 and 407.
[3] Of Shelley's portrait. See Letter 404.
[4] This is the most extraordinary of all Mary's letters. I can find not the slightest clue to the
mystery referred to. Nor can I suggest even an approximate date. Jane Williams (Mrs. Hogg since
1827) lived at 12 Maida Place in July, 1835, and had been there at least since 1832. After March 4,
1836, letters to her are addressed to 12 Maida Vale.

my sending arises from *precaution* more than *necessity*—yet you—indeed you must come.

Do not shew any alarm on arriving at this house—there is no occasion for any—& you would *much gratify* me if you would shew none at *your house*—but let it be only supposed that as I have talked of calling for you in the Fly—that I send in consequence— I shall of course explain all when I see you & you will understand my earnestness to have you here for a day or two—as well as my wish to conceal that any thing extraordinary has prompted me to send for you—till you yourself know the cause

But come—my only Friend come—to the deserted one— I am too ill to write more.

[Unsigned]

ADDRESS: Mrs. Hogg/ 12 Maida Place/ Edgware Road. ORIGINAL: British Museum (Add. MSS 43,805, no folio (34); A.L. (unsigned), 1½ pp. 4to. UNPRINTED and UNPUBLISHED. TEXT: From original letter.

417. *To John Gregson*

33 Somerset St.
Saturday, 1 Dec. [18]32.

My dear Sir,

I send you the usual receipt. If you can give the bearer the cheque in exchange it would convenience me, as I am going out of town for a week on Monday or Tuesday and should be glad of it before I go. Otherwise perhaps you will mention when I can send again.

My Son comes home for his holydays on Dec. 11th and on the following Sunday, if agreable to you, I will call on you with him in Cumberland St.

I am, dr. Sir,
Yrs. Obly.
M. W. Shelley

ORIGINAL: Sir John Shelley-Rolls. UNPRINTED and UNPUBLISHED. TEXT: From copy made by Sir John Shelley-Rolls.

418. *To John Gregson*

[London] Sunday [December 2, 1832]

Dear Sir,

I feel so ashamed to trouble you—but you quite forgot your promise yesterday. Perhaps you will be good enough to send to me tomorrow morning—Otherwise I shall send to Bedford Row early on Tuesday and hope that you will have left the cheque ready for my messenger.

Yrs. Obedly.
M. W. Shelley

ADDRESS: John Gregson Esq./ Cumberland St. ENDORSED: 3 Decr. 1832. Mrs. M. W. Shelley. ORIGINAL: Sir John Shelley-Rolls. UNPRINTED and UNPUBLISHED. TEXT: From copy made by Sir John Shelley-Rolls.

419. *To John Gregson*

[London, December 3, 1832]

Dear Sir,

I send you the receipt as you desire—and will send early tomorrow morning for the cheque—when I shall be so glad if you will give it.

Yours Obly.

M. W. Shelley

ENDORSED: 3 Dec. 1832. Mrs. M. W. Shelley. ORIGINAL: Sir John Shelley-Rolls. UNPRINTED and UNPUBLISHED. TEXT: From copy made by Sir John Shelley-Rolls.

420. *To John Gregson*

33 Somerset St.

16 Dec. 1832.

Sir,

The enclosed papers will in some degree explain to you the nature of my difficulties, and I hope excuse me, for applying thro' you, to request Sir Timothy Shelley to afford me that assistance, without which, I, and, what is of more consequence, my Son will be placed in a situation of great embarrassment.

The letter to Mrs. Paul is one from Dr. Longley, Head Master at Harrow, to whom she wrote last year, at my request, for particulars as to the expence of that school. It was upon the information contained in that letter, that I pressed Sir Timothy to arrange that his Grandson should go to it—he kindly complied, and afforded me the means.

On applying again to Dr. Longley, his numbers are full, so I placed Percy with Mr. Kennedy the Under Master, whose terms are higher than Dr. Longley, but who said that the bills should not exceed £150 per ann.—which I hoped to be able to meet.

You may judge of my consternation on receiving the enclosed account for one quarter. Having had many things to provide for Percy on his first going to a Public School, I am not before hand with the world— I have many things to get for him on his return—he is at home for the holydays—and I have to provide for my own expences till next March—you may judge therefore that it is impossible for me to pay a bill of £75—which must be discharged before the 16th Janry. when the school reopens. I had expected to be called upon for rather less than half that sum— I have no resources except Sir Timothy's allowance, and have no possible means of meeting it. In this emergency I am forced to have recourse to Sir Timothy— I feel great pain in making this demand, and regret exceedingly having been led into false views with regard to the expence of the school, through the representations of its Masters. But there is no use in regret—the bill must be paid. I do trust that Sir Timothy's interest in and kindness towards his Grandson will induce him to assist me on this occasion, and to excuse this inevitable request.

69

What is to be done for the future is another question— On examining
Mr. Kennedy's account I find that I may hope that the future quarterly bills
may fall short of this by about twenty pounds—which yet leaves a sum of £55
which is beyond what I can meet—as thus Percy would cost me very nearly
£300 p. ann. including holydays at home, &c. He must not be taken from Harrow—for having once entered a public school, he cannot leave it without a slur.
There is one expedient, which, with Sir Timothy's leave, I shall adopt. You see
that Dr. Longley says that no objection exists against home Boarders—and
Percy tells me that some of the best and most highly esteemed boys in the school
are home Boarders. My design is therefore to go to reside at Harrow after the
Xmas holydays—the school, the pupil room, which he must attend, books, &c.
would limit the expences to about £50 per ann. and I could meet his other
expences & my own with that respectability, which Sir Timothy must desire
that his Grandson should enjoy. I should have to take a house there, and in
some degree furnish it—however if the present bill be defrayed through Sir
Timothy's kindness, and he does not object to the plan I mention, I have every
hope we shall go on well for the future, without again annoying him.
If he objects, will he be so good as to direct me as to what I ought to do—as I
shall myself be totally at a loss, and deeply anxious on the subject.

I enclose also a note from Mr. Kennedy concerning Percy's character and
progress, which Sir Timothy will perceive to be a favorable report— Percy
went to Harrow at Michaelmas.

I am, dear Sir,

Yr. Obedtly.,

M. W. Shelley

[P. S.] I write this letter fearing that I may miss you again. I ought to
mention that the hosiers, joiners, &c. mentioned in the bill—are for repairs and
furniture for Percy's bed room and study—items I certainly had no idea of
being called upon to defray.

It is impossible to say how exceedingly anxious I feel. To know that here
is a debt I am unable to pay is very painful, but the idea of any injury arising
to Percy in the course of his education, is ten times worse— I hope Sir Timothy will consider these things, and prevent any real harm from occurring.
Allow me to entreat you to use your influence in our behalf.

ADDRESS: John Gregson Esq./ A. ENDORSED: Copy sent to Sir Timy. Shelley,
27 Dec. 1832. ORIGINAL: Sir John Shelley-Rolls. UNPRINTED and UNPUBLISHED.
TEXT: From copy made by Sir John Shelley-Rolls.

421. *To John Gregson*

33 Somerset St., Portman Sq.
2 Jan. 1833.

Dear Sir,

I hope you will not think me importunate if I remind [you] that in a
fortnight Percy's holydays end—and I must come to some decision, as well

[   ] his bill— I am not a little anxious to know the result of
my application to [Sir Timothy. (*MS faded and illegible*)].

Yours obedly.,

M. W. Shelley

ORIGINAL: Sir John Shelley-Rolls. UNPRINTED and UNPUBLISHED. TEXT: From
copy made by Sir John Shelley-Rolls.

422. *To John Gregson*＊

33 Somerset St.
3 Jan. [1833]

My dear Sir,

Your note alarms me beyond measure. My childs respectability through
life depends upon his going on fairly at his school. I will, if you will permit
me, call in Bedford Row tomorrow between twelve and one to ask your
advice as to what I should do. I do not ask this [   ] for any common
[   ] and I must think that upon *some conditions* Sir Timothy will
consent to give me a sum on which the education and welfare of his Grandson
entirely depend. I have no other resource on Earth.

I am, dear Sir,

Yours obly.

M. Shelley

ORIGINAL: Sir John Shelley-Rolls. UNPRINTED and UNPUBLISHED. TEXT: From
copy made by Sir John Shelley-Rolls.

423. *To John Gregson*

33 Somerset St.
13 Janry. 1833.

My dear Sir,

The weather was so bad today that I did not fulfil my engagement—hoping
to see you—and thinking also that by delaying a day, there was a greater
chance of your being able to oblige me without inconvenience. I will call
tomorrow without fail, at half past one—in Bedford Row—as that is the last
day of the holydays.

I am, dear Sir,

Yrs. Obly.

M. W. Shelley

ADDRESS: John Gregson Esq./ Cumberland St. ORIGINAL: Sir John Shelley-
Rolls. UNPRINTED and UNPUBLISHED. TEXT: From copy made by Sir John
Shelley-Rolls.

424. *To Maria Gisborne*

33 Somerset St.
16 Jan^{ry} 1833.

Dear Maria,

I was very glad to receive the Signor Giovanni's invelope (more by far
than the enclosure—which did not amuse me in the least) and to hear that
your silence was occasioned merely by your being the naughtiest person in

the world, and not through any mishap.—This being the case—and being assured that a letter from me will not bore you—I scribble a few lines, being secure of a frank tomorrow— If modesty on the score of postage prevents your writing, you may at any time direct to me (*under cover*) to Major Beauclerk M. P. 12 Chester St. Grosvenor Place, London.

Never was poor body so worried as I have been ever since I last wrote, I think—worries which plague and press on one, and keep one fretting. Money of course is the Alpha and Omega of my tale. Harrow proves so fearfully expensive that I have been sadly put to it to pay Percy's bill for one quarter (£80 soltanto) and to achieve it, am hampered for the whole year— My only resource is to live at Harrow—for in every other respect, I like the school and would not take him from it. He will become an home boarder—and school expences will be very light. I shall take a house, being promised many facilities for furnishing it by a kind friend— To go and live at pretty Harrow, with my Boy, who improves each day, and is everything I could wish, is no bad prospect—but I have much to go through, and am so poor that I cannot turn myself. It is hard on my poor dear Father— And I sometimes think it hard on myself—to leave a knot of acquaintances I like—but that is a fiction—for half the times I am asked out, I cannot go, because of the expence—and I am suffering now for the times when I do go, and so incur debt. No, Maria mine —God never intended me to do other than struggle through life—supported by such blessings as make existence more than tolerable—and yet surrounded by such difficulties as make fortitude a necessary virtue, and destroys all idea of great good luck— I might have been much worse off and I repeat this to myself ten thousand times a day, to console myself for not being better— and it has now and then the desired effect. Had God meant me ever to be well off, he had taken Sir Tim to himself twelve years ago[1]—if decently, *ten*— As it is I shall be *imbrogliata*—e non avrei da vantarmi mai— Pazienza—e basta.

Poor Janey climbing a pair of wooden [? up] steps "on household cares intent"—fell—or rather the steps came in two, and she and they came down *by the run*— She escaped with only breaking the ligaments of her elbow joint, neither dislocating it, nor injuring the bone. It was an affair of a good deal of pain, and much inconvenience, it being her right arm— But she is now perfectly recovered. Jeff is well and flourishing—the children well— Dina is a very nice girl indeed.

My Father's Novel[2] is printed and I suppose will come out soon. Poor dear fellow! It is hard work for him— I am in all the tremor of fearing what I shall get for my novel,[3] which is nearly finished— His and my comfort depend on it— I do not know whether you will like it— I cannot guess

[1] In which case Shelley would not have been drowned.
[2] *Deloraine*, 1833.
[3] *Lodore*, published by Richard Bentley in 1835.

whether it will succeed— There is no *writhing* interest—nothing wonderful, nor tragic— Will it be dull? Chi lo sa! We shall see— I shall of course be very glad if it succeeds.

Percy went back to Harrow today. He likes his school much— Have I any other news for you? Trelawny is gone—to America—he is about to cross to Charlestown—at the moment that there is a prospect of War. War in America! I am truly sorry— Brothers should not fight for the different and various portions of their inheritance— What is the use of republican principles and liberty, if Peace is not the offspring? War not Kings is the [   ] of the world— War is the companion and friend of Monarchy—if it be the same of freedom—the gain is not much to Mankind between a Sovereign and a president.

The Countess Guiccioli is gone at last[4]—what she found to please her in this dingy land, I cannot guess— Not an Amante, I believe—as far as I could judge by the aspect of things. Still she did like it and was sorry to go.

I will write to you soon when I leave this place— Meanwhile you may enclose your letter to Major Beauclerk—writing my name in pencil on the enclosed letter— I may be, and probably shall, in [? Surrey] and [will] receive [it] by the General Post— He will then frank it on to me—and will be sure to know my address as I am in correspondence with his sister, who writes to me in the same way.

I wish I had more cheering news for you—but loneliness—my unsupported situation and the difficulties and annoyances that surround me are not *rallegrante*— Will it ever be better? I despair for myself, and only live again in my child, who is the delight of my heart.

Adieu, dear Friend, send me a few kind words— Present my regards to your husband and believe me—

Ever Affly. Yours
M. W. S.

ADDRESS: Mrs. Gisborne/ 17 Union St./ Plymouth./ A. W. Beauclerk. POSTMARK: London/ JAN.19/ 1833. ENDORSED: London, 16th Jany. 1833. recd 21st do. Ans. 6th July 1833. Mary Shelley. ORIGINAL: Sir John Shelley-Rolls. PRINTED: *Shelley and Mary*, IV, 1173–75; Marshall, II, 254–55 (incomplete). TEXT: From copy made by Sir John Shelley-Rolls.

425. *To Edward John Trelawny*

33 Somerset St.
Friday Even^g, Jan^y [18]33.

My dear Trelawny,

I was very glad to get your letter. I did not suspect your going so immediately—but as you did not come on Sunday, I sent to your lodgings, to ask you to dine on Wednesday with Papa and Jane—but you had disappeared— It is frightful to think of you exposing yourself to that miserable cold—but that you bear a charmed life, you must have died—considering your previous

---

4 She had arrived in England in April, 1832. (See Letter 403.)

indisposition. Nothing harms you however, which destroys others, and I do not doubt that you will return to find me a *Vecchiaccia,* while you still are conquering hearts—and living, like a bee on sweets— What a pity you do not contrive a little wax as well as honey, but that comes from other flowers—and except a Virginian Widow should cede her right of flogging and rearing tobacco, none of the Fredericas, Barbaras, or Katherines can furnish your hive, and turn the Wanderer into a lazy Gentleman in an easy chair.

You will return with a whole life of new experiences—the tale of a thousand loves—the same yet ever new— Dont let them (your Americans) spoil Lady Berghersh's—Lady Dorothea's and the gentle Marchesa's[1] work—and rub off that polish which adorns so well the good strong metal. Jane, whom I saw today, says that she did not wish for a leavetaking but wished much to see you again— She says she will write to you and meanwhile sends her love— She and Mr. and Mrs. Godwin dined here on Wednesday, and your absence was much lamented. The two ladies composed your Elegy—which was as laudatory as an Epitaph ought to be— While the wilds of America were destined to be your untimely grave. For myself, I consign you to the elements you love, believing that they will return you again, all the better in health and spirits for their congenial ministrations.

I will give your message to Mrs. Leicester Stanhope if ever I see her again—but it looks much as if I were going to take an everlasting adieu of London. This house is let—so I cannot prolong my stay— Sir John Paul in the kindest way, offers to furnish the house at Harrow for me. I do not like obligation yet should disoblige if I refused. What a strange position mine is and how annoying—however as it might be worse I will not repine. While Percy continues the blessing and comfort to me that he is, I ought not [*MS torn*]

I have heard and seen nothing of the [   ] or Beauclerks. I cannot tell you how your Lady pales and wanes, and becomes a skeleton. Did you really cause her to grow a little thinner, you would do her a greater service, than you did poor Frederica. I think of going to Ditton for a week or two. When in America you had better direct to me to the care of my father, 44 Gower Place, Euston Sq. Although few, and those slender, ties bind me to London, and I am surrounded by privation and mortification I suppose I should have lingered on for ever but for the wreck of my finances— Reasonably and prospectively speaking, I do not regret going—and yet it is sad to change—to be cut off from the few one likes—It is different in travelling, when the excitement of something new prevents regret for the old.

Pray write again at the moment of sailing— Stay as short a time as you possibly can among the Yankees—so that you may not write "that was" of all your young womankind—not find me with a mask on—for fear of shewing my face. All happiness be yours.   Yours,

                                                    M. W. S.

[1] Jane Boccella, who had adopted Zella.

ADDRESS: Edward Trelawny Esq./ Messrs. Rop & Brothers/ 16 Harrington St./ Liverpool. ORIGINAL: Sir John Shelley-Rolls. UNPRINTED and UNPUBLISHED. TEXT: From copy made by Sir John Shelley-Rolls.

426. *To [Charles Ollier]*

33 Somerset St.
31 Jany 1833

[*Summary:*] Sends Ollier the first volume of *Lodore* and describes the whole work. Ollier is to arrange with Richard Bentley for its publication.

ORIGINAL: Keats-Shelley Memorial, Rome; A.L.S., 3 pp. 4to. UNPRINTED and UNPUBLISHED. SUMMARY: From original letter.

427. *To [Charles Ollier]**

33 Somerset St.
11 Feb^ry 1833

My dear Sir

Would it be possible for Mr. Bentley or Mr. Colburn to oblige me with a copy of any of my books—I have not one in the world—& wish to give them to a friend going abroad—　If you can send me all or any—it must be directly, as my friend Sails this week—

When shall I hear from you on the other subject? soon I hope—as I want things to be settled before I leave town, which I shall do almost immediately— So I commend me to your good offices

Yours truly
M W Shelley

ORIGINAL: Owned by Colbeck Radford & Co., London, in February, 1939; A.L.S., 2 pp. 8vo. UNPRINTED and UNPUBLISHED. TEXT: From original letter.

428. *To John Gregson**

33 Somerset St., Portman Sq.
2 March, 1833.

My dear Sir,

I enclose the usual receipt and will send on Monday morning for the cheque —unless you could be so good as to send it to me tomorrow.

On writing to Mr. Kennedy—he mentioned the Easter holydays as the period when I should be able to take Percy from his house—I shall at that time remove to Harrow. You may have seen in the paper that there was a fire at the house of Percy's Tutor—which taking place in the Boys bedrooms, destroyed them all—　Most unluckily all Percy's clothes which I had just sent, were burnt, so that in addition to my other expences, I have had to refit him entirely.

I am, dear Sir,
Yr. Obly. and obliged
M. W. Shelley

ADDRESS: John Gregson Esq./ 18 Bedford Row. ORIGINAL: Sir John Shelley-Rolls. UNPRINTED and UNPUBLISHED. TEXT: From copy made by Sir John Shelley-Rolls.

429. *To Charles Ollier**

33 Somerset St.
Monday 18 March [1833]

My dear Sir

Can I see you tomorrow morning at *twelve?*—or when do you think it likely that you can do me the favor to call? If not tomorrow, I hope some day early this week

I am

Ys. truly
M W Shelley

ORIGINAL: Bodleian Library (MS Montagu d.3, f.97); A.L.S., 1 p. 4to.
PRINTED: *Bodleian Quarterly Record*, VIII, No. 95 (1937) 417. TEXT: From
original letter.

430. *To John Murray**

33 Somerset St.
15 April, 1833.

My dear Sir

Mr. Finden has succeeded with the engraving far better than could have been at all expected— If it is not every thing that one would wish a portrait of Shelley to be, it is very far superior to any thing one could have hoped, considering the picture.

Mr. Finden mentioned to me your request that I should sit for the purpose of an engraving being made. There is no portrait of me—& it will be necessary that a drawing should be made. I do not quite like appearing in public thus— Still I should be sorry to refuse any wish of yours. What artist would you employ? I must tell you that I am (I don't know why) a very difficult subject for the pencil. There is another difficulty. I leave town on Monday 22d inst. for Harrow—& shall not be in town again for several months—so that what is done must be done quickly.

You told me to write to you if I did not receive the remaining volumes of your Edition of Lord Byron— I did so—but you have taken no notice of my *flapper*. I have only the first 6 volumes—you have never sent the rest. I am the more disappointed because I meant to have asked for something more. When I heard that you had given Mr. Trelawny the Landscape Illustrations, I intended as soon as Shelley's portrait was finished, to ask you to be equally generous towards me.

I am, dear Sir

Yours truly & obliged
M W Shelley

ORIGINAL: Sir John Murray; A.L.S., 4 pp. 8vo. UNPRINTED and UNPUBLISHED.
TEXT: From original letter.

MARY W. SHELLEY

from the miniature by
Reginald Eastman

431. *To John Gregson**

Harrow on the Hill,
1 June, 1833.

My dear Sir,

I enclose you my receipt— Will you send me the cheque—which will be only for £75 I suppose—unless Sir Tim. who is in town I hear should hear of my debt to you, from you—and remit it to me. Harrow I find expensive— though of course in the end I shall find living here the cheapest way of going on—

I am, dear Sir,
Yr. Oblly. & obly.
M. W. Shelley

ADDRESS: John Gregson Esq./ 18 Bedford Row. ORIGINAL: Sir John Shelley-Rolls. UNPRINTED and UNPUBLISHED. TEXT: From copy made by Sir John Shelley-Rolls.

432. *To John Gregson*[1]

2 Melbury Terrace, Dorset Sq.
2 Sep. 1833.

My dear Sir,

I send the usual receipt, to be exchanged for a cheque, which you will oblige me by sending by the 2*d*. post to the above address if you do not give it to the bearer.

I am going to make a request which, when I have explained the cause, I hope you will not think unreasonable—you will oblige me greatly if you can comply.

When I arranged to go to Harrow I could not immediately take my Son from the Boarding House—where I had placed him—this occasioned another heavy bill—which was not delivered to me till the beginning of the present holydays.—My moving and settling at Harrow cost me so much as to prevent my being able to reserve any portion of my income— Mr. Kennedy's bill is £65—if I receive only £75 I shall experience very great inconvenience. At Xmas on the contrary—I shall have only the schoolbill, and be able to spare the £25 far more easily. If therefore you would make it convenient to yourself, and let me have my full quarter now—deferring the payment of the remaining £25 till December you would be extricating me from a great deal of difficulty— The bill at Xmas will not be more probably than £25. I shall be so much obliged if you can favor me as I ask.

Percy is quite well— Mr. Kennedy expresses himself quite satisfied with his industry, and on being removed to a higher form this quarter, he took a high place, although having had the Influenza twice (as well as myself) he

[1] Mary spent the first half of September at Putney with Julia Robinson. (See Letter 437.)

was prevented attending the school quite regularly. I return to Harrow at the end of the holydays which conclude on the 18th.

I am, dear Sir,

Yr. Obly.

M. W. Shelley

ORIGINAL: Sir John Shelley-Rolls. UNPRINTED and UNPUBLISHED. TEXT: From copy made by Sir John Shelley-Rolls.

433. *To Charles Ollier*

Harrow. 10 Feb. [*error for November, 1833*]

[*Summary:*] Invites Ollier to visit her at Harrow. Inquires when her novel, *Lodore,* will go to press.

ADDRESSED: Chas. Ollier Esq/ 8 New Burlington St. POSTMARKS: (1) T. P./ Harrow (2) [1]2.NOON.12/ 11.NO/ 1833. ORIGINAL: Keats-Shelley Memorial, Rome; A.L.S., 3 pp. 8vo. UNPRINTED and UNPUBLISHED. SUMMARY: From original letter.

434. *To John Gregson*

Harrow,

2 Dec. 1833.

My dear Sir,

I send the receipt—will you be so good as to send the cheque— I shall be in town tomorrow and can get the cheque cashed there more easily than when I am here— Will you be so good as to send it as soon as you can to me at 2 Melbury Terrace Dorset Sq. by the 2 *d*. post.

Percy is very well indeed—and getting on very well—he is a good boy—and his Masters are quite satisfied with him.

I am, dear Sir,

Yr. Obly.

M. W. Shelley

ADDRESS: John Gregson Esq./ 18 Bedford Row. ORIGINAL: Sir John Shelley-Rolls. UNPRINTED and UNPUBLISHED. TEXT: From copy made by Sir John Shelley-Rolls.

435. *To Charles Ollier**

Harrow,

*Saturday [March 15, 1834]

My dear Sir

I wish the printers wd. go on a little quicker—I only get two proofs[1] a week & am quite tired—especially as something might take me further from town—I should like at least a proof a day—& so have done with it—will you be so good as tell the Printers to be more expeditious

The Hamiltons[2] is very clever—& the character of Susan very sweet—& true

[1] Of *Lodore.*
[2] By Mrs. Gore, *née* Catherine Grace F. Moody (1834, 3 vols.).

to nature & highly interesting—but how very political—& how very radical—
Nor did the Tory Ladies go out of fashion because the Whigs came in—for
there are very few ladies who are not Tories—

I like Godolphin[3] very much— It is like all his things in a high tone of
feeling & truth & beauty

Ever Ys, Obliged

M W Shelley

[P.S.] I wish you & Mrs. Ollier would contrive to come & see me soon—
one day next week if fine— Why not?—

ADDRESS: Chas. Ollier Esq/ 8 New Burlington St. POSTMARK: 7.NIGHT.7/
15.MR/ 1834. ORIGINAL: Owned by Maggs Brothers in December, 1939;
A.L.S., 4 pp. 8vo. UNPRINTED and UNPUBLISHED. TEXT: From original letter.

436. *To Edward John Trelawny*

Harrow,

7 May, 1834.

Dear Trelawny,

I confess I have been sadly remiss in not writing to you— I have written
once however, as you have written once (but once) to me— I wrote in answer
to your letter— I am sorry you did not get it—as it contained a great deal of
gossip— It was misdirected by a mistake of Jane—who had your letter to me
—and told me that the address given was Brown and Barclay—do ask Brown
and Brothers to enquire after it—it was sent at the end of last September to
New York— I told you in that of the infidelity of several of your womenkind—how Mrs. Robert Stanhope was flirting with Bulwer—to the infinite
jealousy of Mrs. Bulwer and making them thus the talk of the town—how your
little Jewess Miss McEliney was desperately in love with and lately married to
Erskine Perry—how Barbara Cummings was blooming and surrounded by
admirers at Lady Thorold's—how Catherine Perry showed a soft inclination
to the handsome Mildmay who never spoke to her—such and much more tittle
tattle was in that letter—all old news now. Mrs. Erskine Perry has been in
Italy with her husband and returns in June to be confined— The Stanhopes
(Captain Robert and wife I mean) went to Paris and were ruined and are
returned under a cloud, to rusticate in the country in England—Bulwer is
making the amiable to his worn wife who is worth in beauty all the Mrs. R. S.'s
in the world—of Barbara I have no news just now. Jane Perry married Frederic
Elliott last summer—she has had the small pox since and says herself that she
has lost all her beauty—she is indeed sadly disfigured—but I hope it will go
off— Mrs. Crawford always asks most kindly after you— None of the Perry
girls liked Erskine's marriage—indeed there were several things attendant on
it which made it disagreable—but he got a good deal of money (for him—
500 a year and 1500£) and he could not do better. Mrs. Leicester Stanhope is

---

[3] A novel by Bulwer-Lytton (1833, 3 vols.).

one of the Belles this season—she goes out a great deal—acts charades and amuses herself and others—she is a good natured clever woman besides being handsome and I like her very much— Julia Robinson is married and just sailed to India—it was a very happy match; her husband is a Major in the B. A. Company's service, he is a handsome man—of very good family tolerably well off and with great expectations— I liked him much and was sorry to lose them both. Claire is still in a situation at Pisa—she is in good health and grown fat—she always asks after you—she had formed acquaintance with Jane Boccella—whom she likes—and describes as you used, as a most interesting and elegant person—She (Jane B.) was just going to be confined of her first child, when Claire last wrote—she is not happy— Claire describes Zella as very handsome clever and spirited, and very charming when she likes— Laurette and Nerina Mason (Tighe) are both married. Laurette's marriage is not propitious, but Nerina appears matched delightfully to an amiable and cultivated and rich Italian[1]— Sir Tim was intended to die last November—being given over, but he has come out as fresh as ever, on a new lease—he has quarrelled with John, wont see him, and is ruining him as he has done me, cutting down his timber, &c.

Georgina is settled in a little cottage in Sussex—everyone visits her—yet her situation is a painful one— Jane has been a good deal indisposed and is grown very thin— Jeff had an appointment which took him away for several months[2]—and she pined and grew ill on his absence—she is now reviving under the beneficent influence of his presence— I called on your Mother a week or two ago—she always asks after you with empressement and is very civil indeed to me—she was looking well—but Julia[3] tells me, in her note enclosing your letter, that she is ill of the same illness as she had two years ago—but not so bad— I think she lives too well— Julia is expecting to be confined in a very few weeks or even days— She is very happy with Burley— He is a thoroughly good natured and estimable man—it is a pity he is [not] younger and handsomer; however she is a good girl and contented with her lot—we are very good friends. I saw from Lord Wenlock's death in the paper a few days ago—he died at his Villa near Florence— I should like much to see your friend Lady Lowther—but though in Europe I am very far from her. I live on my hill, descending to town now and then; I should go oftener if I were richer— Percy continues quite well and enjoys my living at Harrow, which is more than I do, I am sorry to say—but there is no help. My Father is in good health— Mrs. Godwin has been very ill lately but is now better—

---

[1] Lauretta married a Frenchman named Galloni, with whom she lived a tempestuous life. Nerina (b. June 20, 1815) married Bartolomeo Cini. For a delightful account of the stormy life in the Mason family during the wooing of Lauretta, see Claire's letter to Mary, Pisa, October 26, 1832, in Marshall, II, 249–53.

[2] In 1833 Hogg was appointed one of the Municipal Corporation Commissioners by Lord Brougham. He was away from home most of the time from September, 1833 to April, 1834. (See *After Shelley,* xxiv, 73–87.)

[3] Maria Julia, Trelawny's eldest daughter, married John Burley of the Temple.

I thought Fanny Kemble[4] was to marry and settle in America— What a singular resemblance you have discovered— I never saw her except on the stage— So much for news. They say it is a long lane that has no turning; I have travelled the same road for nearly 12 years—adversity poverty and loneliness being my companions— I suppose it will change at last—but I have nothing to tell of myself except that Percy is well—which is the beginning and end of my existence— I am glad you are beginning to respect women's feelings— You have heard of Sir Harry's death— Mrs. Breredon (who is great friends with Salisbury now Sir William, an M. P.) says that it is believed that he has left all he could to the Catholic members of his family. Why not come over and marry Letitia who in consequence will be rich? and I dare say still beautiful in your eyes, though 54— We have had a mild fine winter and the weather now is as warm, sunny and cheering as an Italian May— We have thousands of birds—and flowers innumerable and the trees of spring in the fields—Jane's children are well— The time will come I suppose when we may meet again more befriended by fortune—but youth will have flown—and that in a woman is something— I do not need [to] remind you to marry because I do not think you would make a good husband—else surely—In marriage and its results we can only hope for happiness— I mean to marry when I find a person I should like to have—not very likely to happen in this place— and indeed I have always felt certain that I should never again change my name—and that is a comfort, if a pretty and a dear one. Adieu, write to me often and I will behave better and as soon as I have accumulated a little news write again.

Ever yours,
M. W. S.

ADDRESS: John Edward Trelawny Esq./ Care of The Honble James Barber/ Barbersville/ Orange Co./ Virginia. ORIGINAL: Sir John Shelley-Rolls. PRINTED: Marshall, II, 256–58 (incomplete). TEXT: From copy made by Sir John Shelley-Rolls.

437. *To Maria Gisborne*

Harrow, Middlesex.
17 July [18]34.

My dearest Friend,

I have just received your agonizing and interesting letter. Often have Jane and I said: "When shall we hear from her again?—She forgets us!"—and last spring we looked each day for your arrival. I cannot tell you of my delight in receiving tidings of you—sad as they are. How your letter reached me I cannot exactly say—you directed it to me to *the care of* Major B[eauclerk] which destroyed the priviledge of franking— Pray do not direct to Chester St. again

[4] She married Mr. Pierce Butler in Philadelphia on June 7, 1834. Trelawny had accompanied Charles and Fanny Kemble and Pierce Butler from New York to Niagara. See Margaret Armstrong, *Fanny Kemble* (New York, The Macmillan Co., 1938), 171–76.

at all on any account—Write to me directly *here*. Your letters are worth far more than their postage—or if your extreme tenaciousness of cost prevent your writing on these terms write to me (*not* to the care of, but) *under cover*— no matter the weight of your letter—to The Speaker G. C. B. New Palace Yard. Indeed I beg of you to write not long letters to injure your delicate nerves—but news of your precious health. May life be prolonged, dearest Maria—for your husband's sake you must desire this. His affection is rare and admirable—you are most happy to possess it— You truly deserve it by your qualities, your talents—your devotion to him—still gratitude and constancy are infrequent and delightful to know of. Do write to tell us of your state— I answer your letter immediately to assure you of having received it—and how dearly I prize any communication from you. I will forward it to Jane, it will touch her to the heart. I congratulate you on your [?   ] your Doctor so virtuous—so attached and thank God so capable—your poor faithful Elizabeth—and I would express to S. G. however feebly the respect I feel for his devotion and affection—What scenes Gracious God—wherefore do your creatures exist!—if not for another world wherefore?—how sure I feel that our being will continue yet how and where who can tell!—

I could go on long remarking on each line of your letter, and dwell on the terrible narrative with all the interest and grief it excites, but it will please you more if I tell you of ourselves— Do you know of my taking up my residence at Harrow? In the Autumn of 1832 I placed Percy to board here—but found it so frightfully expensive, that I could only meet it by taking up my abode here and having him as a home boarder. I did this in April 1833— I am satisfied with my plan as regards him—I like the school, and the affection thus cultivated for me will I trust be the blessing of my life. Still there are many drawbacks— This is a dull inhospitable place— I came counting on the kindness of a friend who resided here—but she died of the Influenza—and I live in a silence and loneliness—not possible any where except in England where people are so *islanded* individually in habits— I often languish for sympathy—and pine for social festivity. Percy is much—but I think of you and Henry and shrink from binding up my life in a child, who may hereafter divide his fate from mine— But I have no resource— Everything earthly fails me but him—except on his account I live but to suffer— Those I loved are false or dead—those I love absent and suffering—and I absent and poor can be of no use to them— Of course in this picture I subtract the enjoyment of good health and usually good spirits—these are blessings—but when driven to think I feel so desolate, so unprotected, so oppressed and injured that my heart is ready to break with despair. I came here as I said in April 1833—and 9 June was attacked by the Influenza so as to be confined to my bed—nor did I recover the effects for several months. In September during Percy's holydays I went to Putney and recovered youth and health— Julia Robinson was with me—and we spent days in Richmond Park and on Putney Heath—often walking 12 or 14 miles—which I did without any sense of fatigue. I sorely regretted returning here— I am too poor to furnish— I have lodgings in the town—disagreable ones— Yet often in spite of care and sorrow I feel wholly compensated by my boy. I will try to describe him to you, though it is difficult—In person he is of a fair height and excessively fat—his chest would remind you of a Bacchus, he has a florid complexion, blue eyes—like his father—and his looks and gestures and shape of his face would remind you of Shelley and his person before he grew fat—he is full of spirit and animation but proud and reserved with strangers— There used to be a great want of sensibility—this lingers about him—but is rather concentrated than slight—he loves me more than he knows himself and would not displease me for the world—if he sees me sad he does all he can to comfort me—and would give up any pleasure for my benefit—his temper is a little defective but he is neither violent nor sulky—but perfect and generous and true—he is trustworthy and thoughtful beyond his years—cautious tho' impetuous—and exceedingly constant, so that he now loves Edward and Dina[1] better than any newer friends. He has the true Shelley hatred of society—he has no ambition and little emulation—yet [is] attentive to his lessons and sufficiently diligent—he is the 20th boy in a form of 50 boys—he has a great respect for truth and good faith—One day I said to him—"Suppose when you grow to be a man—you would leave me all alone."—"O Mamma," he said, "How do you think I could be so shabby—that would be too bad!" To be *left all alone* seems to him the worst evil of all—he does not like any poetry except Percy's Ancient Ballads and Shelley's translation of Homer's Hymn to Mercury and the Cyclops—but he likes romances any marvellous tales—and is a great story teller—he is a little bitten by metaphysics—he is always occupied. He is very handsome—and a perfect child in all his notions and quite obedient— He is better to me than any one, for he has no notion of giving up any whim to any body but me,—besides being very incommunicative except to his intimates— God help me if any thing was to happen to him— I should not survive it a week. Besides his society I have also a good deal of occupation— I have finished a Novel[2] —which if you meet with it—read—as I think there are parts that will please you. I am engaged writing the Lives of some of the Italian Literati for Dr. Lardner's Cyclopedia[3]—I have written those of Petrarch Boccaccio &c. and am now engaged on Macchiavelli—This takes up my time and is a source of interest and pleasure.

My Father I suppose you know has a tiny shabby place under Government[4]—the retrenchments of Parliament endanger [it] and render us anxious — He is quite well—but old age takes from his enjoyments Mrs. G[odwin]

---

[1] Jane Williams's children.
[2] *Lodore.*
[3] See Letter 441, note 2.
[4] In April, 1833, Lord Grey appointed Godwin Yeoman Usher of the Exchequer (a sinecure), with residence in New Palace Yard.

after the Influenza has been suffering with the Tic Douleureux in her arm most dreadfully—they are trying all sorts of poisons on her with little effect— Their discomfort and low spirits will force me to spend Percy's holydays in town to be near them. Jane and Jeff are well—he was sent last Autumn and winter by Ld. Brougham as one of the Corporation Commissioners, he was away for months and Jane took the opportunity to fall desperately in love with him— She pined and grew ill and wasted away for him. The children are quite well, Dina spent a week here lately—she is a sweet girl— Edward improves daily under the excellent care taken of his education—I leave Jane to inform you of their progress in Greek—Dina plays wonderfully well—and has shewn great taste for drawing—but the last is not cultivated— I did not go to the Abbey—nor the Opera nor hear Grisi— I am shut out from all things—like you—by poverty and loneliness— Percy's pleasures are not mine I have no other companion— What effect Paganini would have had on you I cannot tell—he threw me into hysterics. I delight in him more than I can express—his wild etherial figure, rapt look—and the sounds he draws from his violin are all superhuman—of human expression it is interesting to see the astonishment and admiration of Lindley Spagnoletti[5] and [? Nina] as they watch his evolutions— Bulwer is a man of extraordinary and delightful talent—but spoilt by vanity disappointed ambition (for he wishes to be a Parliamentary Leader which his deafness entirely prevents) and a certain vulgarity of fashion, not acknowledged by supreme ton. He went to Italy and Sicily last Winter and I hear disliked their inhabitants—to depreciate is his tone—and then a deaf man without a word of Italian to judge of Italians in a rapid journey, of 5 months—si da retta a un tale force!—Yet notwithstanding I am sure he will spread inexpressible and graceful interest over the Last Days of Pompeii [1834]—the subject of his new Novel— Trelawny is in America —and not likely to return— Hunt lives at Chelsea and thrives I hear by his London Journal—I have not seen him for more than a year—for reasons I will not here detail—they regard his family not him— Claire is in a situation at Pisa near Mrs. Mason— Laurette and Nerina are married—the elder badly to one who won her at the dagger's point—a sad unintelligible story—Nerina to the best and most delightful Pistoriese, by name Bartolomeo Cini—both to Italians— Laurette lives at Genoa, Nerina at Livorno—the latter is only newly a Bride and happier than words can express— My Italian maid Maria says to Claire—Non vedro ora mai la mia Padrona ed il mio Bimbo—her Bimbo!—such a Bimbo as tall as I—and large in proportion or rather [*MS torn*]— He has good health with all—he had a blow on his knee which

---

[5] Robert Lindley (1776–1855), the most celebrated violoncello player of his day. He held the position of principal violoncello at the opera from 1794 to 1851.

P. Spagnoletti (1768–September 23, 1834), a distinguished Italian violinist, who spent nearly the whole of his musical life in England and was for thirty years leader of the King's Theatre orchestra. He directed the orchestra at all of Paganini's thirteen concerts. (*Grove's Dictionary of Music and Musicians.*)

menaced a tumor but did not come to one, so I took him to Lawrence in a fright (such a fright—tho' groundless—as made me pass days of torture) over health he said was all his ailment so forbade him animal food—but the less he eats the more robust he grows—his contrast to Edward is whimsical—both in complexion and stoutness—their height is the same.

I have written this letter immediately on receiving yours that you may be sure that it came safe— I direct it simply to Plymouth— I trust you will receive it duly— Pray write one word of information concerning your health —before I attributed your silence to forgetfulness—but you must not trifle now with the anxiety you have awakened— I will write again soon— With kindest regards to your poor good husband—the fondest hopes of hearing that your health is improved and anxious expectation of a letter,

Believe me,

Affectionately yr.

M. W. Shelley

ADDRESS: Mrs. Gisborne/ Plymouth, Devon./ E. S. Ruthven. POSTMARK: London/ July 19/ 1834. ENDORSED: Harrow, 17th July 1824. recd. 20th do. Ans. 22nd Aug. ORIGINAL: Sir John Shelley-Rolls. PRINTED: *Shelley and Mary*, IV, 1181–85; Marshall, II, 258–61 (both incomplete). TEXT: From copy made by Sir John Shelley-Rolls.

438. *To Douglas Jerrold**

13 New Palace Y[ar]d

9 Aug. 1834

Dear Sir

You would very much oblige me if you would give me admissions for 2 for Beau Nash[1] next Wednesday—If that day is not convenient any day next week—only letting me have them as soon as you can. Excuse the impertinence of this request—but a successful dramatic writer must make up his mind to be the victim of impertinence—as a philosopher he will forgive—as a Xtian he will return good for evil—and I shall get the orders.

Dear Sir I am

Ys truly

M W Shelley

ADDRESS: Douglas Jerrold Esq./ Chelsea./ or at T. R. Haymarket. POSTMARKS: (1) 18.PAID.34/ AU.9 (2) 10.F.NOON.10/ AU.9/ 1834. ORIGINAL: Sylva Norman, Oxford; A.L.S., 2 pp. 8vo. UNPRINTED and UNPUBLISHED. TEXT: From original letter.

439. *To Maria Gisborne*

7 Upper Eaton St.

19 August, 1834.

Dearest Maria,

I feel anxious to know whether you got my last letter safely—and above all how you are— There was a little embroglio with your last, from the letter

---

[1] *Beau Nash,* by Douglas Jerrold (1803–57), was produced at the Haymarket on July 16, 1834.

being too heavy for a frank—but if you enclose under cover to the Speaker, this need not disturb you— Do let me hear how your health is—and whether this warm weather has been too much for you—or revived you with a reflex of Italy. Claire says that it is so hot at Pisa that existence is a burthen—here it is pleasant enough to exist if one has nothing else to do.

Mrs. Godwin is gone to Herne Bay to try to recover a little health after an attack of Influenza and tic douleureux— I am in town with Percy during his holydays—to keep Papa company on her absence— Papa likes the heat—and the few less warm days that interpose he calls quite wintry. Percy is fat and blooming—the acquaintances of the Shelleys find him very like that family— Jane is quite well— She has dined with me frequently lately, to meet Papa with whom she is a great favourite. Dina is grown taller than Percy and is a very fine girl— Edward improves; under Jeff's care he must turn out well— I often wish I had a Dah[1] for Percy, who is [? not] quite amenable to feminine management—not that he is disobedient—and being very trustworthy and childish no evil results as yet—but bad habits of imperiousness and thinking only of himself are difficult to be got over—and will be hurtful to him hereafter—and yet a Dah must be something very wonderful for him to respect and obey—and so perhaps it is best as it is—and as it is likely to be for evermore.

I went to the House of Lords the other night and heard the debate on the Tithe Question— Is Lord Brougham a favourite of yours? *Buffone sublime* the Italians would call him—as with all his powers, he plays the Buffoon in the house— His wit and sarcasms provoke laughter—but his want of dignity ill befits the Ld. High Chancellor. I am very angry with him for his speech on the poor laws.

What would I give could I see you again. If I were able to make a trip to Devonshire you would soon see me in your seclusion—sympathizing with Sig. G. and trying to rally the spirit of life in you. Did I tell you of my misfortune, in my Aunt, my Mother's surviving sister, coming over and settling at Pentonville— Everina was never a favourite with any one—and now she is the most intolerable of God's creatures. The worst is, that being poor and friendless, it is on my conscience to pay her attention—and she is so disagreable to me, that I know no punishment so great as spending an hour in her company— Dont let me lead you into a mistake—others might like her—for she can be amusing and means well—but her queerness—her assumption [of] the right that she thinks she has to annoy me, makes me deplore that I cannot *purchase* exemption from personal attentions—and I do as much as I can— The many sorrows and cares I have—and the very little good that is sprinkled over my melancholy existence, renders me blameably intollerant of annoyance.

Adieu, my dearest Friend—pray write and let me know how you are— My Novel is not published yet and God knows when it will be—it is printed and that is all I know about it— Jane and Papa send kindest messages—

[1] Hogg's pet name in his family.

Make my kindest remembrances to Sig. Giov[anni] and believe me with—
with the greatest anxiety to know how you are,

Ever Affectionately Yours,

M. W. Shelley

ADDRESS: Mrs. Gisborne,/ To the care of Dr. Budd/ Plymouth, Devon./ E. S.
Ruthven. POSTMARK: London/ August 19/ 1834. ENDORSED: Recd. 20th Aug.
1834. Ans. 22nd do. ORIGINAL: Sir John Shelley-Rolls. UNPRINTED and UNPUB-
LISHED. TEXT: From copy made by Sir John Shelley-Rolls.

440. *To Maria Gisborne*

Harrow,
October 30 [18]34.

My dearest Maria,

Thank you many times for your kind dear letter—God grant that your
constitution may yet bear up a long time and that you may continue impressed with the idea of your happiness. Your expression is not ill applied—
the object of tender solicitude—necessary and dear to one whom you love and
esteem, you enjoy a greater portion of happiness than many whose lots are
less beset by pain—to be loved is indeed necessary—sympathy and companionship are the only sweets "to make the nauseous draught of life go down"—
and I, who feel this, live in a solitude, such as since the days of hermits in the
desert, no one was ever before condemned to! I see no one—I speak to none—
except perhaps for a chance half hour in the course of a fortnight. I never walk
out beyond my garden—because I *cannot* walk alone—you will say I ought
to force myself, so I thought once, and tried—but it would not do—the sense
of desolation was too oppressive—   I only find relief from the sadness of my
position by living a dreamy existence from which realities are excluded—but
going out disturbed this—I wept—my heart beat with a sense of injury and
wrong—I was better shut up. Poverty prevents my visiting town—I am too
far for visitors to reach me—   I must bear to the end—when and what will
that be? You say truly that my father-in-law's prolonged life will ruin me—
it has done so—twelve years have I spent, the currents of life benumbed by
poverty—and meanwhile he does all he can to injure the future prospects of
Percy and myself. Of him I think,—life and hope are over for me. You may
guess that absorbed in him, I adhere to your advice of cultivating his affection
—   Fate shews her determination to drive me to him alone—she cuts me off
from love, friendship, society, ambition; she gives me him alone—but there is
no sympathy in a child—and though I look forward to reaping a subsequent
harvest from my sacrifices (how likely to be blighted—he will marry and
there ends a Mother's happiness)—yet for the present something more is
needed—something not so unnatural as my present life. Not that I often feel
ennui—I am too much employed—too much a being of dreams—but it hurts
me—it destroys the spring of my mind; it makes me at once over sensitive with
my fellow creatures, and yet their victim and dupe—it takes all strength from
my character—making me, who by nature am too much so—timid. I need to

have one resource, a belief in *my good fortune,* this is exchanged after twelve years of *one* adversity, blotted and sprinkled by *many* adversities—a dark ground with sad figures painted on it—to a perfect belief in my ill fortune—Percy is spared to me because I am to live—   I should be free and die if——— But no—he is a blessing; my heart acknowledges that he is perhaps as great a one as any human being possesses, and indeed, my dear friend, while I suffer I do not repine while he remains—   He is not all you say—he has no ambition—and his talents are not so transcendant as you appear to imagine, but he is a fine, spirited, clever Boy—and I think promises good things—   If hereafter I have reason to be proud of him—these melancholy days and weeks at Harrow will highten in my imagination—and they are not melancholy—I am seldom so—but they are not right—and it will be a good thing if they terminate happily soon. At the same time I cannot in the least regret having come here. It was the only way I had of educating Percy in a public school—of which institution, at least here at Harrow, the more I see, the more I like—besides that it was Shelley's wish that his son should be brought up at one. It is indeed peculiarly suited to Percy—and whatever he will be—he will be twice as much as if he had been brought up in the narrow confinement of a private school—   The boys here have liberty to the verge of licence—yet of the latter, save the breaking of a few windows now and then, there is none. His life is not quite what it would be if he did not live with me—but the greater scope given to the cultivation of the affections is surely an advantage. Then it cultivates his hospitality, since his friends would rather dine badly with him than well at their tutors—   He has two who frequent the house—he will not extend the number, for fear of their annoying me—but sometimes he gives breakfasts to 6 or 8—and so gets a portion of popularity, despite my poverty—this last has caused him to be quizzed now and then—the character I hear from others that he bears among his companions, is that he is clever, and gives more help than any boy in the school, but is very haughty—it is odd that with me he is yielding either to persuasion or rebuke—but with his boys—their utmost violence can never make him give in a jot—he can say *NO,* which I cannot do—and has lively spirits—and is indeed a strange mixture of Shelley and I—he wants sensibility—but I fancy mine at his age was almost as covert—except that Mrs. Godwin had discovered long before my excessive and romantic attachment to my Father—he is not cruel to animals, and he likes them but has no tender solicitude about them.—But when he has suffered himself he will feel for others—   May that day be far off!

Nov. 17, 1834.

So much was written some time ago, and has been waiting for a frank—now I send it. You heard of the dreadful fire of the Houses of P[arliament][1]—We saw it here from its commencement blazing like a volcano—it was dreadful to see—but fortunately I was not aware of the site—   Papa lives close

[1] On the night of October 16, 1834.

to the Speakers, so you may imagine my alarm when the news reached me—fortunately without foundation, as the fire, did not gain that part of the Speaker's house near them so they were not even inconvenienced. The poor dear Speaker and Speakress have lost dreadfully—what was not burnt is broken smoked and drenched—all their pretty things and magnificent furniture and princely chambers—the house was a palace—for the sake of convenience to the Commons, they are to take up their abode among the ruins.

Why did not G. send his MS. it is sure to interest from the very circumstance you mentioned of its being true. You have awakened my curiosity and I long to see it— Do, dear Signor G. send it. Jane I believe has written to you— She talks of coming here for a day or two— You allude to Henry— Have you news of him? What is he doing and where is he?

Now to your questions— I am reading [?   ]—its being an invention takes from the interest—if it were true, it wd. be a deeply exciting work— It reminds me much of Calderon's La Vida es Sueño— My book is called Lodore— I know nothing of when it is to be published— I have heard nothing of the Booksellers intentions since it was printed—but I suppose it must be published this winter— Papa's Necromancers was published last summer—has it not made its appearance in Plymouth— Percy likes animals and is not cruel but there is a certain indolence in his disposition (which indeed pervades all his actions except when he has a *desire* for a thing, and then he wd. go thro' fire and water—in this he is like me) that renders him inattentive to the wants of his pets—so I have reduced them to one dog—a smooth haired terrier—ugly except in face, sagacious and affectionate— Even with him I am obliged to attend to his wants— Percy is now 15.

You are very good to write so often— I am always anxious to hear of your health, and delighted to get your letters— Reading your letter again I fancy I ought to have sent to S. Curtis's. I have not done so but will— Signor G.'s keeping back his MS. made me neglect it—it was very wrong in him. Adieu, my dear friend, God preserve you and diminish your sufferings. With kindest wishes for you and Sig. G[isborne],   Ever Afftly. Yr.

M. W. Shelley

ADDRESS: Mrs. Gisborne/ Plymouth/ Devon./ A. W. Beauclerk. POSTMARK: London/ 19 Nov/ 1834. ENDORSED: Harrow 17th Nov. 1834. recd. 20th do. Ans. ORIGINAL: Sir John Shelley-Rolls. PRINTED: *Shelley and Mary*, IV, 1185–88; Marshall, II, 261–63 (incomplete). TEXT: From copy made by Sir John Shelley-Rolls.

441. *To Leigh Hunt*

Harrow, 3 Feby 1835

My dear Hunt

Thank you for your kind letter— I hope things are going on as prosperously as you expected— I am glad to hear of dear Henry's destination—he was a very fine boy when I saw him last—and no doubt still *tops* Percy—though for size *round,* I am afraid he must yield—

Believe me I did not think of currying your public influence for my book[1] when I wrote, for valuable as that is—it did not enter my head— Where the book is, I cannot imagine—it has been printed these 10 months but I hear nothing of it & can extract no information from Burlington St.—which I strongly suspect, has become a Ward of St. Luke's. A volume of the Lives,[2] is coming out directly. Is out that is on the 1st. Unfortunately before I was applied to—some of the *best lives* were in other hands— The omnipresent Mr. Montgomery wrote Dante & Ariosto in the present vol.—the rest are mine.

I wish I could look with the indulgence you do on Shelley's relations. Sir Tim indeed, were he alone, I could manage—did I see him—violent as he is—he has a heart & I am sure I could have made a friend of him. It is Lady S[helley] who is my bitter enemy—and her motive is the base one of securing more money for herself and her terror was great lest I should see Sir Tim at one time. Now there is no fear since the old gentleman never comes to town. Besides the sacra auri fames (is that [the] right syntax—I wager not) her conduct having been very open to censure, she naturally attacks me—because those kind of women love detraction.

Janey paid me a visit yesterday   she is looking very well—we talked about you—you know how great a favourite you are with her. I had already got the books you mentioned. However defective these lives are (& I am far from satisfied) I spared no pains to get information & to do my best.

I have not been to town for months, I have no idea when I shall visit it again—I am quite a prisoner. I cant tell you how civil & kind the Conservatives have shewn themselves about Papa's Place which was in jeopardy— The D[uke] of W[ellington] or [and] Sir Robert Peel both have shewn the greatest consideration, besides the *real good* of continueing him in it— They have not the *Morgue* of our Whigs.—Do write & let me know how you all are. It is too late in the day to congratulate Thornton—but I *do* wish him & Kate [Gliddon] all happiness with all my heart— They are both deserving— With love to Marianne & best wishes, I am dear Hunt

Sincerely Ys. ever

M W Shelley

[P.S.] I have mislaid your letter & forget the address— I fear *Chelsea* w[oul]d not be enough so send the letter to Mr. Hunters

ADDRESS: *To be forwarded*/ Leigh Hunt Esq/ Rowland Hunter Esq/ St. Paul's Church Y[ar]d. POSTMARKS: (1) T.P./ Harrow   (2) 7.N[IGH]T.7/ FE.[3]/ 1835. ORIGINAL: Huntington Library (HM 2756); A.L.S., 4 pp. 4to. PRINTED: *Letters*, 176–78. TEXT: From original letter.

[1] *Lodore*, 1835.

[2] Volume I of "Lives of the Most Eminent Literary and Scientific Men of Italy, Spain, and Portugal" (1835, 312 pp.). *The Cabinet Cyclopedia*, conducted by the Reverend Dionysius Lardner. The volume contained lives of Dante, Petrarch, Boccaccio, Lorenzo de' Medici, Ficino, Pico della Mirandola, Politian, the Pulci, Bojardo, Berni, Ariosto, Machiavelli, and others. A second volume of Italian lives by Mary (see Letter 457, note 1) was published by October 13, 1835; a volume of Spanish lives in 1837; and a volume of French lives in 1838.

442. *To Maria Gisborne*

Harrow,
9 Feb. 1835.

My dearest Friend,

I am rendered anxious by your long silence, I fear you suffer through the vile winter weather, yet we have not much cold—and it must be warmer in your Devonshire. Do write— I have no news—I have scarcely stirred from this place since I wrote— I confess that sometimes I am visited by fits of dreadful despair at my exile from all my friends—especially when any circumstance renders me anxious about any of them—and I hear nothing for days and days—and weeks—and sometimes not at all— It is too bad—could I get to town readily I would not mind—but it is always a matter of calculation and fear of spending money &c. &c.

Percy is very well—he is in the 5 form, with a tailed coat and watch, and quite a man—his legs annoy me sometimes, and I think it very hard that I cannot get a horse for him. My father feels the cold weather, but is well. The Conservatives have been very civil and kind to him—and I feel that his income is safe while Sir Robert Peel is *in*— It is strange but so it is—Sir Robert wrote to him to say that a sense of justice as well as of gratitude from the pleasure he had received from his works would make him do all he could—and he wrote to my friend the Speaker at the same time, to say that he did not doubt but that Papa's income would be secured to him. We had a very clever letter from Claire the other day—she describes the annoyances of her life—and her rage at Church, when the Clergyman begins "We have followed too much the devises and desires of our own hearts"—"I," she continues, "who am always forced to do every thing that my heart detests."—Apropos of a little blasphemy, I must tell you of Ld. Alvanley's mot on the *grossesses* of our gracious Adelaide. He says that it reminds him of the psalm, Lord Howe wondrous are thy works!

I must tell you that I have had the offer[1] of 600£ for an edition of Shelley's works with life and notes, I am afraid it cannot be arranged yet at least—and the *life* is out of the question—but in talking over it the question of letters comes up— You know how I shrink from all *private* detail for the public— but Shelley's letters are beautifully written, and every thing *private* could be omitted— You must have many of them. Would you allow the publisher to treat with you for their being added to my edition? If I could arrange all as I wish, they might be an acquisition to the book, and being transacted *through me* you could not see any *inconvenience* in receiving the price they wd. be worth to the bookseller. This is all *in aria* as yet—but I should like to know what you think about it.

Poor Peacock has been dangerously ill of an inflammation of his lungs. He is in the country at Halliford, with his children—his wife in Stamford St.—is not this too good? she must be mad. You know I suppose that when his

[1] From Edward Moxon, which led eventually to Mary's edition of the Poetical Works (1839) and the prose works (*Essays,* &c., 1840).

Mother died in 33, his wife played the same part—and though at the same time her children were ill of the scarlet fever, made her *maid* write word that she was too unwell to join them. I first heard of poor Peacock's danger in a note from his daughter—I told Jane—and Jeff wishing for news, wrote to Mrs. Peacock directing to Stamford St.—fancying that Peacock was there. He gets for answer from the wife, dated Stamford Street, "I am happy to inform that the accounts from Halliford are more favourable—and that our poor friend is pronounced out of danger." And yet her husband is the person in the world she cares for *most*— Do you think that a very powerful magnifier cd. discern her heart?—I think not.

I write all this yet [am] very anxious to hear from you—never mind postage, but do write. Percy is reading the *Antigone*—but he has no talent for Latin verses—he makes sad work— He has begun Mathematics— Mrs. Cleveland and Jane dined with me the other day— Mrs. C[leveland] thought Percy wonderfully improved—he gets more disinvoltura yet that is not his forte— The Vol. of Lardner's Cyclopedia with *my lives* was published on the 1st of this month— It is called Lives of Eminent Literary Men Vol. I— The lives of Dante and Ariosto are by the omnipresent Mr. Montgomery—the rest are mine— How is S[ignor] G.? What are you doing—Do write, my dearest Maria, and believe me Ever and Ever

Affectionately Yrs.
M. W. Shelley

[P. S.] I have just begun the Adone—and like it.

ADDRESS: Mrs. Gisborne,/ Plymouth./ J. Rickman. POSTMARK: London South/ Febry. 1835. ENDORSED: Harrow 9th Febry. 1835. 12th. ORIGINAL: Sir John Shelley-Rolls. PRINTED: *Shelley and Mary*, IV, 1190–91; Marshall, II, 263–64 (incomplete). TEXT: From copy made by Sir John Shelley-Rolls.

443. *To John Murray*

Harrow,
Feb. 10, 1835.

[*Summary*] Will Murray send her a prospectus of his new edition of Boswell's Life of Johnson edited by Croker, whose edition is the best of all editions. She is not "fishing" for a present.

She is sorry Murray would not let her have the "Illustrations of Ld. Byron": "I suppose you *could* not & Finden *would* not—for I could not make up my mind to be exhibited among the portraits I have such a dislike of display."

POSTMARK: 7 Night/ FE.10/ 1835. ORIGINAL: Sir John Murray; A.L.S., 3 pp. 8vo, addressed. UNPRINTED and UNPUBLISHED. SUMMARY: From original letter.

444. *To John Murray**

Harrow, Friday [February, 1835]

My dear Sir

Many thanks for the Illustrations which are so beautiful & interesting— I am delighted at the success of your publication. I have read Boswell I am sure ten times—& hope to read it many more—it is the most amusing book in the world, besides that I do love the kind-hearted wise & gentle Bear—& think him as loveable a friend as a profound philosopher. I do not see in your list of authors whence anecdotes are extracted, the name of Mrs. D'Arblay—Her account of Dr. Johnson Mrs. Thrale &c. in her Memoirs of Dr. Burney are highly interesting & valuable.

I am so unhappy that Sir C. Manners Sutton has lost his election as Speaker[1] — It is not that I am not at Whig—I suppose I am one—but I think the Whigs have treated him most shabbily—electing him themselves as they did last year. They will never have such a Speaker again. I feel particularly kindly towards the Conservatives also just now as they have behaved with the greatest consideration toward my father—preserving him in his place, which was about to be abolished by the Whigs & that with a *manner* as gracious as the *deed*. The Duke of Wellington & above all the Prince of our orators Sir Robert Peel deserves my gratitude & has it— By the way what will the Whigs do for an orator in the Commons— I never heard Canning—& never heard any Speaker who I thought could claim the praise of a good Orator except Sir Robert Peel —his speeches have all a beginning middle & end—he rises with his subject & carries the hearer along with him—Ld. Brougham I only heard in the House of Lords & his want of dignity & his insolent sarcasm towards the Peers annoyed me—

My boy is now in the 5th form & is very promising & clever & *good*— I am dear Sir

Very truly ys.
M. W. Shelley

ORIGINAL: Sir John Murray; A.L.S., 4 pp. 12mo. PRINTED: S. Smiles, *A Publisher and His Friends* (1891), II, 290, 329 (quots., 10 & 15 lines). TEXT: From original letter.

445. *To Gabriele Rossetti*[2]

Harrow, 3 April 1835

Most honoured Sir

Will you excuse with your usual goodness an annoyance which I set before

[1] Sir Charles Manners-Sutton had been elected Speaker of the House of Commons many times (June, 1817; January, 1819; April, 1820; November, 1826; October, 1830; June, 1831). In February, 1835, being opposed by the Whigs, he was not re-elected; James Abercromby (afterwards Lord Dunfermline) was given the office.

[2] The original Italian text of this letter is as follows:

Harrow, 3^{zo} Aprile 1835

Signor Pregiat^{mo}

Vuol scusare colla solita sua bontà un incomodo che la reco intorno al mio vergheggiare? Sto in questo momento scrivendo la vita dell'illustre suo compatriota Alfieri;—e vorrei sapere se inoltre la vita scritta da se stesso, ve ne sono altre vite o altri saggii, che mi daranno notizie pregiabili intorno al medesimo; vuol favorirmi, gentillissimo Signore Rosetti con delle informazioni.

E poi—dopo Alfieri, devo scrivere la vita del Monti—della quale si sa pochissimo qui—chi fra voi altri hanno composto la vita sua?—e dove troverò quelle notizie che mi faranno consapevole degli avenimenti a lui accaduti—lettere scritte da lui, ve ne sono publicate?

Abito sempre questo paesaccio col mio figlio—così non vedo nè Lei, nè nessun de'miei amici

you concerning my [vergheggiare]? I am at this moment writing the life of your illustrious compatriot Alfieri;—and I would like to know whether besides the life written by himself there are any other lives or essays which would give me important information concerning the same; please favour me, my dear Mr. Rossetti, with some information.

And then—after Alfieri, I have to write the life of Monti—of whom very little is known here—who among you people have written up his life?—and where shall I find such notices as will acquaint me with the incidents which befell him—have any letters written by him been published?

I am still living in this dreadful place with my son—so I do not see either you or any of my friends except so rarely that I am really in despair. I hope meanwhile that you are enjoying good health—and that prosperity which your talents and remarkable worth merit.

Excuse this barbarous Italian—I do not feel the language—I do not ever speak it and it is forever since I have done any reading—but after all what will you have! There is a certain unusedness in my mind which is always making me make hundreds of blunders when I try to express myself in a foreign language—however I know enough of it, nevertheless, to assure you that I am always

Your admirer and servant
M. W. Shelley

POSTMARK: 18 PAID 35/ AP.3/ NIGHT. ORIGINAL: Biblioteca del Risorgimento, Rome, package No. 275 of the Rossetti MSS; A.L.S., 3 pp., addressed. PRINTED: E. R. Vincent, "Two Letters from Mary Shelley to Gabrielle Rossetti," *Modern Language Review*, XXVIII (October 1932), 459–61; E. R. Vincent, *Gabriele Rossetti in England* (1936), 186. (Italian text only.) TEXT: Italian text from Vincent, *Gabrielle Rossetti in England*, 186. Translation by Creighton Gilbert.

446. *To Gabriele Rossetti*[1]

Harrow, April 20, 1835.

Courteous Signor Rossetti,

Thank you so much for your amiable reply, and the interest you show in

---

che così raramente, che mi fa proprio disperare. Spera intanto che lei goda una buona salute—e quella prosperità che merita i talenti ed egregii pregii suoi.

Scusa questo Italiano barbarico—non sento il linguagio—non le parlo mai mai ne leggo pur sempre—ma pero che vuole! C'è una certa inusitatezza nella mia mente che mi fa sempre dire cento spropositi, quando tento di esprimermi in una lingua forestiera—tanto ne possiedo, non di meno, che basta per assicurarla che mi ripeto sempre

Ammiratrice e serva sua
M. W. Shelley.

[1] The original letter is in Italian.

Harrow il 20 di Aprile 1835

Gentil^{mo} Signor Rosetti

La ringrazio tanto per la sua amabile risposta e le di lei premure per la interpresa di una penna pur troppo indegna di quei bellissimi nomi che danno un tal lustro alla sua patria. Intanto ho da farla un'altra domanda—ma temo di mostrarmi poca discreta, e la prego di dirmi schiettamente il suo parere—non vorrei avere l'apparenza di far spropositi impertinenti, e se la mia idea le pare impraticabile, non ne dica una parola a nessuno—

Mi dice che il suo suocero, il celebre Polidori può narrare molte circostanze interessanti intorno all'Alfieri. La vita che scrivo sarà stampata nella Ciclopedia del Dottore Lardner—così è

the undertaking of a pen but too unworthy of those great names which give so much lustre to your country. Meanwhile I am about to make a farther request: but am afraid of showing myself troublesome, and beg you to tell me your opinion sincerely. I should not like to seem to take impertinent liberties; and, if my idea appears to you impracticable, don't say anything about it to any one.

I am informed that your Father-in-law the celebrated Polidori can relate many interesting circumstances regarding Alfieri. The Life which I am writing will be printed in *Dr. Lardner's Cyclopaedia:* therefore it is very short, running perhaps to 70 pages—not more. Thus, if I could introduce some details not yet known but worthy of publication, I should be very pleased indeed. I don't know whether Polidori would be willing to give me such details. For example, I should like to know whether Alfieri was really so melancholy and taciturn as is said by Sir John Hobhouse in his work, *Illustrations to the Fourth Canto of Childe Harold;* whether he gave signs of attachment to his friends, and whether he was warmly loved by them in return. Some anecdotes would be welcomed by me; also some information about the Countess of Albany. There is an affectation of silence, as to all that relates to her, in whatever has yet been written concerning Alfieri. But, now that she is dead, this is no longer necessary. Were they married? If not, nothing need be said about it; but, if they were, it would be well to affirm as much.

I shall be in London next Sunday [April 26], and shall be staying there several days. But I am in a quarter so distant from yours (7 Upper Eaton Street, Grosvenor Place) that it would be indiscreet to say that, if Signor Polidori would visit me, he could perhaps tell me some little things more easily than by writing. As the Tuscans say, "Lascio far a lei" (I leave the

corta assai, cioè può fare una settantina di pagine, non più. Però, se potessi introdurre qualche notizie non conosciute, ma degne da essere publicate, mi farà assaissimo piacere. Non saprei se il Polidori volesse darmi queste notizie. Per esempio vorrei sapere se veramente era così malinconico e silenziale come dice il Cavaliere Hobhouse nella sua opera 'Illustrations to the Fourth Canto of Childe Harold'—se mostrava amare gli amici suoi, e se fu riamato caldamente da loro—qualche annetdoti mi sarebbero gradevoli—e poi qualche notizie sulla Contessa di Albany. V'è l'affettazione di silenzio in quanto tocca ad essa in tutto quel che sia scritta finora sopra l'Alfieri ma sicchè è ormai morta, questo non è più necessario. Fuorono maritati? Se no—non sene dice nulla—ma se lo furono, sarebbe bene di dichiararlo.

Sarò in Londra la Domenica prossima, e mi tratengherò costà per parecchi giorni. Ma sto in un quartiere così lontano dal suo (7 Upper Eaton St. Grosvenor Place) che sarebbe indiscreta di chiedere una visita di lei—ed assai più indiscreta di dire che se il Signor Polidori mi vorebbe far visita forse mi dirà più facilmente che scriverà alcune cosine, come dicono i Toscani. Lascio far a lei—farà lei tutto quel che sia convenevole—e mi renderà risposta con suo comodo.

Ripetendo le grazie tante dovute alla sua bontà, Credami

Serva sua obligat^{ma}

M. W. Shelley.

[P. S.] Per quel che ho sentito era intrinseco il Alfieri col Guiccioli di Ravenna essendo l'ultimo giovanotto—ed ebbero insieme l'idea e l'interpresa non riuscita possibile di stabilire un Teatro nazionale in Italia. Forse ne è consapevole di questo il Signor Polidori. Ce n'è qualche opera istorica dove si troverà notizie sugli ultimi anni del real marito della Contessa di Albany—non so io—e sono nel bujo— Fu lui l'ultimo dei Stuardi, non è vero fuorchè il fratello, il Cardinale York? Ah che impegno le do per rispondermi—ne ho veramente una vergogna indicibile adesso—ma è così buono lei!—e poi la grammatica di questa lettera sarà come la Cleopatra del Alfieri.

question to you). You will do whatever is most fitting, and will give me a reply at your convenience.

Repeating the thanks so much due to your kindness, believe me

Your much obliged servant,

M. W. Shelley.

[P.S.] I hear that Alfieri was intimate with Guiccioli of Ravenna, the latter being then quite young; and they had a joint idea and project (which did not turn out manageable) of establishing a national theatre in Italy. Possibly Signor Polidori knows about this. Is there any historical work containing particulars about the closing years of the royal husband of the Countess of Albany? I don't know, and am in the dark. He (is it not so?) was the last of the Stuarts, except his brother the Cardinal of York.

Oh what trouble I am giving you to reply! Really I now feel more than ashamed of it. But you are so kind. And, besides, the grammar of this letter must be like Alfieri's *Cleopatra*.

POSTMARKS: (1) HARROW/ 3py. P.Paid (2) 18 PAID 35/ AP.20/ Night. ORIGINAL: Biblioteca del Risorgimento, Rome, package No. 275 of the Rossetti MSS; A.L.S., 4 pp., addressed. PRINTED: (Translation) *Diary of Dr. John Wm. Polidori*, edited by W. M. Rossetti (1911), 220–21. (Italian text) E. R. Vincent, "Two Letters from Mary Shelley to Gabriele Rossetti," *Modern Language Review*, XXVIII (October 1932), 459–61; and E. R. Vincent, *Gabriele Rossetti in England* (1936), 186–87. TEXT: From (Translation) W. M. Rossetti, *Diary of Dr. Polidori*; (Italian text) E. R. Vincent, *Gabriele Rossetti in England*.

447. *To Mr. Mignot*

May 1 [? 1835]

[*Accepting the dedication of a song:*] I shall never be happy now till it is published. It will be appreciated and liked I am sure. I think Novello would be very glad to publish it. Do let me see it in print.

ORIGINAL: A.L.S., 2 pp. 8vo. Owned in July, 1939, by Bernard Halliday, Leicester; Catalogue 239, Item 586. UNPRINTED and UNPUBLISHED. TEXT: Quotation from Halliday's catalogue above.

448. *To Maria Gisborne*

Harrow,
11 June [18]35.

My dearest Friend,

It is so inexpressibly warm, that were not a frank lying before me ready for you, I do not think I should have courage to write. Do not be surprised therefore at stupidity and want of connection, I cannot collect my ideas— and this is a good-will offering rather than a letter.

Still I am anxious to thank S[ignor] G[iovanni] for the pleasure I have received from his tale of Italy in tale all Italy[1]—breathing of the land I love— the descriptions are beautiful—and he has shed a great charm round the con-

[1] See Letter 410, note 4.

centrated and undemonstrative person of his gentle heroine. I suppose she is
the reality of the story— Did you know her?—it is difficult however to judge
how to procure for it the publication it deserves. I have no personal acquaintance with the Editors of any of the Annuals— I had with that of the Keepsake—but that is now in Mrs. Norton's hands—and she has not asked me to
write—so I know nothing about it. But there arises an stronger objection from
the length of the story— As the merit lies in the beauty of the details, I do
not see how it could be cut down to *one quarter* of its present length, which
is as long as any tale printed in an Annual. When I write for them, I am
worried to death to make my things shorter and shorter—till I fancy people
think ideas can be conveyed by intuition—and that it is a superstition to consider words necessary for their expression.

I was so very delighted to get your last letter—to be sure the *Wisest of Men*
said no news was good news—but I am not apt to think so, and was uneasy—
I hope this weather does not oppress you— What an odd climate! A week
ago I had a fire—and now it is warmer than Italy—warmer at least in a box
pervious to the sun, than in the stone palaces where one can breathe freely.
My Father is well— He had a cough in the winter—but after we had persuaded him to see a Doctor it was easily got rid of— He writes to me himself
—"I am now well—now nervous—now old—now young." One sign of age
is that his horror is so great of change of place that I cannot persuade him even
to visit me here— One would think that the sight of the fields would refresh
him—but he likes his own nest better than all—though he greatly feels the
annoyance of so seldom seeing me. Indeed, my kind Maria—you made me
smile when you asked me to be civil to the brother of your kind Doctor. I
thought I had explained my situation to you—you must consider me as one
buried alive—I hardly ever go to town—less often I see any one here— My
kind and dear young friends the Misses Robinson are at Brussels—I am cut
off from my kind— What I suffer— What I have suffered—I [to] whom
sympathy—companionship—the interchange of thought is more necessary
than the air I breathe I will not say. Tears are in my eyes when I think of days,
weeks, months, even years spent alone—eternally alone— It does me great
harm—but no more of so odious a subject—let me speak rather of my Percy—
to see him bright and good is an unspeakable blessing, but no child can be a
companion especially one whose fault is a want of quick sensibility—he is very
fond of me—and would be wretched if he saw me unhappy—but he is with
his boys all day long, and I am alone—so I can weep unseen. He gets on very
well—and is a fine boy—very stout—this hot weather though he exposes himself to the sun—instead of making him languid, heightens the color in his
cheeks and brightens his eyes. He is always gay and in good humour—which
is a great blessing.

You talk about my poetry—and about the encouragement I am to find
from Jane and my Father. When they read all the fine things you said they

thought it right to attack me about it, but I answered them simply "She exagerates—you read the best thing I ever wrote in the Keepsake and thought nothing of it."—I do not know whether you remember the verses I mean[2] I will copy it in another part—it was written for music. Poor dear Lord Dillon spoke of it as you do of the rest—but "One swallow does not make a summer"— I can never write verses except under the influence of a strong sentiment and seldom even then. As to a tragedy—Shelley used to urge me—which produced his own.[3] When I returned first to England and saw Kean, I was in a fit of enthusiasm—and wished much to write for the stage—but my father very earnestly dissuaded me[4]— I think that he was in the wrong—I think myself that I could have written a good tragedy—but not now— My good friend— every feeling I have is blighted—I have no ambition—no care for fame— Loneliness has made a wreck of me—I was always a dependant thing—wanting fosterage and support— I am left to myself instead by fortune—and I am nothing.

You speak of women's intellect— We can scarcely do more than judge by ourselves— I know that however clever I may be there is in me a vaccillation a weakness, a want of "eagle winged" resolution that appertains to my intellect as well as my moral character—and renders me what I am—one of broken purposes—failing thoughts and a heart all wounds— My Mother had more energy of character—still she had not sufficient fire of imagination— In short my belief is—whether there be sex in souls or not—that the sex of our material mechanism makes us quite different creatures—better though weaker but wanting in the higher grades of intellect.

I am almost sorry to send you this letter it is so querulous and sad—yet if I write with any effusion—the truth will creep out—and my life since you went has been so stained by sorrows and disappointments—I have been so barbarously handled both by fortune and my fellow creatures—that I am no longer the same as when you knew me— I have no hope— In a few years when I get over my present feelings and live wholly in Percy I shall be happier. I have devoted myself to him as no Mother ever did—and idolize him—and the reward will come when I can forget a thousand memories and griefs that are as yet alive and burning—and I have nothing to do here but brood.

Another word of Mr. Budd— I should have been delighted to have been of use to him—but can make no offers—prisoner as I am. Jeff [*MS torn*] flourish—she suffers from his reserves of [   ] but his real good qualities make up for it— Dina is growing a fine girl—Edward as yet does not de-

[2] The verses at the end of this letter. They were published in *The Keepsake* for 1831 (page 85), under the title "A Dirge." Other poems by Mary in *The Keepsake* are: "Absence" (twelve lines), 1831, page 39; "Stanzas" ("How like a star you rose upon my life," sixteen lines), 1839, page 179; and "Stanzas" ("O, Come to me in dreams, my love!"), 1839, page 201. All these poems are on the same theme—the loss of Shelley. Mary is quite right in saying that "A Dirge" is "the best thing I ever wrote."
[3] *The Cenci,* written in 1819.
[4] See Godwin's excellent letter to Mary on February 27, 1824, in Marshall, II, 106–108.

velope much—he is not physically strong— How I should like to see you
and talk to you— I sometimes fancy a journey to Plymouth— What would
you say to seeing me pop in some day— The Countess Guiccioli is in England—I have such a dread of her coming to see me here—imagine the talk.
Adieu—Do write—if you ever want a conveyance—enclose your letter to me
(while the Session lasts) *under cover* to D. Gaskell Esq.,[5] M.P. 5 Parliament
St. but dont let it be above franking weight— O the heat! How overpowering
it is— Percy is gone 2 miles off to bathe— He can swim and I am obliged
to leave the rest to fate— It is no use coddling [   ]—yet it costs me
many pangs—however he is singularly trustworthy and careful—Do you remember 16 years ago at Livorno—he was not born then— Do write and
believe me,

Ever your truly attached friend,
M. W. S.

[P. S.] I sent to Mr. Stephen Curtis for you the 1st Vol. of my Lives of
Italian Poets— The lives of Dante and Ariosto are not mine, return it when
you have done with it—it belongs to Jane.

Do you not guess why neither these nor those I sent you wd. please those
you mention. Papa loves not the memory of S[helley] because—he feels he
injured him—and Jane— Do you not understand enough of her to unwind
the thoughts that make it distasteful to her that I should feel—and above all
be thought by others to feel and to have a right to feel— O the human heart
—it is a strange puzzle.

A DIRGE

This morn thy gallant bark, Love,
Sailed on a sunny sea;
Tis noon, and tempests dark, Love,
Have wrecked it on the lee.

Ah Woe—ah woe—ah woe
By spirits of the deep,
He's cradled on the billow,
To his unwaking sleep!

Thou liest upon the shore, Love,
Beside the knelling surge,
But sea-nymphs ever more, Love,
Shall sadly chaunt thy dirge.

O come, O come—O come!
Ye spirits of the deep!

[5] The Gaskells were introduced by Claire, who wrote from Pisa on March 5, 1832: "This letter
will procure the acquaintance of Mr. and Mrs. Gaskell."—*Shelley and Mary*, IV, 1156. See
Letter 458.

> While near his sea-weed pillow,
>   My lonely watch I keep.
>
> From far across the sea, Love,
>   I hear a wild lament,
> By Echo's voice for thee, Love,
>   From Ocean's caverns sent:
>
> O list! O list! O list!
>   The Spirits of the deep—
> Loud sounds their wail of sorrow—
>   While I for ever weep!

ADDRESS: Mrs. Gisborne,/ Plymouth./ D. Gaskell. POSTMARK: Harrow/ 11
June/ 1835. ENDORSED: Harrow 11th June 1835. rec. 12th do. Ans. 22nd Oct.
1835. ORIGINAL: Sir John Shelley-Rolls. PRINTED: *Shelley Memorials*, 226–27
(incomplete); *Shelley and Mary*, IV, 1192–96; Marshall, II, 267–71. TEXT:
From copy made by Sir John Shelley-Rolls.

449. *To Edward John Trelawny**

Harrow,
Monday [July, 1835]

Dear Trelawny,

I am glad to hear of your safe arrival[1] and wish I could give you an happier welcome. You left me the victim of poverty—you return to find me the same; and in addition a prisoner. My life at Harrow,—friendless alone and poor, has nearly destroyed me—but there is no remedy. I do not repent having come—for it was I still believe, the only thing I could do to give Percy a decent education and save myself from getting into debt, which seemed inevitable on my remaining in London. Still I wish this place were not so odious and that the want of money, always pressing me to the limits of existence, had permitted me to make a home of some comfort here; but every mitigation has been denied me in my exile. I write in low spirits—because I hate having to give a disagreable account of myself—and because I have been very ill lately and am still suffering from the weakness that is its consequence.

Percy's holydays begin in a fortnight when if possible I shall get to town for a few weeks— Shall we meet then? I have a repugnance to your coming here, you would hate it so much—and I hate that a friend should do any thing disagreable. You will see Jane. You will find her in the same house, 12 Maida Place. Will you call on the Godwins? 13 New Palace Yd. Westminster—they will be delighted to see you.

Percy is grown of course—but you will despise him for he is *horrifically fat* — He is the best and dearest boy in the world.

I do not wonder at your hatred of this vile country. To the poor it is a place of perpetual torture—every wish of the heart is denied—every possibility of

---

[1] From America, where he had been since January, 1833.

escaping from ills cut off— I had courage in adversity for a long time—it is gone now.

Adieu—pardon me for croaking and believe me,

Ever truly Yrs.

ADDRESS: E. J. Trelawny Esq.,/ Colonnade Hotel,/ Charles St./ Haymarket./ Sir W. Trelawny,/ 8 Great George St./ Westminster. ORIGINAL: Sir John Shelley-Rolls. UNPRINTED and UNPUBLISHED. TEXT: From copy made by Sir John Shelley-Rolls.

450. *To Charles Ollier**

3 Alfred Place, Dover
6 August 1835

My dear Sir

My Aunt, Mrs. [Everina] Wollstonecraft has *never* received Lodore. You would very much oblige me if you would see to this—as the neglect is a *real* annoyance to me.

In vain all this summer I have looked out for you. I myself have been very ill—& as I could not get well at Harrow, as soon as the holydays began, came here where I am fast regaining health & strength. I shall return to Harrow in September when perhaps the spirit may move you & Mrs. Ollier to fulfil your kind promise.

What of Lodore— Do you remember that when 700 are sold I am to have £50? Will 700 never be sold? I am very unlucky; praised & noticed as it has been. You promised me to look after my interests in this particular and I trust you, because I think you will feel more sympathy with a *poor Author* than a *rich Publisher*. If therefore 701 are sold, have pity on me & let me know, that I may claim a sum, which will pay for my unlucky illness, & do me a world of good. Do pray attend to this, & I shall be so very much obliged—

I hope you are all well at home & am ever

Yours truly
M W Shelley

[P.S.] My Aunt's Address is,–
Mrs. Wollstonecraft
19 White Conduit St.
Pentonville

ADDRESS: Chas. Ollier Esq/ 8 New Burlington St. POSTMARK: 7.Night/ AU.8/ 1835. ORIGINAL: British Museum (Add. MSS 30,262, f.33); A.L.S., 3 pp. 8vo. UNPRINTED and UNPUBLISHED. TEXT: From original letter.

451. *To Charles Ollier*

[London, ? September, 1835]

Dear Sir

I write this in case I do not find you at home. I perceive with a good deal of surprize an Edition of the Younger Son advertized for the Standard Novels

—without any notice being given to me or Mr. Trelawny. The contract was that Mr. Trelawny was to receive £100 more, when a 2d Edition was printed.[1] Pray represent this to Mr. Colburn or Mr. Bentley—& let me or Mr. Trelawny hear from you on the subject.

Mr. Trelawny is at present at Brighton—a letter would find him directed to 13 Cavendish Place Brighton. I heard the other day from him & he is particularly vexed that he was not applied to, as he wanted to make various corrections. As the contract was entered into between you & me it falls to me to remind you of the £100 & to beg of you to take care that it is properly arranged.

You have not answered my question about Lodore & the 700 copies—nor has Mrs. Wollstonecraft ever received the copy you promised to send. I am returning to Harrow directly—so fear I cannot see you unless you will keep your often broken promise & come out there. I am anxious to send a satisfactory account to Mr. Trelawny.

Yours truly
M W S.

ADDRESS: Chas. Ollier Esq/ 8 New Burlington St. ORIGINAL: Owned by B. F. Stevens & Brown, Ltd., London, in 1936; A.L.S., 3 pp. 8vo. UNPRINTED and UNPUBLISHED. TEXT: From original letter.

452. *To Edward John Trelawny*

[? Harrow, ? September, 1835]

Dear Trelawny,

I have just had a note from Charlotte, that tells me you are still in town. I am going tomorrow to [? Adaes] for a day or two— On leaving Putney, I shall stop short at Brompton—for a day or two, not more— On Monday I think I shall be there. Would it be possible that the tiresome business with Bentley could be arranged for next Thursday, as being in town, I can attend to it better. I must be back here on Friday or Saturday—being very busy. Percy is looking so well, grown thinner and taller: it is odd to mark the white down on his face, changing to mustachios the color of his father's hair—he has so much more of his father's blood in his veins than of mine—and yet in many things is so unlike both of us.

I shall hope to see you while I am in town. The journey here is too far and tedious to make for any except—

Adieu—it will be a great comfort to see you—for notwithstanding—tweedledum—I am truly and always attached to you—

Mary Shelley

[P. S.] I had almost forgotten a message to you from Teresa Guiccioli—Byron's [   ] which she sent in a letter I got from her from Paris. She

[1] A second edition was published in 1835, in Bentley's Standard Novels (No. 48).

says "I beg you will say a thousand cordial things to Trelawny from me—
since I really have a great esteem and liking for him—and tell him besides
that I do not need the letter for Lady Blessington, because I am almost sure
that he would not make use of it."

ORIGINAL: Sir John Shelley-Rolls. UNPRINTED and UNPUBLISHED. TEXT: From
copy made by Sir John Shelley-Rolls.

453. *To Edward John Trelawny*

[September, 1835]

[*Mrs. Rossetti's Summary*] We have Mary again writing to Mr. T. with
regard to his book, a second edition being called for, when, to her confusion,
she finds that through her not having read the agreement, and having taken
for granted that the proposal of three hundred pounds on first edition with
one hundred pounds more on second was inserted, she had signed the contract; but now it turned out that what was proposed by letter was not inserted
by Ollier in the agreement, and she knew not what to do.

ORIGINAL: Not traced. UNPRINTED and UNPUBLISHED. SUMMARY: From Lucy
M. Rossetti, *Mrs. Shelley*, 184.

454. *To Edward John Trelawny*

[Harrow, September, 1835]

[*Mrs. Rossetti's Summary*] In a second letter a few days later from Harrow. . . . she wrote in answer to Trelawny, proposing Peacock as umpire
[about the second edition of the *Younger Son*], because, she writes, "he
would not lean to the strongest side, which Jefferson, as a lawyer, is inclined,
I think, to do." Ollier, she writes, devoutly wished she had read the agreement,
as the clause ought to have been in it.

ORIGINAL: Not traced. UNPRINTED and UNPUBLISHED. SUMMARY: From Lucy
M. Rossetti, *Mrs. Shelley*, 184.

455. *To Sir John Bowring**

Harrow—3 Oct. [1835]

Dear Doctor Bowring

You are very kind to answer my letter in the midst of all your important
avocations. One great difficulty seems to be getting books— There is no
Spanish Library—& one wants to turn over so many that the Longmans would
be tired of buying. I own that I depended much on yours—& am disappointed
at what you say—is there no getting at them?—are the cases large & are all
the Spanish books in one case?— Could indeed any but yourself touch them?
—I do not mind trouble—but wish to do my task as well as I can—& how can
I without books?—The difficulty seems to be that from slight biographical

notices one can get the book will be more of literature than lives—& I know
not how Lardner will like that. The best is that the very thing which occasions
the difficulty makes it interesting—namely—the treading in unknown paths
& dragging out unknown things—   I wish I could go to Spain.[1]

   Many thanks for the hints you give   I am, dear Dr. Bowring

Yours truly

M W Shelley

ADDRESSED: Dr. Bowring M.P./ 1 Queen's Sq/ Westminster. POSTMARKS: (1)
T.[ ]/ Harrow   (2) 7.[NIG]HT.7/ OC.3/ 1835. ENDORSED: Harrow [3]
Oct. 1835/ Mrs. Shelley. ORIGINAL: Huntington Library (HM 2767); A.L.S., 2
pp. 4to. UNPRINTED and UNPUBLISHED. TEXT: From original letter.

456. *To Edward John Trelawny*

October 12, 1835.

   . . . I do not wonder at your not being able to deny yourself the pleasure of
Mrs. Norton's society. I never saw a woman I thought so fascinating. Had I
been a man I should certainly have fallen in love with her; as a woman, ten
years ago, I should have been spellbound, and, had she taken the trouble, she
might have wound me round her finger. Ten years ago I was so ready to give
myself away, and being afraid of men, I was apt to get *tousy-mousy* for women;
experience and suffering have altered all that. I am more wrapt up in myself,
my own feelings, disasters, and prospects for Percy. I am now proof, as Hamlet
says, both against man and woman.[2]

   There is something in the pretty way in which Mrs. Norton's witticisms
glide, as it were, from her lips, that is very charming; and then her colour,
which is so variable, the eloquent blood which ebbs and flows, mounting, as
she speaks, to her neck and temples, and then receding as fast; it reminds me
of the frequent quotation of "eloquent blood,"[3] and gives a peculiar attraction
to her conversation—not to speak of fine eyes and open brow.

   Now do not in your usual silly way show her what I say. She is, despite all
her talents and sweetness, a London lady. She would quiz me—not, perhaps,
to you—well do I know the London *ton*—but to every one else—in her prettiest manner.

ORIGINAL: Not traced. PRINTED: Marshall, II, 272–73 (incomplete); *The Letters
of Edward J. Trelawny,* edited by Forman, p. 192n (from and like Marshall).
TEXT: From Marshall.

[1] Having just finished two volumes of "The Lives of the Most Eminent Literary and Scientific
Men of Italy" for *The Cabinet Cyclopaedia,* conducted by the Reverend Dionysius Lardner, Mary
was beginning a volume of Spanish lives. When published (1837), the volume contained the
following lives: Boscan; Garcilaso de la Vega; Diego Hurtado de Mendoza; Luis de Leon;
Herrera; Jorge de Montemayor; Castillejo; The Early Dramatists; Ercilla; Cervantes; Lope de Vega;
Vicente Espinel-Esteban de Villegas; Gongora; Quevedo; Calderon; Early Poets of Portugal (4);
and Camoëns.
   [2] "Man delights not me; no, nor woman neither, though by your smiling you seem to say
so."—*Hamlet,* II, ii.
   [3] *Alastor,* line 168.

457. To *Maria Gisborne*

Harrow,
13 Oct., 1835.

My dear Friend,

I wrote you a long letter about a month ago, ready for a frank—and lo! when I wd. use it—it has disappeared, and I cannot find it any where—this is tiresome—as there is nothing so annoying as *writing* a twice told tale—besides that writing is now a real labor to me—so you must be content with a scrap of a incoherent letter—but I cannot delay any longer asking how you are—and entreating you to let me have a few lines at least to inform us of your state, and that of S[ignor] G.—and also, permit me to say, of your dear good Elizabeth, whom fidelity and zeal, renders very interesting.

I shall begin my own history in an Irish way—by commencing with Jane—for it will please and interest you to know that she expects to encrease her family in Febry. next— She is frightened at danger and pain—and Jeff, I believe, at expence—but I think it is a good thing—especially if it is, as they *both* wish a boy—a girl, in going out into life, is the Mother's care—a boy the Father's— Jeff, I think, will find new feelings—anticipations and even energies develope, when he has a son to think of and provide for. You or at least S. G. must have seen his name frequently in the papers—Ld. Brougham sent him as one of the Corporation Commissioners—but his Tory, or as he calls them high Whig principles, betrayed themselves—he played the Conservative and brought himself into notice— I hope it will do him good in his profession—had the Tory Ministry remained in, it certainly would— He is now gone on a visit home—a visit prolonged by the death of Aunt Jones at Cheltenham— John and Prue went to attend the funeral—he remained to console Mamma and Sarah—which he says is like riding in a mourning coach all day long. Jane's children are well—Dina is a very interesting girl indeed—the talent she has developed for drawing, would be absolute genius, had she imagination and understanding to put soul in the eye she has for form—we shall see; I sympathize much in the pursuit. She is nearly as tall as her Mother — Jane would be well, but that over activity and the want of a sopha (which Jeff cannot *afford*) threaten to make her suffer as she did with her last— I preach and pray but to little purpose.

Of myself—my dearest Maria—I can give but a bad account— Solitude —many cares—and many deep sorrows brought on this summer an illness from which I am now only recovering. I can never forget nor cease to be grateful to Jane for her excessive kindness to me—when I needed it most confined as I was to my sopha, unable to move. I went to Dover during Percy's holydays—and change of air and bathing made me so much better that I thought myself well—but on my return here, I had a relapse—from which now this last week I am, I trust, fast recovering—but I am obliged to take great care of myself—there is something the matter with my blood I fancy;

105

bark and port wine seem the chief methods for my getting well— In the midst of all this I had to write, to meet my expences— I have published a 2nd Vol. of Italian Lives in Lardner's Cyclopedia[1]—all in that Vol. except Galileo and Tasso are mine— The last is chief I allow—and I grieve that it had been engaged to the omnipresent Mr. Montgomery before I began to write— I am vain enough to think that I should have written it better than he has done. I am now about to write a Volume of Spanish and Portugueze Lives— This is an arduous task, from my own ignorance, and the difficulty of getting books and information. The Bookseller wants me to write another Novel—Lodore having succeeded so well—but I have not as yet strength for such an undertaking.

My Father is tolerably well—he is about to move to another public building —and this is a great worry and labor to them both— Mrs. G. was excessively kind to me in my illness. Percy is much grown and very big—he goes on much the same; but I think of taking him from Harrow, as soon as I can find a tutor — In the first place I am killed by inches here—and then he as a home boarder is not enough with other boys—and consequently does not take exercise enough. I shall place him with a tutor who has four or five other boys. I shall leave this place at Easter I think—but poor as I am, a move is a great anxiety.—Sir Tim is quite well and nearly doting— Claire is at Florence, expecting, poor dear, most firmly to die of Cholera.[2] It is very bad at Leghorn —20,000 people fled from the town—the Doctors could afford no help; one, Punta, faceva fiano; the people rose on him, and he ran for his life—the common people expect to be poisoned. At Florence, one man, taken to the hospital, refused every remedy, even a cup of camomile tea—and died of Cholera in 2 hours— At Florence they take every precaution to conceal the state of the disease—and it seems milder than at Leghorn— The Granduke is exerting himself in the most exemplary manner, goes into every squalid hovel—and himself overlooking the cleanliness of the streets— Poor Claire's state of mind is very sad—the family she is with remained at Florence, so she does— fully expecting to die. Jane has seen Weale once or twice—dined there once with Jeff— [? Monnica] flourishes—Trelawny is in England—in America he was enchanted with Fanny Kemble[3]—here he is enchained by Mrs. Norton — I do not wonder at the latter—she is a wonderful creation possessing wit, beauty and sweetness at their highest grade— They say a stony heart withal —so I hope she will make him pay for his numerous coqueteries with our sex— I have not seen Peacock for some time. His wife lives in town—she is quite mad—his children in the country all by themselves except for his weekly visits

[1] This second volume of Italian lives (1835, 394 pp.) contained biographies of Guicciardini, Vittoria Colonna, Guarini, Chiabrere, Tassoni, Marini, Filicaja, Metastasio, Goldoni, Alfieri, Monti, Ugo Fascolo, Galileo, and Tasso—all by Mary except the last two. The life of Galileo was by Sir David Brewster. (See Letter 441, note 2.)

[2] The details about the cholera are from Claire's letter from Florence, September 1, 1835 (*Shelley and Mary*, IV, 1197–1203).

[3] See Letter 436, note 4.

— His eldest girl educates herself and reads Paul de Kock's novels[4] in all innocence. Adieu, my dear friend—pray write soon and believe me ever

Affectionately Yr.

M. W. Shelley

ADDRESS: Mrs. Gisborne,/ Plymouth,/ Devon./ E. S. Ruthven. POSTMARK: Gray Abbey/ 18 OCT/ 1835. ENDORSED: Harrow 13th Oct. 1835. rec. 23rd Oct. Ans. ORIGINAL: Sir John Shelley-Rolls. PRINTED: *Shelley and Mary*, IV, 1205–1206; Marshall, II, 273–74 (incomplete). (Both introduce into this letter 7 lines that belong to the letter of November, 1835, to Mrs. Gisborne.) Grylls, *Mary Shelley*, 196–97, prints 3 hitherto unpublished lines. TEXT: From copy made by Sir John Shelley-Rolls.

458. *To Maria Gisborne*

Harrow,
Nov. 1835.

My dearest Friend,

You are very good to write, but indeed it would be too cruel to deprive us of intelligence about you. The prolongation of your sad disorder—and your prolonged life are matters of the deepest anxiety and interest to us all—to me in particular—for I always fancy something of relationship between us. I wish I could see you. I often dream of a journey to Plymouth—but alas! the operations of the poor are soon stopt.

I fancy our last letters crossed but I do not remember the date of mine— which I sent to Ireland for a frank—as this will go to Yorkshire—away from town, I cannot catch the passing Members as they fly—and therefore use those who are fixtures in their country residences during the recess. The M. P.[1] and his wife to whom this will go are curious people in their way— They are Liberals—have been to Italy (where they formed Claire's acquaintance and got an introduction to me) knew your friend Bentham and are allied to all the other Radical party—but they are country folks in core—he—a plain silentious but intelligent looking man of fifty—she—the Beau ideal of a Country Blue grafted on a sort of Lady Bountiful—Unitarians in Religion— They do a great deal of good in the country about them—and he looks as if he could feel—while she talking of enthusiasm—benevolence and the poor, bears a face, all the time in which such gentle feelings have made small traces— You esteem but cannot love her—and pretention harmless indeed, but still pretention animates her to perpetual talk. The moment the reform bill past the people of Wakefield chose him for their M. P. He attends the house night after night and dull committees and likes it!—for truly after a country town and country society, the dullest portion of London life seems as gay as a masked ball.

I fancy Jane intends to write. She has made herself ill by walking and exerting herself about her brother's children— I think this a great weakness on her

[4] Charles Paul de Kock (1793–1871), a French novelist who wrote numerous novels dealing with middle and low class life in Paris. His novels were more popular abroad than in Paris.

[1] D. Gaskell. (See Letter 448, note 5.)

part—but [I] preach in vain— J[ohn Wheeler] C[leveland][2] says "Do unto others as you would they should do unto you."—It may seem an extension of such charity to say "Do unto others as they would that you should do to them." Yet sometimes it is a narrowing of it—in the present instance Major Cleveland would certainly prefer that Jane should not injure her health and fret her temper about saving him sixpences when he is spending en Prince. When she has her baby this will stop. Her goodness to me in my illness I shall never forget—and I feel the utmost gratitude to her for it. The Godwins are in the act of moving which is a most troublesome affair tho' with them the use of government conveniences facilitates their arrangements.

Did I not write to you about the Literary Lives— You guessed right as to the sex of Dante's Life; it was written by the Omnipresent Mr. Montgomery —as well as Ariosto's— With Evelina, in a few days, I will send you a 2nd vol.—the life of Gallileo is by Sir David Brewster that of Tasso by Mr. Montgomery—the rest are mine and so ends the Italian lives; for which I am sorry. The Spanish and Portugueeze will cost me more trouble, if I can do them at all[3]— There is no Spanish Circulating Library— I cannot while here, read in the Museum if I would—and I would not if I could— I do not like finding myself a stray bird alone among men even if I know them— Nothing could make me voluntarily go among strange men in a character assimilitating to their own— One hears of how happy people will be to lend me their books— but when it comes to the point, it is very difficult to get at them; however as I am rather persevering, I hope to conquer these obstacles after all.

My health has improved much since I last wrote—and I hope to get away from this detestable place in the spring— Liking society as I do—and too much given in the happiest situations to devour my own heart, I endure torture. While day after day books and my own sad thoughts are my only resources, Percy grows—he is taller than I am, and very stout. If he does not turn out an honor to his parents, it will be through no deficiency in virtue or talents— but from that dislike of mingling with his fellow[men] except in the two or three friends, he cannot do without, which he has in common with all the male Shelleys. He may be the happier for it. He has a good understanding and great integrity of character.

How I feel for dear good S. G. in all his anxieties and fears—his attentions to you and affection make him an object of great interest—for as I grow older I look upon fidelity as the first of human virtues—and am going to write a novel to display my opinion. The publishers pleased with the success of Lodore want me to write another—and I want money to get away from here. Have you read Lodore—and can you get it. If not let S. G. or yourself write me three lines *immediately* you can send it (take care it is not too heavy for a frank)

---

[2] He eventually became a general in the Indian Service.
[3] The remaining part of this paragraph is printed in Marshall (II, 274) and *Shelley and Mary* (IV, 1206) as a part of Mary's letter of October 13, 1835.

EDWARD JOHN TRELAWNY

from a sketch by Seymour Kirkup

and enclosed to D. Gaskell Esq. M. P. Lupzet Hall, Wakefield, Yorkshire and if you write directly I shall hear before I send the parcel to Mr. Curtis and will include Lodore in it.—If you did read it, did you recognize any of Shelley's and my early adventures—when we were in danger of being starved in Switzerland—and could get no dinner at an inn in London?[4]

Remember how anxious we are about your health and write when you can. Your remarks about Bulwer, who is my acquaintance but not my friend are just. Vanity is his marked characteristic and this is disappointed in Literature. He wanted to be a Novelist philosopher and poet—in the last he failed. He wishes to be a leader in Politics and fashion—for the last he is voted vulgar —for the first he can neither acquire confidence nor influence— He is distrusted I know not why—for both he is much disqualified by a considerable deafness. He is ill tempered thro' disappointment—and he disliked the Italians in the true, wise English way—who could not speak a word of the language— I could tell you much more of his flirtations &c. by which 2 years ago he rendered himself his ridicule [*sic*]— I am angry with him—I admired his novels so much, I wanted him to be a great man but he is envious as well as vain— after all I am not a fair judge—I know him too little; I judge him by his actions and his conversation and books—and not by the inner man, which intimacy only reveals to one. Adieu, dear Maria   with best and earnest wishes,

Ever affectionately yours,
M. W. S.

ADDRESS: Mrs. Gisborne/ Plymouth/ Devon./ D. Gaskell. POSTMARK: Wakefield/ 8 NOV/ 1835. ENDORSED: Harrow Nov. 1835. rec. 11th Nov. Ans. ORIGINAL: Sir John Shelley-Rolls. UNPRINTED and UNPUBLISHED. TEXT: From copy made by Sir John Shelley-Rolls.

459. *To Maria Gisborne**

Harrow,
Friday [February 5, 1836]

Dearest Maria,

I enclose a note I got today from Jeff[1]— You will rejoice that all is happily over— Jane had been so weak that I much feared a bad time— I shall go up in a day or two to see her—but as I can only go for a few hours I think it best to leave her quiet for a few days.

I have not been very well since I wrote. My fate is so unchangeably sad, that I have not spirits enough to get well after being ill. I leave this place at Easter—having found a tutor for Percy—and I think the change will prove beneficial to him. For myself I hope nothing. The moving will be full of difficulty and annoyance, my residence in London dreary and mortifying; I am friendless and alone!

[4] See Dowden, I, 436–38.

[1] Hogg's letter of February 4 announcing the birth on that day of Prudentia Sarah (named "after her two paternal aunts") is printed in *Shelley and Mary*, IV, 1207.

I long to hear how you are. We have had a little severe weather about Xmas —but otherwise a mild winter— I am busy writing another novel[2]—but the exertion, though necessary to my purse—and not difficult, since my story writes itself—yet is not beneficial to my languid irritable state.

My Father is quite well—and dearest Percy also— The Cholera has disappeared from Florence and Claire escaped—she gives a frightful account of the effects that panic produced.

I have written to Dr. Budd but not seen him— I am not well enough to make myself agreable to a stranger and this place being so far—and so odious in winter—and I am so soon to migrate to London, I thought it best to defer his visit till that time— I never see any one here for I am domiciled miserably.

Do let me hear how you are—it is so long since you have written— I hope S. G. continues well—his asthma mitigated— God bless you.

Ever Affly. Yours,
M. W. Shelley

ADDRESS: Mrs. Gisborne/ Plymouth/ Devon./ M.D. POSTMARK: London/ 5.FEB/ 1836. ORIGINAL: Sir John Shelley-Rolls. UNPRINTED and UNPUBLISHED. TEXT: From copy made by Sir John Shelley-Rolls.

460. *To John Gregson*

Harrow,
1 March, 1836.

Dear Sir,

I enclose the receipt—will you be good enough to send the cheque to me at W. Godwin Esq.—Exchequer, Whitehall Yard—as thus I shall receive it sooner, and get the cash more readily.

I must now mention a change that I have arranged with regard to Percy and his education. At Easter I shall place him with a Tutor. I should have written before, had I believed it possible that Sir Timothy would make any objection. But I feel sure that he will approve this step—which several circumstances render eligible.

I think Percy has been the better for being at a Public School: but Home boarders—and he is one—labor under disadvantages, which encrease as they rise higher in the school— And besides it seems well, since he is now sixteen, that he should be under the care of a man, and at a greater distance from town. I have nothing to complain of in my son—he is obedient and trustworthy—his faults are rather negative than absolute— I think he will exert himself more under a private tutor.

I think I am fortunate in my selection of one. Mr. Morrison is Vicar of Stoneleigh, near Leamington, in Warwickshire. He has been highly recommended to me. The Head of his College, Wadham of Oxford—speaks in the highest terms of his classical attainments. Lady Dorme and Mr. Chandos

---

[2] *Falkner*, published in 1837.

Leigh, his neighbours, give the very highest testimonials of his temper—morals—and the esteem in which he is generally held. Mr. Chandos Leigh in particular will be very kind to Percy— Mr. Morrison has five pupils besides Percy—the son of Sir Guy Skipwith formerly M.P. for Warwick—the son of Lady Chamberlayne—the son of Lady Maxwell—who was at Harrow—these boys are of Percy's own age— There are two younger boys, named Barrett. Percy has been 3 years and a half at this school. At Easter he takes his place in the highest form but one in the school—in another year he would in the usual course of things leave it— I think his going to a tutor now, under all the circumstances to be preferred— I think Sir Timothy and yourself will agree with me. I may add that Mr. Morrison's terms are moderate and within my means.

Percy is in robust health—well grown—he has good spirits and a good temper. I wish Sir Tim would see him—before he goes. It is hard that going to another county, where I am promised that he shall be kindly received—that he should go without any mark of kindness from his Father's family—who were not always so estranged from him. He himself remembers that his Grandfather was at one time kind enough to notice him—and wonders why there should be a change now—when the notice would benefit him more.

I will if you please call on you with him before he goes to Warwickshire.

I am, dear Sir,
Yours Obdly.
M. W. Shelley

ORIGINAL: Sir John Shelley-Rolls. PRINTED: Ingpen, *Shelley in England*, 614–15 (quot., 10 lines). TEXT: From copy made by Sir John Shelley-Rolls.

461. *To Maria Gisborne*

Harrow,
4th March [1836].

My dearest Friend,

I cannot express the deep concern I feel at the sad intelligence.[1] Poor dear S. G. the devoted husband—the kind friend! For him it is a mercy not to have survived you—but for you with your passionate attachments—with your nervous sufferings I know and feel what you must be enduring. I long to be able to hasten down to you— Alas! poverty is a curse indeed when it prevents all possibility of being of use and comfort to those we love. Your good Elizabeth will I trust write to me again. You have a treasure in her—which while it cannot soothe your regrets, yet in part diminishes the so to speak, bodily wretchedness attendant on your loss. She will wait on you and take care of you.

What she tells me of Mrs. Hale is exactly what one might have expected—What right have they to interfere in a question that concerns Henry wholly?—But vulgar spirits are never easy except when they are making their odious

[1] The death of John Gisborne (Signor Giovanni), Mrs. Gisborne's husband.

influences felt. Elizabeth proves her extraordinary worth by her conduct on this occasion—and Henry I dare say will act as he ought. But that she refers by giving up her claim to him, to one as near and dear to you as your son and one of generous feelings—I should have advised her only giving up part of the legacy—she never can be called upon to relinquish the whole. And do not you save and injure yourself by privation—to save for her—for Henry will assuredly do all that he ought. Meanwhile Elizabeth has the strongest claims on your friends—and I do beg she will regard me as one most anxious to serve her— Now my means are limited indeed but it is to be hoped that by and bye I can give more than words to prove my sense of her fidelity.

Jane goes on well. Jeff idolizes his baby—so that Jane says she wonders how he can have endured life so long without one. I envy her even to bitterness in the possession of a little girl. I am not well—but I hope to become so when I leave this place—where my spirits suffer so much and I have no refuge from melancholy thought. Percy is well—and my Father.

You must indeed let me hear often *of* you, if not *from* you— By and bye avoiding a subject which I *know* you will never be able to touch upon you can write to me of your health and other things. Is there any thing I can do for you?

Ah, dearest Maria, what a thing life is! Do you remember our Italian summer—Villa Valsovano—the stream of life runs on us—for us not calmly and kindly, but destructive and turbid, wrecking and leaving us solitary and desolate— Yours is indeed a bitter fate— Would I could be with you to try to comfort you— Adieu, I shall count the days till I hear again from Elizabeth— She will always find a friend in me.

Ever Affectionately Yours,
M. W. Shelley

[P. S.] Jane sends her love and every kind and regretful message—she begs that Elizabeth will call on her if ever she comes to town.

Direct to me at Jane's, 13 Maida Vale, Edgware Road, as I leave this place shortly— I will write soon again and tell you my new address.

ADDRESS: Mrs. Gisborne/ Windsor Place/ Princess Sq./ Plymouth./ W. S. Trelawny. POSTMARK: London/ 5.MAR/ 1836. ORIGINAL: Sir John Shelley-Rolls. UNPRINTED and UNPUBLISHED. TEXT: From copy made by Sir John Shelley-Rolls.

462. *To John Gregson**

14 North Bank, Regent's Park,
8 April, 1836.

Dear Sir,

Will you have the goodness to communicate to Sir Timothy and Lady Shelley the melancholy event of my dear Father's death—it occurred yesterday evening at seven after an illness of ten days—of a Catarrhal fever.

Percy is quite well. He was to have gone to Warwickshire to his tutor next Monday. His going must now be deferred till after the funeral.

I am, dear Sir,
Your Obdly.
Mary W. Shelley

ORIGINAL: Sir John Shelley-Rolls. UNPRINTED and UNPUBLISHED. TEXT: From copy made by Sir John Shelley-Rolls.

463. *To Edward John Trelawny*

[London] Sunday [April (10,) 1836]

[*Mrs. Rossetti's Summary*] . . . there is another letter asking Trelawny if he would like to attend her father's funeral, and if he would go with the undertaker to choose the spot nearest her mother,'s, in St. Pancras Churchyard, and, if he could do this, to write to Mrs. Godwin, at the Exchequer, to tell her so.[1]

ORIGINAL: Keats Shelley Memorial, Rome; A.L.S., 3 pp. 8vo, page 1 having a heavy black border around it. UNPRINTED and UNPUBLISHED. SUMMARY: From Lucy M. Rossetti, *Mrs. Shelley*, 184.

464. *To J. C. Hudson*[2]

[London] Tu[e]sday [April 12, 1836]

Dear Mr. Hudson

Relying on your often proved goodness & needing a friend I am come to you on a very sad affair—my poor dear Father is gone— I am at the door in a fly—pray come out to me— I want to take you to Mrs. Godwin—who prefers consulting you on several things to anyone else—if you can give her some portion of your valuable time—

I am now waiting.

Yours truly
M W Shelley

ORIGINAL: Huntington Library; A.L.S., 2 pp. small 8vo (6½ x 4½ inches), laid into rare book 90327, Moore's *Life of Byron*, Vol. III. UNPRINTED and UNPUBLISHED. TEXT: From original letter.

465. *To Mary Hays*

14, North Bank,
Regent's Park,
20th April, 1836.

Dear Madam,

Having for some months been somewhat of an invalid—the extreme fatigue and anxiety I went through while attending on the last moments of my dearest father have made me too ill to attend to anything like business. By my father's will his papers will pass thro' my hands, and your most reasonable

---

[1] Godwin was buried on April 14. Among those attending the funeral were Percy Florence (as chief mourner), Trelawny, Thomas Campbell, James Kenney, Dr. Uwins, and Mr. Caunter. A brief notice of the funeral appeared in the *Times* for Saturday, April 16.
[2] Of the Legal Duty office.

request will be complied with. There is nothing more detestable or cruel than the publication of letters meant for one eye only. I have no idea whether any of yours will be found among my Father's papers.—But my health is such that I cannot promise when I can undergo the fatigue of looking over his papers.

You will be glad to know that one whom you once knew so well, died without much suffering—his illness was a catarrhal fever which his great age did not permit him to combat—he was ill about 10, and confined to his bed 5 days— I sat up several nights with him—and Mrs. Godwin was with him when I was not—as he had a great horror of being left to servants. His thoughts wandered a good deal but not painfully—he knew himself to be dangerously ill but did not consider his recovery impossible. His last moment was very sudden—Mrs. Godwin and I were both present. He was dozing tranquilly, when a slight rattle called us to his side, his heart ceased to beat, and all was over. This happened at a little after 7 on the even[in]g of the 7 ins.

My dear Father left it in his will to be placed as near my Mother as possible. Her tomb in St. Pancras Church Y[ar]d was accordingly opened—at a depth of twelve feet her coffin was found uninjured—the cloth still over it—and the plate tarnished but legible. The funeral was plain and followed only by a few friends. There might have been many more, but being private, we restricted the number. My son, now sixteen, was among the mourners.[1]

I have written these few particulars as they cannot fail to interest you.

I am obliged to you for your kind expression of interest.—Your name is of course familiar to me as one of those women whose talents do honour to our sex—and as the friend of my parents.

I have the honour to be, dear Madam

Very truly yours
Mary Shelley.

ADDRESS: Miss Hays,/ 11, Grosvenor Place,/ Camberwell. ORIGINAL: Not traced. PRINTED: *Love-Letters of Mary Hays* (1779–80), edited by A. F. Wedd (1925), 246–47. TEXT: From *ibid*.

466. *To Henry Crabb Robinson**

14 North Bank—Regent's Park
27 May—1836

Dear Sir

I am, for the benefit of Mrs. Godwin, who is left unprovided by the un-

---

[1] Godwin wrote in his will: ". . . it is my desire that my mortal remains should be deposited, as near as may be, to those of the author of *A Vindication of the Rights of Woman*."—Ford K. Brown, *The Life of William Godwin* (London, J. M. Dent & Sons, 1926), 372. The monument which stood over the grave of Mary Wollstonecraft and Godwin is still to be seen in the old St. Pancras Churchyard, now a public garden. But the bodies were removed in 1851 by Sir Percy Florence Shelley to the churchyard of St. Peter's, Bournemouth, where they now occupy the same grave with Mary Shelley, Percy Florence Shelley, Lady Jane Shelley, and Shelley's heart. The St. Pancras monument and its inscription are reproduced by Ingpen in *Shelley in England*, 609, 611.

fortunate death of my dear Father—engaged in collecting his papers for publication— There is a portion of autobiography & some interesting Corre-
spondance— Could you assist me in augmenting the latter. It strikes me that
there may be many interesting letters to Mrss. Coleridge, Wordsworth & yourself—which no one would object to seeing published— I have no acquaintance with Mr. Wordsworth nor the Executors of Mr. Coleridge— Would
you kindly interest yourself on the subject—& if there exist letters that would
interest the public & annoy no one to see in print, would you endeavour to
procure them for me

I take a great liberty in asking you—but am inducted by the long intimacy
that subsisted between you & my father & Mrs. Godwin & my belief that you
would willingly to [*sic*] the latter a service

I am, dear Sir

Your ob^t Servant

Mary Shelley

ADDRESS: Henry C. Robinson Esq/ 2 Plowden Buildings/ Temple. POSTMARKS:
(1) Park Terrace (2) My 28/ 1836. ENDORSED: 27 May 1836./ Mrs. Shelley,/
autograph./ No publication took place— All the letters I was in possession of
were applications for money— I wrote in reply that I had none but on
business. ORIGINAL: The Dr. Williams Library, London (H.C. Robinson's
Letters. Volume for 1836–37, f.131); A.L.S., 2 pp. 4to, with seal. UNPRINTED
and UNPUBLISHED. TEXT: From original letter.

467. *To John Gregson*

14 North Bank, Regents Park,
1 June, 1836.

Dear Sir,

I send the receipt   will you send the cheque to me here.

I have frequent letters from Percy. He seems to be getting on very well—
and Mr. Morrison says that in a twelvemonth he will be fit for colledge— I
have reason to be pleased with my selection of a tutor and also—with Percy's
improvement and good qualities. His holydays begin 2nd July.

I am dear Sir,

Yr. Obly.

M. W. Shelley

ADDRESS: John Gregson Esq./ 18 Bedford Row. ORIGINAL: Sir John Shelley-
Rolls. UNPRINTED and UNPUBLISHED. TEXT: From copy made by Sir John
Shelley-Rolls.

468. *To John Gregson**

14 North Bank, Regent's Park,
6 June, 1836.

Dear Sir,

Have you quite forgotten me? I would not write to remind you that I sent the receipt on the 1st, but that if any accident has happened to the cheque it ought to be discovered.

I am, dear Sir,
Yrs. Obdly.
M. W. Shelley

ADDRESS: John Gregson Esq./ 18 Bedford Row. ORIGINAL: Sir John Shelley-Rolls. UNPRINTED and UNPUBLISHED. TEXT: From copy made by Sir John Shelley-Rolls.

469. *To [Henry Colburn]**   14 North Bank—Regent's Park
Wednesday 8 June [1836]

Dear Sir

I have heard that there has been, thro' Mr. Ayrton, some communication made to you—with regard to the intended publication of my Father's Autobiography letters &. I should be glad to see you & converse with you on the subject—   Can you call tomorrow before two—or the next day—but tomorrow would suit me best—   I am, dear Sir

Yours obl.
M W Shelley.

ORIGINAL: Owned by Maggs Brothers in 1936; A.L.S., 1 p. 8vo; paper inside has slender black border. UNPRINTED and UNPUBLISHED. TEXT: From original letter.

470. *To William Hazlitt, Jr.*   4 Lower Belgrave St.
10 Oct. 1836.

Sir,

I am at this moment occupied in editing the Memoirs & Correspondence of my Father, Mr. Godwin.[1] If among your Father's papers, you found any

[1] Mary never completed editing her father's Memoirs and Correspondence, and what she actually wrote is unpublished, except for brief extracts in Kegan Paul's *William Godwin.* (See Letter 472.) The following memorandum was signed by Mrs. Godwin and Henry Colburn:

"London, July 19, 1836.

"Memorandum of an Agreement made and entered into this day between Mrs. Mary Jane Godwin of No. 5 Featherstone Buildings, of the one part, and Henry Colburn, of 13 Great Marlboro Street, Publisher, of the other part.

"The said Mrs. Godwin, for and in consideration of the sum of Three Hundred and Fifty Guineas, to be paid by the said Henry Colburn as hereinafter mentioned, hereby agrees to sell to the said Henry Colburn, . . . the exclusive right of printing and publishing for his own use and benefit, an edition of One Thousand Copies of the Personal Memoirs and Correspondence of the late William Godwin, comprising the most interesting letters that can be selected therefrom, also the autobiography of William Godwin, the whole to be edited by Mrs. Shelley, at the expense of the said Mrs. Godwin. The said selection of letters to be made at the absolute discretion and judgment of Mrs. Shelley.

"The said Memoirs are to consist altogether of not less than two volumes, demy octavo, of thirty sheets, each volume, of the average size, page and print: the first volume to be ready for the press by the 1st of October next; the second volume by the 1st of November next, so as to enable the said Henry Colburn to publish both volumes on or before the 20th of November next, at the latest. . . ."

The original document of the above memorandum was offered for sale by Birrell & Garnett, Ltd., 30 Gerrard Street, London, W. 1, in a catalogue of "Autograph Letters, Documents, and Books by Shelley, Godwin, and their Friends" [November 1936], in which catalogue the extracts above are printed.

letters or notes of his, you would confer an obligation on me by letting me have them. I have a few notes from Mr. Hazlitt to my Father, which I will look out & send you if you wish.

I wish I may perform my task as well as you have done yours. I read your Memoirs of your Father with great pleasure.[2] Mr. Talfourd's Essay is very beautiful & worthy its subject.

As I am leaving town will you direct to me at Hookham's Library, 15 Old Bond St., & oblige me by an early answer.

I am, Sir

Your obt. servant

Mary Shelley

ORIGINAL: Owned by Thomas J. Gannon, Inc., New York, in January, 1937; A.L.S., 2 pp. small 8vo. UNPRINTED and UNPUBLISHED. TEXT: From copy sent me by Gannon, Inc.

471. *To Edward John Trelawny*

Brighton,
3rd Jan. 1837.

My dear Trelawny,

This day will please you—it is a thaw—what snow we have had—hundreds of people have been employed to remove it during the last week—At first they cut down deep several feet as if it had been clay—and piled it up in glittering pyramids and masses—then they began to cart it onto the beach it was a new sort of Augean Stable—a never ending labor— Yesterday when I was out— it was only got rid of in a very few and very circumscribed spots— Nature is more of a Hercules—she puts out a little finger in the shape of gentle thaw— and it recedes and disappears.

When I got your letter I looked and rubbed my eyes and looked again for the little speck you mention—but no it was gone, absolutely gone—and how much I miss the dear entity I need not tell—since you know what a dear thing she is— She has left behind a microscopic something that she calls a Mustachio comb—I wish I could send it you—it is delicate and immaterial as if made by Queen Mab— How she could fancy that it would suit the shaggy hairs of a wolf I do not know—but even now she insists that it will meet with your approbation— We shall see.

Percy arrived only yesterday—having rather whetted than satisfied his appetite by going seven times to the play. He plays like Apollo on the flagiolet —and like Apollo is self taught— Jane thinks him a miracle, it is very odd— he got a frock coat at Mette's and if you had not disappointed us with your handkerchief, he would be complete—he is a good deal grown—though not tall enough to satisfy me—however there is time yet—he is quite a child still —full of theatres and balloons and music—yet I think there is a gentleness

[2] *Literary Remains of the Late William Hazlitt,* With a Notice of His Life, by his Son, and Thoughts on His Genius and Writings, by E. L. Bulwer and Sergeant Talfourd (London, Saunders & Otley, 1836, 2 vols.).

about him which shews the advent of the reign of petticoats—How I dread it—
I hope you will be useful to me when it begins—and let him into a few of
those secrets—which, as he has a horror of risking health or comfort, will I
hope keep him right.

Poor Jane writes dismally— She is so weak that she has frequent fainting
fits. She went to a physician who ordered her to wean the child—and now she
takes 3 glasses of wine a day—and every other strengthening medicament—but
she is very feeble—and has a cough and tendency to inflammation on the
chest— I implored her to come down here to change the air— Jeff gave
leave and would have given the money—but fear lest his dinner should be
overdone while she was away—and lest the children should get a finger
scratched makes her resolve not to come— What bad logic is this—if she got
stronger here how much the better they would be in consequence. I think
her in a very critical state—but she will not allow of a remedy. Claire's direction is 11 Queen St. Mayfair— Mrs. Bennett[1] is better and Claire also. Do
write to her.

I have no other news for you—no news from Mrs. N[orton] or Mrs. G.—
The day before you left Brighton Caroline Aldridge came to it—she staid a
week— She was looking very handsome indeed—and her daughter of 6
years old you would have idolized—a little fair fairy thing, as gay as a lark—
She called on me—and I was glad to see how well, happy, and handsome she
looked.

Poor dear little Zella— I hope she is well and happy— We are such
wandering Tartars that we can be of little comfort to her— Thank you for
your offer about money— I have plenty at present—and hope to do well hereafter—you are very thoughtful—which is a great virtue— I have not heard
from your Mother or Charlotte since you left— A day or two afterwards I
saw Betsey Freeman—she was to go to [? place] the next day— I paid her
for her work—she looked so radiantly happy that you would have thought
she was going to be married rather than to a place of hardship— I never saw
any one look so happy— I told her to let me know how she got on and to
apply to me if she wanted assistance. Jonathan still sails in stately size along
the Parade— I am glad you are amused at your Brother's— I really imagined that Fanny Butler[2] had been the attraction, till sending to the Gloucester,
I found you were gone by the Southampton coach—and then I suspected another Magnet—till I find that you are in all peace—or rather war—Sherfield
House— Much better so.

I am better a great deal—quite well I believe I ought to call myself—only
I feel a little odd at times— I have seen nothing of the Smiths[3] I have met
with scarce an acquaintance here—which is odd—but then I do not look for

[1] Claire was governess in the Bennett family.
[2] Fanny Kemble (Mrs. Pierce Butler).
[3] The Horace Smiths, who lived at Brighton.

them, I am too lazy— Adieu—I hope this letter will catch you before you leave your present perch. Believe me always,

Yours truly,
M. W. Shelley

[P. S.] Will this be a happy New Year? Tell me—the last I cant say much for—but I always fear worse to come— Nobody's Mare is dead—if this frost does not kill—my cure (such as it will be) is far enough off still.

Its a hard [thing], pleasures come singly misfortunes in batallions.

ADDRESS: Edward Trelawny Esq.,/ Sherfield House,/ Romsey--Hants. ORIGINAL: Sir John Shelley-Rolls. PRINTED: Marshall, II, 279–80 (incomplete). TEXT: From copy made by Sir John Shelley-Rolls.

472. *To Edward John Trelawny*

Brighton,
Thursday, January 27, 1837.

Dear Trelawny,

I am very glad to hear that you are amused and happy—fate seems to have turned her sunny side to you—and I hope you will long enjoy yourself— I know but of one pleasure in the world—sympathy with another—or others—leaving out of the question the affections—the society of agreable, gifted, congenial-minded beings is the only pleasure worth having in the world. My fate has debarred me from this enjoyment, but you seem in the midst of it.

With regard to my Father's life—I certainly could not answer it to my conscience to give it up— I shall therefore do it—but I must wait. This year I have to fight my poor Percy's battle—to try to get him sent to College without further dilapidation on his ruined prospects—and he has to enter life at College—that this should be undertaken at a moment when a cry was raised against his Mother—and that not on the question of *politics* but *religion,* would mar all—I must see him fairly launched, before I commit myself to the fury of the waves.

A sense of duty towards my father, whose passion was posthumous fame makes me ready—as far as I only am concerned, to meet the misery that must be mine if I become an object of scurrility and attacks—from the rest—for my own private satisfaction all I ask is obscurity. What can I care for the parties that divide the world or the opinions that possess it? What has my life been? What is it since I lost Shelley?—I have been alone—and worse— I had my father's fate for many a year a burthen pressing me to the earth—and I had Percy's education and welfare to guard over—and in all this I had no one friendly hand stretched out to support me. Shut out from even the possibility of making such an impression as my personal merits might occasion—without a human being to aid, or encourage or even to advise me, I toiled on my weary solitary way. The only persons who deigned to share those melancholy hours, and to afford me the balm of affection were those brave girls[1] whom you chose so long to abuse. Do you think that I have not felt, that I do not feel all this?—If I have been able to stand up against the breakers which have dashed against my stranded wrecked bark—it has been by a sort of passive dogged resistance, which has broken my heart, while it a little supported my spirit. My happiness, my health, my fortunes, all are wrecked— Percy alone remains to me and to do him good—is the sole aim of my life. One thing I will add—if I have ever found kindness it has not been from Liberals—to disengage myself from them was the first act of my freedom—the consequence was that I gained peace and civil usage—which they denied me— More I do not ask— Of fate I only ask a grave— I know what my future life is to be—what my present life is—and shudder—but it must be borne—and for Percy's sake I must battle on.

If you wish for a copy of my novel[2] you shall have one—but I did not order it to be sent to you because being a rover all luggage burthens— I have told them to send it to your Mother—at which you will scoff—but it was the only way I had to shew my sense of her kindness. You may pick and choose those from whom you deign to receive kindness— You are a man at a feast—champagne and comfits your diet—and you naturally scoff at me and my dry crust in a corner—often have you scoffed and sneered at all the aliment of kindness or society that fate has afforded me— I have been silent—the hungry cannot be dainty—but it is useless to tell a pampered man this— Remember in all this, except in one or two instances—my complaint is not against *persons* but *fate*—fate has been my enemy throughout— I have no wish to encrease her animosity or her power, by exposing more than I possibly can—to her cancourous attacks.

You have sent me no address—so I direct this to your Mother's. Give her and Charlotte my love—and tell them I think I shall be in town at the beginning of next month— My time in this house is up on the 3rd, and I ought to be in town with Percy to take him to Sir Tim's Solicitors—so to begin my attack.

I should advise you, by the bye, not to read my novel—you will not like it— I cannot *teach*—I can only *paint,* such as my paintings are—and you will not approve of much of what I deem natural feeling because it is not founded on the New Light.

I had a long letter from Mrs. N[orton][3]—I admire her excessively and I

---

[1] The Robinsons. (See Letter 309, note 2.)

[2] *Falkner,* 3 vols., published by Saunders & Otley, 1837. This novel should have been of special interest to Trelawny, for the chief character (Falkner) is modelled after Trelawny himself, whose appearance, character, and adventures Falkner reproduces.

[3] This letter, dated January 5, 1837, is printed in Jane Gray Perkins's *The Life of Mrs. Norton* (London, John Murray, 1910), 133–36. Mary and Mrs. Norton became fairly intimate. Miss Perkins quotes from eight of Mrs. Norton's letters to Mary written in 1836–38, and from two of a later date.

think could love her infinitely—but I shall not be asked nor tried, and shall take very good care not to press myself— I know what her relations think.

I shall soon be in town I suppose—*where* I do not yet know. I dread my return—for I shall have a thousand worries. Despite unfavourable weather—quiet and care have much restored my health—but mental annoyance will soon make me as ill as ever. Only writing this letter makes me feel half dead—Still to be thus at peace is an expensive luxury, and I must forego it—for duties which I have been allowed to forget for a time—but my holyday is past. Happy is Fanny Butler if she can shed tears and not be destroyed by them—this luxury is denied me— I am obliged to guard against low spirits as my worst disease—and I do guard—and usually I am not in low spirits— Why then do you awaken me to thought and suffering by forcing me to explain the motives of my conduct—could you not trust that I thought anxiously—decided carefully—and from disinterested motives—not to save myself but my child from evil—Pray let the stream flow quietly by as glittering on the surface as it may. Do not awaken the deep waters which are full of briny bitterness— I never wish any one to dive into the secret depth be content if I can render the surface safe sailing, that I not annoy you with clouds and tempests but turn the silvery side outward as I ought, for God knows I would not render any living creature as miserable as I could easily be—and I would also guard myself from the sense of woe which I tie hard about and sink low low out of sight or fathom line.

Adieu. Excuse all this; it is your own fault—speak only of yourself and never speak of me and you will never again be annoyed with so much stupidity.

Yours truly,

M. S.

[P. S.] If you are still so rich and can lend me £20 till my quarter I shall be glad. I do not know that I absolutely want it now, but may run short at last, so if not inconvenient, will you send it next week?

ADDRESS: Edward Trelawny Esq.,/ 16 Michael's Place,/ Brompton,/ London.
ORIGINAL: Sir John Shelley-Rolls. PRINTED: Marshall, II, 282–85. TEXT: From copy made by Sir John Shelley-Rolls.

473. *To Leigh Hunt**

41 d Park St.
Saturday [? February–March, 1837]

My dear Hunt

Your promise for May is very kind & pleasant—though so far off— I shall remind you of it be assured & Jane & I shall be delighted once again to see our unforgotten & dear friend. I am sorry that Marianne cannot join us. I hope all coughs & illness will be well then. You are good & right to be careful—for Jane especially—as she has a little baby.

I hear that some friends Talfourd & Bulwer are trying to get a pension for you—God grant they succeed—no one deserves it more. I am trying to get a small one for Mrs. Godwin[1]—poor as I continue to be through circumstances never changing, I have it much at heart to succeed.

I will tell Dr. Lardner to cause the Lives of the Spanish Poets to be sent directed to you at Hookhams—some day next week send for it— I am sure that of Cervantes will come home to you. Camoens was more unfortunate than he—but does not *come home* to *you* in the same manner. I am now writing French Lives[2]— The Spanish ones interested me—these I do not so much —yet it is pleasant writing enough—[? spurring; ? sparing] one's imagination yet occupying one & supplying in some small degree the *needful* which is so very needful.

With love to Marianne believe me

Ys ever truly

M W Shelley

ORIGINAL: British Museum (Add. MSS 38,523, ff.106–107); A.L.S., 4 pp. 8vo. UNPRINTED and UNPUBLISHED. TEXT: From original letter.

474. *To Edward John Trelawny**

[London] Friday [? May, 1837]

Dear Edward

I have heard from Charlotte & agreed to dine at Brompton on Monday.

I have not yet called on Mrs. Butler.[3] How can I without a carriage? It is too hot to walk— I will on Monday if possible. Send me her address, for I do not know it

Yours Ever

M W S

ORIGINAL: Owned by J. Kyrle Fletcher, Ltd., London, in 1937; A.L.S., 2 pp. 12mo. UNPRINTED and UNPUBLISHED. TEXT: From original letter.

475. *To Sir John Bowring**

24 South Audley St

1 June [1837]

Dear Doctor Bowring

Many thanks for the Del Rios, which is of the greatest assistance— Would it be quite impossible for you to lay your hands on any other of Cervantes's works— I remember you lent me some several years ago—Pellicers' book[4] I want much

Do not forget your promised call—a conversation with you would doubtless

---

[1] In this Mrs. Norton assisted Mary. See Perkins, *Life of Mrs. Norton*, 141–43.
[2] Published in 1838 as Volume IV of the biography part of Reverend Lardner's *Cabinet Cyclopaedia*.
[3] Fanny Kemble (Butler)?
[4] Pellicer's *Vida de Cervantes*, 1800.

be a great help to me, and I count on it—though, it is trespassing on very valuable time

Ever truly yours
M W Shelley

ENDORSED: June 1 1837/ M. A [sic] Shelly. ORIGINAL: Huntington Library (HM 2768); A.L.S., 2 pp. 8vo. UNPRINTED and UNPUBLISHED. TEXT: From original letter.

476. *To Leigh Hunt*

Rock Gardens, Brighton,
June 20, 1837.

I was an exile at Harrow for several years—a more dreary life than that which I lived there cannot be imagined—however, I did not grudge it for Percy's sake.

ORIGINAL: Not traced. A.L. (sig. cut out), 2 pp. 4to. Sold at Sotheby's on July 29, 1921 (as part of a collection of various letters), to Thorpe, for £30. UN-PRINTED and UNPUBLISHED. TEXT: A quotation printed in *Autograph Prices Current.*

477. *To Sir John Bowring**

17 South Audley St
Monday 3 July [1837]

Dear Doctor Bowring

Your labours in P[arliamen]t are closing for the moment—shall I not see you before you quit town—is there the slightest hope of your being able to get at any other Spanish books for me   And will you tell me *what papers* you have written in *what Reviews* on Spanish literature & if there exist any trans-lations by you of Spanish poets besides the volume which I am well acquainted with. Will you tell me if any where I can meet with any translations from Boscan, Garcilaso de la Vega, Herrera, Mendoza[1] &c &c—Do let me have an answer to this question directly—

I am dear Dr. Bowring
Ever truly ys
M W Shelley

ENDORSED: July 3, 1837/ M A [sic] Shelly. ORIGINAL: Huntington Library (HM 2769); A.L.S., 2 pp. 8vo. UNPRINTED and UNPUBLISHED. TEXT: From original letter.

478. *To Sir John Bowring**

24 South Audley St.
Thursday 13 July [1837]

Dear Doctor Bowring

Your note made me melancholy to think how you should be drawn from

---

[1] Spanish poets: Juan Boscán Almogaver (?1495–1542); Garcilaso de la Vega (1503–36); Diego Hurtado de Mendoza (1503–75); Fernando de Herrera (?1534–97).

the studies you loved & adored to the arid business of life. Thanks for all the hints you have given me— I have got Wiffin's Garcilaso[1]—He mentions in that that he meant to publish a Spanish Anthology—did he ever?—or can you tell me if any where I can find translations from Boscan & Hurtado de Mendoza— Did you ever in any Article? Your translations are best of all—they are so easy flowing & *true*.

Would you be so good as to frank & send the enclosed today if possible if not tomorrow

Ever truly ys

M W Shelley

ENDORSED: July 13, 1837/ Mrs. Shelley. ORIGINAL: Huntington Library (HM 2770); A.L.S., 2 pp. 8vo. UNPRINTED and UNPUBLISHED. TEXT: From original letter.

479. *To Edward Bulwer*

41 d Park St.
Sunday [? March, 1838]

Dear Mr. Bulwer—

Do excuse my writing a few lines to say how very much *The Lady of Lyons* pleased me.[2] The interest is well-maintained, the dialogue natural, one person answers the other, not as I found in *Werner* and *Sardanapalus,* each person made a little speech apart, or one only speaking that the other might say something; the incidents flow from the dialogue, and that without soliloquies, and the incidents themselves flow naturally one from another. There is the charm of nature and high feeling thrown over all.

I think that in this play you have done as Shelley used to exhort Lord Byron to do—left the beaten road of old romance, so worn by modern dramatists, and *idealised the present;* and my belief is that now that you have found the secret of dramatic interest, and to please the public, you will, while you adhere to the rules that enable you to accomplish this necessary part of a drama, raise the audience to what height you please. I am delighted with the promise you hold out of being a great dramatic writer. But (if I may venture to express an opinion to one so much better able to form them—an opinion springing from something you said the other night) do not be apt to fancy that you are less great when you are more facile. It is not always the most studied and (consequently) the favourite works of an author that are his best titles to fame —the soil ought to be carefully tended, but the flower that springs into bloom most swiftly is the loveliest.

I have not read your play. I would not till I saw it, for a play is a thing for acting, not the closet.

[1] J. F. Wiffen's English translation of "Garcilaso de la Vega," 1823.
[2] This play was produced by Macready at Covent Garden on February 15, 1838. It was published before March 13, by which date it was in a second edition.

I hope you will remember your promise of calling on me some evening, and believe me—

Yrs. truly,
M. Shelley

ORIGINAL: Not traced. PRINTED: *Life of Edward Bulwer, First Lord Lytton,* by his Grandson, The Earl of Lytton (1913), I, 538–39. TEXT: From *ibid.*

480. *To [George Henry] Lewes**[1]

84 Park St.
26 April [? 1838].

Dear Mr. Lewes

Many thanks— I send you Genl Pèpè's note to me.—He calls his treatise in English "A Political View of Italy with its relations to Great Britain & France"— I shall be very glad indeed to get it printed.[2]

Percy is confined to the house by a feverish attack—or he would call

I am   Very truly ys
M W Shelley

ORIGINAL: Stark Collection, University of Texas; A.L.S., 1 p. 8vo. UNPRINTED and UNPUBLISHED. TEXT: From original letter.

481. *To Richard Rothwell**

41 d Park St.
Friday Evg. [October 5, 1838]

Dear Mr. Rothwell[3]

Will you go to Drury Lane with me & a party tomorrow— If you will, be here at six—or join us at Drury Lane any time in the evening—going to the Private Door—& asking for the Duke of Bedford's box—Eliza Robinson will be with me— She considers that she requires another lesson on the art of [? Singing in Public] & docility in yielding to the requests of others—you giving an example by joining our party at the theatre tomorrow—

Believe me
Ys. truly
M Shelley

ADDRESS: Richard Rothwell/ 31 Devonshire St./ Portland Place. POSTMARK: 12 N[n] 12/ OC 6/ 1838. ORIGINAL: Luther A. Brewer Collection, University of Iowa; A.L.S., 2 pp. 8vo (4¾ x 7⅝ inches). UNPRINTED and UNPUBLISHED. TEXT: From original letter.

[1] (1817–78). Later Lewes became the "husband" of George Eliot. My only reasons for doubting that 1838 is the correct year for the letter are the youth of Lewes and his residence in Germany for a part of 1838.

[2] General Guglielmo Pépé (1783-1855) was a Neapolitan general who served in Napoleon's army. In Naples he organized the Carbonari into a national militia, and had a part in the Revolution there. He led the army against the Austrians, but was defeated; after the defeat he spent many years in exile, in England, in France, and in other countries. During these years he published several books and pamphlets. He returned to Italy in 1848.

His *Political View* appears not to have been published in English. But it was published in French with the title: *L'Italie Politique et ses Rapports avec la France et l'Angleterre, par [le général Pépé], précédée d'une introduction par M. Ch. Didier* (Paris, Pagnerre, 1839). Another edition appeared in 1848.

[3] See Letter 366, note 3.

482. *To Lady Morgan*

41d Park Street [1838–39]

As you return none of my calls I suppose [you] cut me, which I think cross. I send you the relic—you may say that I have never parted with one hair to any one else.

> ORIGINAL: Owned by Walter T. Spencer, London, in 1937; A.L.S., 1 p. 8vo.
> UNPRINTED and UNPUBLISHED: TEXT: A quotation sent me by Walter T. Spencer, who would not permit me to copy the letter.

483. *To Thomas Jefferson Hogg*

41, Park Street, Dec. 11, 1838.

Dear Jefferson,

J[ane] has told you, I suppose, that I am about to publish an Edition of Shelley's Poems.[1] She says, you have not a *Queen Mab*. Yet have you not? Did not Shelley give you one—one of the first printed? If you will lend it me, I shall be so very much obliged; and I will return it safely when the book is printed. [...]

Will you lend me your *Alastor* also? It will not go to the printer; I shall only correct the press from it.

Sir Timothy forbids Biography, under a threat of stopping the supplies. What could I do then? How could I live? And my poor boy! But I mean to write a few Notes appertaining to the history of the Poems. If you have any of Shelley's letters, mentioning his poetry, and would communicate them, I should be glad, and thank you.

I am ever truly yours,
Mary W. S.

To T. J. H., Temple

> ORIGINAL: Captain R.J.J. Hogg. PRINTED: T. J. Hogg, *Life of Shelley* (1858),
> I, ix (incomplete, and with alterations and additions). See letters 6–16. TEXT:
> From T. J. Hogg, *Life of Shelley*.

484. *To [? Charles Ollier]**

41 d Park St.
12 Dec. [1838]

Dear Sir

You would oblige me very much if you could inform me whether you have, or any friend of yours has, a copy of the *original* edition of Queen Mab.

[1] *The Poetical Works of P. B. Shelley,* edited by Mrs. Shelley (London, Edward Moxon, 1839, 4 vols.). As this and the following letters show, Mary had great difficulty in finding a copy of the first edition of *Queen Mab*. She eventually got Mrs. Boinville's copy.

This lady wrote from Paris on January 26, 1839: "I seize an opportunity offered by a very obliging friend, on whom I can depend, to send you my copy of 'Queen Mab.' I confess that I lend it with reluctance, and to no one but yourself would I confide it. I commit it to your care and rest confidently on your promise to return it to me as soon as you have made the use you wish of it. Will you have the goodness to send it when you have done with it in a sealed packet.

"I value highly this copy of 'Queen Mab' for many reasons, which you need not be told. It is a relic of genius, of friendship, of past happy days, which it would really grieve me to lose." —*Shelley and Mary*, IV, 1221.

And if it could be sold or lent to me—as I am publishing an Edition of Shelley's poems & wish to correct the press by the original edition & cannot find a copy. You would greatly favour me— I would take every care of the book & return it.

I am, dear Sir

Yours truly

M W Shelley

ORIGINAL: British Museum; In *The Poetical Works, Letters and Journals of Lord Byron*, in 44 vols., edited by Thomas Moore, London, 1844, Vol. 38, 22. The materials for this monumental set were gathered by Wm. Watts, musician and amateur artist, who died in 1859, aged 81; A.L.S., 1 p. 8vo. UNPRINTED and UNPUBLISHED. TEXT: From original letter.

485. *To Leigh Hunt*

41 Park Street,

December 12, 1838.

My dear Hunt,

I am about to publish an edition of our Shelley's Poems, Sir Tim giving leave if there is no biography. I want a copy of the original edition of *Queen Mab* to correct the press from—it must be the *original*—it would not go to the Printers, but only [be] used to correct from. Have you one—or do you know who has—Has Miss Kent? I should be so grateful for the loan. Moxon wants me to leave out the sixth part as too atheistical. I don't like Atheism—nor does he *now*. Yet I hate mutilation—what do you say? How have you been, and when does your Play[1] come out? With love to Marianne,

Yours ever,

M. W. Shelley.

[P.S.] Let me have the book quickly—if you have it—*as the press is waiting*.

ORIGINAL: Not traced. PRINTED: Ingpen, *Shelley in England*, 619–20. TEXT: From *ibid*.

486. *To Leigh Hunt**

41 d Park St.

Friday [December 14, 1838]

Dear Hunt

Many thanks for your kind note— I have not yet made up my mind. Except that I do not like the idea of a mutilated edition, I have no scruple of conscience in leaving out the expressions which Shelley would never have printed in after life *I* have a great love for Queen Mab—he was proud of it when I first knew him—& it is associated with the bright young days of both of us.[2]

Thanks for your very kind offer of assisting me in my note. But it must rest on myself alone. The edition will be mine—& though I feel my incompetency—yet trying to make it as good as I can, I must hope the best. In a future

---

[1] *The Legend of Florence*. See Letter 510, note 1.
[2] See Letter 495, note 1.

edition if you will add any of your own peculiarly delightful notes it will make the book more valuable to every reader—but our notes must be independant of each other—for as no two minds exactly agree, so (though in works of imagination two minds may add zest & vivacity) in matters of opinion—we should perhaps only spoil both—

Will you look in on me on Tuesday—   With love to Marianne

Ever yours

M W Shelley

[P. S.] I will give your message to Jane but to poor pedestrian ladies Chelsea is *very* far—especially in winter—or we should have called before.

> ORIGINAL: Huntington Library (HM 2751); A.L.S., 4 pp. 8vo. PRINTED: *Letters,* 180–81 (the postscript is printed on page 185 as a separate note). TEXT: From original letter.

487. *To Abraham Hayward**

41 d Park St.

Friday 14th Dec. [1838]

Dear Mr. Hayward

Will you do me the pleasure to drink tea with me on Tuesday next—Will you ask Mr. Sumner[1]—if you think he would like to come

Yours truly

M. W. Shelley

> ADDRESS: A. Hayward Esq./ Athenæum Club/ Pall Mall. ORIGINAL: Harvard University Library; A.L.S., 1 p. 8vo. UNPRINTED and UNPUBLISHED. TEXT: From original letter.

488. *To Thomas Jefferson Hogg*

41 d Park Street, Jan. 12, 1839

[Original letter owned by Captain R. J. J. Hogg. See letters 6–16.]

489. *To Thomas Jefferson Hogg*

[41 d Park Street] Monday Evening [? January 14, 1839]

[Original letter owned by Captain R. J. J. Hogg. See letters 6–16.]

490. *To Charles Sumner**[2]

41 d Park St.

Monday [? January 15, 1839].

Mrs. Shelley's compts to Mr. Sumner & requests the pleasure of his company at tea on Thursday at 5 o'clock

---

1 See Letter 490, note 2.

2 Charles Sumner (1811–74) was in England from May 31, 1838, until March 22, 1839, when he went to the Continent for a year. In a letter to George S. Hillard dated December 4, 1838, he gave this interesting account of Mary: "I did not expect . . . the next evening to be sitting on the same sofa chatting with Godwin's daughter, Mrs. Shelley, the author of 'Frankenstein.' I dined

ADDRESS: Charles Sumner Esq/ 2 Vigo St./ Regent St. ORIGINAL: Harvard University Library; A.L. (3rd person), 1 p. 12mo. UNPRINTED and UNPUBLISHED. TEXT: From original letter.

491. *To [? Charles Ollier]**

41 d Park St.
Saturday [? January 19, 1839]

Dear Sir

I am sorry I could not see you today— Your friend is very vexatious— any one else wd. prefer assisting me in giving out a perfect edition— The press has been waiting some days—and I know not what to do— I have no friend on whom I can put this sort of job—which I wish to do myself—so the agreable result of your friend's want of courtesy is that his offer is of no use at all.—Who is Brookes The press is waiting & all delay is too tiresome rendering success in the end of no avail—*do* tell me who & what Brookes is that I may apply—two persons so uncivilized as to refuse to lend the book to *me* for *such a purpose* cannot exist.

If you will call tomorrow at twelve I will see you—& you will be very obliging—if you cannot, pray let me know who Brookes is.

You do not even tell me who your friend is & where he lives—so that could I send,—this disastrous delay still goes on— Perhaps the Publisher wd. go & look at the copy—did I know where it was to be found—I am heartily vexed that a copy should have got into such churlish hands—

I beg your pardon—but I am vexed & with cause—

Yours truly

M W Shelley

[P.S.] I *must* send the proofs back early on Monday morning[1]—I would give any thing to see the original tomorrow— It is *TOO BAD*

with Theobald . . . and, stealing away from his drawing rooms, repaired to Lady [Sydney] Morgan's. Her Ladyship had particularly invited me to her party on this evening, saying, 'Promise me that you will come on Sunday night, and I will have all the literary characters of London. I will trot them all out for your benefit.' Accordingly, there were Sam Rogers . . . Kenyon, Hayward, . . . Westmacote Young, the retired actor . . . Quin, and Mrs. Shelley. . . . I talked a good deal with Mrs. Shelley. She was dressed in pure white, and seemed a nice and agreeable person, with great cleverness. She said the greatest happiness of a woman was to be the wife or mother of a distinguished man. I was not a little amused at an expression that broke from her unawares, she forgetting that I was an American. We were speaking of travellers who violated social ties, and published personal sketches, and she broke out, 'Thank God! I have kept clear of those Americans.' I did not seem to observe what she had said, and she soon atoned for it. Lady Morgan points every sentence with a phrase in French. She is now engaged upon a work on 'Woman' [*Woman and Her Master,* published in 1840], which will be published in the spring."— Edward L. Pierce, *Memoir and Letters of Charles Sumner* (London, 1878), II, 21.

In a letter of January 23, 1839, to Hillard, he added: "A far different person from Lady Morgan is Mrs. Shelley. I passed an evening with her recently. She is sensible, agreeable, and clever. There were Italians and French at her house, and she entertained us all in our respective languages. She seemed to speak both French and Italian gracefully."—*Ibid.,* II, 46.

[1] Volume I of the *Poetical Works* was published late in January, 1839. *The Spectator* for January 26, 1839, (pages 88–89), contains a moderately favorable review of it, though the omission of parts of *Queen Mab* is regretted. The reviewer's copy was an early one, and was in sheets. Volume II was out by March 5, and Volume III before April 4, Volume IV soon after May 2.

I shall be at home this evening if you called—*do* help me— I know *you* wd. if you could. If I cannot get the book tomorrow—it will be welcome at any time to correct the latter proofs or for an erata—but the sooner the better.

ORIGINAL: British Museum (Add. MSS 30,262, ff.35–36); A.L.S., 4 pp. 8vo. What appears to be an endorsement, though on a different kind of paper, is on folio 37: "1835 Mrs. Shelley, Park St. 13th Dec." The entry in the B.M. Catalogue gives this as the date of the letter and says it was addressed to Ollier; but there is no evidence in the letter itself. UNPRINTED and UNPUBLISHED. TEXT: From original letter.

492. *Two Letters to Thomas Moore*

[41 d Park St., January, 1839]

[Moore writes:[1]] Jan. 18, 19, [1839]: Received a letter one of these days from Mrs. Shelley, who is about to publish an edition of Shelley's works, asking me whether I had a copy of his "Queen [Mab]",—that originally printed for private circulation, as she could not procure one, and took for granted that I must have been one of those persons to whom he presented copies. In answering that I was unluckily *not* one of them, I added, in a laughing way, that I had never been much in repute with certain great guns of Parnassus, such as Wordsworth, Southey, her own Shelley, &c. Received from her, in consequence, a very kind and flattering reply, in which she says,

"I cannot help writing one word to say how mistaken you are. Shelley was too true a poet not to feel your unrivalled merits, especially in the department of poetry peculiarly your own,—songs and short poems instinct with the intense principle of life and love. Such, your unspeakably beautiful poems to Nea; such, how many others! One of the first things I remember with Shelley was his repeating to me one of your *gems* with enthusiasm. In short, be assured that as genius is the best judge of genius, those poems of yours which you yourself would value most, were admired by *none* so much as Shelley. You know me far too well not to know I speak the exact truth."

ORIGINALS: Not traced. PRINTED: *Memoirs, Journal and Correspondence of Thomas Moore*, edited and abridged by Lord John Russell (1860), 647–48 (quot., 15 lines). TEXT: From *ibid*.

493. *To Miss Mary Peacock*[*2]

41 d Park St.
Tuesday [January 22, 1839]

Dear Mary

Engagements of one sort or another have sprung up with the week, so that I find Friday is my only day. I expect Mrs. Hogg & a few people on that day—

1 *Memoirs, Journal and Correspondence of Thomas Moore*, 647–48.
2 Mary Ellen Peacock (1821–61), Peacock's eldest child, who after the tragic death of her husband Lieutenant Edward Nicolls, whom she had married in January, 1844, became the (unhappy) wife of George Meredith on August 9, 1849.

if you will join us I shall be very glad, at dinner. I dine at six—but come when you like

Yours Affy.

M W Shelley

ADDRESS: Miss Peacock/ xviii Stamford St./ Blackfriars. POSTMARK: 6.EV.6/ [?].22/ 1839. ORIGINAL: Owned by The Brompton Bookshop in 1937; A.L.S., 1 p. 8vo, with seal. UNPRINTED and UNPUBLISHED. TEXT: From original letter.

494. *To Edward Moxon**

41 d Park St.

4 March, 1839.

Dear Sir,

Thanks for the second £125—which I have received—

I have heard much praise of the mode the book is got up—but regrets *from all parties* on account of the omissions in Q[ueen] M[ab]. I trust you will not think it injurious to the copyright to insert them in the next edition   I think it would improve the sale—

Thanks for the books—   Have you sent 2nd vols. to those who read the 1st.

I am, dear Sir,

Yrs. truly,

M. Shelley

ORIGINAL: Sir John Shelley-Rolls. UNPRINTED and UNPUBLISHED. TEXT: From copy made by Sir John Shelley-Rolls.

495. *To Edward Moxon*

41 d Park St

5 March, 1839

Dear Sir

Pray do not believe that I intended to express any discontent about the omitted passages—   All I mean is—that as they have been published several times, I should prefer their being published in your edition—unless your doing so injured your interests

You were quite right in not sending Mr. Trelawny a copy of the 2ᵈ vol— I did not mention it—but of course understood that you would not.[1]

Yours truly—

M W Shelley

ORIGINAL: Sir John Shelley-Rolls; A.L.S., 1 p. 8vo. UNPRINTED and UNPUB-LISHED. TEXT: From original letter.

[1] The review of Volume I in *The Spectator* for January 26, 1839 (pages 88–89), disapproved of the omission of parts of *Queen Mab*. The review of volumes I–III in the *Athenæum* for April 27 (page 313) criticized Mary severely for this fault. In her journal Mary wrote on February 12: "I almost think that my present occupation will end in a fit of illness. . . . I *much* disliked the leaving out any of *Queen Mab*. I dislike it still more than I can express, and I even wish I had resisted to the last; but when I was told that certain portions would injure the copyright of all the volumes to the publisher, I yielded. I had consulted Hunt, Hogg, and Peacock; they all said I had a right to do as I liked, and offered no one objection. Trelawny sent back the volume to Moxon in a rage at seeing parts left out. . . .

"Hogg has written me an insulting letter because I left out the dedication to Harriet. . . .

"Little does Jefferson, how little does any one, know me! When Clarke's edition of *Queen Mab* came to us at the Baths of Pisa, Shelley expressed great pleasure that these verses were omitted.

496. *To Mary Peacock**

Layton House
Putney
30 March [1839]

Dear Mary

You will think me very rude not having answered your kind considerate note— But I have been ever since that time so very much indisposed—& as my illness was nervous, could not write. Even now I can only send a shabby letter. The poor girls were quite overwhelmed by the dreadful blow & are by no means recovered from it. Rosa sends her love & thanks you very much for your kindness.

I have got away from town at last & am so *very glad*. I have taken a furnished house on the Upper Richmond Road very near Putney—& if we have a fine summer I hope to enjoy myself greatly. Julia is with me. Percy rows in his boat to Kew & fetches Rosa & Eliza— I hope you will join us in the summer for some days— Meanwhile write & let us know how you get on—& if I am not able to write in answer, Rosa will for me.

Thanks for the Misfortunes of Elphin— Percy claims Melincourt as promised & wants it very much so if you find a copy pray let him have it. He deserves it—as he knows your father's Novels nearly by heart.

Your "Childhood's friend"—has been very ill—indeed poor girl—she was very ill the day you saw her— She had afterwards an inflamation of the chest —but is now quite recove[red.] Adieu, dear Mary— Remember me to your father—   I am

Ever truly ys
M W Shelley

ADDRESSED: Miss Peacock/ Lower Halliford/ Esher. POSTMARKS: (1) PUTNEY
(2) 4 Eg 4/ MR.30/ 1839   (3) G/ MR-30/ 1839. ORIGINAL: Huntington
Library (HM 12874); A.L.S., 3 pp. 4to, with seal. UNPRINTED and UNPUB-
LISHED. TEXT: From original letter.

497. *To Edward Moxon*

Layton House   Putney
4 April   /39

Dear Sir

Thanks for your parcel & the £125—which I received. The 3^d vol is thin— & I have an idea that the 4th will be a good deal thicker, but I could not get the Printers to calculate exactly—& did not like to trust to my own idea— We shall see— I sent a week ago the order of the remaining poems to the printer

---

This recollection caused me to do the same. It was to do him honour. What could it be to me? There are other verses I should well like to obliterate for ever, but they will be printed; and any to her could in no way tend to my discomfort, or gratify one ungenerous feeling. They shall be restored, though I do not feel easy as to the good I do Shelley."—Marshall, II, 289–90.

The omissions were replaced in the next edition, late in 1839. Moxon was prosecuted (see letters 524 and 525). On June 30, 1841, Trelawny wrote Moxon a conciliatory letter (*The Letters of Edward J. Trelawny,* 209–10).

& am in daily expectation of proofs. I told them to send them to me two at a time by the 2ᵈ post.—

Thanks for Miss Martineau's book[1] with which I am highly delighted Her pictures are so graphic & true to nature that they interest highly. Hester is I think very finely drawn indeed. Without Miss Austen's humour she has all her vividness & correctness. To compensate for the absence of humour she has higher philosophical views It is a very interesting & very beautiful picture of life.—I say this having read only two volumes

I hardly like asking you for books—but if I am indiscreet you must let me know. I should like Campbell's works—& Philip van Artevelte[2]— If you can easily spare them, send them to me to the care of Miss Bennet 2 Wilton St. Grosvenor Sq—& they will be brought to me on Saturday.

I am dear Sir Yˢ truly
M W Shelley

ORIGINAL: Duke University Library (formerly in Ingram Collection); A.L.S., 3 pp. 4to. UNPRINTED and UNPUBLISHED. TEXT: From original letter.

498. *To Mrs. Stanhope**

Putney
Friday [April 5, 1839]

Dear Mrs. Stanhope

If you go to town tomorrow & it is not inconvenient to you would you call at 2 Wilton St. (Mrs. Bennet) & ask for some books left there for me I am very rude to ask you to take so much trouble—if inconvenient you will not do it, of course—

I wanted much to call—but have been very unwell.

Ev. Ys.
M W Shelley

ADDRESS: Honbl/ Mrs. Stanhope/ Cedars. ORIGINAL: Owned by The Brompton Bookshop, London, in December, 1938; A.L.S., 3 pp. 12mo, with seal. UNPRINTED and UNPUBLISHED. TEXT: From original letter.

499. *To Edward Moxon**

Putney—2 May [1839]

Dear Sir

There was some delay at the beginning of April through my being too ill to write at all— The Printers were very impatient then— Latterly they have been slower when I was ready. In a few days now all will be finished I very much hope the book will have great success. Remember when you think of another edition to let me know—as for several reasons I shall wish it to pass through my hands.

In a short time I should like to see you with regard to [a] volume of Letters

[1] *Deerbrook* (1839, 3 vols.), a novel.
[2] A play by Sir Henry Taylor, published by Moxon in 1834. The sixth edition appeared in 1852.

& other prose essays—which I believe that the public will warmly welcome.[1]
I will call in Dover St. some day when in town

With regard to the books, you will deduct the price out of the sum I next
receive. Certainly I did not know that Southey's would be so voluminous &
cost so much—& would return them but have cut open two volumes which I
fear will prevent your being able to return them—for you must not lose—if
their being cut open makes no difference I will return them—but keep the
Wordsworth[2] & Coleridge

I send a fresh list for distribution. I should have accepted your kind offer
& delayed finishing till I was quite well— But my illness being chiefly produced by having to think of & write about the passed [*sic*]—it would have
renewed when I return[ed] to it—and I felt that at no time could I do better
than I have done now. It has cost me a great deal.

With fervent wishes for success I am, dear Sir

Ys. truly

M W Shelley

[P. S.] I have done as you asked with regard to mentioning the suppres-
sions[3]—You will find one or two new poems added.

ADDRESSED: Edward Moxon Esq/ Dover Street/ Piccadilly. POSTMARK: T. P./
Putney. ORIGINAL: Henry W. and Albert A. Berg Collection, the New York
Public Library; A.L.S., 4 pp. 4to, with stamped, addressed envelope. UNPRINTED
and UNPUBLISHED. TEXT: From original letter.

500. *To Mrs. Jones**

Putney—12 May [? 1839]

Dear Mrs Jones—

I have been going to write to you every day, to say how truly I sympathize
with you in your sorrow—Lady Morgan tells me you are very unhappy—you
must struggle with your distress however—for I know by painful experience,
how wrong it is to indulge in melancholy—I wish you could come up among us.

Lady Morgan rouses & is in good spirits, when she has a friend or two
about her. She came down to see me with her old Beau, Mr. Halford, & calling
on her the other day, she was kind enough to make me stay to dine—& Sir A—
& Lady Duff Gordon formed her party. I spent a delightful evening Lady
Morgan exerted herself & was very entertaining; I never saw her to greater
advantage.

I hope dear Josephine is recovering her spirits after her long & distressing

[1] Published by Moxon in two volumes as *Essays, Letters From Abroad*, &c., 1840.
[2] The books may have been volumes I–III of Southey's *The Doctor*, reprinted in 1839; and
The Poetical Works of Wordsworth, A New Edition, 6 vols., advertised by Moxon in Volume IV
of Shelley's *Poetical Works*, 1839, as "Just Published."
[3] *Poetical Works*, 1839, IV, 226, footnote: "I will add in this note that no omissions have
been made except in the Cantos of 'Queen Mab.' Some asterisks occur in a few pages, as they did
in the volume of Posthumous Poems [1824], either because they refer to private concerns, or
because the original manuscript was left imperfect." This is about half the note. The "Note on
Poems Written in 1822" is dated "Putney, May 1, 1839" (page 236).

attendance—it will be a great consolation to her to feel that she had the comfort of being a help & support, during so much suffering—& to feel that she fulfilled a dear & sacred—though most sad duty.

I can only repeat my wish that you were here—yet perhaps you desire, for a time at least, that quiet & privacy—which affliction naturally seeks, but which would certainly not accord with Lady Morgan Still, as I said—pray do not indulge in grief—fight against it— Come up here as soon as you can— You are ever wished for.—

My best remembrances to Mr. Jones—I am

Affectionately Y^s

M Shelley

ORIGINAL: A.L.S., 4 pp. 8vo. Owned by Raphael King, Ltd., Museum Street, London, in November, 1939. UNPRINTED and UNPUBLISHED. TEXT: From original letter.

501. *To Mrs. Alexander Berry*[1]

Putney—3 August 1839

My dear Cousin

Mr. Charles Robinson carries with him a recommendation to you from our Aunt Everina.—I will add that I have known him from boyhood that he is a most honourable kind hearted excellent young man—so he goes out for the purposes of advancement & any advice & kindness you & Mr. Berry shew him will oblige me deeply—& be well bestowed.

[1] Mrs. Berry, Mary's cousin, was Elizabeth Wollstonecraft, the daughter of Edward Wollstonecraft, a London attorney. She married Alexander Berry between 1815 and 1819. Her brother, Edward, was born in 1783.

Alexander Berry (1781–1873) was a very remarkable man. Born in Fifeshire, Scotland, and educated at the University of Edinburgh in surgery, he made three or four trips to India and China as ship surgeon. Some commercial ventures having succeeded, he abandoned medicine for commerce. He and Edward Wollstonecraft met aboard a Spanish ship in 1810 at Lisbon, where Edward had a business connection with the Spanish firm of De Zasel. Berry and Wollstonecraft (a "tall, formal-looking young man, dressed in black") at once became associated in business, Wollstonecraft undertaking to act as Berry's agent in London. From 1815 to 1819 Berry lived in London with Wollstonecraft and his sister, Elizabeth. In 1819 they went to Australia as partners, arriving in Sydney on September 1. Here they set up the firm of Berry and Wollstonecraft and were very successful. Wollstonecraft became senior director of the Bank of New South Wales and chairman of the first Chamber of Commerce in Australia. The government granted Berry 10,500 acres and Wollstonecraft 500, the latter being along the northern shore of the harbor, where Wollstonecraft built a cottage called the Crow's Nest. This district is now a residential suburb of North Sydney and still bears Wollstonecraft's name. Berry's grant was in the Shoalhaven district, south of Sydney. Further purchases of large tracts of land in the Shoalhaven district created the great Coolangatta Estate. Wollstonecraft saw only its early development; he died on December 7, 1832. His sister, Mrs. Berry, died on April 11, 1845. They were both buried in the family vault in St. Thomas's burial ground, West Street, North Sydney. When Berry died in 1873 at the age of 92, he was the proprietor of sixty-five thousand acres, an area of one hundred square miles. Berry was both a pioneer and a man of wide and deep culture. In 1912 the *Reminiscences of Alexander Berry* [edited by Alexander Hay] was printed privately in Sydney by Angus and Robertson. (Materials for this note were sent me by the late Mr. Alexander Hay, manager of the great Berry Estate. They consisted of Alexander Berry's reminiscences, newspaper articles, proofs of a brief history of the "Coolangatta Estate, Shoalhaven," and notes by Mr. Hay himself. In addition, the following have been useful: James Collier, *The Pastoral Age in Australia;* an article by J. H. Watson in the *Scottish Australasian,* April 5, 1919; and the *Journal and Proceedings* of the Royal Society of N. S. W., 1921, Vol. 51, xxxiii–iv, xlii–iii.)

I saw our Aunt yesterday—she is infirm—but is [in] tolerable health—she is with very good people & well taken care of. I wish I could do more for her— I do what I can, but while my father-in-law lives I have little to command. Charles Robinson will describe us to you—he knows Percy well, so if you have any curiosity about us, you have but to see & question him. I am sure you will like him—every body does—for he deserves it. He has a good mercantile connection in this country & if put in the right way will I hope get on.

Ever, dear Cousin
Truly Y^s
Mary Shelley

[P.S. *at top of page*] If you write to me direct to me at Hookham's Library —15 Old Bond St. London

ADDRESS: Mrs. Berry. [The letter evidently was delivered personally by Charles Robinson.] ORIGINAL: Mr. Alexander Hay, Coolangatta, Berry, N.S.W., Australia; A.L.S., 4 pp. 8vo (4⅜ x 7⅛ inches), with envelope. UNPRINTED and UNPUBLISHED. TEXT: From original letter.

502. *To Leigh Hunt**

Putney—Friday [August, 1839]

Dear Hunt

I am about to publish a vol. of Prose of Shelleys[1]—   This will please you I am sure—& it will not be painful to me as the other was. But I want your advice on several portions of it—especially with regard to the translation of the Symposium. I want also to know whether you would assent to the letters you published in your recollections[2] being joined to such as I shall publish—

I expect you on Wednesday & will dine at 5—but if you could [come] a little earlier to discuss these things I shall be glad. Do not disappoint me on Wednesday or you will disappoint Mr. Robinson who *almost* worships you—besides two pretty daughters who have inherited his feeling—   You need not be at the trouble of answering this letter—I only write that you may come, if you can, a little earlier, for the reason I have mentioned.

I have read your play[3]   It is admirably written. It is full of beautiful & elevated & true morality clothed in poetry—   Yet I can under understand [*sic*] Macready's not liking to identify himself with Agolanti—his conduct —true to nature & common, being redeemed by no high self forgetting passion would not I think interest in representation as much as in reading. I long to hear of your new play—

Ever truly ys.
M W Shelley

[1] *Essays, Letters from Abroad, Translations and Fragments,* by P. B. Shelley, edited by Mrs. Shelley, published by Edward Moxon in 2 vols., 1839 (dated 1840).
[2] *Lord Byron and Some of His Contemporaries, with Recollections of the Author's Life,* 1828.
[3] *The Legend of Florence.* On August 1, 1839, Hunt wrote to Southwood Smith: "I am expecting to send you news daily from Macready, who said he would write to me, and of whom I have still hopes."—*Correspondence of Leigh Hunt,* I, 315.

ORIGINAL: Huntington Library (HM 2757); A.L.S., 4 pp. 8vo. PRINTED: *Letters,*
181–82. TEXT: From original letter.

503. *To Mary Peacock**

[London] Thursday 29 Aug. [1839]

My dear Mary

This letter is more for your Papa than you—but I want an answer—& that
is not to be hoped for from him—& so I trespass on your good nature to make
you read my letter & get you to answer me. In the first place is there any chance
of my getting the papers I so much want— I should have thought that all
my papers would have been together & form a largish packet easily discernible
I should be *so* glad of them.

I must tell you that this being Thursday I have been to the India house
hoping to find your father I got there by 2—but the bird had flown. I wanted
to speak to him about the plans & prospects of a young friend[1] of Percy—who
thinks of trying his fortunes in the Military service in India— I wanted to
know whether your father could & would serve him—even advice is service—
so if you & yours do not object Percy will take him down to Halliford on
Sunday or any other day when your father is there & introduce him. He is
English but has been educated in France—he is a good fellow & I should be
very glad to serve him. Let me have an answer about this visit by return of
post—as Percy thinks it would be to[o] intrusive to take down a stranger
without previous permission.

I write in a hurry in Hookham's shop— Rosa *talks* of writing to you every
day— Mr. Campbell is in Wales— We went to Kew the other day & were
caught in the storm. Adieu dear Mary— I wish we were nearer & that you
could pop in on us now & then. Percy was enchanted with every thing at Halliford except the Cats— In haste

Y⁸ Ever

M W Shelley

ADDRESS: Miss Peacock/ Lower Halliford/ Chertsey/ M.S. POSTMARK: H/
AU-29/ 1839. ORIGINAL: Bodleian Library (MSS Autogr. c.9, ff.143–44);
A.L.S., 4 pp. 4to. UNPRINTED and UNPUBLISHED. (Maggs Brothers print about
a third of the letter in their *Catalogue of Autograph Letters and Historical
Documents* (1929), 215–16. TEXT: From copy made by Professor Elizabeth
Nitchie, Goucher College.

504. *To [? Gideon Algernon Mantell]**

Layton House Putney
Sep. 5—1839

Sir

I am going to publish some more Works of my husband which will include
some letters. Mʳ H. Smith tells me that some time ago he gave you one of
Shelley's letters, & he gives me leave to ask you for a copy of it—You will very

---

[1] Probably Charles Robinson.

much oblige me by letting me have it—& it will add to your kindness if you will let me have it soon.

As Mr Smith says that you are an enthusiastic admirer of Shelley—I am sure these volumes will please you. The first piece A defence of poetry, is the only entirely finished & corrected prose essay left by him—but it is truly magnificent & places him very high in the scale of prose writers. Its diction is exquisitely harmonious & the imagery grand & vivid.

Hoping soon to hear from you—I am

> Your ob^t Servant
> Mary W. Shelley

ORIGINAL: Alexander Turnbull Library, Wellington, New Zealand; A.L.S., 3 pp. 8vo (4½ x 7¼ inches). UNPRINTED and UNPUBLISHED. TEXT: From copy made from original letter by Professor Waldo H. Dunn.

505. *To [? Gideon Algernon Mantell]**

> Layton House
> Putney
> 18 Sep. [1839]

Sir

I must appear very rude—but it was only on returning from Sussex today, after nearly a fortnight's absence that I find your very acceptable present & note. The books are delightful—of course I have only *looked* into them yet—but they treat on a subject, which has always greatly interested me.

I am sorry for your Son's departure[1]—& regret the absence of the letter—perhaps some time hence both may be restored. I will take an early occasion of asking your acceptance of the volumes of Shelley's poems published by me.

If ever you come this way I hope you will kindly call on me.

> I am dear Sir
> Y^s truly
> Mary W. Shelley

ORIGINAL: Alexander Turnbull Library, Wellington, New Zealand; A.L.S., 3 pp. 8vo. (4½ x 6¾ inches). UNPRINTED and UNPUBLISHED. TEXT: From copy made from original letter by Professor Waldo H. Dunn.

506. *To Edward Moxon**

> Putney
> 30 Sept. [1839]

My dear Sir

Will you dine with me next Wednesday at 5 o'clock   I expect Leigh Hunt —& I have asked Mr. Campbell—persuade the latter to come—& tell him how to find my house.

I have told the printer to send me the proofs in slips at first to save expense from alterations—I got a note from them as if they meant to be furiously quick

---

1 Walter Baldock Durant Mantell emigrated to New Zealand.

—& they sent with it a proof without copy—so I am waiting for the copy to come before I return it

Yours truly
M W Shelley

ORIGINAL: Owned by the Brick Row Book Shop, New York, in September, 1936; A.L.S., 2 pp. 12mo. UNPRINTED and UNPUBLISHED. TEXT: From original letter.

507. *To Leigh Hunt**

Putney Sunday [October 6, 1839]

Dear Hunt

I send you the rest of the Devil that you may judge better— You see I have scratched out a few lines which might be *too shocking*—and yet I hate to *mutilate*. Consider the fate of the book only—if this Essay is to preclude a number of readers who else would snatch at it—for so many of the religious particularly like Shelley—had I better defer the publication, till all he has left is published— Let me hear what you think as soon as you can

Remember Wednesday

Ys.
M S.

[P. S.] Remember *I* do not enter into the question at all. It is *my* duty to publish every thing of Shelley—but I want these two volumes to be popular —& would it be as well to *defer* this Essay?[1]

Send back the slips.

ADDRESS: Leigh Hunt Esq/ 4 Upper Cheyne Row/ Chelsea. POSTMARKS: (1) P u t n e y/ 3 py P Paid   (2) PD/ OC 7/ 1839/ 4 Eg. ORIGINAL: Huntington Library (HM 2758); A.L.S., 2 pp. 4to. PRINTED: *Letters*, 179. TEXT: From original letter.

508. *To Leigh Hunt**

[Putney] Thursday [? October, 1839]

Dear Hunt

You have puzzled me much. What you *said* convinced me. You said: "Do as Mills, who has just phrased it so that the common reader will think common love is meant—the learned alone will know what is meant." Accordingly I read the Phaedrus & found less of a veil even than I expected—thus I was emboldened to leave it so that our sort of civilized love should be understood— Now you change all this back into friendship—which makes the difficulty as great as ever. I wished in every way to preserve as many of Shelley's OWN *words* as possible—& I was glad to do so under the new idea which you imparted—

[1] The "Essay on Devils" (or "On the Devil, and Devils") was not included in the *Essays,* although actually put into type. A copy of the proof, corrected by Mary, is in the Bodleian. Forman printed the essay from the proof-sheets in the *Prose Works* in 1880 (H. Buxton Forman [ed.], *The Prose Works of P. B. Shelley* [London, Reeves and Turner, 1880, 4 vols.]). The text in the Julian edition is taken from the MS owned by Sir John C. E. Shelley-Rolls (Julian edition, VII, 346).

but your alterations puzzle me mightily—   I do not like *not* to abide by them—
yet they destroy your own argument that different sexes would be understood
& thus all is in confusion

Accordingly I have left some & not others—where you seemed very vehement—& your p. 192 I have altered & omitted as you mention—but I could
not bring myself to leave the word *love* out entirely from a treatise on Love.
With regard to your verbal corrections—this was no hasty translation—   Shelley read it over aloud several times—so some things that look uncouth, I suppose he thought, as you phrase it—*more Greek*—and I like to leave it as he
left it as much as possible.

After all the beauty of the piece consists in Agathon's, Socrates, & Alcibiades
speeches—the rest are of minor importance. It is puzzling—*That's a fact* as the
Americans say.

I shall have other sheets so[on]—so hope you will come to look at them.
Will you dine here next Wednesday—or Thursday—if Thursday *write* directly   if I dont hear from you I shall expect you on Wednesday.

Ever truly Ys.
M W Shelley

ORIGINAL: Luther A. Brewer Collection, University of Iowa; A.L.S., 4 pp. 4to
(7¼ x 8⅝ inches). UNPRINTED and UNPUBLISHED. TEXT: From original letter.

509. *To Leigh Hunt*

[Putney] Monday [? October, 1839]

Dear Hunt

When I told Percy you were coming next Thursday he said "What a bore!"
He being engaged to dine out that day in town—   Can you make it Friday?
If not let it still stand for Thursday—but let me know how it is decided—   It
was a most lovely night—I hope you got home well—   With love to Marianne

Ever ys.
M W S.

ORIGINAL: Henry W. and Albert A. Berg Collection, the New York Public
Library; A.L.S., 1 p. 8vo. UNPRINTED and UNPUBLISHED. TEXT: From original
letter.

510. *To Leigh Hunt**

Putney—Wednesday [October 1839]

Dear Hunt,

I hear from Mrs. Carlyle that your play was accepted—but your note gives
me the further pleasure of the agreableness of its reception—the Green Room
that purgatory before this or the other thing, to Saturnine & umbragious spirits,
will be a milky way, all sprinkled with dancing stars to your free hearted disposition & witty mind—   God speed you through all.

I send you a letter I got from Percy to-day—he thinks the Pit the most influential position I fancy. Rothwell resolves to go & to give the aid of his Irish enthusiasm— You must and will succeed.

I will let you know about Claire when the time comes. I delight in your having got among these kind friends but don't wonder— Carlyle says you read your play so exquisitely, so much better than anyone ever read before, that you must enchant.[1]

Let me hear how you progress & believe me

Your[s] truly

M Shelley

[P.S.] Percy when he says he was bigotted means that he would not be persuaded to have any more lessons from Nichols having spent so much already.

ADDRESS: Leigh Hunt Esq/ 4 Upper Cheyne Row,/ Chelsea. ORIGINAL: Lady Dorothea Charnwood. PRINTED: Lady Charnwood, *Call Back Yesterday* (2nd ed., 1938), 205. TEXT: From *ibid.*

511. *To Leigh Hunt**

Putney 14 Nov. [1839]

Dear Hunt

I have desired to fix a day when you will meet Claire but have not yet been able— I hope I shall soon— Meanwhile I wish much to hear of your play— and when it will appear— Percy is very anxious to learn.

I see a few asterisks & omissions in the letters of Shelley you published— were these wholly private & indifferent or did some temporary or modest personal reason cause them— If the latter pray let me replace them—let me have the originals for a few days—but then it must be *directly*—as they are printing fast off—tomorrow it ought to be I hope you have been quite well all this time—

Yours truly

M W Shelley

ORIGINAL: Huntington Library (HM 2750); A.L.S., 2 pp. 8vo. PRINTED: *Letters*, 179–80. TEXT: From original letter.

512. *To Leigh Hunt*

[Putney, ? November, 1839]

Dear Hunt

I write in haste— Will you come here & talk over your finale with me— flint & steel knocking a dormant spark may come out[2]

---

[1] Hunt wrote *The Legend of Florence* in 1838, and kept on altering it and reading it to his friends until it was finally produced at Covent Garden on February 7, 1840. In October, 1839, he read his play to a group of friends, including Carlyle, Dickens, Procter, and Sheridan Knowles. They applauded it. Shortly after this Hunt read it again in the Green Room to the Covent Garden management. "Accepted" means "accepted to be read before the management." After the reading in the Green Room, Madame Vestris, who controlled Covent Garden, suggested that Hunt change the last act. It is this proposed change that Mary probably alludes to in her letter of [? November, 1839] (Letter 512). The play was published in 1840; a second edition, with a preface, appeared in the same year.

[2] See Letter 510, note 1.

I send you a book you will be glad to have— Let me have the letters as soon as you can even if too late for this—they will only be *time enough* for another edition—so let [me] have them *as soon* as you can— I have it at heart to replace these passages—why not—we write to shew *him* not ourselves—& each word of *his* is *him*—besides one does not get so much earthly honey to spare confessing that a bit of ambrosia was once on a time put in ones cup by heaven

Ys

M S

ORIGINAL: British Museum (Add. MSS 38,524, ff.201–202); A.L.S., 3 pp. 12mo. UNPRINTED and UNPUBLISHED. TEXT: From original letter.

513. *To Leigh Hunt**

Putney
Wednesday [1839–46]

My dear Hunt

I am *strongly* against Julia's[1] learning from an English teacher Singers *never* get over their abominable style— Mrs. A. Thaw with her superb contr'alto voice, has a something of *unrefinement* that deteriorates [sic] from her singing—got by English teaching at the beginning. Why not have recourse to Percy's master old Negri—who will give lessons for 5 shillings at his own house— It is true he can only speak Italian—but this I think will be an advantage, forcing Julia to learn Italian & I should advise her interspersing her lesson[s] with some instruction on counterpoint & thorough bass— She is quick & by help of the instrument wd. make out what he meant—& doing Italian exercises & reading it at home—she wd. soon get on with him. Henry shall speak about it and introduce her if you like—or we will have old Negri here to meet you & your daughter— Negri is the father (& of course teacher) of the most fashionable Italian singing master of the day—& of one of the masters at the Academy— Julia cannot injure herself by learning from him— Tell Julia that if by any chance her voice will not do for concerts—yet if she will be industrious—& put her heart in it—& her time & industry, she will by learning singing & thorough bass & Italian, acquire independance as a teacher — We wd. talk to Negri of only 12 lessons to begin with that if some other teacher or methods arose she wd. be free to follow it— Meanwhile she is so far advanced in the good style—which with an English master she never wd. be— She cannot begin too soon— I will talk to Percy & he shall settle with Negri the next time he goes— Meanwhile tell Julia to put herself hard to reading Italian & writing exercises—& to practising the scales—& accompaniment— If she is industrious—all will go well—

What do you say? Shall it be so?

Yours ever
M Shelley

ORIGINAL: British Museum (Add. MSS 38,524, ff.197–200); A.L.S., 8 pp. 12mo. UNPRINTED and UNPUBLISHED. TEXT: From original letter.

[1] Hunt's daughter.

514. *To Edward Moxon*

[Putney] Dec. 19, 1839.

The Examiner was *really* good—*very*—the Athenæum creditable.—*But* the Spectator!¹—its editor must be both a goose and a coxcomb—the notion that L[ord] B[yron] had any hand in the Peter Bell is half-witted—the incapacity of appreciating the Defence of Poetry betrays a degree of ignorance rarely to be parelleled in the whole circle of criticism—to so foolish and uneducated a person the Fragments of Metaphysics must indeed appear devoid of meaning—he does not know his a.b.c. of the language in which they are written.

ORIGINAL: Not traced. PRINTED: H. Buxton Forman, *The Shelley Library* (1886), 121 (quot., 9 lines). TEXT: From *ibid*.

515. *To Abraham Hayward*

Putney,
Dec. 22 [? 1839]

Dear Mr. Hayward,

I give you great credit for your tact yesterday in disclaiming the connoisseurship you possess.² Thus you enable me to look back upon past dinners without too much dismay—to future ones without overwhelming terror. You give proof of a friendship rare and to be valued in thus trying to decrease rather than to increase my anxiety when I may have the pleasure of entertaining you. I will try to reward it in some measure. Alas—I am an Ignoram*a*. In my father's house we might eat, but were never allowed to talk of eating. Shelley had no dislike to seeing women eat (with moderation), but he thought it a blot on Julie's character to be *gourmande* and was himself so very abstemious that I could never exert more cookery for him than making a pudding. I really

---

¹ The review of the *Essays* in the *Examiner* (No. 1663, December 15, 1839, 788–89) was extremely favorable. The lengthy review in the *Athenæum* (December 14 and 28, 939–42, 982–85) was rather severe on Mary as an editor. *The Spectator* (December 14, 1186) was very severe. The reviewer wrote: "The time has been when a literary executor examined the papers of the dead with some degree of critical care, to prevent the publication of any thing inconsistent with the reputation of the deceased, or that respect which is due to the public taste, at least from third parties. But circumstances have changed all that; and now the chief consideration with any one possessing manuscripts seems to be whether the author's name is enough to sell them.

"This remark applies to a good part of the volumes before us, except in so far as it may be modified by Mrs. Shelley's relation to the writer, and the circumstance of her taste harmonizing with the weakest and most defective parts of his mind. The whole of the first volume consists either of translations from Plato, or of essays, sometimes incomplete, or of fragments of tales, too visionary to inspire interest had they been completed, but not intelligible in their *disjecta membra*, and which their author appears to have hopelessly abandoned.

"The principal Essays are a Defence of Poetry. . . . The Defence of Poetry appears to have been written in the heyday of the Utilitarians and Political Economists, but is scarcely needed now. The basis of its argument is sound—the superiority of the poetical faculty, or rather of its perfect exercise, to all other intellectual human qualities. Some of its positions and critical decisions are just, others questionable. The style frequently possesses clearness and easy strength; at other times it is remarkable for puerility and feeble prettiness. . . . "

The reviewer was much better pleased with Volume II and praised Shelley's letters highly.

² In the *Quarterly Review* for 1835–36 Hayward had published two articles on the Art of Dining ("Gastronomy and Gastronomers," July, 1835; a review of Walker's *Original*, February, 1836). These articles were printed separately in 1852, 1853, and much later (*c*. 1890), by Murray.

scarcely knew what a dinner was till with(in) a very few years, and now am at once dazzled and confounded by any display of learning; but as far as a partridge-pie with beef-steak *over* as well as under, the birds placed with their breasts downwards in the dish (469) or Surrey capon (466)—(a propos to that page—Hat Joliffe says that pheasants to be good—and no bird is so variable— ought to be fed on hurtleberries)—or any little esoteric but simple dish you may communicate—I will try that you shall be pleased. And are you not pleased with the promise? . . .

Yours truly,

M. W. Shelley.

ORIGINAL: Sir John Murray; A.L.S., 4 pp. 8vo. PRINTED: George Paston, *At John Murray's 1843–1892* [1932], 68–69 (almost complete). TEXT: From *ibid*.

516. *To Charles Ollier*

[? December, 1839]

My dear Sir

Have you any letters addressed by Shelley to you which you could let me have to publish— You will see that I have published such as I have been able to collect and I should like to add any that you will furnish me with.[1]

I asked you to ask Mr. Bentley to give me a copy of Lodore—if he will will you send it to the care of Honbl. Mr. Stanhope—at Mrs. Woods—27 Charlotte St Portland Place.

Would Mr. Bentley like to include Valperga in his standard novels? That novel never had fair play; never being properly published— I would write a preface for it—

Ys truly

M W Shelley.

[P.S.] Could Mr. Bentley also let me have a copy of Frankenstein published in the standard novels?

ENDORSED: (No date) Mrs. Shelley (Application for Shelley's Letters to me) [Ollier's notation on the MS:] I did *not* accede to this request, because no money was offered me, and I felt the letters were valuable to me.—Chas. Ollier, the publisher of Shelley's Works. ORIGINAL: Huntington Library (HM 10797); A.L.S., 3 pp. 8vo. UNPRINTED and UNPUBLISHED. TEXT: From original letter.

517. *To Leigh Hunt**

[Putney] Thursday [January 30, 1840]

My dear Hunt,

If possible Percy will stay till after Wednesday—rather than journey to & fro from Cambridge.[2] It however by any chance your play is put off longer than one day next week let me know as soon as you possibly can

---

[1] As Letter 512 shows, Mary anticipated a second edition of the *Essays* even before the first was out. The second edition came out in 1841; this letter may therefore have been written later than December, 1839.

[2] Percy Florence graduated A. B. from Trinity College, Cambridge, in February, 1841. Sir Timothy Shelley then made him an independent allowance of £400 a year without the condition of repayment.

Many thanks for the tickets. Will not Henry come to see us—

Yours Ever
M W Shelley

ADDRESS: Leigh Hunt Esq/ 4 Upper Cheyne Row/ Chelsea. POSTMARKS: (1) Putney   (2) Ja 30/ 1840. ORIGINAL: Huntington Library (HM 11633); A.L.S., 1 p. 8vo. UNPRINTED and UNPUBLISHED. TEXT: From original letter.

518. *To Leigh Hunt*

Putney—Thursday [February 27, 1840]

My dear Hunt

Thanks for your beautiful play[1]—so full of poetry & philosophy and all the loveliest things of this (when you write about it) lovely world.

Could you manage that I should see it again. Mrs. Stanhope borrowed her sister-in-law's, the Duchess of Bedford's box last Saturday to see it—& then was grievously disappointed that it was not acted. Could you ask your Charming Manager (geress I mean) to give her & me a box some day next week— the one she gave us the first night was perfect— It will be very kind of her— & you—& very delightful to us.

Will you also put down the name of Mrs. Larkins & 4 friends (five persons altogether) for any day next week when your play will *certainly* be played—

And let me have as *early* notice as possible of both things—especially the *box,* as I shall ask two or three friends to go with me who will appreciate your merit

Adieu dear successful Dramatic-Poet

Ever Yours truly
M Shelley

[P. S.] Tell Marianne how I sympathize in her pleasure on this occasion— when are we to see you   not this week but some day next—

ORIGINAL: Luther A. Brewer Collection, University of Iowa; A.L.S., 4 pp. 8vo (4½ x 7 inches). UNPRINTED and UNPUBLISHED. TEXT: From original letter.

519. *To Everina Wollstonecraft**

Putney—1st March [1840]

My dear Aunt

The name of Mrs. Larkins with 4 friends—5 in all—is down on the free list for Tuesday Night 3d March. Let her know this.

I will see you if possible this week—   God bless you.

Yours affly
M W Shelley

ORIGINAL: J. H. Coste, Coverside, Smallfield, Horley, Surrey, to whose father the MS was given (with a copy of the 1840 edition of Shelley's *Essays,* &c.) by Everina Wollstonecraft herself; A.L.S., 1 p. 4to. UNPRINTED and UNPUBLISHED. TEXT: From original letter.

[1] See Letter 510, note 1.

520. *To Abraham Hayward*

Putney,
March 3 [1840]

Will you join me at Covent Garden tomorrow. Leigh Hunt has sent me
a box.

ORIGINAL: Owned by Walter T. Spencer, London, in 1937; A.L.S., 1 p. 8vo.
UNPRINTED and UNPUBLISHED. TEXT: A quotation sent me by Walter T.
Spencer, who would not permit me to copy the letter.

521. *To Leigh Hunt*

Monday Ev^g [April 6, 1840]
3 The Rise
Richmond

Dear Hunt
Could you without inconvenience get the name of Mrs. Blood & two friends
3 in all—put down on the free list of C.G. any day *before Friday* & let me know
in time.
I expect Percy tomorrow—when shall we see you—
With love to Marianne

Yrs. truly
M W Shelley

[P.S.] If pressed for time write in a note "Mrs. Blood & two friends are
put on the free list of C. G.—for *such a* night"—& send it directed to

Mrs. Wollstonecraft
12 Copenhagen St
Pentonville

This will save your note coming first to me & then going to town.

ORIGINAL: Huntington Library (HM 12361); A.L.S., 4 pp. 16mo. UNPRINTED
and UNPUBLISHED. TEXT: From original letter.

522. *To Marianne Hunt**

Brighton,
6 June [1840]

Dear Marianne—
It was you wrote to me last—so I write to *you*. Henry told me that Hunt
talked of calling on me at Richmond—but lo! I am here—whished off— It
seems as if I were never to be stationary—I, who long so for a home. I am
going for a few months abroad with Percy—perhaps as far as Milan. I shall
be back in the Autumn.[2]

---

[2] According to Mary's *Rambles in Germany and Italy* (I, 2–3), she remained at Richmond
until near the end of May, going then to Brighton. About the middle of June she and Percy
sailed from Dover to Calais. After a week in Paris, where they were joined by two of Percy's
college friends who, with him, were to take their degrees the next February, they left on June 25
to make their way to Cadennabia, on the Lake of Como, where the college boys were to study
diligently. "I was shown our way on the map—Metz to Treves; then down the Moselle—un-

How delighted I was at the success of *The Play*—The Players I hear did not take to his comedy[3]— I think there ought to be a dash of romance in all Hunt writes—he being so romantic—so let him not cast aside pretty names— romantic adventures & the adjuncts that enliven his imagination. The piece of which he sketched the plot to me would I am sure delight his audience.

May you and he prosper! It is a hard world—& there are some Immortals in it—yet, as I wrote word to Jane today the Shuldbrugg Lady Cork is dead at 95—so I have only 8 years more to wait[4]—Meanwhile Percy is the comfort & charm of my life—& if my friends were well off I should deem myself happy.

Adieu, dear Marianne

Ever years
M W Shelley

ORIGINAL: British Museum (Add. MSS 38,523, ff.219–20; A.L.S., 3 pp. 8vo. UNPRINTED and UNPUBLISHED. TEXT: From original letter.

523. *To Abraham Hayward*

Rue de la Paix, No. 15, Paris,
October 26 [1840]

Dear Mr. Hayward,

After a very pleasant tour, I am returned here, where I hope to stay till Xmas. I left Italy with infinite regret. Many a long year had elapsed since I had last seen it, but its aspect, its language, its ways of going on, its dear, courteous, lying, kind inhabitants, and its divine climate were as familiar to me as if I had left them yesterday, and more welcome and delightful than I can at all express; it was returning to my own land, a land and a period of enjoyment, and I was very happy during my two months' residence at Cadenabbia, on the shores of the lake of Como, opposite to Bellagio, and close neighbour to Tremezzio, names rendered classical by our dear Rogers.[1] He must be in grief for his friend's death. The loss of Lord Holland will be deeply felt, for no man was ever better loved. I had some hopes of finding both Rogers and you here in October, as you were last year, but I suppose the threat of war has frightened you. I let H. Bulwer know I was here, and he in return left his card, which is a curiosity: it was so dirty I could scarcely read his name. I have two or three old friends in Paris,[2] but I have not been here long enough to make

hacknied ground, or rather water—to Coblentz; up the Rhine to Mayence; Frankfort, and the line South through Heidelberg, Baden Baden, Freyburg, Schaffhausen, Zurich, the Splugen, Chiavenna, to the lake of Como. These are nearly all new scenes to me."—*Rambles*, I, 9. Arriving in Cadennabia on July 14, they remained there until five A. M. on September 9. On September 11 they entered Milan. Mary was forced to remain here until the twenty-eighth because of the failure of an expected letter containing money for the return journey to arrive. Percy and his friends left her there to await the letter, and went rapidly back to Cambridge. Money came at last, and Mary departed on the twenty-eighth and returned by way of Geneva to Paris, where she arrived on October 12, to visit a while with Claire. (*Rambles*, I, 1–152.)

[3] After the successful production of the *Legend of Florence*, Hunt wrote several other plays, which never reached the stage.

[4] Sir Timothy Shelley was born in 1753; he would be 95 in 1848.

[1] Samuel Rogers (1763–1855). *Italy; A Poem*, Part I was first published in 1822; Part II, in 1828.

[2] Claire and Mrs. Boinville were two of them.

a society. A thousand thanks for your kindness. M. Buchon, from your account, I should really like to see. I like a man who talks me to death, provided he is amusing: it saves so much trouble. Sainte-Beuve[3] I like in his way. French people of a certain kind all know how to talk, and I can always get on with them. He, like all his countrymen, sighs to wash out Waterloo; they will not remember that they brought Waterloo on themselves; besides they think War will prevent Revolution, but I believe Louis Philippe thinks that his dear subjects will beg to have both. How can they have too much of so good a thing as *gloire* of all sorts, foreign and domestic?—*les jours glorieux de la France dehors et les jours immortels dedans.* The Chambers, however, seem in a body pacific. Louis Philippe was much better received than he expected, which touched him to the heart, so that when he alluded to the attempts made against his own life his voice was broken by tears, and the Chambers had the civility to cheer him. It was strange to see a king upon his throne cry. Fifty years ago Europe had rung with the expressions of sympathy. The French take it quietly. I know not why, but tears came warm and quick into my eyes, and I thought as I looked at weeping royalty of the verse of Manzoni:—[*Mary omits quotation.*] but you will not recollect the context perhaps; it means, others besides oneself are and have been unhappy, and that is a kind of left-handed comfort now and then to the suffering. I went to see Soult's Gallery the other day. Have you ever seen it? There is an "Assumption of the Virgin," by Murillo, worth ten thousand pictures such as one usually sees. She does not look so beautiful as Raphael's. She looks more like a martyr received into heaven; her almost tearful eyes, soft, upturned, imploring, her parted lips full of sensibility, all appear expressive of painful impressions of horror and death, and gratitude at the reward she is rising to receive; the figure is floating upwards, surrounded by all those foreshortened baby-angels Murillo delights in. She is dressed in white, not usual in a picture, but the colouring is glowing, and, like all Murillo's, is as satisfactory to the eye as harmonious music to the ear. There is a "Birth of St. John the Baptist," exquisite from the colouring and truth, but without ideality in the people; a little dog is sniffing at and going to play with a young angel's wing, who turns round to see who is taking the liberty. I should like to see the Quarterly and am impatient to see Mrs. Norton's poem.[4] Give my love to her; I like her letters and herself, dearly, as the children say. Adieu! My love to dear Rogers. . . . Percy is at Cambridge, he takes his degree this January, after which it seems decided that he will study the law. [Mary is wretched to think this will cause her to live in London. She prefers travel to anything.] Teresa is enriched a good deal I believe by her husband's death.[5] [The Simplon Pass is in a wretched state.]

[3] Charles Augustin Sainte-Beuve (1804–69), literary critic.

[4] *The Dream, and Other Poems* (London, Henry Colburn, 1840).

[5] Evidently Teresa Guiccioli's Italian husband. Later (?1851) she married the very rich Marquis Hilaire de Boissy (d. 1866). (Mayne, *Byron*, 430–31.)

ORIGINAL: Owned in 1937 by Walter M. Hill, 25 E. Washington St., Chicago. Sold by him to an unidentified buyer; A.L.S., 4 pp. Small 4to, with postmarks. PRINTED: *Correspondence of A. Hayward,* edited by Henry E. Carlisle (1886), I, 82–84 (incomplete). TEXT: From *ibid.* (The last lines, beginning "Percy is at Cambridge," are added from the private notes of Professor N. I. White, who once saw the original letter.)

524. *To Edward Moxon*

Penmaen
Dolgelly—N[orth] W[ales]
28 June [1841]

Dear Mr. Moxon—

I meant to have called in Dover St before leaving town last Tuesday [June 22]—but poor Mrs. Godwin's death prevented me.[1] I did not get a newspaper till yesterday when I was deeply distressed to find that the trial had come on[2] —& its result. I have only seen the report in the Examiner & should be very glad if you would let me have a good report—if you have one. I cannot judge of Talfourd's eloquence by this curtailed account—but it seems to me that he took the right view—and [Lord] Denman's summing up appears excellent. Pray let me know something about it. I will write to Lord Normanby as soon as I hear from you—& I hear whether there is any thing you wish me to say.

The spirited & generous temper in which you have taken this persecution brought on you first by the Liberals, who urged you to publish, & secondly by that disgrace to his party Mr. Roebuck, does you the greatest honor—& you must not be a sufferer if it can in any way be prevented.

If you get any book[s] for me keep them till I return to town at the end of August—any letters send here

I am Ever ys. truly
M W Shelley

ORIGINAL: Huntington Library (HM 10798); A.L.S., 3 pp. 8vo. UNPRINTED and UNPUBLISHED. TEXT: From original letter.

[1] Mrs. Godwin died on June 17, 1841, aged 75.

[2] On June 23, 1841, Moxon was tried before Lord Denman for blasphemous libel in the Court of Queen's Bench, as a result of the publication of the full text and notes of *Queen Mab* in the second edition (one volume) of *Shelley's Poetical Works* in November, 1839. Moxon was indicted by Henry Hetherington, a radical printer and bookseller whose purpose was not to injure Moxon or Shelley, but to establish the right of free and unrestrained publication of opinions concerning religion. Moxon was eloquently defended by Thomas Noon (Sergeant) Talfourd, who published his speech as *Speech For the Defendant, In the Prosecution of The Queen v. Moxon, For the Publication of Shelley's Works. Delivered in the Court of Queen's Bench, June 23, 1841, And Revised,* by T. N. Talfourd, Sergeant at Law (London, Edward Moxon, Dover Street, 1841). Moxon was pronounced guilty, but judgment against him was never passed, the prosecution having accomplished its main purpose by securing the verdict. The trial was reported in the *Examiner* for June 26, 1841, 412, under the heading "Courts of Law. Court of Queen's Bench. Shelley's Works.—The Queen *v.* Moxon." This case is reviewed in an illuminating article by Newman I. White, "Literature and the Law of Libel: Shelley and the Radicals of 1840–42," *Studies in Philology,* January, 1925, 34–47. See also Thomas J. Wise (ed.), *A Shelley Library* (London, Printed for private circulation only, 1924), 113–14.

525. *To Edward Moxon*

Dolgelley, N.W.,
14 July [1841]

Dear Mr. Moxon

I know not what to say to your refusal of compensation for all the expence which the Liberals have put you to. Since the evil sprung from them solely— I think you ought to let them repair it—not by a formal subscription—but by allowing them to take the fine &c on themselves. Thanks for Talfourd's speech —it is very eloquent—& so conclusive that I wonder that the Jury was not persuaded by it, they ought to have been— But I suppose there was some bigotted fool among them who made them go wrong. I like *some* things he says about Shelley very much—& he makes out an admirable case for you— You must receive some comfort from the kind & just representation he makes of your character & position.

I shall certainly add a postscript with regard to the trial. I will send [it to] you in a day or two. I must mention that by an unaccountable oversight a poem of Shelley, printed in the Posthumous Poems is omitted in my editions   it [is] the one beginning

> Rough wind that moanest loud

I think the title is a dirge— It can now be added. As to filling up the vacant space of Queen Mab—it is difficult. I object to Leigh Hunt's account—because it looks like patchword taking [*sic*] a thing already printed & published. I should like what was inserted to be original. What I should like would be if Mr. Hogg would write an Essay on Shelley's life & writings—original—though it might embody the substance of his articles in the New Monthly.[1] This would cost something. Perhaps you would see him & learn what it would cost & then I would write to him & arrange it on my own account. Let me know what you think of this—

Let me have 25 copies of Talfourd's speech—send one to Miss Clairmont— 3 Gordon Sq—one to Mrs. Hogg   12 Maida Vale Edgware Road—one directed to Mrs. Boinville to the care of J. Flather Esq Lincoln's Inn 24 Old Square—written outside from Mrs. Shelley, to be forwarded.

I am dear Sir

Ys. truly

M W Shelley

ADDRESS: Edward Moxon Esq/ Dover St./ London. POSTMARKS: (1) DOL-GELLY (2) A/ 15 JY 15/ 1841. ORIGINAL: British Museum (T. J. Wise Collection); A.L.S., 4 pp. 8vo, with stamped envelope. PRINTED: *A Shelley Library* (1924), edited by Wise, 113–14 (not quite complete). Dated July 16 by Wise. TEXT: From original letter.

[1] On "Shelley at Oxford," 1832–33. These articles were incorporated into Hogg's *Life of Shelley*, 1858.

526. *To Claire Clairmont*

Friday 4th March [1842]

Dearest Claire—

I was indeed surprised at your not appearing on Friday & still more to get your note & to find you gone. I congratulate you that you are now free. Let me entreat you to devote all your attention to making yourself *comfortable.* You neglect that too much. Hitherto you have been unable to do otherwise— but when you talk of not getting a bed &c I fear you will not take care of your physical comforts as you ought— Make your home snug—& all will gather cheerful & pleasant about you. You do not mention your health in your letter— tell me whether you feel as well as when last in France.

I will do as you ask with regard to Miss Descon. Will you do me a favour. I have subscribed to Dr. Constancio's periodical[1]—& by some oversight never paid will you pay 22 francs for me for a year's subscript[ion] and will you tell Cornelia[2] I am not rich enough [to] continue it. I promised Dr. C. a set of Shelleys works I will send them by Miss Descon if she will take them Give my love to Cornelia & tell I her [*sic*] I would have answered her letter directly—but that you having gone to Paris intanto would tell her all about us better than a letter. Tell her I should be very glad to visit Paris—but do not see any chance for the present. What you say of the Farrers not quitting Paris is what I expect. I shall have to fight against & be crushed by a thousand ob- stacles in trying to get the society I desire for Percy—such is my fate—yet more than ever I wish that he should see the society of women of his own rank— Would we could set out for Florence directly—but one can never do what one judges best. You remember Helen Shelley's flaming letter to me with regard to Percy— Percy himself got no letter from her till about two days ago when he received a letter so singularly angry, spiteful, & bitter concerning his not paying them sufficient attention when at Field Place, that there must be some reason for their wishing to pick a quarrel. Mrs. Paul says that Sir Tim has taken a fancy to Percy & the women are outrageously jealous. There seems some colour for this, as Percy had several long talks with his Grand- father last time. Percy will return a mild answer—& probably not go to Field Place again in a hurry. Percy is much better indeed I believe quite well— I am well & continue riding—though how long I shall be able to afford it I know not—it costs so much. We go on just as usual. Knox[3] is neither well

[1] Probably Francisco Solano Constancio.
[2] Cornelia Turner, Mrs. Boinville's daughter.
[3] Alexander Andrew Knox (1818–91), who appears so often in Mary's letters hereafter, was born in London on February 5, 1818, the son of George Knox, a landed proprietor in Jamaica who lost most of his large fortune before his son, with whom he was never intimate, had made a place for himself in the world. George Knox was dead by 1843. Young Knox's mother had died at his birth, and in 1843 his only living relative, an aunt, died. He went to Trinity College, Cam- bridge, on a scholarship. Ordered to go south for his health, he went to Italy with Mary and Percy in June, 1842. In 1844 he graduated A. B. without honors; M. A., 1847. In 1844 he was called to the bar as a member of Lincoln's Inn, but did not practice. In 1846 he became a writer of leading articles for the *Times,* and remained on the staff until 1860, when he accepted from

not in spirits—the sun does not shine on him poor fellow—it never does on my friends. Jane is well & going on *al solito*. Col. Hervey[4] (Mrs. Goring's father) is dead. I have no news of any one— I do not see the Sanfords— Rawlinson called— Mrs. Sanford has taken a stall for her hubby at the French Play—& tells him that he need not stay & fill up her box since she has treated him to a stall. Give my love to the Farrers— Thank Annie very much for the handkerchiefs which are perfect— Tell them how glad I shall be to meet them this summer in Germany— They must go there I will write again before we go to the Isle of Wight— I dont know yet when we go. With the exception of a fine day or two rain is the order of the day I am so sick of it. I will send you the 22 francs by Miss Descon Percy sends his love God bless you dear Claire—let me hear from you

Ys. Ever
M S.

[P.S.] You promised to give me my Father's desk. Where is it?—at Golden Sq.?[5]

> ADDRESS: Miss Clairmont/ aux soins de/ M^m Farrer/ Rue Lavoisier No. 19/ à Paris. POSTMARK: 4 MR 4/ 1842. ORIGINAL: Huntington Library (HM 12177); A.L.S., 2 pp. 4to. UNPRINTED and UNPUBLISHED. A copy in Claire Clairmont's handwriting is in the Berg Collection, the New York Public Library. TEXT: From original letter.

527. *To Claire Clairmont**

Cowes [Isle of Wight]—11 May [1842].

Dear Claire—

I just write a few words to say that I have got the handkerchiefs. They were left at Hookhams & Knox brought them down yesterday— Tell Annie & give her my love & thanks for all the trouble.

Sir George Cornwall Lewis the office of police magistrate at Worship Street. In 1862 he was transferred to the Marlborough St. Court, where he remained until in 1878 he was compelled by a paralytic stroke to retire on pension. He performed his duties as magistrate with distinction. In 1857 he married Susan, daughter of James Armstrong of the Bengal Civil Service. Knox was a man of wide culture, knew many distinguished people of his day, and wrote articles for the *Edinburgh Review, Blackwood's,* and other periodicals. In 1881 he published *The New Playground, or Wanderings in Algeria.* He died in London on October 5, 1891. (See *D.N.B.* and "Alexander Knox and His Friends," by Mrs. Andrew Crosse, *Temple Bar* magazine, April, 1892, 495–517.)

Mary became very much attached to Knox, who spent much of his time in her house and whom she assisted in many ways, financially as well as otherwise. Her interest in him was stimulated partly by Knox's desire to write. In 1842 he published *Giotto and Francesca and Other Poems* (London, Edward Bull, 19 Holles Street, 142 pp.). He also wrote several plays, which evidently were neither acted nor printed. His one great service to Mary was the recovery (1845), with the aid of the Paris police, of the overly-ardent letters which she had written to the Italian Gatteschi. Mary never forgot this kindness, even though she suffered much financially at the time from Knox's poor management in leasing and furnishing an expensive apartment, for which she had to pay. Knox and Percy Florence did not get along well together, but this in no way cooled Mary's interest in him.

4 Colonel Hervey (or Harvey), of Thorpe Hall, Norfolk, was the father of Lady Vane Goring, who became Trelawny's third wife in 1847.

5 Where Claire lived for a while in 1841 (July) at No. 3.

Knox will go abroad with us & stay at least during the summer— It is the best thing he can do—& so Dr. Watson told his Aunt—as he must not apply himself—& ought as much as possible to be prevented thinking of his illness— He takes digitalis & wears a bella-donna plaister— He believes that already he has derived benefit from these medicaments & suffers less pain. I told him you thought him lucky—which comforted him. We have not yet decided *where* we go for the summer—did I tell you that Mrs. Hare is not coming to England yet— She is now at Florence I have written to her asking where she will be. We shall cross the Alps at the end of August & go to where Laura may be at once— I enclose a note for Marianna[1]—will you put it in the post for her.

We shall leave this place about 1st June, spend a week in town & then cross to Ostend.

Percy is well—my head is not quite right. I often feel frightened at our proposed trip—but that feeling will disperse when I am once on the other side of the water. Percy sends his love—& Knox his kindest remembrances— No doubt we shall meet in Paris before we recross the channel. Did I tell you the Gaskell's are in town— She wrote to me here asking me to dinner—& asking where you were— I sent her your address.

God bless you

Ys. affly

M S.

[P.S.] Have you called on Lady Canterbury? You ought.

ADDRESS: Miss Clairmont/ Rue Neuve Clichy No. 3. ORIGINAL: Huntington Library (HM 12351); A. L.S., 3 pp. 8vo. UNPRINTED and UNPUBLISHED. TEXT: From original letter.

528. *To Claire Clairmont*

Exberry—2 June [1842]

Dearest Claire—

We do not very often write to each other—and my excuse must be the discomfort writing always inflicts on me, from which I have suffered far more than usual this spring. This will probably be the last letter you will get from England—if our plans are not disarranged in some unforseen manner—our coming here has indeed delayed us somewhat. Percy's visit being always put off, at last I wrote to the "Squire"—he called directly—asked us over here for a night only—but has shewn himself so amiably unwilling to part with us, that

---

[1] Marianna Hammond, known also as Hammy. Just who she was is not clear, but she was a friend of Claire's, served at times as a governess, and had a sister who had been dangerously ill shortly before March 11, 1844. It is quite evident that she was in some way connected with the Masons, Shelley's English friends at Pisa. In February, 1844, Mary wrote to Claire: "I told you Laura [Mason] had got £100 of her fathers fortune saved out of Galloni's [Laura's husband's] hands & had sent 100 crowns to Hammy." To Marianna Hammond herself Mary wrote on June 20, 1843: "I heard from Laura the other day. You of course hear constantly." And again in a letter of October 18 or 25, 1845, Mary links Miss Hammond's name with that of the two Mason girls.

I suppose we shall remain out the week; then we go to Half Moon St—for a few days in our way to cross to Antwerp— I hope to fine [find] Marianna still at Francfort— [I thin]k I told you that Knox goes with us—he is completely [inca]pable of exertion from the tendency to complaint of the heart—it will fall rather heavily on my purse as he will not pay *all* his expences—but I must weather it as I may; it is a great good for Percy, & for me too, to have him with us & Percy *promises* to be economical— All I know of our plans yet is that we go to Francfort—& then on somewhere. There is no chance of our encountering Mrs. Hare I fancy—she *ought* to come to England to settle her affairs at once.

The Squire is infinitely amiable—he has taken a great fancy to Knox—He speaks with tender recollection of Annie but with great asperity of Mrs. Farrer— The history is this—& I mention it, as Mrs. F. told me that Mr B[rett] had behaved very ill—& I dare say she has said the same to you. I know you are not much inclined to give heed to what she says but you might as well hear *his* story. He took Exberry for 3–5 or 7 years optionally—he believed at *his* option—but he received notice of encrease of rent or being turned out at the end of 3 years— As he had spent a great deal of money (£600 he says) on improving the place, which had gone to great ruin under the regime of mere annual tenants, he thought this very unfair—the matter was referred to L[or]d Redesdale (a relation of Mr. Mitford) who decided at once in the Squire's favour— This decision proves that *he* is right & [it] being referred by mutual consent—however unjust Mrs. F. may consider the decision, she has no right to say that Mr. B[rett] behaves *ill*. The pretence now is that Mr. M[itford] wishes to live at Exberry which is quite ridiculous—for no one could live here without a large income;—in the first place to keep it up, & secondly for the sake of seeing his friends. Mr. M[itford] is not likely to like the life of a recluse. The place is very pleasant—thoroughly a gentleman's place—very cheerful—kept in excellent order—& so quiet— Mr. Burgass is here—& Mr. Irby the clergyman of Hilton— We drive about a great deal & it is very pleasant. The weather is becoming warm. I dare say it has been warm inland ere this—but we have had too much wind. I am not very strong— I believe the German Baths will do me great good. I have no further news. Percy sends his love—Knox his best remembrances—I dare say we shall see you before we return to England. Pray write. I will write on the day previous to our sailing that you may be sure of our whereabouts—but if you get this soon let us hear from you next week— We shall leave London I fancy Tuesday week. What an abominable thing is this attack on the Queen—she is a brave little thing having received a threatening letter on Tuesday she would not put off her drive but would not let any lady accompany her—the man seems a mere fool—God bless you dear Claire

Affly. Ys.
M S.

154

[P.S.] Have you seen Bacciochi   he is in Paris—& will be a great resource to you I should think

ADDRESS: Miss Clairmont/ Rue Neuve Clichy No. 3. ORIGINAL: Huntington Library (HM 3899); A.L.S., 2 pp. 4to. UNPRINTED and UNPUBLISHED. TEXT: From original letter.

529. To [? *Monsieur Galloni*]*[1]

34 Half Moon St.
London.
5 June [1842]

I flatter myself that you will remember my name—since you and Madame [? Galloni d' (*name scratched out*)] were good enough last year to invite me to visit you in Venice—and I still regret that I could not accept your kind invitation.

I hear that you are now in Paris. It is possible that you will come to London —I should be so happy to make your acquaintance and be of service to you in London. Please come to see me immediately—come as soon as you arrive.

In a very short while I am going to leave London. I have not decided where I am to spend the summer—it is possible that I shall be in Brussels soon or on the Rhine—do me the favor of letting me know where you are and where you will be—and I shall make it a point to see you.

Remember me to my dear Laura—I wish so much to see both of you— It would be such a great pleasure if only you would come to London— If that should happen, I beg you to treat me as a friend and to command my services if I can be useful to you.

Forgive me if the French that I write is faulty—and believe me always your obliged

Mary Shelley

ORIGINAL: Owned by Maggs Brothers in 1936; A.L.S., 4 pp. 8vo. (in French). UNPRINTED and UNPUBLISHED. TEXT: French text from original letter. Translation by Dr. Nancy Stewart, Mercer University.

[1] Husband of Laura Mason. The Gallonis lived for a while in Venice, as Mary's letter of [August 16, 1842] shows: "My companions desire to sojourn a few weeks at Venice— Oh if Laura had only been still at the Palazzo Cavalli!" The original text is as follows:

Deja je me flatte, Monsieur, que vous vous resouviendrez de mon nom—voyant que vous et Mme. [? Galloni d'   (*name scratched out*)] avez le grand bonté l'annè passè de m'inviter à vous faire visite à Venise—et je regrette toujours que je ne pouvois accepter votre aimable invitation.

On me dit que vous êtes a present à Paris. Ill se peut être que vous viendrez à Londres—je serais si charmèe de faire votre connaissance et de vous etre utile à Londres. Venez donc chez moi de suite je vous prie—venez des le moment de votre arrivèe.

En trés peu de temps je quitte Londres. Je n'ai pas decidèe ou je dois passer l'etè—il se peut que je serais avant peut à Bruxelles ou sur le Rhin—faites moi le plaisir donc de me faire savoir ou vous êtes et ou vous serais—et je me ferai un devoir de vous voir.

Bien des choses à ma chere Laure— Je desires tant vous voir tant les deux— Çe serait trop de plaisir si sielment vous viendriez à Londres— Si cela devrait arriver je vous supplie de me traiter en amie et de commander mes services si je pouvais vous etre utile

Excusez si le Français que j'ecris soit un peu à travers—et crayez moi toujours votre obligèe

Mary Shelley

34 Half Moon St.
Londres
ce 5 Juin [1842]

530. *To Leigh Hunt**

34 Half Moon St.
Monday [June 6, 1842]

My dear Hunt

I am too happy to be able to do as you ask— I send a cheque for the exact amount of the writ.

I hope things will be arranged as you wish— You meet our scruples & wishes with so frank & manly a spirit that it renders the very endeavour to serve you agreable— We can seldom do that which we wish—& often we cannot do the little we can do in the manner we wish—but you will excuse all this—& allow us to regulate both the thing & the manner by what appears the necessity of the case

Ever yours
M Shelley

ORIGINAL: Bodleian Library (MS Shelley Adds. d.5, ff.95–96); A.L.S., 3 pp. 8vo (watermark 1841). PRINTED: *Bodleian Quarterly Record*, VIII, No. 95 (1937), 417. TEXT: From original letter.

531. *To Claire Clairmont*[1]

Kissingen—Bavaria,
28 June [1842]

My dearest Claire—

I have been intending to write to you every day but my eyes are weak (a most annoying discomfort) so even now I cannot write a long letter— I will get lazy Percy to write to you ere long— Hammy told you of our arrival at Franckfort & of our misadventures—the worst being having two purses, each containing £8 stolen out of Percy's & Knox's sleeping room.[2] I found Hammy looking very well—the effect of the waters which she has been drinking She was in a state of great doubt & struggle with regard to the plan you suggested to her— I did the same as all her friends—advising her strongly to accept

[1] Mary's *Rambles in Germany and Italy* (1844, 2 vols.) gives a detailed and interesting account of her travels abroad in 1842–43. The *Rambles* is one of the best things Mary ever wrote; its style is simple and sincere, whereas the style of her novels is usually strained and artificial. On June 12 Mary embarked for Antwerp. She was accompanied by Percy and Knox (see Letter 526, note 3); Henry Hugh Pearson (see Letter 532, note 1) joined the party at Dresden. By way of Liege, Cologne, Coblentz, Mayence, and Francfort, they went to Kissingen, where they spent a rather pleasant month (June 21–July 18) drinking the medicinal waters and trying the *Kur*. From July 27 to 30 they were in Berlin, going thence to Dresden, where they remained until August 27. They then made the long journey to Venice (arrived September 19) by way of Prague, Mulchen, Budweis, Lintz, Salzburg, the Tyrol, Inspruck (September 10), Riva (September 13–14), and Verona (September 15–17). On October 19 they left Venice for Florence (arrived October 30), taking lodgings there for four months. Leaving Florence (without Pearson) on March 20, 1843, they went to Civita Vecchia by boat and on to Rome by diligence. Quitting Rome on May 10, they went directly to Sorrento, a village near Naples, where at the "Cocumella" they resided until July 10. On July 19 they were at Marseilles on their way back to England. Mary stopped in Paris (about July 25–August 26), while Percy went on to England. By August 30 Mary was in London.

[2] Unexplained references to the *Rambles* hereafter mean that the subject is also to be found in Mary's published account of her travels. The stolen purses are recorded in *Rambles*, I, 156, 164–65.

your offer. I think her very fortunate in having it made her—& in having you
for so kind & good a friend. It is true that you will reap great benefit from
her being with you—two together with much the same tastes & pursuits you
will escape from that dreadful voiceless solitude—which I know so well &
hate so much She will not hang a dead weight, nor inflict the same responsibility as Dina[3]—You will at once be independant & yet have a helpmate in all
your pleasures & troubles. But if you gain this—how much more does she gain
by your generous & kind friendship— She quits the irksome position & hard
labour of governess for comparative leisure & independance. All indeed depends on her getting lessons—for if she did not, she would suffer *care*—which
w[oul]d be worse than the present annoyances—but as there is plenty of time
to look about, I doubt not but that by the autumn (& she cannot join you before) your zeal will have made a beginning for her & all will go well. I should
so like to visit Paris & find you comfortable together—perhaps I shall next
year.—

For ourselves I have nothing new to tell you— Mr. Brett was very sorry
to let us go—he took a great fancy to Knox—& kept Turpin under his care—
Turpin made up to him with such delicate flattery that he arrived at the post
of favourite at once— I saw Gregson in town—& found nothing new except
that I am poorer than I supposed—nothing underhand—so dont be alarmed—
but so it is— I have very little left. Sir Tim [is] excessively well. Jane was well
—& quite taken up with Henry[4]—Dina returns home when Da[5] goes to the
North— She corresponds with H[enry] H[unt]—& he has prevented her
accepting your kind invitation—& thus she has lost her last chance. I saw Mrs.
Paul—but heard no news. Mrs. Hare is at Geneva. Rogers was very kind—
He is the *only* person in London who shews me any attentions. He invited
Wordsworth to meet me at breakfast. Old Aunty[6] was not well—I wish you
would write to her it would amuse her.

Enough of England—over our departure from which Mr. Bretts hospitality
shed a sunnier gleam than I had hoped.[7] We remained two days at Franckfort
& came on here by voiturier in two days. The road passes through the valley
of the Maine & the scenery was very beautiful—vast forests of oak & beech
covering the hills that shut in a fertile *riante* valley. The vale of Kissingen[8]
is pretty—& of the same character on a smaller scale— We have pretty lodgings a little out of the town— We dine at the Table d'Hote of the kur saal—
which is at 1 o'clock—& crowded & hot & not good—however we are getting
accustomed to it— Also we are fighting our way at our own lodgings to getting breakfast & tea— We none of us speak German which is a great draw-

[3] Jane Williams's daughter.
[4] Henry Cleveland, Jane Williams's nephew.
[5] Hogg.
[6] Everina Wollstonecraft.
[7] Mr. Brett lived "near Southampton, on the skirts of the New Forest."—*Rambles*, I, 156.
[8] Many of the details about their first experiences are in *Rambles*, I, 179–83.

back— Knox is getting on fast—my eyes have been an hindrance—& Percy does not take to it—our great fight was for water to wash—as they only gave us a pie dish & a caraffe as our apparatus—however we established a tub in each of our rooms— The servants are willing & good humoured—but slow & dirty— We unluckily engaged a bad German master & have been forced to get rid of him— He had no idea of teaching & was so rough & so filthily dirty that we could not get on.—As to health we see a German doctor of the place, a gentle civilized being— Knox must not drink the waters—Percy is still indisposed as in the winter—having neglected himself—so he is not allowed to drink the waters—but is under process of cure— Marianne our greatest invalid, was disgusted by the first effects of the waters—making her feel ill— They agree perfectly with me—I go to drink them between 6 & 7 every morning. I do not take much as yet—& feel no effects except feeling better in health & spirits. We have taken our lodging for a month— What we shall [do] afterwards is not yet settled— There are num[bers] of English—but as far as outside goes no attractive persons of any nation (plenty of Russians) and we as usual know no one—which I am sorry for— Knox is a good hand at making acquaintances—but he has only been able to *lier* conversation with two stupid Englishmen as yet Percy you know has no talents of the sort—& I must be attracted to exert myself—and as yet have seen nothing to please me— The foreigners all look vulgar & dirty—& these Bavarians are without exception ugly— There are some half hundred Graffs among them we hear—but they are indistinguishable. The Queen of Wirtemburg is expected this week— I had expected to see a better style of people than those at Baden Baden—but on the contrary they are more dowdy—

Can you do us a great favour order Galignani to be sent us. Can you pay our subscription for a month—or ask if we can pay it at the post office here— we see no paper & begin to want a little news— If you are good enough to do this make the act trebly kind & useful by doing it *directly* Galignani will send it if you give our direction

Pray write to me & tell me your news— Percy sends you his love—& Knox also— He is not well, I am sorry to say—but I hope quiet & regularity & good hours will benefit him at last. Percy means as soon as he is well to take plenty of exercise & get thinner—Dieu le veuille— God bless you

Affly ys

M S.

ADDRESS: Miss Clairmont/ Rue Neuve Clichy No. 3/ Rue Clichy/ ou chez M^m Farrer/ Rue Lavoisier No. 19/ à Paris. POSTMARKS: (1) KISSINGEN/ 28/ 6 (2) PARIS/ 2/ JUIL/ 42. ORIGINAL: Huntington Library (HM 12157); A.L.S., 4 pp. 8vo and 2 pp. 4to. Copy by Claire Clairmont, Berg Collection, the New York Public Library. UNPRINTED and UNPUBLISHED. TEXT: From original letter.

1 Henry Hugh Pearson, who later changed his name to Henry Hugo Pierson, was a musician of considerable importance. *D.N.B.* and *Grove's Dictionary of Music and Musicians* give substantially the same account of his life. Born at Oxford on April 12, 1815, the son of Hugh Nicholas

532. *To Claire Clairmont*

Kissingen 17 July [1842]

Dearest Claire—

I own your silence amazes me— You have received my letter—for we receive the Galignani—but not a word from you. I conjecture that you may have gone to M^m de Mestre still your entire silence is strange & uncomfortable. We have been here now nearly a month & on the 19 set off for Dresden. There is a railroad from Leipsic to Dresden which tempts us to visit that capital. Pearson[1] is there & will give us a welcome It will be something new—

Pearson, dean of Salisbury, he was educated at Harrow and Trinity College, Cambridge (A. B., 1830, says *D.N.B.*), Percy Florence's school and college. In 1839 he went to Germany to study music. In 1842 and 1843, after joining Mary Shelley and her party at Dresden, he accompanied them on their travels to Florence. But he proved to be an uncongenial companion; he kept the party constantly embroiled. It was therefore with great relief that they parted from him about November 11 at Florence, whence he went to Vienna. In 1843 he became professor of music at the University of Edinburgh, but soon resigned, to make his permanent home in Germany, where he won for himself a great reputation—a reputation not so generously accorded him by his own country. He played the organ and piano with great skill and composed a great deal of music, much of which was still unpublished at his death at Leipzig on January 28, 1873. Among his many compositions are: operas, *Leila,* 1848, and *Contarini,* 1872; an oratorio, *Jerusalem,* his best work, first given at Norwich in 1852; orchestral overtures (posthumous) to *Macbeth, Romeo and Juliet,* and *As You Like It;* and many songs, wherein perhaps his best work is to be found.

In the *Rambles* (I, 233–34) under the date August 1 [1842], Mary wrote of Pearson: "Here [at Rabeau, near Dresden] our friend had betaken him to compose his opera.... When we arrived he was absent; he had gone with his note-book to study among the pines. You know and admire his compositions. Thanks to them, Shelley's Poems have found an echo of sweet sounds worthy of them. The fanciful wildness, the tender melancholy, the holy calm of the poet, have met a similar inspiration on the part of the musician. They have as much melody as the Italian, as much science as the German school—they appertain most, indeed, to the last; but the airs themselves are original. The song of 'Arethusa', and that entitled 'Spirit of Night', are perhaps the best. The one, light and fanciful; the other, solemn and impassioned; both beautiful. The rest are second only to these."* [*Footnote: *Characteristic Songs of Shelley,* by Henry Hugh Pearson, Esq. Published by Alfred Novello."] The British Museum has no copy of this book, nor have I been able to find a copy anywhere. Neither *D.N.B.* nor *Grove's Dictionary* mentions this publication.

Pearson also honored Mary by setting one of her poems to music. The composition was published with the title: " 'Oh Listen While I Sing to Thee,' Canzonet, With Accompaniment for the Harp or Piano Forte, Composed and Inscribed to his Friend Berry King, Esqr. by Henry Hugh Pearson, Professor of Music in the University of Edinburgh. London. D'Almaine & Co., Soho Square." [British Museum, H. 1692 (7).]

Since Mary's poem has not been reprinted, and is not known today, it will be worthwhile reproducing it here.

O listen while I sing to thee,
My song is meant for thee alone,
Thy thought inspires the melody,
And gives the soft entrancing tone.

I sing of joy and see thy smile,
Which to the swelling note replies—
I sing of love, and feel the while
The gaze of thy love-speaking eyes!

If thou wert far, my voice would die
In murmurs faint and sorrowing,
If thou wert false, with agony
My heart would break—I could not sing!

O listen while I sing of thee,
My song is meant for thee alone,
Thine eyes inspire the melody,
And give the soft entrancing tone!

By the help of our German master here we have made a bargain with a voiturier to take us to Leipsic in 5 days for something under £5. The waters have agreed with me excellently & I trust to derive future benefit from the nach kur— They agreed also with Percy—& would have made him thinner but he got tired of the place & is gone on in advance of us on foot— We shall catch him up in a day or two. The weather latterly has been perfect—& this is a very pretty place—the forests affording pleasant walks— There are a great many English here. We talk to a few—but it is stupid & I shall be glad to get away—The living (doctor-directed) is poor & not cheap— There is no gaiety. Last year they say there was a good deal— There is a Reunion once a week in the Conversation House—but it is stupid— Percy means to take lessons at Dresden in German walzing [*sic*] & so be prepared for the Carnival balls at Florence. If this weather continues we shall have a pleasant journey.

I got a letter from Laura yesterday—but there is nothing new. I promise myself great pleasure from being in the same town with her & Nerina this winter.[2] I got a most dismal letter from poor Jane—Henry [Cleveland] sailed 1st July—& she is in despair— Dina talks of coming back as soon as Jeff goes to the North—as she corresponds with Henry H[unt]—& will see him again, I fear the absence has done no good.[3] It is a thousand pities she did not go to India— I got a letter from Hunt—& any thing more distressing it is impossible to imagine. He occupies himself by writing poems for which he gets scarcely any thing—& the blindness with which he goes on is inconceivable These are the only letters I have had from England— Poor Marianna is there now— I shall be very glad to hear that she is with you— Poor Jane, her position is indeed melancholy— Jeff's conduct eats into her— It is one of those things which must prey upon her—& grows worse by thinking on— He got very annoyed at Jane's giving so much of her time to Henry but he is one of those persons who never try to win though they would grasp tight. —Knox does not get better—his side still pains him very much.

I scarcely know, in your silence, what to write to you about—our life here is monotonous— I should like to hear of the Boinvilles—Farrers &c—& above all how you get on in Paris My health is much better—though my head is far from well—& feels strangely when I use it— I can study very little German therefore—which is a great disappointment— I wanted to make good use of my time while here. Knox works at it—it is slow work at the best—

Adieu my dear Claire— I hope to get a letter from you while we are at Dresden. We purpose staying there about a month—& then proceeding southward—a long long journey to Florence. Pray write soon to us therefore—

Ever Yours

M S.

---

[2] Laura and Nerina Mason, of Florence, Italy.
[3] The attachment of Dina Williams and Henry Hunt (Leigh Hunt's son) caused much disturbance in the two families. They married on October 21, 1842. (See Letter 535.)

ADDRESS: Miss Clairmont/ Rue Neuve Clichy No. 3/ ou chez Mᵐ Turner/ Rue
Clichy No. 74/ à Paris. POSTMARK: KISSINGEN/ 18/ 7. ORIGINAL: Huntington
Library (HM 12140); A.L.S., 3 pp. 8vo. UNPRINTED and UNPUBLISHED. TEXT:
From original letter.

533. *To Claire Clairmont*

Palais Garni—Altmark [Dresden]
[August 16, 1842]

Dearest Claire—

I do not know how it is with you—but here it is too warm to live. Had I
anticipated the heat we have got I should never have placed myself in a town
—but have taken refuge in some corner of the Saxon Switzerland or the Tyrol.
Every day is hotter than the day before—& no rain has fallen during the whole
summer—so every thing is dried up & baked. For 3 days I took refuge in a
village 8 miles off[4]—but having taken this place I could not afford to pay
double rent—& besides the accomodation was so bad that one had no rest nor
comfort. You talk of our excursions as if I were millionaire—   We are obliged
to be very economical—& going about costs—   I have seen no one at Dresden.
Pearson having made up his mind to go to Italy with us, is earnest to work at
his opera—& went into the country to work; besides though he knows every
one here—every body is out of town—& for those that remain—he is that sort
of laisser aller, indolent procrastinating person, that he talks of introducing
one—but he never does—so I have seen no one—& it is far too warm to care
about that or any thing. Dresden is a beautiful town—the immediate environs
—that is within a walk—are not pretty—one must drive to get at the pictur-
esque country—   Perhaps we shall take a drive or two before we go—but
I know not—   We are comfortably lodged—rather high up—but so much
the more airy, in one of the best houses of the Altmarkt, & we have got the
apartment cheap. The youths bathe—& I contrive to get to the Terrace over
the Elbe in the evening—but there is scarcely any water in the river—the nights
are as hot as the days—   It cannot be hotter in Italy—& there one would have
stone floors & blinds to keep out the sun & the light.

I am sorry for what you say with regard to Hammy   I am sorry you sacrifice your personal independance—it [is] the last dearest good of those who
have no other. You have I know thought me selfish for clinging to mine—   I
could not help it—the sentiment was plus fort que moi—   It is hazardous for
a woman to marry a woman—   Even if a wife does not get on quite well
with her husband different avocations separate them—   They separate at times
they are of mutual aid at others—two women are ever together & never help
each other. With the Robinsons I struggled hard to retain personal independance—   I did so till the last year or so—when I got so impatient &
wretched in my fetters that I burst away from them—& they could not forgive
me. My temper being at the same time quick & brooding, I am not an example

---

[4] Rabenau. See *Rambles*, I, 240–42.

I allow—but still what you say makes me feel that you will experience annoyance & repent the epicene marriage you contemplate. Au reste Hammy *does not intend* joining you until the New Year she will not mind putting it off longer—lett your apartment & join us at Florence. You can easily get there by Marseilles & a steamer I do not know exactly when we shall arrive there— My companions desire to sojourn a few weeks at Venice— Oh if Laura had only been still at the Palazzo Cavalli! But in October we shall be there [in Florence]—so come—it will be a frisk that will do you good—& not cost you much—& you will be able to lett your apartment for the Autumn.

I dont quite understand all you say about Jane She used to talk of H[enry] C[leveland]'s passion, but with perfect indifference—before & after she knew H[enry] H[unt]. She used indeed to laugh at his jealous annoyance because she kissed H. H.—she said "there are some people one *cannot* kiss"! When H.H. began to be restive towards her, then she took to H. C—& certainly has betrayed a degree of interest & passion which her children think strange— Your expressions in your letter seem to say that this passion has carried her *very far*—& caused her to permit Dina to get out of bounds also—but I suppose you do not mean that either of them have passed all limits— Certainly she has given up more of her time to her nephew than she ought—even to making Da jealous—but he is so totally careless of her comforts & feelings on all points—maternal as well as others—that I do not wonder at her feeling indignant & careless with regard to him. But she looses the respect of her children—& with that the power of guiding & controuling them, which is sad. What I like least is her complaints of Dina's violence & duplicity. Complaining of her even to the Hunts.—Poor Dina—she is in herself uninteresting to me—inasmuch as I always found her silly—so a mere bore, that her society was incomparably tiresome to me. But I thought her sacrificed when her mother threw her at the head of H[enry] H[unt] & have deeply pitied her. I quite hate Jeff when I see how utterly careless he is of her welfare— He sees the evil—he knows & reprobates Jane's conduct with her children but to keep scaitheless himself—to have his dinner & not be bored is all his object in life— & having told Dina that she throws herself away—he adds that she ought to live without object—or pleasure or occupation (for he will not even give her scope to cultivate her extraordinary talent in drawing) in the cabin in which they are all cribbed in so disgusting a manner.

Pray write often—it is so easy to answer a letter so difficult to write de son chef. Percy wrote to you the other day. Dresden *is* a beautiful town—but I cannot exercise my imagination about the Germans—they are so ugly not one pretty or handsome German male or female have I seen—so destitute of grace—so ill dressed—so dirty & as far as I can make out with few qualities to render their society agreable— They are simple hearted I dont doubt—& I am sure they are good humoured & willing—but they have nothing to elevate or brighten one's imagination.

I met yesterday a person I used to meet at Rogers a Breton[5]—who had entered into la petite Chouannerie of 1819— He is married [to] a Welch lady—he is an agreable man—they leave Dresden tomorrow—but I shall meet them again in Italy I believe

O the heat—the heat! It is overwhelming— I never felt any thing like it before— I understand what you say now of # 74 Rue Clichy[6] much better than when you lauded them more— Oswald's beard always repelled me It *was* the outward & visible sign of such intence inward & spiritual vanity— The others I have not studied but I agree with you—deliver me from the intolerance, vanity & bigotry of [perverts,] Of Campbell I know nothing— Percy saw him in the street with Miss Stone whom he thought a very nice looking girl— Percy breakfasted at his rooms several times during our last week in town but Campbell never called on me even to say good bye— I am under ban now he is to be married be assured

God bless you—write—

Ever Yours
M S.

[P.S. *at top of page 1*] We leave this the 27 Aug.—direct to Inspruck or Venice

ADDRESS: Miss Clairmont/ Rue Neuve Clichy No. 3/ Rue Clichy/ à Paris. POSTMARK: DRESDEN/ 16 Aug. ENDORSED: About Mrs. Williams and her nephew Henry Cleveland. ORIGINAL: Huntington Library (HM 12136) A.L.S., 4 pp. 4to. UNPRINTED and UNPUBLISHED. TEXT: From original letter.

534. *To Leigh Hunt*

Dresden 17 August [1842]

Dear Hunt—

I was delighted to get your letter—it relieved me from great anxiety. I can only say if Lord Leigh will join us it will go hard with Percy & me but that we will contribute our share to so dear & honorable a work— You may count on £10 for the Xmas quarter. I wish that I heard of other success & prosperity for you. I saw advertized, that your Poem[1] was reprinted in Galignani's weekly journal to which he transfers what he considers most worthy of our literature— When I get to Florence I shall try to see this & read your poem.

We have made a long journey since I wrote— We found here Pearson, who has set several of Shelley's poems most beautifully to music (Novello published them)[2] & has a great musical genius. He is very German in his music—

---

[5] Monsieur Rio (see Letter 545). *Rambles,* I, 245: "One day, while wandering about the gallery, I saw a well-known face. It was more than a pleasure; it was indéed a gain to meet the accomplished Author of 'La Poésie Chrétienne' in the very spot where his knowledge and taste would inform my ignorance and correct my judgment; still more agreeable it is to learn that he is also bound for Italy. His animated conversation and refined society will add more than I can express of interest and pleasure to our rambles."

[6] Where Mrs. Boinville and her daughter Mrs. Turner lived.

[1] *The Palfrey; A Love-Story of Old Times* (London, How and Parsons, 1842).

[2] See Letter 532, note 1.

but there is much & beautiful melody in some of these songs—in the Arethusa for instance & in the Spirit of Night—but they are very difficult to play. He is now writing an opera which he hopes to have brought [out] at Vienna. Meanwhile he talks of accompanying us to Florence—towards which we shall make progress (it is a long way off) in about 10 days. The Elbe has no water for Steamers—or we had hoped for a beautiful Voyage to Prague. The drought in this part of the world is become disastrous— Every[thing] is dried up— the heat is oppressive beyond description— It is impossible to go to galleries or sights— Doing so in some small degree the other day I was knocked up & quite ill. No rain—no clouds—each day the sun makes its progress through the sky scorching & stewing—a thunderstorm never intervenes to check or change the heat— Water is sold about the town—& the people are forbidden to wash their houses, not to use the water—a superfluity of caution, I should imagine, for the Germans are not given to much washing—& there is still water in the Elbe, though it may be walked across.[3] We regret not being among mountains—but after spending last year in a Welch Valley, rained on the whole time, it did not occur to us that we should be in danger of being broiled alive in Dresden in the month of August.—We visited (helped by the railroad) Berlin on our way hither. The gallery there is a very good one & admirably arranged. All things in Prussia you know are so arranged as to half convert a republican—all is done by the king in the best way. There is free ingress to the gallery to every one   Among all the pictures none delighted me so much as the adoration of the Kings by Raphael[4]—a large picture in his first style—the colors all faded—yet what is left, the expression of the faces— the grace & simplicity of the figures, are quite matchless—one kneeling angel in particular— There is adoration humility & perfect self forgetfulness & such inexpressible sweetness that none but Raphael could have put on canvas. The "Mother & Child" (di San Sisto) here are very fine—but quite different— There is much more majesty & grandeur but less simplicity & sweetness. The Magdalene you mention is very lovely—so tearful yet composed—hoping yet regretting. There are other fine Correggios in the gallery.

As I said we go towards Florence. One of our party is ordered a warm climate—I fear Florence will be scarcely temperate enough for him. Percy's friend Knox—(whom you met at our house) has a complaint of the heart— a painful disorder attended by great nervousness & distress—requiring great quiet & composure—and he has many things to worry him. He is writing & will bring out a volume of poems this autumn[5]—a copy shall be sent you—get

---

[3] *Rambles,* I, 256.

[4] In the *Rambles* Mary gives a good deal of space to descriptions of paintings and other works of art, which she had a real love for and which she strove earnestly to understand and appreciate. But she lacked the power of transmitting her deep impressions, and these accounts tend to be tiresome. The Raphael in Berlin (I, 221–22), the "Madonna di San Sisto" by Raphael, in Dresden (I, 236), and the four Correggios (I, 237–38), all appear in the *Rambles.*

[5] *Giotto and Francesca and Other Poems* (London, Edward Bull, Publisher, 19 Holles Street, 1842, 142 pp.). The leading poem is called "A Tale from Boccaccio" and is in two cantos of

it well noticed if you can—and do it all the good you can. He has a true po[etical (*the cutting out of the signature has mutilated several lines of the text*)] great sensibility—infinite facil[ity   ] deep classical knowledge & other qualit[ies   ha]ppy inspiration to verse—with a great dislike to common place— I hope you will like his volume.

Percy desires to be most kindly remembered I shall hope to hear from you—& to hear that Marianne is well & that some prosperity shines on you— Believe me dear Hunt

[*Signature cut away*]

[P.S.] My letter is very stupid but you must forgive [me] as I am only convalesc[ing] from the illness the [   ]—still very weak

ADDRESS: Leigh Hunt Esq/ Edward Square/ Kensington/ London. POSTMARKS: (1) DRESDEN/ 21.Aug.42   (2) HAMBURG/ 23/ 8.   (3) J/ 26 AU 26/ 1842   (4) 10 Fn 10/ AU 26/ 1842. ORIGINAL: Stark Collection, University of Texas; A.L. (signature cut out, affecting 7 lines of the text), 4 pp. 4to. UN-PRINTED and UNPUBLISHED. TEXT: From original letter.

535. *To Claire Clairmont*

Venice 1 Oct. [1842] | We leave this on
the 19th

Dearest Claire—

Percy got your letter at Inspruck & I have been hoping to receive another from you here as you said you would write—a letter is always a comfort—when from a friend—& I get so few— Jane never writes—though I left all my little affairs in her hands when I left England— Percy hears from his Aunt—& that is all. Ianthe had a boy—at which the Esdailes rejoiced—but poor thing, she lost it immediately after—& is by no means in strong health.[1]—We had a desperately long journey from Dresden here—3 weeks & we never (with the exception of Prague) slept two nights in one bed— We traversed a vast variety of scenery—& saw certainly some of the [most] beautiful spots in the world—in the first rank I should place Salzburgh—yet the grandeur of the Danube that sweeps by beneath the mountains in majestic stream, renders Lintz wonderfully beautiful. I did not take to the people—ugly, dirty & sullen there is nothing in them attractive—the Tyrolese are better—but still they seem to want life & spirit & above all the courtesy of the Italians. Venice has excessively charmed my companions—& we remain here in all a month. Thanks to some introductions Laura sent me, we had useful acquaintance, & got comfort-

ottava rima. Mary quotes eight lines from Knox's volume in the *Rambles* (I, 240) with the comment: "In such and other verse has the 'valley of beauty, sunny Rabenau,' been celebrated by one of my friends, who visited it with us, and whose ardent and poetic imagination was warmed by inspiration in this lonely spot." One of the poems was addressed to William Charles Macready, who wrote in his diary (William Toynbee [ed.], *The Diaries of William Charles Macready, 1833–1851* [London, Chapman and Hall, 1912, 2 vols.], II, 185): "Oct. 5, 1842: A volume of poems from Knox, with a sonnet to myself."

[1] On September 27, 1837, Ianthe Shelley married Edward Jeffries Esdaile. They had two sons, Charles and William. (Ingpen, *Shelley in England*, 514–15.)

ably lodged—a little expensive for us—but still very comfortable—with so large a party it is difficult to find comfort without spending a good deal, for that greatly depends on the independance of each member of the party—both Knox & Pearson are invalids—both suffer a good deal from depression & are irritable —They both are ill in somewhat the same way— Knox has an enlargement of the heart, which threatens ultimately ossification, & added to this an irritation of all the nerves in the region of the heart, the most violent. He ought to be kept quiet—but as he will write—& indeed in a certain sense he must—quiet he cannot have, & his spirits fluctuate with his success in composition— He, as you may know, is proud & sensitive to a fault still we get on very well— Pearson is quite different—the illness that threatens him is aneurism—he is much better—& I think his malady will be subdued; it affects him most by encreasing his natural indolence, which is excessive—he is much more openly irritable than Knox—but it is all on the surface—he has no pride—& the fit of annoyance over he is as gentle as a lamb—beg[g]ing one to excuse him & try-ing to make it up in a thousand ways— He has no more reason in him than a child—but like a child is très raisonneux—as he is utterly incapable of taking care of his own money—I have to take care of it for him—& he wants to buy a thousand things—& I wont let him, & one argues & goes over the same ground a thousand times—& when you think he is persuaded, like a child he comes back to the same point & it is all to do over again. He is a little taller than Knox—an air of indolence is diffused over all his person—his complexion is that muddy one you hate—he has a great deal of hair—about Shelley's color— only yellower where the light catches it—his eyes are grey—his nose aquiline —his features prononcer, but his face is narrow—& his chin, while it supports his face, does not deviate into width of jaw—he is as simple as a child, & to be managed like one. I like myself to have to deal with those exceedingly open characters, without stain of sullen[n]ess or concealment—still 3 young men will draw various ways at times, & I have quite enough to do to keep all well. Percy is my delight—he is so good & forbearing & thoughtful for me, that he is the greatest comfort in the world. Knox is writing a tragedy. When it is finished—& (as we have every trust it will be) accepted, he will go over to England to bring it out. I dont think we shall go so soon. Helen Shelley plainly shews she is glad that Percy is away—& though that may mean that they are afraid that Sir Tim may take to him—yet they would hinder that by quarrel-ling with him, so it is as well that he is away on good terms.

I have made a new acquaintance here that will a little surprise you. Milnes & Leader[2] came together here—so knowing one we know both I cannot make out whether Leader is enclined to be civil. his manners are rather cold

[2] Richard Monckton Milnes (1809–85), later the biographer of Keats, left Venice for Egypt. John Temple Leader (1810–1903), a Liberal politician very active at the time and with a very wide acquaintance among important and influential people in public life. He had gone to Christ Church, Oxford, but had taken no degree. Trelawny was his guest for a long time at his house at Putney. (See *D.N.B.*, Second Supplement.)

& repulsive, but I in a measure wish to cultivate him, because Percy wants to ally himself to the liberal party in England & Leader, if not the wisest, is one of the most respectable among them. They asked Percy & Knox to dinner one day—& yesterday they dined with us— Milnes is gone; he set off by a steamer for Constantinople last night, & Leader remains. He tells me that Trelawny goes on just the same, never going out & building & cutting down trees at Putney. Augusta[3] lives in a cottage near—so the stories told of her going back to her family are not true—perhaps she went to see her father before his death.

This is all my news. Pearson is writing an opera for a German libretto—but he wishes to write for an Italian, & I hope he will get one at Florence. He is very clever— His music is a great resource to Percy—who has added a trumpet to his stock of instruments—& is taking lessons & a pretty noise is made at times—to be heard at Lido.—To Lido, by the bye, they go every day to write & bathe— I have been obliged to fight a great deal to prevent them having a gondola apiece— We have two in our pay as it is— If I saw them all happy I should be content—but I fear poor dear Knox can scarcely be so in the present position of his affairs & health—if his play succeeds, it will be a great thing & I feel sure it will—he writes the dialogue very well—with strength feeling & poetry— A volume of his poems—including the poem you read (which I persuaded him to take back, it was too silly to allow it to be published as written by another) are now being printed & published in England. By the bye I trust that your debt to George R—is now paid I sent the money for the purpose. You have heard I suppose of Mr. Robinson's death,[4] poor man—he seems to have gradually become extinct without suffering. The last I heard was that Mrs. Alfred R—had gone to Boulogne & that Julia was with her poor Julia—she seems to have gained nothing by the changes in her family— Percy has rather a prejudice against her, which has prevented my wishing to see her—& besides her having told you that they had sacrificed a brilliant society for my sake utterly prevents my ever associating with her again on terms of friendship—poor thing—what benefit can she see in covering the truth with false tinsel—one cannot guess—but it is nature with some people. There was a paragraph in Galignani to say that Mrs. Norton's youngest child was killed by a fall from a poney I hope it is not true.[5] Charles Dickens has come home in a state of violent dislike of the Americans—& means to devour them in his next work[6]—he says they are so frightfully dishonest. I am sorry for this—he has never travelled, & will write with all that irritation inexperienced travellers are apt to feel—such as I felt in Germany—& I do dislike the Germans—& never wish to visit Germany again—but I would not put this in print—for the

[3] Augusta Harvey, Lady Vane Goring, who eloped with Trelawny and married him in 1847 after her divorce.

[4] For the Robinsons, see Letter 309, note 2, and Letter 533.

[5] It was true. Early in September William Norton, eight years old, died of blood-poisoning, which resulted from a fall from his pony. (Perkins, *The Life of Mrs. Norton*, 165–66.)

[6] Dickens was in America in January–May 1842. His *American Notes*, which fulfilled Mary's fears, was published in October, 1842.

surface is all I know—& that does not deserve commemoration & vituperation. He is very angry because they refuse to make a law of international copyright —a law that would make his fortune—& his vehement seeking for it when in America Washington Irving says will retard its being passed for ten more years. Pray write dear Claire if by return of post direct here—if not to Florence—& tell me what you are doing about Dina—& what you are doing yourself

Ever Affly

M W S.

(*2nd Oct.*) This letter was just going off, when I received yours. Poor Dina —I pity her for her bringing up—her total want of self command—& above all for her attribute of fibbing—which this story about you displays so glaringly— and much I pity her for her mother's speaking so ill of her— I confess Jane's conduct has shocked me much. She brought it all on her child— We are all liable to do wrong & I would have forgiven that if she had borne her share of the misfortune she brought on Dina. There is no help now—Dina is married by this time[7]—she must give lessons & get on as she can—her character may strengthen & purify under adversity; at any rate this is [the] time to shew her kindness, & would I could serve her—but money matters go against me. It is my fate always to have poor friends— I had hoped when he came with us, that poor dear Knox would have been better off than he is—as it is my purse is exhausted—& my darling Percy's too—who is so good—however one must not complain. I shall be glad if you can lett your house & come to Florence for two months—do if you can.

I have seen nothing of Rawlinson— We frequent the piazza & some of us would be sure to see him if he made his appearance

Writing to you about Knox of course I write in the strictest confidence. He is writing a tragedy which I think will be very fine & its success make all right & well with him [*there follow a few words deleted probably by Claire; they seem to be as follows, though the reading is by no means certain:* & then his grand intention is to pay us off soon] I must tell you by the bye that Percy & I pay half Hunts rent—& I believe L[or]d Leigh will pay the other half— He is dreadfully off—writes poetry by which he gets nothing—hopes about a play, which is never acted & lives on Henry's £100 a year— I wonder if Edward [Williams] will help his sister— It was a great pity that so much money was spent in sending Dina out of the way—to no purpose.

You are right in saying Venice might make me melancholy—it did excessively at first—but I have so much to think of to keep my companions comfortable that the impression is worn off—& my great endeavour is to be in good spirits— I was a good deal worried & careworn & ill from the heat at Dresden —but I feel well here Adieu, dear Claire, I hope Percy will write to you soon

7 Dina Williams married Henry Hunt on October 21 (see Letter 532, note 3).

168

—he sends his love— I hope he will get into no love scrape here to hurt his health—that is the thing to be dreaded in this country— Adieu

Ever Ys.

M S.

ADDRESS: Miss Clairmont/ Rue Neuve Clichy No. 3/ Rue Clichy/ Parigi à Paris. POSTMARK: VENEZIA/ 3 OTTE. ORIGINAL: Huntington Library (HM 12143); A.L.S., 4 pp. 4to. UNPRINTED and UNPUBLISHED. TEXT: From original letter.

536. *To Claire Clairmont*

Casa Quadri—Firenze

4 Nov. Friday [1842]

My dear Claire

Percy wrote to you to tell you of our arrival here—& talked of your coming; this depends apparently on your letting your apartment— Is there any chance of this? & do you still think of coming? Pray write *directly* & let me know.

Did fate allow things to take the usual commonplace course with me, I should say all I could to persuade you to come—for I think the being in Florence would be agreable to you & it would certainly add to our pleasure. But my old destiny pursues me unrelentingly & my spirit is never allowed to repose. I wrote from Venice to my Banker telling them to send me here £100 in Coutts's notes— I ought to have received the money last Monday—no letter has come yet— The cause I cannot divine The worst is that if the letter is stolen, the signature for the notes may be forged & I lose the money altogether — What it all means I cannot guess— I shall be able to get some money here, I suppose, to go on with—but with this doubt hanging over me of the total loss of £100 you may guess that I am uneasy & depressed beyond expression. Nor is this all—but it is useless speaking of one's annoyances at such a distance—& this is the chief.—It is too hard that do what I will, I must forever be oppressed by care & anxiety & have to struggle on with the sense that fate is always at work doing her worst against me

You will be anxious to hear something of Laura & Nerina [Mason]. I see very little of them. Nerina is a complete invalid—she never goes out & sees no society except in the evening between 9 & 10—when having no carriage it is not pleasant to leave one's fireside. Laura's time is devoted to a sick & I believe a dying Cousin so that one can only see her by calling on her in the morning. Were I free from care I would devote myself to overcoming these difficulties & see both the Sisters in spite of them. But I am so crushed & dispirited by anxiety that I have no heart for society. Percy is so shy that he always thinks that he is not wanted & had better not call, so heaven knows how it will all be. But if I can get him to go to Laura in the morning & Nerina in the evening without me I will. It is very foolish to be as cast down as I am—but I cannot help it—the perpetual recurrence of money care puts to flight every power of enjoyment—do what I will it is the same thing, & I am thoroughly tired out.

Nerina has no fever now but a constant pain in her side—she is lamentably thin & weak— I have not yet seen her children. Laura has the same face I remember as a child but she looks sad & worn, poor thing—& her beauty has faded. The Sanfords are here—we dined there once Percy & I. I have seen no one else. Mrs. Hare (the only person who ever treated me kindly) has sent me some letters of introduction— I have had no heart to send them yet— I must for Percy's sake—for myself I have no wish for society. Knox is writing his play— When it is finished he will I fancy return to England. I have great hopes from it—heaven grant it succeed. Pearson is a very great care & even burthen—unless you knew him you could not understand this—he has many charming qualities but he has others which are very unendurable— Forgive this stupid letter—& pray let me hear what your plans are at once— We have a pleasant appartment & if you càn come we shall all rejoice to see you

Ys. Affly
M S.

ADDRESS: Miss Clairmont/ Rue Neuve Clichy No. 3/ Rue Clichy/ Parigi à Paris. POSTMARKS: (1) FIRENZE (2) 11/ NOV/ 42/ PONT-DE B. ORIGINAL: Huntington Library (HM 12174); A.L.S., 4 pp. 4to. Copy by Claire Clairmont, Berg Collection, the New York Public Library. UNPRINTED and UNPUBLISHED. TEXT: From original letter.

537. *To Claire Clairmont*

Casa Quadri
Firenze 5 Nov. [1842]

I wrote you so uncomfortable a letter yesterday dear Claire—that I now send you these words to say that I have received the letter with the money. The post kept it back 3 days in some extraordinary manner.

We are anxious to know what you think of doing—& if there is any hope of seeing you in Florence. Laura & Nerina desire so very much to see you—& the Sanfords are very desirous that you should come. I do not know how it is but I do not get on with Laura— She has not the frank easy manners I expected—& I have lived always so retired a life that I require to be met halfway— Nerina is more practicable—but her recluse life & Laura's devotion to this Cousin—& the distance at which they live renders it difficult If you were here I dare say things would go easier

I will not write to you about my other worries. I think Pearson will soon leave us. I am very sorry he came with us—for with all his genius & good qualities it is neither agreable nor safe to have him so intimate & he keeps us all in hot water. The Sanfords took me to the Opera last night & Percy & I go there [to the Sanfords'] on Sunday Ev[enin]g so they mean to be very civil. Percy is very willing to go into society & I hope I shall be able to arrange that he shall see some. Do come if you can & write & let us know your intentions.

I got a letter from Jane. She is very angry—but speaks less angrily of Dina. She says that Hunt promised for his son that the young people should be

separate for a year—& that after that he ought not to have written as he did to
Dina. His motive was that Henry contrived to have it believed that his life
was at stake—of which I do not believe one word—he was only resolved to
triumph over Mrs. Hogg. Have you seen Bacciochi remember me to him
when you do—

Ever affectionately ys.

M S.

ADDRESS: Miss Clairmont/ Rue Nᵉ Clichy No. 3/ Rue Clichy/ Parigi à Paris.
POSTMARKS: (1) FIRENZE   (2) T.S.1. ORIGINAL: Huntington Library (HM
12342); A.L.S., 3 pp. 4to. Copy by Claire Clairmont, Berg Collection, the New
York Public Library. TEXT: From original letter.

538. *To Everina Wollstonecraft*

Florence. 24 Nov. [1842]

My dear Aunt—

I send Mrs. Hogg some money by this post, so you will receive what you
asked. I am sorry I cannot do more—I should much like to have sent Margaret
a little present, that I might shew my sense of her Mother's kindness to you—
but I cannot— I hope you will be very comfortable when you get the £100
a year regularly— The tombstone is quite out of my power to pay, as I explained in my last—it is a pity you did not keep your promise, on which I relied

We are living here very quietly & know one or two agreable people. The
weather is as bad as it can be in England—so we have not gained in that. We
live quite near the gallery, & often visit it to see the beautiful pictures & splendid
statues it contains. We are near also to the Pitti palace, which has a very fine
gallery. The other day we made an excursion to Vallombrosa, a convent seated
high among the mountains.[1] The season was too far advanced, & we were
caught in a storm, as we were toiling up the ravine, on our ponies— A monk
received us at the convent & took us to the stranger's room & lighted a large
fire, which was very welcome. The sun came out afterwards, & we descended
the mountain in comfort—but had a very rainy drive back to Florence. Lady
Mountcashell's two daughters by Mr. Tighe[2] are here. The Eldest is a very
beautiful woman, with the sweetest face in the world, so kind & gentle—she
made an unfortunate marriage, & has a good deal to go through—but she bears
all with great fortitude & good sense. The youngest is married to an Italian—
a very sensible, good man—she has two young children—& is very lively &
agreable but unfortunately she has very bad health They are the most pleasant people we know here—& we often spend our evenings with them— The
eldest sings beautifully

Percy has bought a trumpet so now he has three musical instruments to
play upon. My health is a good deal improved—my long journey, though
fatigueing at the time, has strengthened me. I hope my stay in Florence wont

[1] Cf. *Rambles,* II, 136–39.
[2] Laura and Nerina (Mason).

hurt me—for I am never so well in any town as in the country—a great deal of fresh air & exercise are quite necessary to me. I hope you creep out in your chair on fine days, & find it a comfort to you— I should be very glad to hear that you & your room looked the picture of tidiness & comfort—& that gentle exercise in your [? chair (*MS torn*)] was giving you strength

Ever affly ys.

M W S

ORIGINAL: J. H. Coste, Coverside, Smallfield, Horley, Surrey, to whose father the MS was given by Everina Wollstonecraft; A.L.S., 4 pp. 12mo. UNPRINTED and UNPUBLISHED. TEXT: From original letter.

539. *To Claire Clairmont*

Casa Quadri—Firenze
25 Nov. [1842]

My dear Claire

We are quite tired of expecting in vain a letter from you— What are you about that you do not write?—Are you in hopes of letting your apartment, & then joining us?—I hope this is the case—but do write— If you come can you find in Paris & bring with you a most unpoetical thing—a corn rubber— or two, if you can—or tell me where you get yours in Florence—for I have sought all over the city & cannot find one. Also when you write to Marianna ask her to get from Hookham 100 of my cards & 100 of Percys—& bring them with her to Paris, when you may find some opportunity of sending them here —or I can find one & let you know through a *Modista* here—if you do not bring them yourself. You will greatly serve & oblige me if you can manage that I should receive these things pretty soon.

Our weather here is odious—an absolute English November—nebbia instead of fog—much rain & great mud & dirt so that I am very much confined to the house. Pearson left us about a fortnight ago to our infinite content. He kept us in such very boiling water while he staid—doing all the mischief he could, trying to set us all by the ears & when he could not succeed, being so savagely cross that he was quite intolerable. It is always a great risk to receive a new inmate— I acceded to his joining us in fear & trembling—but I fancied that he had many good qualities & would be of great good & pleasure to Percy through his music—but his temper spoilt all— He is gone & we are at peace— I wish I could contrive more amusement for Percy—but it is difficult to do all for one who will do nothing for himself—not being musical I cannot help him in that—& he will not cultivate society, though he has sufficient openings here— He has not been well—the effect of indolence & inactivity—he has seen a doctor, who insists on early rising & exercise—& Percy obeys his behests for the present, having been unwell enough to make him wish to recover health. Laura, taken up with her sick Cousin, visits us seldom & then only in the morning & Percy is too shy to call often on her—she has had a cold lately, which interrupts her singing— I dined at Nerina's once—& indeed nothing can be kinder than they are—& Percy likes them—but does

JANE WILLIAMS

from the painting by
George Clint

not cultivate them so as to have a resource in them. Nerina suffers a good deal
— They are of course by far the . . . [*At this point two inches of the upper
part of the second sheet are missing, occasioning the loss of about six lines.*]
. . . his being presented here— I shall try to get over this by the time of the
Carnival balls. I saw Mrs. Smith at Mrs. Sanfords the other day—she was full of
eager & affectionate enquiry about you—but she seems a tiresome old woman.
I mean to see Mr. Kirkup[1] by & bye, but have not yet— The *very* bad weather
is, as in London, a great clog to one who has no carriage— We get on pretty
well—but houserent is so dear that I am driven to the utmost economy in other
respects, & several disasters have happened with regard to money to impoverish
me. Knox has not yet finished his play—heaven knows what will be the result
of that, & whether he will leave us— He is much oppressed by a sense of adversity, so as not to be the Companion to Percy I had hoped. Did I tell you
that I got a ridiculous letter from Gee some time ago, asking me to confide
to her my marriage with Knox—& talking of *surmises*— Surmise could only
come through Julian & whatever gossip his sisters may have founded on his
communications. Of course . . . [*Here again some six or seven lines are missing,
from the same cause mentioned above.*] . . . course that Dina was married
the 21 Oct. Jane is naturally reconciled to her & will do all she can for her
comfort—& so dear is liberty that Dina in Hunts squalid home will rejoice
at having escaped Dah's iron rule—his answer to Jane's announcement of the
marriage was quite fierce—she copied his letter to me— However if she had
married an Angel—& that angel had been poor, he would have [been] equally
averse to serving them. I wish I could write you a more amusing letter—but
my life is passed almost entirely in seclusion— I wish so very ardently that
Percy would get intimate with young people—he seems to me to get shyer—
but I believe he is less so when I am not there—so I draw back & wish him to
go out alone—but then he will not go out at all. He ought to be thrown entirely
on his own resources in some strange wild place where he would be excited
to activity of mind & body— I am bitterly disappointed at the sort of separation there is between Knox & him—a good deal of Pearson's making—but not
altered now he has gone—so that Percy has little or no companion in him—&
all my sacrifices for the sake of giving him one are come to nought. I have
but one wish in the world—to give Percy a cheerful home—it is hard not to
succeed. Adieu dear Claire—pray write directly—

Ever yours

M S.

ADDRESS: Miss Clairmont/ Rue Nᵉ Clichy No. 3/ Rue Clichy/ Parigi à Paris.
POSTMARKS: (1) FIRENZE (2) 3/ DEC/ 42/ PONT-DE B. ORIGINAL:
Huntington Library (HM 12173); A.L.S., 4 pp. 4to (2¼ inches of the top part
of the second sheet is torn off, affecting pages 3–4), with seal. UNPRINTED and
UNPUBLISHED. TEXT: From original letter.

[1] Seymour Stocker Kirkup (1788–1880), artist. He attended the burial of Keats and that of
Shelley in Rome, was a friend of R. B. Haydon, and settled in Florence, where he was a leader of
a literary circle. Among his close friends were Trelawny, Landor, Severn, and the Brownings.
(See *D.N.B.*)

540. *To Claire Clairmont*

(Direct Casa Quadri—it is best)
Casa Quadri—[Florence]
29 Nov. [1842]

Dearest Claire—

I have just got your letter & will answer it at once though I wrote but the other day—do not talk of stupidity, you write the most amusing & clever letters in the world—I mean this au pied de la lettre— If your letters are ever published, all others that ever were published before, will fall into the shade, & you be looked on as the best letter writer that ever charmed their friends— Is this glory? Will it please you? At any rate do write as often as you can. I am so delighted always to get your letters. I am disappointed though, & greatly at not seeing you— The autumn was the time to lett your house—you may find more difficulty in the spring. What we shall do I know not— I am quite ruined by the heavy rent (£4 per week) I pay here— We live quietly, never have any one to dinner I never have a box at the opera & spend as little as I can but I am quite ruined—£400 is so very little to housekeep, pay rent & dress myself on—I am obliged to draw a little on Percy—but even so, I am obliged to economize & to think of economy all day long.—What you say of the expences of a house is all very true & for those very reasons I have never ventured to rent a house. When spring comes on I must diminish the article of rent— I dont much like Florence—the season here is as gloomy & rainy as in England—there are no pretty walks that I can reach (we are close to Ponte Vecchio & too far from the Cascino)—I long to get further south—but shall dislike leaving the Sisters—nor indeed can I set out travelling again in so large a party —it costs too much. Accordingly brooding over these thoughts, I remain in entire uncertainty of what we shall do in the spring—but that is a good way off yet.

I feel what you say of Laura to be true—but the difficulty is to get at her— There is a soggezzione in morning calls that stands in the way of intimacy other visitors being often there—she will not dine with us & calls very seldom —her evenings are spent between her sick Cousin (a M^m Pozzo) & her sister. Nerina receives in the evening—but her hours especially for an invalid are so late—10 o'clock—& having no carriage it requires energy to tear oneself from one's fireside to encounter dirt or cold between 9 & ten at night. Poor Nerina is in a miserable state of health—it is sad to see her—but she is full of life & spirit—generally there are two or three Italian men at her house in the evening— You see thus there is a sort of clog on our intercourse—however it goes on better. M^m Pozzo is if possible to go to Pisa next month & then Laura will be more free—& I trust she will dine quietly with us now & then—& I hope before the winter is over that all ice will be thawed— I want to have her with us in the summer—but how to manage & afford it I know not—

She says she will not spend another summer in Florence. I have thought of
Lucca as a cheap & healthy place—but that w[oul]d be dull for Percy—in
short all is obscurity—by & bye light will struggle through, & we shall do—as
now we are doing—the best we may—tho' that best just now is not quite what
I like. Mr. Rawlinson had left Florence before we came & returned home by
Venice—Munich & the Rhine. The Sanfords have no news of the Lennox's
& have some idea that they are together again. We dont see much of them—
for rich & poor dont get on well together— If Percy would cultivate them
without my intervention, he might—but he wont—he is in the wrong—but I
cant alter it. Their English set is by no means good— The Crawfurds are
very civil & Nerina says that Kitty Crawfurd (the eldest daughter—about six
& twenty) is a very nice girl— I have some idea that Percy may get on
intimate terms there—where he could get singing & dancing quietly to prepare
him for the balls.

I told you what Jane wrote to me. It seems after Dina's return to England
she wrote her mother (she says dictated by Hunt—but I doubt) a short laconic
note asking for clothes—the tone so cold that Jane took no notice of the letter—
a day or two after a letter came from Dina all affection & Jane instantly went
to her—& Dina moreover persuaded her mother to see & forgive Henry. Jane
says she furnished Dina's bedroom—& will provide her always with clothes
& pay her washing bills so that she shall have necessaries & comforts about her.
She says she shall not see Henry probably more than twice or thrice a year—
so she hopes to keep on decent terms with him.

Your account of the discomforts brought on you by your Russian reminded
me of our sufferings through P[earson] Not that he opened letters &c—but he
made all the mischief he could— He has a bad temper—egged on by a self
conceit that makes Jane's look pale, & an envy & jealousy of every one quite
painful— His object was to get Knox out of our house & establish himself
instead—so he told Knox that we looked on him as a travelling tutor without
pay—& told us that Knox's temper was so bad (& he contrived to irritate him
into misery & bitterness) that we must choose between him P., & him   K.—
As with you & M^m I—our intimacy with Knox caused us one fine day to
compare notes & clear up his devices. Another notion of his was that he was
such a first rate genius that I ought to be too happy to go to any expence on his
account—& not a little, to my great vexation & discomfort, he did make me go
to—for I made a great sacrifice at last to facilitate his going to Vienna— It
is hard not to love the author of "Arethusa"—but alas!—and I feel, I think, less
resentment towards him than either Percy or Knox— You will not mention
these things of course—you are the only person out of our own house to whom
we have hinted that all was not bright—however I a li[ttle?] fear his tongue—
for he does not care what he says when he is angry—& by no means is a disciple
of truth. It was a great misfortune to have known him— He will abuse us
for not erecting him on a pedestal & worshiping him   that he expects—with

full liberty to grumble & rail at his worshippers all the time— He was too disagreable [*written* disableable] as well as unsafe a companion.

Your account of the Turners is very amusing— Well I wish you were among us—you would enjoy yourself with Percy & the Sisters— Write soon —& dont forget the things I asked you to do for me in my last letter—the corn rubber—& the cards from England if you can— Percy says he is so sorry you do not come. He is in no humor to return to England—& wants to visit Rome & Naples if not Greece first— I dont know how its to be managed—but I myself want much to visit Rome—when once I return to England heaven only knows whether I shall ever revisit Italy. I have no more news— Knox is going on with [his] play—whether this will cause him to return to England one cannot tell. Adieu— Percy has had no letters from his relations for a long time

Affectionately ys.
M S.

[P.S.] Nerina lives at Casa Leonetti di la d'Arno near the ponta S. Niccoli — Laura—at Casa Mazzain via dei Tonicelli—di que d'Arno & close upon it —a pleasant situation—but not a good house—we had nearly taken up our abode in the same street—but it is a long way from every one—far above the last bridge— You must always direct to Laura to Cinis' care as thus she gets her letters free.

ADDRESS: Miss Clairmont/ Rue N^e Clichy/ Rue Clichy/ Parigi à Paris. POSTMARKS: (1) FIRENZE (2) 6/ [DE]C/ 42/ PONT-DE B. ORIGINAL: Huntington Library (HM 12133); A.L.S., 4 pp. 4to, with seal. UNPRINTED and UNPUBLISHED. TEXT: From original letter.

541. *To Claire Clairmont*

Casa Quadri—Firenze
3 December [1842]

My dear Claire

You will be surprised to get another letter from me so soon—but my motive for writing explains itself.

Mr. & Mrs. Sanford called on me today & asked about the likelihood of seeing you— I told them there was no chance of your coming till the Spring. And then they told me that a Mr. Macdonald (a resident here, whom perhaps you know) had gone to Paris in his carriage to take a daughter (I think they said) to school— But the thing certain is, that he is returning alone— and they propose your coming with him—he has a carriage which will contain himself only unless you accompany him. They say he will arrive in Paris on about this day week (Dec 9) Mrs. Sanford will write to him, to propose the matter to him—so do pray communicate with him. He will be at Hotel Aguardo— Rue Grange Batelier—He will remain in Paris only *one week* & then return here. You will come thus franked here and Mrs. Sanford offers to take you back free of expence, when they return to England.

These offers are worth accepting saving you money—giving you companions—& offering, instead of the diligence, easy & luxurious conveyances. With regard to your house that need not detain you—as if you leave it empty it will not cost you anything—as your journey will cost you so little. The only objection is Hammy—you must judge of the obstacle she places. Whether by writing to her—she can prolong her stay in England till you return in the Spring.—Mrs. Sanford talks of returning in April or early in May—perhaps earlier or whether she cannot install herself & take care of your house till you return. You must determine on all this—but really the opportunity of coming here & returning to Paris so comfortably [at] so little expence is not to be despised— Hammy is no stranger in Paris—& I think she might manage without you till your return.

We were at Casa Cini last night. Laura said she had got a letter from you —both Sisters were most eager to see you—they will be enchanted if you come — We can accomodate you tant bien que mal—in this house— I advise you to overcome obstacles & come— Reflect, at least—& communicate with Hammy—there is plenty of time for that before Mr. Macdonald sets out on his return—

If you come, bring with you (if you do not send by Mr. Macdonald, sealed up a *corn rubber*—carefully packed with wool round the stone part not to rub—& if you can in any way get 100 or 50 of mine & the same number of Percy's cards from Hookham I shall be glad

I shall of course hear from you as soon as you decide—

Ever Ys.

M S.

[P.S.] Today has been absolute June—a clear sky a bright sun—a fresh pleasant air,—no fire, & I hope it will last!

[*Written in another hand* (Laura's or Nerina's)] My dear Claire this is a dispensation of providence—you know who she is, in your behalf and ours— so if you don't come it will be set down by him or her as a contempt for their endeavours to get you here—you had much better *come*

[*Mary Shelley's hand again*] If you do come—& in the carriage & can bring it with *comodo*—& can make a tolerable bargain you may bring me a nice warm—dark-colored cloak with *sleeves* to it—for travelling— However dont trouble yourself much about it If it is not a cold winter I shant want one— so unless both pretty & cheap dont get it—

If you come (& I feel sure you will) bring *Towels* enough for your own use as we are a little short

Also get 6 pocket handkerchiefs—such as Annie Farrer got for Percy & Knox last year— These are for Knox—perhaps dear Annie would get these. Remember me kindly to the Farrers.

Address: Miss Clairmont/ Rue Nᵉ Clichy No. 3/ Rue Clichy/ Parigi à Paris. Postmarks: (1) FIRENZE (2) 10/ DEC/ 42/ PONT.DE B. Original: Huntington Library (HM 12347); A.L.S., 4 pp. 8vo. Copy by Claire Clairmont, Berg Collection, the New York Public Library. Text: From original letter.

542. *To Leigh Hunt*

Casa Quadri Firenze
Dec. 15]1842]

My dear Hunt

I had intended writing to you this very day—when your letter comes—& at once pleases & displeases me by the chequered nature of its contents. I wish I could make the cheque larger, but if you knew the many drains I have on my small means you would see at once that I am obliged to be economical in every way. I hope & trust that Ld. Leigh will provide for your March quarter & that you will be freed from all disturbance & care on the one subject of rent —& though you have so many more, yet that is so impe[*MS torn*] necessary that your mind [   ] by not being obliged to pro[vide for the] next [? quarter]

Of course [I am in the] dark on the subject to which you allude— I know when I first heard of the projected marriage I thought Jane mad—but I understood on reflection what had occasioned so imprudent a step as encouraging so *very* youthful a person as poor Henry, who being only a few weeks older than Percy seemed to me a mere boy. She had lived so unnatural a life under the iron rule of one [Hogg] who seems to think that warm pulses & kindly feelings & social intercourse, at least under his own roof, as vulgar & vicious impulses that no one with a proper moral sense & a gentlemanly education can possibly encourage— Thus poor Jane ground down to sordid economy, & her children to the most hopeless dulness [*MS torn*] the delight of a new tie [   ] whom she conceived a great [   ] as sorry for all their sakes—[   ] with you [   ] the match & [   ] had been permitted to consider themselves as [   ] thing to be tried upon the idea of [   ] good to result to both—but it w[   ] or rather quite impossible, if [   ] attached that it should prove [   ] [? small] the conclusions can I [   ] sorry if any motives [   ] of awakened terror for the [   ] child moved Jane— Give my [   ] & tell her how very sincerely I [   ] happiness. I hope things will [   ] by & bye & under your [? patern] [   ] have [   ] a refuge—but I grieve [   ] how much you have to bear [   ].

You know that in th[   ] possible world [   ] reading Period [   ] for a man at Florence by [   ] soon but that women are [   ] such things—I fear the Edu[   ] a sealed book to me while al[   ] soon however to have a [   ] me & if you can give Jane [*about five lines missing here*] in it I shall be very glad. [   ]ly has been very fine & I am writing [   ] the sun pouring in. Percy takes long [   ] not found out Maiano yet. He [   ] the enquiries you mention. We live [   ] his— I wish the Arno wd. carry it away [   ] it mar our prospects much. We see [   ] trying to get Percy to throw off his shyness & go out—it wd. be easy enough for him [to] make acquaintances if he wd. He goes to the opera every night when there is one—& when there is not, he goes to the [? coconeis] & sees Goldoni's comedies & is much amused.

I can't help hoping & thinking that we may do a little good in China—a nation that shuts itself up in that way is a Briarean Jeff—& I am glad to have them shaken a little out of their bad habits—& I am doubly glad of the peace which prevents any more [? Fins] being sawed in two & so great an effusion of blood—[? Affanghistan] was a sad mistake

Give my love to Marianne   Heaven prosper you & send you some prosperity

Yours Ever

M Shelley

ADDRESS: Leigh Hunt Esq/ Londres   Edward Square/ Kensington/ London/ Inghilterra. ORIGINAL: Owned by Francis Edwards, Ltd., in 1936; A.L.S., 4 pp. 4to (MS is quite imperfect: part of the lower fourth of the first sheet is torn off; the second sheet has the lower fourth and the outer third missing). UN-PRINTED and UNPUBLISHED. TEXT: From original letter.

543. *To Claire Clairmont*

Florence,
Feb. 20 [1843]

Percy is become desirous of returning to England—he takes no interest in pictures and antiquities and scenes that speak of past ages. Still he wishes to visit Rome before we return. . . . Percy goes out a great deal here—but he does not enjoy it.

ORIGINAL: Not traced. Sold at Sotheby's, March 15, 1922 (with 2 other auto-graph letters to Claire), to Phorzheimer [sic], for £12. UNPRINTED and UN-PUBLISHED. TEXT: Quotation from *Autograph Prices Current.*

544. *To Claire Clairmont*

Rome   Via Sistina No. 64[1]
23 March [1843]

Dearest Claire—

My last letter was a most uncomfortable one. I know not why, but the climate of Florence agreed with none of us— It made me suffer in my head, as it were pressure on the brain, more than I had ever done before—& that ac-companied by mingled agitation & depression of spirits. At length a Tramon-tana came, & I got well directly. However Percy was tired of Florence & said he never felt well—so we came away—& have come hither—which is a place full of melancholy at once & delight to me. We were obliged to take lodgings in a hurry—& also cheaply, for we had spent so much money in Florence that I was quite ruined. Percy took a fancy to these rooms, which are in the same house where Miss Curran lived—& though it put me out of spirits at first— still we do very well— The worst is our rooms are somewhat dingy, so that I feel backward in seeking acquaintance— And I am sorry for Percy's sake,

[1] See Letter 531, note 1.

& must get over it—for myself, I care not the least for society, being too poor to enjoy it in any comfort, & have indeed quite lost my zest for it. I enjoy beyond expression—beyond what I thought I was now capable of doing, the galleries & ruins here—& we know one kind & agreable family whom I knew in England.—Knox has taken lodgings separate from us. Poor fellow his lot, from excessive ill health, is a hard one—and it depresses me—now that I have exhausted myself to be useful to him—& though I feel I have done good—it is hardly felt—now that I can do no more. Percy is well— I wish he would write to you—but he is very lazy.

We left poor Nerina very far from well—her own doctor, even while he was frightened by her spitting blood one day, calls her maladies nervous—& does her no good— Nervous no doubt much of her weakness is—but so much pain must have other cause— She & Laura are both dying of Ennui & hope-lessness—& there is no help. I feel now that I could never be of any use to dear Laura, who wants exactly those things of which I by my position, am totally deprived. At Florence I was of no comfort to her whatever— Her resolution not to dine with us—the absence of that sociable spirit that alone can draw poor people together—her not sympathizing in the only pleasures the poor have—the greatest and almost the only ones I enjoy—walks & the sight and influence of nature—joined to the detestable climate & my ill health made me quite useless to her—& Nerina's extreme illness caused the same with regard to her— There is a charm & sweetness about Laura quite indescribable—& a resolution the most admirable—but she is frank—gentle—captivating— One mourned over her—but unless one could by magic have placed her in prosperity one could give her no pleasure & render her no service. She suffers incalculably. Her resolution to endure without stooping or flinching is not accompanied by resignation or one particle of content—& the sight of her sis-ter's suffering adds to the perpetual depression & irritation of her spirit. She mourns over herself helplessly, bitterly—while she sternly shuts every avenue to any transitory amusement. They both long to see you—I wonder whether you will visit Florence this spring. Nerina says she would contrive to receive you in her house. The Sanfords remain in Florence till 10 July—& she told me the last thing that if you came in time, you could always return to Paris with them free of expence. On the 10th April they remove to a sort of villa in a garden within the walls of Florence.

I do not know that I have any other news. Poor Horatia is too silly—as to the notion of a marriage between her & Bentivoglio (the son of Me Ricci by a former husband)—the Sanfords deny it utterly—nor does there seem the smallest foundation except that upon its being reported to Horatia that it was said she was to marry him, she assumed the drollest airs. He has (on dit) a liaison with a very handsome & very silly Englishwoman a Mrs. Bruce— And Horatia turns up her nose about this, to him himself in a way the most *in-conceivable*— She is really too silly to be let loose in society. Thro' Mrs. Hare we knew a very agreable Scotch family at Florence—& Percy formed some acquaintance with some agreable English people—so we did very well—except that———*suffit*———the climate was the worst—& we have found Rome agree with us much better. M^m Boutoulin is in Florence—& asked particularly after you through a lady I knew— I did not see her— I saw nothing of Mrs. Smith after the first evening I met her— Thank you for your wishes about coming to Paris But Percy hates Paris— We shall pass thro' it I dare say on our return—but I know not when that will be— It depends on Percy—who wants companions here sadly if we find any to his mind we may stay longer than I at present anticipate— Pray write you are very lazy

Ys Affly

[*Unsigned*]

[P.S.] Do you hear from Jane? Have you heard that poor Everina [Wollstonecraft] is dead— She died without pain, of natural decay aided by her determination to do nothing she was told— I get no letters & hear no news from England. Poor Dina—that Hunt should have allowed that marriage seems to me absolute & frightful insanity or fearful blindness [? to] what life is & its hard realities in spite of all he has endured.

ORIGINAL: Huntington Library (HM 12327); A.L. (unsigned), 4 pp. 8vo. Copy by Claire Clairmont, Berg Collection, the New York Public Library. UNPRINTED and UNPUBLISHED. TEXT: From original letter.

545. *To Claire Clairmont*

Rome—15 April [1843]

My dearest Claire—

I am sorry you write so seldom & I am sorry when you write, that you adjure me not to do the thing I wish to do. Unluckily I always fear to do the thing that w[oul]d give me pleasure— Still, unless forced, I would not spent the summer in *any* town; for I enjoy fine scenery beyond any thing else in the world—& have a horror of towns—& of society—under the conditions annexed to it with me. We mean to spend the summer at Sorrento—if we find it too hot we shall set sail north by a steamer—but they tell me that the climate at Sorrento is not excessive & by taking care as we intend to do, we need not suffer. I trust things will go well—tho' I confess the plan offers too many charms for me not to be in a fright. I should I confess be delighted to spend next winter in Italy— I have a horror of an English winter—but Percy has not my tastes—& our present idea is to stay at Sorrento till the heats abate & then spend a month at Naples—& then return northward—about the beginning of October— We shall return by Paris—but Percy hates Paris & wont stay there— He will go on to England & leave me at Paris perhaps for two or three weeks. I shall be very glad to see you & stay with you—but I cannot imagine being any support to you. My experience of the mortifications to which I am exposed has determined me never to enter *society* as it is called— If I

181

have a very small circle of friends—*tant mieux* but I cannot stand the impertinence of acquaintance. The rudeness of the Hollands & others shews me that the *great* will not receive me—& I don't like underate gaieties. I am very comfortable here. My chief friends are a Breton gentleman whom I used to meet at Mr. Rogers'—& his Welch wife   M. & M^m Rio[1]—   They make Rome pleasant by going about with us—& being poor—like ourselves we share coach hire—when we venture on any—& she & I have gone together to the Ceremonies of the present week. Mr. Milnes is here—just returned from Upper Egypt—that is where I should like to spend next winter—no clouds nor cold there. I have been quite well since I left Florence—& so has Percy; & Knox feels much better here. Macready will act his play in the autumn, & he must return at that time to bring it out.

I have not heard from Laura. It is a thousand pities that she is given up to despair—   I can understand her being unhappy—but I cannot her total incapacity for enjoyment—   To go to a gallery—to take a walk—to do anything in an English & sociable way are wholly unintelligible to her—   She must be a la Princess or alla Monaca—   She leads the sort of life I did at Kentish town when I first returned to England twenty years ago—& God knows the tears I shed & the lonely misery I endured—by [but] I enjoyed some things & my imagination gilded at times the poverty stricken solitude to which I was doomed—but Laura has no resource in her imagination nor in her tastes— Thus I understand Nerina much better, though her excessive ill health renders her so deplorably a victim—but she has *elans* of enthusiasm—   Laura has none —there is no reaction—no spring. Unless one murdered Galloni[2] & married her to a Prince I do not see how one could render her happier—

Rome is delicious—without a carriage one sees little & one suffers great fatigue—still it is so beautiful & I love so much the sight of its ruins & the tranquility of its churches & the sight of its works of art that I enjoy myself extremely. Had I a carriage of any kind & if Percy enjoyed the same things I do, I should be quite happy—   However one must be content—   The Rio's are a great resource. He is a man of talent & taste, & of the greatest service in going with us to the galleries—   She is a dear good unaffected privitive [*sic*] Xtian (a pious Catholic) who from her facility & cordiality & good nature is a great resource by going about with me—   If Laura had but a tithe of [her] easiness I should never have been able to tear myself from her—& should adore her— but it was irritating to find one so fascinating so perfect & so ready apparently to be friendly, & yet to feel a wall of separation in tastes, in ideas in power of enjoyment that nothing could surmount. To be sure I was very unwell at Florence—& could do little else but suffer & be dull & shut up myself all the time.

[*The following is deleted, probably by Claire:*— I hope you will get rid

1 See Letter 533, note 5.
2 Laura's husband.

of your odious Russian—] Now fine weather is come (& you also have fine
weather I believe) I feel as if all the malignity of the world was harmless—it
is cold & cloud that makes one so dependant on ones fellow creatures & therefore I hate winter—& adore the free delights of summer I am glad to hear
that poor Dina calls herself happy— With fair play, she might be rich here
with her wonderful talent. I am convinced she could copy the old masters as
no one ever did before—& so make a handsome income. I have not heard from
Jane these 6 weeks & more— I hear indeed from no one. I will write again
soon direct to me at Mr. Freeborn's Bank 7 via Condotti Roma Percy is
shockingly lazy— Adieu

Ever Yours
M S.

[P.S.] I owe you 12 francs for a months Galignani— I have told Marianna
to pay you 10 francs I have spent for her. Will you remember me to Louisa
Campbell & say how glad I should be to renew the acquaintance she so kindly
commenced when in England.

ORIGINAL: Huntington Library (HM 12326); A.L.S., 4 pp. 8vo. Copy by Claire
Clairmont, Berg Collection, the New York Public Library. UNPRINTED and
UNPUBLISHED. TEXT: From original letter.

546. *To Claire Clairmont*

Alla Cocumella—Sorrento
Napoli—17 May [1843]

Dearest Claire—

You will be anxious to hear of our movements— here we are. We left
Rome this day week & came directly here. We must stay a month here till we
get money from England— How much longer we shall stay is yet uncertain.
Percy sighs for England so much that we may return before I calculated. I am
very comfortable here—& I trust without any cause for fear—Percy promises
not to make any extensive boatings without me— Dear darling, he is so very
good—I wish I could make him happy— But that he is not just now— He
wants a companion sadly— Knox is not the companion to him I had hoped
& expected— But it is useless filling up a letter with my annoyances—life is
made up of these miscalculations & disappointments— The truth is with
Percy he is dull from not being in love—but how & when that will happen—&
whether more ill will not thence arise, who can tell! As I have said I am comfortable here—but it reminds me too much of Lerici for me not to feel a weight
on my spirits. The weather is cool—but the constant Scirocco we have had
both here & at Rome is very oppressive—there never was such a year for Scirocco. The place is wonderfully beautiful & we live in the midst of orange
groves—the night's rain has filled the air with odours— I think I should like
a villa at Castel a Mare better—they say the air is lighter there—& there are
chestnut woods which must afford pleasant walks. Here there are no walks

except between walls, which is the great drawback of the place— Of course as yet we know little about it.—An excursion or two on mules will tell us whether open country can be found anywhere near.[1]

I am half afraid you will scarcely be able to read this written with Sorrento ink—it seems so pale. Do pray write to us directly—& tell us all the news you can. If Percy should resolve on returning before September to England—do you think I could get a cottage for a month or so at Montmorency or any pretty French village—as he would go over first—and I *must* be in the country in summer. Perhaps I might stay at Fontainebleau—but all this depends on what stay we make here— God grant no evil event happen, & if money does not fall too short I shall make up my mind not to care where I am. When I return to England we must *settle* somewhere—& I want to earn a little money to facilitate this—

I hope you have got over your annoyances with your odious Russian— It seems strange that such things should be— I suppose Paris is getting empty now— Have you any idea of going to Me de Maistre? Where is her chateau? I had a letter from Laura just before I left Rome but you hear from her as much as I do— She thinks the South quite necessary for her in the winter— but the truth is that the summer heats weaken her so much that she becomes an exotic & unable to endure the visitation of winter. Had things gone as I hoped & more than half expected we should have passed the summer in her society—but things are seldom so smooth & practicable in reality as in one's dreams.

Adieu dear Claire—you see we shall certainly meet this autumn—perhaps before— The nervous terrors to which I am a prey here will prevent my regret at leaving this place—and I must put all my thoughts to making a comfortable home for Percy in England. Adieu—pray write

Ever affectly ys
M S.

ORIGINAL: Huntington Library (HM 12324); A.L.S., 4 pp. 8vo. UNPRINTED and UNPUBLISHED. TEXT: From original letter.

547. *To Claire Clairmont*

Sorrento—5 June [1843]

My dear Claire—

It is settled now, as much as human things in prospective can, that we leave this place this day month, Monday 3 July—weather permitting we shall stay a few days at Naples & then proceed northward by steamer to Marseilles —& so on. What we shall do when we get North is not yet decided— I *will* not, if I can help it, stay in any town during the summer & therefore cannot stay with you in Paris. Percy will I suppose pursue his way to England—& I may also—but whither I know not— I shall settle when I get to England—

[1] Sorrento is described in *Rambles*, II, 262–67.

take some cot if I can get it near Putney or Wimbledon—the air of these places agreeing with me so much—but whether I shall delay on my road thither depends on many things. If Percy is to visit his relations on his return I am not wanted in England— I might delay in the neighbourhood of Havre— I would go to the Isle of Wight—but cottages there are dear just at that season. It is a blank for me I care not where I am, so that the scenery is pleasant— beautiful if so it could be—& Percy is content. Had one money to go a little out of the way it were all easy—but this being constantly on the move exhausts one's means utterly— If you were not to be at Paris, I do not think I should cross France—but get to the Rhine & linger somewhere there till Percy paid his visits & summer drew to its close. Could you go to the Rhine—take a lodging in some nook & we join you there, & Percy go over & I remain till I heard from him—or now that the railroad is open are there not beautiful spots about the Loire. You see what my heart is set on—passing the summer—the all of the year in which one can get pleasant sensations, in a pretty spot— I wish you would think over this & write me word— I found my notions first on having very little money to spend & 2^{ly} on Percy's visiting his relations during the month of August. Suppose I went to the same Norman town, where the Farrers have taken a house—the girls w[oul]d amuse Percy if he staid awhile— Would that succeed? Pray let me know what you think.

This place is quite adorable. It has but one drawback (when I am not frightened about Percy's boating—which is not often—he is so good) the Scirocco—which is blowing now, & is very oppressive. To us it has another, shared by every other—that we have no money for excursions & that therefore Percy finds life very monotonous—& longs to be away. When once I have a home in England & feel settled I shall be content—& I trust all our journeying has done Percy good— It seemed to me very necessary to get him out of England when we left it. Things have not gone as I hoped & thought I had a right to expect—but still he has seen various scenes—& mingled in society—& might much more but for his distaste to the same My way just now from being poor is [? fear]fully sown with difficulties—but I must [? do] as well as I can.

Let me hear from you—direct to the care of M. Cotterell & Co—Bankers— Naples— Let me know what you are doing & what you may think we had better do. Write *immediately* that if you suggest any thing your letter may arrive in time to guide us. Knox has been much better lately. He is very busy writing— Our travels have not been thrown away on him—& I trust have been highly advantageous— Adieu—love to my dear Hammy—

Ever ys.

M.

[P.S.] If next month a letter comes to you directed to Knox—take it in & keep it till we arrive. I think your going to the Rhine—some Brunnen prettily situated—Schlagenbad for instance, w[oul]d be best—it would suit our healths —but then *our purses!!!* Mr. Hare talks of spending the winter in Paris.

ADDRESS: Miss Clairmont/ Rue Neuve Clichy No. 3/ Rue Clichy/ Parigi   Paris.
POSTMARKS: (1) NAP. 1843/ 6 GIU   (2) 17/ JUIN/ 43/ PONT-DE-B [   ].
ORIGINAL: Huntington Library (HM 12168); A.L.S., 4 pp. 8vo. UNPRINTED and
UNPUBLISHED. TEXT: From original letter.

548. *To Claire Clairmont*

La Cocumella, Sorrento
17 June [1843]

Dearest Claire—

I have just got your letter— I wrote the other day—so that you have had an answer to your questions— I am truly sorry to interfere with your plans— & it is so little worthwhile as my stay in Paris will be so *very very* short. I cannot stay in a town during the summer— I had too much of that last year at Dresden— Percy is dying to be in England & hates Paris—so we shall not stay more than two days there. I suppose Percy will visit his relations when he gets to England— I shall not be wanted there immediately—but wish to be within call. My plan will certainly be to stay a month at Trouville or St. Valerie— I encline much to the latter if the Campbells are there & you think she would be civil to me. Could you risk a letter to her at St. Valerie & ask if rooms could be got for me in the *country* near— In a town I will not be—my health & spirits entirely depend on spending most of my time in the open air— & that cannot be done in any town. We think of leaving this place the first days of July— We shall spend a few at Naples to see the galleries &c—but I will write to you again when the day of our starting is fixed— Shall I drive at once to you when I arrive in Paris?—rooms can be got for Percy & Knox on the moment at an hotel—& for me too if you have not room but I had better drive to you at once. We shall after two days proceed to Havre—& Percy & Knox will cross & I shall stay at Trouville or Saint Vallerie till 1st September — By which time Percy will have seen some house—my quarter will be due— & I shall go over to settle— What a pity—now there is such easy communication that you could not go too to the sea side. I grieve I shall be so penniless after my journey, & can do nothing to lighten your expences.—Still would it not succeed to go to Me de Maistre by the end of July? you would have more than two Months—& country air is more necessary in the Autumn than at any time. Percy's chief object in England is to see the model of the Flying Machine.

I will not begin other subjects I shall see you so soon—& can talk them over. I grieve you are not more comfortable—but as to society, my experiences in London & Florence & wherever else I have been has determined me never to seek it more—but rather to avoid it as the plentiful source of mortification & disappointment. What a pity Galloni is not hung—poor poor Laura—how I wish—but wishing with respect to her is so useless—things went so contrary to my hopes—

Write & direct to me, *not* to this place—the post is so uncertain—but to the care of M. M. Cotterell & Co Banquiers   Napoli

Percy is very well just now— I have asked Percy if he has any message for you—he bids me tell you that he has made up his mind never to fall in love except in a proper way—he sends his love—& Knox desires kindest remembrances.

Adieu

Ys.

M S.

ORIGINAL: Huntington Library (HM 3898); A.L.S., 4 pp. 8vo. UNPRINTED and UNPUBLISHED. TEXT: From original letter.

549. *To Marianna Hammond*[1]

[Sorrento, June 20, 1843]

Dearest Marianna—

It seems likely that before much more than a month is passed I shall see Paris & you.—I shall indeed be glad to see you—though I grieve so soon to turn northward. This place is quite a Paradise—& suits me excellently. The climate of Florence disagreed with me— The country-town second-rate tone of society was hateful & sweetest Laura was very impracticable while my health spirits & purse did not enable me to make due battle [w]ith her modes of going on. Rome I [*MS defective*] but having no carriage I was in a constant state of self denial with regard to visiting the places & objects I wished to see—but here all is smiling. The place is beautiful beyond expression— The weather exactly one's *beau ideal*—warm & no heat—We live comfortably & well & with economy & I have no trouble. I go about on mules in the evenings —Percy walks by my side—& the exercise does him good—sometimes we go on the sea— We should make a few more excursions if we had more money —& then Percy would be content & I should be quite happy— But alas! we leave this place—too soon—& I plunge again into the shadows & worries of life!

I heard from Laura the other day. You of course hear constantly—so know that she spends the hot months among the mountains near Ar[*Ms torn*] & intends coming to Palermo this winter. How I wish she were with us here The sea-bathing would have strengthened her—&—but wishes are all vain— to England I must go—dark, friendless, ungrateful England!—where I have not a tie—not a friend—not an attraction. I shall as soon as I can get a house at Putney or Wimbledon—for I cannot live in town, it makes me so ill—& the air of those places has always agreed with me so very well—and if I *can* get a house at all to my mind at my price—I shall cultivate my garden—& wish it

1 See Letter 527, note 1.

were finer weather—& be as happy as I can— Adieu dearest Hammy— We shall meet soon   Ys. Affectionately

                     Mary Shelley

ADDRESS: [Cancelled] Monsieur M. Edwd. Williamson/ Employe a l'Amiens Wateau Generale/ Parigi des Postes, Paris. POSTMARK: 20.GIU. ORIGINAL: Huntington Library (HM 12343); A.L.S., 2 pp. large 4to. UNPRINTED and UN-PUBLISHED. TEXT: From original letter.

550. *To Claire Clairmont*

Sorrento   30 June [1843]

My dear Claire—

I hope in heaven this will still find you in Paris— I am more distressed than words can express by the letter I have just got. You say I gave you *carte blanche*—yes to *discuss* plans—but not to *execute* them without the interchange of a line to know whether they are feasible. The foundation of all my plans— & the reason of our leaving this Paradise is that Percy *will* return to England. I told you that I did not mean to cross the channel immediately—but that I must be within call—& wished to be in a place near. Had I money I would follow your lead & go to Geneva—but it is *IMPOSSIBLE* We have barely enough for our journey in the most economical manner across France. I have discussed with Percy how far we could turn aside at Lyons—go to Geneva, & so down the Rhine— WE CANNOT, we have no money— Could I do it, be assured I would, for your sake—but there is no struggling with an empty purse.

We leave this place 10 July— We shall stay a few days at Naples—& then go by sea to Marseilles, thence up the Rhone to Lyons. Could I, as [I] have said go thence to Geneva I should be too glad—but our finances will oblige us to proceed by diligence across France to Havre where I shall stay living on as little as I can till my September quarter— Percy *will* go to England. Otherwise we should have staid here—where I am happier & better & far more economically than I could be elsewhere.

Let me find a letter from you at Marseilles directed Poste Restante & chance a letter to Lyons also. I shall go at Lyons to l'Hotel de l'Europe—but we cannot stay there for every day's delay at an Hotel costs more than we have to spend. You cannot guess—you never remember that we are so very poor that we can never indulge when we travel—but get on as cheaply & directly as possible

My dear Claire, I end as I begun—words cannot express my annoyance & distress—my wildest dreams could never have suggested that without a word of communication you would set off expecting me to follow—because I asked your advice & invited discussion— I will never do so again be assured— Meanwhile God send this finds you still in Paris— If not—I know not what to say or do—but I have no money & can do nothing

                     Affly Ys.

                     M S.

[P.S.] I trust Geneva is not much out of your way to Me de Maistre—What can be done? When I land at Marseilles I will write to you directed to Geneva but let me find there a letter from you.

ADDRESS: (to be forwarded as quickly as possible/ Mlle./ Mlle Clairmont. ORIGINAL: Huntington Library (HM 12325); A.L.S., 2 pp. 4to. UNPRINTED and UNPUBLISHED. TEXT: From original letter.

551. *To Jane Williams Hogg*

Sorrento, 9th July 1843

Dearest Jane—

I am much shocked at the account of yourself contained in your last letter. I hope, my poor thing, that you have got rid of that terrible pain & are better. I can well understand how a serious attack of this sort renders you more sensitive to Jeff's want of sympathy. When thus ill you naturally feel all the more keenly that desire for support, & yearning to be taken care of which all feel—but he cannot understand this—& as money before life & health is his maxim, there is no hope there. Would I could be of use to you. Of use! that will of the wisp that I have hunted so long & all that ensues is, that those I would serve get so far beyond any power of mine to help them. As we are leaving this [place] directly—& about to journey Northward I had hoped to get to the seaside & I had intended to insist on your coming to me for a month & recruiting—but things are going so badly with us that I fear—however we shall see— Whether I stay at, or rather near, Havre—or cross to England, I will see whether I cannot have you & your child for a month—it would do you great good—so try to arrange it.

We have had a sad blow here—in the sudden announcement of the unexpected death of poor Miss Mackay—Knox's aunt—his only relative & friend in England. His affairs are in a very bad way—and this will fall heavily on us for the journey. His health is very much improved by his stay here—so I hope he returns better able to struggle with the hardships of his lot, & that he can follow a profession. All his interest unfortunately lies in the church—but his conscience will not permit him to enter that; so that he has a fearful struggle before him. If his health holds, I doubt not he will do well—but that is for him a fearful question & doubt.

I am grieved beyond measure to worry you about getting the property for me I left with Miss Mackay but I can trust no one else. I have written a line on the other side which will authorize you to take them. I hope Miss Mackay's maid, to whom they were entrusted & who is a very trustworthy person, will have taken care in case there has been any sale—to preserve my things. If you do not see her directly—PRAY go to Doughty St. for I should not like to lose them. The chairs & table are those I bought with you at the sale in the Addison Road. There is too much for your little house—so you had better send the greater part at least to the Pantechnicon— Pray take care the pictures are not hurt.

We leave this place one day this week. We go by sea to Marseilles—traverse France to *Havre*—let me find there a line from you pray, & send the Examiners there—directed Poste Restante. In September I must settle myself in a house. It must be as you say a furnished one— O if I could get one to suit me—the rent not high—a small house—but comfortable— It is difficult—but I must do it somehow—& pitch my tent for a long time. It would have been better to have furnished two years ago. Yet then I thought—& I still think it was best for Percy that he left England as he did for a little while—& if best for him, best for all. I hope so I am sure, for I anxiously act for the best for him, as well as my judgement directs.

What a fearful account we have of your spring—it comes strangely here where we have had perpetual sunshine—this spot is indeed Paradise— Yet this blow coming on poor Knox makes me anxious to get away. Strange I always leave Italy under the pressure of some blow. I shall be afraid to come again. Percy is quite an angel—never was any one so kind & considerate & good. Thank God he is in good health— God preserve him to me & I must be happy. He takes a good deal of exercise among these mountains, which agrees with him. I am much better than I have been for a long time & Knox has lost his pain in his side—if he only continue well he will do well.—

I shall hope to see you before very long—God send us safe to England. We shall arrive as poor as rats. We hear (not from him) that Julian R[obinson] is going to marry a girl with some money—her father a clergyman—so he will get on— Adieu dear Jane I do nothing but give you trouble for which I hate myself— My fond hope one day is to be of use to you   Adieu

Ever Thine

Mary Shelley

[P.S.] Of course I mention Knox's affairs in strict confidence—dont speak of them to Edward or any one   Knox has directed Mr. Lane to send all my things to the Pantechnicon except *the pictures*. He has directed Fanny Ireland to put these in a hackney coach & to bring them at once to you—pay the fare of the coach—& give her half a crown for her journey back. Pay also for the carriage of the things to the Pan^n. If however you do not see Fanny in a day or two—pray go to Doughty St. & make enquiries of Mr. Lane. The sooner my things are under your care & in the Pantechnicon the better.

[*The appended "line" and list referred to above*] Will you, my dear Jane attend to these instructions carefully. I left some property at 13 Henrietta St under the care of the late Miss Mackay. I wish you to have this under your care; it had better be removed at once. I send a list on the other side. In the course of a day or two you will probably see Fanny Ireland, Miss Mackay's confidential servant—or hear from her on the subject   If you do not I must

ask you to call on Mr. Arthur Lane 9 Doughty St. Mecklenburgh Sq—tell him
your name, & that you come from me, & wish to know when you can remove
my things. Say you wish to see Fanny Ireland who by this same post will
receive directions on the subject, from Mr. Andrew Knox. The things are

My Piano—which is a small cottage one of Werner
2 Arm chairs— 1 writing table
5 deal packing cases of various sizes
2 framed pictures (portraits of my father & Holcroft
4 framed prints (portraits of my father & mother—of Shelley & the tomb
3 unframed pictures—(portraits of my William, of Trelawny & L[ord]
B[yron]
1 small blk. trunk— 2 boxes— 1 Band box & a hip Bath

M. Shelley

ADDRESS: Mrs. Hogg/ 12 Maida Vale—Edgware Road/ London/ Londres
Inghilterra. POSTMARKS: (1) [   ]1843/ 11 LUG (2) SARD./23/ GUIL/ 43/
PONT-DE-B (3) 10 Fⁿ 10/ JY 25/ 1843/ H (4) B/ 25 JY 25/ 1843.
ORIGINAL: British Museum (T. J. Wise Collection); A.L.S., 4 pp. 4to. UN-
PRINTED and UNPUBLISHED. TEXT: From original letter.

552. *To Claire Clairmont*

Marseilles 19 July [1843]

My dear Claire—

I find no letter from you here—and cannot guess where you are— I hope
you did not go to meet me at Geneva— Our going there is more impossible
than ever. Knox's Aunt has died unexpectedly—so that he can pay nothing
towards our expences & we must get on as quickly as we can—& spend as little
as we can—for we have little to spend.

We had a fine passage—but I had an attack of illness on board which has
weakened me very much—& makes me fear the heats & fatigue of our wretched
journey. Oh to leave a Paradise—at this moment of loveliness to travel scant
of money I know not whither.

I shall be so glad to find you in Paris—but your notion of going to G[eneva]
& your not writing makes me quite at a loss. I send these few words just to
say that we shall be in Paris in a few days—
Adieu

Ever Ys.

M S.

[P.S.] I know not where we shall go—or what do in Paris—not hearing
from you—puts me quite to sea—

ADDRESS: Miss Clairmont. ORIGINAL: Huntington Library (HM 12345); A.L.S.,
3 pp. 8vo (4¼ x 5⅜ inches). UNPRINTED and UNPUBLISHED. TEXT: From original letter.

553. *To Claire Clairmont*[1]

[Putney] Thursday Morn[g] [September, 1844]

Poor little Guitera[2] seems [? abused, absurd] enough—his heart, from things I heard him say, is bent on entertaining a passion—and I have no doubt he thinks he may inspire one—   However I do not think he will go to Hythe— Mrs. Sanford said something to me about Lady Sussex thinking of having a tutor—but, she said, that was all at an end, & the boys gone to school—   It will be very easy for you to get to Hythe—from Dieppe to Brighton From Brighton to Reigate by railroad—where you join the other road & can go at once to Folkstone. I got a note from Lady Sussex asking about you & what you intended to do; she seemed anxious that you should come to Hythe—   So the sooner you leave your solitude the better—

Adieu   You know, I suppose that the elder Murray is dead.[3]

ORIGINAL: Huntington Library (HM 12366); A.L., 2 pp. (4½ x 4⅝ inches); possibly a postscript to Letter 590. UNPRINTED and UNPUBLISHED. TEXT: From original letter.

554. *To Claire Clairmont*

London 30th Aug. [1843]

My dearest Claire—

I found fine weather when I quitted Paris—the day was pleasant & the journey not too fatiguing—only one person in the coupeé with whom I barely exchanged a word—a good voyage of 2 hours & 3 quarters—rain in England of course—I kept up my spirits however—& found Percy at the station well & in good spirits—   This ought to suffice—but alas! I cannot resist the frightful impression I receive from the gloom & desolation of London—   Oh how often I have left it, striving for something to gladden & inspirit & am dragged back here again!—The lodgings Percy took I am sorry to say are gloomy & shocking —still with him I ought to be content; and yet from him springs so much of my discontent—   He is happy—I believe that he is utterly free from vice— he has a thousand precious virtues—he has good sense, a clear understanding a charming temper. Ought I not to be blest? Yet you know well what disquiets me—   He will live at Clarkes seé Med—go on the river & except an idea of music, which he will never follow up to any real study—there is no aim—no exertion—no ambition. I spent more than I ought trying to form a society in which he might improve himself—but the ban under which I am prevented my doing more than introducing him to a few distinguished people whom he refuses to cultivate & when he did go into society he put on an air of stupidity anything but attractive—   Then I took him abroad—all in vain—so I am dragged back again to this prison house where humiliation, scorn &

---

[1] This letter has, unfortunately, been misplaced. It should follow Letter 590, to which it is probably a postscript.

[2] See Letter 554, note 1.

[3] John Murray died on June 27, 1843.

exile are my portion—with the surcroit of ingratitude This is all horribly selfish & distorted—forgive me for writing it—but there is something in this wretched lodging—in the darkness of the atmosphere—in the sense of wrong which clings to me in my own country which plunges me in despair— I shall be better soon—but it is a grievous trial to *acclimater* oneself to this place.

. I do not mean to take Layton House [at Putney], it is too dear— I must look for others. As Percy has been so unlucky in his choice of lodgings & London is so unspeaka[bly] dark & wretched—I am going today to look for a Lodging in the neighbourhood of Putney— I shall remove to it at the end of the week—& look about when there for a place to fix in.

I saw Jane yesterday—she still suffers from rhumatism, but looked well & in spirits—her room & flowers & her own appearance in high order. Percy sees & likes Henry Hunt—he has an exquisite voice—& their musical tastes bring them together. He says Dina is very much improved; so far less egotistical & silly—but that poor Med has deteriorated— She is very large indeed— I shall call on her soon. Knox seems to be arranging his affairs satisfactorily— He is to take his degree—go to the bar—& hopes to get on—if his health will allow his ambition full room to spring up he will distinguish himself— Heaven help him! He finds himself obliged to give up the idea of going to Paris—as persons whom he wished to propitiate looked upon it as idling—& extravagance—though in truth it w[oul]d have been nothing of either—as he cannot go to Cambridge till October— But he means seriously to apply himself & to get on— I have little other news except that poor Aubrey has lost a child—his eldest by Ida—of the same illness as Ld. Hinton— Cecilia Gore is dead—suddenly at Dover— Lawrence seeing her at a party a year ago said she could not live—the tight lacing must kill her—so much for a small waist— but poor child I fear her course in life would have been a sad one—full of disappointment— I got a note from Hammy—she is near London—& I hope to see her before I leave it.

I am very anxious to hear whether you sent to that poor Unfortunate [Gatteschi][1]—pray let me know— I will pay you faithfully that & all else

---

[1] When in Paris in July–August, 1843, Mary was introduced by Claire to a group of young Italian political exiles, chief among whom were Gatteschi, Martini, Guitera, Mazzi, and Carlo Romano. Mary immediately felt a very strong interest in Gatteschi, who, she thought, had in him "the materials of greatness." Gatteschi evidently came from a family (possibly of Bologna) of some rank and wealth; Mary speaks of his earlier life of opportunity and luxury. But at that time he was suffering the usual exile's fate, penury. Mary took him under her wing at once and attempted to make his life tolerable. Before leaving Paris she gave him 200 francs, which she borrowed from Claire. Until Gatteschi attempted to blackmail her in 1845, Mary continued to supply him with money and to devise means for his earning more. She procured pupils for him, engaged him to supply her with materials for the political parts of her *Rambles* (1844), and tried to get him to come to England and earn a living by tutoring and writing. Gatteschi did not know English, however, and would not come. But Guitera and Martini were for a while Mary's guests in England; Guitera also seems to have tutored Lady Sussex Lennox's boys at Hythe for a while. All these exiled Italians apparently belonged to the Carbonari.

Before leaving Paris in 1843, Mary had already determined to write the *Rambles,* and had arranged with Gatteschi that he should supply her with information about political affairs in Italy. The proceeds of the book (£100 or more) were to be devoted to the payment of Gatteschi's

of money—by degrees but as soon as I can—a debt will still remain of all I owe you for your kind welcome & the calm & repose I enjoyed at your pretty house I hope you have left or are leaving Paris—for though Paris is Paradise compared to England yet change of air is so very good & you will enjoy coming back to your home again. Tell me shall I send the £10 to Lewell or to you?

I gave to *little Marie* a pair of stockings to mend & the *metre* of my gown which I cut off for sleeves to hem—of course she never did it nor brought them back—& unluckily I forgot to ask for them—do, on the first opportunity send me these things especially the *metre* of mousseline de lain as that is of great consequence perhaps it could come by the Russian Embassy or someone will be coming—take care of it meanwhile. I left behind my old pink gown—& old embroidered skirt— I dont want them—in fact they are only good to be thrown away— The only thing I miss is a flannel petticoat—& that I cannot account for. Get from Jolly the cape & cuffs of my gown & send them when you can.

Percy sends his love Give my love to Mme Ivanhoff—remember me most kindly to Alexy to Gatteschi & Mazzi. I hope to manage something for G[atteschi] with Moxon, if his attempt at writing succeeds— I mean to write also

---

debts. Although Mary wrote [July, 1844] of the *Rambles* that "the best parts were furnished by Gatteschi," her statement probably exaggerates his contributions to that book. The book itself and Mary's statement (July 1, 1844) that Gatteschi "has furnished me dayly with materials for my book" show well enough that whatever Gatteschi may have supplied was thoroughly digested, rearranged, and rewritten by Mary. Gatteschi's contributions are probably to be found almost entirely in Volume II, chapters xiv, xx, xxi, which treat of "The Carbonari," "The Pontifical States," and the "Insurrection of 1831, and Occupation of Ancona by the French."

After the publication of the *Rambles* in July, 1844, Mary's correspondence seldom mentions Gatteschi until September, 1845. But it is quite evident that she had continued all this time to correspond with him with enthusiasm and frankness, and that she had supplied him with money more or less regularly. By September, 1845, however, Gatteschi had proved himself a villain. For one thing, Mary had discovered that he was carrying on an affair with Lady Sussex Lennox, apparently a flighty woman. Lady Sussex was infatuated with Gatteschi, who succeeded in extracting most of her money and in adding considerably to her reputation for instability. Mary's letters evidently expressed her disapproval of his betrayal of her trust and affection (for Mary seems to have been jealous; Gatteschi had even talked of marrying Mary), and Gatteschi wrote passionate and threatening letters to her. Realising her mistake and that Gatteschi might do her great damage by publishing parts of the many letters which she had written to him with great freedom, Mary became frightened. She put the matter in the hands of Alexander Andrew Knox, who went to Paris with instructions to use any means necessary to procure the letters Mary had written to Gatteschi. Knox, by the use of a considerable sum of money, persuaded M. Delessert, the prefect of the Paris police, to seize Gatteschi's papers and to allow him to take Mary's letters from among them. This was effected by October 10, to the infinite relief of Mary, who was then at Brighton. Mary's sufferings had been especially great because the whole affair had been concealed from Percy. Mary's rescued letters (which must have been written in Italian) were probably destroyed. It is very unlikely that any will ever come to light.

It was, however, some months before Mary's agitation was allowed to die away. Claire (in Paris) was constantly alarmed at the danger of Lady Sussex and Gatteschi conspiring to publish something to embarrass her and Mary. Her letters recovered, though, Mary refused to allow herself to be upset again, and gradually Claire's agitation subsided.

One other blow yet remained, however. When in Paris, Knox had leased an expensive apartment for three years and had filled it with expensive furniture which he did not pay for. Mary had to pay out at least £100 in order to free Knox from debt. This came particularly hard after the expense of recovering her letters. Already, too, she was half supporting Knox. So depressed was she with the feeling that she was wasting Percy's fortune, none too large at best, that momentarily she wished she were dead. By January, 1846, all these troubles were matters of the past.

myself—for I must get some money, though I die for it— Adieu dear Claire pray write & tell me of the 200 frs. [for Gatteschi].

Ever Affectionately Ys.

M S.

[P.S.] I send the Examiner—will you forward it to Mrs. Woulfe—, not throw it in the hole— What news of Galloni

I almost forgot to say that Sir Tim had a severe attack—but is recovered— he is still weak & will not receive visitors— John has not the natural sense of propriety to invite Percy—manco male—he says.

Direct to Hookham's 15 Old Bond St

ADDRESS: Mademoiselle/ Mlle. Clairmont/ Rue Nᵉ de Clichy No. 3/ Rue de Clichy/ à Paris. POSTMARK: (1) T/ PAID/ 30 AU 30/ 1843 (2) 1/ SEPT/ 43/ BOULOGNE. ORIGINAL: Huntington Library (HM 12170); A.L.S., 8 pp. 8vo, with envelope containing an added note inside the flap. Copy by Claire Clairmont, Berg Collection, the New York Public Library. UNPRINTED and UNPUBLISHED. TEXT: From original letter.

555. *To Edward Moxon**

11 Portugal St. Mount St.
Grosvenor Sq.
Wednesday   30 August—[1843]

Dear Mr. Moxon—

I am arrived from my rambles—& should be very glad if you would call— I shall leave town probably next Monday—so call soon— You will find me before 12—or pretty certainly in the Evening— Could you drink tea with me tomorrow at 9?

Ys. very truly

Mary Shelley

ORIGINAL: Huntington Library; A.L.S., 1 p. 8vo, laid into rare book 109638, Wm. Graham, *Last Links with Byron, Shelley,* &c. UNPRINTED and UNPUB- LISHED. TEXT: From original letter.

556. *To Edward Moxon**

Putney—2 Sep. [1843]

Dear Mr. Moxon

A few words you let fall made me reflect & look over some notes I made. And the spirit moves me to put together a journal of my late tour[1]—which long and varied affords scope— Many facts of expences I can tell which will be useful—but above all—my 6 weeks tour[2] brought me many compliments & my present twelvemonths tour will, I feel sure, procure me many more. This sounds vain, but is not. I distrust myself & often lose advantages natural to

[1] Published in July, 1844, by Moxon as *Rambles in Germany and Italy in 1840, 1842, and 1843,* 2 vols.
[2] Mary's *History of a Six Weeks' Tour,* 1817.

me thro' this distrust— The 6 weeks tour—& among my novels Lodore—
were written off hand & have pleased most.— I mean therefore to make my
present work as light—as personal to myself—& as amusing as I can. I think
you will like it as a reader—as a publisher I hope it will meet your approbation.
I am working fast—but then I work best—since fast ever comes with me from
the inspiration of & pleasure I take in the subject— I told you I wanted money
—not for myself—but for a purpose[3] most urgent & desirable I want it— I
shall work fast therefore—& I hope you will prepare to receive the offered MS.
graciously & generously—*as usual.*—

Ever truly Ys
Mary Shelley

ORIGINAL: Luther A. Brewer Collection, University of Iowa; A.L.S., 3 pp. 8vo
(4½ x 7¼ inches). UNPRINTED and UNPUBLISHED. TEXT: From original letter.

557. *To Leigh Hunt**

11 Portugal St. May Fair
3 Sep. [1843]

My dear Hunt

I am arrived at last—yet I confess that *last* is too soon— I could not leave
Paradise without a sigh— I am looking out for a house—& my time is so occupied, that I do not attempt to seek my friends till I am more quiet. This uncertainty hurts my health & my head is just now very bad.

If you ever venture to town in the evening—you will be pretty sure to find
me— I trust you are pretty well—& [I] should be so very glad to hear that
things were more prosperous with you

Affly Ys.
Mary Shelley

ORIGINAL: Luther A. Brewer Collection, University of Iowa; A.L.S., 2 pp. 8vo
(4½ x 7 inches). UNPRINTED and UNPUBLISHED. TEXT: From original letter.

558. *To Claire Clairmont*

My new address is
White Cottage
Lower Richmond Road—Putney.

———————

London. 10 Sep. [1843]

My dearest Claire—

You are very lazy & do not write—& have not answered my question as to
how I should send you the money. I send therefore a Bank post bill— I would
have paid it to [? L]ewell—but he is not a banker—& attorneys are so stupid—
& make such mistakes from multiplicity of affairs that I think it best to send

[3] The relief of Gatteschi.

it to you. I direct to Alexy—as he will best know whether you are in Paris. I much fear your country plans are gone away in smoke—which I shall regret—as bad for your health—but as you may not be at home [I] direct to Alexy— I send £10—another £10 you shall have in December—& even before if I can I will repay the 200 fr. you advanced the day I left.—

We have taken a house at last & go to it tomorrow. It is just one of those found by Percy—which I would not take on account of the high rent— But we could not positively find another on the river. We found a very pretty secluded one near Mortlake—which unfurnished will only be 50 or 60£ a year —but we cannot have it till next September—our cot is on the banks of the Thames—not *looking* on it—but the garden gate opens on the towing path. It has a nice little garden—but sadly out of order—it is shabbily furnished—& has no spare room—except by great contrivance—if at all—so perforce economy will be the order of the day. It is secluded but cheerful—at the extreme verge of Putney close to Barnes Common—just the situation Percy desired. He has bought a boat— God preserve him—& all will go well—I trust— I have many fears & tremblings on the score of expence—but I shall do my best to economize.

Do you see G[atteschi] often? He wrote me a letter so full of bitter misery that I am glad it[1] all came from me—for I believe he could not have prevailed on himself to see you with such a weight of humiliation on him— I am far away—& the emotion will wear off—besides that I shall take care that it shall wear the semblance of a debt that will be acquitted. I hope he will write for I am very uneasy about his future, & how to be of use I know not— There is something in his position that makes me *frisonne*—born to all the luxuries of life & to want bread—one's blood runs cold at the idea. Could you not contrive that some governess took lessons from him & we—or I—advance money to pay for them? The governess might think it all done from interest for *her* on your part, & his pride not hurt.

Heaven help me I have been in the midst of all this embroglio of Jane & Hunt— But I perceive there is a secret— I have no wish to know it— You do—from what I guess Jane was mad to endeavour to prevent the marriage—& Hunt thoroughly honourable & right—but mine are all guesses—and I wish for no explanations. As to Dina's being forced to leave the house—Hunt gives his own account in which I think Marianne's misinterpretations are discernable. You know the certain want of modesty of speech even of Jane—& Dina copying her mother carries it to a strange extent—this want of modesty being strictly confined to speaking without restraint or blush about every thing physical or moral that concerns themselves—because all that appertains to them ought to be written in letters of gold & read in the market place—while if it concerned others—it would [*from this point a 1¾ inch strip is torn from the right side of the sheet, affecting pages 3 and 4.*]

1 The 200 francs.

be deemed incorrect & shocking—   The [   ]
the fibbing of which Jane herself accu[   ]
nothing of it) appears to have annoy[   ]
Hunt—while he positively denies t[   ]
—nay unhuman manner with w[   ]
cund of accompanying his acts. In sh[   ]
deceit has been pro[   ]
Jane & Dina are accused, it mu[   ]
cult to mix intimately in their affa[   ]
judgement & wish to form none— [   ]
separated now—& they had better not me[   ]
past impressions—& then only on terms [   ]
& acquaintanceship. You know Hunt's se[   ]
bears the stamp of truth & benevolen[ce   ]

help believing him. He spoke very kindly of you—& was much pleased when I told him that you thought that his conduct with regard to the marriage was generous & honourable.

Percy is very well—   He goes to Henry—& they sing together—Henry having a fine voice. He thinks Dina very much improved—she suffers a good deal from her situation being near her time. Jane is very good to them.

[   ]self the victim of every body. She denies
[   ]ny violence to tear Dina away—or that Dina
[   ]—quite satisfied to go to you—   Good God if what
[   ]ue what an act to send her—without
[   ]n with the truth how inexcusable—& how
[   ] the marriage—but I make be mistaken in my
[   ] dearest Claire—quiet at my lot I will

write—& do you write—above all let me know that you get this money safely directly. I remember with gratitude the quiet month spent under your pleasant roof—

Affectionately ys.
M Shelley

[P.S.] I have just had a visit from Cha[   ]
uncle—several things we talked out gave m[   ]
ing to serve Gatteschi—   I shall see—& do my best—[   ]

I had a very nice letter from Laura the other day

I have seen Marianna—she is looking so wonderfully well—her lips coral —her eyes diamonds—all the effect of early rising & cold water. She is at Edmonton   What news of Galloni—do tell me.

ADDRESS: Miss Clairmont/ Rue Nᵉ Clichy— No. 3/ Rue de Clichy/ à Paris. ORIGINAL: Huntington Library (HM 12355); A.L.S., 4 pp. 4to; a 1¾ inch strip is torn from the lower right side of the second sheet, affecting pp. 3–4. UN- PRINTED and UNPUBLISHED. TEXT: From original letter.

198

559. *To Claire Clairmont*

Direct to me White Cottage
Lower Richmond Road
Putney
London   Monday   11 Sep. [1843]

Dearest Claire

Just now I sent you a letter under cover to Alexy—containing a bank post bill for £10— I did that before I got your letter. I hope all will be safe—another time I will send bank notes—cut in half—half to you & half to Alexy—that I have found the best way.

I write in all the hurry of moving & can say but a few words. My house for a year is taken. Of course before I got your letter. You must not however exclaim about the ill luck—because I cannot see how it would have been possible to do as you ask. I am not alone—or I would not hesitate to make a sacrifice even if it were one, to comply with a request put as you ask me. But you know Percy hates Paris— He *will* be in England. Could any persuasions of mine have kept him abroad we should still be in Italy. Nothing could induce him—he said he should die if kept out of England— You know how much I lament this both for his sake & my own—but I could not resist his wishes. As to leaving him for four or six months, I see not how I could do it. You know also how poor I am   that is how I am pushed to meet my expences.— If it would serve you that I should spend a month with you I would try to do it when Percy goes to Ianthe [Shelley]   I am afraid you will say this is useless — I would—if by any means I can afford it spend a month in the autumn—another in the spring— Though how to afford it I know not—we pay an oddiously high rent— You must write to me further on the subject. But to leave my house & Percy—& Percy will not go to Paris—for a longer period I could not & even for that it will be with great difficulty on account of money. I am going to economize à l'outrance—but the expences of a house are so heavy I am terrified. Can you not tell me why you wish me to come— I would be as secret as the grave—& knowing the cause, might see better what to do. I cannot bear to refuse you anything *really useful*.

Dear Claire take my advice—never acknowledge you have money—never *lend a rich* person—poor people have consciences about money—a rich person none.—A person alone is always a victim unless strictly on the defensive.

Gatteschi is writing & collecting materials   at least he said so—but the recollection of past troubles thus recorded makes him miserable[1]— Poor fellow—I dare say he spoke as he did on account of Mazzi— If not inconvenient see him when in Paris & tell me how he goes on. I write in great haste   let me hear from you—& how far my offer of a month would be of service to you— On a matter concerning your whole life—I would do all I could—& if on a

---

[1] Gatteschi was writing (for Mary's *Rambles*) about the Carbonari and the Insurrection of 1831, of which he was a victim.

marriage or any event of equal importance of course I would try to manage the impossible & stay two—but it would be a great sacrifice to leave Percy for so long—

Ever affly ys.

M S.

[P.S.] If I had money to come & go—I would not mind the fatigue of travelling & go & come more than once on a matter of such importance but my purse will with difficulty allow one visit—pray write immediately

ADDRESS: Madlle./ Mlle Clairmont/ Rue N^e de Clichy/ Rue de Clichy/ à Paris. POSTMARK: 11 SP 11/ 1843. ORIGINAL: Huntington Library (HM 12176); A.L.S., 4 pp. 4to. Copy by Claire Clairmont, Berg Collection, the New York Public Library. UNPRINTED and UNPUBLISHED. TEXT: From original letter.

560. *To Edward Moxon*

White Cottage
Putney
20 Sep. [1843]

Dear Mr. Moxon

I wrote to you soon after my return—but learnt afterwards that you were out of town— I hope when you return you will come down & see us. You are pretty sure to find me. I seldom go out.

You asked me about writing—it is a serious question to me—but I hope as winter comes on to have strength—& dont despise me if I say I wish to write for I want money sadly I dont want it for myself—that is I dont want it so much as to impel me to write—but I do for another purpose—which will make me exert myself. But now—Is it a novel or a romance you want?—I should prefer quieter work, to be gathered from other works—such as my lives for the Cyclopedia—& which I think I do *much* better than romancing— Something, God willing, I must do, if you fancy it worth your while to set me to work.

Will you thank Mr. Talfourd for the kind present of his pleasant book[1]— Where is Mr. Rogers? I will visit town to see him though for no one else.

Did I tell you. There were no letters of Mr. Southey among Shelley's papers —he destroyed those he received— I should be glad of those Mr. Taylor can find.[2]

I hope you & yours are all well

Ever truly ys.

Mary Shelley

ADDRESSED: Edward Moxon Esq/ Dover Street/ Piccadilly. POSTMARK: 4 EG 4/ SP 21/ 1843/ B. ORIGINAL: Henry W. and Albert A. Berg Collection, the New York Public Library; A.L.S., 3 pp. 8vo, with stamped addressed envelope, seal. UNPRINTED and UNPUBLISHED. TEXT: From original letter.

[1] This was probably T. N. Talfourd's *Recollections of a First Visit to the Alps, in August and September, 1841* (Privately printed [?1842]).
[2] This inquiry after Southey's letters is probably related to J. W. Robberds, *A Memoir of the Life and Writings of the Late William Taylor, of Norwich*, Containing his Correspondence with Robert Southey and Other Eminent Literary Men (1843, 2 vols.).

561. *To Claire Clairmont*

White Cottage, Putney—20 Sept. [1843]

My dearest Claire,

To begin—dont cross your letters when you write on such very thin paper —it becomes very difficult to read them. I am glad you have got quiet at last— The weather here also has been very warm—but I keep quite quiet—more so than would suit you—for I see scarcely any one—& my time is spent in my garden for the most part alone. Percy has bought a boat, & is very happy—he amuses himself by trying to compose music— He goes to town now & then. I am very content as far as I am concerned— Just now I have no wish for any thing but the quiet of the country—to try to get my luckless head a little more serviceable than it now is. I shall try cold water or homeopathy. The fashionable quackeries of the day—which consisting chiefly of diet & exercise, are just suited to me—but get better I must—it is so ridiculous helpless & stupid to feel ill.—So really I am to visit you in December? I shall not be sorry to do so if I can afford it for Percy will be away for a month—& it will be cold & lonely here—and Mrs. Hare will be in Paris—& I shall be so very glad to be near her— She is so kind to me & so fond of me that I find her friendship a great happiness. But if really I am to come I must settle some preliminaries with you. As to being comfortable with you I have no doubt of being that—I was so before. I shall bring Marianne[1] with me—& she will make us both comfortable. I certainly, I allow, should like being more in Paris—moreover— don't think me ungrateful—but I should prefer being in rooms of my own. I am sadly & savagely independant—& this arises from defects in my character I cannot surmount. And, dear Claire—being with you, I must be thoroughly independant. When last with you as one was in Paris, I was averse at first to society, & you were so *aigue* with your neighbors of Rue Clichy—that I saw no one & did nothing, & was very content— I could not do this again. As to Rue Clichy—the set are indifferent to me but I like the society of Mme de B[oinville] and it is a privation to me not to see her when in Paris— She may be deceitful & ce m'est egal— I do not seek her for friendship & sympathy— but because there is something in her society & conversation that animates & pleases me—& I find this so seldom among my fellow creatures—& finding it enjoy it so seldom, that it is privation not to get it when I can. I made a law when last with you not to call on her without you—because I thought it due you—you know I differ with you as to how such people as Mlle K——— ought to be treated. I think silent contempt and utter indifference is all they should get— At any rate on my return to you you must trust to my judgement & affection to do by you what I consider best to raise & support you—and leave my actions unshackled— I shall be a great deal at Mrs. Hares— But my

[1] Mary's maid, who had accompanied her on the tour of 1842–43. She should not be confused with Marianna Hammond.

visits—goings out & comings home must be left independant & unshackled—
Dont say that I am unjust to you in making these conditions & of course they
will be so— I am guarding against the results of the defects of my own
character, not of yours—a defect that made the Robinsons living with me
intolerable as a necessity. I am very easily put under *soggezione*—but while
under it I hate it—and if I fancied any of my goings on annoyed you I should
alter them to please you—but I should go away & regain my liberty with all
speed. We should both be happier could I afford a place of my own in Paris—
but I cant—& this leads to the other question— I can only pay you as I did
before—but I sincerely trust that that covers my expenses; or I could not come
for I will not cost you any thing 50 fr. a week for myself & 12 for Marianne—
£10 a month is all I can do having a house here—of course I dont include wood
for my fire— That of course I should pay extra—does this suit you? I sincerely hope you wont take any thing amiss I have said— It is necessary for
people who are to be together to understand each other—and I must feel free—
& that you are not annoyed by anything I do—or I must run away— I should
prefer coming late in November—because of tempestuous weather for the voyage—but however that one must trust to fate— I would not attempt to cross
in bad weather. It is strange indeed that I am to come for an important object,
& am to be kept in [*Something seems to be missing here; in her copy Claire
has a line of dots.*]

Poor Gatteschi— He wrote to me telling me that he has prepared some
papers & I have told him to send them if possible through Alexy. He is mad
to join the insurgents in Bologna—and I do not wonder— It is more manly
& natural to desire to be in arms & in danger than to be dragging out the
miserable life he leads at Paris. I gather from what he says joined to what you
tell me that he thinks that he cannot leave Paris with honour while in debt.
Poor fellow, for how much better a lot he was made. I hope to be able to get
some money to meet the 400 fr. All depends on the papers he sends me, so you
may guess therefore how anxious I am to get them. If they are what I want
my plan is to make a volume & make a £100 if possible more by it for him—
but meanwhile if the volume promised well & Moxon agreed to take it he
would advance me £20. [I k]now it all depends on this—but I hope & will
do my best. You certainly have a most active imagination. The moment you
think of doing any thing you figure to yourself the worst possible evil that can
accrue to you from your action, & then believe it must happen. You will trust
nothing to steady quiet conduct—which (even if for a moment you are mistaken) sets all right in time. Your notion that you must leave Paris because
if you try to serve G[atteschi] it will be supposed by himself & others that
you are in love with him appears to me as if you should rush out of doors the
moment you lighted a candle for fear your house should catch fire & you be
burnt alive. Curtains have caught at candles & people been burnt—but if you

hold a candle steadily, & dont, like Pearson,[2] drag a curtain into it, there is no danger. I am never afraid of loving a man who does not love me—and if I am suspected of liking him—maneo male steady conduct soon puts that out of people's heads—& if it does not—I am not the less indifferent. [*Two lines are missing here.*]   life is too short—& the stream of time carries all too rapidly away for one to care about any of the talk of people—all one can care for is ones own feelings & what one really does and suffers. If I saw any opening for G[atteschi] I would have him over here & serve him all I could—& what should be said about it would be supremely indifferent to me—but I do not say this for you—we must all judge for ourselves—   I am so entirely exiled from the good society of my own country on account of the outset of my life that I *can* care for nothing but the opinion of a few near & dear friends—& of my own conscience.—With regard to the 200 fr. As G. received it from me I think I ought to pay it all—& wish to do so—I leave it to you—but I think it would be *just* that I should pay it—& that you should give the 100 you meant [to] give as I said to a governess—make her pay 4 or 5 francs a lesson if you can—& that will be doing present good.—But if you think any evil is to accrue to yourself do nothing as you say you can do little—& it would be very hard that you should do any thing that would disturb your peace of mind & the quiet you have earned so hardly & gained so late. I will exert myself strenuously for him in every way I can possibly—for I have a very high opinion of him.

I have filled my paper. I will learn what I can of Sartoris. I see scarcely any one—but when Rogers is in town I shall see him—poor Natasch—I am truly sorry. The gown & skirt I left *knowingly* in my room—meaning to mention it to you but forgot. The flannel petticoat is missing—but not *left* in my room—perhaps the washerwoman did not send it back. I wish you could get a metre and a half of the blue stripped white mousseliné de lainé I bought for a dressing gown. I want a cape to it.—My cot is comfortable—my servants I hope good and economical & I hope to get on well—

If I dont come to you to Paris—that is if you change your mind, I shall try to join Mrs. Hare who will be there in a fortnight about. I have no room for more—but I have no news of any one or any thing. Yours

M W S.

[P. S.] *dont* send the Examiner to Mrs. Woulfe any more—[*From Claire's copy:*] Percy will call on the Sanfords soon—Mrs. Paul tells me she sees Trelawney now & then looking so very dirty & old. I have heard nothing else except some new people are in the *Farm.* So Augusta is not there—   I cannot learn anything of the Sartoris yet—no one is in town to ask.

ORIGINAL: Huntington Library (HM 12175); A.L.S., 4 pp. 4to. Copy by Claire Clairmont, Berg Collection, the New York Public Library. UNPRINTED and UN-PUBLISHED. TEXT: From original letter.

[2] Henry Hugh Pearson. See Letter 532, note 1.

562. *To Claire Clairmont*

Saturday—7 Oct. [1843]—Putney

Dearest Claire—

Hammy has left her letter open that I may write a word to you—but I have nothing new to say. She has spent two or three days with me—but I have not been well. Warm muggy weather makes me feel ill—I was alive during the cold—so I must welcome it, though I hate it.

Gatteschi tells me he has sent me an M.S. through Alexy—this was nearly a fortnight ago but I have not yet received it. I hope to turn it into a good article—& if I am lucky enough to get it into the Edinburgh—I shall get a good price. Dio volesse. I wish it would come. Hunt was here the other day & very amiable—but I have no explanations about Jane. She——but never mind—till we meet I shall say nothing—Only I think you ought to have answered her letter. I mean—I should—for I think it is always best to be amiable & facile in ones *procedeés* when one possibly can.—Percy's visit to his sister [Ianthe] he mentioned for the end of November—he has had no answer—to go later than the beginning of December would not I fear suit me— I cannot leave him here any time alone—he is so good to me— I ought to do all for him—however I will do my best for you—if you still wish it.

Have you heard from Mrs. Hare? She must be in Paris now— I gave her your address—she asked for it. She is very anxious I should visit Paris—dear thing—she is surprisingly fond of me— It does surprize me when any one belonging to the world can care for such an outcast—her welcome was so affectionate—it warmed my heart—& set Mrs. Paul on being affectionate too— Rosa[1] is in the family way again—as yet she has only had one child—a girl.—

Hammy has quite made up her mind not to go to you. She does not like the worry & care attendant on giving lessons in Paris. If B—— takes a house, & has his father & mother with him—I see no earthly objection to her taking the charge of his little girl—he must have a governess—why not her? It seems to me one of those bits of good fortune, that the unfortunate, rendered timid through adversity & "advice of friends"[2]—are forever throwing away—& then they complain of fate. The Sanfords are gone to Tunbridge Wells for 15 days I have not seen them—farewell—write

Ever ys

[*Unsigned*]

[P.S.] Percy heard from Hellen— Sir Tim is *quite well* but does not feel equal to having company in the house—, so Percy does not go— From others I hear that he is quite recovered.

ORIGINAL: Huntington Library (HM 12329); A.L. (unsigned), 2 pp. 4to. Copy by Claire Clairmont, Berg Collection, the New York Public Library. UNPRINTED and UNPUBLISHED. TEXT: From original letter.

[1] Probably Rosa Robinson, who married Aubrey William Beauclerc.
[2] An adaptation of Macbeth's (V, iii, 25) "troops of friends"?

LEIGH HUNT

*from an unfinished painting by
Samuel Laurence*

563. *To Claire Clairmont (a fragment)*

[Putney, October 9, 1843]

... plan for serving our friend [Gatteschi]— When I think of his birth—the habits of his youth—his just expectations—& compare these with his sufferings & the noble way in which he apparently beares them I feel the most earnest desire to extricate him It is, & has been, the curse of my life to have this desire to serve others without the means—however one must try & be patient— Meanwhile there is measure in all things—a measure which you owe it to me not to go beyond—that of your own self preservation—& the keeping up your position by being *settled* in one spot—& known as an established person.

What you can wish for me in Paris for—passes all my guessing. Had I a little space money & that my presence w[oul]d bring with it a little amusement à la bonne heure but I am wretchedly poor— To get on at all with house & servants needs all I have— I spend not a penny on myself— How can I do you any good?— Oh how my own plans for Percy are brought to rack & ruin by this detestable want of means— However he is happy now—that is much— He studies harmony—takes long walks to & from town & now and then a friend or two of his dine here— I wish I could make him read—or bring round him the society of women—& have music for him &c—it is all vain— Old Tim or rather Eternity will not let us & will live long enough to ruin us & destroy all my hopes— Thus is it to be!—

[P.S.] I will get cement & send it—

ADDRESS: Madll./ Mll. de Clairmont/ Rue Nᵉ Clichy No. 3/ Rue Clichy/ à Paris. POSTMARKS: (1) F u l h a m (2) 9 OC 9/ 1843. ORIGINAL: Huntington Library (HM 12365); A.L., 2 pp. 8vo (a fragment), with envelope. UNPRINTED and UNPUBLISHED. TEXT: From original letter.

564. *To Claire Clairmont*

[Putney] Friday 13 Oct [1843]

My dear Claire

I am going to town & will get & enclose cement. I will send the £5 in a short time, if you do not get your money from the Princess— I had arranged in my own mind to send £10 in December only—necessary expences on getting into a house have drained me—but I am fortunate in an economical cook—& spend as little as I possibly can—

I am afraid I may have written hastily— I was hurt by the way you put what I said about Rue Clichy. If you had quarrelled there—I would not go— yet why not trust to me why distrust me so much— I love & esteem you— Why not allow me to act as I think best for you? This uneasy sense you have, that you are illused if your friends act upon their own judgement, not upon yours—is natural—but it is a painful shackle to them. I give you a proof of friendship in coming over at your wish, to do a service, the nature of which is not imparted to me—ought not this to satisfy you?—

Knox is gone to Cambridge to prepare for his degree. I am going to ask Coulson to take him as he took Edward [Williams]— I fear he will not—& that makes me nervous. Dina is not confined yet—but expects daily. Percy flourishes

One thing I want you to do DIRECTLY— I am writing some thing that requires that I should refresh my memory with regard to our tour in 1840.[1] If you have any descriptive letters from Percy & myself at that time I wish you would send them to me with all possible speed.

My dear Claire—I wish to say a few things to you on the subject of your plans—which I hope you will take in good part— When you made the sacrifice you did & secured yourself a small income—I considered much how you could be really comfortable on it— You could not in England—your income was very small—you could not keep a house & if you paid [? £8 or 8/] for lodgings they are almost equally detestable— Besides you wanted society —which was impossible in London unless you were far richer— Paris seemed to me far preferable—it does still— I should choose it for myself—were I not bound here, & did not my likings carry me to Italy— To have society & to have a good position there also; you must be *settled*— I gave you therefore £100 that you might secure these advantages—little enough, but by your excellent management, you accomplished it— But now you must remain & be steady—you need not be chained there—

Sunday—15 Oct. Dont let me forget to tell you Dina was confined yesterday—she suffered beforehand & had several false alarms but like our little Queen, she had no trouble or pain at last at all & has a boy.—I say nothing of the former history of this message—& reserve it till we meet. Percy likes Henry & goes there often to practice singing &c Edward has been taking a holiday colla sua Bella at Ramsgate & enjoyed the sea breezes mightily He is the same as ever.

We have quite winter here fine days now & then—but so cold—today a fog—

Gatteschi's papers do not come it is too tiresome— Do find out & tell me to whom they were addressed in London that I may enquire for them— Let my letters that I have asked for come by a better channel

Monday Mrs. Paul has just called asking after you & full of your praises —"so clever so fascinating"—comme de saison— She *opportunely & comfortably* said to me "I hope you are not writing—whats the use of your writing —it does no good to any body—neither to yourself nor any one?"

Why is it that when thus spoken to I can never assert myself— I only feel guilty & wretched— I long to run away & shut myself up yet more entirely (& heaven knows here I am as nearly as may be) apart from every body. I own myself I am sorry I am writing— But I feel that I shall save poor G[atteschi] from starvation—from desperation & the lowest depths of misery—

[1] The *Rambles* (1844).

206

I know this—& write when otherwise I never would—that never my name
might be mentioned in a world that oppresses me   I mean to have sent this
cement before but did not go to town & have just received it—   I shall go to
town on Thursday & will send you more—   Adieu—

Ys. affectionately
M S.

[P.S.] If you do not hear from the Princess I will send £5—somehow, but
you know Percy goes to Ianthe at the beginning of December—so this will
just suit you for me will it not.

> ADDRESS: Miss Clairmont/ Rue N^e Clichy No. 3. ORIGINAL: Huntington Library
> (HM 12353); A.L.S., 8 pp. 8vo, with envelope. Copy by Claire Clairmont, Berg
> Collection, the New York Public Library. UNPRINTED and UNPUBLISHED. TEXT:
> From original letter.

565. *To Claire Clairmont*

[Putney] Saturday   28 Oct [1843]

Dearest Claire

I answer a note from Alexy today to acknowledge the receipt of Gatteschi's papers—so enclose a scrap for you. It *is* odd that my plans for economy
never succeed. Had I asked Gatteschi to send his MS. by post—he could have
made the packet as light as may be & I should have had to pay 3 or 4 shillings—
As it was he naturally was careless about weight, & the whole was un[n]eces-
sarily bulky—   Heaven knows what it all means—but I got a letter from Mr.
Hervey to say that the Russian vice Consul had sent a packet for me to him
& the postage was 9/7—true enough he sent the envelope—with the Paris
postmark & 9/7 to pay.—I had to send my servant to town also to get it—
however it is no use worrying Alexy—as of course I shall never dream of
troubling him again; & above all dont say anything about paying money to
poor Gatteschi—   Except that the whole thing has been managed stupidly
I dont grudge the shillings for the papers are well worth much more. They
are admirably written—   Had poor G—— fair play & repose of spirit he might
make a name for himself—   His style is perfect—& his essay full of vigour;
his details vivid & well arranged—& the whole eloquent—   What a wonderful
people the Italians are—   Would I were rich to free this poor devoted struggler
amidst the strangling waves of poverty—   He must in self-defence of the
slights that his relations would cast on his name do something to shew what
he is—he has the materials of greatness in him—& his talk of his powers of
mind being gone is all delusion. He wants ease of mind & encouragement. He
must *do* something. What a shame Mr. Hare has not sent my note.

My life goes on in perfect solitude—& I use my eyes till they get weak &
inflamed which is a great discomfort. Percy is very happy—& that is much—
Dina is doing well. Henry was here the other day—   I think there is much
good in him—poor boy—no wonder his passions were excited to madness—

207

yet so incapable is Jane of putting herself in the place of another that she sees only self-will & wicked desire of revenge in what was evidently the rebellion of nature against the outrage perpetrated on it— Remember I only know Jane's own account—so judge impartially enough—but it is best not to talk of these things till we meet.

What are you doing? Have you been paid by the Princess? Do you still wish me to visit Paris— I should enjoy the holyday were I richer—as it is I fear being only a bore to you

Adieu

Affectionately ys
M S.

ADDRESS: Miss Clairmont/ Rue Nᵉ de Clichy No. 3. ORIGINAL: Huntington Library (HM 12330); A.L.S., 4 pp. 8vo, with envelope. UNPRINTED and UNPUBLISHED. TEXT: From original letter.

566. *To Claire Clairmont*

Friday—Putney [? Nov. 1843]

My dearest Claire

Winter is come now with snow— I hope the change does you good— I have been thinking of a thing that I suggest to you— You can think of it yourself. Miss Maberley asked Mrs. Hare about getting a situation for a Protegeè of hers— She had lived in their family (I think) & wanted a place as Bonne d'Enfant. The poor thing is exceedingly deformed—but she is respectably born (Swiss or German) & left her home because her father married again & her mother in law made her unhappy—she works like a fairy—is an excellent creature—the objections to her are first that she is deformed—second tho' not a governess she objects to eating with the servants She asks 500 fr. a year but would take less— Now it has struck me that as she has not a place —& would be (as I think I understood) on the pavé when the Maberleys left Paris—whether you would not like to have her about you—you need not engage yourself to take her nor tie yourself—but engage her only till she found a place or you went into the Country—& she w[oul]d come for almost any pay—& work for you & put all your things in order—& wait on you—& you could try her— If you like the idea speak to Mrs. Hare about it— Her not being French is a comfort— I shall feel much easier if you have a respectable person of this sort about you—

I write in a hurry just to mention this— We are all well here— Percy flourishes & Campbell came to see us yesterday. He is getting almost out of patience waiting but hopes it will not last longer than this session— Ianthe is very unwell indeed—confined to her bed or sopha with cough & great weakness— I have seen no one else— Adieu let me hear from you.

Affly. ys.
M S.

[P.S.] I hear that Eliza R—— is to marry Henry Perry—they are now on a visit at St Leonards together.

ADDRESS: Miss Clairmont/ Rue Nᵉ Clichy No. 3 bis/ Rue de Clichy. ORIGINAL: Huntington Library (HM 12341); A.L.S., 4 pp. 8vo. Copy by Claire Clairmont, Berg Collection, the New York Public Library. UNPRINTED and UNPUBLISHED. TEXT: From original letter.

567. *To Claire Clairmont*

[Putney] 10 Nov. [1843]

You do not say whether you want more cement— I send some—thro' Alexy also—to save you postage—is this right? Percy is gone to spend one day at Field Place— Sir Tim is better—tho' they say he is much altered latterly— Percy dines afterwards at St. Leonards.

It is true I am writing—there were certain things I could not manage without it—nor with it indeed well— It does not hurt my health—yet I am sorry so to do— I earnestly wished never again to publish—but one must fulfil ones fate— However I dont work hard—& by twelve my task is always over— When with you I shall probably write in my own room—which being *from* the street—is quieter than the drawing room.

On Monday I saw Nerina's friend Mayer—who I like excessively—better than I did at Florence—for in truth tho' I delight in Nerina's talk, yet she rather makes every one else silent— I got a letter from her she says she is sorry almost for G's[1] acquittal & Laura says she is glad for now she can hate him again to her heart's content.

I cannot fix the day for my coming—for Percy's for going to his sister is not settled—& at this time of the year it must be somewhat regulated by weather — I do not mean to cross in a storm— I would rather it should freeze— I will write again at the end of this month. I wish you w[oul]d write & tell me a word of fashions— I must get a thing or two from Miss Descon—for I have no money to buy in Paris & should just like to hear a word of colors &c— my bonnet however I shall get in Paris

You saw in the Examiner the death of poor Charles Hopwood (they called him Orpwood in the paper) poor William—whose whole life has been devoted to his brother to be censured because he chose to commit suicide[2]—such is the world's justice—

Send me also when you write Mrs. Hare's address. I hear nothing of the Sanfords & have not received my metre.—

[1] Galloni, Laura Mason's troublesome husband?

[2] In the *Examiner* (No. 1866, November 4, 1843, 700) under "Suicides" is an account of an inquest held at Railway Tavern, Hampstead Road, for the purpose of inquiring into the death of "Mr. Charles Orpwood," Harmood Street, Camden Town, whose death resulted from taking prussic acid. His brother William testified. Charles had been a cripple for sixteen years. The jury thought William should be censured for placing prussic acid into Charles's hands, even though Charles was accustomed to mixing his own medicine and to putting a little prussic acid in it.

I have no more news— We shall soon meet when we can talk of things & it is useless writing— God bless you

Affcly. Ys
M S.

ORIGINAL: Huntington Library (HM 12359); A.L.S., 4 pp. 8vo. Copy by Claire Clairmont, Berg Collection, the New York Public Library. UNPRINTED and UN-PUBLISHED. TEXT: From original letter.

568. *To Marianne Hunt**

Putney
21 Nv. [? 1843]

My dear Marianne

I grieve very much at the state of things which you describe—& wish it could be altered. Believe me it is not unkindness but a knowledge of what money transactions are that leads me to consider your plan impracticable.

I remember well the circumstances to which you allude. Some letters passed between your sister & me & it was suggested that some *friend* of Hunts might lend him money on a post-obit on Sir Tim's life. It was a foolish impracticable idea—but I did not then know as much as I do now of these things. Hunt called on me with a Solicitor. This was not what I expected—but the matter was fully talked over, & the difficulties found to be insurmountable. Exactly the same exist now, nor can I raise money for myself, as you suggest. My security—as my claims during Sir Tim's life are contingent—is not worth [? having].

If I had money I should as I have done before have tried to be of use to you; but I have none till Xmas—when you will have £10 as usual.

Things are indeed hard—& my hopes of serving you have been balked by the extreme prolongation of Sir Tim's life—a thing never calculated upon—as it always seemed highly improbable. I deeply regret this—& still more that you suffer so much difficulty— The time is not far off *now* I verily believe— when there will be a change—though it is *unlucky,* I fear, to express the opinion— I am

Very truly yr. friend
M Shelley

ORIGINAL: Bodleian Library (MS Shelley Adds. d.5, ff.91–92; A.L.S., 4 pp. 8vo. PRINTED: *Bodleian Quarterly Record,* VIII, No. 95 (1937) 417–18. TEXT: From original letter.

569. *To Claire Clairmont*

[Putney] 5 Dec [1843]

Dearest Claire

My letters seem to say very different [things] from my thoughts   you say I seem to think you not sincere in your annoyance about Miss K—— I only think you *too* sincere & too deeply annoyed. You beg me to beleive that her calumnies are a misfortune   I do believe it—& therefore I wish you to dismiss them from your mind. We should go mad if we brooded over all our misfortunes as you do over this one. Above all, having bitterly suffered from calumny myself, the only cure I have found for its venom is resolutely to dismiss all consideration & thought of it from my mind. The sort of annoyance the sense of it produces is so irritating & so destructive of peace, that we owe it to ourselves not to allow our thoughts to dwell on it at all When I am with you I shall not as I did before allow you to dwell for hours on this odious subject but try to draw your mind from it—I do most seriously assure you that this is the only means of saving you from a sort of monomania on the subject.

I am very sorry for your toothache— I have suffered from the same so much myself that I truly pity you— The only cure I found was to lose my teeth till lately when creosote has killed the nerve.

I shall be glad indeed if I can do you good by going to Paris—*ma ascolta*— & dont think me mean. I can manage the journey there & back—but I must not spend more from being there I have calculated my expences here—& what they ought to be there to equalize the sum— Will 50 fr[ancs] a week cover Marianne's & my expences with you? That makes £8 a month—& two more for wood making £10 a month in all—if this will cover our expences I shall be glad—if not let me know. I mentioned this sum before exclusive of wood— now I say inclusive— I must not cost you any thing that is certain—but if you can contrive that I shall not cost you more, it will be an ease to my mind in going.

I send you now £10 & now only owe you the sum you advanced for me to poor G[atteschi]—

9 Dec.

I hope to send this off today but I am waiting for the money. I send the other half of the notes under cover to Alexy. I send £10—& only owe you now the money you advanced for me to poor G[atteschi].

I intend to set out next week— The day depends on the weather—if it be fine I shall go to Folkstone on Monday next. If it be rainy I shall wait— in that case I shall write to you again— At any rate I hope [the] weather will favour me, & that I shall see you *next week*— I should have written before but waited to send the money. Adieu— I will bring the books

[*Unsigned*]

ADDRESS: Miss Clairmont/ Rue N^e de Clichy No. 3/ Rue de Clichy/ à Paris. POSTMARKS: (1) 1/ 7 DE 7/ [184]3 (2) 9/ DEC/ 43/ BOULOGNE. ORIGINAL: Huntington Library (HM 12332); A.L. (unsigned), 5 pp. 8vo, with envelope. UNPRINTED and UNPUBLISHED. TEXT: From original letter.

570. *To Joseph Severn*

Reu Neuve Clichy.
No. 3 Rue de Clichy, à Paris.
15th Dec. 1843.

Dear Mr. Severn,

It is some months now since, with the deepest regret, I left Italy. I have been in England since, and continually intended seeing you; but, not remaining in London, I have not been able. I am now come over here for a few weeks. When I return I shall hasten to see you and Mrs. Severn. I can never express how much obliged I was to you both for the letters you sent to me for your acquaintances at Rome, who showed their respect to you and their own goodness by the very great attention they paid me. I had hoped to spend this very winter in the Eternal City, but I must wait for other days before I revisit it. I now write to you on a subject in which I am much interested. I shall be truly obliged to you if you will consider it and give me counsel and information. Do you know the picture of Titian—the 'Woman taken in Adultery'— did you ever see it? It was in the Galleria Calderara at Milan: the print at least you know, made from it by Anderloni (Colnaghi, the printseller, has an impression). Is it not the second best of that admirable master? The 'Assumption' being the best? Is it not worth a very large price? Would it not be an excellent thing that our National Gallery should possess it? A Milanese nobleman possesses it, who does not consider himself rich enough to retain a *capo d'opera* of such great value, and wishes to sell it. He expects to receive, of course, several thousand pounds. It is established genuine by incontestable evidence, and is in excellent preservation. In size it is eleven feet by five. How could it be brought before the consideration of those who might propose it to Government for the National Gallery? Or indeed what is the right way to bring it before the consideration of Government? The difficulty seems to be that the picture is at Milan. To bring it away will cost some hundred pounds, and its possessor wishes, before he spends these, to have knowledge of how far it is probable that it can be sold in England. As far as I can judge by the print, and as far as I know the value of so great a work of Titian, it seems to me that we English ought to possess it, and that our National Gallery, not over rich in first-rate paintings, would acquire great glory from possessing this one. Its originality is, I am told, incontestable. Let me have a line of advice, and telling me your ideas on the subject, as soon as you can.

> Ever yours,
> Mary Shelley.

ORIGINAL: Not traced. PRINTED: William Sharp, *Life and Letters of Joseph Severn* (1892), 204. TEXT: From *ibid.*

571. *To Claire Clairmont*

[Putney, February, 1844]

. . . more serious & painful than you can now. I own I think her being withdrawn for you "a blessing disguised"—as they call it with regard to yourself —nor ever had you cause to trust Jane——you always knew her—& Dinas total want of strength of character or of want of real heart could never render her one to be deeply regretted. I cannot help seeing the thing in this light—& I earnestly hope that time will enable you to view it dispassionately & calmly.

Believe, dear, if there is one person in whom you can place trust, & I hope you ever will in me, it is as much as falls to the lot of most—still your days are companionless & dreary—here is the sting—would it could be altered.

You ask me to write but my eyes are still ailing & nothing hurts them so much as writing.

I am sure those poor people of Rue de la B——can not mean to be cold. Guitera really likes you & has a taste for you—but his time is not his own—Unfortunate G—— tells me that his foot is so bad he cannot get out at all—& he hopes que vous ne lui voulez pas for an appearance of neglect that is not & cannot be real. His intense suffering at present results from total absence of *money* from which he is suffering severely—at the same time that he cannot controul himself to write as I wished him—by which means some supply might have been got for immediate use. He has a roof & other comforts—but Mme G. & himself find it hard to procure food often— Martini being careless in paying Guiteras pittance—he does not mention these things in his letter, but I know it from what I saw in Paris. God send there be a turn in his fate—but I see it not—so far at least as his getting employment & so being rendered independant & secure of daily bread. Poor fellow—he has a princely spirit—but an *impressionability* & a sense of wrong that eats into his life—

I will send a letter for Mrs. Vivian— Think however about Mrs. Dunbar —& tell me what I ought to say. Remember that introduced by me, they will know at once who you are—that ought not to be against you—will it be? if it is not Miss Stewart will want to talk of Shelley & Lord Byron—you must deliberate as to the tone to be assumed & what to say— And do tell me how you wish me to write & how to mention your name &c— Shall I say that in my absence she can from you learn many things about Shelley, such as she wishes to know— Answer me this & you shall have letters directly. I encline to saying this—as if she thinks you will be useful & if you *are* useful to her she will be more likely to be useful to you—such is the world. Study peoples weak points either of character or necessity & prop & help those—& you will get on.—

I write in a hurry on account of my eyes—A thousand thanks for your long letter— Percy sends his love. Campbell is in high hopes just now of a place—Knox's position makes me truly unhappy & is one of several thorns that stick into me & make my solitude not a bed of roses— Percy, thank God, is well—& as usual the comfort & joy of my life. I wish he would write to you He devotes himself exclusively to practising the piano—

Adieu— I send this thro Alexy to save postage do I do right— I will send the letters by the Russian Embassy—but that is slow—& I thought you may like an immediate answer about Charles

Adieu
                                        Affly ys
                                        M S.

[P.S.] Send by Guitera (Percy asks) several pieces of *Savon Ponce premier qualitè*— I will pay him.

I will write soon again but let me hear from you— Remember me kindly to Mrs. Ivanoff I told you Laura had got £100 of her fathers fortune saved out of Gallonis hands & had sent 100 crowns to Hammy—

> ADDRESS: Miss Clairmont. ORIGINAL: Huntington Library (HM 12363); A.L.S., 8 pp. 8vo (incomplete). UNPRINTED and UNPUBLISHED. TEXT: From original letter.

572. *To Abraham Hayward*

Putney,
Feb. 16 [1844]

Do you object to my alluding to your delightful little account of your passage over the Splugen in /34 & mentioning your name.[1] . . . I am always sorry when lady authors make their heroines so very sentimental.

> ORIGINAL: Owned by Walter T. Spencer, London, in 1937; A.L.S., 4 pp. 8vo. UNPRINTED and UNPUBLISHED. TEXT: A quotation sent me by Walter T. Spencer, who would not permit me to copy the letter.

572A. *To Thomas Moore*

[Putney, March, 1844]

[From *Memoirs, Journal, and Correspondence of Thomas Moore,* edited by Lord John Russell, VII, 365:] [March] 10th and 11th. . . . I received a letter from Mrs. Shelley, whom I had not seen or heard of for many months, and she, too, is pleased to be pleased with my Ireland.[2] "But you do not," she says, "come to town, so I write at last that I may not be quite dead to you. You cannot be so to me; for your delightful volumes on Ireland would remind me, even could I forget your kindness in old times."

573. *To Claire Clairmont*

Putney 11 March [1844]

My dear Claire—

Though my eyes are better—I cannot spare them to write more than a few lines— Percy says he *will* write—but he is such a procrastinator that I fear. I mentioned to him you wished to have the prose works—so he sends you a copy— I send also the enclosed letters, which you will send or not as you like—but I *hope* you will— I think Miss Stewarts circle will be something new, & alive & agreable.

Ianthe has been very much indisposed with cough & weakness—but she is now better. Sir Tim was for some days confined to his bed by a bilious attack

---

[1] Mary crossed the Splugen in the tour of 1840, and gave an account of the experience in the *Rambles,* I, 56–61. On page 58 she refers to Hayward's *Some Account of a Journey Across the Alps in a Letter to a Friend* (London, Printed for Private Circulation), a pamphlet of 44 pages. Hayward crossed the Alps in August, 1834. His principal aim is to give an account of the great storm that had occurred earlier in August and had produced such extraordinary results. His letter is dated October 14, 1834.

[2] Moore's *History of Ireland* (1835–46, 4 vols.).

which almost looked dangerous—but he is now quite well again— Percy heard from Hellen today—who says he is daily gaining strength— My good child, you did well indeed to secure your annuity—you will enjoy it ten years longer.

I hope I shall not inconvenience you not sending the 5 immediately as I hoped & intended— I cannot tell you how I am harassed— I scarcely know what to do—or to what to look forward— Our present style of life is too expensive for us—yet I am as careful as I can [be]— I never go to town—& except Martini have received no guests except Percy's friends— I must be more careful however or I cannot get on. You shall have the money soon—the moment I can—be sure—& I wont get into debt with you again.

When Martini came the Sanfords were in Wiltshire, on a visit to Mrs. Long (a lady we knew in Florence)—on their return they left Horatia behind — I have not seen them; Heaven knows when I shall!—the weather is strangely boisterous & does not entice people here. I met Mr. Leader the other day who talks of calling— I should not have been civil to him (I think the whole clique so odious) but Percy wishes it. I hear from people who have met Trelawny (I have not Dieu merci) that he looks inconceivably shabby, dirty & *old*.—Dina is not well—& having seen a Physician is ordered to lye up as much as possible— I have seen none of them except Henry who came down once.—He complains of Jane, so I keep Percy out of the way as much as I can that he may not be accused of *mischief making*—& praise Jane systematically. Martini might have amused himself very well here I fancy—L[or]d Brougham being particularly civil—but he has avoided society—except ours, to whom he has taken mightily— I have been as civil as I can—he is agreable but an *enfant gaté* & not to be compared to our poor Gatteschi from whom I have not heard a long time. L[or]d Brougham really seems mad—he has gone on in the funniest way with Martini but Guitera can tell you all about that. Mrs. Paul is still all kindness to me—they have come into some money lately. The affair of the picture is sadly balked by its non arrival— It ought to have been sent before Martini set out—it was sent after—it was too large to *go below* in the steamer—so they were obliged to wait for calm weather which was long coming. I have not seen it yet—but hope to do so tomorrow—& to take Mrs. Rogers to see it— Every one tells Martini that he could not do better than as I have counselled, which is a comfort.

Am I ever to hear from you again?— Have you done any[thing] with regard to your brother—how is dear Mrs. Ivanhoff— I have not seen Hammy — Her sister has been dangerously ill— How is 74? Letting you alone I trust,—& if I could believe, forgotten by you also, I should be quite content. Pray do not be so lazy—write—tell me how you are—whether Robecchi succeeds in vanquishing your illness. My eyes these last day or two are better— I hope it will continue. If Mrs. Vivian gives you the lace, simply give it to Mrs. Hare as for me, & she will I am sure be kind enough to bring it over—

Adieu, my dear Claire— I am anxious about you—& you are very unkind not to let [me] hear often from you—

Ys. affly.

M S.

[P.S.] Kind things many from me to Mrs. Ivanoff & Alexy. Marianne sends her duty & hopes you are quite well.

ORIGINAL: Huntington Library (HM 12132); A.L.S., 6 pp. 4to, with seal. UNPRINTED and UNPUBLISHED. TEXT: From original letter.

574. *To Claire Clairmont*

[Putney] Friday [April 12, 1844]

Dear Claire—

I congratulate you on your recovered health— I hope you will find in it the source of good spirits & quiet feelings. I am very sorry you are going to Mme. de Maistre—as I fear you will not be comfortable with her, though the change of air will, I doubt not, benefit you. I am sorry to have to report an event which will distress you, tho it does not touch you nearly—poor Mary has lost her husband.[1] They were stationed you know, in the south of Ireland —going out on some act of duty in an open boat, during one of the late terrible storms—on the 11th of this month, the boat upset & he & another were drowned.—Peacock I believe has set off for his unfortunate daughter— It is most sad!—I saw Dina yesterday—the poverty, the penury there is very painful —though what strikes me as so wretched—their bare uncomfortable rooms, Dina, I fancy, feels far less than one does for her. She is rather better, but is kept back by the illness of her child who has had convulsions & she lives in terror— Jane devotes herself to her but such excessive narrow means must bring a thousand misfortunes in their train.

I am very comfortable in my cot & *so* glad not to be in town. The misfortune is that being at *a convenient distance,* Percy's friends come down, & we cannot afford it, & so care is born & will not die!—

I heard an account of Mr. D. L's ball in a letter, I forget from whom, to Mrs. Stanhope, it said it was a failure, for we knew no one, so the invitations were entrusted to an English-Lady who has— [*Letter breaks off abruptly.*]__

(The rest enclosed with the other half of the 5£ to Alexy.)

[*Unsigned*]

ORIGINAL: Not traced. A copy in Claire Clairmont's handwriting is in the Berg Collection, the New York Public Library. UNPRINTED and UNPUBLISHED. TEXT: From Claire Clairmont's copy, as above.

575. *To Claire Clairmont**

[Putney] 19 April [1844]

Dear Claire—

Guitera tells me that you are not gone to Me de Maistre—that you are *going*

[1]Mary Ellen Peacock had married Lieutenant Edward Nicolls in January, 1844.

to Saint Germains, so I dare say this will reach you— I have not sent the Examiners lately—not knowing where you might be.—

I do not know how far this letter is worth while—but the reports from Field Place seem dubious. Ever since the bilious illness attack I mentioned Sir Tim, though nothing ails his health, has never recovered his strength or appetite—whether he will rally (but that is not much expected) or all terminate in a few months or a few weeks is doubtful—but his family do not expect him to last more than a few months more or less, as nature hold[s] out— In this state of things John & his wife have had the *good taste* to go [to] the opera— He has always been a too good father to him at least—

Heaven preserve my Percy—every time he goes on the water—& he will go —is there now— I have a fear of a Parthian kick from fate at the last instant — It seems too blessed a thing that all should be well at last— Percy [is] too dear an angel—he is so perfectly good— I have had such fearful letters about our poor friend G[atteschi]'s state of destitution—that I felt it quite necessary to try to do something— Nothing *could* I do except send some of what we have in hand—& Percy has complied & helped me in the most angelic manner— God preserve him!

If any thing happens, you need not be in a fever but arrange as you judge most comfortable—four *years* are given us to pay the legacies—they may & probably will be paid sooner—— but till we can raise the money so to do— you will have nothing to do except receive fair percent on your legacy— I dare say it will be better that you should come over *soon*—but there will be no need of hurry or disquiet—

My head has been *far* from well lately— Our weather is like June—sunny & delightful— I have no news of poor Mary—except that she begged her father not to go over to her—but leave her to manage every thing herself— this was at first— I should think by this time [?] she is over—some day soon I shall go by steamer & pay Peacock a visit at the I[ndia] H[ouse]— Dina is well I hear & the child also— Have you seen Hammy she is in Paris now I suppose

Adieu—writing is so painful to me that I will at once conclude

Ys. affly

M Shelley

ADDRESS: Madlle./ Mlle. de Clairmont/ Rue N^e Clichy— 3 bis/ à Paris Rue de Clichy/ [*Redirected to*] chez M. du Bertrand, à St. Germain en Layes. POSTMARKS: (1) Putney (2) 19 AP 19/ 1844. ORIGINAL: Huntington Library (HM 12171); A.L.S., 6 pp. 8vo, with envelope. Copy by Claire Clairmont, Berg Collection, the New York Public Library. UNPRINTED and UNPUBLISHED. TEXT: From original letter.

576. *To Leigh Hunt**

Putney
20 April 1844

My dear Hunt

The tidings from Field Place seem to say that ere long there will be a change—if nothing untoward happens to us till then,—it will be for the better.[1]

Twenty years ago in memory of what Shelley's intentions were—I said that you should be considered one of the legatees to the amount of £2,000.[2] I need scarcely mention that when Shelley talked of leaving you this sum he contemplated reducing other legacies—& that one among these is (by a mistake of the Solicitor) just double what he intended it to be[3]—

Twenty years have of course much changed my position— Twenty years ago it was supposed that Sir Tim[thy] would not live five years. Meanwhile a large debt has accumulated—for I must pay back all on which Percy & I have subsisted as well as what I borrowed for Percy's going to college. In fact I sca[r]cely know now how our affairs will be. Moreover Percy shares now my rights—that promise was made without his concurrence—& he must concur to render it of avail—nor do I like to ask him to do so till our affairs are so settled that we know what we shall have—whether Shelley's uncle may not go to law—in short till we see our way before us.

It is both my & Percy's great wish to feel that you are no longer burthened by care & necessity—in that he is as desirous as I can be—but the form & the degree in which we can do this must at first be uncertain.

From the time of Sir Timothy's death I shall give directions to my banker to honour your quarterly cheques for £30 a quarter—and I shall take steps to secure this to you & to Marianne if she should survive you—

Percy has read this letter & approves— I know your *real* delicacy about money matters & that you will at once be ready to enter to my views—& feel assumed that if any present debt should press if we have any command of money, we will take care to free you from it.

Anxiety we shall not have for neither Percy or I will allow ourselves to be *anxious* where matters of necessity or [are] not concerned—but worry & business enough we shall have.

I believe we are going into Hampshire on Monday— When we return we hope to see you—& Percy will call to see how you are, and I hope find you all better

With love to Marianne

Affectionately ys

Mary Shelley

ORIGINAL: Stark Collection, University of Texas; A.L.S., 4 pp. 4to, with note at top of page 1 by Thornton Hunt. (A transcript by Vincent Hunt— 4 pp. 4to— was owned by the Brick Row Book Shop in September, 1936.) PRINTED: *The Correspondence of Leigh Hunt*, II, 10–11; Marshall, II, 302–303 (not quite complete); *Letters*, 183–84. TEXT: From original letter.

[1] Sir Timothy Shelley died on April 23, 1844.

[2] Mary had written on October 30, 1826 (Letter 267).

[3] Claire received two separate legacies of £6,000 each. The will shows plainly that this was Shelley's intention and not a lawyer's mistake. One legacy seems certainly to have been intended for Allegra and would probably have been cancelled after her death had Shelley lived longer. (See John Cordy Jeaffreson, *The Real Shelley* [London, Hurst and Blackett, 1885], II, 324–27.)

577. *To Thomas Jefferson Hogg*

Putney, April 24 [1844]

[Original letter owned by Captain R. J. J. Hogg. See letters 6–16.]

578. *To Claire Clairmont*

Putney
24 April [18]44

My dearest Claire

Poor Sir Tim is gone at last— He died yesterday morning at 6 o'clock He went gradually out & died at last without a sigh.

As yet we are in all the quiescence of having nothing to do—worry enough will come—& money too I trust—seeing that we have none just now.

Of course the Insurance people owe you up to the present time & you had better write to your solicitor telling him to claim & send it[1]—

The moment we know what is doing or to be done I will write again— Meanwhile I think you had better write to Peacock & tell him who your Solicitor is

Percy sends his best love—

I say no more now but will write in a day or two more at length

Ys. affectionately
M Shelley

ADDRESS: Madlle./ Madlle de Clairmont/ Rue Neuve Clichy No. 3 bis/ Rue de Clichy/ Paris [*Redirected to*] St. Germain. POSTMARKS: (1) Putney (2) 25 AP 25/ 1844. ORIGINAL: Huntington Library (HM 12169); A.L.S., 3 pp. 8vo, black border. UNPRINTED and UNPUBLISHED. TEXT: From original letter.

579. *To Claire Clairmont*

Saturday—Putney 27 April [1844]

Dearest Claire

I saw Gregson yesterday & all things seem to go smoothly enough— Only I think it will be necessary for you to come over very soon. Gregson can borrow any sum of money for us at 3½ percent—& therefore we shall raise money for the legacies &c & pay every thing off directly. You must be here soon to settle what to do with your money—which will require great consideration & care You are *very* prudent in money matters—in all matters of self denial— but do not fall into the Charybdis which has swallowed so many fortunes & ruined so many *lone females*—trying to get a large percentage for your money. However that is all matter for after consideration. How do you stand now— do you want money for your journey?— If so let me know & I will send some. We have had none yet but on Monday must get some.

Gregson thinks it a great shame that Percy is not named in Sir Tim's will— at least that he did not leave him the securities I signed— I did not expect it

[1] Claire had bought an annuity during Sir Timothy Shelley's lifetime.

& therefore we are not disappointed. The *good* of our position is that money can be got now on such easy terms of interest Percy goes down to the funeral with Gregson on Monday—

I am very anxious to know *when* you can come—we have absolutely not room in this house— I cannot bear for a minute that you should be in wretched London lodgings—what *can* be done?

Do write & tell me that you get my letters—for since you wrote to tell me you were going *directly* to Me de Maistre you have not written—from Me Ivanoff I hear you were gone to St. Germain—But whether you are there now or whether you have received my letters I cannot tell.

Lady Shelley is left sole executrix— The girls have made up to them about £2500 each & all that Sir Tim could leave he has left to Lady Shelley during her life—strictly entailed on John & his children afterwards— John grumbles excessively at his mother having every thing for life—but as he comes in for a good fortune & she is above 80—no great harm is done— But it shews the fruits of a *heartless* bringing up.

I am truly anxious to know when you can come— Would you like a lodging near us?—but that is so far from town— It is *too bad* not having a room to offer you—but such is the case—as you will see when you come.

Percy has bought a half decked sailing boat for the river & is deep in her rig—& happy.

God bless you dear Claire—answer this letter directly— Percy is happy to think he shall see you, without going to Paris which he detests.

Adieu

Affly. ys
M Shelley

ADDRESS: Madlle./ Mlle de Clairmont/ Rue N^e Clichy No. 3 bis/ Rue de Clichy/ à Paris [*Redirected to*] St. Germain. POSTMARK: Putney. ORIGINAL: Huntington Library (HM 12134); A.L.S., 8 pp. 8vo, with envelope. Copy by Claire Clairmont, Berg Collection, the New York Public Library. UNPRINTED and UNPUBLISHED. TEXT: From original letter.

580. *To* [*Miss Marianna Hammond*]*

Monday [? May, 1844]
Putney

I never heard of any thing so abominable—& do not imagine that I mean to endure this treatment—a few hours! My dearest Marianna—you are crazy — Reform your notions of things— You *must* come & spend a few days with me before you go. Choose your time only I shall be out of town for a few days—*I believe* next week— This week would suit me—but well you will—and we will go to the Opera & French play & you shall have a little fun before you are buried— Make what arrangements are most convenient— I will let you know when the day is fixed (but it will not be till next week) for my going into Sussex—it will only be for a few days—if you like to come on Wednesday—do—let me know & we will go to the French play in the Even[in]g

  Be a good girl & dont be troublesome

Affectionately ys.

M Shelley

ORIGINAL: Owned by B. F. Stevens & Brown, Ltd., London, in April, 1937; A.L.S., 3 pp. 8vo; page 1 has a heavy black border around it; at top of page 1 in pencil and in another hand is written "To Miss Hammond." UNPRINTED and UNPUBLISHED. TEXT: From original letter.

581. *To Claire Clairmont*

Putney   4th June [1844]

Dearest Claire—

I am very sorry to hear you are so ill—especially as I had flattered myself that you were getting better— I hope being with Lady Sussex suits you & does you good.

I fear, my dear Claire—we cannot serve you about your money & that you must come over. The burthens on the estate amount to £50,000—if money were *scarce* this w[oul]d pretty nearly ruin us—as it is—it is necessary to pay them in such a way as will fall lightest. The thing we are advised to do is to raise the whole sum at once on [a] mortgage which we can do at 3½ percent —even so we have to pay nearly 2,000 a year interest—& 500 a year Lady Shelley's jointure—this joined to the necessary expences attendance on the *care of an estate* leaves Percy any thing but rich. A second mortgage is always to be greatly avoided & is very expensive. When we have raised the £50,000 to pay all—what could we do with four of yours?—only put it in the funds; which you can do as easily as ourselves— I am afraid dear Claire you must be satisfied with receiving at once the legacy of £12,000—& though just now money brings a low rate of interest—things may change & you may do better by & bye. Mrs. Hare talks of putting some portion of her money in the Austrian funds which give 5 per cent— I am far from advising this or any thing that MAY not be safe. But there could be no harm in writing to your brother & asking his advise as to placing say £2,000 into Austrian funds. I sincerely wish I had a room to ask you here—but we have not. You talk of coming to Boulogne in August—that is in your way here—& the trip may do you good.

    The £50,000 is now *being raised*— I cannot tell you when it will be done— as these things are uncertain— A month or six weeks, I imagine is the time— By that time you ought in some way to understand what to do. Write to Mr. Amory—to Mr. Rawlinson to Mr. Sanford. I will myself speak to the two latter, if you like, & hear what they have to say. *You* ought to write at once to Amory— It will cost you no trouble just to say "I expect my legacy to be paid in about a month can you advise me how to invest the whole or a portion in a *safe* manner at tolerably good interest—better that is than the funds." Coming over here might do your health good— If you could continue to be anywhere at all comfortable. You are within 6 hours of us at Boulogne—& if you came here, at any time you might be at Boulogne in 6 hours. From the little I have seen it looks as if our rents were more likely to be *lowered* than raised—at least the leases of two of the best farms end at Michaelmas & the tenants ask to pay a less rent—& the farms are to be surveyed to see whether that is fair.

We are at this moment returned from Field Place where we were invited— They were all immensely civil—& Lady Shelley told Percy that she was sorry she did not know me before— Why then did she not? Hellen however seems to have some heart, & speaks of her brother with enthusiasm. Field Place itself is desperate—it is so dully placed—& so dull a house in every way. Lady S. does not stay there—& people say (London people I mean) that I ought to persuade Percy to live there—but how can I?—he would either spend all his money in going away from it—or be forced from sheer ennui to make love to the dairy maid. He shrinks from it—& no wonder—& for me, it would avail little whether I had 300 or 3,000 a year if I am to vegetate in absolute solitude— I have had too much of that. We shall see what we shall do. Lady S[helley] has taken it till Michaelmas at all events, so we have time to reflect.

Percy is very well indeed— Mrs. Nicholls [Mary Peacock] is still in Ireland. Edward [Williams] is rather a despair—however Peacock will get a place for him in the India House—& he it is to be hoped will work.

John Shelley has quarrelled with his mother because Sir Tim left her so much. This of course renders her more enclined to be civil to us.

(I have heard that the Belgian funds give 4 or 5 percent & are safe—but I cannot advise on these funds— What is safe for a man, is often so unsafe for a woman—because he hears more what is going on & can be more on his guard.) I think that you had better at once make arrangements to come over here in 3 weeks—and take advise at [as] to what to do with the money—but I would have you write to Amory in the way I mention *directly*. You may remember when in Paris I spoke about your leaving some of your money with us—which you negatived *then* in the most decided manner. Now that the 50,00[o] is raised, it is impossible—besides you must imagine that with such a burthen of debt, we must be very careful

Adieu Claire—kind Compts to Lady Sussex.

Affly. ys
M S

ORIGINAL: Huntington Library (HM 12346); A.L.S., 8 pp. 8vo. Copy by Claire Clairmont, Berg Collection, the New York Public Library. UNPRINTED and UNPUBLISHED. TEXT: From original letter.

582. *To Marianne Hunt**

June 25 [1844]
Putney

Dear Marianne

I explained to Hunt that nothing was done at present, & that we had only

enough to go on with. Out of this we reserved the quarterly payment to your-
selves. This was due on the 26th July—but it seems best that you should receive it at the proper quarter days. Instead of July October Jany & April—you
will receive it 24 June—Sep. Dec. & March. Percy is gone up about it today.
The people at the Bank said that the first time, Hunt must be good enough
to go himself, when they would arrange with him about its being drawn—
They want to *see* him write his name. If therefore Hunt will be good enough
to go tomorrow & draw for £30 it will be paid.

I am sorry to say it is not in our power to do more till the will is proved—
no legacies are yet paid nor can till then—

As to my looks, dear Marianne—Hunt is a friend—& also near sighted—
& my glass tells me a different tale. However I am well in health. I hope with
this arrangement you will be able to arrange matters. Something Moxon told
us the other day made me easy about you— I was glad to hear from Hunt
that you were better. Poor Henry is laid up with an erisipylas—aggravated it
would seem by his dislike to medicine—but now he is *really* laid up & must
do as the doctors order

Yours truly

M Shelley

[P.S.] Hunt will remember that *we* pay the income tax on the 30 a quarter
—so you need make no return.

> ORIGINAL: British Museum (Add. MSS 38,523, ff.249–50); A.L.S., 4 pp. 8vo;
> heavy black border around page 1. UNPRINTED and UNPUBLISHED. TEXT: From
> original letter.

583. *To Claire Clairmont*

Putney   1st July [1844]

My dear Claire—

I have just got your letter (I wish you would not cross them)   Percy will
call today on Gregson, & hear when it is likely that the mortgage will be signed
& all settled.—You appear to me to take all I say & do in such bad part that
I feel averse to advise—*all* I can say is, that I think it probable that in the course
of this month the money will be raised & the legacies paid—& that for *your*
OWN *sake,* I think you ought to be on the spot *before* that time, that you may
arrange how to dispose of your money. This appears to me the more necessary
from another circumstance. Emily[1] wrote to me in distress—it seemed to me
right to assist my brother's widow & I have promised her £50 a year. She camed
[*sic*] to see me—& in the course of conversation mentioned that a rich stock
jobber of her acquaintance spoke of Amory as not quite honest. This excessively surprised me—& I do not know what to think—for I never heard any
thing against him & in 1841 my affairs were very nearly being put into his
hands & Coulson whom I then saw said nothing against him. I think you

[1] William Godwin, Jr.'s wife.

ought to be *here* to consult as to the placing of your money—& this is the opinion of all the persons who know about your affairs. It takes time to place money properly—& till you are on the spot nothing can be done. If, all at once you hear from your lawyer that your legacy is paid, & asking your directions, what to do with it—what will you reply? If you are not prepared you will lose—& perhaps largely. As to economy dear Claire, it is a foolish economy which leads you to neglect the future. Your not liking to spend for the purpose of learning how to place your money to the best advantage is as if a horse were given you & you refused to incur the expence of keeping or selling him & let him die. Be assured in matters of business the person interested must *be on the spot*—no person however capable & zealous can do business for another —& as far as I know you have not even consulted any one here capable of giving advise. You must see & talk to men of business conversant in such matters— You must, however disagreable to you, take some trouble. I write this with a very painful feeling—as you appear to look suspiciously on all I say. But I conquer this to do what is right & give you the best advise I can.—You *ought not* to wait till your legacy is paid (*which will be ere long*) but be prepared where to place your money *the moment it is paid.* This I have written to you over & over again. I only repeat my words. Much time has been lost by you— Whether this will injure your interests I cannot tell; I fear so— I have feared this so much, that as you did not heed me, I asked several of your friends to represent the matter to you & beg you to come—but you have not listened to us.

I am a good deal surprised at the sort of insinuation contained in your letter, with regard to your Italian friends— You say "Before you came, they talked in the most open confidential manner to me, especially about their affairs—when they had you for a friend they pretty nearly cut me." With regard to Gatteschi, all I know is, that the first evening of my arrival in Paris, you said he was so strange & appeared so annoyed when you mentioned his affairs to him that you never meant to speak of them again to him—more I know not— I hear from him—for he has furnished me dayly with materials for my book— I dont write often—for I am occupied with my book—& cannot write to any one. With regard to Guitera—I have not written to him these 3 months—not having answered his last letter, which I ought to have done— but writing hurts me. I will copy a passage from this last letter which will shew you how he feels towards you "Da gran tempo non vedo la Cliara— So essere a St. Germain—ma non mi ha dato il suo ricapito. Sento che ella mi manca—amo molto la sua conversazione—sopra tutte quando si discorseva intorno alla filosofia Germanica. Perche mi ha ella cosi completamente obliato? Non so—E dopo tante promesse di amicizia. Cosi sono da tutti abbandoneto —meno che da Ferdinando."

I would entreat you to banish the suspicions you too readily entertain with regard to your friends—but it is constitutional. Besides you do not consider any one a friend who is not willing to abandon all their ideas, habits & plans of life to adopt yours & unite with you— It appears to me that persons may be very dear & real friends who differ wholly in tastes & theories, & who could not be happy constantly under the same roof—but who feel & shew mutual esteem & affection

The marriage of Horatia is broken off I am sorry to say—& poor Mrs. Sanford much cut up— Mrs. Long I much dislike.—But except that the rupture is of course a bad & painful thing, it was not suited for any youth not one & twenty to marry Horatia She wants a guide—a person to take care of her—as Mr. Rawlinson said no girl ever needed 35 years in a husband so much. This does not diminish the odiousness of Mrs. Long's conduct. I am glad you are comfortably placed with Lady Sussex—very glad—nothing could be more against my notions than the discomfort & solitude you chalked out for yourself at St. Germains. I will learn & let you know whether Lord Sussex is in town.

I lead a very quiet life for the most part—& feel uncomfortably uncertain about our future plans. It is useless to fill my letter with pros & cons— Lady Shelley will never leave a *sous* to Percy—her money will go to her daughters—& some perhaps to John's children— I will get some cement tomorrow & send it with this letter.

Tuesday [July 2]

Gregson told Percy yesterday that *things were going on*—& might be expected to be soon ready—that is all he could get. You say in yours "Tell me when you want me." Pray understand, dear Claire, you are not wanted for me or Percy at all—it is simply to place & arrange for placing your own money that you are wanted as I think—& as others think.

Do not think any thing I say unkind. But your letter seems to me written in a tone as if you were offended. I hope I am mistaken for I am sure you have no cause. I am earnest you should come for your own sake—because if all of a sudden your money is paid you may lose if not prepared to place it on the instant. I certainly believe it will be paid this month— I may be mistaken — Gregson may drag on till August—but if you settle what to do that is the great thing

Affly ys
M S.

ADDRESS: Madlle./ Mlle. de Clairmont/ 2 Rue des Gardes/ Bellevue/ à Paris. POSTMARKS: (1) []landford St. (2) 1844/ JY 3/ 8 MG 8/ A (3) JY—2/ 1844 (4) 4/ JUIL./ 44/ BOULOGNE. ORIGINAL: Huntington Library (HM 12180); A.L.S., 8 pp. 8vo, with black bordered envelope. UNPRINTED and UNPUBLISHED. TEXT: From original letter.

584. *To Claire Clairmont*

Tuesday [July, 1844]

My dear Claire—

I answer your letter directly to say that *I* have nothing to do with paying your money. The will is proved Peacock is executor & means to act. You must write to him & give directions— I have no authority or power over it. There has been no delay that could be helped. Gregson *instantly* found a mortagage— but to draw up so large a mortgage takes it seems some months—[*The following is cancelled, apparently by Claire:* Your brother is insane to expect to reap any good from that sort of bullying.]

I called on the Sanfords today— Lady Sussex called while I was there— I did not see her. They consider her quite mad to have refused a cadetship for Berkely—indeed from all I hear the boy's safety consists in *roughing it*—but of course I *know* nothing never having seen him.—As for Lady S— herself she seems to me half mad poor thing—constitutionally so I should say, considering her whole career. I should be very sorry to be mixed up with her. Guitera is a goose par excellence— I guess from your hints he has spoken to her of us—particularly of me—who am the most committed with regard to what has been done for poor Gatteschi— If he has done so, it is infamous— more so towards his friend than us—but infamous towards both—& did I *know* he had done so I would entirely cut his acquaintance— I never mention these things (I mean things done for G——) in letters to you—because it is useless writing about things of this sort. Knox says that he might make £200 a year (not Guitera he thinks him to[o] wild & strange, but an educated gentleman such as from me & Martini he considers Gatteschi to be) as Italian master here— I told this to G—— but he appears averse to leaving Paris— though he seems to be doing nothing there. Not knowing English is a great— & if he will not learn it, an invincible objection—so I have said nothing more about it.

I am sorry I was unjust in my letter—it seemed to me that you were unjust *to me*. If you come to Boulogne if you wont come here, I will try to run over there for a day or two at least—just now I cant go for long—for we have no house & are quite unsettled— We shall have not quite 3000 a year—out of this there are many necessary expences agents &c—& the worst is that no furniture or plate—or any thing except this income comes—so that we have to buy every thing. I went to Field Place for a day or two—but milady does not renew her invitation. Percy goes on Wednesday for business, leases falling in—tenants wanting rents lowered &c— Percy wont think of Field Place—indeed on our small income to go to live there would be burying us both alive.

I hear Lady Sussex returns tomorrow—my book[1] is not out I fear— I will write for a copy to go by her but fear it will not be ready—it is a poor affair— I am sorry to say—the best parts were furnished by Gatteschi[2]— He seems mad to have talked the nonsense you say—but it is so unlike him that I suppose it was only a whim for the moment. Some people if in good spirits shew it by talking nonsense. From all I hear I think Horatia had a good escape in not

---

[1] The *Rambles in Germany and Italy* was published at the very end of July. The Advertisements are dated July 30. The book was reviewed in the *Athenæum*, August 10, 1844.
[2] See Letter 554, note 1.

marrying Walter Long. She would have been much in Mrs. Long's hands, & she I think is capable of any thing— The Sanfords heads were turned with the idea of the heir of 1800 a year—but I dont think the rupture has injured Horatia—the Longs—I know not why, are neither liked nor respected—& people think she had an escape.

Julian Robinson has accepted a chaplaincy to Bengal—& goes in about 6 weeks— This is a good thing—if the climate does not disagree with him—his fortune is made.

Peacock has been ill with sciatica—he is now better. Jane is in a very bad state of health. Percy is quite well & gay—dear child, he is so easily contented —& never repines— Mrs. Hare is here & a great happiness to me— Percy dances the Polka with little Tigress who is charmed. I fancy you will have Mrs. Hare in Paris again this winter.

I am so sorry to hear you continue so very ailing—pray try the sea This warm weather is just the thing. If you want money & wrote to Peacock I feel pretty confident he could get an advance from Gregson for you

Our weather is beautiful— I hope to be better now my book is finished—but it was doing me a serious injury— Adieu my dear Claire—pray forgive me if I said any thing to annoy you—let us see each other soon & be friends

Affly. ys

M S.

ORIGINAL: Huntington Library (HM 12368); A.L.S., 8 pp. 8vo. Copy by Claire Clairmont, Berg Collection, the New York Public Library. UNPRINTED and UN-PUBLISHED. TEXT: From original letter.

585. *To Edward Moxon*

Putney [? July, 1844]

You were good enough to say that I should have 12 copies, I received a parcel yesterday containing 4 . . . the book is very nicely got up.

ORIGINAL: Owned by Walter T. Spencer, London, in 1937; A.L.S., 1 p. 8vo. UNPRINTED and UNPUBLISHED. TEXT: Quotation sent me by Walter T. Spencer, who would not permit me to copy the letter.

586. *To [Leigh Hunt]*

Tuesday [? August, 1844]

I was sorry you did not come yesterday—but I hope next week to fix a more propitious day.

I am really frightened when I think that you are reading my book critically. It seems to me such a wretched piece of work—written much of it in a state of *pain* that makes me look at its pages now as if written in a dream. The second volume only tells any thing new— I fear I shall be very much ashamed of it—

Ys. truly

M Shelley

ORIGINAL: British Museum (Add. MSS 38,524, f.205); A.L.S., 2 pp. (3⅛ x 9 inches, a slip of paper). UNPRINTED and UNPUBLISHED. TEXT: From original letter.

587. *To Leigh Hunt**

Putney
Thursday [1844]

My dear Hunt

It was surely an hallucination of a very extraordinary kind to rate yourself as receiving above £150 per ann[1]—when the income tax was imposed—when Marianne used to assure me that you never got £100 *Now* there can be no help I fear— But I really thought that your absence of means did not expose you to the tax— I fear your scrupulous conscience cheated yourself—& thus your family also— It is very *possible* to have too good a conscience—a truth pressed upon us daily— You can have no idea of the letters we get, to which it is heart breaking to send refusals—while at the same time we feel that our income is very far short of any thing we at all expected.

I grieve to say that I am quite exhausted—& Percy has been calculating how much he *could* send to an unfortunate relation in absolute want. I will shew him your letter We cannot get our lawyer to move quicker & are inconvenienced by the delay.

Forgive me if the most painful regret at your having brought this claim on yourself, by the excess of injustice *towards yourself* makes me strongly express this regret You were not amenable to the income tax decidedly having at that time so to speak no income—

Percy will not return till late this evening.

Again forgive me but I am truly sorry & deeply pained

Affly. Ys.

M Shelley

ORIGINAL: Luther A. Brewer Collection, University of Iowa; A.L.S., 7 pp. 12mo (3 x 4¼ inches). UNPRINTED and UNPUBLISHED. TEXT: From original letter.

588. *To Leigh Hunt*

[Putney] Thursday Evg. [1844]

My dear Hunt

I write to rectify a word in my note of today I said, I feared there was now no remedy with regard to the income tax—which will certainly not be repeated— I was thinking of the £120 per ann But I recollect that *we* pay the tax on that sum—so that it is not to be counted in your income (we never paid any tax on what Sir Tim allowed us—& yours stands in the same category)—so that, as I cannot help believing that you have not been in the receipt latterly of £150 per ann. I think you may save to your family a sum which legally you have no call to pay.

Pray understand that the £120 is not to be twice paid for

Very truly Ys.

M S.

[1] That is, a total income of £150, including the £120 given him by Mary and Percy.

Friday *Morng*

I have been talking with Percy—& have settled that I must manage to send you £10 on account of what you will receive when our affairs are settled—but till they are settled your creditors must wait—

And pray, dear Hunt, do not put this down as income—presents from friends are *not income*

ORIGINAL: Luther A. Brewer Collection, University of Iowa; A.L.S., 4 pp. 12mo (3½ x 45⁄8 inches). UNPRINTED and UNPUBLISHED. TEXT: From original letter.

589. *To Joseph Severn*

Putney, Sept. 5 [1844]

The picture is at your service . . . the next time I drive your way into town I will leave it.[1]

ORIGINAL: Carl H. Pforzheimer, New York; A.L.S., 1 p. 12mo. Professor Herbert Hartman, Bowdoin College, who gave the MS to Mr. Pforzheimer in the autumn of 1936, says it contains only two sentences. UNPRINTED and UNPUBLISHED. TEXT: Quotation from catalogue No. 20 (1936) of Dobell's Antiquarian Bookstore, Tunbridge Wells.

590. *To Claire Clairmont*

[Putney] Wednesday Evg. [September 11, 1844]

My dear Claire—

I grieve very much at the account you give of yourself—   You write as if you thought it necessary to use much reasoning to convince me you are in bad health—but I assure you I am most sadly convinced of it—   Your countenance alone bespeaks that you suffer—   I hope that as the illness seems chiefly to depend on one thing, that it will pass away after a time.

I wrote to you only yesterday telling you that affairs are still unsettled—my belief however is that they will not be protracted much longer—and I think it unadvisable that you should return to Paris. I mentioned in my letter how these delays hampered us in getting a house—& there are other obstacles that make me desirous not to change immediately, which it would be long to mention on paper—however it is not [a] matter of choice   I *could not* move now if I *would*. I think under the circumstances you had better join Lady Sussex—   Guitera is not with her—as well as I can learn, there is no intention of his going there. The boys are all gone or to go to school—there wd. be no pretence for his going—nor is it I think at present in contemplation. If he did come & continued to worry you you could come away directly but I feel sure that he will not—   You would thus be near the sea & within a few hours of London—   You *must* be here ere long—so this seems to me the best plan and something may be arranged afterwards for your comfort when obliged to come up to town and if Guitera came over & annoyed you, you might leave

[1] Early in January, 1845, Severn finished the portrait of Shelley. He painted from Miss Curran's portrait, which was in Mary's possession. See Letters 594 and 596.

Hythe at once—for your affairs would always give a pretext—but I feel sure from all I hear that there is no such idea on the *tapis* at present.

I did not see the advertisement you mention & fancy it is all a newspaper paragraph founded on nothing— I *know* Ld. B[yron] left no MS. with Teresa [Guiccioli] except letters to herself—which I have seen & in which you are not alluded to. But I will make every enquiry; so set your mind at ease— I will do every thing to learn what this publication is, & prevent any thing being printed that can annoy you.

I am afraid if you had been at Hythe you wd. have been dreadfully worried. Sussex & Charley are away at school—Berkeley with his mother—his first exploit was to fight with the nurse, which so disturbed her milk that Lady Sussex brought her & Consuelo up to town & left them at Connaught Place—where they are now—& Lady Sussex is obliged to devote herself to her scape grace of a son— I fancy by this time she thoroughly repents having prevented his having the cadet ship. He will very soon in a few days leave her for school.

I wish you had poor dear Hammy with you—or some one to take care of you— Pray escape from your solitude with all haste—it is too dreadful— To a person in health that sort of loneliness is misery, what must it be when a person is suff[er]ing so much bodily ailment— I had not the slightest idea that the H's were not still with you so I comforted myself with thinking that you were taken care of by people you liked.

I have no further news— Percy is quite well & sends his love— Rest satisfied that I will immediately take measures with regard to the publication you mention.

Ys. Affly
M S.[1]

ADDRESS: Madll/ Madll Clairmont/ Chez Mme Billotét/ Rue de la Barre— No. 35/ *Dieppe France*. POSTMARKS: (1) T.P./ P u t n e y   (2) PAID/ 12 SP 12/ 1844   (3) DIEP[PE]/ 14/ SEPT/ [44]. ORIGINAL: Roe-Byron Collection at Newstead Abbey, near Nottingham; A.L.S., 4 pp. 8vo, with black-bordered envelope. Letter 553 is probably a postscript to this letter. UNPRINTED and UNPUBLISHED. TEXT: From original letter.

591. *To Claire Clairmont*

Sandgate—Friday [September 27, 1844]

Dear Claire

I hope you are still at Dieppe & bathing this enchanting weather. I ran down here yesterday to see the Beauclerks— I only stay 3 days—but am delighted I came   the sea is so sunney & fresh. I went into it this morning & found it delightful

I called on Peacock— I told him to write to Gregson for money for you —but he wants to know where to send it—whether you are still at Dieppe— When I return home which will be early in the week I will call on Gregson—

---

[1] Letter 553 should follow this letter, to which it is probably a postscript.

meanwhile pray write a line to say whither your money is to be sent to Peacock.

I saw Mr. Methuen for a moment—he might be 30 or 32 but he is only 26—he is a tall big man & looks excessively good humoured—& your theory you know is that fat people are *true*— Horatia is full of her trousseau which is to be splendid— It seems an excellent match & I truly hope it will turn out well. Percy is gone to shoot in Sussex while I am here. I sincerely wish any thing could be done to draw Knox out of the slough of despond in which poor fellow he is sunk— I am sure *smoking* unmans & un[n]erves—for surely I never knew men—courageous to dare & expose themselves—so little able to cope with adversity as my smoking young friend I saw Consuelo who is lovely— Lady Sussex had left her cottage for the hotel—& is probably in town now—they were expecting her daily. Adieu my dear Claire This fine weather & bathing must do you good. It is rumoured that one of Lady Dorothea's daughters Nanky—is going to be married—is this true & to whom—A french vicomte!

Yours affly.
M S.

ADDRESS: Madlle./ Mlle. Clairmont/ Rue de la Barre/ France Dieppe. POST-MARKS: (1) SANDGATE (2) FOLKSTONE/ SP 27/ 1844 (3) DIEPPE/ 29/ SEPT./ 44. ENDORSED: Talks of Knox and of his smoking and want of manly courage. ORIGINAL: Huntington Library (HM 12138); A.L.S., 3 pp. 4to, with seal. UNPRINTED and UNPUBLISHED. TEXT: From original letter.

592. *To Claire Clairmont*

Putney, 27 Oct. [1844]

My dear Claire—

Percy saw Gregson the other day & he said he would write to you—perhaps you have heard—however I shall see him tomorrow & learn whether he has written to you— If not, he shall do it at once while I am there. His dilatory ways of going on are trying enough—but it [is] useless tormenting oneself, it does no good. I am indeed very much out of spirits—for in every way our affairs are not sunshiney—a burthened estate is always a great evil—nor shall we, by any means, have the income I supposed. The rent roll I saw was £5,000 a year—but it seems a portion of this, about 4 or 500, is derived from farms that Sir Tim bought & they go to Lady Shelley; & then there is Lady S[helley]'s jointure of 500 a year—We have to pay nearly 2000 interest on the mortgage to pay off legacies, younger children fortune & debt to Sir Tim—& when you add to this that our income is derived from rents—frequently in arrear—paid at uncertain periods—while we must pay regularly—you may guess that our income will neither be large nor on a pleasant footing— All dreams of being a good landlord & taking care of ones tenants vanish—& indeed one has always heard that to be a tenant on a burthened property is always a great evil.—As to Lady Shelley—she affichies not liking Percy—so there are no hopes in future from her—& her conduct is grasping & mean beyond expression. The furniture at Field Place is hers— She has bought another house—but not content with taking all the furniture of any use to herself away, which with her large fortune she ought not to have done—for the best was not worth removing—but she makes a sale of all she leaves behind & even grasped at things fixtures &c—to which she has no right.

In the midst of these vexations—Percy is my comfort. You say you should like to see him worried by the lawyers. He is never at all worried— He takes all with the utmost equanimity— I should have liked to have made him more a man of business—but for his own happiness he could not be altered for the better. Moderate in his wishes—& ready without a murmur to resign those wishes, when obstacles of prudence occur—always cheerful—always occupied, he is the dearest darling in the world—the sheet anchor of my life. When he marries—but I will not think of a time yet uncertain & perhaps far off.—It was fortunate we determined to remain here—for we must study economy, especially in the commencement. I should like to go abroad—but as Percy does not like that we must look for & take a house better suited to us than this, but not requiring a larger establishment than what we now have. I should like to build a cottage on a part of our property close to the London & Brighton railroad— Field Place we are trying to let—& on some sort of terms I suppose we shall soon. Forgive this long account—but you would wish to know the state of things, which is not so bright as I imagined— We must make the best of it—& the great thing is to diminish our expectations & keep ideas within the actual fact—but still for Percy to live as a gentleman on £2,000 a year is only barely possible, & as his nominal income is much larger of course our modes of going on will surprise people. We have the property in the most uncomfortable position possible—a title, a nominal large inheritance—coming after a much richer man—& heavily burthened with debts.

I suppose you have seen Mrs. Hare. She is at Maison Valin. I gave her a letter for you—& mentioned in it an investment she had found for property—for which she is to get something more than 4 per cent— I do not know whether you will find it worth attending to.—You find difficulties in your arrangements—& annoyances—such is the universal law of life—& we must submit. For myself my time is spent in nearly complete solitude— I do not see my way at all as to what is best & practicable for Percy—which is all I look to—for myself—I would go to Italy or Greece if I could, & enjoy the delights of a fine climate—to me the dearest pleasure of life—not doing that—to keep out of debt is my aim & for the rest I have little care or hope. I am not well just now & that also puts me out of spirits

(*Monday*) Peacock had not written to Gregson—but it is all arranged now —he w[oul]d have sent today—but it is a holyday over the Queen's visit to the City. But tomorrow he will send you 3 Bank post bills of £50 each—which is the sum you mentioned to me.—Let him know that you get it safe.

Ys. Affy.

M S

ADDRESS: Madlle/ Madlle Clairmont/ Rue Nᵉ Clichy No. 3 bis/ Rue de Clichy/ à Paris. POSTMARKS: (1) Oxford St. W.O. (2) PAID/ 28 OCT 28/ 1844. ORIGINAL: British Museum (T. J. Wise Collection); A.L.S., 4 pp. 4to, with envelope. UNPRINTED and UNPUBLISHED. TEXT: From original letter.

593. *To Claire Clairmont*

Putney. 6 Dec^ber 1844

My dear Claire

I have just seen Gregson— We sign the Mortgage on Tuesday next, on Wednesday the money will be ready for you. It will be necessary that you should receive this directly & Gregson begs you will write to him to tell him what to do with it. A release on the estate will be drawn out for you to sign which will be sent to you in Paris—unless you come over at once to dispose of your money. Gregson told me a strange thing that Peacock is not executor of the will except as it concerns the personal estate—of which there is none— You must come over or write to a solicitor giving a power of attorney to receive your money—as interest will not be paid after the money is ready for you—that is, next week— It can be paid for you into the bank of England, which is safe—but then you get no interest on it. In fact all this time you ought to have prepared how to dispose of your money—perhaps you have. Gregson begs you will write to him without delay telling him what to do with it.

Heaven help us—the burthens on the estate legacies & debts &c &c amount to so much that if we get £2,000 a year we may think ourselves lucky— My poor Percy is quite ruined—for after all receiving only 2000 a year—we have to pay out of it the expences of the estate—& to suffer from any non payment of rents—a large estate burthened to the amount of more than half its rent roll is a very troublesome thing

I write these lines in haste to save postage— I will write again tomorrow a in [*sic*] answer to your last

Ever Ys.
M Shelley

ADDRESS: Miss Clairmont/ Rue Nᵉ Clichy No. 3 bis/ Rue de Clichy/ à Paris. POSTMARK: 6 DE 6/ 1844. ORIGINAL: Huntington Library (HM 12158); A.L.S., 6 pp. 8vo, with envelope. UNPRINTED and UNPUBLISHED. TEXT: From original letter.

594. *To Leigh Hunt**

Putney
23 Dec [1844]

My dear Hunt

I have not seen Gregson since your visit—& do not know any thing— When I saw him last he said it was best *to do no* thing— This however will scarcely be—for Peacock is going on a visit to Sir John Hobhouse—& the affair for better or worse will be discussed— Some lawyers say that L[ord]

B[yron]'s disclaimer[1] being in a letter to a third person is absolutely null— I cannot say I hope much

Meanwhile I wish you would send me *directly* another copy of the disclaiming paragraph—dated &c—like the last that I may forward it to Peacock— Do this at once

Ys. truly
Mary Shelley

[P.S.] Go & look at a picture Severn is painting of Shelley amidst the ruins of Rome   Your & Marianne's criticism will be very acceptable & useful.

ORIGINAL: Bodleian Library (MS Shelley Adds. d.5, ff.97–98); A.L.S., 4 pp. 12mo. PRINTED: *Bodleian Quarterly Record*, VIII, No. 95 (1937), 418. TEXT: From original letter.

595. *To* [*Nerina Mason Cini*] (*a fragment*)

[Putney, January, 1845]

. . . to have tightened round it. You have heard no more probably—if you have pray tell me all. And give me news of darling Laura.—I might write 20 half excuses why I delayed sending the poplins as I did—but the truth is—it was more laziness & procrastination—they went however with your silk a month ago—and I have sent the bill of lading to Laura so I hope she will get all safe— I will send you the money on the 1st Febry.—will that do?—

I believe Claire will soon come over about her affairs— Her money is ready for her—but the trustee is bound by the will to see that a portion of it is placed *securely*— Shelley's intention being that she should not have it in her power to speculate & lose it— The misfortune is that *safely* so little interest can be got for money just now—& Claire wishing to get more wants to get her money into her own hands that she may place it (& perhaps lose it) as she likes. Accordingly she is coming over to throw the affair into Chancery, as a remedy —Heaven help her— *I* have nothing to do with all this—& only hope I need not be implicated in a Chancery suit— Alas, when cruel destiny has linked to one such a mauvaise tête as Claire, it is very difficult to steer clear of annoyance.

I don't think I have any news for you. Mr. Drake is in town just now & asked about Laura He was at Naples & Rome in the summer—but getting a touch of fever at Rome he was obliged to come back in a hurry. Julian Robinson is gone out as Chaplain to India—perhaps I told you— Tell me your news—& what you think of doing this New Year   do write to me & believe

Ever Affly. Ys
Mary Shelley

[1] Concerning Shelley's will, of which Byron was one of the executors, Byron wrote to Hunt on June 28, 1823: "There was something about a legacy of two thousand pounds which he has left me. This, of course, I decline, and the more so that I hear that his will is admitted valid; and I state this distinctly, that—in case of anything happening to me—my heirs may be instructed not to claim it."—*Correspondence of Leigh Hunt*, I, 203.

ORIGINAL: Owned by Francis Edwards, Ltd., London, in 1937; A.L.S., 5 pp.
12mo (a fragment). UNPRINTED and UNPUBLISHED. TEXT: From original letter.

596. *To Marianne and Leigh Hunt**

Putney   Friday [January 9, 1845]

My dear Marianne

I wish you could be persuaded to go *tomorrow* to Severns to see his picture
of Shelley. The *nose* is any thing but right—if you wd. only cut out one with
your scissors you would set it right—   The mouth is defective—& so is the
shape of the face—do look at it, if you *can* contrive—   He goes out of town
on Monday[1]

In haste

Yours truly
M Shelley

Dear Hunt

Would you be so good as to give Knox an introduction to Charles Mathews
—   He wishes to see him on the subject of a Comedy & wd. be greatly obliged
of a line from you as introduction. Will you send it *here* tomorrow if you can
—by post—   Do you know where he is living at present

Yours truly
M Shelley

[P.S.] Knox says he will walk over to you with this himself

ORIGINAL: Bodleian Library (MS Shelley Adds. d.5, ff.93–94; A.L.S., 4 pp.
8vo. PRINTED: *Bodleian Quarterly Record*, VIII, No. 95 (1937), 419. TEXT:
From original letter.

597. *To Claire Clairmont*

[Putney] 15 Jan. [1845]

My dear Claire

I have just got a note from Gregson—   I told you, as Peacock demurred
about paying you the £6,000, & as he thought that Peacock *might* be in the
right—he was to take Counsel's opinion on the subject. He now writes "The
learned are of opinion that you & Sir Percy & your Mortgagees will be discharged by the payment of the 2^d £6000, to Mr. Peacock, with the concurrence
of Miss Clairmont—& that Miss Clairmont may, at any time before marriage,

[1] Bodelian MS Shelley Adds. d.5, f.65 has the following letter from Severn to Hunt:

21 James St., Buckingham Pal
Mon. Jan. 5th 1845

Dear Hunt

I am most anxious to have your opinion of my picture of Shelley which will be finished tomorrow—next week I go to Scotland, but before I leave I am most desirous to compleat my work,
even including your valuable hints so if you can oblige me with a visit by the middle of the week
I shall be very glad

Yours very truly
Joseph Severn

make an absolute disposition of the fund. The whole is therefore within her power."

If you come over it will therefore be simply to receive your money, & if you like you can carry [it] over with you as you asked me to do. My objection to your plan of buying in Austria rests upon your *not* being an Austrian— there are many difficulties connected with possessing land in a country of which one is not the subject, nor naturalized— As you are prudent you take care to understand the Austrian laws with regard to foreigners possessing land, before you do any thing— I write thus shortly as I write only on the chance of this finding you & beleiving [*sic*] that in fact you will not get it— but are on your way to England— I am

[? ys truly]

M Shelley

ADDRESS: Miss Clairmont/ Rue Nᵉ Clichy— 3 bis/ Rue de Clichy/ à Paris.
POSTMARK: UQ/15 JA 15/ 1845. ORIGINAL: Huntington Library (HM 12163);
A.L.S., 4 pp. 16mo (3⅜ x 5⅛ inches), with envelope. UNPRINTED and UN-
PUBLISHED. TEXT: From original letter.

598. *To Claire Clairmont*

Putney 14 May [1845]

My dear Claire

Your letter seems in better health & spirits— I hope you will not be worried about any thing & that you find comfort in the society of your friends— keep out of the way of storms—if they approach, treat them as Ulysses did the Syrens—stuff cotton in your ears—& they will blow by, & you remain unharmed. I am somewhat out of spirits—our money affairs look gloomy—so much, so very much to pay away—& very little in comparison coming in— the result is economy & solitude   Percy did not like his going to court at all— poor child, how should he? He never looked better—the court dress became him—but he went alone & knew no one— Lord de Lisle had sent civil messages, & I thought some kindness & countenance might be shewn him—but no—this friendlessness is partly Percy's own faul[t]—the result of a modesty that looks like pride—but this results also from feeling that he has always been unkindly treated by his family—& is in a false position.

With all her annoyances Lady D[orothea] C[ampbell] regrets & likes Paris— She says this is her last visit to London—her daughters like Paris— by the bye do learn one thing for me without using my name—are the *Willats* not [in] Paris?— Lady Canterbury tells me that she heard that they had removed to Bath— I cannot help thinking that if they did leave Paris for Bath, they have not given up their house in the former place—& have returned or will return— Their house is 6 or 4 Rue Royale.

You are very good to say so many kind things about your stay here— I only wish I could have made your visit pleasanter—but your troublesome business—wintry weather & my secluded way of living made it anything but amusing I must hope it will be better another time— Poor Dina has lost her little girl—she died on the 28th April—of inflam[m]ation of the bowels I believe— she suffered a great deal so that death was a release— I see little of the family —there is always so much tittle tattle afloat, that it is best to keep aloof. The little boy is a very nice child—& Prudentia is vastly improved. She has grown now into a very nice looking child—having lost her contortions & affectations I fancy poor thing she suffered from *worms* which gave her the strange un- natural look she had—she looks thriving & pretty. I have not seen or heard any thing of Marianna, & have just written to her brother to ask how she is

[*The letter is incomplete*]

ORIGINAL: Huntington Library (HM 12146); A.L., 4 pp. 8vo (incomplete). Copy by Claire Clairmont, Berg Collection, the New York Public Library. Claire, rightly perhaps, makes the letter of May 23 a part of this letter. UNPRINTED and UNPUBLISHED. TEXT: From original letter.

599. *To Claire Clairmont**

[Putney] 17 May [1845]

My dear Claire—

I will send your pens & write to you on Monday or Tuesday— I write now to ask you whether you will go shares with me in an opera box— This opening will surprise you— I will explain. Lord Lonsdale has bought a 30 years lease of the opera house—& is selling some of the boxes— Mr. Sanford has bought one for £3500—which will lett for £300 a year at least or £350— I would buy one directly if I had the money (& could get one—that is if all are not already sold)—but if you will go shares with me this will cost you £1750—or if the price be raised as it may be to 3700—£1850 & you will get at least £150 a year. People concerned with the opera consider it so good a bargain that Mr. Sanford has been assured that he can 6 years hence sell it for what he gave for it— You must decide at once—& let me have yes or no by return of post—as you think Percy & me lucky—& as you know Mr. Sanford is a careful man about money I think you will say yes—& then I will let you know whether the purchase can be made—& for what—& then you can direct Mr. Ellis to sell out your long annuities to the amount—you only get 8½ percent for those & they last only 15 years—this will pay you 10 & last 30—I w[oul]d buy it myself had I the money—but have only £2000 to share But I must have an answer by return of post as Lord William Lennox[1] is to exert his influence about it—& I must give an answer *directly*— I would not ask you I did not thing [think] it good—as you may guess—

If you prefer you can sell your railway shares—but I advise the long an- nuities—& if you give absolute directions to Mr. Ellis, I do not doubt he can sell out—& at no loss—

[1]Lord William Pitt Lennox (1799–1881), miscellaneous writer. See *D.N.B.*

The boxes in the chief tier all let for £350 a year

Yours Afly

Mary Shelley

[P.S.] Mr. Sanford says it will be just the thing for you—as you want encome

ADDRESS: Mlle./ Mlle. Clairmont/ Rue Nᵉ Clichy— No. 3 bis/ Rue de Clichy/ à Paris. POSTMARK: JS/ 19 MY 19/ 1845. ORIGINAL: Huntington Library (HM 12144); A.L.S., 6 pp. 8vo, with envelope. UNPRINTED and UNPUBLISHED. TEXT: From original letter.

600. *To Claire Clairmont*

[Putney] May 23 [1845]

Your letter & consent dear Claire has come very unexpectedly—not having heard from you immediately I imagined that you declined—& now I feel uncertain— In fact Percy is against the investment—since the lease is for 30 years—& it will be sinking the money—

You know we have only £2500 at our disposal & this we have looked on as money to furnish a house.—There is a talk of our selling Castle Goring—if we did that we should have money in hand—but Percy now thinks of not selling it, but living in it—whether this is feasible on his income I dont know—but if [that] took place, it would not do to be drained of all ready money—as then furnish we must— This renders us uncertain— Percy is *against* the opera box for these reasons

Moreover probably it is too late now—no more in all likelihood are to be sold.

As to your buying the whole box yourself nearly 4000 sunk & lost after 30 years— I do not advise that—

I am very sorry to torment you about these uncertainties— I shall see the Sanfords tomorrow & hear more about it— Meanwhile I write that you may not take any step with Mr. Ellis till you hear from me again I am sorry you are worried—but these sort of worries form life—& all one can do is to steel oneself not to be worried— It is indeed a duty not [to] let the affairs of others—especially people one has no affection for annoy one.—

If you think of buying the whole opera box yourself, write at once to Mr. Sanford—but I do not at all advise that—& for us—we must consider—& Percy must know more what his plans are with regard to Castle Goring— As I said if we got a good offer for that & determined to sell—I would close about the box directly—but as it is I am afraid we cannot—

I will write again soon

Affly Ys

M S.

[P.S.] I am still for the box I confess—but Percy is against it—& the reasons given above make me hesitate—besides I like him to decide

ADDRESS: Mademoiselle/ Mlle. Clairmont/ Rue Nᵉ Clichy No. 3 bis/ Rue de
Clichy/ Paris. POSTMARK: 1/PAID/ 23 MY 23/ 1845. ORIGINAL: Huntington
Library (HM 12364); A.L.S., 4 pp. 8vo, with envelope. Copy by Claire Clair-
mont, Berg Collection, the New York Public Library. Claire makes this letter
the latter part of the letter of May 14, rightly perhaps. UNPRINTED and UNPUB-
LISHED. TEXT: From original letter.

601. *To Claire Clairmont**

[Putney] Saturday [error for Friday—May 23, 1845]

Dear Claire—

I sent off a letter to you just now—but wish to add a few words— You
may imagine the delicacy that makes me wish Percy to decide— He looks
forward to the lapse of 30 years— I do not—& therefore the benefit to me is
something—to him perhaps a loss— When I wrote first to you, I fancied he
liked it— As I said I do not advise your buying a whole box—still if you
choose to have two thirds—I think it w[oul]d not be imprudent for us to take
a third—when I say imprudent I am thinking of the inconvenience that may
result from parting with ready money if we have to furnish Castle Goring—
However I think it may be saving £200 which w[oul]d otherwise perhaps be
spent if we bought a 3ᵈ—

I am so sorry to have annoyed you by these troubles

I have just called on Lady D. Campbell—old Lady Dillon was there &
cut me—you may guess how gladly I shelter myself in solitude & Putney from
these pieces of impertinence—at Castle Goring certainly one would be out of
the way of all— Percy however is the person to please—

Affly Ys

M S.

ADDRESS: Mlle./ Mll./ Clairmont/ Rue Nᵉ Clichy— No. 3 bis/ Rue de Clichy/ à
Paris. POSTMARK: NW/ 23 MY 23/ 1845. ORIGINAL: Huntington Library (HM
12151); A.L.S., 4 pp. 8vo, with stamped envelope and seal. UNPRINTED and
UNPUBLISHED. TEXT: From original letter.

602. *To Claire Clairmont**

27 May [1845]

Dear Claire

I write from Mr. Sanfords It is possible that more must be given for the box
—£3600—or 3700—

You cannot count on its making more than £300 a year— I still think
you ought not to risk more than the 2 thirds & we will gladly take the 3ᵈ—
This will give us authority & interest to treat for you Mr. Sanford wants
particularly Sir Percy Shelley's name to be as the buyer, as he thinks he can
manage better the sale with L[or]d William Lennox— If L[or]d William
thinks he is obliging Sir Percy & if we have a 3ᵈ—that will do— You had
better wait till I hear the price agreed upon—& then write to Mr. Ellis to
realize the proper sum & place it at Percy['s] disposal—

Let me hear directly— If the theatre be burnt down it must be built up in a year—& you only lose the years income—but as accid[e]nts may happen any one year to diminish the worth I think you ought not to place so much of your income on it—

Whatever I hear I shall act on nothing till I get an explicit reply to THIS LETTER—write at once & say whether you like us to take a third If you do not —& choose the whole—I think you had better write direct to Mr. Sanford—

Mention whether you will go as high as £3700—

I write in haste & have no news

Ever ys
M S.

[P.S.] Mrs. and Mr. Sanford both think it most prudent for you only to take two thirds in case of any circumstances making the price of box[e]s fall— I should like to have one third.

> ADDRESS: Mademoiselle/ Mlle. de Clairmont/ Rue Ne Clichy No. 3 bis/ Rue de Clichy/ à Paris. POSTMARK: 27 MY 27/ 1845. ORIGINAL: Huntington Library (HM 12147); A.L.S., 4 pp. 8vo, with envelope. Copy by Claire Clairmont, Berg Collection, the New York Public Library. UNPRINTED and UNPUBLISHED. TEXT: From original letter.

603. *To Claire Clairmont*

[Putney] Friday [June, 1845]

Dearest Claire—

I wrote to Mr. Sanford on getting your letter to decline the opera box at the advanced price— I said you would give £4,000 for one on the grand tier— this was rather more than you said—but I thought you would go so far & might— I have had no answer—so that means that the negotiation is at an end The Sanfords have been spending the last week at Corsham.

Warm fine weather has come at last which I enjoy—& now am so glad to be out of town—for London is an oven— I hope the heat does not disagree with you— I am anxious to hear that you are taking care of yourself & reposing—the beginning & end of what will cure your maladies— What news of Natalie's marriage— I do not understand people of a certain age fuming & fretting after the past as you relate of your friends. While young & life stretches out before us long—long—all seems so momentous—so real—so desirable, so sensible but time makes life appear but a passing scene, & so that one does not do any thing to occasion one to reproach oneself while one tries to do good to others—it will so soon become a quoi bon fume & fret— I do not include in this Me K——'s anxious fears for her daughters welfare—*that* feeling must endure to the last & Me I.'s for her sons—but to regret for oneself when all is nearly over ne vaut pas la paine— God put us here—one is sorry one has not done better—but it is all over— To be sure one suffers from ennui sometimes if left too much alone—but vehement regrets & desires have faded away—& the calm of years is a comfortable port to reach at last. To do a little good—to watch over those dear—to enjoy quiet—& if one can be a little amused *voila tant*—after passion & youth are gone & life is pretty well over—

I have not been down into Sussex yet— I go at the end of this month or about the 1st of July— I hope this weather will last—but our English summer is not a stable thing like an Italian one and rain & cold may return I hope not— I shall not go down in bad weather—

I saw Jane the other day—the theme *al Solito* self laudation—& accusations of Henry— She cannot imagine one's being quite apart from all this & indifferent—so fancies that Percy & I occasion his being away from home & God knows what—it is very droll—when Henry is as much out of my horizon as Cape Horn can be—

Hammy came here the other day & I gave her your letter. She is looking very well—but bored of course— The people she is with are Irish but they are ultra English in being inanimate & dull—her pupils are very good but very slow—& amusement & animation are a thousand miles off— Laura is better & in better spirits—but poor Nerina is to be réliquée at San Marcello which wont suit her at all.

Percy's time is pretty well taken up with his yacht—he is to sail in her for the first time next Monday— My life is *very* quiet—& now warm weather is come I do not mind its solitude— Mrs. Paul is returned so I am not quite so lonely—she is very much better— Pray write to me & tell me how you are & what doing

Affly. Ys
M S.

[P.S., *at top of page 1*] Do let me hear about the Willats

[P.S., *at bottom of page 6, cancelled*] Put the enclosed in an envelope & in the petite poste

ORIGINAL: Huntington Library (HM 12357); A.L.S., 6 pp. 8vo. UNPRINTED and UNPUBLISHED. TEXT: From original letter.

604. *To Claire Clairmont*

[Putney] Monday [June, 1845]

My dear Claire—

I send you a letter I got on Saturday from Lord William [Lennox]— I replied that I would write to you & that the money would be forthcoming with regard to your having the whole box— I should have liked to have a 4th but do as you like—je n'y tiens greatly—& above all even if I had it, I should be obliged to ask you to pay the whole just now—as beleiving [*sic*] the whole thing at an end, I invested our money in railway shares—but not being in the luck you ascribe to me—& not having been treated quite well—they are fallen— I have no fear of ultimate loss, but we should lose considerably if we sold out just now. The enclosed came for you—seeing that it was a printed paper, I opened it, to judge whether it was necessary to forward it to you— I see it is the usual form (we have had the same) for asking for a power of attorney you must fill it up with Mr. Ellis's name the proper sum & the name of the stock to be sold out—& sign your name—as it is directed to you & send it—back, not to me—but simply turning it round the printed direction suffices. You say you will write to Gregson— You know how expensive he is —& in many respects tiresome—especially he w[oul]d be, I should think in an affair like this, out of his usual line of business—but he is safe. Another thing is that Lumley & Lord Lonsdale have not yet acquired a *title* to the Opera House— The affair has been for years in Chancery—& the *title* is not yet properly made out. However Mr. Sanford paid his money, secure that if the title were not made out it would be returned to him. He paid it last May & has been in possession of his opera box ever since—he sold it to Mitchel for the subscription nights for £180.—reserving the Thursdays for himself— But May & June are the best months for the opera— As soon as your money is paid you will have the box— I should judge at the lowest it would be worth during July £5 a night, 3 nights in the week—making £60 for the month——& then there are some more nights in August— You had better sell the whole at once to a library—Mitchell or some one else. At the beginning of the season it would be better I think to advertize it & get if possible a private purchaser— But for the end of the season, when people have all made their engagements— a library only would treat— It would certainly be more satisfactory if you would come over & manage things yourself—at any rate write without delay & take measures—for every days delay lessens the worth of your box for *this* year—

You understand the opera season is always divided into subscription nights —Tuesdays & Saturdays with about 4 Thursdays & you may pretty well count on £300 for those—& the extra nights & benefits—to which you, holding a property box, are also entitled—which Lumley makes as attractive as possible & are counted this season as being worth £80 additional.

I certainly should like you to come over about it— Write however to Gregson—& I would advise your asking Mr. Sanford to see Gregson to explain the grounds he went on in paying his money.

When I got your last note I wrote to Lord William copying your words that you w[oul]d give £4000 for box 23 on the grand tier.——If you had been here the whole thing w[oul]d have been done long ago—& you have had the box for this season—therefore if you could start & come & at once I should advise it.——My paper is full—I have only a tiny bit in which to say that giving a party for the Regatta, I invited Ada R—who is coming with her sister Mrs. G. W[ilhaman?] Adieu I am so sorry to hear you are ill— I fear the heat for you

Ever

M S.

ORIGINAL: Huntington Library (HM 12354); A.L.S., 4 pp. 8vo. Copy by Claire Clairmont, Berg Collection, the New York Public Library. UNPRINTED and UNPUBLISHED. TEXT: From original letter.

605. *To Claire Clairmont*

[Putney] 5 July [1845]

My dear Claire—

Gregson wrote to me asking to whom the money was to be paid—& I sent him Lord Williams' note—to Lord Lonsdale's banker. At the same time I wrote to Lord W. to say that you ought to have your box directly, that you might make a little money by it this year. I send you his answer—& he is in the right, though it is hard you should give your money before /46— I have heard no more from Gregson—but I trust all is going right—a line from you will make me attend to anything you want done directly.

My last letter was grumbling enough—it is foolish to grumble—but being minus nearly £1,000 in our rents is not pleasant— I suppose it will all come right in time—& one always hears that people never get rents regularly—but as we are obliged to pay the interest of our mortgages regularly we must suffer much annoyance— Percy's contented mind—his cheerfulness—his total absence of all repining is compensation to me for every evil—& heaven knows I only repine *for him*. To add to our embarassments I am afraid we shall have to pay Willats £4500[1]—or rather I feel sure that we shall—so poor we must look on ourselves—& people must not look up to us, as they do now in crowds, for help & support. Basta Percy is my comfort in all—any thing so unselfish, singleminded & noble I never met in my life—

Tomorrow he tries his yacht again— I will tell you more when he returns — I must get to see her— I should like much to go to Cowes when she is there—but it would cost too much—& Brett has been so shabby to me— Percy has a German music mistress—did I tell you?—recommended by the Novellos —so ugly & so clever he is getting on very nicely. Mrs. Hare will cross with her boys today I believe—the weather is perfect—so I hope she will have a fine passage— I am always in a fright after the measles, so warned her much not to begin on her journey—she is looking very well—she wanted me so much to return with her—but that is impossible. I have delayed my going into Sussex till Percy goes to Cowes—at the end of this month I hope to go—& then I shall pay the Shelleys a visit—& then—if such happiness be permitted, prepare to go abroad.

Miss Ada R—— called to take leave—& Colonel Pringle called too he seems a most good humoured agreable man—they will be back in Paris before this letter— I shall call today on Mrs. Wilhaman, with no hope of finding her pero, for every one must be out [on] so fine a day— Mrs. Paul is not so well again poor thing. I sent you Nina—& a novel of the Countess Hahn Hahn[2] by Miss R—— her best, I believe— I am reading another now that I do not like so well—Faustina is very clever—all about Clement is excellent—

---

[1] See Letter 632, note 2.
[2] Countess Ida Maria Hahn-Hahn, author of many books. Her novel *The Countess Faustina* was twice translated into English, and published in London in 1844 and 1845.

two things I think erroneous—one is bad management on the part of the authoress the other unnatural— She ought to have accounted better for the absence of Audlan— In the situation she describes, he w[oul]d have come back or sent for her—never have al[l]owed so long a separation—the unnatural thing is Faustina ever wishing to leave her child—a woman of that directness of feeling is always I think maternal but I like the book & it is clever—lend it to Knox when you have read it— Adieu—pray write— I hope you continue better; affectionately ys

M S.

ADDRESS: Miss Clairmont/ Rue Nᵉ Clichy 3 bis/ Rue de Clichy/ à Paris. POST-MARK: (1) P u t n e y—S O/　(2) N/ PAID/ 5 JY 5/ 1845. ORIGINAL: Hunt-ington Library (HM 12344); A.L.S., 4 pp. 8vo, with envelope and seal. Copy by Claire Clairmont, Berg Collection, the New York Public Library. UNPRINTED and UNPUBLISHED. TEXT: From original letter.

606. *To Claire Clairmont*

[Putney] Monday, 7 June [(*error for July*) 1845]

My dear Claire—

　Your letters are so amusing & clever that I thank you much for writing them—& am sorry that I send such stupid ones in return—but I never was a good letter writer & you always were— I have heard nothing more about your box—but as you are not to be put in possession till 46/ delay is of no consequence— I shall see (or Percy will) Gregson soon & make enquiries— Poor Emily[1]— I hope she is not very ill— She wrote some time ago asking me if she could pay us a visit—but rainy weather came on to prevent it—& now she writes she is too ill— One gets odd [? fancies] in this wicked world— but it is no business of mine— I would get to her but she does not ask me, & I fancy it might be indiscreet— What a terrible picture you give of Casa Kaisaroff— I own I have a terror of the French, & Galloni & Laura w[oul]d make me forgive a mother's most panic terror for a daughter, especially one so unprotected as poor Natalie by nature as well as relatives—but I cannot at all sympathize even with a mothers jealousy & pain at losing the first place in her child's heart—for there is nothing so foolish, so hurtful & unsympathetic as repining at a plain necessity—as well make scenes because one day one must die— The inevitable must be submitted to, & a person who cannot submit to a law of nature, however good in other respects, is to a certain degree insane, & insane in a manner that robs them of ones esteem. It w[oul]d indeed be well if people did not interfere so much—Rogers says—the world would go on much better if the old did not interfere so much with the young. De Romand I know nothing of—if I saw him I might see (or I imagine I saw) sincerity in his face & pity him—a bit of distrust will creep in as it is—but Natalie has all my pity   no situation can be so terrible so agonizing as hers—between a lover

---

[1] Widow of William Godwin, Jr.

& a parent— Running away is a thing people may do—*but* no one can ever advise it. To you this must be very painful.—

I suppose our income will come round & get right—but retrench we must— I cannot accuse myself of any extravagance except that we have given away more than we ought   This last year—I calculated as I was told, I might that we should each have £1200 a year—my [? house] was [?   ] so as to amount (houses, rent, & everything) to £1200 a year— Each contributing our quota we should each have £600 for other expences—but we cannot spend so much—we must as they say, get beforehand with the world— Paying Willats too will be another drag on our income. I am glad to hear that Knox is so happy—but I am very anxious about him—for he must help himself— I do not see that he is in the way so to do.

The Sanfords consider that Lady Sussex did not like to have the charge of Berkeley in Paris & so determined to take him away—she took places to go the day when he said he was to arrive—he did not come—but the places being taken she went   telling him to follow—but as he delayed, there was no time for him to go as far as Lucerne— As you say, would that Gatteschi redeemed himself by becoming independant & industrious— In all things a person must have a place to stand on—a little room & space or energy is of no avail—but this appears to be given him now—& it will give me the sincerest pleasure to know that he avails himself of it— I had an high opinion of the independance & uprightness of his character, which I shall be too delighted (after being forced to doubt) to find well founded— The Guiteras I fancy are most wretchedly off & Guitera has so lost his head that there is no help— Baloschi tells me that he has accepted a bill for 500 fr. fr[om ?] a man he knows nothing of— as Guitera had such a horror of bills & debt, this is very weak. Baloschi is consceited & dictatorial— I dont like him at all—he bores me—& I grow icy as he lays down the law, & turns up his nose at every thing he sees. Marianne says she does not remember the lace—so probably it is your own after all—however I shall not send it back—but make use of it.—Mrs. Hare had a most beautiful lace mantilla but it cost 250 fr.—which is too much for me— If I could get one her shape—but not so long I should think for me— not so expensive, I should be glad—but dont give yourself trouble— I hope the children will reach Paris well

I must tell you I am told that the Berry's have 12,000 a year I have heard nothing from her—but still cannot think that she can be so heartless to Mrs. Larkins even if she were so shabby to me.

                                                                        10 July

I hear nothing of your box—if you feel at all anxious I will call directly on Gregson.—Percy is not well—he has not felt the thing lately—& it has turned to a violent bilious attack, threatening jaundice—so now he is obliged to lay aside boating for some days & keep quiet— I hope he will all the more enjoy Cowes in a week or two— I have not seen Marianne a long time I asked her to come here but she could not—she is entirely disgusted with her mode of life & quite out of humour with things in general— Were I richer I would take her to Italy with me—but such pieces of agreable generosity are quite out of the question.

You will have seen Ada R—— —she is a nice frank agreable looking girl— but I have scarcely exchanged two words with her— I called again on her sister the other day— I dare say it is not rouge—but it is the prettiest softest carmine looking color in the world— She has a very fine spirited little boy— O when I think of the past & my Percy's childish days—so cramped by my poverty how I hate the Shelleys— Percy has set his heart now on going abroad —so I trust we shall—but it requires great present economy & shutting one's heart against those who really need one's assistance—but I must do *that*—for I have done far too much— Adieu—pray write often your letters are so very amusing—

Ys. affl.

M S.

ADDRESS: Miss Clairmont/ Rue Nᵉ Clichy No. 3 bis/ Rue de Clichy/ à Paris. POSTMARK: ANGL./ 12/ JUIL/ 45/ BOULOGNE. ORIGINAL: British Museum (T. J. Wise Collection); A.L.S., 8 pp. 8vo, with envelope. PRINTED: R. Glynn Grylls, *Claire Clairmont* (London, Murray, 1939), 197 (4 lines); otherwise unpublished. TEXT: From original letter.

607. *To Claire Clairmont*

[Putney] Thursday [July 17, 1845]

My dear Claire—

I called on the Sanfords yesterday—& asked him what he had done with regard to securing the purchase of the box He had done nothing, except paying his money into the hands of Lord Lonsdale's banker—not getting a receipt or any thing else except possession of his box— I saw Gregson & he said he had not liked to do the matter so—& he got a paper from Lumley promising to grant you a lease as soon as the title is secured in chancery— Gregson says that this paper is good in equity he keeps this paper to refer to when the lease is to be drawn out— You will have possession of your box in /46— A score of noble purchasers have paid their money & are placed exactly as you are—so that I do not doubt it will all go right—& I believe you will be able to make £400 by it next year at the lowest calculation it is £300 for the subscription & £80 for the extra nights—but next year you will get more than that. I should advise your advertizing it—& letting alternate weeks of the subscription to different parties & then seeing what best you can do with your extra nights— I am very sorry you have lost by your money transactions—prudence does not avail without knowledge—& it is amazing how difficult it is to get at other people's knowledge— With the idea [of] selling out again good railways was the best investment—but to learn which were good is impossible without patience & study & understanding what they all mean— Ellis did not act well by me in buying for me— The shares were fluctuating & he told me he would watch them   The prices varied from 104—to 106, 7, 8   I told him I would give 105—or 106—but not more—he bought them for 106—tho the day before & the day after they were 104   besides his buying cost me in commission 15 shillings more than my bankers—   I applied to him because my bankers would not give advice—but was no better off with him—my shares are in the Hull & Selby. I hope the opera box will set all your affairs right—ours will get right in a sort of way—but we must be economical because we have not £2,000 a year nor any thing like it—I am sorry to say—much more like £1500—& we must manage on that—   We go abroad I believe *pour sur* Percy wishes it as much as I do—   It is likely enough to be our last long absence—for when we have a house we shall not be able so readily to get away — Percy is much better—he had no fever & was not out of spirits—but was very obedient to his doctor & kept quiet   Next Monday we go into Sussex—& the Polka goes to Cowes & Percy will join her there Monday week. It was very sad he could not go to see the sailing of the experimental squadron on Tuesday—but he could not.

Mr. Sanford tells me that Lady Sussex has been seen in London   She wrote as I told you to Berkeley to meet her at Lucerne—he did not—but on his return to London got another from her saying she w[oul]d be at Ostend & telling him to come there—but he did not go—today he goes to join his regiment in Ireland. —— I have been reading another translation of Faustus, a better one—& wonder you read it in English at all—for translations are always bad—   The one I sent you is very inelegant—   I have another of the Countess von Hahn Hahn & will send it you by Natalie if she comes—   I am glad they are to be married at last & if after marriage Mme K. is cross, it will result from temper & selfishness—joined to a total want of common sense—dont think of buying me a lace cloak—unless you happened to pounce on a wonderful bargain. I have no more news—our weather is bad & I have suffered lately in my head a good deal—

Ys

M S.

[P.S.] I dont grudge paying for your letters however long but I do paying for the thick half sheet of blank paper in which you wrap them—your last letters have been very heavy & *dear*

ADDRESS: Madlle./ Mlle. Clairmont/ Rue N^e Clichy No. 3 bis/ Rue de Clichy/ à Paris. POSTMARKS: (1) T. P./ P u t n e y   (2) 17 JY 17/ 1845. ORIGINAL: Huntington Library (HM 12145); A.L.S., 4 pp. 8vo, with envelope and seal. Copy by Claire Clairmont, Berg Collection, the New York Public Library. UN-PRINTED and UNPUBLISHED. TEXT: From original letter.

608. *To Claire Clairmont**

Putney
5 August [1845]

My dear Claire—

I was beginning to wonder at your silence & going to write to you—   I

congratulate you on your brothers[1] arrival—it must be a great pleasure to you
— Say everything that is kind to him from me—& how glad I shall be to see
him here— I wish I had a room to offer him—but I can get him one at Avis's
— Pray let me know the exact date when he comes— The very bad weather
has prevented my going to Balcombe—& I *must* go this week or next (it depends on the weather)—but I cannot possibly avoid it— I shall only be away
however two days— I do not know what plans Charles has in coming to
England—does he mean to go to see the Hodgetts? if he does he can go while
I am at Balcombe & thus I should not lose any of his society. I w[oul]d put
off going but from a concatenation of circumstances I *must* go at the time I
mention. Percy & I go to Elcott[2] on the 20th (tomorrow fortnight) for a week
—after that I shall be quiet here, during the rest of my time as [at] this house
(11 Sep.). Percy must run up from Cowes to see Charles. He is now there
with Aubrey Paul. The weather is very much against their enjoying themselves—so stormy & rainy—he says his boat is a capital one in a storm—so steady
& serviceable. It is not a racing boat—& has no dazzling qualities— I have
not been on board—for it was painting while here. I should like to go to Cowes
—but cannot afford it— Our affairs are just the same—the only difference
being that we see clearer into them & have made up our minds to the very
limited income we have—it will mend by & bye—& at present we must use
every economy. I am retrenching all I can— I have dismissed Edwin—never
go to the opera—see no company— Percy has set his heart on going to Naples
—so, I believe we go—on our return I shall settle in Sussex—unless indeed
Percy goes into parliament—in which case I shall only have a pied à terre on
our estate (that we must have) & take a small house in town. This uncertainty
—& the uncertainty also about our selling Castle Goring, makes our going
abroad prudent—as we must defer a little our plans for settling We did very
wisely in remaining here so that tho' this year has been expensive to us, we
have done nothing that we could avoid—& can retrench at a moments notice—
as I am doing.

Knox is coming back— I am very uncomfortable about him—& see not
what the future will be for him

I congratulate you on Natalie's marriage— I hope Me Kaisaroff will find
that instead of losing her daughter—she has gained a son— If de Romand
has conduct & common sense—& she has the latter also—she will find that a
man in the family is a great advantage & encreases the comfort—& above all
expels a great many annoyances

I shall be delighted to see you my dear Claire, though as you say it will
only be for a moment Percy does not like Paris & will be in a great hurry to
get away. However we shall not be long in the South—& when we are settled
—& you have your opera box to look after— I look forward in future to our

---

1 Charles Clairmont, who was living in Vienna.
2 Evidently the home of Lady Shelley and her daughters after they left Field Place.

seeing much more of each other & I assure you the anticipation affords me great pleasure You do not mention your health so I hope you are pretty well —& with health you will no longer suffer so keenly from those annoyances which latterly have poisoned your peace—

The Sanfords are much tormented by Lord & Lady Methuen's conduct— they want to turn their son out of Corsham. Unfortunately Mr. Bailey being Mr. S's friend & Lord M's also—Mr. Sanford, in his joy at the match, trusted much of the future to spoken instead of written words, & the stay at Corsham was not put in the settlements.— The fact seems to be that Lady Methuen is pursued by envy—& always disliked her son—& delights in injuring him & worrying him while L[or]d M—— is pretty well doting & does not know what he says or does. Horatia remains to be confined at Corsham—because she is afraid that if she left it, she w[oul]d never return— L[or]d M—— writes to say that after her confinement they must go, as he means to occupy it himself which is nonsense; he has not lived there these 9 years & Lady M is in such bad health that she is carried up & down stairs & is always on the sopha —in fact the probability is that she can never recover—& will not last very long. Mr. Methuen is much annoyed—& Horatia frets at the idea of leaving Corsham. As a bystander I cannot help feeling that life is *herissée des peines* and it is far better that Methuen & Horatia should have one in common—than that he should get disatisfied with her, or quarrel with the Sanfords. The Sanfords are reconciled to their not coming to town now that they fear that if they did they could not return. Mr. Bailey does what he can to smooth matters but Lady M's mischief making and L[or]d M's irritability & folly render his task difficult.—

Our summer is indeed detestable— I dont remember such continued rain since 1816—& if it goes on the harvest is spoiled—& what will be the result heaven only knows—*our* prospects will not brighten in a scarcity.

Again pray let me have a line before Charles's arrival & let me know his plans. Give him my love

Affly. Ys

M S.

ADDRESS: Mlle./ Mlle. Clairmont/ Rue Nᵉ Clichy No. 3 bis/ Rue de Clichy/ à Paris. POSTMARK: VH/ [5] AU 5/ [18]45. ENDORSED: [*On back of envelope*] Says she is very uncomfortable about Knox. ORIGINAL: Huntington Library (HM 12161); A.L.S., 7 pp. 8vo, with envelope and seal. Copy by Claire Clairmont, Berg Collection, the New York Public Library. UNPRINTED and UNPUBLISHED. TEXT: From original letter.

609. *To Claire Clairmont*

Putney—Tuesday [August 12, 1845]

Dearest Claire—

I am truly sorry that Charles does not come—yet as his time is so short

I allow it would have been scarcely worthwhile— I wish he could have contrived to have given us some time— As it is I will hope that he will come some other time at [&] that we shall meet in my house & pass a few pleasant weeks together. Your expressions towards me are very flattering—dear Claire — I have been pursued all my life by lowness of spirits which superinduces a certain irritability which often spoils me as a companion— I lament it & feel it & know it—but that does not suffice— To be as I ought to be towards others (for very often this lowness does not disturb my inward tranquillity) I need to be a little tipsy—this is a sad confession but a true one;—any thing of emotion that quickens the flow of my blood makes me not so much a happier as a better person. I wish I were made otherwise—but so alas it is—& I hate & despise myself for it—without being able to bring a remedy.—

I am grieved you do not get the papers so regularly—they now go to Percy —however I will cheat him today & send it to you instead. Buying & selling in Railroads is an art & requires an apprenticeship. You must study the prices —trust to no broker & give orders yourself— You must always say to your broker buy or sell when the shares are at such a price—never leave it to him When you bought shares unfortunately railways were screwed up to their highest— Will you tell me what yours are in; for I have a friend who (tho now drawing in) has trafficked a good deal & will tell me what to think of your lines & whether it is better to change into others—at any rate I will get you good information as to your shares—& you can judge—there are some from which you can get 4½ percent & these are the best to choose as a steady investment—they may rise or fall, but when once you have bought they will not diminish as to the percentage you get—

Poor Knox—would that your view of his position were the true one!— If really he will have courage & resolution & industry I trust with his talents he will do well—but as yet these have failed him—but he writes now in a good tone & I hope it will go on.— He might have secured a real friend in Percy, but young people are not apt to make allowances—and he at one time behaved ill—& at no time acted well towards Percy—

Rubio from what I saw I should think can never succeed—as you say his works are stamped with mediocrity— I can not think that Mrs. B——forgets or ceases to grieve bitterly for Oswald—but I do not like to think of them— If they committed one act I must always dislike & disapprove of them—I mean if they talked of your private history to Miss K——

[*Written under the envelope flap*] I have heard nothing of Mr. Bouboukine.— Percy is still at Cowes—his boat is quite a failure & is a very great pecuniary loss—he wants to sell it if he only gets half what he gave I shall think him lucky—but he will not—that is certain. This pains me particularly now— that besides many calls, I should so like to shew myself generous— You have not the money now but I wish you could give Charles £10 out of the £50 you owe me—perhaps you can by & bye— If you do, give it him with every affec-

tionate expression of regard from me—or buy some presents that will please
Tom & the girls[1] with it   Adieu—

Ys Affly

M S

[P.S.] Mrs. Sanford says you must send her stays by the first opportunity
she must wait for them.[2] Lady Sussex is gone to Sandgate.

> ADDRESS: Mademoiselle/ Mlle. de Clairmont/ Rue Nᵉ Clichy—3 bis/ Rue de
> Clichy/ à Paris. POSTMARKS: (1) STRAND   (2) T/ PAID/ 12 AU 12/ 1845.
> ENDORSED: [*On back of the envelope*] says Knox acted ill towards Percy.
> ORIGINAL: Huntington Library (HM 12167); A.L.S., 4 pp. 8vo, with envelope.
> PRINTED: Dowden, II, 355 (quot., 8 lines), otherwise unpublished. TEXT: From
> original letter.

610. *To [Alexander Andrew Knox]*

[Putney, ? September, 1845]

My dear Friend—

Putting the thing into the hands of you and your legal adviser—I shall of
course be guided by you.[3]

Certainly it looks as if they would make no great use of my letters—but
who can tell? They were written with an open heart—& contain details with
regard [to] my past history, which it wd destroy me for ever if they saw light
—possibly even if left to themselves they never may.

I suppose M Delessert objects to acting unless you are well recommended—
but I feel very doubtful of getting the letter from Trelawney—he is in Devonshire I write to him by today's post & will get the procuration—yet if my name
is not to be used—wherefore?—   Indeed I feel puzzled—but I put myself in
yours & M. Peronne's hands—only keep my name secret I conjure you.

I do not understand what you mean by my leaving Putney. Since you have
decided to act in this way—I shall certainly open no more of his letters, but
forward them to you—but if I left Putney the letters wd be forwarded—you
say *dont start without consultation*— consultation with whom? I have no
human being to speak to—   You fear perhaps his coming over he has no
money for such a trip. However as soon as I have got Trelawney's answer
—& got the procuration I think I will go—   In one way I dont think Claire's
notion of my coming boldly to Paris a bad one—only it costs money—& might
cause me to be talked of. I think therefore I shall take a trip as soon as I get
your answer to this—explaining what you mean by *consultation*. —I will calm
myself—the feeling that I shall open no more of his letters nor answer any
is very calming

[1] Charles Clairmont's children.
[2] The various notes made by Claire on the back of the envelope show that she took care of
Mrs. Sandford's request and did other shopping at the same time.
[3] This and the following letters deal with Gatteschi's attempt to blackmail Mary and with
Mary's successful efforts, through Knox and Delessert (the prefect of the Paris police), to repossess
the letters she had written Gatteschi. See Letter 554, note 1.

I think with Claire that his debts are not much—except a quantity of trifling to trades people but he wants the means of subsistence—& could not come over here I guess—　However I shall go when I get an answer to this—perhaps before—but when you tell me to do a thing let me have an [? inkling] *way*—or I hesitate　Especially when you add dont start without consultation—　My idea is running with Percy to Broadstairs where Mr. Rogers is—to stay a few days　or more as I may like—

I think my plan as detailed wd succeed—but I leave it to you—　You speak dreadful things of G[atteschi]—that he is a villain & only wants money of *course*—but do you know that his acts are so infamous as you say?

I am better in my head—my general health is suffering somewhat from the past suffering but not having to read any more nefarious letters or to write to him quiets me much—　Dont forget to have the portrait sent back—just done up & directed & sent without a word

M. Delessert & no Frenchman ought to see what he has written about expected commotion in Italy—　It is a falsehood of course—but one's conscience must be clear of any betrayal of that sort—

It is all very dreadful—but being out of my hands, I will do my best not to think of it—　Only as my name is not to be mentioned I do not see the use of the procuration—but you shall have it.

How kind—how more than kind you are—　Heaven bless you—dont wrong yourself too much—　I will take it all quietly now—　I was reading the other day—the worst part of any evil is the fear of it—& fear too[k] so violent a possession of me—but I am better [*letter incomplete*]

ORIGINAL: Huntington Library (HM 12348); A.L., 8 pp. 8vo (incomplete).
UNPRINTED and UNPUBLISHED. TEXT: From original letter.

611. *To Claire Clairmont*

[Putney] Monday [September 15, 1845]

My dearest Claire—

I will only write a few words—for I am too agitated—　I am indeed humbled—& feel all my vanity & folly & pride—my credulity I can forgive in myself but not my want of common sense—& worse—my self reproaches are indeed keen—　If my folly causes you annoyance in Paris—will you come to me　my heart & house are open to you—

The blow was so terrible—for yours—my childs my name's sake—& in truth because to feel one has come in contact with a villain—& from the bitterness of my self reproaches—that my reason almost gave way—never did poor wretch about to be tried for murder suffer more but I will take courage & calm myself—& collect my thoughts

Your views in many things are just—　A good appearance is G[atteschi]'s desire above all—& for this he insults & abuses me that he may preserve a good appearance of being wronged—& revenge is justifiable to an Italian. It w[oul]d

ruin me forever in every point of view for Knox to come into personal contact
with him—no one must do that but a lawyer—in short your quotation about
Talleyrand is excellent. I also do think that he still gets money from Lady
Sussex or he w[oul]d not be so patient—but she does not meddle in this plot
to extort money—& as to my marrying him—why he would not thus insult
me if he thought of that now. ——I cannot fathom his designs—it may be
only that he is waiting to threaten again through Guitera & get more money
for he manages himself never to ask or even to hint at getting any. Enough—
only pray my Knox to precipitate nothing—to do only what is most prudent—
most well advised— I shall be calmer after this.

My own Percy is quite well—he was at Balcombe all last week with Fergusson—& is gone today again with Med— I want much to leave this house—
but our plan of going abroad being I fear upset all is uncertain. I say, I fear—
for tho' I should be well content to stay in my own country among my own
people—I do not well see how Percy can spend the winter to so much advantage as in joining in the gaieties of a foreign city—

God bless you dearest Claire

Evr Ys

[*Unsigned*]

[P.S.] Dont think of going to Martini—it is better to do nothing—than to
shew fear & fail— As you say no money must be *offered*— Knox must not
get it talked of among the English—my name get wind at least—the English
are the people to avoid.

> ADDRESS: Mademoiselle/ Mlle. Clairmont/ Rue des Maronniers No. 8/ Passy
> à Paris. POSTMARK: PAID/ 15 SE 15/ 1845. ENDORSED: [*On envelope, under
> seal*] She calls Mr. Knox my Knox. ORIGINAL: Huntington Library (HM
> 12335); A.L. (unsigned), 4 pp. 8vo, with envelope and seal. UNPRINTED and
> UNPUBLISHED. TEXT: From original letter.

612. *To Claire Clairmont*

Broadstairs
Wednesday [October 1, 1845]

Dearest Claire

I just write a line to say that I write by this post— There is no such luck
as that all should be over & Knox have left Paris—but were it so you w[oul]d
call for my letter at his lodgings—it contains one from G[atteschi] which I
have not opened It could [do] no good my reading it, & might drive me
crazy. Another thing, dear Claire, Knox lays great stress on getting a letter
from L[or]d Brougham & Trelawny has written such a letter to Leader that
I think he will get it—but Knox has a feeling of dignity which makes him
hang back—he has left his card on Leader—& L. has taken no notice & a
million to one never will. I would not on any account that Knox should do
anything to lower him in any one's eyes—but Leader is so accustomed to be
acted for—& never to put out a little finger—that Knox will never get the letter

unless he sees Leader—this T[relawny] declares—has nothing to do with presumption or pride but simply from indolence & pray if necessary speak so to Knox as to shew that he will not do an unbecoming or lowering thing by calling & seeing Leader.

Knox says he is justified by facts he has discovered in saying the horrible things he does of G[atteschi]—at my worst I always thanked God that your present happy pupil did not get entangled with him & I should be glad indeed to find that Lady S[ussex] had escaped out of his hands—under these circumstances I do not feel enclined to give him another franc— O what an easy dupe I have been—& worse—but never mind. Knox seems haunted with the fear that he may have secreted elsewhere my letters I do not think this likely —& even if in the letter I send he should intimate that he had made some use of my letters & they were no longer in his hands I should not believe him (all the less for his saying so—) & search for them all the same—

Dear Claire I am odiously selfish & never speak of your affairs & of your brother & your having a niece with you— I will write about this another time — I now write in a hurry—just leaving Broadstairs for Tunbridge Wells—a fine day for a wonder—& very welcome I hope you continue better I am so glad you are with your kind friends— Be kind to dear good Knox

Affectionately ys
M S.

ADDRESS: Madlle./ Mlle. Clairmont/ Rue des Maronniers No. 8/ Passy [*Redirected to*] Paris. POSTMARKS: (1) BROADSTAIRS   (2) RAMSGATE/ OC 1/ 1845. ORIGINAL: Huntington Library (HM 12178); A.L.S., 4 pp. 8vo, with seal. UNPRINTED and UNPUBLISHED. TEXT: From original letter.

613. *To Claire Clairmont*

[Brighton] Wednesday [October 8, 1845]

I wrote you a wild letter yesterday, dear Claire full of impossibilities—yet so it is—my brain is so weak, that when a thought touches it, it absorbes it & deprives me of my reason. But I have no right to worry you—you who have ever shewn me so much kindness & whom I have so ill requited throughout. Forgive me—I see now—all—all I see of injury I have done of pride & folly. My heart is burthened with anguish—at my age too—& all this will add years instead of days to my life. Yet I meant no ill—I thought I was doing so kind so good an action—comforting an angel—till I found he was not one—but still I would have succoured & befriended him—but he would not—till his affair with Lady S[ussex] alienated me from him entirely. Still I wish him good not evil— I do not wish him to be injured & insulted—though my fears with regard to my letters—when excited renders all justifiable Even after his threats I wrote to him kindly, but he answered by new threats & insults.—

If I were alone I would creep away somewhere & get over the days as I might till some light dawned on the storm—but my child—my adored—for whom I alone would live—& so I always told him. We are not so rich as he thinks & this year I have lived in so retired & economical a manner tho' that has not helped us much— Were Percy going about & amusing himself I could manage better—but his life is centred in home—he sees a change in me —he says—I look so subdued— I attribute it to my health, but this cannot last. I cannot bear seeing any one— I feel as if soon they will be pointing at me. The only thing that quiets me is a friendly voice to speak comfort—but that have I not near me— I do not wish him to be injured— I wish I knew what would be right—to take him from debt is nothing unless one placed him in a position to earn money—& could awaken that which once I thought his peculiar & glorious characteristic—independance of mind. Forgive me, dear Claire, that I unburthen myself to you—but Knox has spoken to you— Knox in his zeal, in his contempt for my enemy, does not perhaps make necessary allowances—& you as a woman may calm him—

The weather is dreadful—this is the third day of perpetual rain—it will do more injury to the farmer than any thing— You have heard that Horatia has a boy a little Hercules, they say—& she behaved so well in all— Mrs. Paul is in Cumberland at her sister's–Lady Vane— I must be away ere she return—for I could not see her as I am—there is that in innocence——but no more of this—but when I think what I ought to be to my darling child & how the poisoned arrow may reach him thro' me—remorse & terror possess me

Dear Claire farewell all seem happy except myself—but I have no right to complain— I might be in heaven—& have placed myself in a torture of my own making— I accuse only myself—but I heartily pray for release.

God bless you—

It is most true Lady S[ussex] L[ennox] is (or was lately) at Boulogne—if G[atteschi] is there or they are friends, I can understand not hearing now—as he is getting money from her. Knox might learn whether he is at Boulogne— or has been there. He must not try to corrupt Carlo Romano—he is a carbonaro —& sworn to obedience but a spy in the enemies' camp were much—he might call on Martini & hear something but I leave that to him. I will write tomorrow to Knox— If G[atteschi] is away he had better come back—& I wait for a new attack oimè—but he must leave *pour sur*

[Unsigned]

ADDRESS: Miss Clairmont/ Rue des Maronniers No. 8/ Passy. ENDORSED: [*On page 4*] She confesses her remorse and how ill she has requited my kindness. ORIGINAL: Huntington Library (HM 12333); A.L. (unsigned), 4 pp. 8vo. Copy by Claire Clairmont, Berg Collection, the New York Public Library. TEXT: From original letter.

614. *To Claire Clairmont*

Brighton—Thursday [October 9, 1845]

I wrote to you yesterday, dearest Claire directed to Passy—& sent an Examiner also send for them How I pity you worried by your two foolish

friends—& they in real & excessive danger—but dont go to Lady S[ussex].
You could do her no good—your being there w[oul]d encrease her danger—
She must get some man to help her, & be under the protection of some man—
You do not know G[atteschi]—see his hideous letters—& how they act like
poison—if I read them I should go mad again— I am only saved by sending
them unread to dear Knox—but poor Lady S[ussex] irritable alone terrified
—I feel for her—but you could do her no good—fear is the only thing that can
act on him— Lord S[ussex] took the right way—would he could take it
again for it is only thus he can be treated—do not for gods sake go to her—
you would be killed—his vile letters must make her wild with horror &
terror— He is an Italian & would stab either of us willingly—but without
us he has no money & cannot stir a step—remember that tho' his vast debts
are fictitious his daily wants & trifling debts are not & when a man has *nothing*
this becomes horrible—no money at all is worse a great deal—far more apalling
than a little money & large debt—dont think I pity him or w[oul]d help him—
by threatening Lady S[ussex] (whom he has entirely drained & who acted by
him with far more generosity than myself) he has quite hardened me—but we
must not forget that he is vindictive unprincipled, & when desperate will stick
at nothing he *can* do. Dear Knox fears the prefêt will not do as we wish—if
threatening letters will induce him I have little doubt I shall get enough of
those soon—but I fear this will not succeed—to buy the letters from G[atteschi]
will be our last necessary resort & I think this can be done at no enormous
sacrifice by shewing courage—taking very little notice about them but shewing
some pity for his situation—but saying that I cannot shew that pity nor help
him till my letters are given up— All this Knox must think over— Getting
no money from Lady S[ussex] he is now becoming desperate, & weak as he
is from position the weakest turning to bay are mischievous. Dear Knox must
act with consummate prudence & keep strict watch over him. I wish Lady
S. could be told to write to the Prefêt enclosing a threatening letter & throwing
herself on his protection—or get the English Consul at Boulogne to do it for
her— She is in France & under the protection of French laws—& I think if
M. Delessert found what the wretch was doing on all sides he would put a
summary stop to the whole—but my detestable letters must be got in the first
place or he will do me a harm with them be sure

Let me implore you to follow your doctor's advice When we are settled
come over to us— I dont understand a Maison de Santé—but do keep at
peace—they wont touch you they want money to extort that they will do
any thing—but from you they will not hope it.

God bless you dear Claire pray take care of yourself & dont be induced
to go to Lady S[ussex]. Your advice to her was excellent

[Unsigned]

ADDRESS: Miss Clairmont/ Rue Neuve Clichy No. 3 bis/ Rue de Clichy/ Paris.
POSTMARKS: (1) BRIGHTON/ [9 OC] 9/ [18]45 (2) 11/ OCT/ 45/

BOULOGNE. ENDORSED: [*On back of envelope*]. Describing Gatteschi's character. ORIGINAL: Huntington Library (HM 12367); A.L. (unsigned), 5 pp. 8vo, with envelope and seal. UNPRINTED and UNPUBLISHED. TEXT: From original letter.

615. *To Claire Clairmont**

Brighton   Sunday [October 12, 1845]

Dearest Claire—

Knox writes as if he *may* have left Paris before this gets there— God grant indeed that he may have left it—for then all will be well—but I dare not hope so much good—so I write, & if he be still in Paris put my letter into the *petite poste* if he be gone—put it into the fire. I say no more on this odious subject, for at this critical minute what can I say? You & Knox will take counsel together in my behalf if the *requisition* is refused—but I shall so deeply grieve that Knox should be further worried on my stupid account—yet——but——I leave it to you & him—& I know you will not leave me aground tho' I deserve it. —I shall leave this place next Thursday— I am sorry to go—& would stay longer but—there is ever a but— The Smiths are very kind & civil—& have a pretty nice little daughter[1] about Percy's age—they sing—they dance & are merry— Percy has lately so shut himself out from all girls society that this could not go on for any time without his falling in love—if he did so, she is a good little thing—& I could not oppose it—but I cannot *wish* the match—& above all not throw them thus together, so as almost to take his freedom of choice from him—so I shall go back to Putney—for which I grieve —as Brighton agrees with me & I like it— When in London I must get other girls about me—& then his heart will not be so tindery— I shudder when I contemplate London—but it cant be helped— This is a most lovely day— You must regret Passy.

I dont see how Lady S[ussex] can be helped—the only good advice is for her [to] leave France—never write to him & do nothing—& he will prove innocuous to her—as I trust he will to me when once my letters are safe out of his hands

I can feel for her distress of mind—for without a friend to whom to apply one feels in the hands of a villain & that ruin must ensue— It is so difficult to advise her—that I do not see how you can help her— Adieu, dear Claire— I confess I do not hope the blessed end for which Knox has laboured will so readily be attained so a failure will not depress me so much—only it will be difficult to know what to do next

Aff ys

M

ADDRESS: Madlle./ Mlle. Clairmont/ Rue Ne Clichy No. 3, bis/ Rue de Clichy/ Paris. POSTMARKS: (1) BRIGHTON/ OC 12/ 1845   (2) Z/PAID/ 13 OC 13/ 1845. ENDORSED: [*The endorsement, though appearing on this letter, seems to have been meant for the next letter, of October 13.*] Written upon receiving the news that Knox had got a promise from M. Delessert the Prefet of Police at

[1] Horace Smith's daughter Rosalind, born April 6, 1821.

Paris, that he would seize all Gatteschi's Papers, bring them to the Prefecture, and that Knox should take from them all Mrs. Shelley's letters to Gatteschi and return them to her. ORIGINAL: Huntington Library (HM 12172); A.L.S., 2 pp. 4to, with seal. UNPRINTED and UNPUBLISHED. TEXT: From original letter.

616. *To Claire Clairmont*

Brighton, Monday [October 13, 1845]

My dearest Claire—

Is not Knox a darling— I never expected after all that he would succeed in this way. How clever—how more than clever he is— Even now I can scarce believe that all is well—my letters my stupid nonsensical letters really rescued from such villainous hands— I still almost fear—& yet if they are not to be found among his papers I shall think them already destroyed— I write to K[nox] but fancy he may have quitted Paris before this reaches it and [in] which case throw the letter into the fire—

And now dear Claire if you fear or are annoyed by this shocking person come over & I will try to compensate to you for all you have suffered of anxiety on my account.

It is an awful power this seizure—& but for the villainy one would shrink from having put it into exercise but it never was better employed to defeat villainy & save one whose only aim & thought was benefit & kindness— Poor Lady S—— I pity her—but could she do as I have done & be wholly silent—all would go well with her— I will write again more at length in a day or two— I can never do enough for Knox to reward him for his kindness & shew my gratitude & I thank you also for your sympathy & great kindness I shall never forget it.

[*Unsigned*]

[P.S., *Monday Night*] After all I will not write to Knox for this will not reach Paris till Thursday & then he will surely be gone How happy he must be to have succeeded yet his trouble, his anxiety, his labour have all been so great he is indeed an angel

I think we shall leave this place on Thursday—for Putney tho I begin to think Percy's heart not in so much danger—but still I think we shall go— Fine weather has begun I fancy— We went to the theatre here tonight with two daughters of H[orace] Smith & in the box next us were Mr. and Mrs. John Shelley—he is nice looking & young looking—but took no notice of me—

I will write again I wish Knox w[oul]d arrive before we leave it

[P. P. S. *on inside flap of envelope*] Wednesday [*error for Tuesday*] I have just got Knox's other letter—poor Lady S—how advise & comfort her? it is difficult without betraying a fact that must not be whispered to the winds—if only she stopt short & never wrote again—

Poor wretch—he might have contrived a respectable livelihood thro' us—but I cannot help thanking God he did not marry Natalie—he w[oul]d have spent her fortune, broken her & her mother's heart by infamous usage & cruel conduct & you would have been miserable.

ADDRESS: Madlle/ Mlle Clairmont/ Rue Nᵉ Clichy No. 3 bis/ Rue de Clichy/ Paris. POSTMARKS: (1) BRIGHTON/ OC 14/ 1845 (2) London/ OC 14 (3) BOULOGNE/ OC 16. [ENDORSED: See endorsement of the October 12 letter.] ORIGINAL: British Museum (T. J. Wise Collection); A.L. (unsigned), 4 pp. 8vo, with wrong envelope; and Huntington Library (HM 12352), 2 pp. 8vo (with envelope), a postscript to the Wise portion of the letter. UNPRINTED and UNPUBLISHED. TEXT: From original letter.

617. *To Claire Clairmont*

Brighton　Tuesday Evg. [October 14, 1845]

My dear Claire—

Is it not all wonderful? Knox's firm & admirable conduct—his success—the authorities consenting to so desperate a step—all—all is wonderful—& the more I hear the more I admire & am grateful—tho' too humiliated by the part I played, & by being the cause of so much disagreable labour to exult. Poor Lady S[ussex] what can become of her! poor poor thing—what a situation —he cannot hurt her but who will help her? for she is such an enemy to herself—how much she must now be enduring What a monster it is— His conduct to her is so a thousand times worse than all. How did he make the acquaintance of Lady M Germains? And how idiotic has been his conduct; but lying & driving to desperation those whose services he wanted—& falling into utter ruin— It is dreadful to think that such a wretched being exists. It is strange—how strange the whole thing next to the immeasurable comfort of getting out of such nefarious hands. I rejoice for Knox's own sake that he succeeded—poor fellow worrying himself about my money &c—certainly I regret the large sums spent on so worthless an object—for I would so much prefer that [they] were spent so as to benefit the deserving—but in escaping from such snares one cannot count pence I do not write to Knox because I imagine he will have left Paris—if not tell him what I say— How glad I shall be to see him—what a change in me— I was nearly out of my mind when he went.

We leave this place on Thursday— I dont think now Percy's heart in danger but he wants to be occupied & following up his plans—the weather is warm & fine. The sea beautiful & so healthy—but we must go—& I am not in the humour to repine at anything just now

Martini too ruined! What can be the end of all this? & he might have been respectable surrounded by friends—& even with this tie between him & Lady S— he might always have been above want—but he could not be satisfied— You may imagine that as yet every new account sent by Knox fills me with surprize & conjecture— I shall be glad to hear from you— I sincerely hope you will not be worried—if you are, you must come over, till the storm passes —for your sake it were better he were conducted to the frontier—& really when a man thus turns to stab with poisoned daggers those who desired & exerted themselves to benefit him, pity is a sin—besides he will not be worse off in one place than another   he must fall into ruin on all sides—for he brings ruin on himself by his crimes—poor Lady S[ussex]—   She indeed I do pity—I run on dear Claire saying nothing to the purpose—but can not compose my thoughts it is all so strange—but after a time his affairs will run in a new channel & he will forget the wild dreams awakened by foolish kindness—& sink far below our level—   Meanwhile if you are annoyed or frightened come over would I could say to my house—but you know I have no room—still if you can come we could get a room near—& you could have the little room next my bedroom to sit in—at any rate you would be among us all—goodnight—   Percy is gone to a ball tonight   I am afraid it will be stupid—he sadly wants to marry—I wish I could find a wife for him meanwhile *occupation* is the best thing—he feels this & wishes to occupy himself—he is so *right-minded*—he ought to be happy—if he gets a tolerably good wife he will be—   God grant that he find such a one

Nothing can be so ridiculous as the newspapers—the *bubble* of the day is to project railroads—not a quarter of the number (not a tenth) can be executed. Meanwhile they are the subject of gambling & will be the ruin of thousands—for no one but a person versed in the science & on the spot can do other than *lose*—the papers meanwhile publish 3 & 4 *sheets* of advertisements about them & this brings in a large sum to *them* & to the revenue—

[Unsigned]

ADDRESS: Madlle./ Mlle. Clairmont/ Rue Nᵉ Clichy No. 3 bis/ R[u]e de Clichy Paris. POSTMARKS: (1) BRIGHTON/ OC 15/ 1845   (2) P[AID]/ 15 OC 15/ 1845. ENDORSED: On receiving the news that her letters had been got back. ORIGINAL: Huntington Library (HM 12142); A.L. (unsigned), 8 pp. 8vo, with envelope and seal. UNPRINTED and UNPUBLISHED. TEXT: From original letter.

618. *To Claire Clairmont*

Putney—Saturday [October 18 or 25, 1845]

Dearest Claire—

I have just got your kind letter—I [? dread] Lady S[ussex] for you—   She will worry you to death—cling to you when G[atteschi] treats her ill—when he is gracious she will betray you to him—   If she comes to Paris she will be in his hands again—every thing you say will be reported   you will be kept in hot water & made ill—   You cannot hope that when G—— is driven to desperation—with no resource *for bread* except Lady S[ussex] that he will not humble himself to her—& if she is in *that* situation, he will do what he will with her—you can be of no use to her—   I wish he were well out of Paris if she comes to it.—

I am returned to this place bien contre gré—the sea did me good—but there is no help the money I have squandered on that wretch forces me to be careful —   My poor Percy is very economical—   His heart is still set on the plan of his— He is so tired of having no end or aim—travelling does not seem one to him— No—I must take & furnish a house in town— I wont repine for it is, I trust for the best,—but I am so nervous that all things seem fraught with evil just now Thanks for your promise about the cloak & bonnet— I am sorry shawls are not worn— I prefer them for myself but you get what is worn— Mrs. Hare wrote to me—"Go for bonnets to Me Seguin of Rue des Capucines—she will make you the prettiest bonnets possible for 35 fr—which will pack in a box of 25 centimetrs high—a wonderful invention."

I want to write to her—but have not yet mustered spirits

I am so glad you are under a physician in whom you have confidence & whose directions you follow. Marianne says Laura is very well & is at Florence she is to join Nerina at Pisa in November Nerina is very well & amusing herself having made a conquest of the grand-duke—

You do not mention in what way Lady S[ussex] speaks of the seizure of his papers. I fear her for you beyond words—& if she come to Paris I fear for her with him

I cannot write more I feel so nervous— I hate this London plan for my-self—& for Percy I confess I dont think it good—but ill will result tell Knox what it is—but he thinks differently & thinks it the only thing that will give him occupation & a career he must begin in November— God send it—my brilliant star— What a mockery—however did I not still fear from that wretch & were I not so unwell I should feel the blessed effects of dear Knox's generosity & success God bless you—farewell dont talk to me about going here & there—I cant— Percy is anxious to get settled—going about with him when he is not amused or interested is impossible—no—I will hope that what I dislike will end well—since so much ill is come from what I sought

I do *so* fear Lady S. for you—& if she is in Paris you *can* do her no good.

[*Unsigned*]

ADDRESS: Miss Clairmont. ORIGINAL: Huntington Library (HM 12356); A.L. (unsigned), 4 pp. 8vo. UNPRINTED and UNPUBLISHED. TEXT: From original letter.

619. *To Alexander Berry*[1]

Putney
Oct. 24 1845

My dear Sir

I was much grieved to hear of my poor Cousin's death— Some years ago our Aunt Everina told me that she did not consider herself in good health— but in these days, life is so prolonged, that I hoped she would be long spared to you. Such a companion, the friend & wife of years, is never to be replaced— & so good a woman is a loss to the world. My regrets will reach you so long, long after the event that I will not prolong them, to renew in you painful

[1] See Letter 501, note 1.

impressions. I had hoped that my Cousin would have come over here, & that I should have seen her.

I am afraid that many of my letters are lost.—I never received any answer from my Cousin to any of the letters announcing poor Everina's death, which took place in the Spring of 1843. Your & her kindness to her was indeed great, and a comfort to me, who would otherwise have been quite overwhelmed by the demands of one who had no consideration for others. As it was she died a good deal in debt—as I wrote to poor Mrs. Berry, and I was much inconvenienced & should have been far more, had it not been for the kindness of the very excellent women in whose house she died—who waited long for their money—tho' they could ill afford to do so. I wrote also last year to announce the death of my father-in-law; I cannot now exactly remember the date of my letter—some time in September /44, I think. Perhaps the letter has reached you since you wrote. You will see by that, that my Son has indeed inherited the family honours, but only a small portion of the family wealth—it would be a long story for a letter—but it is enough to say that by the exceeding injustice of his Grandfather, his estate is burthened by a heavy mortgage, & his means lessened more than one half of what they ought to be. He is of a happy cheerful disposition—& feels no discontent—tho' I do for him. I am in hopes he will get into parliament at the next election—but we are obliged to be very moderate & modest in our way of life. He has lett the family seat in consequence, & lives quietly in my cottage. He is upright, intelligent & amiable— so I have every reason to consider myself blessed—since with opposite qualities his fortune, were it even such as he is duly entitled to, would avail nothing either to happiness or honour.

I have to thank you for kindness to my friend Charles Robinson. Percy heard from him not long ago (he also appears by no means to receive all the letters written to him) he is much discontented with his lot—& in this shares the feelings of the whole colony—but the Governor is recalled, so it is to be hoped things will go better—

Thank you for your kind promise of writing to me again. If there is any thing I can do for you in this country pray command me. I hear your colony is reviving— We here are on the eve of changes. Sir Robert Peel is most ready to make them if his party would let him. While crops & harvests went well he could do nothing. But this disease among potatoes will famish Ireland. It can no longer send over its corn to us—& they say the ports are to be opened in England to foreign corn—but it is said that the supply from the continent (the demand not being expected nor provided for) will be very small. After a very wet, cold, dreary summer, I am in some hopes that we shall have a mild winter—that will lessen the sufferings of the poor—but if hunger is felt more than usual in Ireland, the coming months will prove critical—& must curb a party who forces the government to be illiberal—it may occasion my friends the Whigs to return to power— Every party is obliged to confess that the Whig administration in Ireland was singularly wise & successful.

I have written a long letter for me—for I suffer much from nerves, & am obliged to refrain almost entirely from writing. I shall hope to hear from you —& am, dear Mr. Berry

Yours truly

Mary Woll^{ft} Shelley

[P.S. *at top of page 1*] Direct to me at Hookham's Library

15 Old Bond St. London

ADDRESS: Alex^r Berry Esq/ Sydney/ New South Wales. POSTMARKS: (1) PAID/ OC 2[4]/ 1845 (2) SHIP LETTER/ FE * 20/ 1846/ SYDNEY. ORIGINAL: Alexander Hay, Coolangatta, N.S.W., Australia; A.L.S., 4 pp. 4to, with envelope and seal. UNPRINTED and UNPUBLISHED. TEXT: From original letter.

620. *To [Addressee Unknown]**

Putney

24th Oct. [? 1845]

Percy & I have been gadding, so that your note did not reac[h] us in due course. We shall be very happy to dine with you on the 30th at 7 o'clock, I think you mentioned—but I am ashamed that I have been thus prevented answering you before

I am   Truly ys

Mary Shelley

ORIGINAL: A.L.S., 2 pp. 12mo, inlaid into a 4to sheet. Owned by Suckling & Co., London, in March, 1940. UNPRINTED and UNPUBLISHED. TEXT: From original letter.

621. *To [Thomas Hookham]**[1]

Putney Oct. 28 [1845]

My dear Sir

From what Mr. Finch said I hoped to fine [find] a line from you telling me what you thought of the man [G. Byron] who called on you & the letters

[1] This is the first of several letters relating to "G. Byron." Much publicity has been given to the Shelley letters forged by G. Byron and sold to William White in 1848. (See Seymour de Ricci, *Bibliography of Shelley's Letters*, [Bois-Colombes (France), privately printed, 1927] 245–46, 293–95.) Some of these were published in 1852 by Edward Moxon as *Letters of P. B. Shelley*, with an introductory essay by Robert Browning, but the volume was suppressed when it was discovered that the letters were spurious.

G. Byron's dealings with Mary Shelley in 1845 and 1846, however, have heretofore been only vaguely hinted at. The letters printed here lack much of giving a full and clear account of these transactions, but they unquestionably add important facts to the history of G. Byron's activities, and also suggest some conclusions not hitherto drawn.

When G. Byron approached Thomas Hookham late in October, 1845, on the subject of Shelley letters in his (Byron's) possession, Hookham wrote to Mary, who was excited over the possibility of regaining letters long lost. She suspected that Byron had discovered the letters and papers which had been lost in Paris in 1814, letters precious to her and by all means to be kept out of print because they were the earliest letters Shelley had written to her. She had also lost many letters when the desk which was left at Marlow in 1818 disappeared. But she evidently did not think it possible for Byron to have recovered these.

The business developed rapidly. On October 28, 1845, it was quite new; by November 12 it

in his possession. Can they be any among those lost with other things in Paris in 1814— I should like to know what you think about the matter. He did not call today. Does he want the letters bought of him—or what?

Yours truly
M Shelley

---

was concluded temporarily when Byron addressed to Hookham the following letter (A.L.S., 2 pp. 8vo. All the letters relating to G. Byron, both in the text and in this note, are in the Henry W. and Albert A. Berg Collection, the New York Public Library):

Sir

I beg to acknowledge the receipt of thirty Pounds and most solemnly declare once more that I cannot receive that sum otherwise than as a loan to be repaid in the course of twelve months. Please to give this assurance to Mrs. Shelley. Circumstances prevent me from signing my name in full, but I trust you will mention to Mrs. Shelley (*as far as circumstances admit of it*) the conversation I had with you.

G. B.——

London
Novbr. 12, 1845.

It is evident that Mary did not get all the letters he had, as she had so much insisted upon.

Mary expected Byron to show up again, which he did in 1846. This part of the narrative is by no means clear, but the following reconstruction of what happened may be ventured.

In August or early September Byron again informed Hookham that he had some Shelley letters or copies of letters, and probably intimated that if he were not sufficiently paid for them he would sell them to a bookseller named Memon, who might be expected to publish them. Hookham probably threatened legal difficulties if Byron disposed of the letters without Mrs. Shelley's consent. Byron then sought Mr. Thomas Holcroft, the solicitor, and placed the letters or copies of letters in his hands. Holcroft wrote to Hookham, who in turn took instant action. He wrote first to Mary, abroad then at Baden-Baden, enclosing Holcroft's letter and telling her that he had written Holcroft not to return any letters to Byron or in any other way to dispose of them except upon the written permission of Mrs. Shelley, who claimed the letters as her personal property which had been stolen. Hookham then asked Mary to give him a written statement directing him to take possession of the letters. Upon receiving Hookham's "legal interdict," Holcroft wrote to Byron or Memon (A.L.S., 3 pp. 8vo):

3 North St.
Tuesday
15/8 [*error for* 9]/46.

My dear Sir

Acting on the maxim, "Fas est ab Hoste doceri" I copy for your guidance the legal interdict wch I recd from TH.

Byrons Solicitor in re Shelley Papers—

15 Old Bond Street
Sept: 15. 1846.

"Sir

I hereby give you notice not to deliver the letters, copies of letters, or any other papers you obtained (received) from Mr. Byron to that person or any other person or persons without the written authority of Mrs. Shelley, her heirs representatives or other persons authorised to act on her behalf, the said copies of letters &c—being her sole property—

I am Sir
Your obed^t Ser^t
(Signed) Thos. Hookham.

I have slightly modified the terms [received *for* obtained] to suit the circumstances—

I need not say how sincerely I appreciate your prompt and efficient service yesterday— I write this in case when I call you should be out or engaged—

Yours faithfully
Thos. Holcroft

Byron resisted these high-handed measures by having the question reviewed in the magistrate's court in Bow Street. Holcroft wrote to Hookham in this connection (A.L.S., 2 pp. 8vo):

3 North Street—
Friday [*1846*]

Dear Sir—

A Summons has issued from Bow Street out of this Byron-Shelley business— It is returnable on Monday at Two— Can you by any means conveniently attend? as it is possible the question

[P.S., *all of which except the last sentence is stricken out*] Do you know whether Macaul[a]y has written in the Edinburgh—any paper about the breaking of the peace of Amiens—or are there any good political articles in the Edinburgh (on our policy with France) relative to the years 1800 to 1805? If so would you be good enough to send them.

ORIGINAL: Henry W. and Albert A. Berg Collection, the New York Public Library; A.L.S., 3 pp. 8vo. UNPRINTED and UNPUBLISHED. TEXT: From original letter.

622. To [*Thomas Hookham*]

Putney—30 Oct. [1845]

Dear Sir—

I have written to Mr. Peacock about this affair— Did you give his address in John St—for as our friend B[yron] prefers the dusky hours he may not find him [Peacock] at the I[ndia] H[ouse]—

Most likely he will call on you again—& then the best possible thing wd be for you to possess yourself of the letters at once. As to his saying he wd *give* me mine that is all talk—he wants to sell them & to get money—he knows they are stolen—& my property, & he is afraid they will be taken from him—& yet he cannot make up his mind *how* to ask or *what* to ask. In treating with a fellow of this sort a 3ᵈ person is so much better If you can get the letters at once for £20 get them & I will pay it at once— I dont think he ought to have more—& should be glad if half the sum sufficed.

We must not shew any great desire The man must feel that he can get something, but not much.

may turn upon your former agency in the matter. I am at Hampton Court fishing which will account for the tardiness of this notice—

Your ob. Sᵛᵗ
Thos. Holcroft

Evidently Byron did not get legal authority to repossess the letters, which Holcroft must then have turned over to Hookham, who in turn sent them to Mary, as her grateful note to Hookham shows. Whether, as Mary prophesied, Byron came again, we do not know. He probably found William White and others better customers.

In these letters two things are very striking: (1) Mary's conviction that Byron had actually found a considerable lot of letters and papers which she had lost or which had been stolen. (2) After seeing the first lot of eight letters in November, 1845, Mary said nothing whatsoever about their being forgeries. Instead, she kept insisting that Byron had many more letters, and when she saw the letters which Hookham had seized in 1846, she expressed only pleasure and evidently had not the least suspicion that they were forgeries. It is true that the letters printed here do not prove conclusively that Byron ever sold to Mrs. Shelley anything except copies of Shelley's letters; but that seems hardly credible, for Mary insisted upon *bona fide* letters and would certainly have expressed dissatisfaction with mere copies, as indeed she did when it was not known whether the letters Holcroft had were original letters or only copies.

If one person in the world was capable of detecting a forged Shelley letter, Mary Shelley was that person. Her memory of Shelley's handwriting did not date back to 1822; she had literally lived with Shelley's manuscripts. It is also incredible that she could have been deceived even by a copy. No other conclusion is therefore possible than that Byron did have at least some of Shelley's genuine letters, and that everything he offered to Mary was either an original manuscript or a correct copy. He probably resorted to forgery when he had disposed of most of the original letters in his possession. It should be remembered that the letters published by Moxon in 1852, after Mary's death, were almost instantly condemned as forgeries, by people who knew infinitely less about Shelley than Mary herself.

As those he shewed you are only a small portion of those lost, has he any more?

I should be very glad indeed if he saw you that you should settle it all yourself— I dont like seeing him—for he seems a disreputable person—and with such a third person manages things so much best [*sic*]— He wont *give* any letters—of that be assured.

I leave it to you to judge how to manage him if you see him—but it would be a very good thing if you got the letters out of his hands at once. I am so very truly obliged to you for the trouble you have taken

Ys truly
M Shelley

ORIGINAL: Henry W. and Albert A. Berg Collection, the New York Public Library; A.L.S., 4 pp. 8vo. UNPRINTED and UNPUBLISHED. TEXT: From original letter.

623. *To* [*Thomas Hookham*]*

Putney
Friday Evg. [October 31, 1845]

Dear Sir

You are very good to take all this trouble— The Rascal's notes make me sick

I went to see Peacock today—& meant to see you tomorrow, but I fear I shall not be able—so I write & being very tired will just succin[c]tly say what I can on the subject.

Peacock says I did wrong to give any money— I am sure I did so in offering so much so readily. I am far poorer than any one knows or this rogue cd be made believe—not that he would care, so he got the money, whether I could well or ill afford it—but fancying me richer than I am makes him exorbitant.

Peacock says the fellow has brought himself within the law—he had better take care—he does not live at Greenwich certainly (for *whatever he says must be false* of that be sure) I wish he could be followed.

However to the [?] of course I would give £5 for the letters—but to offer this would be unavailing—& besides I fear he has *many more*—to offer so much per letter (one pound for instance) wd. be the only way—but this I would only give for *Shelley's own*—for the rest a pound a dozen wd. he give *all*—but as I doubt Shelley's are bona fide letters to me—in which case I wd. only give £5 for all—but it is better to treat at so much per letter—

Above all let me beg of you to shew every *backwardness* to treat at all. I am not afraid of the rogue—he has more cause to fear me—& I would buy them simply for the pleasure of having them—but cannot afford to pay high for any pleasure & must therefore go without if he prove impracticable.

At so much *per letter* remember—as he has more & will come again—& not more than I mentioned before.

And do not go so far as assenting even to this arrangement for 10 days
or a fortnight

Ys Truly

M S.

[P.S.] You say "Why take more trouble if he will give up those on the
list for £5—certainly not— I would give £5 & have done—but has he said he
will? I fancy not—& wd. at first scout so small a sum— And have you seen
the letters? I will call on Monday & hear about all this

I only got 8 2^d letters this afternoon

[P.S. *at top of page 1*] The poems you talk of are mere copies of course

ORIGINAL: Henry W. and Albert A. Berg Collection, the New York Public Library; A.L.S., 8 pp. 8vo. UNPRINTED and UNPUBLISHED. TEXT: From original
letter.

624. *To* [*Thomas Hookham*][1]

[Putney, October 31, 1845]

2

Dear Sir

A few more words—I mentioned £1 a piece for my letters of Shelley—
[*5½ lines are stricken out*] one or two things themselves to me on this.
I see you mention 8 letters of Shelley dated 1816— Are these to me? because
otherwise I would not treat in the same manner or on these terms—they must
be *bona fide* letters to *me*.

As to a payment on an unpublished poem it is of course only a bit of copy
—& not worth regard

(Except that I desire to possess every scrap in Shelley's hand—& if you
treat, you wd. bargain for ALL)—

2 letters of Mrs. S—do you mean Harriet—I doubt that they are hers—

In fact the rest are mere private papers—of which the rascal could make
no possible use—but he must *give all up* or he will receive *no money*.

I fear he has *many more*

The way we must manage is to demand all at so much a letter— *Nothing
unless mine by law. His not giving his name shews his designs to be bad &
the means he would take unscrupulous—*

My seeing him would put me in a position at once improper & useless—
If I see him I shall adopt the conduct you point out—but conduct & manner
of mine will avail nothing against a man of this sort trying to make money.

I am sorry to trouble you so much—but if he comes again it would be as
well to lead him to think that he had better arrange the barter of the affair
with you or Peacock. However if you see him again in talking he may shew
his designs further, & what his pecuniary hopes are   Whatever they are he had
better be let understand that he will get something—but nothing immense—

[1] This letter was probably enclosed in the same envelope with the preceding letter.

He *can* make no use of the papers in this country— I should think £10 or £20 would suffice—I hope so—for there is nothing so mortifying as to have to give money to a rogue—when there are so many honest persons one is pining to benefit

Very truly ys
M Shelley

[P.S.] He said he would give me *my* letters. He will not—or if he did it would be because he thinks them the least valuable portion & giving him besides a right to ask more for the rest. Mine by themselves I dont think I wd. accept. I must not *treat* with such a fellow *alone* altogether I shrink from him—

> ORIGINAL: Henry W. and Albert A. Berg Collection, the New York Public Library; A.L.S., 8 pp. 8vo. UNPRINTED and UNPUBLISHED. TEXT: From original letter.

625. *To* [*Thomas Hookham*]

[Putney, November 1 (?), 1845]

Dear Sir

You are very kind— I dare say it seems odd to you how I bargain with this fellow—but not only we are far from rich—but I have been so imposed upon & pillaged that I have laid down a *moral law* to myself—never to part with a guinea to an unworthy object—

There were 8 letters I suppose 6 only to me—he will bring the others some day. I *dont believe in the original poem* I believe it to be merely what printers call a bit of copy

[*Unsigned*]

> ORIGINAL: Henry W. and Albert A. Berg Collection, the New York Public Library; A.L., 3 pp. 12mo. The signature "Mrs. Shelley" is in the middle of the sheet between pages 2 and 3 and is not in Mary's hand. UNPRINTED and UNPUBLISHED. TEXT: From original letter.

626. *To* [*Thomas Hookham*]*

[Putney] Monday [November 3 (?), 1845]

Dear Sir

I am in bed far to ill to attend to business—

The letters were stolen—they were entrusted to a [*word illegible*] we thought honest & stolen.

No bookseller could publish poem or letter— They are all my property— the will is now proved—I should take out an injunction directly—

The fellow is a rogue & has more letters so a £1 [a]piece is safer & better— he will find more

I cannot write more— You are very good to take so much trouble

Ys.
M Shelley

Brighton   Tuesday Eve^g

My dear Claire — Is it not all wonderful? Knox's firm & admirable conduct — his success — the authorities consenting to so desperate a step — all — all is wonderful — & the more I hear the more I admire & am grateful — This 'too humiliated' by the part I played, & by being the cause of so much disagreeable labour to exult. Poor Lodge — what can become of him. Poor poor thing — what a situation — he cannot want — but who will help him? for she is such an enemy to

First page of Letter 617: to Claire Clairmont
[October 14, 1845]

ORIGINAL: Henry W. and Albert A. Berg Collection, the New York Public Library; A.L.S., 3 pp. 8vo. UNPRINTED and UNPUBLISHED. TEXT: From original letter.

627. *To* [*Thomas Hookham*]*

[Putney] Monday Evg. [November 3 (?), 1845]

Dear Sir

I send you the rascal's letter. This is the note that we wish you to send the man.

15 Old Bond St.

Sir

If you will call here on Monday Evg. at 5 o'clock—I will communicate further with you on the subject of the Shelley Letters & you will most probably receive the assistance you require on your giving up *all* the letters you had when you called upon me before—be so good therefore [as] to bring them *all* with you.

I will call on you on Monday about one—but send this letter as soon as need be before 8 Monday A.M.

Ys. truly
Mary Shelley

ORIGINAL: Henry W. and Albert A. Berg Collection, the New York Public Library; A.L.S., 3 pp. 8vo. UNPRINTED and UNPUBLISHED. TEXT: From original letter.

628. *To* [*Thomas Hookham*]

[Putney, November, 1845]

Dear Sir

The man has not come—& now some days are gone by—he will doubtless shew himself again. It may be too much to call him a rogue—but he is a fellow desirous of making money in a disreputable way— He wont at all care for my politeness—he will only think of what he can get—& how to augment his demand—

Whether I am at home when he calls (as my hours for exercise vary) is very doubtful—but if you see him, it were much better if *you* could settle the matter. You know what letters or letter he has—& how improper as well as disagreable it would be for me to haggle about the price to be given for them: improper & indiscreet in the highest degree— A third person can do this so much better—& this he felt, perhaps, when he called on you— The thing would be for a third party to bring him to terms. If he calls again, it were best to say that the letters were stolen & that I shall be very glad to possess myself of them & any trouble & expence he had been at I should be very glad to remunerate. If he talk of seeing me, make him understand if to give me the letters & to be sure they come into my hands it would be well—but that *I* could not enter into [the] question of price—& that he had better treat it with you or Mr. Peacock. He is a low fellow obviously—but the papers were stolen & are [*a four-page folder may be missing here*] —enough.

Still we must not offer— He must be told that I demand all the letters as mine—or say what you will— I wish him to be made [to] understand that I consider that he is playing the rogue & that he will make nothing by me— Thus he may be brought to the terms I have mentioned. I cannot afford to give more or I might be fool enough to do it—but I *cannot*

Have an eye to any auctions of autographs—will you be so good.

One pound per letter of Shelley's own for all others half a crown—but do not *offer* this I entreat. Let him bully & threaten a little more, & feel that I will do nothing & then he may avail himself of what I will do. The more letters he writes us & the more blackguard & threatening they are, the better

I dont believe he has the impudence to take the name of Byron generally—tho' a swindlers name is only an alias of course

Ever ys.

M. Shelley

ORIGINAL: Henry W. and Albert A. Berg Collection, the New York Public Library; A.L.S., 8 pp. 8vo. UNPRINTED and UNPUBLISHED. TEXT: From original letter.

629. *To Claire Clairmont*

[Putney] Wednesday [November 5, 1845]

My dear Claire—

To begin—when it happens that you have no thin paper by you—write upon thick & do not mind what it costs—now pray attend to this & do as I say—never mind postage.

The tone of your letter is alarming—but I consider you have just escaped from a horrible moral tempest & till you have recovered yourself, you naturally feel more dismay than is necessary. It would be very ruinous for Knox to leave certain arrangements he is making for himself to go to Paris again. Let us know *any facts*. Knox is writing to you. His feeling is that you ought to leave Paris—not to be worried; & what can G[atteschi] & Lady S[ussex] do—? Write a memoir against me & get it published in England or France that is all they could do to hurt me—for anonymous letters & spoken calumny from them could do me no real injury. It is indeed infinitely to be regretted that he has the support of that unfortunate woman for without her, he would be crushed.

Pray dear Claire, write to Knox or me the details of what you fear on my account. He could be sent out of Paris—but she w[oul]d follow him & it w[oul]d do no good.

Always dear Claire, be explicit when you write on this—say exactly *what* you fear & the foundations of your fear—

Would you were away, or here or going with the Princess— I dont under-

stand what you mean in allusion to Lady Dorothea if they are spreading
calumnies in Paris about me, it cant be helped My absence—my having
scarcely ever been in Paris renders their poison nearly innoxious I think if
Lord Sussex had an intimation it were best. If M. Delessert would write to
him to tell him the hands his wife is in—if Delessert were to send for her or
to her & tell her that he is a villain surveillé by the police. Peronne is out of
Paris just now but his goings on must be looked to—

When you receive this you will be calmer— You will look back & consider
& then to me or Knox write in a detailed & circumstantial way what you fear
that G[atteschi] is plotting against me—& Knox will then judge what he
ought to do

As to our house, it is all uncertain for the present— Things with regard
to Castle Goring are going ill instead of well— I fear *care* so much that I
would willingly rent a smaller house—but Percy cant bear it.

It was quite *too* sure that if Lady Sussex could be saved, it was not after
she came to Paris—it was scarcely to be expected in her position— Could she
have been kept away—would she go away—

He is only drawing ruin on his own head—

When is the Princess C—— going? could you not go with her & get out of
the way of this web of mischief? What do you mean about Lady D?—"base
slanderous nature of hers" alludes I suppose to Lady Sussex.

[*Written under the flap of the envelope*] You see what Knox says—take
care of yourself he is not well—poor fellow—writing does not agree with
him nor does England Adieu

[*Unsigned*]

ADDRESS: Madlle./ Mlle. Clairmont/ Rue Nᵉ Clichy—No. 3 bis/ Rue de Clichy/
à Paris. POSTMARK: A/ PAID/ 5 NO 5/ 1845. ORIGINAL: Huntington Library
(HM 12362); A.L. (unsigned), 4 pp. 8vo, with envelope containing the final
words of the letter on the inside of the flap; seal. UNPRINTED and UNPUBLISHED.
TEXT: From original letter.

630. *To Claire Clairmont*

[Putney, November 10, 1845]

My dearest Claire—

We can only entreat you to be firm— If they are plotting—*really* plotting
& not talking of it only, your going to her w[oul]d be most dangerous. While
she sees G[atteschi] she has her consolation—& you only embroil yourself—
You ought to leave Paris—that would settle the thing—but of course you are
the best judge of how you can.

The first thing we have to do before we frighten ourselves is to consider
what they can do—even if aided by the people you mention (which if mere
conjecture I cannot myself think likely—G's insolent [tone] is his natural one)
what can they do? talk against me—of course G—— & whoever joins him
does that a *l'outrance* it cant be helped & therefore I will not make myself

unhappy about it. Publish against me—there indeed they might stab me mortally but I trust nothing of the sort will happen— G[atteschi] cannot do it by himself—Lady S[ussex] scarcely—& the B—— could of course, but is there likelihood or appearance—& how could I hinder them—if they chose to do it—they could not be prevented—but *why* should they?—in short, dear Claire, I may be wrong, but I will not be driven to the verge of madness, as I was before, by fearing a thing which when I reason calmly, I do not see I have any reason to fear—namely that the B——s will exert themselves to publish calumnies against me,—& therefore I follow Knox's advice by dismissing so shocking an idea from my mind— Knox will write to Peronne to excite him to look after G's goings on— Poor unfortunate Lady S[ussex]—could you serve her I would not say a word—but you cannot while she sees him—while you may do yourself & all of us irreparable mischief. She asks you to save her *from them* from the Gs—I presume. You do your best to do that when you make your visits depend on her not seeing them—how can you save her from them while she sees them.

That they plot day & night & are bent on mischief, we are well aware—it is not what they *wish to do*—but what they *can do,* that we must consider— They can calumniate me & they do, everywhere they can—I cant help it—& must banish the thought for the sake of peace. I have brought it on myself by my foolish confidence in the excellence of one I really knew nothing about— I must bear it—as long as nothing is printed I must forget the rest—& I must hope for the best on that score—because I can *do* nothing—& apprehension is the worst part of all evil. I suffered so fearfully not long ago—& could so easily, if I permitted my thoughts to dwell on the subject, terrify myself again —that I make our kind friend my guide in the difficult path—& am resolved not to fear till he tells me that I ought. W[oul]d you were away—that were indeed a good that would put me in good spirits—depressed as I must be by knowing that you are exposed to so much annoyance Knox desires his kindest remembrances & will write to Peronne.—We have no news The Pechells cannot persuade themselves to make an offer about Castle Goring & worry us exceedingly—Captain P— is the most tiresome person to deal with in the world— Our house taking is stopped meanwhile—but patience is the only weapon we have for it. Percy is very well—& is to go to the Conveyancer tomorrow with James Campbell. Percy has seen William Campbell— I have not—nothing new there [*the last three lines are deleted and are unreadable*].

[*Unsigned*]

ADDRESS: Mlle./ Mlle. Clairmont/ Rue Nᵉ Clichy No. 3 bis/ Rue de Clichy/ Paris. POSTMARKS: (1) Putney (2) UM/ 10 NO 10/ 1845. ENDORSED: [*On the last page*] Lady Sussex Lennox was hinting that Gatteschi knew also that Mrs. Shelley had been plotting against him, and had paid a large sum to the Prefet Delessert to bribe him to seize Gatteschi's papers—and also hinted that Gatteschi had friends who would avenge his injuries— I informed Mrs. S of it and this is her answer. ORIGINAL: Huntington Library (HM 12181); A.L. (unsigned), 4 pp. 8vo and 2 pp. 4to, with seal. UNPRINTED and UNPUBLISHED. TEXT: From original letter.

631. *To Claire Clairmont*

My dearest Claire—   [Putney] Friday [November 14, 1845]

How I wish you were over here— Every thing proves that I can only be hurt thro' you—& were you away it would all die like a straw fire—but you are exposed to worry which injures your health so much & deeply distresses me.—To harden ones heart is a sore but necessary trial—& I beseech you not to expose yourself again to the risk of encountering G[atteschi]—how can you help Lady S[ussex] by being there? You cannot send him out of the house— or in any way protect her— If she really wished to be out of his way she w[oul]d never have come to Paris— But you know her well—she must either be darting along railroads or in scenes— She cannot be quiet & all her exertions are directed to implicating others in her worries— She & G[atteschi] are well pitted—he has the best of it as a man—but she has the real power in her hands—she can absent herself—never read another letter never write—& he *can* do her no harm— Timid as I am I do not fear him—if ever I do it is when a mysterious silence is observed whenever any plan is discovered I perceive how futile their endeavours are—such as their getting a deputy to speak about them—no deputy could do this without its being known before hand what he was about to do—& then he w[oul]d receive such information of his protégées as w[oul]d stop him at once—foolish people—their only safety is in taking the thing quietly—& every step they take for publicity is a step towards their own entire ruin. As you wrote to me the thing is taken up by those well able to protect themselves & me also— Would you were here— yet as you say how uncomfortable you would be— Our affairs are still waiting—my dearest Percy goes every day to town to read at a conveyancers with James Campbell—for his sake I wish we were in town & am only stopt by obstacles I cannot controul—but next week I hope to be able to do something— Winter is coming now with cold fogs after a fine Martins summer— Is there no means by which you can stop communication between you & Passy— O would indeed that you were over here—if you could come I w[oul]d exert myself to the utmost to make you comfortable & you would have no business to torment you. You should have the little room adjoining mine to sit in—& only sleep out of the house—& having no going to the city or business you might keep well—& Knox being here the house is much more cheerful— I will send you £5 for your journey if you will come

ADDRESS: Mlle./ Mlle. Clairmont/ Rue Ne Clichy 3 bis/ Rue de Clichy/ Paris. POSTMARKS: (1) Putney (2) 14 NO 14/ 1845. ORIGINAL: Huntington Library (HM 12339); A.L. (unsigned), 4pp. 16mo (3⅞ x 4¾ inches), with envelope containing an added note on the inside; seal. UNPRINTED and UNPUBLISHED. TEXT: From original letter.

632. *To Claire Clairmont*

Putney Monday [December 1, 1845]

You will think me lost, dearest Cl[aire]—you have not heard from me

so long   I have been employed by the sale of Castle Goring—& looking for a
house—& then when I was a little in repose Mrs. Paul entreated me to go
into Sussex with her for a few days—& I can never write comfortably except
at home. We have taken a house—we are to buy it—we give a great deal for it
—& it is not very large—   We could have got a larger one in Eaton Sq for the
same price—indeed less—but I had a great fear of a large house with a number
of servants—the lighting & warming—the expectation created that we should
entertain—   Our present house is exceedingly pretty—it is situated in Chester
Sq[1]—Belgrave Sq [a] quarter which you will disapprove; only two quarters
were open to us—that & the quarter you prefer near the Sanfords—but I know
no one there—you must remember *why* I go into town—with a hope of improving Percy's circle of acquaintance & his going into parliament—so I could
not bury myself in a part of the town where we should have been quite lost.
My grand aim after this is to get a little cottage—I dont care how small, on our
estate at Balcombe—& there I am not afraid for my health—for that situation
is so high & the air so bracing—that when once I can run down there every
now & then—I must be well—however I must not go too fast—we give a
great deal for our house—& then we have to furnish—   If it were not for the
claim of the Willats[2]—I should see my way very well—but that hangs over
our heads—£2500 must be paid—I fear £4500—& that will drain us & leave us
poorer than we were before selling Castle Goring—   However I wont grumble
—I must do my best to give Percy a comfortable home as economically as I
can—   If I can only see him in parliament all will go well—for then his set
of acquaintance must improve. Meanwhile, say what you will, my position in
society is very bad—it could not well be worse & as we are not rich enough
to give dinners—it is only by Percy's being in p[arliamen]t that I hope to get
a set such as I should like about us—   I have no pleasure myself in the idea
of town—far from it—when in bad spirits I foresee the mortifications & annoyances with horror—when in good, I hope to acquire in time a few friends
& agreable acquaintances which will compensate for the rest—but it will take
time.

The house is not ours yet—when it is I furnish—but shall not be in a hurry
to complete furnishing it till the year advances—as it will be better to save
our furniture from the great smoke of London in this season. There is a room
which is not as large as I should wish but which I will make as comfortable
as I can for you—   I will have it ready by the middle of January by which
time I hope to be settled—& I trust you will then pay us a long visit—   I am
anxious that you should find the comforts of a home—not the discomforts of
your last trip. I am very glad you talk of coming without Stephanie—   She
would keep the house in one continual bustle of attendance on her—& excite

---

1 The house at 24 Chester Square is still there.
2 In January, 1818, Shelley borrowed £2,000 from William Willats of Fore Street, Cripple-
gate, agreeing to pay in return, three years after Sir Timothy's death, the sum of £4,500. (Ingpen,
Shelley in England, 528.)

all kinds of ill feeling & dislike by her pretentions— You know how kind
Marianne was to her— Stephanie has written to a person she formed acquaintance with in Putney—but never sent a civil message even to Marianne.
Then for any length of time a strange servant always makes a tumult in a
house—especially a French one so I am quite pleased that you do not bring
your Stephanie with you   Tell me that I may expect you at the time I mention.
Indeed, dearest Claire, I can never sufficiently repay you for your exceeding
kindness during my late unhappiness—& I rejoice very much in the prospect
of having you among us this winter when in my house you may repose a little
—& even enjoy yourself a little after all you have had of disagreable to encounter. I hope you have no more been annoyed by the people at Passy— To
accuse—to abuse—to create storm is that poor woman's element. Nothing you
could do for her would prevent her turning on you & injuring you deeply—
You cannot benefit her (except by opening a wider field for her maleficence)
& you may & indeed must greatly injure yourself if you come into contact with
her—PRAY keep away.

And now, dearest C[laire] to worry you— I want your kind assistance
in settling Knox's business in Paris[3]—no small thing as you will see by the
account he sends you. After all he achieved for me, I would fain repay him
by freeing him entirely from annoyance but the sum is too large. Besides that
I must serve him here also— I am deeply grieved that he so foolishly involved himself—why he did so, I can only darkly guess—but so it is—he has
his apartment & furniture on his hands, & exertion must be made to get rid
of it. He ought to have done this himself before he left Paris—but young, indolent & impressionable, he left it with the vague hope that he might get rid
of it during the Parisian season— Why he took a bail[4] for 3 years is quite
inexplicable to me— His great horror is that his credit & good name should
be hurt in Paris. It has sometimes struck me whether the apartment would not
suit you— He would underlet it to you for something less than he pays—
I hear that it is an exceedingly pretty apartment delightfully situated— This
would take you from a quarter full of painful association to you & where you
are at a distance from all your friends—& place you in the pleasantest part
of Paris— Your bail is out I fancy & you could leave your rooms at a quarter's notice— What do you say? otherwise it had better be advertized in
Galignani— Some English person might take a fancy to so pretty a set of
rooms & even buy the furniture—now is the season & it is better to lose no time
— I leave to Knox to explain particulars— I have great hopes that he is
now on the road not only to create a comfortable independance for himself—
but even to distinction & a brilliant career—but it takes time & money—& it
is very vexatious that while I wish to do my best to help him forward, serious
sacrifices must be made to defray past debts incurred to no purpose & to a

[3] See Letter 554, note 1.
[4] Lease.

large amount. Indeed for myself & my friend, *care* I fear is my destiny. I knew he had an apartment in Paris that hung on his hands—but was not aware till yesterday of the great extent of the debt incurred—no time must be lost in setting all right— If your name & security can obtain better terms & longer time for him to pay the tapissier &c pray give it—for you may [be] sure I will not let you suffer but in time he will be able to pay the debt himself I trust—& just now with all the expence I am going to in this tiresome London house (how I should like to bury myself & economize for a year & so pay off without imprudence money that I am expected to pay—but this w[oul]d not do for Percy & would be quite unfair toward him)—with the money spent on that wretched mistake of mine—& the large claims that cluster round me— it is absolutely impossible that I can meet & pay at once this debt of dear K[nox] desirous as I am to serve him   In managing this business you will do a good action & you will benefit me more than I can express— I am quite ashamed to put this on you—but you see how large a sum is at stake & how necessary for the sake of his good name it is that something should be ar- ranged with the landlord & tapissier—I think the furniture taken back, so much being paid on it & the bail given up is the best (unless you would rent the rooms)   if this cannot be done they must be advertized in Galignani—but as it is slippery work treating with the English it is far preferable that the tapissier should have the furniture back & the rooms let *un*furnished.

Campbell has got an appointment as commissioner for Lunacy—it is £1500 & travelling expences paid—he will now marry & be happy— I have not seen him.

Knox says he will write to you about his rooms by tomorrows post— I cannot say how annoyed I am to trouble you—how doubly annoyed that he should be so involved   God bless you dear Claire— We are all quite well— I hope you are better—

Affly Ys
[*Unsigned*]

ADDRESS: Mlle./ Mlle. Clairmont/ Rue Nᵉ Clichy—No. 3 bis/ Rue de Clichy/ à Paris. POSTMARKS: (1) UE/ 1 DE 1/ 1845   (2) 3/ DEC/ [45]/ BOULOGNE. ORIGINAL: Huntington Library (HM 12179); A.L. (unsigned), 10 pp. 8vo, with envelope and seal. UNPRINTED and UNPUBLISHED. TEXT: From original letter.

633. *To Claire Clairmont*

Putney. Thursday [December 11, 1845]

Dearest Claire—

Your letter—with the pages numbered was none the worse for your mis- take. I send the £5 K[nox] says that he owes Pierre something like £3 but that he does not remember any other *little* bills—as he took great care to pay up every thing— It will be indeed a great good if you can settle the affair of his apartment— He is engaged in an arduous struggle for a career; it involves a good deal of expence, which for the present must fall on us—& it is hard that something so useless & foolish as this Parisian burthen should fall also. The best thing to do w[oul]d be to get some one who w[oul]d take the bail—& the furniture too & settle with the tapissier for a *little less than his bill* & K[nox] pay the difference as soon as he can This is the *best*—but what *can* be done is another affair— You will, I am sure, judge correctly & act judiciously & with zeal.

You will ask, are we ever to move?—We ask it ourselves— The lease is in the hands of lawyers every day. We expect to be called on to sign & then we can take possession—meanwhile we must wait. You will like the house it is so pretty & cheerful. I should have preferred Mayfair—but we were obliged to take what we could get—for economy's sake I chose a smaller house to a larger one for the same price—as easier lighted & warmed & necessitating fewer servants—however Percy Mrs. Paul & Knox no sooner saw the house than they were wild we should have it. Your room is a pleasant one—& there is one for a maid—for though you may not bring Stephanie you may like to have one— I am afraid I shall not be ready for you till the end of January—proceedings are so hopelessly delayed.

Percy is gone into Sussex today about his sitting in Parliament. He is gone to ask the Duke of Norfolk's support. The Duke is a Whig & yet like all landed proprietors a Tory with regard to the corn laws. Just read a speech I have marked of his making in the paper I send today—& say, What pity that England's first nobleman should choose to declare himself fool, rather than yield on a point, in which he thinks his interests concerned—a pinch of curry powder in hot water to comfort the empty stomach of a labourer— This far outdoes the famous question of the French Princess—when told the people had no bread—"Why dont they eat cakes"—curry powder! It looks like a joke—but it is a sad one. The Times they say is the parent (for the purposes of speculation) of the reports that the cornlaws are to be abolished— No one can really tell how it will be—but for selfish motives I sincerely hope they will be done away with before the next election—as they form so difficult a bit for a candidate—& once done away with & there is an end of them. I got Charles' letter & shall answer it. His whole soul is in his children, poor fellow. Your account of Clairkin[1] is singular. I think Charles did quite right to put her attachment to the proof—but after a year she might have her own way— Strange world —where children are sometimes forced by worldly parents to this sort of unequal match—& here is a father who prevents his child from making it. I dont wonder the old gentleman runs after her. Unfortunately I never saw a German who did not seem to me the Antipodes of Romance—tho' in fact they are so romantic—but then it is [in] so slow, methodical & heavy a manner—scented with tobacco smoke—& shut up in close stove heated rooms. The wild valley of the Tyrol a little helps it—but from Prince Albert downwards they all seem to have the same type.

[1] One of Charles Clairmont's children.

I am so very glad that that shocking [? Lady S.] leaves you quiet— I cannot help thinking that that £150 has something to do with it. I am so glad you keep firm in your determination to keep aloof from two persons—one acknowledgedly (as Knox says) disliking you— The other of so frightful a disposition, that she turns like a wild cat upon any one who opposes her in her wildest & most unjustifiable attacks. You do quite right to keep her letters against her own family—some day she may write in the same way of you to them—& they may not have the sense to disbelieve her (tho' I should think they w[oul]d) & then her letters to you will shew them how double tongued she is.

I grieve for what you say about your money— I hope all will go well this spring. Remember that just now nothing can be done with advantage—all is unsettled & a[t] low ebb— In the spring—especially if the corn laws go— there will [be] a swift & prosperous advance in all things concerning *trade,* among which are railways. You cannot do better than keep quiet just now— Things are reviving, as you may judge by the prices of shares—but they are still very low—every body who can afford to wait, is waiting till they rise, as they will. I only tell you what I hear said all around me. It was abominable your having to pay for your opera box[2] & not to receive any interest this year— had you been on the spot it would not have been— However Lumley is making great exertions for the opera—& I feel sure that you will realize the sum mentioned £380 if not £400—or more—for the season.

The papers today declare that Sir Robert Peel has resigned   there *may* be a dissolution—& Percy stand on this very cornlaw question an arduous think [thing] for a young man. The article in todays Chronicle about the curry powder is by Knox— I got a letter from Percy today which shews the Pechells very kind to him— He has not yet seen the Duke The curry powder speech bids fair to make him a but for many a long day for the shafts of ridicule—it goes *far beyond* any thing of the kind ever before recorded in the history of the government of the aristocracy—& must bring conviction to many that the corn laws must go since they are to be upheld only by such support— I am very political—but you would not wonder if you knew the atmosphere of politics around me—& I confess Percy's getting into parliament is very near my heart.

I finish my letter—you will hear from Knox tomorrow in answer to yours of today—[*This part of the letter shows, in the handwriting, considerable agitation.*] Of course I dont send the £5 all will be settled together. I am overwhelmed. What am I to say to Percy— What am I to do? & then to live (for K[nox] I mean) to make the present struggle— I must meet it—& it is heavily expensive at [present] to give £150 for this affair this senseless mad affair—it is too—too cruel— God help me whenever I try to do good it returns on my own head in too frightful a manner—[*The following is scored*

2 Claire had invested in an opera box at Covent Garden. The investment was not successful.

through, probably by Claire: Considering my obligations to K[nox]—money seems of no consequence]—but Percy does not know of these & what am I to do? I am quite lost— You shall hear from us about it tomorrow

Ys.

[*Unsigned*]

[P.S. *under the flap of the envelope*] I have given Knox a cheque for £100 —even that I have not—but the bankers will advance it— My poor poor Percy w[oul]d he had no mother to rob him in this wicked manner—[*six or seven words, containing something about Knox, are here scored through*] who is help win [*sic*] when money that would have been the making of him is thrown into the gulph—a thousand tim[es] w[oul]d I were dead. This 100 must do for I can give no more

ADDRESS: Mlle./ Mlle. Clairmont/ Rue Nᵉ Clichy—No. 3 bis/ Rue Clichy Paris. POSTMARK: 11 DE 11/ 1845. ENDORSED: [*On outside of envelope flap*] She says would she were dead for robbing Percy her son of money to give Knox! ORIGINAL: Huntington Library (HM 12153); A.L. (unsigned), 8 pp. 8vo, with envelope containing a note on the inside of the flap. UNPRINTED and UNPUBLISHED. TEXT: From original letter.

634. *To Claire Clairmont*

[Putney, December 12, 1845]

My dear Claire—

I gave £100 to Knox yesterday to send you to settle his affairs. I do not know in what way he has written to you about them—but let me implore you not to listen to any of his sayings that he will pay the *rest* at such or such a time— for he cannot—he will have no funds—& this his anticipation that he will have some at some future day has ever been his ruin.

Thus I understand the business though having seen no accounts, I can not be sure I am right—he owes 3,000 fr[ancs] for furniture—& in Jany will owe some thing like 500 fr[ancs] for rent. A person is ready to take his bail & will pay a third of this 500—the hundred sent are 2500 fr. It strikes me that if this is paid the furniture may go for a little less than a 1000 (perhaps the new tenant, though you say he refused it—yet seeing it almost all paid for will take it for that sum) & this 1000 will do more than pay for the residue of the tapissier's account & the portion of rent Kn[ox] is to pay: indeed a little more may remain to pay some other of his Parisian debts—

I will not say more of this to me deeply distressing subject except again to implore you to settle the thing *completely* so that my poor £100 may not be thrown in the dirt like so much more & yet is [it] is thrown in the dirt—for if I know my own heart tho' ill able to spare it—I would cheerfully for a real good—to place him in an honorable position—to enable him to bear the brunt of his present struggle—but to go for so vile a purpose—as I must call furniture taken at an exorbitant price God knows when to be paid for— And now

279

I can do no more—all my plans for his advantage are crushed   I *can do no more*—& he—what can become of him—

I write in great distress of mind—   This affair makes me miserable—any thing more [*three lines are crossed out*] but whenever I desire to serve it returns as a curse on my hand—   What will my Percy say! Economy I must practice of the most rigid kind but of what avail? [*Three other lines are crossed out*] half is all thrown into the waste gulph of prodigal useless expenditure   Enough—I shall never another word on the subject—nor do you to me—it can do no good—   The blow is given—the evil done—& there is no help—only do your best I entreat to settle all *completely* with the sum sent   God bless you   Adieu   Pray burn this.

[Initialed signature probably obscured by the seal]

ADDRESS: Miss Clairmont/ Rue Nᵉ Clichy No. 3 bis/ Rue de Clichy/ Paris. POSTMARKS: (1) PUTNEY   (2) M/ PAID/ 12 DE 12/ 1845. ORIGINAL: British Museum (T. J. Wise Collection); A.L. (signature probably obscured by seal), 4 pp. 4to, with envelope and seal. UNPRINTED and UNPUBLISHED. TEXT: From original letter.

635. *To Claire Clairmont*

Monday [December 22, 1845] Putney

Dearest Claire—

After writing to you on Saturday, I went up to town & called on Mrs. Sanford—& asked her to ask Michell the present price of boxes—   She said (as indeed I had heard from others) that it was useless asking till Lumley published his programme since the price of boxes depended on that—   Lumley is away now getting his company—the programme wont be published probably till the beginning of February—& till then you would get no offers unless by chance from any private person you knew. The usual prices are such as I sent in my last—the subscription for a box such as yours is £300. The extra Thursdays are of Lumley's own manufacture—he crams them full of attractive bits both operatic & from favorite balléts—& they let to occasional visitors at a high price. Mrs. Sanford has let her Tuesday nights to a friend for £120   She means to let her Thursday to Michel—& to keep her Saturdays for herself. She is gone today to Corsham for a week—We dine there on the 2ᵈ Janʳʸ so if there is anything you w[oul]d like me to ask I can. Lady S[ussex] was not mentioned—   Sussex & Charles are there for their Xmas holydays—   I saw Sussex   he looked to me much improved in his appearance & they praise him —division from his mother & elder Brother affords a chance for their turning out well.

You see the change again on the scene of politics. Ld. John can not make a ministry—   I understand from good authority that the reason is that Lord Grey (son of the great Ld. Grey—& known as Lord Howick as a crochetty man) insisted that Ld. Palmerston should not be foreign minister—& Lord P. would not give up his old post—so the ministry could not be formed. As to

Percy's election I have no hopes myself— As he has never cultivated any acquaintance with any one in his own rank of life—he finds himself quite alone in this first step in life—the only person to stand by him (& a totally inexperienced young man cannot move alone) is Aubrey Beauclerck & he is in Ireland & likely to stay there. And Percy himself is so thoroughly without address or quickness—that I quite despair— He is willing to exert himself by fits & starts but——however it is useless worrying you with all this— I dont see my way & that makes me despond—but I trust it will [be] clearer by & bye—

The weather has become thoroughly wintry wind rain & snow— We hear nothing of our house—& being here is very inconvenient to Percy— I have no more news— It is a million of pities that we are not in town just now— I hope Knox's affair is being terminated to our satisfaction—it is very good of you to take so much trouble. Adieu

Affly. Ys
M Shelley

ADDRESS: Mlle./ Madlle. Clairmont/ Rue Nᵉ Clichy—3 bis/ Rue de Clichy/ Paris. POSTMARKS: (1) P u t n e y N.O.   (2) PA[ID]/ 22 DE 22/ 1845. ORIGINAL: Huntington Library (HM 12141); A.L.S., 4 pp. 8vo, with envelope and seal. Copy by Claire Clairmont, Berg Collection, the New York Public Library. UNPRINTED and UNPUBLISHED. TEXT: From original letter.

636. *To Claire Clairmont*

[Putney] Monday Evg. 29 Dec. [1845]

Dearest Claire—

I have just got your amusing letter (no one writes such good letters as you do) & I begin to answer it at once—& will finish my letter by & bye— I hope you will burn my letters— I should be very sorry they ever saw light— I have not the art of letter writing— You have to an eminent degree— My Percy has—but it is lost—like so many of his excellencies—in a sort of indolence—yet he ever endeavours to do well—& there never was so kind, so feeling—so perfect a son.

We are assured that we shall have our house this week—I hope so—& the upholsterer talks of our being able to get in in a month— I shall try my very utmost to be ready to receive you early in February but I shall not be settled by that time, & I fear I must defer all hope of your having any enjoyment in my house till next year— This time it will only be a better sort of lodging— All English people do not live as I do—the rich live otherwise but you contrast justly my quiet life with a Parisian one— Thank God I am at last *acclimatié*—besides my interest in Percy prevents ennui— What years I have spent!—The years in Somerset St alone in London— The years at Harrow—quite alone— Well, it is over now & with years comes liking for quiet— All I ask is to be free from care—& for that with our fortune, to give Percy his fair chance & station one must be so dreadfully selfish & spend all on oneself—a thing I have not yet been able to do, poor or rich.

What you say of Sir Robert is just—& I hope from him in spite of the Examiner— I think after our (i.e. the Whigs) disgraceful break up we have no right to find fault. The Whigs pretend to place themselves between the Radicals & Tories—yet are unable to manage between the two— The corn laws will doubtless go under Sir Robert's guidance—& I sincerely believe that there will be no such excessive change in the state of things as is usually anticipated

Mrs. Paul has just & somewhat suddenly lost her father— It is a loss to me—for ever since he knew me he liked me—and I was ever welcome at his house—he had a violent bilious attack—which at his age (74) not being strong, affected the functions of his heart—he suffered severely for a time poor fellow — I am very sorry he is gone.

Your picture of Octavia is to the life & your account of the B's mournful in the extreme—are they not all mad in their way? This subjection to impulse looks very like it—one is not apt to call error madness—but when it is in the family it looks like it—& now having filled my sheet pour le moment—good night

Friday— I finish my letter— I have not been well— I have suffered from rhumatic pains which leave me weak— Percy is quite well & flourishing— I fancy the agreement for our house will be signed this week so that during the next I shall really be at work to get into it—how I dread the sea of expence— What I misspent this autumn is a sad drag & loss to us; but it cant be helped—

3 Dec. [*for Jan.*] *Saturday* I did not feel well yesterday so left my letter there—& the more readily as we were to dine at the Sanfords & I thought perhaps I might learn some news—but there was none— Mrs. Sanford is remarkably well. Mr. Sanford not so—for some months he has been troubled by lumbago which wears him much by continual pain. They had just returned from Corsham Bessy Althart had been with them; they all say that no happiness was ever so great as Horatia's—she only lives in her husband's presence— & annoys Mrs. Sanford by sitting on his knee & kissing him continually. He is very fond of her—she obeys his slightest look & is much improved in manners & temper Her child is a very nice one but quite secondary in her eyes to her husband. I told you she is in the family way again

I have no news— Percy is going to Gregson today & hopes to find the agreement ready to be signed. The weather has become cold—which I think more healthy— I am very much better today—& am going to walk over to see Mrs. Paul— I told you her poor father is dead—I am very sorry—

You will find London very dull after Paris— I am now quite content with solitude—so that I have a domestic circle however small. Adieu dear Claire—

Affly. ys.
M Shelley

[P.S.] No news about the opera yet

ADDRESS: Mlle./ Mlle. Clairmont/ Rue Nᵉ Clichy —3 -bis/ Rue de Clichy/ Paris. POSTMARKS: (1) Putney   (2) 3 JA 3/ 1846. ORIGINAL: Huntington Library (HM 12328); A.L.S., 7 pp. 8vo; lower half of last leaf is cut away. UNPRINTED and UNPUBLISHED. TEXT: From original letter.

637. *To Leigh Hunt*

[Putney, 1846]

My dear Hunt

You must be tired of my ugly handwriting—yet your book[1] is so suggestive that one wants to talk about it—the more I read the more I am enchanted by it.—I have been struck however by your mention of Dante—which seems founded entirely on the Inferno—a poem I can only read bits of—the subject being to me so antipatetica but the Purgatorio & Paradiso—the Poet revels in beauty & joy there to the full as much as in the horrors below—and some of his verses & even whole cantos rap one in a gentle sort of Elysium—or carry one into the skies— Can any thing be so wondrously poetical as the approach of the boat with souls from earth to Purgatory—Shelley's most favourite passage— The angels guarding Purgatory from infernal spirits—the whole tone of hope—& the calm enjoyment of Matilda is something quite unearthly in its sweetness—& then the glory of Paradise— I do not rely on my own taste but the following verses appear to me to belong to the highest class of imagination; they occur in the last Canto of the Paradiso after the vision he has of beatitude

> —— il mio veder fu maggio
> Che 'l parlar nostro, ch'a tal vista cede,
> E cede la memoria a tanto oltraggio
> Quale è colui che soguando vede,
> E dopo 'l sogno la passione impressa
> Rimane, e l'altro alla mente non riede,
> Cotal son io, che quasi tutta cessa
> Mia visione, e ancor mi distilla
> Nel cuor lo dolce, che nacque da essa.
> Cosi la neve al sol si disigilla;
> Cosi al vento nelle foglie lievi
> Si perdea la sentenzia di Sibilla[2]—

Will you think me hypercritical about a most beautiful stanza of Keats[3]—It was the sky lark not the nightingale that Ruth heard "amid the alien corn"—the sky lark soars & sings above the shearers perpetually— The nightingale sings at night—in shady places—& never so late in the season— May is her month—

[1] *Stories of the Italian Poets*, 1846.
[2] *Paradiso*, XXXIII, 55–66.
[3] *Ode to a Nightingale*, stanza VII.

Excuse all this

Ever ys.
M Shelley

ORIGINAL: Owned by Walter M. Hill, 25 E. Washington St., Chicago, in 1937; A.L.S., 4 pp. 8vo, black-edged paper. UNPRINTED and UNPUBLISHED. TEXT: From original letter.

638. *To Edward Moxon*[*]

Putney   Friday Evg. [January 30, 1846][1]

Dear Mr. Moxon—

How good of you to send me these books. I am ashamed to say that I forget whether I thanked you for the last—but I *do* thank you. I liked the 3ᵈ tale, "Maude Chapel Farm" very much.

We expected long ago to have removed into town—but there has been a spell—I cannot tell why, on our proceeding—however I believe that we do proceed & that early in February we shall be in *Chester* Sq. I should have preferred other things myself—only if Percy gets into Parliament, I shall prefer *this*.

I have been so busy with our house that all, combined with short & rainy days, & above all, with uncertainty (for every week I have thought that *next* week we should move) that I have seen nobody—not even Mr. Rogers— I hope he is well— Give him my love when you see him & say I hope to see him soon.

Ever truly
M Shelley

[P.S.] When do the Minor poems come out? How detestably Sir Edward Bulwer speaks of Shelley in his life of Schiller.[2]—he thinks to gain popularity by truckling to the times—& mistakes the spirit of the times, & casts an indelible stain on his own name, as long as it survives.

ORIGINAL: Henry W. and Albert A. Berg Collection, the New York Public Library; A.L.S., 4 pp. 8vo. UNPRINTED and UNPUBLISHED. TEXT: From original letter.

639. *To Claire Clairmont*

Putney   Friday [January 30, 1846]

My dearest Claire—

You ask me to do the impossible That is, to fix the day when my house

---

[1] The date "31 Jan. 1846", added by someone to the MS in pencil, cannot be right since Friday was the thirtieth. It was probably taken from a postmark on the now lost envelope.

[2] Sir Edward Bulwer-Lytton's translation of the *Poems and Ballads* of Schiller, with a brief sketch of Schiller's life (1844, 2 vols.). In the last chapter of the "Brief Sketch" Bulwer-Lytton wrote: ". . . amongst us, of late years, everything that can pervert true taste in poetic diction, has been elaborately and systematically done; and most of our young poets vie with each other who can write the most affectedly: masculine thought is dwindled into some hair-breadth conceit; the wording is twisted into some effeminate barbarism called 'poetic expression': a poem is not regarded as a whole, but as a string to hold together glittering and fantastic lines which, as in Shelley, only distract the reader from the comprehension of the general idea,—if, indeed, any general idea is to be found buried amidst the gaudy verbiage."—page xcix, Tauchnitz Edition, 1844.

will be ready to receive you. This morning I got a letter from the landlord
who says that he has no doubt we can send in the upholsterer early next week;
from the time I get possession I must count a fortnight before I can receive you.
If your health permit I should advise your coming to Boulogne immediately
& one day next week coming to the Sanfords. You wont like it—but you can
be quiet there in your room if you like—   There will be none of the worry
of a lodging. Avis is impracticable. The *fracas* that goes on continually would
drive you wild. This is the best thing that can be done. Meanwhile you must
not stop too long about your box—send me word whether I shall discuss the
price with Hookham & Mitchell—& see what will be offered—a very good
season is expected—   You would hear what the libraries offered & judge
whether you would advertize it. The danger is in letting it to gentlemen &
ladies of [&] never getting paid. Hookham is sure pay & so I fancy is Mitchell.
Let me hear from you directly.

I am sorry to hear of poor Robecchis' death. You must indeed be nervous
to be deeply impressed by that & the other. The impression it makes on me
is to think, wherefore worry oneself about enmities &c—when we and others
so soon pass away—& all is changing & shifting—if we fear a person today, they
are gone tomorrow—& it is the only philosophy not to trouble oneself with
what turns out so evanescent. I know that *on the spot* one cannot do this quite
—but any excess of emotion about people who were really nothing to you can
only be caused by your nervousness & ill health.—A thousand thanks for
getting our things   If you want more money to pay I will send it directly.
I heard from Knox & believe that he has now an engagement that puts an
end to excessive anxiety—   I hope & trust he will rise & succeed & become
if not a great man—yet a distinguished one—   I see him seldom now—as he
has no time to spare—   But when we are in London I shall hope to do so
oftener. I write in a hurry dear Claire, going to town about this eternal house
which I hate with all my heart—a life in London is antipathetic to me, but
it cant be helped

Affly ys

M.

[P.S.] I have been frightfully nervous during the warm weather it is colder
now & I am better.—[*Under the envelope flap*] You say, I think you do not
bring a maid with you—which is a great comfort the more so that I should
have no room for her—   We will take care of you

ADDRESS: Madlle./ Mlle. Clairmont/ Rue Ne Clichy 3. bis-/ Rue de Clichy/
Paris. POSTMARKS: (1) PAID/ 30 JA 30/ 1846   (2) ANGL./ 1/ FEVR./
46/ BOULOGNE. ORIGINAL: Huntington Library (HM 12358); A.L.S., 4 pp.
8vo, with envelope containing an added note under the flap. Copy by Claire
Clairmont, Berg Collection, the New York Public Library. UNPRINTED and UN-
PUBLISHED. TEXT: From original letter.

640. *To Claire Clairmont*

[Putney, February, 1846]

My dear Claire—

The last words are merely an excuse for idleness, so dont think I robbed you of any portion of a letter. I saw Hookham yesterday—he said Lumley was very cautious, & said nothing nothing was known yet about the opera, except that the house was being finely decorated. I will call on the Sanfords. Through Ld. William they may know more nothing being yet publicly known   No one yet will offer for your box, but the moment some thing is known—if you should not have arrived—I will if you please advertize it. You will get plenty of offers doubtless, but the great thing will be, to be sure of being *paid,* & for this it is better to deal with a responsible tradesman, than with ladies & gentlemen unless well known as regular pay.

I send you a note from Mme. Rousseau, but I do not send you the money as I have no expectation that the shawl will be ready. Miss Descon says she has written to her to let you have it—take care of the note as it is a memorandum.

Adieu   let me hear from you

Afftly Yrs

[*Unsigned*]

ORIGINAL: Not traced. A copy in Claire Clairmont's handwriting is in the Berg Collection, the New York Public Library. UNPRINTED and UNPUBLISHED. TEXT: From Claire Clairmont's copy, as above.

641. *To Claire Clairmont*

Putney—   Monday 9 Feb. [1846]

Not hearing from you, dearest Claire, I write but on the chance of your having set out—to Boulogne—   Mrs. Crisnet has she says cured the chimney of smoking. She has adjoining to the bedroom you had a small room with a window on the *staircase*—their servant has slept there—& yours *could*—or if you liked her to be in your room, all her things could be in this other room—& she could dress there—so you would not be troubled with her dressing or her things lying about—   I am afraid you must have the drawing room too— they cannot separate the rooms   I shall tell Mrs. C—— that she must settle terms with you—but take it only for a week for you. Perhaps when we leave Putney you may like to pass the week that must elapse before I can receive you, at the Sanfords.

Do not think me unkind for urging you not to bring a French Servant— Stephanie made herself so odious that every one is frighten[ed] at the idea— & as you said you would not bring one I have made arrangements to have an extra one so that there will be no room in my house for her. Marianne will do her best to make you comfortable

Things progress—but *so* slowly—   It is very provoking.

I write no more for I cannot guess when you will receive this—   I think the change will do you good & we shall be delighted to have you. ——Percy is just now gone to see his aunts at Cheltenham.

Affl. Ys.

M

[P.S.] I have just seen the rooms—the plan mentioned above wont do at all—so I think of taking for you the drawing room floor a bed put for you in the drawing room—& a room for the servant on the same floor. If I dont hear from you tomorrow—I shall take these at once by the week.

I must, tho in a hurry, add one word to say how very sorry I am things happen so crossly—about my receiving you—but it has arisen from circumstances over which I have no controul whatever—however I most earnestly trust that the change to my house & London will calm & do you good—& I will do my utmost to make you comfortable— At the Sanfords you must keep quiet during the morning & dine in the afternoon & when well enough come to help put my house in order It is an arduous undertaking & hangs like a mill stone round my spirits— God grant things go better than I anticipate

ADDRESS: Madlle./ Mlle. Clairmont/ Poste Restante/ France   Boulogne.
POSTMARKS: (1) Putney (2) 9 FE 9/ 18[4]6. ORIGINAL: Huntington Library
(HM 12339); A.L.S., 4 pp. (4 x 6⅛ inches), 2 pp. (3½ x 5¼ inches), 2 pp.
(5¼ x 4⅜ inches), with envelope. UNPRINTED and UNPUBLISHED. TEXT:
From original letter.

642. *To [Addressee Unknown]**   Putney
                                                     9 Feb. [1846]

Dear Sir

The lady[1] to whom the box belongs is coming over to manage the matter herself— I therefore have no directions— I think the number is 24 at least I have been told that it is at about the bend (or nearer the side) of the house on the Queen's side. The number of tickets are four.

If I hear any more or have the matter at all committed to me I will see you directly.

I am, dear Sir,   Yours truly
                                   Mary Shelley

ORIGINAL: British Museum (Add. MSS 38,510, f.61); A.L.S., 2 pp. 8vo.
UNPRINTED and UNPUBLISHED. TEXT: From original letter.

643. *To Thomas Medwin*

[May, 1846]

Dear Captain Medwin

Your letter has surprised and pained me—I had no idea that you contemplated the work you mention.[2]

[1] Claire, now in possession of her box at the Opera House.
[2] Medwin's *Life of Shelley.* To Mary's letter Medwin replied (*Shelley and Mary*, IV, 1241–42):

Horsham, May 17, [*1846*]

Dear Mrs. Shelley,

You tell me that my letter has surprised and pained you. Why it should pain you, I am at a

As you remark I had said, the time has not yet come to recount the events of my husband's life. I have done all that can be done with propriety at present. I vindicated the memory of my Shelley and spoke of him as he was—an angel among his fellow mortals—lifted far above this world—a celestial spirit given and taken away, for we were none of us worthy of him—and his works are an immortal testament giving his name to posterity in a way more worthy of him than my feeble pen is capable of doing.

In modern society there is no injury so great as dragging private names and private life before the world. It is one from which every honourable and up-right mind shrinks—and your does—I am sure, for you have always been careful not to injure others in your writings.—But the life of dear Shelley—the account of the Chancery Suit above all, would wound and injure the living —and especially Shelley's daughter who is innocent of all blame and whose peace every friend of Shelley must respect.

---

loss to guess, and had thought that it was pretty generally known that I had long been engaged in this work.

When you say that you have vindicated the memory of Shelley, and spoken of him as he was, you seem to *imply that I shall take a different course.* I have latterly met with "Gilfillin's Gallery of Literary Portraits", and De Quincey's review of the same. I am disgusted with your English writers—with their accursed cant—their cold, false conventionalities—their abominable clap-trap. They should take a lesson from the Germans. I should like to show you a book just published, entitled "Burger Ein Deutscher Dichterleben." Poets are not to be squared by the rule and measure of ordinary mortals. But how bright does Shelley's character come out. What a glorious creature he was! How infinitely above all those methodical hypocrites that bow-wow at him.

I remember seeing, when we were at Pisa, a book of considerable length, that Shelley wrote, a book of "History of Christ" [the *Essay on Christianity*], why do you not publish it? How did he differ in his opinions from Paulos and Strauss and the   , who felt the theological chains in Germany, and drag from them the Divinity of Christianity. What does Rouge, the new Luther, teach? Why you are 100 years behind the Germans. I speak not of my own profession of faith. Every man has his own, and should have—a bit of narrow-minded intolerance that reigns here. Every visit I make to England disgusts me more and more with it, and were it not that I come to see my dear old Mother, I would never set foot in it again. Germany is my foster mother, and there I have passed the happiest part of my existence; there I mean to lay my bones. It is cheap also to be buried there.

But to return to your letter. You cannot suppose that I shall undo the arrangement I have made for the publication, which will take place in about a month, or six weeks at latest, and you shall have a copy among the first. It will be translated in German by a friend of mine, a most accomplished person, a lady, who has done more justice in her translations, to our lady poets, than any I know of—Madame de Ploennium—who has admirably rendered some of Shelley's minor poems.

My hands are so cold, that I can scarcely write, and this is the middle of May.
Yours truly,
T. Medwin.

To this letter Mary made no reply. Medwin wrote again a week or two later (*Shelley and Mary,* IV, 1237):

Will's Coffee House, Serle Street,
Lincoln's Inn,
Saturday.

Dear Mrs. Shelley,

I have found in the Record Office, and made extracts of the proceedings in Chancery regarding Shelley's children, which I have deemed an indispensable passage in his life. There are also other passages, I fear, whose discussion you would not approve of, but which justice to his memory has obliged me to dilate on.

It pains me much that I could not at once, on receipt of your letter, suppress the "Memoirs." The book occupied me eight months, and I have taken an expensive journey (have an expensive

I must therefore in the most earnest manner deprecate the publication of particulars and circumstances injurious to the living. That such is the feeling of Shelley's friends their common silence shews. You have been long in Germany and forget what our English world is—when you reflect, I am sure you will feel as we all must do— In these publishing, inquisitive, scandal-mongering days, one feels called upon for a double exercise of delicacy, forbearance—and reserve. If you were to write to Mrs. Hogg on the subject I am sure you will find that her feelings coincide with mine.

I had a severe attack of illness this spring—and both before and since I have been very unwell. I went to Cowes for change of air—and am now on a visit to a friend. My address in town is 24 Chester Square—for the present—but I hope (though disappointed last autumn) very soon to be on my way to Italy—as a Southern climate is absolutely necessary to my health for some little time. I have not been to Horsham for a long, long time. As to any sort of writing even a short letter is a most painful effort to me—and I do not know when I have written as much as now.

I am, dear Capⁿ Medwin

Yours truly

M Shelley

ORIGINAL: Owned by H. Buxton Forman in 1913. (See his edition of Medwin's *Life of Shelley* (1913), 504.) PRINTED: *Medwin's Life of Shelley,* edited by H. B. Forman (1913), xviii–xix. TEXT: From *ibid.*

644. *To Jane Williams Hogg*

[London] Saturday Evg [May or June, 1846]

Dearest Janey

I have received the enclosed pleasant epistle from the precious writer—What do you think of him—£250 for his book!!!—had he said £100 there had been a semblance of truth— Booksellers are not so generous now-a-days

I think I told you I did not answer his last—nor of course shall I this—

journey back), to bring it out, and have now disposed of it for £250. You are, I am sure, too reasonable to ask me, poor as I am, to make this great sacrifice. If you are desirous that the "Life" should not be published, and will make me some indemnity for the losses I should sustain, I will give you up the MS., stipulating at the same time never to write anything more about Shelley.

This sacrifice of my own fame, and, in some degree, of Shelley's fame, I am ready to make, solely with a view of complying with your wishes.

As we are going to press immediately, let me have a reply by return of post.

Yours truly,

T. Medwin.

To this blackmailing letter Mary made no answer, nor to any other letter written by Medwin. The *Life* was not, as Medwin implied, published immediately. Mary heard nothing of it for more than a year, when Medwin wrote again. Realizing from the advertisement in the *Examiner* of August 21, 1847, that the *Life* was actually to be published, Mary wrote to Hunt to ask his and Thornton's help in suppressing it if possible. But all this was in vain. Medwin's *Life of Shelley* was published in two volumes late in August or early in September by Thomas Gautley Newby, 72 Mortimer Street, Cavendish Square. It was reviewed in the *Athenæum* of September 18 and 25 (pages 971–73, 1002–1004). The review says nothing about Claire, and the Chancery suit is referred to as something only too well known. (See letters 644, 645, 669, and 671.)

Return me this letter of his by the bearer, but be so good as to let Jefferson see it—& return me also this man's two former letters which I sent you

I continue very uncomfortable—unable to walk or make any exertion— The doctor declares it to be all Neuralgia— I am well in all respects except it is as if the spine were injured the nerves are all alive—the pain thank god— not great but if I lift any thing or walk or do any thing—it is as if the spine w[oul]d altogether give up the ghost— You may think this wretched fellow's nefarious attempt at extortion does me no good

I will if possible get to you on Monday (driving does me good)—but let the bearer have the letter back with him—

Thine

[Unsigned]

ORIGINAL: British Museum (T. J. Wise Collection); A.L. (unsigned), 4 pp. 8vo. PRINTED: *A Shelley Library*, edited by Wise, 115 (quot., 6 lines). TEXT: From original letter.

645. *To Leigh Hunt*

[May or June, 1846]

An attempt to extort money finds me quite hardened. I have suffered too much from things of this kind not to have entirely made up my mind. I told Mrs. Hogg, because as she had known Captain Medwin it was possible that he might make some sort of Communication to her—but I never dreamt of answering his letter or taking any notice of this threat. The fact is, he couldn't find any bookseller to publish his trash, so he thought, by working on my fears, to dispose of it to me. Unfortunately for his plan and for my own comfort I have had too much experience of this sort of villainy, and his attempt is quite abortive. He may certainly find a bookseller to publish a discreditable work— but really I cannot bring myself to care the least about it.

ORIGINAL: "Her letter was sold at auction a few months ago and passed into the hands of Messrs. Maggs Bros. of No. 109 in the Strand, who have included it in a recent catalogue of autographs for sale, quoting the salient sentences."— H. B. Forman, *Medwin's Life of Shelley* (1913), xix–xx. PRINTED: *Medwin's Life of Shelley*, edited by H. B. Forman (1913), xx (quot., 12 lines). TEXT: Quotation from *Medwin's Life of Shelley*.

646. *To Walter Savage Landor*

[1846][1]

[From John Forster, *Walter Savage Landor*, 1869, II, 453:] Again the widow of Shelley, to whom he sent the volumes [Landor's Collected Works, 1846], took occasion to tell him how endeared to her by old associations all his early poetry had been; to relate that her husband's passionate love for *Gebir* had outlived his young college-days, remaining with him to the last; and to

[1] Landor's Collected Works, according to John Forster, *Walter Savage Landor, A Biography* (London, Chapman and Hall, 1869, 2 vols.), II, 447–48, was published in two volumes "a few weeks subsequent to" July 6, 1846.

add for herself that she had thus been led, since his death, to Landor's later works, in which she had ever found "the noblest sentiments, the most profound remarks, and the most exquisite imagery, expressed in words that ought to be studied for the welfare and cultivation of our language."

647. *To Claire Clairmont*

Baden-Baden

Thursday [(*error for* Wednesday) August 26, 1846]

Dear Claire

I write in great haste to save the post—if Mr. Rawlinson comes will you ask him (& lose no time, please) to bring a pair of black boots with him for me—these boots are either in the cupboard of the washstand stand in my room or in my wardrobe of which Mary has the key— I want them much—they are a NEW pair of black—& send also a 6ᵈ foreign Railway guide to be bought at Hookhams

If Mr. R. could learn what is charged for a carriage from Malines to Cologne by railway—& from Cologne to Manheim by steamer, I should be glad—

Tell him to come by the Dusseldorf boats they are several hours the quicker.

I am writing in the dark—& have hurt myself by a walk & am not well— I hope my Percy takes care of himself

I will write soon again & only write now for my boots   The Sanfords have come looking well.

Ys

M S

ADDRESS: Miss Clairmont/ 24 Chester Sq/ *Londres*   London. POSTMARKS: (1) BADEN/ 26 Aug 46 (2) BP/ 1 SP 1/ 1846. ORIGINAL: Huntington Library (HM 12156); A.L.S., 4 pp. 8vo. Copy by Claire Clairmont, Berg Collection, the New York Public Library. UNPRINTED and UNPUBLISHED. TEXT: From original letter.

648. *To Leigh Hunt*

[? August, 1846]

That we have not the wealth of Croesus—alas!— We borrowed the £200 you had last year for the D. of D—& we have not yet paid it— We have a bond of dear Shelley for £3,800 to pay,[1] besides repairs on the estate to the amount of £1,000 & starving villagers— We have sold some property[2] to meet these necessities which will all go as soon [as] we get it— My dear Hunt—I grieve beyond expression but I cannot conjure impossibilities tho it cuts me to the heart to say Nay

Forgive me—& again beg Marianne to forgive me—but I could not see her

ORIGINAL: Luther A. Brewer Collection, University of Iowa; A.L., 4 pp. (incomplete), 12mo (3½ x 4⅜ inches). UNPRINTED and UNPUBLISHED. TEXT: From original letter.

1 To William Willats. See Letter 632, note 2.
2 Castle Goring, sold in 1845 to Captain Pechell for £11,250 (Ingpen, *Shelley in England*, 17).

649. To *Claire Clairmont*

Baden Baden
30 Aug. [1846]

My dear Claire—

I am truly grieved by what you tell me of the opera house— I hope there is exaggeration—doubtless the Italian Opera in its glory must soon return to the Queen's Theatre, even if for a season it is forced away— I do not doubt that you will get a good sum for your box after all, when the time comes.— Lumley will do something to awaken curiosity—& a box on the grand tier will always fetch its regular £300 per an[num] price—though the extra nights may not be so good.

When I wrote about shutting up my house (I sincerely trust you did not take my writing [as] unkind—if it seemed so forgive me—it was not so meant) I was so eager to get my Percy here—& so I am still for I want him to consult Dr. Guggert for the sensation in his back—& I thought William[1] must go—/ [*Inserted between lines:*] I sent your message afterwards thro' Percy. I hope they ans[wer] it/ There is no hurry now—unless indeed Percy bring William with him—at any rate you will probably like to stay longer suit your convenience tho' certainly by the end of September I should like the house shut up.

For myself I fear my *kur* will not be so quick as I expected—through my own fault— The long walk I took has brought on a state of extreme suffering; & severe pain with excessive nervousness have been my portion ever since —dont alarm Percy—for I do not doubt I shall get over it again in a few days— but I cannot move about the least at present & suffer a great deal— No doubt this will retard my *kur*.

I am so glad to hear any good tidings of dear Knox,—he writes to me in such dreadful spirits.

I cant look forward to my return or any thing till I get a little better. Percy says you meditate establishing yourself in London— I often wonder whether you would be happier—it would be a great gain to us to have you among us— but I hate London so much myself that I cannot fancy any one being happy there

Monday   I have just got a letter from Percy saying that he will leave town on Tuesday—tomorrow so it is useless writing to him If you got my letter about asking Mr. Rawlinson to bring some things—you have probably been good enough to charge Percy with them. I feel very uncertain about the length of time my kur will occupy—as I have been so suffering these last days—at last I trust I am slowly getting over the harm I did myself—but I fear the kur will be retarded by it. Had I thought that Percy would have set out so soon I should have written about several things—bringing his gun &c—but it is too late now.

[1] A servant.

The secession from the opera house will certainly only be temporary—but it is most unfortunate—you do not mention your brother—have you better news of him?—Can anything be so shocking as these applications by Hunt for money!—in 44 they had £200 to pay *all* their debts   in 45   200 more—& now urgent distress—one must harden ones heart—for this is the most fearful insanity or worse—& take care that they shall have bread. I believe that thro' Henry & Dina they heard of the sale of C[astle] G[oring]—& wanted to come in for a slice; it is too shocking. Lucky he still writes for the Daily News & has not for years been so well off—but they have been counting on a pension & spending it before they got it. Poor Mrs. Pringle has had a sad visit to her sister. Adieu my dear Claire—believe me

Ever Affl. Ys.
M W.

[P.S.] My birthday—helas! not a very gay one—but I hope I shall be better soon

ADDRESS: Miss Clairmont/ 24 Chester Sq/ Londres   London. POSTMARK: BADEN/ 31 Aug 46. ORIGINAL: British Museum (T. J. Wise Collection); A.L.S., 6 pp. 8vo, with envelope. UNPRINTED and UNPUBLISHED. TEXT: From original letter.

650. *To Claire Clairmont*

Baden-Baden—5 Sep. [1846]

My dearest Claire—

I fear I worded my letter about shutting up my house unkindly—for you seem hurt—& I am so, *so* sorry—God know[s] I am the last person who ought to inflict the smallest pain on you—I to whom you have ever been so kind—forgive me if it is so—I entreat you— When I wrote I was very ill—& excessively disturbed by Percy's having been so ill—longing for him here—expecting William to go—not liking the house to be kept open without him—I wanted Percy to come to consult Dr. Guggert—& William going I did not feel the house safe with the maids if kept ope[n]   I know you w[oul]d have taken every care—but—in short—I should (you not being their mistress & not going down stairs) have been very uneasy had the house been kept open without William— I hope I did not write unkindly—nothing was further from my thoughts—As soon as I heard of Lady's S's death I wrote to Percy [to] tell him to ask you whether you would not like to stay till the end of September— I mentioned this in my last— I hope you are still in Chester Sq.—

I must ask my friends to have patience with me in all I go through.—After that long walk I mentioned, I suffered a martyrdom in mind & body—a nervous sciatica kept me in frightful pain & my nerves were shaken most dreadfully—the s[c]iatica is now gone—but my nerves will not be calm—& your letter today awakening the fear that I had hurt your feelings distresses me beyond measure.—I have full trust that I shall get well here—but as yet I have not advanced much— I have been so thrown back by the last attack—

I do not venture on the smallest walk—still I believe the *cur* to be in progress but more rooted & difficult to get rid of, than my doctor thought at first. I have not yet been able to talk to him about you—but I will— I was in hopes from Percy that your spirits were better—but you do not write so. This opera house &c must weigh on them— The evil will not last—the Opera must return in glory to the Queen's theatre—there is not such another house for the voice in the world—but I fear next winter you will not get so much—& it will be against your selling it—how deeply does all this grieve me.

Mr. Rawlinson arrived a few days ago—he seems well— Mr. Sanford is better the last day or two—& think[s] the Wisbaden waters did him good— he is now under Dr. Guggert as well as Bessy— Mrs. Hare's boy's go back next week— I do not know when to expect Percy as he seemed to think that he should loiter with Mr. Burgass on the way— it will be such a happiness to see him—it is so long since I saw him— I have now no news for I never hear from anyone— I wish the bill of Mr. Berry had been sent me here—I should have signed it & sent it to the Pauls—it must wait now & I cannot advance the money to Mr. L—— for I have none— Adieu dear Claire pray forgive me—if I hurt you—you must attribute it to the sufferings of an invalid & the anxiety excited by the state of things—to any thing rather than being criminally unkind to so good a friend as you have ever been to me. Pray write to me & take care of yourself

Ev[er] Affl. Ys.

[Unsigned]

ADDRESS: If gone, to be/ forwarded/ Miss Clairmont/ 24 Chester Sq/ Londres London [*Redirected to*] 3 bis Rue Neuve Clichy/ à Paris. POSTMARK: (1) BADEN/ 5 Sep 46 (2) B Y/ 10 SP 10/ 1846 (3) 12/ SEPT/ 46/ BOULOGNE. ENDORSED: Saying how very kind I had been to her. ORIGINAL: Huntington Library (HM 12135); A.L. (unsigned), 6 pp. 8vo. UNPRINTED and UNPUBLISHED. TEXT: From original letter.

651. *To [Thomas Hookham]*

[153 Promenade, Baden-Baden]
Saturday 12 Sep. [1846]

Dear Sir

I of course expected this sort of thing to happen— And you know how totally hardened I am against this species of rascality. Mr. Byron has of course got other[s] & will get other copies—& to keep these is of no avail— I am not sure that the best mode of action is not to let him have them again (except that one wd. not voluntarily put them in his hands)—& defy him to make any use of them—but of what use is it to make a fuss about keeping one set of copies, when having another, he can make as many as he likes? Of course I wish you in my name to relieve Mr. Holcroft from all onus on the subject. It is very disagreable to be brought into contact with Mr. H— whose letter is disgusting to me. Tho the feeling that dictated it had something of good in it—he is not of course such a person as Mr. Memon—but he is one with whom I do not wish to come in contact— Say every thing civil from me to him—& tell him that I hold the efforts of such swindlers as Mr. Memon in such contempt that my impulse is to defy them, without more comment or care.

I have written to a young friend of Percy's & mine Mr. Knox with whom I wish you to talk over the matter before you act— He is a lawyer very clear-sighted—& I should depend on his advice on the subject. I fancy he will counsel defiance merely—as wd. Peacock & Jefferson—and indeed under the circumstances it seems, in the *last* resort, ones only resource—so it may be better to begin with it.

I am very much obliged to you for your kindness in all this. Your friendship for Shelley naturally leads you to wish to serve his name—and I am obliged to you for all the zeal & kindness you have shewn me.

The great thing [is] will he avoid police reports & police magistrates—

                    I am dear Sir
                         Yours very truly
                              M Shelley

[P.S.] My health is, I trust slowly mending—but I am still far from well— I will preserve carefully Mr. T. Holcroft's letter Do not let him come in contact with Mr. Knox.

Dont put via Belgium or via any thing out side your letter
My address is
          153 Promenade
          Baden-Baden

ORIGINAL: Henry W. and Albert A. Berg Collection, the New York Public Library; A.L.S., 8 pp. 8vo. UNPRINTED and UNPUBLISHED. TEXT: From original letter.

652. *To Thomas Hookham**

                              153 Promenade
                              Baden-Baden
                              12 September 1846

Dear Sir

I authorize you to possess yourself of & to keep possession of the copies of letters (my property) which you mention to me as they are mine by law & cannot in any way be published by any one else. I will of course take care to guarantee you against the consequences of your acting in this manner for me.

    I am dear Sir
                    Yours truly
                         Mary Shelley

ADDRESSED: Thos. Hookham Esq/ 15 Old Bond St. ORIGINAL: Henry W. and Albert A. Berg Collection, the New York Public Library; A.L.S., 3 pp. 8vo. UNPRINTED and UNPUBLISHED. TEXT: From original letter.

653. To [Thomas Hookham]

24 Chester Sq
Wednesday [? October–November, 1846]

Dear Sir

I cannot express the great pleasure it has given me to have the letters you last sent. I have much to say—but am still confined to my bed by serious illness—but this I want to say—*I am sure* this man has *many more others*—in time I hope to get them—he will come again—& you can say that there were *many* more of Shelley's letters. I cannot write more. Dont raise the mans hopes about money or he will become impracticable—A[t] first he hoped for hundreds had he got them he would have grasped at thousands now he is obliged to content himself with units   he has *many more*   manage to get them

Ys. tr.

M W S

[P.S.] I am so much obliged to you

ORIGINAL: Henry W. and Albert A. Berg Collection, the New York Public Library; A.L.S., 4 pp. 8vo (written in a very unsteady hand). UNPRINTED and UNPUBLISHED. TEXT: From original letter.

654. To Alexander Berry

24 Chester Sq London
12 Nov. [1846]

My dear Mr. Berry

I cannot express how I am obliged to you for the £20 for Mrs. Larkins— It was too much to ask you to send it—but your affectionate recollection of my Cousin was the impulse— Mrs. Larkins begs her most grateful thanks—she asked me whether she should write to thank you—but I suppose my conveying them will do as well. You may have the satisfaction of feeling that the money was most opportunely & worthily bestowed—& dearly earned also, by her unwearied & kind care of a very recalcitrant & exigeante patient—poor thing.— I should have written ere this to thank you & in answer to your letter, but I was abroad when it arrived—& by a mistake it was not forwarded to me & I waited also to see Mr. Robinson— He speaks most gratefully of your generous kindness to himself. He has arrived unluckily, when the Ministry which he served is *out,* & the people who are *in* may not consider that they owe him any thing— He has hopes however which I sincerely hope will be realized— he is very deserving—& would be a useful & faithful servant to the Queen however he may be employed.

I was interested to hear of the monument you have erected to my Cousins. —The necessity of Churchyards in this country removes these affectionate tokens of memory away from the haunts of the living, & by crowding many together interferes with the feelings of the survivors. Mr. Robinson says that you have selected a favourite spot—& that the monument does credit to your taste & affection.

As yet there has been no election—so whether Percy will become M.P. I know not—Horsham, the borough which he ought to represent, is so exceedingly venal, that he is strongly advised to have nothing to do with it. A contested election would cost too much; for he is far from rich—& he is desirous by care & economy to re-establish his fortune, so grievously injured by the injustice of his grandfather—& not by any act of extravagance (& a contested election w[oul]d be one) to do it further detriment. Time & care may do something—& *luck* w[oul]d do more—as his Estate is open to very great improvements in various ways—had he capital—   He is told he must look out for an Heiress—   Did he meet with one—& were there a mutual attachment it would certainly be a desirable event—but he is not venal in any respect

It is impossible to say what the present government will do about the Colonies. The English are so engrossed by their own affairs—which, by help of rail:roads, are so exciting, that they will scarcely even think of near Ireland— And the Colonies are so far off that it is quite an affair of luck when they are well governed—   I hope prosperity is dawning on you—& that you are better satisfied with the state of things.

My health has not been good lately. I went to Baden:Baden this last summer & have returned better, tho' not quite recovered—but I think I shall by degrees get better of my ailments & be restored to my natural good health.

It interests & pleases me very much to hear from you—so I hope that you will occasionally write to me. Percy desires his best compliments—& believe me dear Mr. Berry,

Yours very truly

Mary Woll^{ft} Shelley

[P.S. *at top of page 1*] This is Percy's Birthday   He is 27

ADDRESS: Alexander Berry Esq/ Sidney/ New South Wales. POSTMARKS: (1) PAID/ 14 NO 14/ 1846   (2) SHIP LETTER/ MR * 28/ 1847/ SYDNEY. ORIGINAL: Alexander Hay, Coolangatta, N. S. W., Australia; A.L.S., 4 pp 4to, with envelope. UNPRINTED and UNPUBLISHED. TEXT: From original letter.

655. *To Marianne Hunt**

Brighton

17 Nov. [1846]

My dear Marianne

I deeply grieve over the account you send—we all hoped that Hunt was made comfortable for life—   However he has an income—& the alternative you mention need not be recurred to—   For ourselves I am sorry to say that we can do no more than pay the annuity regularly—we have no command over sums of money—& just now are very much hampered by having to pay £500 for Percy's election expenses—when he thought of standing last spring— which must be paid out of what we may receive at Xmas—& will leave us quite bare—   The estate is so much mortgaged & needs so much to be spent in repairs, totally neglected by Sir Tim, that it requires the utmost prudence to get on— I am truly sorry to hear so bad an account of your health. I have long been a sufferer & am so still my illness having fallen on the nerves which gives me a great deal to bear—

How I rejoiced for you last Autumn surely so much good cannot be quite without avail. I am

Ever truly ys
M Shelley

[P.S.] Percy & I have all in common— I have *nothing* of my own exclusively.

> ORIGINAL: British Museum (Add. MS 38,524, ff.23–24); A.L.S., 4 pp. 8vo. UNPRINTED and UNPUBLISHED. (Grylls, *Mary Shelley*, 248, quotes 1 line.) TEXT: From original letter.

656. *To Mrs. Milner-Gibson**

24 Chester Sq
Friday [1846–48]

Dear Mrs. Gibson

Since meeting you at Lady Morgan's[1] I have been confined by the vile Influenza & could not therefore join your party—

As to Percy he is quite ashamed but till yesterday he believed your party to be for this Evening— He hopes you will forgive him

I am

Ys. truly
M Shelley

> ORIGINAL: Library of Trinity College, Cambridge University, in the Milner-Gibson-Cullum Collection of Autographs; A.L.S., 2 pp. 12mo (3½ x 5½ inches). UNPRINTED and UNPUBLISHED. TEXT: From original letter.

657. *To [Addressee Unknown] (a fragment)**

24 Chester Sq
3 Jan. [1847–48]

. . . harm done was loss of time—in time I now feel I shall be well—but it requires patience—and I cannot leave the neighbourhood of my doctor— Were it still warm autumn or cheering spring, instead of pinching winter, I should feel much enclined to run down for a day for "a sniff of the briny" & to see you all—but I must wait.

I am very glad to receive so good an account of you all. My kindest regard to your family circle & believe me

Very truly ys
Mary Shelley

> ORIGINAL: Owned by J. Kyrle Fletcher, Ltd., London, in 1937; A.L.S., 2 pp. 8vo (a fragment). UNPRINTED and UNPUBLISHED. TEXT: From original letter.

[1] Lady Sydney Morgan (1789–1859), author of poems, novels, and books of travel.

658. *To Alexander Berry*

24 Chester Sq—London
29 March 1847

Dear Mr. Berry

Charles Robinson dined with us today—& I enquired whether he had heard from you—he had not—so it is a long time since a letter has reached us. Charles remembers your kindness with much gratitude & I am thankful to you for being so good to a friend of mine so that we both wish you not to forget us—& Charles looks forward to the time when he may have the pleasure of seeing you again— His plans are still uncertain—for he has not yet got a place & feels very impatient—tho' his friends bid him be patient & that he will be sure to get one— Had he arrived while the Tories were in office he would not have had to wait so long—but the Whigs are noted for only giving places to Greys & Howards—people of their own kin— Still Charles is so well recommended both by his own personal character & by the influential friends he has that I sincerely trust that there is no doubt but that he will be recompenced as he deserves.

Just now indeed politics are in a strange position & the famine in Ireland engrosses the attention of government— The universal scarcity felt on the continent of Europe as much as with us—has so raised the price of corn that the fears of the Protectionists are for the present allayed—but it is fearful to think of Ireland & the million a month sent her from England—& the unfortunate propensities of the people who, in the hopes of money from this country, can scarcely be induced to sow seed for next harvest. All parties here shrink from the load of responsibility—in Government & no one I fancy envies Ld John Russell—not even Sir Robert Peel—

I sincerely hope that Percy will get into parliament next election—but the dissolution will not take place till next Autumn.—Your late governor Sir George Gipps is dead you see—but before this he had lost the power of injuring the Colony— The recall of Sir Eardly Wilmot is now a principal *colonial* subject. Lord Stanley having moved that Mr. Gladstone's dispatch recalling Sir Eardly should be printed. Lord Stanley's own speech is looked upon as doing Sir Eardly no good—& Mr. Gladstones dispatch recalling him is, I am assured, a curious specimen—he tells Sir Eardly that he has been accused—& that he has been defended—& that he does not know which is the true statement—but "there is something between certainty & uncertainty" & on that he founded his recall. There are rumours of changes in the modes of governing the colonies—& Lord Grey is very active & intends to be very reforming— You will know best whether he will do any good. Charles Robinson tells me he got a Sidney newspaper the other day—if it came from you he thanks you. How does the plantation round Mrs. Berry's & her brother's tomb thrive? I am interested on that subject & shall be very glad to hear from you—

I am ys. every truly
M Shelley

[P.S. *at top of first page*] Percy desires to make your acquaintance at least by a friendly message. We hope all is going on well with you

[P.S. *written inside the envelope, which is sealed in black*] The mourning seal is for Lady Shelley—Percy's grandmother. Her death makes him some what richer.

ADDRESS: Alexander Berry Esq/ Sidney/ *New South Wales*/ Australia. POST-MARKS: (1) PAID/ 30 MR 30/ 1847 (2) T.P./ Ebury (3) SHIP LETTER/ JY * /2[6]/ 1847/ SYDNEY. ORIGINAL: Alexander Hay, Coolan-gatta, N.S.W., Australia; A.L.S., 4 pp. 4to, with envelope and seal. UNPRINTED and UNPUBLISHED. TEXT: From original letter.

659. *To Claire Clairmont*

[? April, 1847]

Dearest Claire

Percy has asked several men to dinner so as I do not go down stairs you will not like to dine alone with them—   But come here to a 2 o'clock dinner with me—& we will drive afterwards—& I mean to see the party—which con-sists of Coulson Peacock—Burhel—[   ]ugh—J. Campbell—Knox,—after din-ner—

So I expect you today before 2

Ys. Affl
M S.

ADDRESS: Miss Clairmont/ 26 Osnaburgh St. ORIGINAL: Huntington Library (HM 12331); A.L.S., 2 pp. 8vo, with envelope. UNPRINTED and UNPUBLISHED. TEXT: From original letter.

660. *To Leigh Hunt**

24 Chester Sq
Friday [c. April, 1847]

My dear Hunt

I congratulate you on the news you so kindly send me. I hope this turn of fortune will make you easy—& that better will come this summer—& the pen-sion granted. This fine weather will do your health good too.

I am almost entirely confined to my room at present—but I am getting better—

Percy is in Sussex   He, with me, will be delighted to hear that we shall [have] more books of yours[1]   Nothing can be more welcome

I suffer a good deal—so you will excuse a short note

Ever truly ys
M Shelley

ORIGINAL: Frank J. Hogan, Washington, D.C.; A.L.S., 3 pp. 8vo. UNPRINTED and UNPUBLISHED. TEXT: From original letter.

[1] Hunt's *Men, Women, and Books* was published in 1847.

*Mary W. Shelley's house, 1846–51, at
24 Chester Square, London*

661. *To Mr. Halford**

24 Chester Sq
18 April [? 1847]

Dear Mr. Halford

I delayed answering your note for a day or two with the idea of obtaining better information from a medical gentleman of this neighbourhood—I have been disappointed—so can only now tell you my experience of this Square. The houses are well built on 20 feet of gravel—well drained & the whole vicinity very airy. It is not a bracing air—but I never heard of fevers prevailing —I have had nothing of the kind [? in] my household—which has been very healthy ever since I came here   I think it quite as healthy a spot as any part of London. Tiburnia is said to be more bracing—but it is cold being on clay— The only part of town I should prefer as more bracing is Kensington Gore— but that is scarcely London.

I hope you will not think that I take too great a liberty in sending the enclosed account of an hospital in which I take great interest. It is a most excellent institution—carried on by medical gentlemen *gratuitously*—with a humanity—a skill & a sedulous attention quite unequalled.—Nor do they seek remuneration   they only anxiously deplore that the funds are so very low. I know that you are a munificent patron of several charitable institutions— that very circumstance may disable you from extending relief to any other— but we should be very thankful for even a small donation.

Pray excuse this liberty & believe me

Very truly ys
Mary Shelley

ORIGINAL: Owned by Francis Edwards, Ltd., London, in 1937; bought by Dr. Herman T. Radin, New York, in 1943; A.L.S., 6 pp. 8vo. UNPRINTED and UNPUBLISHED. TEXT: From original letter.

662. *To Richard Monckton Milnes, Lord Houghton**

24 Chester Sq
20 April [? 1847]

Dear Mr. Milnes

When you dined here I was very suffering—& have been almost confined to my room ever since. I am now better & get out for an airing—but I am still quite an Invalid tho' with the prospect of good health before me to cheer me. I shall be very glad to see you whenever you can call

Percy thanks you for remembering him—he is now gone to Mitchells—

I send a Stanza of the Revolt of Islam which I hope will serve your friend —   I have lately sometimes expected to rejoin the beloved Writer—if such grace would be afforded me—which I scarcely dare hope—   if I did—what were death? a Blessing—

Ever truly yours
Mary Shelley

ORIGINAL: Preussische Staatsbibliothek, Berlin (in the Varnhagen Collection); A.L.S., 3 pp. 12mo (3½ x 5⅛ inches). UNPRINTED and UNPUBLISHED. TEXT: From original letter.

663. *To Claire Clairmont*

[? April 27, 1847]

My dear Claire

All you say puts me so in mind of myself, that a thousand times over I feel the most anxious wishes about you—not that I think your illness just like mine —but I feel convinced that [yours] arises from the same organ— When I think how you enjoyed your health a year ago—how I wish you were brought back to the same state. I know the long protraction of my illness acts as an argument against me with you—but mine was so fearful—so fatal it w[oul]d soon have been—that it is quite a miracle of art my cure— Just now I am much of a prisoner from a cause I will explain when I see you—a most provoking freak on the part of nature to put me to pain, when in the order of things I ought to be well & can take a little drive but not so far as you

Percy is not well   I am sorry to say just now

Your account of Jane is heart breaking   Life is such a struggle & warfare— that if you put yourself in a wrong position you must be the victim— Poor Jane with that lump of self-concentreted flesh beside her!

The weather now is changing for the better, I trust—   What is poor Henry C[leveland]'s illness?

I shall be very glad to see you when you can come—a line would always bring you the Brougham and I will get to you the first day I can go so far

Affl Ys

M S

ADDRESS: Miss Clairmont/ 26 Osnaburgh St./ Regent's Park. POSTMARKS: (1) E b u r y/ 1ᴰ· PAID   (2) [   ]/ [   ]7/ 1847. ORIGINAL: Huntington Library (HM 12334); A.L.S., 6 pp. 8vo, with envelope. UNPRINTED and UNPUBLISHED. TEXT: From original letter.

664. *To Leigh Hunt*

Chester Sq.

10 June [1847]

Dear Hunt

Your kind present[1] was most welcome—how much more in a sick room— as I must call mine—for tho' much better—I still suffer a great deal—& am almost entirely confined to my sopha—in a few days I am going to Brighton —& after the sea air & baths have given me a little strength I hope to get further off, & to the real country.

I grieve very much to receive so bad an account of your health—we have all I suppose our theories about health—mine is that change of air is the best

[1] The two volumes of *Men, Women, and Books* (1847), selections from Hunt's uncollected prose works.

remedy—& it is therefore to be deplored that you cannot avail yourself of opportunities offered for this purpose

I have read a good deal of your volumes with great pleasure recognizing old friends— Percy who is just setting out on a yachting expedition[2] takes them with him & thanks you very much.

I was pleased to see in the Examiner a mention of the pension— The Whigs are a shabby cold-blooded set— I hope they may redeem themselves by doing as they ought towards you— Remember me to Marianne— I write lying down— I should be so glad to hear that you are better

Affly Ys
M Shelley

ORIGINAL: Bodleian Library (MS Shelley Adds. d.5, ff.89–90); A.L.S., 4 pp. 8vo. PRINTED: *Bodleian Quarterly Record*, VIII, No. 95 (1937), 419–20. TEXT: From original letter.

665. *To Leigh Hunt*

13 Bedford Sq
Brighton
29 June [1847]

Dear Hunt—

I congratulate you very sincerely on the pension granted.[3] It ought to have been three—but the Whigs must be shabby. You will now be able to give your head rest—& I hope you will change the air. If you go to the sea—the best place for us is [? Candus]—*dont* go to Southern the air is [? low] & bad— Broadstairs or Sandgate are nice places—particularly Sandgate for there are very pretty walks about & it is a pretty quiet place— Now your money troubles are, I hope, at an end— Percy is on a cruize, or he would join in my congratulations. It is delightful to know that you are at last enjoying peace of mind— I hope the amateur play[4] will go on & make you a rich man—in which character it will be charming to see you—

I am getting strong by slow but I trust sure degrees— With love to Marianne

Ys truly
M Shelley

ORIGINAL: British Museum (Add. MSS 38,524, ff.203–204); A.L.S., 4 pp. (4 x 6¼ inches). UNPRINTED and UNPUBLISHED. TEXT: From original letter.

666. *To Claire Clairmont*

[Brighton, July 28, 1847]

My dear Claire

I shall be very glad to see you for a fortnight but as just now your little room

---

2 To Norway.

3 Hunt's pension of £200 was granted on June 22, 1847.

4 On July 26 and 28 Charles Dickens's amateur company acted Jonson's *Every Man in His Humour* in Liverpool and in Manchester for Hunt's benefit, Dickens himself taking the part of Bobadil. Hunt was presented with 400 guineas.

is occupied by a lodger you must put it off till towards the end of next week when fix your own day & come— I remain here—for the trouble of moving is great—& the weather is not by any means too hot— I must move when Percy returns so that one move will do. You are very good to give poor little Dina a holyday.

After I wrote to you about poor E[mily] D[unston] I reflected that her brother w[oul]d certainly be bail for her, so I wrote to Sarah, saying I could not command so large a sum, but that of course her brother would be bail—& then the debt need not be paid for some weeks—not to appear too hard hearted —& as indeed I felt they might want money, I sent a cheque for £10—which I grudged I own—however I got the enclosed answer from Sarah returning the cheque—it is the letter of a lady certainly—tho' it may hide anger at my not doing more. I must tell you in answer to Emily's asking me about a physician of enlightened mind—I said, tho' I was not acquainted with him I had heard that Dr. Southwood Smith was both clever & liberal— Poor Emily! I am anxious to know how she is— I answered Sarah's note but have not heard again.[1] I do hope they are in Amory's hands—for he will give them good advice in every way—

I heard from my Percy yesterday—he was at Copenhagen on the 22d— their voyage was slower than they expected but they seem to enjoy themselves

I have had somewhat of a stomach attack which pulled me down—but am better—

What does W. C. say & do?

Affly Ys
M Shelley

ADDRESS: Miss Clairmont/ 26 Osnaburgh St./ Regent's Park/ London. POST-
MARKS: (1) BRIGHTON/ JY 28/ 1847/ E   (2) KM/ 28 JY 28/ 1847   (3)
8 NT 8/ JY 28/ 1847/ D. ORIGINAL: Huntington Library (HM 12155); A.L.S.,
8 pp. 16mo (3¼ x 5¼ inches), with stamped envelope. Copy by Claire Clairmont, Berg Collection, the New York Public Library. UNPRINTED and UN-
PUBLISHED. TEXT: From original letter.

667. *To Claire Clairmont*

Sunday [August 1, 1847]
Brighton

My dear Claire

I have Mrs. Booth with me & it is quite uncertain when she will go—so it

---

[1] In September, 1936, I saw in the Brick Row Bookshop a letter from Sarah E. Dunston to Mary Shelley and a letter from Emily Dunston to Mary. Sarah's letter, dated July 23, 1847, and beginning "Dearest Madam," says that she is returning a note for £10; she had already borrowed money and therefore had no need for it. The money was required to bring her sister home from prison; the sister was desperately ill and would have died if not removed from prison. Her brother would give nothing.

The letter from Emily (A.L.S., 4 pp. 12mo), dated August 28, 1848, tells Mary that Emily had sent a book to Field Place for Mary, that Emily had taken Mary's advice about her affairs and was much happier. She wished to know if Miss Clairmont was offended; she had not answered her letter.

will be better that you defer coming till tomorrow week Monday 9th August—
& then come for my last fortnight in Brighton

The weather is fine—but I have not been well with a stomach attack & am,
I confess—sadly bored—

Percy writes to me from Copenhagen—he is now on the shores of Norway
—he enjoys himself much—

As you like to have your friends' letters I send you one received today—
Have you been to Maidstone?—

Mrs. Paul improves in health here—

I got a note from S[arah] D[unston] saying E[mily] D[unston] wished
for a lodging here that she might enjoy my society Poor thing I can be of
no use to her & said that my stay here was uncertain (true enough for 20 times
I have planned going away) & that Brighton (truer still) was the last place
to bring an invalid to on account of the hideous unceasing noise—the glare of
light & heat &c &c &c— I pine to leave it—

I hope you will be able to come on the day I mention the 9th

Ys. affly

M S—

ADDRESS: Miss Clairmont/ 26 Osnaburgh Street/ Regent's Park. POSTMARKS: (1)
BRIGHTON/ AU 1/ 1847/ A (2) C O/ 2 AU 2/ 1847. ORIGINAL: Hunt-
ington Library (HM 12149); A.L.S., 4 pp. 8vo, with envelope. Copy by Claire
Clairmont, Berg Collection, the New York Public Library. UNPRINTED and UN-
PUBLISHED. TEXT: From original letter.

668. *To Alexander Berry*[1]

Brighton—17 Augt 1847

My dear Mr. Berry—

I wrote to you last October & last March—& was in hopes to have heard
from you ere this—as the last letter I have received contained your generous
remittance of £20 to poor Mrs. Larkins. When I last wrote I was confined to
my room by illness—for many months I have been very indisposed—but
getting better, my physician sent me here for bracing air—& I am getting
strength & hope in the end quite [to] recover my health—which after so long
a time will be a very great blessing. Percy I am daily expecting back from a
trip in his Yacht to Norway, by which he has been amusing himself this summer—he has an hereditary passion for the sea—which he thus indulges. He
has not endeavoured to get into Parliament this General Election—for at no
period has there been more bribery & corruption—so that if he had tried to get
in for either of the two places Horsham & Shoreham for which he w[oul]d
naturally stand—the contest would have cost 2 or 3 thousand pounds—more
than he could afford to spend—above all for an uncertainty—however a delay
of a year or so will do no harm—& there is likely enough to be a vacancy for

[1] In the original letter someone has inserted (in ink) a dozen or more punctuation marks.
These are not reproduced here.

Shoreham when he will try for it I hope with better prospects than would have been the case this time. When he returns from Norway—we meditate a trip to the West of England—as it is necessary for me to remain near the sea. I think that this is all the news I can give you of ourselves—for indeed my painful & long indisposition has made a great recluse of me & caused me to lead a dull life.—But I hope I shall hear from you & how you are—now recovered from that sense of isolation which you described as coming over you after your sad loss. Do you ever think of England—& finding friends here? You are of too much consequence in your adopted country to think of this—or I need not tell you how glad we should be to see you.—As for public news there is little that you will not find in the newspapers—   What chance there is of the Whigs remaining long in office I cannot say—the feeling is that they are there till Sir Robert Peel has consollidated his plans—when he will return—& the mercantile interest of the country have confidence in him—while the state of England in one way or another is becoming more mercantile every day. Your being in N[ew] S[outh] W[ales] makes me regard with interest that part of the world—   I remark that your Surveyor General Sir T. Mitchell arrived in England a few weeks ago—   Do you not want him?—or what does he do here? Perhaps you have no objection to his absence—but absence & his place seem at variance—   One w[oul]d think there was plenty of occupation for him. How do you like the successor of Sir G. Gripps—whose measures you disapproved—Does Sir C. FitzRoy act with more enlightened views for the c[o]lony—   A colony—if we comprehend all Australia growing in importance—the Copper mines in the South (is it true gold is also found?)—the new country discovered by Dr. Leichhart north of you—all these excite attention here but are of vast importance & will—if only indeed you were preserved from drouths—make a fine & rich country of that large continent—   Is it getting better peopled—& do squatters flourish—I hope you & your property are free from them.

Charles Robinson was absent for some months in France negotiating for the N[ew] Z[ealand] Company the purchase of the French Co'y's land in Banks' Peninsula—he is returned but I have not seen him—   I heard from him the other day & he asked if I had heard from you—mentioning as he always does, your great kindness to him with warm gratitude—he says that he has not concluded the affair above mentioned but hopes he shall by & bye—The English C— have offered £10,000 for the peninsula—   He says he shall probably return to N. Z. as agent to the Co. G. if the Government do not give him a situation. What a change for the better has Captain Grey operated in a country which lately seemed devoted to ruin—prosperity, security return—C^n Grey is a good genius & has remedied the mischief inflicted by C^n FitzRoy —as he had before in S. A. that brought about by C^n Grawler—   Charles looks forward with hope for himself—& for the country—& he approves highly the new system of Government in sending out pensioners, who are to have a kind

of Military tenure of their land, better than keeping them idle here—& it will
to be a means both of provinding [*sic*] for their families & protecting N. Z.
against the natives

I am writing a long letter—a thing *very* unusual for me—for my illness
being much on the nerves makes me use my pen as little as possible. I hope
I have not wearied you— If you feel as I have felt when on the continent a
letter from England will be welcome. If I can afford you any entertainment I
shall be happy—& very glad to hear from you—as I trust I may—as a near relation of your beloved wife   I hope I do not take up your time disagreably by
sending these more than a few lines. Your kindness to poor Everina & to
Charles Robinson must ever command my gratitude & thanks—

Believe me to be

Very truly yours
Mary Shelley

[P.S. *at top of page 1*] My address is 24 Chester Square, Pimlico, London.

ADDRESS: Alex^r Berry Esq/ Sydney/ New South Wales. POSTMARKS: (1)
[BRIGHTON]/ AU 18/ 1847/ C   (2) PAID/ OF/ 19 AU 19/ 1847   (3)
SHIP LETTER/ JA * 3/ 1848/ SYDNEY. ORIGINAL: Alexander Hay, Coolangatta, N.S.W., Australia; A.L.S., 12 pp. 8vo, with envelope and seal. UNPRINTED
and UNPUBLISHED. TEXT: From original letter.

669. *To Leigh Hunt*

Friday M[ornin]g [August 27, 1847]

My dear Hunt,

I am very grateful to you and to Thornton.

I am led to believe on reflection that the book[1] may not be so utterly abominable—tho' still painful to many. The history is—last year, more than a year
ago he wrote to me for materials about the Chancery suit— I wrote to say
that the subject was one if minutely treated that would be so painful, among
others to Ianthe, that it was altogether improper to dwell on it.

A week or two after I had the letter I think you saw it—saying that he had
obtained details which wd. be disagreable to me—that he wd. suppress the life
if I wd. pay him—that he had just had an offer of £250 and had been to expences &c.

I discovered that *on the very day* he wrote thus, Colburn returned his MS.
positively refusing it—he had had it returned from several booksellers, all de-
clining it unless I approved— I did not answer his letter and heard no more
till the other day when came another letter saying that it was on the eve of
being published and talking of its being *slashing* and the hubbub it wd.
make, and saying that money forced him to write—but proposing to let me
see [it] if I liked before publication, but saying it was printed. Of course after
his previous attempt to extort money I did not answer his letter—and will cer-

[1] Medwin's *Life of Shelley*. See Letter 643, note 2.

tainly never address another line to him— A fellow I know to be a villain will never have any thing but silence from me.

Still on thinking over his saying he wd. send me his book and that I should see it at once, it would appear that it is likely enough not to be so odious as he threatened—but so many people can be injured poor C[laire] for instance whose best years were past in so laudable a struggle for independance—and never injured any one—suppose *she* were mentioned—and as I said, Ianthe's Mother in short a fellow of this sort goes about dealing wounds with a poisoned dagger—and being beneath injury himself—(yet he would not like his history to be known among his friends, if he have any in Germany), can inflict the most cruel wounds— Thus it is not merely for myself—but who can tell how many he will pain and injure. This will add zeal to dear good Thornton—and if he speak to Newby—he need not *think* only of me—but of Claire Mrs. Esdaile (Ianthe) and who knows how many whom the wretch with what he calls his slashing may inflict misery upon.

Strange enough if the book be not *in the press*— He says in his note (I sent the note to Jane—but you shall have it) he is correcting his last proof— Till I saw the book advertized in the Examiner[2] the next day, these words made me think that every word was still in Manuscript—the moment I saw the advertisement I wrote to you.

Certainly if the publication could be wholly prevented so much pain wd. be spared to so many innocent persons—and the wretch prevented so bad a triumph in evil, that the endeavour is worthy of Thornton's best endeavours— God speed him in it—the bad seldom succeed in open wickedness—so I will hope that Newby will repent and refrain from publishing so nefarious a production— It has already been refused by at least half a dozen Booksellers—so Newby takes the refuse and will attain a bad notoriety together with the author.

I was in hopes to hear that you were at the sea side. I grieve at giving you all this trouble but when I think of the many hearts to be wounded, I cannot help urging it and I verily believe I am likely enough to be the least injured —and yet enough—

Affectionately yrs.

M. Shelley

[P.S.] The day for these sort of libels in England is over—and it is strange any respectable bookseller will look at it or disreputably hope to gain by it.

ORIGINAL: Sir John Shelley-Rolls. PRINTED: *Shelley and Mary*, IV, 1238–40; *A Shelley Library*, edited by Wise, 116 (quot., 24 lines). TEXT: From copy made by Sir John Shelley-Rolls.

[2] *The Examiner*, August 21, 1847, 544: "Mr. Newby will Immediately publish. . . . In 2 vols. post 8vo (now ready) *Life of Shelley* By Captain Medwin, Author of 'Conversations with Lord Byron,' &c."

670. *To Claire Clairmont**

24 Ch[ester] Sq
Tuesday [August 31, 1847]

My dear Claire—

I was in hopes we should after all have seen you yesterday— Hunt was here & it would have been pleasant— As it is we do not go till tomorrow— for Percy has just on a sudden been asked to go & help keep Emily Aldridge's birthday today—& could not well say nay—& I was glad to have a day of rest for my Monday's drive did not agree with me the streets are so rough—& I have suffered tortures— But Doctor Smith has settled that now it is entirely neuralgia—as the growth I mentioned has quite disappeared—& there is nothing the matter with me any where except this vile pain—and Brighton evidently irritated my nerves most fearfully I am better today & hope the attack is gone off— I suppose there is no chance of seeing you today but if you do come I shall be very glad I have done nothing but suffer pain since I came to town— I hope you got the cheque safe I left at your house on Tuesday. Adieu my dear Claire—I hope your Sunday's visit amused you pray write to me at Elcott if you do not come this ev[enin]g & believe me

Affly yours
M Shelley

[P.S.] Foster says Jenny Lind *is* coming back!![1]

ADDRESS: Miss Clairmont/ 26 Osnaburgh St./ Regents Park. POSTMARK: 1 An 1/ AU 31/ 1847/ E. ORIGINAL: Huntington Library (HM 12360); A.L.S., 4 pp. 8vo, with stamped envelope. UNPRINTED and UNPUBLISHED. TEXT: From original letter.

671. *To Leigh Hunt**

13 Bedford Sq
Brighton
Thursday [? September 2, 1847]

Dear Hunt

You are very kind indeed—I believe, as you say, the Life was never so injuriously written but for the sake of extorting money, he tried to frighten me—& a man who could commit that sort of low crime is capable of any thing. Tho' not so injurious—I am sure the book will be a disgrace to dear Shelley's name & an annoyance to all connected with him—& that it should be passed over in silence is the most honorable way in which the press can act.

For the rest, dear Hunt, I leave it to you— I agree with you that pushing the matter is only to awaken attention. For myself the man's letter & the advertisement disturbed me greatly & nervous as I am made me ill—but having

[1] Jenny Lind (1820–1887), the famous Swedish singer, created a sensation in England during the summer and autumn of 1847. Her first appearance was on May 4. Bishop Edward Stanley of Norwich persuaded her that she ought to give up acting and opera; but this she did not do until after performing during the 1848 season and giving five farewell performances in May, 1849, the last being on May 10. Her later years were devoted to concert and oratorio singing.

got over that I shall dismiss the whole affair from my mind & shall only be too grateful if it is not dragged before my eyes by articles in the newspapers. I will not read a line— I will not look at the book if I can help it. I hope Mr. Newby will not send it to me—for I dislike doing a rudeness but I should send it back directly— The attempt to extort money *outlaws* the Author in my eyes—but I *do hope* the book will not be sent me. I should counsel you not to read it—I am quite sure that it is a vulgar disgusting production. He said that it is slashing—& will make a hubbub— O the delight & joy of *Silence*. If only I could command that with regard to it— It is all I ask.—I leave it all to you —but would not give the book the importance of your taking too much trouble or notice.

I hope Marianne is fast recovering, & that I shall soon hear of your changing the air which is the best remedy for all illness—especially to convalescents.

Ever truly ys

M Shelley

ORIGINAL: British Museum (Add. MSS 38,524, ff.102–104); A.L.S., 6 pp. 8vo. UNPRINTED and UNPUBLISHED. TEXT: From original letter.

672. To [*Addressee Unknown*]

Dec. 4 [1847]

I am gratified by the terms in which you speak of my Husband. In what I have already published I have said all that I think should be said while those live who are nearly related to him. The custom of publishing biographies totally careless of the feelings wounded or privacies invaded is I think, most censurable . . . [Mary goes on to say that she has not seen Medwin's *Life of Shelley* and does not expect to do so.]

ORIGINAL: Owen D. Young, New York, in 1937; A.L.S., 3 pp. 8vo. UNPRINTED and UNPUBLISHED. TEXT: A quotation sent me by Mr. Owen D. Young (from his catalogue slip).

672 A. *To Mr. Blewitt*

Elcott House,
Hungerford,
4 Dec. [1847]

Dear Mr. Blewitt

I enclose you a note such as you suggested from Mr. Bethune—I most earnestly hope it will be of service. I have not yet received the paper back from Mrs. Booth. If by any chance she should send it to you, would you want Sir Percy's signature? He is with me here, so pray forward it to me. With thanks for the kind trouble you take.

Yrs. truly

M. Shelley

ORIGINAL: Sold by City Book Auction, New York, in October, 1942; A.L.S., 1 p. 8vo, with black border. UNPRINTED and UNPUBLISHED. TEXT: From copy made from the original letter by Dr. Herman T. Radin.

672 B. *To* [? *Mr. Blewitt*]

24 Chester Sq.
13 Dec. [? 1847]

My dear Sir:

Many thanks for your communication which gave me great pleasure— I am truly obliged to you for the trouble you have so kindly taken.

Sir Percy desires his compliments. I am

Yrs truly
Mary Shelley

ORIGINAL: Sold by City Book Auction, New York, in October, 1942: A.L.S., 1 p. 8vo, with black border. UNPRINTED and UNPUBLISHED. TEXT: From copy made from the original letter by Dr. Herman T. Radin.

673. *To* [*Addressee Unknown*]

Dec. 23 [? 1847]

I have mentioned to Mr. Hookham that I do not object to his shewing you any of my Husband's works that he possesses . . .

ORIGINAL: Owen D. Young, New York, in 1937; A.L.S., 1 p. 8vo. UNPRINTED and UNPUBLISHED. TEXT: A quotation sent me by Mr. Owen D. Young (from the catalogue slip).

674. To *Claire Clairmont*

Sunday [December 26, 1847]

My dear Claire

You will be sorry to hear that I have lost my dear kind friend[1] She was ill just a week & suffered dreadfully at first but her last moments were as easy as such a fearful struggle as death is in one so strong, even unto the last —could be

The disease was obstruction—but of what nature the medical men are totally ignorant—they acted in the dark

She shed a charm over my life by the lively & affectionate interest she took in all that belonged to me that I shall miss at every hour, in every act. How many poor will mourn her loss—how bereft her poor son will feel—

Ys Affectionately
M S

ADDRESS: Miss Clairmont/ 26 Osnaburg Street/ Regent's Park. POSTMARKS: (1) 10 FN 10/ DE 27/ 1847/ A (2) 12 NN 12/ DE 27/ 1847/ C. ORIGINAL: Huntington Library (HM 12162); A.L.S., 4 pp. 16mo (3½ x 5⅜ inches), with stamped envelope. UNPRINTED and UNPUBLISHED. TEXT: From original letter.

675. *To Claire Clairmont**

24 C[hester] Sq
Thursday [February 10, 1848]

My dear Claire

I talked to Hookham today about the Opera—he says it is to open on the

[1] In Mary's letter of June 10, 1848, to Mrs. Trelawny, this friend is called Georgina.

22^d & there is to be no programme— I asked if any boxes had been taken by the libraries—he said Lumley asked such a prices [*sic*] that he had not taken any but that Mitchel & Sams had— I asked "Do you know what they give?" —he said "No"— I said "Is it fair to ask what he wanted from you?"—He said £300 & £320 for boxes on the Queen's tier—only for the *subscription* nights —as much in short as was ever given & more. Mitchel you see wants to give you considerably less than he gave Lumley— Lumley cannot give you less than he has asked from others—

I cannot get over this little attack—it keeps me very weak—I hope to see you soon—

Affly Ys

M Shelley

[P.S.] I thought it best to send you this account from Hookham—tho' perhaps not worth much

> ADDRESS: Miss Clairmont/ 26 Osnaburgh Street/ Regent's Park. POSTMARKS: (1) T.P./ Ebury (2) 10 F^n 10/ FE 11/ 1848/ E. ORIGINAL: Huntington Library (HM 12148); A.L.S., 4 pp. 8vo, with stamped envelope. Copy by Claire Clairmont, Berg Collection, the New York Public Library. UNPRINTED and UNPUBLISHED. TEXT: From original letter.

676. *To Mary [Peacock Nicolls]*

24 Ch[ester] Sq

March 15 [1848]

My dear Mary

Mr. Charles Beauclerk said that Lord Sefton had received a letter from M. de Lamartine telling him to advise every one in whom he took interest to leave Paris & withdraw their property[1]— I asked him if this were only an *on dit*— he said no—it was the fact—& I have never found him enclined to say *the thing that was not*—

It is a matter of disposition not to believe in any future warnings—we should *all* have been incredulous if forwarned of the fall of L. P.— At present it seems to me that it requires a great stock of credulity to believe that the present state of things in France can last—& the manner & measure of change may or may not be destructive to an extent that would render it very desirable to be absent— Who can tell!—the worst feature in all French changes is, that all people of any birth, station fortune or influence fly at once— No one makes fight for order; the field is quitted at once—but what can foreigners do when all natural stays & supports of the fabric of society shrink into nothing? —personally probably they may only have a[n] unendurable difficulty in getting supplies, to contend with—but *some* English houses have been entered & every thing burnt. At any rate I am glad that you are by good luck here—&

---

[1] This refers to the Revolution of February, 1848, in France.

I scarcely think your father wd. wish you in France again till we see what turn things take during the next month or two

Ever Ys.

M Shelley

ORIGINAL: Luther A. Brewer Collection, University of Iowa; A.L.S., 4 pp. 8vo (4½ x 7⅛ inches). UNPRINTED and UNPUBLISHED. TEXT: From original letter.

677. *To Charles* [*Robinson*]

Monday [March, 1848]

Dear Charles

Percy called yesterday, but did not find you. Will you dine here one day this week (but tomorrow) & you will see Mrs. St. John[1] who is a prize indeed in the lottery being the best & sweetest thing in the world— She is not however nearly as rich as Rosa was told

I have had long letters from Mr. [Alexander] Berry, which I shall answer at the end of the month[2]

Ys. truly

M Shelley

ORIGINAL: Frank J. Hogan, Washington, D. C.; A.L.S., 3 pp. (3½ x 4½ inches). UNPRINTED and UNPUBLISHED. TEXT: From original letter.

678. *To Alexander Berry*

24 Chester Sq

28 March [1848]

My dear Mr. Berry—

You are very kind to write to me. It always gives me great pleasure to hear from you. It is pleasant to know that I have a connection so far off who takes interest in my fortunes. Sometimes I have thought that the feeling of solitude with which you felt assailed after losing your dear wife might impel you to revisit this country—& I should have been delighted to give you a cordial welcome. This feeling has probably worn off by this time, & you are too great a man in Australia—& your interests & influence there are too great, to allow of your coming home—is it so? or is it possible that I may see you? Percy & I are the nearest relatives of Elizabeth[3]—indeed I believe her only ones left (for I think our Uncle Charles, who went to America, left no family) & we should be most happy to welcome you under our roof—if the epidemic of revolutions leave us one.

It is terrible to write such words half in jest—but these are awful times. The total overthrow of law, the dislocation of the social system in France presents a fearful aspect. In Italy & in Germany the people aim at political rather

---

[1] Jane, widow of Charles Robert St. John, daughter of Thomas Gibson, and to become, on June 22, 1848, the wife of Percy Florence Shelley.

[2] Because mail to Australia did not leave England until the first of April.

[3] Elizabeth Wollstonecraft, Mr. Berry's wife, who died in 1845.

than social change—but the French will spare no pains to inculcate their wicked & desolating principles—& to extend the power of their nefarious Provisional Government all over Europe. At first indeed the P. G—— was looked on with favour, as standing in the gap to prevent worse anarchy—but their measures are so tyrannical—so ruinous that they must be looked upon as the worst engines of a bad system. There is no doubt that a French propoganda is spread among all the nations—they are rousing the Irish & even exciting the English Chartists. Ireland is fortunate in having Lord Clarenden, a man of courage & wisdom—but will he be able to repress all the risings with which that country is menaced?—who can tell? One half of Ireland detests the other half—nor have the Irish any political grievance (for they have not the burthen of our taxes) except that the Catholics are forced to support the Protestant Church— With us—the Chartists are full of menace—covert & secret—but not the less to be guarded again[st]— I do believe that in England law & the orderly portion of the community will prevail. God grant it—God preserve us from the tyranny & lawlessness now oppressing France—

I write seriously—perhaps too much so—I perpetually see & hear of people ruined by this late French revolution— Many English have invested funds in the French railways & funds—& London is also crowded [with] runaway French— Suppose here also we should be runaways— We would make fight first—but if Percy & I ran to Australia would you allow us to *squat* on your land?— We would pay you a fair rent, as soon as we could raise crops & sell them

Public matters are thrusting private ones from this letter; but I must say something of what *is* with regard to us— Percy is just now a candidate for a seat in Parliament. The bribery & corruption practised in the last election for Horsham has caused the parliament to declare it void—& Percy was entreated to come forward & to try purity of election— He has a fair chance— of course I am anxious for his success— He is at present at Horsham canvassing—it will be decided next week—but I believe letters for Australia must be posted before the 1st of the month. It will cost a little money & that we can ill afford—but it is right that Percy should enter into active life—& tho' I do not expect that he will make a *brilliant* figure—I am [s]ure that his good understanding—[h]is stainless integrity & uprightness will command for him respect from all.

Our friend Charles Robinson I am sorry to say has failed in procuring employment in this country. He has relations who could have served him—but they are inconceivably selfish—& have done nothing He talks of taking Sidney in his way back to New Zealand. I shall send by him a book for you, which I published a few years ago[4]— He tells us that you smoke, & find difficulty in getting cigars to your liking— Percy intends to ask your acceptance of a few,

4 *Rambles in Germany and Italy*, 1844.

which he hopes will please you. Charles deserves a better fate— I hope he will have better success in this his second emigration

Believe me, dear Mr. Berry

Very sincerely yours—
M W Shelley

March 30th. Percy is still canvassing—he has a fair chance— We are all quiet here—but sad tidings are expected sooner or later from Ireland— It is the fashion here for Gentlemen of London to swear in as special constables— & enrol themselves under the Commander of their district but this is all done quietly & I trust there will be no active need for them. I am dear Mr. Berry,

Ys. very truly
Mary Shelley

ADDRESS: Alexander Berry Esq/ Sidney/ New South Wales. POSTMARKS: (1) PAID/ 30 MR 30/ 1848   (2) SHIP LETTER/ JY * 19/ 1848/ SYDNEY. ORIGINAL: Alexander Hay, Coolangatta, N.S.W., Australia; A.L.S., 6 pp. 4 to, with seal. PRINTED: Grylls, *Claire Clairmont* (London, Murray, 1939), 281–84. TEXT: From original letter.

679. *To Claire Clairmont**

Saturday ¼ past 5 [April 8, 1848]

My dear Claire

I was disappointed not seeing you yesterday when we made that long journey—which I should scarcely have had the courage to take if I had not hoped to find you— Mrs. St. John is still with us— She stays longer than I expected— Hellen having delayed her visit—I wish you could come here tomorrow— If possible I will get to you tomorrow—but perhaps if I do not come, you may be better & can get here   I have only *just* received yours— If I do not see you tomorrow I will get to you *early* on Monday— I shall not be at liberty till Friday   But any day you can come here I shall be delighted to see you— On Monday I hope all will be quiet—so many precautions are being taken.

How much I wish you were nearer to us.

Affcly Ys
M Shelley

ADDRESS: Miss Clairmont/ 26 Osnaburgh Street/ Regent's Park. POSTMARK: BC/ AP——8/ 1848. ENDORSED: This letter was written Sat—8–April 48— when fears were entertained that a Chartist meeting to be held on April 10th would produce [*sic*]. ORIGINAL: Huntington Library (HM 12154); A.L.S., 4 pp. 8vo (4 x 6 inches), with stamped envelope. Copy by Claire Clairmont, Berg Collection, the New York Public Library. UNPRINTED and UNPUBLISHED. TEXT: From original letter.

680. *To [Addressee Unknown]**

24 Chester Sq.
4 May [1848]

My dear Sir

It was very provoking that during your short stay I should have been so engaged or I should have hoped to see more of you— I hope you will revisit London before long and that I shall see you again in a more hospitable manner. I believe Percy and his Bride have no idea of visiting Scotland at present— if they did, I know from experience how bounteous is Scotch hospitality & I am sure they would be delighted to have an opportunity of making your acquaintance, & Percy w[oul]d be glad to see his old friend Mrs. Stuart.

With love to her

Ys very truly
Mary Shelley

ORIGINAL: National Library of Scotland (MS 582, No.632); A.L.S., 3 pp. small 8vo. UNPRINTED and UNPUBLISHED. TEXT: From copy sent me by the National Library of Scotland.

681. *To Mrs. E. J. Trelawny*

24 Chester Sq.
10 June [18]48.

My dear Augusta,

Trelawny told me when I saw him in the winter that you would be glad to see me if I visited your neighbourhood (as I did last autumn—but was then too ill to seek anybody) and therefore I think you may not be displeased to hear from me. This is a most interesting moment for me, for Percy is about to be married. He is most fortunate in his choice— She is a young widow, she married 7 years ago one of the St. Johns—she says one devoid of the defects of the family—perhaps Trelawny knew him at Florence—Charles a younger brother of Ferdinand—however he was in ill health all their married life and lived in the country in England—he died 5 years since.

She is in herself the sweetest creature I ever knew—so affectionate—so soft —so gentle with a thousand other good qualities—she looks what she is all goodness and truth. She has no taste for society and will thus participate in Percy's taste for a domestic quiet life and now as a married man he will settle at Field Place. She has a little money.

When I saw Trelawny I fancied another match might have come about which would have suited him as little as this suits him well—for he is not fitted to guide and tutor a young girl—while his present choice is but little younger than himself.

I have often heard of you from James Campbell—your present house is beautiful I hear—and I well know in what a lovely county it is placed—your children thrive and are beautiful—and all goes well with you.

You will even after so long a time have lamented dear Georgina. She was a great loss to me and her death was a cruel one—arising from accidental causes —and taking her from us, just as we were rejoicing to think that her health was restored. Her son was away at the time—he is now travelling in the east— I could write you a long gossipping letter about old acquaintance if you cared to receive it— I shall be glad if ever I am able to make a trip to Chepstow again—I liked it so much when I was there.

You know of course that James Campbell's projected marriage is quite off. I believe now that he could even see the young lady without danger—so completely is the spell broken—but he will not be exposed [to] that danger.

Remember me kindly to Trelawny and believe me to be

Affectionately Yr.
Mary Shelley

ORIGINAL: Sir John Shelley-Rolls. UNPRINTED and UNPUBLISHED. TEXT: From copy made by Sir John Shelley-Rolls.

682. *To Alexander Berry*

24 Chester Sq
30 June [1848]

Direct to me at
  Hookham's Library
    15 Old Bond Street
or to Field Place—Horsham

Dear Mr. Berry

You are very good to write me such long & really interesting letters. You live, you say, a hermit's life—but your writing has all the vivacity of youth—& shews the deep interest you take in your Country & its welfare. A Colony—where one can at once perceive the operation of the social laws—presents a wide field for enquiry & the acquisition of knowledge. At the same time there is melancholy attached to it—the melancholy spectacle of misgovernment. This is particularly mortifying in the cases of such men as Sir G. Gipps & Lord Grey—for they mean well, while they do so much mischief. We boast of our improved lights—& our books overflow with philosophical principles, yet our public men perpetually make the grossest mistakes, & all they do, had better be left undone. Lord Grey has always been called a crochetty man—a man of schemes, who will neither hear nor see reason (speak it ever so loud, look it ever so big) against his own preconceived ideas. At the present moment he has given a grievous specimen of this defect with regard to the West Indies. You will see the details in the papers, so I need not fill my paper with them. The matter will, it is beleived ruin him as a public man. The Whig ministry are likely to resign, when left in a minority on the sugar question—probably no other ministry will be formed, & after 24 hours they will return to office—but Ld Grey, it is to be supposed will be left on the way side. And who will be his successor? & what new plans will he try to work out. He will not be a Saint, it is to be hoped for Saints are most of all to be dreaded from their fatal habit of always confiding in men who talk their talk, however incapable or dishonest they may be— Our colonies are just now of the mightiest import, while strange & fearful events are in progress in Europe. Barbarism—countless uncivilized men, long concealed under the varnish of our social system, are breaking out with the force of a volcano & threatening order—law & peace. In Germany the bands of society are entirely broken—no rents are paid—the peasant invades the Chateau—& would take it—were it worth his while—as it is, he demands a dinner & it is given him. In France how unscrupulous was the flattery that turned the heads of the working classes & produced the horrible revolt just put down. With us the Chartists have lowered themselves greatly for the present—but tho' their demonstrations are at an end, their numbers are on the encrease & before many years there will be surely great great changes in England. (I have just seen the Times—the ministry have a majority about the sugar, so there will be no change yet)——But now let me turn to private matters. You say in your letter "Were you a young man of Percy's age & fortune you w^d devote yourself to scientific pursuits & the improvement of your estates, instead of embroiling yourself in politics." These words have reached us at an opportune moment— When I wrote last in March, Percy was canvassing the boro of Horsham—he was then a single man, now he is married—he has given up politics & is about to settle in the country— on his estate. He has made a most happy marriage. The lady was a widow. She was a Miss Gibson—married to the youngest son of the late Lord Bolingbroke[1] Her husband was an invalid & died after 2 years a period she spent nursing him with the tenderness of a mother— She had no family. She is very pretty—but that is her least merit. I never knew any one so good, true & affectionate. She never thinks of herself—all her thoughts are spent on those she loves—her tastes are quiet & domestic. Percy deserves so good a wife—& please God they will be long happy together & I hope to share their happiness living at Field Place with them occupied by improving the estate & being of use to the tenants She has a fortune of £15,000 which will lighten our odious mortgages—which are a sad obstacle to our plans of improvement— However living on the estate is the best way of improving one's income & serving those dependant. The present Lady Shelley has no expensive tastes—& has no love for company. They were married on the 22^d June—& are now gone to the lakes in the North of England for their wedding tour.

Charles Robinson says he will write to you by this months post; so he will explain his silence himself— He has so often intended to write, & delayed until he had some positive news to tell—& the moment has perpetually retreated before him— I hope this is over now—he is greatly esteemed & loved by all who know him, & deserves the good fortune which at last I hope he will obtain.—— You do quite well to look upon a return to England as possible—for by accustoming yourself to think about it, some day, it is to be hoped, you will come, & we shall be very glad to see you— You will find us quietly settled in our Country house. I am much obliged to you for your Sidney papers—and shall hope to hear from you soon again—perhaps new measures will soon prevail & you may have better accounts to give of your

---

[1] Charles Robert St. John.

Colony— What a pity we do not send thousands of our suffering workmen to you— I am dear Mr. Berry

Ever truly Yours

Mary Woll^ft Shelley

[P.S.] Percy's Country House is distant 40 miles from London & there is a rail road station within 3 miles of it—in my next letter when I hope to be living there I will tell you more about it.—

ADDRESS: 30th June/ 1848/ Alex^der Berry Esq/ Sydney/ New South Wales. POSTMARKS: (1) PAID/ 30 JU 30/ 1848   (2) [SHIP LET]TER/ OC * 24/ 1848/ SYDNEY. ORIGINAL: Mr. Alexander Hay, Coolangatta, N.S.W., Australia; A.L.S., 6 pp. 4to, with seal. UNPRINTED and UNPUBLISHED. TEXT: From original letter.

683. To John Gregson

24 Chester Sq.
7 July, 1848.

Dear Mr. Gregson,

I find it somewhat difficult to answer your question as I do not know where all this money is to come from—it being so far greater a sum than I contemplated.[1] Percy parted with half his Hill & Letty shares this spring—the others can be sold immediately that is £500 which can be paid next week—as soon as Percy can write, that is—and give his orders and the shares sold—another £1,000 we have in Eastern Counties—not worth that now—but the shares are rising I hope in the course of this month they will be worth £700   I should not like to sell them before August.

As for the rest you told me not to be frightened about the valuation for the farm but I was and am frightened. I will write to Percy tomorrow on the subject; who may understand this subject better than myself I suppose you may say the end of the year as the furthest date as something must be contrived by that time and [I] hope before.

Yours truly,

Mary Shelley

ORIGINAL: Sir John Shelley-Rolls. UNPRINTED and UNPUBLISHED. TEXT: From copy made by Sir John Shelley-Rolls.

684. To Claire Clairmont

Sandgate
Monday [July 24, 1848]

Dearest Claire—

I promised to tell you when the Pair w[oul]d be in town—they arrive today —to busy themselves about moving—as I am quite incapable of attending to it— I am pretty well—but the least exertion brings on a renewal of my illness which besides has left [me] so weak that I am fit for nothing but perfect

---

[1] Percy meant to live at Field Place after his marriage. It cost him £2,000 to get it back in his hands, as Mary explains to Claire on July 28.

quiet— Marianne has had a sharp attack of English Cholera & has not left her bed these 5 days— She is, I trust, convalescent now—but she has suffered a great deal & is very weak—

Knox is gone back to town— I hope to get to Field Place on Saturday— Nothing has gone as I hoped. I wished to enjoy myself with my friends during the last few weeks of my stay in town—& to have made things comfortable for Percy & Jane—now they must do all this themselves—& perfect quiet is my refuge—

Adieu— I hope you are well—

Affectionately Ys
M Shelley

ADDRESS: Miss Clairmont/ 26 Osnaburgh St./ Regent's Park. POSTMARKS: (1) SANDG[ATE]   (2) FOLKSTONE/ JY 24/ 1848   (3) [   ] L/ JY 25/ 1848. ORIGINAL: Huntington Library (HM 12150); A.L.S., 4 pp. 8vo, with stamped envelope. UNPRINTED and UNPUBLISHED. TEXT: From original letter.

685. *To Claire Clairmont*

Sandgate
Saturday [(*error for Friday*) July 28, 1848]

Dearest Claire

How grieved I am to hear of poor Charles's illness— Poor fellow—I hope your next letters will bring good tidings of his recovery.

I leave this place tomorrow for Sussex— I am glad you are going to Brighton—and shall be very glad to see you at F[ield] P[lace]. I should think the time you mention would be excellent—there was a talk of our going in August to Elcott—but that w[oul]d not be for long— I will let you know when things are settled—

I write nervously & hurri[e]dly now-a-days—but I am certainly peculiarly unlucky in my expressions—when I mean kindness & affection—& they convey another meaning. The phrase you quote certainly does not look pretty all by itself—what I meant was that you seemed angry with me when I disagreed with you in opinion— As to any one speaking against you to me—no one w[oul]d venture on that. The person to whom you allude did not mention your name during the few times I have seen her lately. Talking over one's friends to other friends is a practice I have in abhorrence, except indeed with praise & affection—

Poor G[eorge] Sand— No doubt she has lost by the Revolution—all *artistes* must[1]— And how can she expect the preaching of Equality to excite any thing but dislike of the preacher who thus arrogates superiority in Wisdom. I stumbled on the following in a work of Bulwer's published in /41—it is curious.[2] Speaking of France he says: "The vast masses of energy & life broken up by the great thaw of the imperial system floating along the tide,

[1] George Sand took an active interest in the Revolution of February, 1848.
[2] *Night and Morning,* in 3 volumes, was the only book by Bulwer published in 1841.

are terrible icebergs for the vessel of the state. Some think Napoleonism (he ought to say revolutionism) over—its effects are only begun. *Society is shattered from one end to the other, & I laugh at the little rivets by which they think to keep it together."* —The last is curious.

I heard from E[mily] D[unston] the other day—nothing new—she is going to Ireland on a visit.[3]

And now for F[ield] P[lace]— Percy takes the farm into his own hands —& God send he attends to it & will not lose. It costs us immensely to get the house & farm into our hands, more than £2000— We have not that nearly on hand & where we are to get it I dont know—but we need not pay the whole directly— I will write to you the moment I am a little settled at F.P.

Ys Affectionately

M S.

[P.S., *under the envelope flap:*] I have got quite well—a little warm winter cloathing drove away the remnants of my illness— Marianne is convalescent —she had a sharp attack

> ADDRESS: Miss Clairmont/ 26 Osnaburgh St./ Regent's Park. POSTMARKS: (1) SANDGATE (2) FOLKSTONE/ JY 28/ 1848. ORIGINAL: Huntington Library (HM 12336); A.L.S., 6 pp. 16mo, with stamped envelope containing added note on inside of flap. UNPRINTED and UNPUBLISHED. TEXT: From original letter.

686. *To Claire Clairmont*

Field Place

Monday [August 14, 1848]

My dear Claire

This is indeed weather! It completely puts an end to every occupation & amusement— It can't be helped & cant last for ever—that is all one can say for comfort

While I was at Sandgate I heard from Mrs. Sanford wondering what had become of you. Mrs. Hare writes in the depth of the Blues & hatred of this climate For myself I am delighted to be here So many mortifications attended all my attempts to form an agreable society in London—that I am quite relieved to be away— Whether I shall feel ennui hereafter I dont know— I hope not— It entirely depends on others If Percy & Jane are happy, I know I shall be so—if they were to feel bored—I should be miserable —but I have every hope that they will continue satisfied & happy. They are gone to town today to see Mrs. Hare & shop—they return home tomorrow— I confess I do not wish you to come while this vile weather lasts—but it cannot for ever & by the time you have paid your visit to Brighton it will be fine & then I am sure you will like this place— It is indeed quite a change of life for us—but we have as yet scarcely begun an apprenticeship—it is a trade to learn—& if as the difficulties attendant on & the attention required by farming

---

[3] See Letter 666, note 1.

& taking care of a place, open on Percy, he takes to it I have no doubt we shall do well & be happy—as to money matters—I am as careful as I can [be]—& for the rest will not think about them—for the prospect is gloomy—

I send you a County paper which will give you the hours for this month— When you fix to come, write me a line & the carriage shall go to the station for you. Come in fine weather & I trust you will enjoy yourself & not mind our stupid life—for such it is, there is no doubt—but thank God I am at present perfectly happy—& only pray things may continue as they are— I am not very well—but still have no great reason to complain. I sleep in the room you mention—

Knox came here yesterday for the first time—& is gone—he tells me the Campbells are going to get rid of their house if they can—at any rate they are going away Percy & Jane *do not* go to [? Marnbull]—I am glad to say.

Knox saw Jenny [Lind] in the Sonnambula[1] & is quite a convert to her— he says he never saw such acting—he cried like a child—

Adieu, my dear Claire— You will write to me from Brighton—Remember me most kindly to the Pringles— We are not yet settled enough for visitors—but by & bye I hope to see them— When you are here they can come easily by a day ticket, if they will & spend nine hours with us—by & bye we hope to be settled & more hospitable

Affly. Ys

M Shelley

ADDRESS: Miss Clairmont/ 26 Osnaburgh St./ Regent's Park/ London. POST-MARKS: (1) HORSHAM/ AU 14/ 1848/ B (2) 15 AU 15/ 1848. ORIGINAL: Huntington Library (HM 12164); A.L.S., 12 pp. 12mo (3½ x 8⅜ inches), with envelope. UNPRINTED and UNPUBLISHED. TEXT: From original letter.

687. *To Claire Clairmont*

Field Place

Wednesday [August 30, 1848]

My dear Claire

We held conclave over your letter & decided that we should be most happy to have you for a LONG visit in November but shall be much disappointed if you do not come before—both that we may see you—& that you may see Field Place before the leaves are gone— The journey is not expensive—for you to come for a few days & return to town—or if you liked it better when you go to Brighton come here on your way— Come by the 10 o'clock A.M. Brighton train & take your ticket for Horsham & then after a few days you can take a ticket from Horsham to Brighton—& this will only add 4/- to the expence of your Brighton journey. The workmen are hammering in your room now— but it will soon be ready Let us know when you fix that we may send the carriage to the station for you

---

[1] One of her greatest rôles was in Bellini's *La Sonnambula*.

Jeff [Hogg] is inimitable

Affectionately Ys
M Shelley

ADDRESS: Miss Clairmont/ 26 Osnaburgh Street/ Regent's Park. POSTMARK: HORSHAM/ AU [30]/ 1848/ B. ORIGINAL: Huntington Library (HM 12165); A.L.S., 4 pp. 16mo (3½ x 5⅜ inches), with stamped envelope. Copy by Claire Clairmont, Berg Collection, the New York Public Library. UNPRINTED and UNPUBLISHED. TEXT: From original letter.

688. *To Claire Clairmont*

Pier Hotel, Brighton
Thursday [October 19, 1848]

Dearest Claire

We were all so sorry you did not accompany my Children to F. P. I hope you were detained for *good* & got your money. Jane says you talk of coming here while we are here & then coming to F. P. later—this will be a good plan— I do not know when or how we shall fix ourselves—but with the Pringles, Sanfords & ourselves you will have a little society—& go to F. P. when it is frost bitten & healthy—

No further news in this mornings Times from Vienna— I am very anxious for Charles—

I am troubled with a most odious malady   attacks of dizziness in the head which leave me so very low. Calomel is it is true a divine medecine—   But I am Semele to Jove—it would soon send me to the other world—like poor Lady Canterbury—

I hope you will come here soon—and let me hear from you what your plans are—

Ever Affcly. Ys
M Shelley

ADDRESS: Miss Clairmont/ 56 St. John's Wood Terrace/ St. John's Wood/ London. POSTMARKS: (1) BRIGHTON/ OC 19/ 1848/ E   (2) 8 NT 8/ OC 19/ 1848/ L   (3) RH/ 19 OC 19/ 1848. ORIGINAL: Huntington Library (HM 12152); A.L.S., 3 pp. 8vo, with stamped envelope and seal. UNPRINTED and UNPUBLISHED. TEXT: From original letter.

689. *To Claire Clairmont**

[Brighton] Thursday [November 23, 1848]

My dear Claire

I suppose it was the excitement of seeing Percy, but I had a violent nervous attack yeste[rday] ev[enin]g   more violent than I have had yet—   I have written to Dr. Smith about it—   I was so very well on Tuesday and yesterday m[ornin]g   Percy is very well—but they will not return here just yet—   I do not know what I shall do—perhaps Brighton air is too much for me—   Perhaps I shall see you today   I hope you are well

Ys Affly
M S

ADDRESS: Miss Clairmont/ 11 Waterloo Street/ Brighton. POSTMARK:
BRIGHTON/ NO 23/ 1848. ORIGINAL: Huntington Library (HM 12139);
A.L.S., 2 pp. 8vo, with stamped envelope. Copy by Claire Clairmont, Berg Col-
lection, the New York Public Library. UNPRINTED and UNPUBLISHED. TEXT:
From original letter.

690. *To Claire Clairmont*

[Brighton] Friday [November 24, 1848]

Dear Claire

I am better today—no pains or aches—only the feeling as if the spine were all alive up to my head—which makes me feel *very* weak still.

I hope you did not think me unkind yesterday— You were so good—but I was in a state that the smallest effort of mind or body overcame me. I shall stay quite quiet today—& hope to be better tomorrow.

I have sent for some flannel drawers!!—but I have no pains—only this overwhelming run of weakness the whole length of the spine

Being so ill I could attend to nothing I have settled to stay in this house till Monday—so I shall hope you will dine here either tomorrow or the next day.

God bless you

My children will return to F. P. I suppose in a fortnight— When they are settled there why should you not go to them?—I shall go to London for a short time then (thus I plan—if plans can be made)—& then, especially if it be frosty I shall be so eager to return home—if my health permits—as please God, it will

Ever Affly Ys
M S.

ADDRESS: Miss Clairmont/ 11 Waterloo Street/ Brighton. POSTMARK:
[BRI]GHTON/ NO 24/ 1848. ORIGINAL: Huntington Library (HM 12159);
A.L.S., 4 pp. 8vo, with stamped envelope. UNPRINTED and UNPUBLISHED.
TEXT: From original letter.

691. *To Claire Clairmont*

77 Warwick Sq
30 Nov. [1848]

My dear Claire

Percy told you I was quite well— I am glad when he thinks so as it spares him anxiety—which I should certainly have spared you had I thought you w[oul]d have been frightened at the account of my last illness—but though all disease is, Thank God, cured (Dr. Smith has assured himself of that) it has left deep *wrinkles* in my constitution—which the same doctor hopes to eradicate—tho' I did give them extra depth by the use of Calomel— He says it is all debility—having produced a slight inflammation of the mucous mem-brane—& besides a great inclination on my part to neuralgic rhumatism—all things by no means dangerous—but certainly distressing— However I am better—not so all over pain in my nerves—& I am trying Cod's liver oil—&

hope for the best results— I must keep very quiet & not go out till a little stronger— I found my Janey[1] much better I hope she will soon be well— In a little time I hope to tell you more about ourselves

I hope you are well & so love the Pringles for the comfort they are to you. I will write soon again—now I send the P.O. order—remember it comes *from Percy*—& is *for* Miss Claire Clairmont Adieu

Affly Ys

M Shelley

[P.S.] Charles Buller's[2] death is a great loss to his party

ADDRESS: Miss Clairmont/ 11 Waterloo Street/ Brighton. POSTMARKS: (1) DE——1/ 18[4]8 (2) BRIGHTON/ DE 2/ 1848. ORIGINAL: Huntington Library (HM 12349); A.L.S., 4 pp. 8vo, with stamped envelope. UNPRINTED and UNPUBLISHED. TEXT: From original letter.

692. *To Claire Clairmont*

77 W[arwick] Sq. Sunday [December 10, 1848]

My dear Claire

At length I can give you news of your box—the Carrier took it away from Chester Sq yesterday—& in due course it must have arrived at F[ield] P[lace] this morning—the delay has been the fault of the Carrier not ours

I am grieved to receive a letter from you in such bad spirits—I am afraid any thing I can write will not tend to raise them— Our dear Jane continues to suffer from her throat— I trust that at last it is better but she has not been allowed to leave her room— It seems that every winter she has had bad attacks in the chest—it is better in the throat—the tonsils are still much swollen but less sore— For myself I am much the same—stronger as to dizziness &c— & the nerves calmer— I have been ordered perfect quiet—& Dr. S[mith] says it agrees with me— I had a little drive today—but the carriage was rough & it brought on pain—but not much—however my back is weak & sensitive—& I am very good for nothing—tho' much better than at Brighton— I am to go on encreasing my dose of C[od] L[iver] O[il] & it is to cure me at last please God— I hope it may—fine weather w[oul]d be the best cure & we have had two days very fine (how the sea must sparkle) after several very stormy

I have absolutely no news— Charles & Nita B. called one day & these are the *only* persons I have seen since my arrival— Percy takes lessons in turning in the morning & spends the Evenings with his wife— Knox has his usual work & they both see nobody—neither King Cole—nor H. H.—nor have I written to any one to say I am here—the idea of visitors frightens me— I only thirst for quiet—& having it drink it in, & like it. I am not yet well enough

[1] Lady Jane Shelley, Percy's wife.
[2] Buller (1806–48), a liberal politician.

to want amusement— I only wish Janey were well it is dispiriting that she should be ill as well as myself—but I trust her attack is on the turn—

The Shelleys' asked us to Elcott for Xmas; but we cannot go—I fear your plans are deranged by our goings on—but I will not apologize—we are too bitterly the sufferers by the sad necessity that keeps us away from home—

I know of no public news but what you see in the papers— The servants at F[ield] P[lace] shall be told that you will go over there soon to your box— If you liked to take a friend & sleep there they could manage I dare say to make you comfortable

Percy & Jane send their love

Affectionately Ys

M Shelley

ADDRESS: Miss Clairmont/ 11 Waterloo Street/ Brighton. POSTMARK: DE 11/ 1848. ORIGINAL: Huntington Library (HM 12340); A.L.S., 8 pp. 8vo, with stamped envelope. Copy by Claire Clairmont, Berg Collection, the New York Public Library. UNPRINTED and UNPUBLISHED. TEXT: From original letter.

693. *To Claire Clairmont**

[London] Friday Ja⁷ [1849]¹

My dear Claire

The people at F. P. shall be written to today as you desire— It is indeed a misfortune that we cannot be there such a misfortune that I dare not think of it. I am going on exceedingly well—tho' as you say this weather is not good for me (nor indeed the situation of the house—so good as it might be—the house itself has been built 4 years & is airy & dry) & worse than the weather is the great anxiety I suffer—but I am forced to banish that as much as possible from my thoughts or I should be laid up in half an hour— I am really getting on wonderfully on my medecine—tho' I do not get out—*faute* of getting a machine to suit me—if I had only a Brighton Chair they are hung on C. springs & easy—the others & [? bumping] &c—all bring on pain through the ceaseless jog of eliptic springs.

Much of my anxiety arises from dear Jane If she is not better tomorrow we shall call additional advice—her malady is so obstinate— The other day there was a change that gave me hopes—but she is worse & feels ill now which she did not before—as then she felt in great pain at times but otherwise well She does not leave her room, scarcely her bed My poor Percy when not out for exercise, is always with her. I will write immediately when she gets a little better. I grieve deeply for your disappointment about F. P. only the cause of it, dear Jane's illness—is so much more grievous

I am anxious also very about poor K—— after vows & letters that were more than vows—a giving of her heart & faith with such tenderness & passion that one could not believe that a girl could retract—after advising him about taking this house & plunging him into an ocean of expence Mary coolly writes

¹ In the MS, *Friday* appears at the top, *Friday Jay* at the end.

to say that her mother was so unhappy she must give up her engagement—as if Mrs. W's dislike for & avowed unhappiness at the match were a new thing— Mary ought to have been guided by that a year ago if ever—& her mother's un-ladylike & brutal way of treating her lover ought to have raised her indignation —but she coolly dismisses him— On the first burst K—— was off to Kingstown to resolve to see her & I thought that she would herself have only wished to be urged—but she has written to me since & I see she is so weak as to be utterly faithless— I dread the effect on our friend—& his misery will be most painful to witness— It is not more than a fortnight that he got a line from her speaking with certainty of their marriage and [?   ] as undoubtedly to happen It is weakness—& an incapacity to resist the influence immediately at work over her—

I hope Mrs. Pringles arm is better— You too I hope are not suffering The weather is changed to cloudy & in a week or 10 days I hope for frost— O if our Janey were only getting well

God bless you

Affl Yours

M S.

ADDRESS: Miss Clairmont/ 11 Waterloo Street/ Brighton. ORIGINAL: British Museum (T. J. Wise Collection); A.L.S., 10 pp. 8vo, with envelope. UNPRINTED and UNPUBLISHED. TEXT: From original letter.

694. *To Claire Clairmont*

[Field Place] Sunday [February 11, 1849]

My dear Claire

I write seldom & shabby letters—for writing is the one thing, that makes me uncomfortable. I am much better—especially on such a fine frosty day as this— I am very glad to hear from you—and very anxious to hear all is well with your [opera] box.— Have you not written to Mrs. Sanford as you said you would? She must know all about the opera. I wrote to her about a cook a little while ago—the Methuens had been staying with them but are gone. There is a story about that the Bishop of Norwich (Stanley) had been persuading Jenny Lind that it was sinful to sing on the stage—& that she was only to sing at concerts By the accounts Percy gave of Mitchell it was evident he would not make up his mind at present to a large sum—he said he must wait till something was decided about the opera—& Knox saw Hookham the other day—who said that nothing was yet decided How fearfully things have worked against you my dearest Claire but it will all get right again with regard to the opera—for C. G. is quite done up—

I differ so entirely with you about Willy's[1] going to California that I scarcely know what to say— You say that there is plenty of gold, so no need of law— but there is (as we are told) a deficiency of food— All is scramble—a

1 Charles Clairmont's son.

scramble for actual food & life—with Americans—savage lawless—brutal—& without check—how could gentle Willy fight with them? I may be mistaken but such is the picture represented in the papers—& it seems likely— A general rush to a wild country—*all* picking gold—how to get food is the difficulty —vessels have been sent with cargos but all the sailors desert—troops have been sent—soldiers officers—general all desert & pick gold—it seems to me for a gentle youth of 16 to go out among them would be like a butterfly in a wasps nest. We see no one—nor does Knox except the people concerned with the Times—& this is the view they all take—perhaps we are all wrong—but as yet I have not heard a word in favour of California for individuals— As to a Company—we burnt our fingers in Railways & I am now convinced of what I thought before that only men of business can make money (except by the rarest chance)— A company by & bye may do something—but now it is a mere scramble.

I am very glad to hear Willy is better— Why not come here? At present our house is vacant— Knox is here now—he goes tomorrow & will not be back for a fortnight The weather is fine— Do come—you might run up to town for a day or so (to the Sanfords) & leave Willy with us You had much better come— Write & say that you will.

I actually know nothing of Coulson We led a shut up life in town—all the time I was there I had a succession of attacks that quite confined me—& dear Janey being ill Percy never went out— I asked Knox if he had seen Coulson lately—he said—no— In fact as at present he is not going on with the law he does not like seeing him—

We know nothing of H. H[unt].—I have not written to Mrs. H[unt] since I came back.

Adieu dear Cl[aire]   this is a great effort—let me hear from you

Ys. Affly

M S

ADDRESS: Miss Clairmont/ Post Office/ Town Malling/ Maidstone/ Kent. POSTMARKS: (1) HORSHAM/ FE [ ]/ 18 [ ]   (2) MAIDSTONE/ FE 12/ 18[4]9   (3) 12 FE 12/ 1849. ORIGINAL: Huntington Library (HM 12137); A.L.S., 10 pp. 8vo, with stamped envelope. Copy by Claire Clairmont, Berg Collection, the New York Public Library. UNPRINTED and UNPUBLISHED. TEXT: From original letter.

695. *To Mr. Touchet*

Field Place,
Friday [? March 16, 1849]

Dear Mr. Touchet,

I came back on Wednesday for a day or two. Dr. Prout saw Jane and pronounced that there was a slight improvement but he says it is very serious —he says she is like one on the verge of a precipice—the slightest touch would throw her over—but if that touch does not occur—she may turn and walk back in all safety— It makes me so anxious, that often I cannot command the great distress of mind I feel— She is so perfect, and so very dear to my child and to myself. But no more of this—I trust in God she will be quite well soon. They have taken very nice lodgings at 25 Upper Seymour Street, Portman Square.

Poor Bennet is dead, he died yesterday afternoon. He wished to see me, but when I saw him he could say nothing—he was too weak, he said, he would another time— He was sensible to the last—but he struggled with death—for it is hard even for disease to drive life out [of] one so young.—His poor wife behaved with great fortitude and the neighbours were very kind to her. Bostock saw him twice every day.

Thanks for the address. I wish you were returning to town as your visits would be a great comfort to us. Percy does not fear for her, happily—and is thus spared many of what will I hope prove useless pangs, which sad experience of past sorrows force upon me. I intend going back to them on Tuesday Morning.

Yours truly,

M. Shelley

ORIGINAL: Sir John Shelley-Rolls. UNPRINTED and UNPUBLISHED. TEXT: From copy made by Sir John Shelley-Rolls.

696. *To Claire Clairmont*

F[ield] P[lace]

Monday [March 19, 1849]

Dear Claire

I was grieved to hear from Percy that [you] had been obliged to take so much less for your box— It is too bad just now that you are making so generous a use of your money—

You will be glad to hear that Prout pronounces Jane to be very much better —it will be long ere she is well—but Thank God we are relieved from our cruel fears.

I cant say much for myself—the Neuralgic pains in my limbs are gone— but I suffer in my head & in other ways at times in a manner that makes all things a burthen—& brings on a trembling alarm which they call nervous— fortunately I have days of [? interval] when I am well—otherwise I am sure I should soon become idiotic—I am any thing but well just now— I am going up [to] town to see my Children & as every change seems to do me temporary benefit, I hope the journey will rid me of the present attack—

It will be long before Jane returns to F. P. without them the place I fear would be too dull—still I do hope that you & Willy will come here yet I can hardly hope it while they are away & I am often but half alive

Let me hear from you I write this letter with difficulty but would not remain silent longer love to Willy

Ys. Affly

M Shelley

ADDRESS: Miss Clairmont/ West Malling/ n[ea]r Maidstone/ Kent. POSTMARK:
O H/ 20 MR 20/ 1849. ORIGINAL: Huntington Library (HM 12160); A.L.S.,
4 pp. 8vo, with stamped envelope and seal. UNPRINTED and UNPUBLISHED.
TEXT: From original letter.

697. *To Claire Clairmont*

F[ield] P[lace] Sunday [April 15, 1849]

My dear Claire

I am very glad that you had this pleasure & that a lump of sugar tumbled into your cup. I hope the relish of the sweetness still continues—& that another lump will come soon. I am obliged to you for your prompt and kind answer to my last—but Man proposes & God disposes—the aspect of things is changed since I wrote— I will tell you how they are—& you will see what you think best— When I wrote I believed that my children would be away for another month—or if they came would speedily leave me again— They returned—& it appears likely that they will not go again for a couple of months—although till Jane is quite well we can be sure of nothing— She is much better, thank God—though this weather is much against her—& she feels herself all the better for being in the Country— Had I been as I expected—alone—I should take care, after the frequent observations you have lately made, that my one or two intimates (I have no more I think) should not come here during your visit— I cannot promise this while Jane & Percy are here—for of course they do as they like—& I cannot interfere with their plans & pleasures.

There is an obstacle at this moment to your coming with Willy. There is a lad[1]—a near relation of Jane's first husband—of whom she is guardian—he made choice of the sea as his profession & went to Sidney last year & returned only a few weeks ago—soon he is going on another long voyage—but for about a fortnight he will be here— He is not attractive & would not be in yours & Clairys[2] way for the few days he might stay after you came—but I do not think that he would be an eligible companion for Willy.

There would be nothing to prevent your staying as you express it "a month & a day"—but that the Shelley's talk of being in town in May & of paying us a visit—& you know how little room we have—they w[oul]d not stay more than two nights—& I dare say will not be here till June—at any rate not till quite the end of May—so that I hope they would not interfere with you— but it is settled that they are to come—however we need not look forward so long— If you & Clairy would come on the 1st May it would be very nice; & I sincerely hope that we should have the room free for you for 4 weeks— Indeed nothing but "les tantes"—would prevent it—& as I said they will probably not come till June for they only talk of going to town in the middle of May—& they will amuse themselves there for at least a fortnight & not come to us till afterwards— I would take care of that.

1 Named Roberts.
2 Another of Charles Clairmont's children.

Now as to your rooms—you talked of a servant sleeping in your room   I think it will be best to put up a little bed for Clairy (unless she sleeps with you) in your room & she can have the little room adjoining for her dressing room. That will [be] much pleasanter than a servant.

Let me know how all this suits you & whether you will come on the first of May. Willy can come over some Saturday till Monday & join us.

Jane is much better but suffering a little now I fancy with the weather   I have been better lately. By Dr. Smith's orders I have not touched potatoes for more than a year—   Percy & Jane send their love & hope to see you here— My love to Willy

Affly. Yours
M Shelley

[P.S.] Writing is so bad for me that I only scrawl with some difficulty

ADDRESS: Miss Clairmont/ West Malling/ n[ea]r Maidstone/ Kent. POSTMARKS: (1) O E/ 16 AP 16/ 1849   (2) MAIDSTONE/ AP [ ]. ORIGINAL: Huntington Library (HM 12350); A.L.S., 8 pp. 8vo, with envelope and seal. UNPRINTED and UNPUBLISHED. TEXT: From original letter.

698. *To Claire Clairmont*

F[ield] P[lace] Thursday [April 26, 1849]

My dear Claire

By this time Cleary I hope is with you—& her journey safely over. Pray come with her as soon as you like—just writing the day before—that your room may be ready. You say—"perhaps you will let her come without me," & Willy with her that he may not be left alone—   Certainly if you like—arrange it just as you like—& as you & she will sleep together after your visit to town come here & join them—after or before, just as you like.

Young Roberts is still here—but he can do Willy no harm—he is unrefined & has no general notions nor much education—so not enticing. We are trying to find a Naval Academy where he may board for a month or two till he goes to sea again—for he is only idle here & ought to be learning his profession— But it is difficult to get a *boarding* Academy of the sort. Did you ever hear of one?

Make it all convenient to yourself—only the sooner you come the better, as we are now quite free.

I was astonished yesterday to see in the Times (I send it) the advertisement that Jenny Lind, after all, is to come out in the Lucia—   This changeableness on her part is too bad[1]—& is the cause of great injury to every body—to you above all—   But it will make Lumley flush, & able to pay you.

I wish there were furniture &c for you in Chester Sq. Knox is still in his house & James Campbell with him—they remain there till the beginning of

[1] See Letter 670, note 1.

June when Campbell goes into his house—& Knox's furniture will for the most part be moved there

Give my love to Clairy & Willy—this dreadful weather must be bad for him as to every body— Every day one says, *it must change*—& every day continues the same—yet May is coming so one hopes.

If you could come or they come *next Monday* so much the better—The Shelleys say they will come in May to spend *two days* with us—I hope not till the end of May—but if before we can manage something just for that time—it is so provoking that one can never arrange things exactly as one likes. But some time in the summer I shall be left quite alone here and then I hope to have you all in more freedom & quiet

I should certainly think that Willy were better South in the winter—but remember this endless winter or rather this wintry spring is unusual even in this climate—

Adieu dear Claire I may expect you on Monday I hope— You ought to let me know the train you will come by that we may send the carriage for you— Could you join the train from London to Brighton, at Reigate, that leaves London at 10 A.M. or at 4 P.M. those are the best trains

Affcly Ys
M Shelley

[P.S.] I look at your letter—you seem much to want to go to London & to leave Willy & Cleary with us. Pray then send them here *at once*—we shall be very glad to see them—and I will take all possible care of them

ADDRESS: Miss Clairmont/ West Malling/ n[ea]r Maidstone/ Kent. POSTMARKS: (1) HORSHAM/ AP 26/ 1849 (2) MAIDS[TONE] AP [ ]/ 18[4]9. ORIGINAL: Huntington Library (HM 12166); A.L.S., 8 pp. 8vo, with stamped envelope and seal. Copy by Claire Clairmont, Berg Collection, the New York Public Library. UNPRINTED and UNPUBLISHED. TEXT: From original letter.

699. *To Thomas Love Peacock**

Field Place,
6 Sep. [1849]

My dear Friend,

I do not by any means yield to your arguments— Long habit makes slight things difficult—you might spend a few days with us, at least, while this lovely weather continues; escape the atmosphere of Cholera, and leave your workmen to proceed a little way with your roof, without any harm resulting from your not touching the trowel— Think over all this—the weather here is really delightful.

I know Southend—and it merits much of what you say—what I liked best was the perpetual passing of crafts, large and small, at all times—in storm and calm—evening and morning—night and day—when at moonlight or twilight, they looked like spectres—shadowy—and twice their real size. One thing I disliked much—at ebb of tide, a large extent of mud was left—and at that

The Grave of Mary W. Shelley, St. Peter's Churchyard, Bournemouth.

*In the same tomb are buried William Godwin, Mary Wollstonecraft
Godwin, Sir Percy Florence Shelley, Lady Jane
Shelley, and Shelley's heart*

time I began to think of the heavy air of Essex.—There was something in it
that put me to sleep and drew all life out of me, my sensations told me in-
fallibly when the flowing tide covered the mud, for then I came to life again—
the walks are pretty—but once I went some miles by the side of the river sea-
wards—hoping to make discoveries, and to find an inland way home—there
was nothing but desolation, and we got entangled in the ditches and canals—
and were lucky in getting back to the beach, and so home by light of the
setting moon.

Pray tell me the address of Mrs. John Williams as she must be answered—
I wish I could pay her back the sum absolutely raised and lent— I will some
day if I can— You wd. be very good if you wrote as executor to say how
diminished and burthened Percy's inheritance came and how impossible to
pay P[ost] O[bit] bonds[1]— Now we are (through Jane's illness and its expences) most sadly hampered and can do nothing—nor promise—as in these
days of cheap corn one scarcely knows what one's income is—but if any wind-
fall happens I will remember her (i. e. Percy will) and do what he can—(let
me have her address).

Many things render our going abroad particularly inconvenient—and I do
not yet see our way—yet it must be— Jane had an attack—brought on by a
cold the other day, which frightened us, and Doctor Prout strongly urged her
being saved a Northern winter—a winter at F[ield] P[lace] would not do—
it is charming in weather like this summer—but the damp is absolutely fabu-
lous in rainy weather—and the cold moist and penetrating. I have but one
thought to get her well—for she is the sweetest wife to Percy and the most
loving daughter to me; a woman such as poets love to paint.

If it be possible, if you continue to abide dully by your notion of not being
able to get here (I wish on the spurt of the moment you would walk over
London Bridge some day at 5 min. to 5 P.M. you would be here at 20 mins.
past 6) I shall call at the India House before I go.

Ever Yours,

Mary Shelley

ORIGINAL: Sir John Shelley-Rolls. UNPRINTED and UNPUBLISHED. TEXT: From
copy made by Sir John Shelley-Rolls.

700. *To Mrs. E. J. Trelawny*

Field Place, Horsham.

24 Sep [18]49.

My dear Mrs. Trelawny,

You must think me very rude to have remained so long without writing—
I would not fill my letter now with excuses but that my excuse lies in the history of this year. As soon as I came here last year I fell into a bad state of health,

---

1 The post-obit bond referred to is probably that about which Hugh Owen wrote to Peacock
on December 12, 1844 (Ingpen, *Shelley in England,* 635). If so, it was for £200. See also Shelley's
letters to John Williams, Julian edition, IX, 50, 54.

which in particular attacked my nerves and rendered me absolutely good for nothing and above all disabled me from writing. I have been getting gradually better since the spring and am now in better health than I have been for years —though still damp weather affects me disagreably. But a greater misfortune than my own ill health, has been the serious illness of my Percy's dear wife. She was in apparent health—tho' the doctors now think there must have been a slight affection of long standing—a bath in a cold taken during the first month of her marriage brought on symptoms which for a long time were mistaken by the doctors—but which at last was seen to be an acute affection of the kidneys. I shudder to think of the danger she was in last winter, while being treated in an absolutely wrong manner— Since then she has been getting better—but a winter in a warm climate is considered as absolutely necessary to her— Thus when I thought I was fixed in a home, I am to become a wanderer again— But her health is our first consideration—for indeed she is to us as the dearest portion of ourselves. Warmly affectionate, sweet tempered—true and kind these sterling qualities are adorned by a vivacity and a winning softness that renders her the most perfect woman it was ever my fortune to meet. Percy is most fortunate—and ill to happen to her, would be a misfortune from which we should never recover. God grant our cares, our hopes be crowned with success. It is particularly inconvenient to us to go abroad just now—but everything fades into nothingness before the object we have in view.

This is a particularly damp place—the first day of rain, a fortnight ago, quickened our movements; and ten days ago Percy took his wife to Paris— I shall follow some day this week, towards the end. We shall then proceed to the South of France—and then to Spain or Sicily—Italy is not warm enough to do the benefit required.

You asked me some questions in your last which it would be difficult to answer in a letter—you asked whether poor dear Mrs. Paul's reconciliation to her husband succeeded—yes—and no— She was happier than in her cottage—she entered warmly into his religious views—and the helping and instructing the poor at once satisfied an instinct of her kind heart, and was in accordance with the governing mania of the Beauclerks—yet she was not happy in her husband—nor was this all his or her fault— He has now married again—I fancy for money— I have not seen her, but have heard nothing agreable about her—she is (I am told) plain and in bad health—not a lady by birth and without the ease and agreable manners of one. I have not seen much of our neighbours— Mrs. Aldridge goes as usual, Aubrey's health is very bad, and he gives himself up to despondancy and self neglect. Charlotte has grown up a fine girl but not so pretty now as she was a few years ago. Miney is pretty and has much of the arch sweet look she had as a child—both she and Augusta are pleasing—and Rosa says they are perfect tempers sensible and good. Little Aubrey is not robust—he is at a tutor's in Leicestershire.

We live very quietly. Jane dislikes society—tho' she likes to have friends about her, and Percy has the same tastes— We have our garden and our farm —our dogs, our birds, our doves. We want indeed a rising family—if my darling Jane gets well and gives us that—but alas! we must not dream—if she be preserved to us, we shall be content.

I should be very glad to hear from you—when we are settled in our winter quarters—especially if we prosper, you shall hear from me. I envy you your beautiful Monmouthshire— I wish I could transplant Field Place to the Vale of Usk.

Remember me to Trelawny,

Believe me, Ever Yours,
Mary Shelley

ORIGINAL: Sir John Shelley-Rolls. UNPRINTED and UNPUBLISHED. TEXT: From original letter.

701. *To Mrs. E. J. Trelawny*

Maison Serrat, Nice,
24 Febry. 1850

My dear Mrs. Trelawny,

I received your letter just as I was leaving England, and it gave me great pleasure—being a sincere proof that it gives you pleasure to hear from me— and that you have not forgotten me. I had always, so to speak, a natural inclination for you—and though I appreciated the motives that made Trelawny and yourself keep me at a distance, I was not reconciled to the fact— To hear that all is well with you is a happiness which I hope you will frequently let me have.

I should have written to you before but I have suffered so much anxiety and ill health all the winter, that I for ever deferred writing until a better day. The winter every where has been severe; and from all I hear was worse at Rome and Naples than here—the peculiarity of the Nicard climate is the absence of rain and the extreme dryness of the atmosphere which renders it exciting—I felt this very painfully when I first came; but the effect has worn off—and I am getting my health and strength again— The Spring has come on us like a sudden leap to summer, so bright and warm. We had not settled whither to go when we left England and were most inclined to the south of Spain—but travelling made Jane suffer so very much, that we were soon forced to select the nearest spot that promised a mild winter—this place is as far south as Tuscany—and though I should not recommend it to a consumptive person, it has suited us.—Jane is now much better and we begin to hope—what we long despaired of—that she will entirely throw off her illness. She and Percy amuse themselves by painting and sketching, and are as happy as possible. They suit so entirely—both being absolutely devoid of every tinge of worldliness and worldly tastes—both having cheerful tempers and affectionate hearts— Indeed Jane is the very ideal of woman, gentle, soft—yet very vivacious—when well even to high lively spirits—both wearing the heart upon the sleeve—but both having the precious instinct of avoiding pecking daws—and of keeping off ill conditioned wasps. I never deserved so much peace and happiness as I enjoy with them—illness has been the dark shadow;—I tremble to think what other may cover our sun when that, as looks likely, is withdrawn—We think of returning in April—for we left England at a very inconvenient time for our affairs— I only wish I could look forward to a stationary abode at Field Place,—but it is so low and damp that it requires to have been born there to flourish. I own I envy you your country— Ill as I was when in Monmouthshire, I never enjoyed a place more—the scenery is so lovely and so cheerful— The Vale of Usk appeared to me a spot to choose out of all England to live in—and then I was quite ignorant of your being there.

I do not know that I can amuse you with any gossip about acquaintance for indeed one does not like to put in writing the little fault finding and *tracassierie* that rises up in social intercourse— I can only say that Sussex offers no charms to us whatever in the way of society, but then we have had little to do with it—you must not think with all this that we dislike Field Place — It is any thing but a country seat of any mark whatever; it is old fashioned and with few rooms—so better suited to our fortunes—but it has a home and comfortable feeling about it—that makes it very pleasant—we have but one objection to it—its being in a hole, in a clay soil.

I enclose 3 lines to your husband to ask him to do something for me which I wish to be done *very much*[1]—and what more do I say—this seems so selfish a letter—let yours be the same, as regards yourself—tell me of your house—your children, your garden, your occupations. I hope the sun is shining on you as cheerfully as it does on me—beaming on the bright sea—the excursions about here among the hills and by the shore are very beautiful, it has not the verdure of Usk—Olives being the chief tree—but they are large and tall here—and the pure bright atmosphere gives colors to all that compensate for the absence of emerald green. Adieu.

Affly Yours,
M. Shelley

ORIGINAL: Sir John Shelley-Rolls. PRINTED: Grylls, *Mary Shelley,* 250–51. TEXT: From copy made by Sir John Shelley-Rolls.

[1] The three lines to Trelawny requested him to return to her the portrait of her painted in Rome by Miss Curran in 1819. Mary wished to present it to Lady Jane Shelley. Trelawny refused. In a letter to the editor of *The Athenæum,* August 3, 1878, Trelawny wrote: "Mrs. Shelley said, 'I have written to Miss Curran to give you the portrait she did of Shelley. . . . There is one of me too, but now no one will value that.' I said, 'Yes, I do.' 'You can have it, but it is unfinished, and she has made a great dowdy of me; I care nothing about it' . . . I executed this commission. From this time Mrs. Shelley never saw her own portrait, nor expressed any wish to see it, until fifteen or twenty years after. She then asked or wrote that she wished I would let her have it, as a particular friend of hers was very anxious to see it. To this verbally or in writing I refused, and she never afterwards alluded to it."—*The Letters of Edward J. Trelawny,* 263.

On April 11, 1823, Trelawny wrote to Claire from Rome: "Dearest, I have got possession of a portrait of you—it is an excellent likeness."— *Ibid.,* 46–47. He doubtless secured Mary's portrait at the same time.

702. *To Mr. Touchet*

F[ield] P[lace]
2 August [1850].

Dear Mr. Touchet,

I am very well pleased to write and send you news—since all our news is good. Lady S[helley] has been spending a week in town under the care of Dr. Lowry who has dismissed her as being perfectly well— She is indeed quite herself again—as plump as a partridge and as gay as a lark no headaches and no pains—it is so great a pleasure to see her so blooming and frisky. I am also so well that at present I have nothing to complain of—my nerves are tranquil and indeed I am so much better than you ever saw me, that I have misgivings, that in spite of apparent non-success while at Nice, little sips may not share with the absence of anxiety on Janey's account, in restoring me to health.

Our visit to Elcott was very pleasant and the Vicar amiable and agreable— there was besides another visitor so clever and amusing, that our visit was particularly pleasant.

Jane was very sorry that you missed Mr. St. John—he is gone—he has promised to look out for shooting for you in Scotland next year, and he says that he does not doubt but that he shall be able to get what you want on reasonable terms. I found the Knox's flourishing while I was with them for a few days— I have one bit of news that I do not like—tho' it is not bad news. Next week Percy and Jane are going to Newcastle and then to her brother—they will be away above a fortnight—I do not know what I shall do— I have an idea that Charley will come over with Harry on his return—but Charley will find it very dull with only me.

Carlo is quite bankrupt in all good—his misdeeds are too numerous for a detail— He refused to come here for a couple of days— His heart was set on getting an allowance given him for clothes, &c.— Lady S[helley] made the allowance but placed it at the disposal of Mr. Wiggins, as Carlo had given every token that he was not to be trusted— He was furious—and desired to go before the Mast, to punish Lady S. and then that his indentures should be cancelled, that he might engage himself elsewhere—to all this he received no answer— He then saw his old Captain, Titman, who has always shewn him so much kindness—Ctn. Titman was going a voyage to China for [*MS is incomplete.*]

ORIGINAL: Sir John Shelley-Rolls (MS incomplete). UNPRINTED and UN-PUBLISHED. TEXT: From copy made by Sir John Shelley-Rolls.

703. *To Mr. Touchet*

Field Place,
Friday M[ornin]g [? August 9, 1850].

Dear Mr. Touchet,

Lady Shelley received a letter a day or two ago to announce that Harry and

Charley would be in town on the 12th. I suppose that they will come down here directly—so we consider that if you have the proper feelings of humanity you will come up to see Harry before he goes.

I am sorry to say that our dear Janey has not been so well these last few days—she has been doing too much—and her attack is nervous—we believe that it will pass off soon— I am very well.

Percy, in great tribulation, has just told us, that until this moment he has quite forgot all about the £5 he ought [to] have sent you—you will receive it by this post.

Mrs. Hare and her daughter have been spending two days with us—they are now gone via Baden to Rome— Please God we see the former again— she is looking dreadfully ill—but she [is] so strong that one cannot but hope that a good climate will restore her.

Harry's destination is Gibralter. We do not know how long he will stay with us—but a day or two, we fear.

Adieu—with love from all,

Ever Yours,
Mary Shelley

ORIGINAL: Sir John Shelley-Rolls. UNPRINTED and UNPUBLISHED. TEXT: From copy made by Sir John Shelley-Rolls.

704. *To Mrs. E. J. Trelawny*

Field Place,
12 August, 1850.

Dear Mrs. Trelawny,

I wrote to you from Nice but have not heard from you since— Your last letter however makes me think that this has been accidental, and that you would like to hear from me— We staid 6 months at Nice; at first Lady Shelley continued ill and gave us great anxiety; at length we fell in with a clever German homaeopathic doctor, and she got much better. Such is the force of prejudice (or reason) that I cannot bring myself to believe in homaeopathy—though the experience I have had of it, is in its favour. The doctor was a clever man—and acted boldly—and the bold measures (changing hot water for cold being the chief) succeeded—and she has got over her alarming illness. This place being very damp, does not agree with her—when she gets into dry air she is as blooming and bright as ever. Nice did not agree with me—it kept my nerves in a state of irritation indescribable— I could not walk— I was kept on the sopha nearly all the time; now I am here I am much better—but I half think that I ought to ascribe the *very* much better that I am than last year to homaeopathic medicine as my health and nerves have not been so well for years. With all the drawback of much suffering I like Nice— The climate *to look* at is the loveliest I ever knew—and the donkey rides ever varied and ever beautiful. We returned by the Riviera but unfortunately we got rain when we left Nice, and did not enjoy it as much as we otherwise should. The spring was very tardy—and we were delayed in crossing the Alps—but as we spent the time on the lake of Como we did not regret it. We only returned 17 June.

We all of us like Field Place if it wd. be dry—if weather like this continued —but there is no help—and we must spend the time of the fall of the leaf elsewhere.

On our return we find things as we left them— Aubrey Paul is going to be married this winter to a very pretty girl Laura Lister Karge— I have heard of no particular admirer for Emmy Aldridge. James Campbell has disappeared —he went yachting with his mother and sisters to Constantinople—and we have not heard from him since— He had settled to return during the month of August, but he has neither come nor written.

I wrote a line to Trelawny when I wrote to you, begging him to let me have a portrait painted by Miss Curran which was placed in his hands in Italy for me— It was left at Florence, I believe, and I was in hopes he would have ordered it to be sent me while I was at Nice. I wish he would order it to be sent me by sea to London.

We live very quietly and happily— Jane's health is our only real evil— When she is well all is bright and gay— She is the sunshine of our house. The dearest, gentlest, truest, most perfect creature I ever knew. I wish they had a family and as her health improves and she becomes strong, we hope it will arrive.

I confess I wish Destiny had placed Field Place in the Vale of Usk—at least in a dry soil—the country here is sufficiently pretty and I would be content with that—though Usk I thought extremely lovely—and I delight in mountains and torrents, especially when mitigated so as to bear the aspect of cheerfulness and life as is the case in Monmouthshire.

Aubrey Beauclerk and his family are at Ardglass and mean to spend the winter there—he was sadly ailing while in Sussex, but is much better now, I hear—and does not shut himself quite so much up.

I hope you will write and believe me,

Ever truly yours,
Mary Shelley

ORIGINAL: Sir John Shelley-Rolls. UNPRINTED and UNPUBLISHED. TEXT: From copy made by Sir John Shelley-Rolls.

705. *To Mr. Touchet*

Field Place,
8 Sep. [1850].

The "fairest Fair" arrived today in all her miniature and ivory beauty— She is very welcome—and casts a halo round her, attracting the gaze and admiration of all. I am very much pleased with your present, which is quite divine in its perfection— Jane is glad also of her silk—it all came safe and well—all right, except one thing, that *you* did not bring them— Are we never to see you? The weather is fine and partridges many (poor things— they are already fewer), and are you to have no share? We live here in great ignorance. The Knox's leave town tomorrow whether for Dorset or Devon-shire I do not know. Aubrey Paul stays with us till the end of the week— Charley is here rejoicing and yet anxious— He wishes for some certain pros-pect and that might be afforded him, if there were as much care for his future as of present enjoyment— He is a good little fellow and we are all fond of him.

Field Place, tho' become cold, is dry at present—so Jane keeps well—and I hope this weather will last. I could not have believed any air to be so per-nicious as that of beautiful Nice to me. A sermon might be written about it— yet I remember it with affection; it was so very beautiful, and I enjoyed the donkey rides so much. We had a letter the other day from Penelope—she and her husband passed the summer at the Chartreuse—and had just returned to Nice, when she presented him with a boy— No news whatever of the Camp-bell's— I should believe in a Calypso, but that wd. only account for him—so they must all [have] eaten of the fatal plant—burnt the yacht and have mar-ried— I forget the name of the Lotus eaters.

Adieu we are impatient for a letter—if that is all we are to have—My children send their love.

Ever Yours,
M. Shelley[1]

ORIGINAL: Sir John Shelley-Rolls. UNPRINTED and UNPUBLISHED. TEXT: From copy made by Sir John Shelley-Rolls.

[1] Mary Shelley died at 24 Chester Square, London, on Saturday, February 1, 1851, and was buried in St. Peter's Churchyard, Bournemouth, with her father and mother, whose bodies were removed at this time from the old St. Pancras Churchyard. In the same grave now are her son, Sir Percy Florence, and his wife, Lady Jane Shelley. Shelley's heart, snatched from the flames by Trelawny and preserved by Mary Shelley, was placed in Sir Percy's coffin and buried with him. (See Appendix IV.)

Appendices

Other Mary Shelley Letters

Most of the following letters have not been traced to their present owners. A few early auction sale records and booksellers' catalogue items have been omitted as too vague for identification even if the MSS were available. There are probably some duplications in the list.

1. 1817, Jan. 17. Bath. To Shelley. (Beginning: "You were born to be a Don Quixote . . .") A.L.S., 4 pp. 4to, with postmarks. Owned by Mr. A.S.W. Rosenbach, in August, 1937.
2. [1818, Feb.–Mar. 1] 119 Great Russell St. To Isabel Booth. A.L.S., 1 p. 4to. Owned by Walter T. Spencer, in 1937. Spencer's note: "about a letter directed to Marlow while Mary Shelley was in London."
3. 1818, March 22. Lyons. Shelley to Leigh Hunt. According to de Ricci *(Bibliography of Shelley's Letters,* 149), "Across the pages [of Shelley's letter] is a letter by Mary Shelley." This has never been printed with Shelley's letter; the MS was once in the Frederick Locker-Lampson Collection.
4. [1822 or 1823] Saturday. [Albaro] To Lord Byron. (Beginning: "Your Lordship's MS. was very difficult . . .") A.L.S., 1 p. (4 x 5 inches), addressed. Owned by Sir John Murray.
5. [1822 or 1823] To the Countess Guiccioli. (Beginning: "Mia Cara—Sono disperata accioche . . .") A.L.S., 3 pp. (4 x 6 inches), addressed; written in Italian. Owned by Sir John Murray.
6. [1823] Aug. 13. Paris. To William Godwin. A.L. (unsigned), 4 pp. 4to. Sold at H[odgson's], June 22, 1922, for £4.12.0.
7. 1823, Nov. 19. Lamb's Conduit St. To Charles Ollier. A.L.S., 1 p. 8vo. Sold at Sotheby's, December 4, 1916, to Dobell, for 4s. Refers to the publication of her works.
8. [1824–32] To J. H. Payne. A.N. on small fragment of paper. Sold on February 26, 1917, by the Anderson Galleries (1013: Duplicates and Selections from the libraries of Henry E. Huntington and Wm. K. Bixby), for $5.
9. [1824–32] To J. H. Payne. A.L.S., 1 p. 8vo. Sold on November 7, 1902, by Bangs & Co., N.Y. (297: A Miscellaneous Collection), for $6.50.
10. [1825] Nov. 29 Kentish Town. To J. H. Payne [at Paris]. A.L.S., 4 pp. 4to; a small piece torn out, where sealed, slightly affecting the text. Sold on April 9, 1929, by the Anderson Galleries (166: Americana, Selections from the library of Francis A. MacNutt, Brassanone, Italy, &c.), for $170.

11. [1825] Dec. 5. Kentish Town. To Charles Ollier. A.L.S., 1 p. small 8vo, addressed. Sold on May 7, 1901, by Bangs & Co., N.Y. (395: Collection of Wm. Harris Arnold), for $25. Mary asks Ollier for Keat's "first publication."

12. [1826] Jan. 29. Kentish Town. To J. H. Payne. A.L.S., 4 pp. 4to. Sold on February 20, 1905, by the Anderson Auction Co. (7840: Library of the late Thos. Jefferson McKee, Pt. VIII), for $6.59. The letter mentions her husband, father, mother, Mr. Elliston, Trelawny, and others. Probably the same as the letter sold on March 18, 1910, by the Anderson Auction Co. (236: Collection of Books, Letters, MSS of the late David Pell Secor, Derby, Conn., Pt. I), for $15. And probably the same as Letter 259 of the text, dated January 28, 1826.

13. 1827, Aug. 22. Near Shoreham, Sussex. To J. H. Payne. A.L.S., 3 pp. 4to. Sold on May 27, 1921, by Stan. V. Henkels, Philadelphia (295: Library of Dr. Herman Seidler, N.Y. City), for $29.

14. [1827] Aug. 30. Sompting. To J. H. Payne. A.L.S., 3 pp. 4to. Sold on April 9, 1929, by the Anderson Galleries (167: Americana, Selections from the library of Francis A. MacNutt, Brassanone, Italy, &c.), for $130.

15. [1827] to J. H. Payne. A.L.S. (initials), 2 pp. 4to, addressed. Sold on January 26, 1914, by the Anderson Auction Co. (420: Autograph Letters, MSS, and Documents including the collection of the late I. Remsenlane, Orange, N.J.), for $24.

16. [1828] Park Cottage. [To   ?] A.L.S. (initials), 1 p. 8vo. Sold on February 26, 1917, by the Anderson Galleries (1008: Duplicates & Selections from the libraries of Henry E. Huntington and Wm. K. Bixby), for $5.

17. [1828, March 26] To J. H. Payne. A.L.S. (initials), 1 p. with letter cover. Sold on November 24, 1913, by the Anderson Auction Co. (1254: Collection of the late Douglas Taylor, Pres. of the Dunlop Society, N.Y.), for $9.75.

18. [1828, June 8] Sunday. Dover. To J. H. Payne. A.L.S., 3 pp. 4to, small piece torn out where sealed, slightly affecting text. Sold on April 9, 1929, by the Anderson Galleries (168: Americana, Selections from the library of Francis A. MacNutt, Brassanone, Italy, &c.), for $110.

19. [1829] [To Henry Colburn ?] A.L.S., 2 pp. 4to. Sold on April 19, 1904, by the Anderson Auction Co. (730: Collection of Autographs, &c., by the late John H. V. Arnold of N.Y.), for $5.25.

20. [1830–35] March 21. London. [To Charles Ollier?] A.L.S., 4to. Sold on January 8, 1915, by the Anderson Auction Co. (244: Autographs, mainly American, collection of Gen. Horatio C. King, Brooklyn, N.Y.), for $3.75. The letter refers to the sales of *Lodore*.

21. [1834] To Charles Ollier. A.L.S., 3 pp. 4to. Owned in July 1939 by Bernard Halliday, Leicester: Catalogue 239, item 587, price £5. Catalogue notation: "One of her MSS has been lost in the post, gives a full account of posting, etc."

22. [1835, March 25: pstmk.] [To ?] A.L.S., 8 vo. Sold at C[   ], April 4, 1917, to Sabin.

23. [1828–39, Dec.–Feb.] 41 d Park St. To Mr. Perry. A.L.S., 1 p. 8vo. Owned by Walter T. Spencer, London, in 1937. Spencer's note: "Writes of her son Percy being engaged today."

24. 1839, May 27. [To ?] A.L.S., 2 pp. 4to. Sold on March 29, 1922, at Sotheby's, to Edwards, for £1.12.0.

25. [1839–46] Monday. Putney. To Abraham Hayward. A.L.S., 1 p. 8vo. Owned by Walter T. Spencer, London, in 1937. Spencer sent me this odd excerpt: "As you know, to learn a thing is not detailed—to be found is next in importance to finding the details."

26. [1839–46] July 2. Putney. [To ?] A.L.S., 2 pp. 8vo. Sold on October 10, 1906, by the Merwin-Clayton Sales Co. (294: Collection of Autograph Letters, MSS, & Documents), for $6. Letter evidently written to an Italian; it gives the years in which *The Triumph of Life* and *Prince Athanase* were written and mentions Byron three times. Probably the same as No. 27.

27. [1839–46] July 2. Putney. [To ?] A.L.S., 2 pp. small 8vo. Sold on May 7, 1901, by Bangs & Co. (396: Collection of Wm. Harris Arnold), for $6. Probably the same as No. 26.

28. [*c.* 1840] Nov. 21. Putney. [To a publisher (? Moxon)] A.L.S., 4 pp. 8vo. Sold on June 3, 1914, by the Anderson Auction Co. (194: Literary & Hist. Letters & Documents, collection of the late Rev. Edwin F. Hatfield), for $5.50.

29. 1843, Oct. 8. Putney. To Edward Moxon. A.L.S., 3 pp. 8vo. Sold on March 22, 1915, by the Anderson Auction Co. (492: Library of the late Adrian H. Joline, Pt. IV, Eng. and Continental Autographs), for $16 (with another letter).

30. [after March, 1832] To Mrs. Gaskell. A.L.S., 1½ pp. 8vo. Sold at Sotheby's, December 22, 1919, to Dobell, for £5.

31. [?   ] Richmond. [To   ?] A.L.S., 2 pp. 12mo. Sold on March 22, 1915, by the Anderson Auction Co., with another letter (492: Library of the late Adrian H. Joline, Pt. IV, Eng. & Continental Autographs), for $16.

32. 1859 [*sic*] Aug. 28. To Leigh Hunt. A.L.S., 4 pp. 8vo. Sold on January 26, 1921, by Stan. V. Henkels (507: Autograph Letters from Several Collections), for $30.

33. [?   ] To Sir Walter Scott. One of two letters from Mary to Scott in the great Letter-Books of Sir Walter Scott, owned by the late Sir Hugh Walpole. The other letter is printed in this volume.

34. [?   ] To Mr. Thompson. A.L.S., 2 pp. 12 mo. Owned in July, 1939, by Bernard Halliday, Leicester: Catalogue 239, item 585, price 25/–.

35. [?   ] [? To Mrs. Matthews, wife of the Actor.] A.L.S., 1 p. 8vo. Owned in July, 1939, by Bernard Halliday, Leicester: Catalogue 239, item 588, price £3.10.0.

36. Two Letters: to Edward Moxon and Isabel Booth. A Collection of 8 A. Lrs. S., 1795–1866: 2 by Godwin; 2 by Mary Shelley to Moxon and Isabel Booth; 1 by Shelley to Godwin; 1 by Everina Wollstonecraft; 1 by Sir Percy F. Shelley; 1 by T. J. Hogg. With 6 portraits, together 14 pieces, tipped or inlaid to 4to sheets, with typed transcripts, and tipped to binding of lev. morocco, by Grabau. Sold on February 14–16, 1927, by the American Art Ass'n. (1129: Library of Major W. Van R. Whitall, Pelham, N.Y.), for $1400.

37. Letters to Jane Williams. Some six to ten are owned by Lord Abinger, I am told by one who has seen them.

38. Mr. Carl H. Pforzheimer of New York has many Mary Shelley letters; particulars concerning them will not be available until the catalogue of Mr. Pforzheimer's Shelley Collection is completed. Most of the letters are probably from the H. Buxton Forman Collection.

39. Letters to Sophia Stacey. Miss Stacey's "correspondence, with various other papers relating to her family, was sold at Puttick & Simpson's, 24 Dec. 1857. In this sale came to light three letters addressed to her by Shelley, together with various letters from Mary and Godwin."—S. de Ricci, *Bibliography of Shelley's Letters* (1927), 48.

40. Letters to Mrs. Gisborne. "A considerable body of Gisborne papers were sold at Messrs. Puttick & Simpson's, on 27 May 1878 (pages 46–48, nos. 650–75) as 'Shelleyiana formerly the property of Mr. and Mrs. Gisborne.' . . . lot 656 (page 47: £10.5.0 to Ellis and White) would be interesting to trace: 'Transcripts of letters (1819–22) of Percy B. Shelley, Mary Shelley, and Claire Clairmont, including the long letter in verse addressed to Mrs. Gisborne; Shelley speaks of the Queen as the vulgar cook-maid.' "—S. de Ricci, *Bibliography of Shelley's Letters* (1927), 57.

41. Three Letters to W. T. and Christie Baxter. The Property of a Gentleman living at Leamington, sold at Sotheby's on December 8, 1911, item 300, page 38: Mary Shelley to W. T. Baxter and his daughter Christie, 3 A. Lrs. S., 6½ pp. 4to. Bought by Maggs for £11.

42. Three Letters to A. Brooke. The Shelley-Whitton Papers, sold at Sotheby's on July 24, 1918, lot 703; page 70: 3 A. Lrs. S., 6 pp. 4to, two of 1824, to A. Brooke, editor of the Kent *Herald*, one most interesting letter acknowledging a gift of his own poems, and speaking of Shelley's *Posthumous Poems*. Bought by Francis Edwards for £1.6.0.

43. Twenty-four Letters to Leigh and Marianne Hunt. Sold at H[odgson's], June 22, 1922, to Chaundy, for £10. Only description: Putney, undated. (From *Autograph Prices Current*.)

Mary Shelley, John Howard Payne
and Washington Irving

Mary Shelley's long friendship (1824–32) with John Howard Payne and her brief interest in Washington Irving have yet to be properly evaluated by one sufficiently acquainted with Mary's life and character. The world knew nothing of these matters until her correspondence with Payne was printed in 1907 for the Boston Bibliophile Society, with "remarks" by F. B. Sanborn.[1] The editing of this volume is mediocre, and the remarks are lacking in sympathy and understanding. More unfortunate still, all subsequent comment has taken its tone from Sanborn. Gribble's *Romantic Life of Shelley* (New York, G. P. Putnam's Sons, 1911) makes good use of the possibility of scandal; Massingham's biography of Trelawny (*The Friend of Shelley*, 1930) is ferociously hostile to Mary. Stanley T. Williams's *Life of Washington Irving* (1936), though scholarly and impartial, could give only a limited space to so small an event in Irving's life.[2] Miss Grylls, Mary Shelley's latest biographer (1938), dismisses the whole affair with a contemptuous reference to Payne.[3] It is hardly possible briefly to set this important matter in its proper light, but a few facts will help the reader to draw his own conclusions.

Just when Mary met Payne is not known. It is possible that she met him in Paris at the Kenneys' in August, 1823, but not likely. Her letters[4] for that time (August 12–20) give a rather complete account of her activities, and they say nothing at all of Payne. Nor did she meet Irving in Paris. Irving's *Journal* for 1823–24 gives a daily record during Mary's visit of 1823. It appears that, though visiting the Kenneys on the very evening of Mary's arrival in Paris, Irving was absent from Paris for the remainder of Mary's stay. While Mary was in Paris, his journal makes no reference to the Kenneys, Horace Smiths, or anyone else that Mary was then associating with. Thus Mary's first meeting with Payne and Irving was doubtless during Irving's visit to England from May 30 to August 14, 1824. The Kenneys were probably responsible for both introductions. We know positively that Mary met Irving at least twice; that they met on other occasions as well may be regarded almost as a certainty. In

---

[1] *The Romance of Mary Shelley, John Howard Payne, and Washington Irving.*
[2] I, 286–88.
[3] *Mary Shelley*, 181.
[4] Hitherto mostly unpublished.

his *Journal* Irving wrote:[5] "Saturday 17th July [1824] Sat to Newton to alter my portrait—Mr. Foster came in—Lake also—Moore, Kenney, Miss Holcroft & Mrs. Shelley—came in—" Again on Tuesday, August 10, he wrote (page 244): "Kenney breakfasted with me. In good spirits anticipating the success of his piece this Evg— . . . Went to Haymarket—Private Box with Miss Holcroft—Mrs. Shelley Mrs. Linton . . . Kenneys piece went off bravely."

According to Payne's own statement,[6] after meeting Mary, he for a considerable time refrained from indulging in her society because he was afraid of falling in love with her. He nevertheless corresponded with her and frequently supplied her with theater tickets. Their acquaintance was then interrupted for several months by a misunderstanding brought about by young Thomas Holcroft's error in transmitting a message from Payne to Mary. The error having eventually been discovered and rectified, they resumed corresponding early in April, 1825. Payne then broke his resolution and allowed himself often to enjoy Mary's company. Up to this time Payne's relationship with Mary had been rather formal, but now it rapidly became warmer. Payne continued to furnish Mary with theater tickets for herself and her friends, and the two exchanged numerous hasty notes, most of which are undated. Payne often accompanied Mary to the theater, or met her there. His growing admiration and affection for her, which she observed with some alarm, led him, on June 25, to declare himself. During the course of the conversation Mary made it plain that, having been the wife of Shelley, she could not bring herself to an alliance with anyone whose genius could not in some measure match Shelley's.[7] Washington Irving, she hinted, was such a person. That Mary had an extraordinary interest in Irving and desired to develop a real friendship with him, and even dallied with the thought of marrying him, cannot be denied. In his disappointment, Payne remembered the many instances of her strong interest in Irving—her requests to see Irving's letters, her comments on his books—and concluded, hastily perhaps but surely lover-like, that Mary was seriously in love with Irving. He soon determined to do the heroic thing: to give to the friend he loved the woman he loved. It is a truly noble action in the life of this man of talent who often came near to success but never reached it. That it was all wrong makes no difference. Certain it is that Mary Shelley knew nothing at all about Payne's heroic resolutions.

When again in August, 1825, Payne was in Paris, he gathered together and arranged Mary's letters and copies of his letters to her. He thought that a perusal of them would show plainly that Mary was in love with Irving and that she hoped through him (Payne) to bring Irving within her orbit. On the evening of August 16, 1825, he wrote and dispatched (or handed) to Irving the following letter.[8]

5 *Journal of Washington Irving* (1823–24), edited by Stanley T. Williams (1931), 229.
6 *Romance*, 72.
7 *Romance*, 61.
8 *Ibid.*, 17–20.

My dear Irving,—I have reflected a long time before I determined to show you this correspondence, because from its nature it might appear indelicate to expose the letters, especially to you, as you are more involved in it than you even appear to be. It was some time before I discovered that I was only sought as a source of an introduction to you [*an odd statement, for Mary had already met Irving at least twice*]—and I think you will, on reading the papers, feel that I might have mistaken the nature of my acquaintance with the writer, without any gratuitous vanity. But at the same time you will admit that she is a woman of the highest and most amiable qualities, and one whose wish for friendship it would be doing yourself injustice not to meet. Of course, it must be a perfect secret between ourselves that I have shown the letters. They are at present not known to any one. You must not look upon the affair in a ridiculous light, as, if you should, I shall never forgive myself for having exposed so fine a mind to so injurious a construction.

I really wish you would see and know Mrs. S[helley] whenever you go to London. I am not in the least dissatisfied with the way in which she considers me, however difficult an affair so little flattering to one's pride and affections is to endure at first. But I felt from the beginning that I had been too deeply galled ever again to be let in among the herd—however much individuals might pity me at a distance.

No doubt it will cost you some reflection fully to appreciate the trouble I am taking to make you well acquainted with one whom I have known so well —to transfer an intimacy of which any one ought to be proud. I do not ask you to fall in love—but I should even feel a little proud of myself if you thought the lady worthy of that distinction, and very possibly you would have fallen in love with her, had you met her casually—but she is too much out of society to enable you to do so—and sentiments stronger than friendship seldom result from this sort of previous earnestness for intimacy when it comes from the wrong side.

The letters were generally scribbled off on scraps of paper, as soon as those which prompted them came. These scraps I kept by me—accidently—or rather, most of them; when the communications grew a little serious, I kept them on purpose. I have been taught great distrust of my own impressions on such matters by experience, and hence felt the propriety of retaining all the materials for a future opinion. After I found which way the current ran, I copied all I could make out, fairly—that you might understand the matter thoroughly. I am a little proud of having acted, in the main, with so much consistency.

I have felt myself in honor bound to withhold nothing from you, and you must judge of what I now do, not from your own uninterested views of the subject, but from those by which I have been guided and the strong feelings I have sacrificed.

I think the rest will explain itself. It may help your understanding of the early part, to know there was some blunder made by Thomas Holcroft in a message, which for a long time stopped all correspondence with Mrs. S., who some months before had written to me frequently for orders.

Yours ever, J. H. P.

Irving read the packet that same night. His only recorded comment is his journal entry for August 16: "Read Mrs. Shelley's correspondence before going to bed."[9]

When Payne returned to England a year later (October, 1826), whatever romantic dreams he or Mary may have had had long ago faded into tranquil memories. Steady friendship, untroubled by vain hopes, they both enjoyed until Payne returned to America in 1832.[10]

What does Mary's connection with Payne and Irving teach us about Mary Shelley? To the casual observer it shows nothing except a woman who was quite willing to use friendship to forward her own purposes and pleasure, and who was unwilling to make any returns. To one who seriously attempts to understand Mary Shelley, it shows every element of importance in her character. Mary had an insatiable desire to associate herself with people of talent and

---

[9] S. T. Williams, *Life of Washington Irving*, I, 286.

[10] A few facts about Payne and Irving may be useful to the reader. Long before Mary met Payne, he was well known in the English theaters. (Shelley refers to him in the preface to *Adonais*.) Born in New York on June 9, 1791, and becoming an actor in 1809, he sailed for England on January 17, 1813, sent by friends who wished to have him try his fortunes on the London stage. He was a fair success until the summer of 1814, when he became jobless and penniless. He turned to writing and adapting plays for the stage. In 1814 his *The Maid and the Magpie* (adapted from a French play) was acted at Covent Garden. During the seasons of 1818 and 1819 he conducted the correspondence of Covent Garden, read MSS, etc. His *Brutus* (December 3, 1818) was his first genuinely successful play.

In 1820 he leased the Sadler's Wells Theatre, but failed, and at the end of the season was sent to Fleet Street Prison for debt. The success of his *Thérèse* (Drury Lane, February 2, 1821) was responsible for his release. He fled to Paris, and there wrote *Clari, or The Maid of Milan* (Covent Garden, May 8, 1823), which he turned into an opera. It is this play that contains the famous "Home, Sweet Home."

In the summer of 1823, Irving came to Paris. He and Payne arranged to collaborate in supplying the English and American theaters with translations and adaptations of French plays. Payne went to England in the autumn of 1823 to negotiate with the theaters, and remained there until August, 1825, when he returned to Paris. *Charles the Second* (Covent Garden, May 27, 1821) was the first successful play of collaboration. *Richelieu, A Domestic Tragedy* (Covent Garden, February 11, 1826) was not so fortunate; it ran only six nights.

By October, 1826, Payne was back in England, where he continued his dramatic activities until June 16, 1832, when he sailed for America. In 1842 he was appointed American consul at Tunis. Recalled in 1845, he was reappointed in March, 1851. He died at Tunis on April 9, 1852. His successor found the packet of correspondence with Mary Shelley among his papers.

Payne wrote eleven tragedies, nine comedies, twenty-six dramas and melodramas, seven operas, and ten farces. The most popular of all his plays was *Brutus, or The Fall of Tarquin*, a tragedy, produced by Kean at Drury Lane, December 3, 1818. It held the stage until the 1870's. *Thérèse* (1821), *Clari* (1823), and *Charles the Second* (1824) were also among his most successful plays.

During the short time that Mary was interested in Irving, he was, except for a period of three months, physically beyond her reach. He was in Paris from the summer of 1823 until May 30, 1824, when he went to England. In Paris he was intimate with the Kenneys and often saw Thomas Medwin. In England he associated with Thomas Moore, Samuel Rogers, and John Murray (his publisher). He also visited Godwin. He returned to Paris on August 14, 1824. On September 22, 1825, he went to Bordeaux for four months. In February, 1826, he went to Madrid, and remained in Spain through June, 1828. There is no evidence to show that Mary's interest in him extended beyond 1825.

genius. She could never forget that she was the daughter of William Godwin and Mary Wollstonecraft and the wife of Percy Bysshe Shelley. Though she liked society, it was the society of intellectual people that she preferred: Hunt, Lamb, Coleridge, Hazlitt, Procter, Novello, Bowring, Tom Moore, Samuel Rogers. She liked Payne because he was a man of talent if not of genius; she admired Irving excessively for a while because, personally, he struck her imagination and because she thought him a man of genius.

Mary's craving for friendship is likewise forcefully exhibited. Throughout Mary's whole life, her constant cry was for friendship. There is even something morbid in her desire for affection—a certain lack of self-confidence, of self-sufficiency. Isabel Baxter, Claire, the Hunts, Jane and Edward Williams, Trelawny, the Gisbornes—to these she clung, almost desperately, as long as it was possible to cling. After Shelley's death her idealization of Jane Williams, who she well knew did not return her passionate devotion, appears repeatedly in her letters and her journal. Trelawny she addressed in most affectionate terms until he gradually withdrew himself from her and became harsh and critical. One so sensitive to friendship must necessarily meet with bitter disappointments. Hunt's coldness of 1822–23 wounded her most painfully; Jane's unfeeling tattling in 1827 was almost like a death blow.

And yet with all her passionate desire for friendship, her loyalty to those friends to the last, her willingness to serve them, to give as well as to take,—with all this, Mary was not on the whole successful in holding friends. One reason for this failure is probably her possessiveness. Most people do not care to feel that they belong to their friends; the weight of friendship is often heavy. But that is not all: Mary had two unpleasing qualities of which she could not rid herself. From Godwin she inherited an exterior coldness, a serenity and severity of countenance which belied the warmth of her heart. She impressed others as being reserved and self-sufficient. Again and again she confesses to her journal that her friends think she has a cold heart. This haunted her to the grave. The second quality came to her from the mother she idolized. Mary Wollstonecraft was given to melancholia, which often lent to her letters a wailing tone. Such people lament too much; the slightest disappointment, vexation, or apprehension sets them off. Their lack of cheerfulness makes them unpleasant company at times. Their friends neglect them when they do not care to be doleful. In Mary Wollstonecraft this unhappy quality was partially offset by strength of character and forcefulness of personality; but Mary Shelley lacked these redeeming qualities, at least in their redeeming quantities.

Being such an epicure for friendship and having an affinity for people of talent, Mary Shelley could not do otherwise than accept gratefully the worship which Payne offered her. But from him she wished no more than warm and sincere friendship; he was no match for her Shelley, and besides he was improvident. She accepted theater tickets from him because she thought it gave him pleasure to serve her. But always she was careful not to overstep the bounds of friendship, and it was with dismay that she saw his admiration ripening into love.

Still another element in Mary's character clearly demonstrated by her friendship with Payne is her dependence. Mary Wollstonecraft could stand alone, although she preferred the support of a greater and stronger person. Mary Shelley could also stand alone, but to do so was contrary to the very bent of her character. She was made to lean upon another, to look up for direction and sympathy. To be independent was agony; her very nature rebelled against it. For twenty-two long years she did make her way alone, looking after her aging father and educating her son, determined that these duties should not in any way be neglected. She might wail through the years the want of affection and understanding, but this did not hinder her a particle from making every sacrifice for those she loved. Writing novels and articles and lives of Italian and Spanish and French notables, contributing whenever she could to the annuals, editing under tremendous strain Shelley's poetry and prose— these she may not have done cheerfully, but these she nevertheless did with the single purpose of providing comfort for her father and opportunity for her son. And because all this was done against the grain, the more admirable her success, the more noble her triumph. It was one of her great disappointments that her son, though affectionate and docile, did not take the family affairs into his strong hands and afford her the support she needed, but instead depended upon her, even to the choosing of a wife for him.

Trelawny rightfully taunted Mary with being no match for the rebel and reformer Shelley; for Mary was no rebel at heart. But Trelawny was wrong in insisting that it was Mary's love of conventionality that made her an insufficient mate for Shelley. Mary did not have the desire or the ability to champion a cause on her own account. However, she had the rare power of assisting the strong soul who is aflame for a cause. Her reflection of Shelley's enthusiasm for freedom in Spain and Naples and Greece is only an example of many possible examples. The society that Mary most enjoyed was far from being conventional.

Mary's friendship for Payne shows another fact about Mary that is not to be found in *Shelley and Mary* or Mrs. Marshall's *Life and Letters*. From these one gets the impression that Mary's last twenty-nine years were devoted to a constant and all-absorbing worship of Shelley, that a thought of marrying again could not possibly have entered her mind. This was by no means the case. Mary often considered the possibility of marrying again, and had the man of genius who was at the same time a man of ample means approached her under pleasing and proper conditions, she would have married him. But such a one under such conditions never appeared. The conditions were right for Payne, but Payne had neither the requisite genius nor the ample means. Had Payne possessed ample means, it is quite possible that Mary could have brought herself to be satisfied with his amount of talent.

Marriage with Payne was, of course, impossible. With a son to rear and educate and an aged father to support, she would have been a very weak woman to make impossible the performance of these duties by joining herself to one whose whole history proved him to be improvident. Sir Timothy Shelley, who already had an ill opinion of her, would instantly have stopped her meager income of £200 per annum. To Mary the whole matter must have been as clear as day; to Payne it probably was by no means clear. But Mary did enjoy Payne's adoration, and if she could enjoy it while she performed her duties and after she had made known to Payne her position on the limits of friendship, who can blame her? The sneering of Sanborn, the smirking of Gribble, and the Trelawnyean ferocity of Massingham have injured the name of a good and brave woman; the levity and unsound scholarship of these authors should not go unchallenged.[11]

[11] It is regrettable that Payne's letters to Mary cannot conveniently be included in these volumes, for they are necessary to a full understanding of the course of the friendship between Payne and Mary. These letters can be found in the *Romance*. Unfortunately, that volume is not edited with the care so important a collection deserves. Many of the letters are improperly dated. The staff of the Huntington Library (where the MSS now are) have taken great pains to date the letters, and I have also wrestled with the problem of dating them. The results of this double effort to put them in their proper order will, it is hoped, be found to be at least an improvement over the *Romance*. That there are no errors remaining is too much even to be hoped for.

Mary Shelley's Second Defense of Velluti[1]

Sir

It can only be considered as a continuation and a summing up of the letter I had before the honour to address to you, if I now add to what I then said on the subject of Velluti, the conclusions drawn from an attendance at his benefit on Thursday night [June 22, 1826].

Madame de Staël has observed, that there are many things, and those among the most lovely and delightful in the world, which unless we admire with enthusiasm we do not admire at all: we must be, as it were, instinctively attracted and charmed, or the spell is wholly without avail, and there is no medium between fervent admiration and cold distaste. From the extreme contrariety of sentiments expressed concerning the subject of this letter, it would seem that he is thus circumstanced; so that it is merely justice that when his censurers are so eager to come forward to express their disapprobation, that his admirers should be permitted to record their approval with that zeal which this accomplished singer has found means to inspire. Having however already expressed my opinion concerning him, an opinion, which founded on sentiments imbibed at the eye and ear, is not to be overthrown by a mere battery of words, it is needless to reiterate assertions, to be opposed by counter : assertions. Leaving therefore the general discussion to the arbitration of each individual who has heard him, I will confine my remarks to the representation of the night of the 22nd.

The opera then selected, Aureliano in Palmira, was, it seems, composed by Rossini expressly for Velluti, and brought out twelve years ago at the theatre of La Scala at Milan, and has never since been sung by him. It bears marks of its design and would be better understood in Italy, where the audience pay no attention except to particular airs, carrying on during the rest of the piece all the small talk of a private converzazione in their respective boxes, and do

---

[1] Enclosed in a letter to Charles Cowden Clarke, dated June 23 [1826]. It was not printed. See letter 262. The MS (3 pp. 4to) is in the Luther A. Brewer Collection, University of Iowa.

not labour like the audience of Thursday to attend to the heavy intermediate scenes with which the composition abounds. The house was well filled and Velluti on his appearance was greeted with an enthusiasm which did honour to the audience, and was acknowledged by him with that grace peculiar to him, and with that mixture of gentle timidity and mild consciousness of desert which always animates him. His most pleasing airs occur in the second act. I will freely allow that those who were not delighted with the soft expression and perfect taste displayed in his execution of the air "Soave immagine," can never be converts to his style. The compass of his voice was be [*sic*] particularly to be remarked in it, and the immediate transitions from his clear upper notes to the mellow sweetness of his lower ones was affected with the greatest flexibility and command of voice. It was rapturously received and that as well as the lighter movement of "Sorgete miei cari," and the terzetto "Vive saran nostr'anime" would have been encored, had not the house reluctantly yielded to manifest tokens of weakness on his part. He is labouring under a severe cough; the result we fear of our ungenial climate. But if he returns for the winter to restore his health in his native country, we trust that his friends here will secure his re:appearance in the spring, and that during next season our opera will not be deprived of its bright ornament. To avoid the usual and annoying ceremony of being called for after the piece, at the close of the finale, before the curtain fell, he came forward to make his acknowledgements to the audience. But that was not allowed to suffice and he was forced to appear again. This fervent desire to express approbation was not confined to a mere knot of partizans. It partly sprang from the general determination to protect and encourage a gifted stranger, who had been oppressed, and who yielded himself to their award: but it chiefly arose from the interest and admiration spread universally around, his critics were invisible, and the whole audience shewed themselves eager to confer upon him the honours of a well earned triumph.

Though I am afraid that I transgress my limits, yet I must add one word more. I would ask why so much carelessness has been shewn in the getting up of the piece, the more remarkable from its contrast with the perfection which Medèa was first exhibited. Velluti is not to be blamed for this. He has been indefatigable in his exertions; as one token of them he delayed his night a week, when the town was emptying, and each day must have been attended by a pecuniary loss. He also suspended his Academia for the sake of bestowing more time on its preparation; is this to be called over anxiety? If it were so, it must be attributed to the opposition which he has encountered, and is the reverse of all sordid feeling. He had wished to have the rehearsals carefully attended; but this desire excited the resentment of the gentlemen of the orchestra; they considered it an encroachment on their freedom; war was declared, and if they came it was only to disappear again, and to leave the most important *spartiti* to shift for themselves. I believe that of all little worlds, the little world of the Italian Opera House is without exception the most perfect specimen of the evils of anarchy.

I am, Sir, Your obedient Servant,
Anglo : Iatalicus.

Londone 23. June. 1826.

Mary Shelley's Last Illness and Death[1]

1. *Sir Percy Florence Shelley to Mrs. Isabel Booth*

Dear Mrs. Booth

On your second letter arriving my mother asked me to write to you. She has been very ill indeed, and is still in the same state. She had been attended till within the last fortnight by a homeopathic doctor—who did not do her the least good—and at last—last Saturday week—she got a numbness in her left leg, which gradually increased to paralysis— She is ordered not to read or write, so that she did not read your last letter. The medical people look very favourably on her case—but of course we are very anxious indeed. I will let you know directly [if] any change for the better takes place which I hope will be soon.

At one time her speech was a little affected but that has entirely gone off. I hope you are well. I hear good accounts of the weather in the North. Here it is very bad—the thermometer has been at 60 for the last ten days—and this state of heat is very prejudicial to my mother's complaint. Pray remember me to Catharine

Believe me
Yours faithfully
Percy Shelley

24 Chester Square
Jan. 3, 1851

2. *Sir Percy Florence Shelley to Mrs. Isabel Booth*

Dear Mrs. Booth,

I write a hurried note to tell you that my mother is still very much in the same state. The Doctors are very sanguine about her—and as she is no worse—

---

[1] The three letters by Sir Percy Florence Shelley to Mrs. Booth are in the Bodleian Library (MS Shelley Adds. d.5, ff.105–106, 107–108, 109–10). I failed to make a note on the MS of the first letter; but the second is 2 pp. 8vo, and the third 3 pp. 8vo, with a heavy black border. The fourth letter (3 pp. 8vo, black border) is owned by Mr. Frank J. Hogan, Washington, D. C. The letter from Lady Jane Shelley to Alexander Berry was owned by the late Mr. Alexander Hay of Coolangatta, N.S.W., Australia.

they think it tantamount to being better. We are very much obliged to you for your offer of coming up—but there is no danger now, so I should not at all like you to make so long a journey—When my mother is well we shall be very glad indeed to see you

Yours sincerely
Percy Shelley

[P.S.] I will send you another bulletin soon.

3. *Sir Percy Florence Shelley to Mrs. Isabel Booth*

My dear Mrs. Booth—

You will be very much shocked to hear that my dear mother died last Saturday [February 1]. Her illness puzzled the doctors so long, and presented so many different appearances that they could not make out what was the matter with her. At one time before and some time after I last wrote to you I was very hopeful about her—but about a fortnight ago she had a succession of fits, which ended in a sort of stupor in which she remained for a week—without any sign of life but her breathing which gradually ceased without any pain. And now she has left us most mournful and wretched.

One morning sometime before she was very ill she made her wishes known to us—and though she has left no will, still I shall be glad to comply with them. She wished you to have £50 per annum, and also that you should have a suit of mourning sent you. In a short time, as soon as her affairs are arranged—which will be in about a fortnight from this time—I will send you £25—as the first half year which will date from the 1st Feb. 1851, and as I could not send you things to fit I think it better to send you £10 that you may provide yourself with mourning if you think fit. I hope at some future time to have the pleasure of seeing you again.

Ever yours faithfully
Percy Shelley

4. *Sir Percy Florence Shelley to Leigh Hunt*

My dear Hunt—

I am sure that you will be much grieved to hear that my dear mother died last Saturday night. I will write by & bye and tell you more of it. I had intended writing to you before—but I have been unable to do so, and now you are one of very few that I have written to.

I assure you I am quite unconscious of the irritability on the part of my mother that you allude to. She and I had ordered the "journal" some time previous to it's appearance—and have been subscribers to it to the present time   unfortunately I have not had much time or inclination during the last few weeks to read any thing—you may be assured that my mother did and I always shall think everything good of you

Yours affectionately
Percy Shelley

24 Chester Square
  Feb. 6 1851

[P.S.] I leave London tomorrow—we have given up this house now—& do not intend to live in London again—but whenever I come I shall be glad when you can manage it to see you again—

5. *Lady Jane Shelley to Alexander Berry*

| I send an Athenæum newspaper— | 24 Chester Square
March 7th 1851 |

Dear Mr. Berry

I trust the newspapers may not have already acquainted you with the sad intelligence I have taken upon myself to communicate to you—

Five weeks ago dear Mrs. Shelley breathed her last—

She had been for some weeks suffering greatly from pains in her head & from what appeared the entire destruction of the nervous system—at last paralysis gradually came on & we were naturally greatly alarmed—Dr. Bright whom we called in thought seriously of her from the first & considered that paralysis had been caused by something going wrong in the brain— Alas! it was too true— On the 23rd of January she was seized with a fit after which she fell into a kind of stupor in which she remained eight whole days—apparently not suffering, thank God—and on the first of February with those she had dearly loved and who idolized her standing by her side, her sweet gentle spirit passed away without even a sigh—

I have undertaken to write to you on this occasion for I was anxious to spare my dear Percy the pain of doing so— Our sorrow is a terrible one!— No mother & son were ever bound together by such ties of love as my husband and such a mother as she had been to him, and to myself the loss is indeed a fearful one— For three years she had been to me more than a mother, sister friend—my daily & hourly companion—it was impossible for any living thing to approach her & not love her & Heaven knows no words can express what my love for her was— Some weeks before her death she felt convinced she could not recover, & had then told me all her wishes— It was her desire to be buried by her father & mother who were laid in St. Pancras Churchyard— however it would have broken my heart to let her loveliness wither in such a dreadful place—we have therefore removed them to a vault in the churchyard at Bournemouth, a lovely spot in Hampshire & about a mile from a little place

359

we have taken & which we intend to make our future residence— There she rests with her father on one side of her & her mother on the other, & in a year or two should we be spared, we intend to make a pilgrimage to Rome to bring home the Urn containing the ashes of her beloved husband which we shall place in her grave—

We have left Field Place, forever I hope, and this house we have sold—& have taken a very small but very pretty little place quite on the Coast—and so near the resting place of our beloved one that my own hands can tend the flowers around her grave— Should you ever return to old England, I hope you will come & see us there & we will do our best to make you happy & at all events can promise a warm welcome— My poor Percy has suffered greatly & I am very anxious to take him into the country, where we hope to go this next week— Our future address will be

Boscombe Lodge
Christchurch
Hants

Believe me dear Mr. Berry

Yrs. very truly
Jane Shelley

[P.S.] Sir Percy desires all kind regards.

Owners of the Original Letters[1]

(By Letter Numbers)

Lord Abinger: 147, 161, 305
Bibliothèque et Musée Calvert d'Avignon: 304
Frank B. Bemis Collection: 2
Bodleian Library: 1, 3–5, 17, 20, 21, 29, 32–42, 45, 50, 52–55, 57–59, 61–63, 66–71, 74, 76, 77, 79–84, 87–94, 96–100, 103, 104, 106, 108, 117, 120, 122, 126, 127, 130–32, 135, 137, 141, 143, 145, 146, 150, 155, 159, 184 (a copy ?), 188, 190, 196, 266, 279, 352, 429, 503, 530, 568, 594, 596, 664
Boston Public Library: 261, 263
British Museum: 102, 112, 192 (part in Huntington Library), 203, 221, 334, 407, 409, 410, 416, 450, 473, 484, 491, 512, 513, 522, 582, 586, 642, 655, 665, 671. Ashley Library of Mr. Thomas J. Wise: 109, 144, 257, 260, 312, 525, 551, 592, 606, 616, 634, 644, 649, 693
Lady Dorothea Charnwood: 73, 510
Mr. J. H. Coste: 519, 538
Duke University Library: 497
Harvard University Library: 291, 487, 490
Mr. Alexander Hay: 501, 619, 654, 658, 668, 678, 682
Mr. Frank J. Hogan: 178, 660, 677
Captain R. J. J. Hogg: 6–16, 169, 198, 205, 210, 217, 218, 220, 343, 483, 488, 489, 577
Henry E. Huntington Library: 24–28, 49, 51, 64, 65, 72, 75, 78, 85, 95, 101, 107, 192 (part in British Museum), 193, 204, 209, 226–56, 258, 265, 269, 275, 288, 295, 296, 308, 318, 322, 323, 326, 328, 330, 332, 333, 335, 337, 351, 375, 383, 441, 455, 464, 475, 477, 478, 486, 496, 502, 507, 511, 516, 517, 521, 524, 526–28, 531–33, 535–37, 539–41, 544–50, 552–55, 558, 559, 561–67, 569, 571, 573, 575, 578, 579, 581, 583, 584, 591, 593, 597–605, 607–15, 617, 618, 629–33, 635, 636, 639, 641, 647, 650, 659, 663, 666, 667, 670, 674, 675, 679, 684–92, 694, 696–98
University of Iowa Library, Luther A. Brewer Collection: 31, 262, 481, 508, 518, 556, 557, 587, 588, 648, 676
Jacquemont Family Archives: 311

[1] In this list all booksellers have been omitted. Those permitting me to use letters in their possession are listed in the Acknowledgments and in the record after each letter concerned. Letters owned by private persons are also liable to change hands at any time. In fact, the Bemis, Newton, Hay, Walpole, and Wise letters have already met with varying fortunes since the deaths of their owners.

Keats Museum, Hampstead: 415
Keats Shelley Memorial, Rome, Italy: 138, 142, 214, 224, 329, 426, 433, 463
Miss Kelsall: 211
Pierpont Morgan Library: 170, 180, 223, 270, 393, 402
Sir John Murray: 23, 56, 153, 154, 156, 157, 160, 164, 165, 168, 171–74, 176, 181,
    212, 213, 298, 313, 317, 339, 341, 347, 349, 354–58, 360, 363, 367, 369, 370,
    373, 390, 403, 404, 430, 443, 444, 515 (*also* Appendix I, Nos. 4, 5)
A. Edward Newton Collection: 48, 110
New York Public Library: 382. Henry W. and Albert A. Berg Collection: 148,
    271, 499, 509, 560, 574, 621–28, 638, 651–53
Miss Sylva Norman: 345, 378, 438
Historical Society of Pennsylvania Library: 272, 289, 290, 292, 366, 374
Mr. Carl H. Pforzheimer: 30, 46, 116, 589
Preussische Staatsbibliotheke: 662
Dr. Herman T. Radin: 377, 661
Biblioteca del Risorgimento, Rome, Italy: 445, 446
Roe-Byron Collection, Newstead Abbey: 590
John Rylands Library: 405
National Library of Scotland: 680
Sir John C. E. Shelley-Rolls: 163, 167, 175, 177, 179, 186, 189, 194, 195, 199, 201,
    202, 206, 215, 216, 219, 222, 225, 267, 280–82, 285–87, 293, 297, 299, 301, 302,
    306, 307, 309, 314–16, 319–21, 325, 336, 338, 340, 346, 359, 361, 362, 364, 365,
    368, 371, 376, 380, 381, 384–86, 388, 391, 392, 394–401, 406, 408, 411–14,
    417–25, 428, 431, 432, 434, 436, 437, 439, 440, 442, 448, 449, 452, 457–62, 467,
    468, 471, 472, 494, 495, 669, 681, 683, 695, 699–705
University of Texas Library, Miriam E. Stark Collection: 22, 121, 124, 324, 353,
    480, 534, 576
Trinity College Library, Cambridge University: 656
Alexander Turnbull Library, Wellington, New Zealand: 504, 505
Sir Horace Walpole: 331 (*also* Appendix I, No. 33)
Dr. Williams Library: 466
Williams College Library, Chapin Collection: 274
Mr. Thomas J. Wise: (*See* British Museum.)
Owen D. Young Collection (now in Berg Collection, New York Public Library):
    672, 673

Table of Correspondents

(With Letter Numbers)

Bartlett, Mrs.: 279

Baxter, Christie: 43 (*see also* Appendix I, No. 41)

Baxter, Isabel: *see* I. B. Booth

Baxter, Wm. T.: 44, 46, 47 (*see also* Appendix I, No. 41)

Berry, Alexander: 619, 654, 658, 668, 678, 682

Berry, Mrs. Alexander: 501

Blewitt, Mr.: 672 A, 672 B

Booth, Isabel Baxter: 309 (*see also* Appendix I, No. 2, 36)

Bowring, Sir John: 260, 308, 326, 330, 332, 333, 335, 337, 351, 455, 475, 477, 478

Brooke, A.: Appendix I, No. 42

Bulwer, Edward: 479

Byron, Lord: 23, 56, 153, 154, 156, 157, 160, 164, 165, 168, 171–74, 176, 181, 184 (*see also* Appendix I, No. 4)

Campbell, Thomas: 310

Cini, Nerina Mason: 595

Clairmont, Claire: 109, 110, 116, 121, 133, 148, 162, 526–28, 531–33, 535–37, 539–41, 543–48, 550, 552–54, 558, 559, 561–67, 569, 571, 573–75, 578, 579, 581, 583, 584, 590–93, 597–609, 611–18, 629–36, 639–41, 647, 649, 650, 659, 663, 666, 667, 670, 674, 675, 679, 684–94, 696–98

Clarke, Charles Cowden: 262

Colburn, Henry: 269, 270, 344, 469 (*see also* Appendix I, No. 19)

Curran, Amelia: 71, 74, 84, 97, 99, 122, 141, 143, 222

Editor, An: 266

Galignani, W.: 324, 353

Galloni, M.: 529

Gaskell, Mrs.: Appendix I, No. 30

Gibson, Mrs. Milner-: *see* Milner-Gibson

Gisborne, John: 92, 94, 103

Gisborne, Maria: 52–55, 59, 63, 67–70, 76, 79–83, 87–91, 93, 94, 96, 98, 100, 104–106, 108, 111–14, 117, 118, 120, 123, 125, 126, 129, 130, 132, 135, 136, 139, 144, 145, 150, 155, 159, 177, 410, 424, 437, 439, 440, 442, 448, 457–59, 461 (*see also* Appendix I, No. 40)

Godwin, William: 45 (*see also* Appendix I, No. 6)

Gregson, John: 395–401, 406, 408, 411, 412, 414, 417–23, 428, 431, 432, 434, 460, 462, 467, 468, 683

Guiccioli, Countess: Appendix I, No. 5

Halford, Mr.: 661

Hammond, Marianna: 549, 580

Hanson, John: 212, 213

Hays, Mary: 465

Hayward, Abraham: 487, 515, 520, 523, 572, (*see also* Appendix I, No. 25)

Hazlitt, William, Jr.: 470

Hessey, J. A.: 207

Hogg, T. J.: 6–16, 147, 169, 198, 205, 210, 217, 218, 220, 343, 483, 488, 489, 577

Hogg, Mrs. T. J.: *see* Jane Williams

Holcroft, Louisa: 197, 223

Hookham, Thomas: 621–28, 651–53

Hoppner, Mrs. R. B.: 128

Hudson, J. C.: 464

Hunt, Leigh: 24, 26, 28, 30, 48, 49, 51, 60, 65, 75, 77, 95, 101, 107, 119, 131, 137, 140, 186, 188–90, 192–96, 199, 202, 204, 215, 216, 225, 243, 257, 265, 267, 441, 473, 476, 485, 486, 502, 507–13, 517, 518, 521, 530, 534, 542, 557, 576, 586–88, 594, 596, 637, 645, 648, 660, 664, 665, 669, 671 (*see also* Appendix I, No. 3, 32, 43)

Hunt, Marianne: 22, 25, 27, 28, 30, 31, 49, 51, 64, 72, 73, 78, 85, 102, 131, 134, 186, 192, 201, 209, 219, 522, 568, 582, 596, 655

Jacquemont, Victor: 311

Jerrold, Douglas: 438

Jewsbury, Maria: 366

Jones, Mrs.: 500

Kelsall, Thomas F.: 211

Kenney, James: 327

Knox, A. A.: 610

Lamb, Mary: 283

Landor, W. S.: 646

Lewes, G. H.: 480

Manners-Sutton, Mrs.: 402

Mantell, Gideon A.: 504, 505

Mason, Nerina: *see* N. M. Cini

Matthews, Mrs.: Appendix I, No. 35

Medwin, Thomas: 138, 142, 643

Mérimée, Prosper: 304

Mignot, Mr.: 447

Milner-Gibson, Mrs.: 656

Milnes, R. M.: 662

Moore, Thomas: 492, 572 A

Morgan, Sydney Owenson, Lady: 482

Moxon, Edward: 494, 495, 497, 499, 506, 514, 524, 525, 555, 556, 560, 585, 638 (*see also* Appendix I, No. 28, 29, 36)

Murray, John: 273, 298, 303, 313, 317, 339, 341, 347, 349, 354–58, 360, 363, 367, 369, 370, 373, 390, 403, 404, 407, 415, 430, 443, 444

Nicolls, Mrs.: *see* Mary Peacock

Novello, Vincent: 203, 300
Novello, Mrs. Vincent: 221
Ollier, Charles: 200, 274, 345, 348, 350, 352, 377, 378, 382, 393, 426, 427, 429, 433, 435, 450, 451, 484, 491, 516 (*see also* Appendix I, No. 7, 11, 20, 21)
Owen, Robert Dale: 292, 374
Owenson, Sydney: *see* Lady Morgan
Parke, John: 146
Payne, John Howard: 226–42, 244–56, 258, 259, 261, 263, 264, 271, 272, 275, 277, 284, 288–91, 295, 296, 318, 322, 328, 375, 383 (*see also* Appendix I, No. 8–10, 12–15, 17, 18)
Peacock, Mary: 493, 496, 503, 676
Peacock, T. L.: 50, 57, 58, 61, 62, 66, 115, 151, 699
Perry, Mr.: Appendix I, No. 23
Portman, George W.: 294
Procter, B. W.: 208
Redding, Cyrus: 323
Reynolds, Frederic M.: 334, 409
Roberts, Captain Daniel: 178
Robinson, Charles: 677
Robinson, H. C.: 466
Rossetti, Gabriele: 445, 446
Rothwell, Richard: 481
Saunders, Mrs.: 170
Scott, Sir Walter: 331 (*see also* Appendix I, No. 33)
Severn, Joseph: 570, 589
Shelley, P. B.: 1–5, 17, 20, 21, 29, 32–42, 127 (*see also* Appendix I, No. 1)
Shelley, Sir Timothy: 280, 362
Stacey, Sophia: 86 (*see also* Appendix I, No. 39)
Stanhope, Mrs.: 498
Sumner, Charles: 490
Taaffe, John: 124
Thomas, Mrs.: 166, 180
Thompson, Mr.: Appendix I, No. 34
Touchet, Mr.: 695, 702, 703, 705
Trelawny, E. J.: 158, 163, 167, 175, 179, 182, 206, 224, 276, 278, 329, 336, 346, 372, 379, 387, 389, 391, 392, 413, 425, 436, 449, 452–54, 456, 463, 471, 472, 474
Trelawny, Mrs. E. J.: 681, 700, 701, 704
Unidentified: 18, 19, 342, 620, 642, 657, 672, 673, 680 (*see also* Appendix I, No. 16, 22, 24, 26, 27, 31)
Via Reggio, Authorities at: 149
Watts, Alaric A.: 268, 405
Whitton, William: 281, 282, 285–87, 293, 299, 301, 302, 306, 307, 314–16, 319–21, 325, 338, 340, 359, 361, 364, 365, 368, 371, 376, 380, 381, 384–86, 388, 394
Williams, Jane: 152, 161, 183, 185, 187, 191, 297, 305, 312, 416, 551, 644 (*see also* Appendix I, No. 37)
Wollstonecraft, Everina: 519, 538

Index

See Appendix VI, Table of Correspondents, volume II, page 363,

for letters indexed under names of addressees.

A

Abercromby, James: II, 93 n

Abinger, Lord: I, *vii, xxvi* n; II, 345

A'Court, Sir W.: I, 148

Adams, J. Q.: I, *x*

Adelaide, Queen of England: II, 91

Æschylus: I, 126

Aimée (daughter of Elise [Foggi]): I, 26 & n, 49 & n

Albany, Countess of: II, 95 & n, 96

Aldridge, Emily: II, 309, 339

Aldridge, Mrs. (*née* Caroline Beauclerc): II, 24, 41, 334

Alexander, Dr. (Byron's physician): I, 217

Alfieri, Count Vittorio: I, 232; II, 93 n, 94 & n, 95 & n, 96, 106 n

Ali Pashaw: I, 125, 164

Althart, Bessy: II, 282, 294

Alvanley, Lord: II, 91

Ambrogetti, Giuseppe: I, 295

Amory, Mr. (Mrs. Shelley's solicitor): I, 358 & n, 360 & n; II, 48, 221, 223, 304

Anacreon: I, 76

Anderloni (engraver): II, 212

Angeli, Mrs. Helen Rossetti: I, *x*, 88 n, 92 n, 117 n, 190 n; in bibliographical notes, I, 100, 130, 168

Annunziata: I, 108, 109, 112

Antonio (servant of Countess Guiccioli): I, 163 n, 167, 169

Arblay, d', Mme.: *see* Burney, Fanny

Argiropoli, Princess: I, 125 n, 137, 161

Ariosto: I, 53, 54, 55, 56, 60, 227; II, 90 & n, 92, 99, 108

Armstrong, James: II, 152 n

Ashton, Mr.: I, 135

Aspiwall, Col.: I, 365

Athenæum, the: II, 131 n, 143 & n, 336 n; in bibliographical notes, I, 157, 342

Austen, Jane: II, 133

Autographic Mirror, the: in bibliographical note, II, 22

Ayrton, Mr.: II, 116

Azzioli: I, 85

B

Bacciochi, Signor: II, 155, 171

Bacon, Francis: I, 120

Bailey, Mr.: II, 249

Baird, Mrs. (sister of Jane Williams): I, 291

Baloschi, Signor: II, 245

Bandeloni, Signor (Claire's music master): I, 79

Barff, Samuel: II, 50

Baring, George: II, 36

Baroni, Sig. Stephano: I, 196 n

Barretts, the: II, 111

Barry, Charles F.: I, 291 n

Bartolo: I, 295

Baxter, Isabel: *see* Booth, Isabel Baxter

Baxter, Mr. W. T.: I, 5 n, 30, 32, 39, 44; admiration of Shelley, I, 30 n, 32

Beauchamp, Robert Farthing: I, 206 & n

Beauclerc, Aubrey, Jr.: II, 334

Beauclerc, Aubrey William: I, 378 n; II, 193, 204 n, 281, 334, 339

Beauclerc, Augusta: II, 334

Beauclerc, Caroline: *see* Mrs. Aldridge

Beauclerc, Charles: II, 312

Beauclerc, Charlotte: II, 334

Beauclerc, Ida (first wife of Aubrey William Beauclerc): II, 193

Beauclerc, Major: II, 72, 73, 81

Beauclerc, Miney: II, 334

Beauclerc, Mrs.: I, *xxxii,* 156 n, 166 n, 167; II, 24, 49 & n, 74, 230

Beauclerc, Rosa (second wife of Aubrey William Beauclerc); *see* Robinson, Rosa

Beddoes, Thomas Lovell: I, 264 n, 292, 297 & n, 302 & n

Bedford, Duchess of: II, 145

Beethoven, Ludwig von: I, 268

Begnis, Claudine de: I, 295, 328, 343 & n

Begnis, M.: I, 295

Bell, Mr. (English surgeon in Rome): I, 72, 75 & n

Bellini, Vincenzo: II, 322 n

Bennet: II, 329

Bennett, Grey: I, 125

Bennet, Miss (*or* Mrs.): II, 133

Bennett, Mrs.: II, 118 & n

Bentham, Mr.: II, 63, 107

Bentivoglio, Signor: II, 180

Bentley, Richard: I, 371 n; II, 26, 45, 52 n, 72 n, 75, 102, 144

Berghersh, Lady: II, 74

Berkeley, Col.: I, 311 n

Bernardini, Marchesa Eleonora: I, 127 & n, 128

Berni, Francesco: II, 90 n

Berry, Alexander: I, *xxxii;* II, 135 & n, 245, 294, 313 & n, 357 n

Berry, Mrs. Alexander (*née* Elizabeth Wollstonecraft): I, *xxxii;* II, 135 n, 245, 261, 262, 296, 299, 313 & n

Bethune, Mr.: II, 310

Biagi, Dr. Guido: I, 196 n

Bielby, J.: I, 56

Biondi, Luigi: I, 160 & n

Birbeck, Morris: I, 82 & n

Blackwood's Edinburgh Magazine: review of *Alastor* and general attitude toward Shelley, I, 90 & n

Blessington, Lady: II, 66, 103

Blessington, Lord: I, 291 & n

Blood, Mrs.: II, 146

Bloomfield, Captain: I, 136

Blunden, Edmund: I, *x,* 121 n

Boccaccio: I, 77, 117, 227; II, 83, 90 n

Boccella, Marchesa Jane: II, 51 n, 74 & n, 80

Bodleian Quarterly Record: I, *xxvii;* in bibliographical notes, I, 54, 55, 61, 63, 70, 72, 80, 83, 87, 88, 90, 92, 93, 94, 101, 102, 103, 104, 105, 106, 107, 110, 112, 115, 120, 121, 126, 135, 138, 143, 196, 200, 207, 241, 348, 358; II, 28, 76, 156, 210, 234, 235, 303

Boinville, Mrs.: I, 66 & n; II, 126 n, 147 n, 150, 151 n, 160, 163 n, 201, 250, 272

Boinville, Alfred: I, 66 & n

Boinville, Cornelia: *see* Turner, Cornelia

Boissy, Marquis Hilaire de: II, 148 n

Bojardo, Matteo: II, 90 n

Bojti, Professor: I, 126 n, 151 n

Bolingbroke, Lord: II, 318

Booth, Catharine: I, 378; II, 357

Booth, David: I, 5 n, 30 & n, 32, 46, 378

Booth, Isabel: I, 378

Booth, Isabel Baxter (Mrs. David): I, 5 & **n**, 30 & n, 31 n, 32, 45, 46, 262 & n; II, 3 & n, 304, 310, 351, 357 n

Boscán Almogaver, Juan: II, 104 n, 123 & n, 124

Bostock: II, 329

Boswell, James: I, 228; II, 92

Bouboukine, Mr.: II, 250

Boutoulin, Mme.: II, 181

Bowen, Captain John: I, 131

Bowring, Sir John: I, *xxx,* 300 & n, 316 n, 317, 339, 340, 342 n; II, 19 n, 27 n, 63 & n, 351

Boyd, Julian P.: I, *x*

Breredon, Mrs.: II, 81

Brett, Mr.: II, 153, 154, 157 & n, 243

Brewster, Sir David: II, 106 n, 108

Bridgwater, Lieutenant Colonel: I, 255 n

Bright, Dr.: II, 359

Broglie, Duc de: II, 31

Brookes, Mr. (banker): I, 165

Brookes, Mr.: II, 129

Brough, William and Robert B.: I, 259 n

Brougham, Lord: II, 51, 84, 86, 93, 105, 215, 253

Broughtons, the: I, 225

Brown, Charles Armitage: I, 69 n, 211 & n, 252, 282; II, 12 n, 40

Brown, Charles Brockden: I, 335 & n, 336, 337

Brown, John: I, 25 n

Brown, Ralph: I, *x*

Browne, Hamilton: I, 289 & n, 290, 291, 314

Browning, Elizabeth: II, 173 n

Browning, Robert: II, 173 n, 263 n

Bruce, Mrs.: II, 180

Brugière, Amable G. P., Baron de Barante: II, 17 & n

Brunelli, Mr.: I, 175 n, 215

Bryant, the Misses: I, 257 & n

Buchanan, George: II, 15 & n

Buchon, M.: II, 148

Budd, Dr.: II, 110

Budd, Mr.: II, 97, 98

Buller, Charles: II, 325 & n

Bulwer, Sir Henry: II, 147

Bulwer-Lytton, Edward George Earle Lytton, First Baron Lytton: II, 40, 43 & n, 52 n, 66 & n, 79 & n, 84, 117 n, 121, 320 & n; on Shelley, II, 284 & n

Bulwer-Lytton, Mrs.: II, 79

Burdett, Miss: II, 41

Burdett, Sir Francis: I, 125

Burgass, Mr.: II, 154, 294

Burgess, Rev. Richard: I, 190 n

Burhel, Mr.: II, 300

Burley, John: II, 80 & n

Burney, Charles: I, 259

Burney, Dr. Charles: II, 93

Burney, Fanny (Mme. d'Arblay): I, 213; II, 93

Burns, Robert: quoted, I, 356

Bury, Lady Charlotte Maria: I, 346; II, 26 n

Butler, Mrs. Pierce: *see* Kemble, Fanny

Butler, Pierce: II, 81 n

Byron, G.: I, *xxxi;* II, 263 & n, 265, 270; his Shelley letters, II, 263–70 & n, 294–96

Byron, George Gordon, Lord: I, *vi, xxix,* 13 n, 14 n, 18 n, 25 n, 26 & n, 27, 36, 37 & n, 43, 50 n, 53, 56 n, 57 n, 59 n, 67 n, 69, 79 n, 82 & n, 103 n, 106 n, 128, 144 n, 149, 152, 155 n, 158, 160, 161, 162 & n, 163, 165, 166, 167, 168, 169 n, 170, 182, 183, 185, 188, 191 n, 192 n, 193 & n, 195 n, 198 n, 199 n, 200 & n, 203, 204, 210, 217 & n, 218 n, 236, 247, 250, 258, 260 & n, 262, 268, 278, 285, 291 & n, 297 n, 310, 311, 314, 315, 317, 333, 338, 345, 348 & n, 371 & n, 376; II, 17, 24, 29, 49, 57, 58 & n, 59, 76, 92, 102, 124, 143, 191, 213, 230, 345; dissipation in Venice, I, 67, 70; ascription of *Vampyre* to, I, 70 & n; Claire wishes to remove Allegra from, I, 140–41; Mary's opinion of, I, 140, 141, 208, 265; II, 29; and the Hoppner scandal, I, 146 n, 147 & n, 149; takes Casa Lanfranchi, I, 150 & n; and Hunt, I, 151 n, 153, 200–203 & n; the Bolivar, I, 155 & n, 189; and Allegra's death, I, 169; and the name of Shelley's boat, I, 170 n, 171; services to Mary, I, 195, 208 & n, 212, 213 & n, 215 & n, 217 n, 218, 220, 224, 229; and the Greek expedition, I, 225, 226, 228, 231, 236, 246 & n, 265, 304 n; his wager with Shelley, I, 229 & n; and J. Hunt's trial, I, 286 n, 301–302; death and funeral, I, 292 & n, 294, 297, 298 & n, 299, 301 & n; burning of memoirs, I, 298; Med-

win's *Conversations*, I, 308 & n, 315; Moore's life of, I, 298–99, 313 & n, 371 n; II, 13 n, 24, 25, 28–29, 30, 31, 34, 35, 37, 60; plan for performance of *Othello*, I, 316; characters in his poems, II, 60–61; influence of environment on poems, II, 61; mode of composition, II, 61; and Shelley's will, II, 234 & n

——, Works: *Childe Harold,* I, 25 & n; *Manfred,* I, 26 & n; *Beppo,* I, 49, 50; *Don Juan,* I, 70 & n, 198 & n, 251, 290; II, 36; *Cain,* I, 150, 153; *Vision of Judgment,* I, 198 & n; *Heaven and Earth,* I, 212

Byron, Lady Annabella: I, 298

C

Calderon: I, 120; II, 89, 104 n

Cam, Mr.: I, 16

Camoens: II, 104 n, 122

Campbell, James: II, 272, 273, 300, 316, 317, 331, 332, 339, 340

Campbell, Lady Dorothea: II, 74, 231, 236, 239, 271

Campbell, Louisa: II, 183, 186

Campbell, Nanky (daughter of Lady Dorothea): II, 231

Campbell, Thomas: I, *xxxii;* II, 10 n, 113 n, 133, 137, 138

Campbell, William: II, 163, 208, 213, 272, 276, 322

Campetti, Æsop: I, 131–32

Camporese, Mme. Violante (*misspelled by Mary* Camporeri): I, 48, 51

Canning, George: I, 290; II, 93; refers to *Frankenstein,* I, 291

Canova, Antonio: I, 27

Canterbury, Lady: *see* Manners-Sutton, Mrs. Charles

Caradja, Prince: I, 125 n, 137

Caradori, Mme.: I, 294

Carlisle, Henry E.: in bibliographical note, II, 149

Carlyle, Mrs. Thomas: II, 140

Carlyle, Thomas: II, 141 & n

Caroline, Queen of England: I, 114 n, 116–17 & n, 121 n

Carter, Mrs.: I, 364

Cartin: I, 252

Castellani, Signor: I, 61

Castillejo, Christoval de: II, 104 n

Castlereagh, Lord: I, 96 n, 97, 98

Catalini, Angelica: I, 295

Caunter, Mr.: II, 113 n

Cervantes: II, 104 n, 122

Chamberlayne, Lady: II, 111

Chapman, R. W.: I, *x*

Charlemont, Lady: II, 60

Charnwood, Lady Dorothea: I, *x;* in bibliographical notes, I, 78; II, 141

Charters (coachmaker): I, 3 n

Chaworth, Mary: II, 60

Chiabrere (Chiabrera), Gabriello: II, 106 n

Cini, Bartolomeo: II, 80 n, 84

Cini, Signora Bartolomeo: *see* Mason, Nerina

Clairmont, Allegra (*or* Alba): I, 18 n, 23, 26
& n, 28 & n, 30, 31, 33, 34 & n, 35, 36, 37,
38, 39, 40, 41, 42, 43, 44, 47, 56 n, 57 n, 59,
79 & n, 140 n, 146 n, 149, 317; II, 218 n;
birth, I, 18; compared to Fanny Imlay, I, 39;
christened, I, 47 n; sent to Venice, I, 52 & n;
in care of Hoppners, I, 58 n, 67 & n; in convent, I, 140–41; death, I, 169–70 & n; grave,
I, 198 & n

Clairmont, Charles: I, 3 n, 26 & n, 80 & n, 87
& n, 92 & n, 191 n, 194, 211; II, 24, 41 & n,
52, 213, 226, 248 & n, 249, 250, 251 n, 277
& n, 293, 320, 323, 327 n, 330 n

Clairmont, Claire (*also* Jane *and* Clare): I, *vi,
xxix, xxx, xxxi, xxxii,* 3 n, 5 n, 7 n, 8, 13 n,
14 & n, 15, 16, 17, 20, 22, 23, 24, 26 & n,
27, 28 n, 29 n, 30, 31, 32, 33, 34 & n, 35,
36, 37, 38, 41, 44, 45, 46, 47 n, 49, 50, 52
& n, 53, 55, 56, 57 n, 58, 59 n, 61, 64, 69,
72 n, 79, 81, 83 & n, 86 n, 101, 102, 103,
104, 106 n, 109, 114, 118 n, 119, 121 n,
127 n, 140, 142 n, 143 & n, 146 n, 147 & n,
148, 151 & n, 155 n, 181, 187, 197, 211 n,
212, 214, 215, 243, 289, 294, 298, 303, 308,
315, 316 n, 317, 319; II, 36 & n, 41 & n, 46,
51, 52, 64 n, 80 & n, 84, 86, 91, 99 n, 106 &
n, 107, 110, 118 & n, 141, 147 n, 150, 152 n,
153 n, 193 n, 194, 219 n, 251 & n, 252, 278 n,
287 & n, 289 n, 304 n, 308, 319 n, 346, 351;
and birth of Allegra, I, 18; on the opera at
Milan, I, 48–49 n; goes with Shelley to Venice, I, 56 & n; lessons in singing, I, 65, 77,
85, 88, 89; letter on William's illness, I, 72
& n; and Reveley, I, 83 n; portrait by Miss
Curran, I, 73 n, 111, 114 & n, 215 & n;
changes in name, I, 85 n; departure for Florence, I, 126 & n; plan to remove Allegra from
convent, I, 140–41; plan to set up a school,
I, 141; plan to leave Italy, I, 157; and the
death of Allegra, I, 169–70 & n; returns to

Florence, I, 169 n, 170; goes to Vienna, I,
191 n, 192, 194; translates Goethe, I, 192 &
n; on Mary's character, I, 216 n; in Moscow,
I, 300, 310; legacy from Shelley, I, 300; II,
218 & n, 219, 221, 223, 224, 233, 234, 235–
36; returns to Germany, II, 14, 17, 24;
stories circulated about her, II, 49 & n; article on Italy, II, 66 & n

Clairmont, Clairkin (daughter of Charles Clairmont, *also called* Clairy *and* Cleary): II, 277,
330, 331, 332

Clairmont, Tom (son of Charles Clairmont):
II, 251

Clairmont, Willy (son of Charles Clairmont):
II, 304, 327, 328, 329, 330, 331, 332

Clare, Lord: I, 203 n

Claremont, Mrs. (Mrs. Clermont, Lady Byron's governess): I, 298

Clarendon, Lord: II, 314

Clark, William (publisher of *Queen Mab*): II,
131 n

Clarke, Charles Cowden: I, *xxx,* 261 n, 268,
271, 274, 304, 309; II, 192, 354 n; in bibliographical notes, I, 372

Clarke, Mr.: I, 29

Clarke, Mrs. Charles Cowden (*née* Mary Victoria Novello): I, 261 n, 271, 309, 330, 372 n;
in bibliographical notes, 372

Claude Lorrain: I, 295

Clementis, Mr.: I, 198

Clermont, Mrs.: *see* Claremont, Mrs.

Cleveland, Henry (nephew of Jane Williams):
II, 157 & n, 160, 162, 302

Cleveland, John Wheeler (brother of Jane Williams): I, 289 n; II, 3 & n, 4, 108

Cleveland, Mrs. (mother of Jane Williams): I,
322, 326, 346; II, 92

Cobbett, William: I, 18, 37, 46, 82 & n; Mary's
comment on, quoted in *Examiner,* 41 & n

Cochrane, Lord: I, 355

Cockburn, General: I, 190 n

Cogni, Margaretta ("la Fornarina"): I, 59 & n

Colburn, Henry: I, *xxx,* 256 & n, 287, 306,
341 n, 351 n, 353, 371 n; II, 23, 26, 27, 28,
29, 31, 39 & n, 40, 45, 49, 52 n, 75, 102,
116 n, 307

Coleridge, John Taylor: I, 66 n, 90 n

Coleridge, Samuel Taylor: I, 255, 260, 269;
II, 10 n, 115, 134, 351

Collyer, Rev. William Bengo: I, 262 & n

Colnaghi (printseller): II, 212

Colonna, Vittoria: II, 106 n

Comines, Philippe de: II, 5
Constancio, Dr. Francisco Solano: II, 151 & n
Constant de Rebeque, Benjamin: II, 31, 34
Cook, Rev. W.: I, 190 n
Cooke, T. P.: I, 259
Cooper, James Fenimore: I, 321 & n; II, 39 n
Cooper, Mrs.: I, 362, 364
Cork, Lady: II, 147
Correggio: II, 164 & n
Correspondence of Leigh Hunt: I, *xxv,* 64 n, 66 n, 78 n, 138 n, 154 n, 201 n; in bibliographical notes, I, 22, 78, 125, 158, 258, 272, 350; II, 218
Coulson, Walter: I, 66 n, 271 & n, 272, 281, 284, 307; II, 206, 223, 300, 328
Courier, the: I, 97, 99
Crabbe, George: I, 260
Crawford, Mrs.: II, 79
Crawfurd, Kitty: II, 175
Crawfurds, the: II, 175
Crisnet, Mrs.: II, 286
Croker, J. W.: II, 92
Croker, Thomas Crofton: II, 7
Croly, George: I, 290 & n
Cummings, Barbara: II, 79
Curran, Amelia: I, 72 n, 73 n, 143 n, 178 n, 199, 205, 305 n, 307, 311 n; II, 179; portraits of Mary and Claire, I, 73 n, 111, 114 & n, 175 n, 215 & n; II, 336 n, 339; portrait of William, I, 73 n, 175 n, 176 n, 310; portrait of Shelley, I, 73 n, 175–77 & n, 178–79 & n, 199, 205, 215, 281, 284, 287, 297 & n, 302, 305, 310 & n; II, 10, 229 & n; and William's grave, I, 74, 79 & n, 94 & n, 110–11, 113
Curran, John Philpot: I, 43 & n, 73 n, 111 & n
Curran, William Henry: I, 111 & n
Curtis, Stephen: II, 89, 99, 109

D

Dabbitt, Miss: I, 313
Danieli, Francesco: I, 142
Dante: I, 77, 123, 129, 310; II, 90 & n, 92, 99, 108, 283
Davide, Giovanni: I, 51 & n, 128–29 & n, 249
Davidson (pawnbroker): I, 4 n
Davis, Jackson, I, *x*
Dawkins, W.: I, 166, 190, 191
Del Chiappa, Signor G. B.: I, 53 & n
Delessert, M.: II, 194 n, 251 & n, 252, 256, 271
Delicate, Signor: I, 175 n
Della Mirandola, Pico: II, 90 n

Della Robbia, Marchesa E. Viviani: I, 117 n, 118 n
Del Rosso, Federico: I, 108 & n
Denman, Lord: II, 149 & n
De Quincey, Thomas: II, 288 n
Descon, Miss: II, 151, 152, 209, 286
Desse, Mr. (Mr. Westbrook's solicitor): I, 17
Devonshire, Duke of: I, 342
Dickens, Charles: II, 141 n, 303 n; and America, 167 & n
Dillon, Lady: II, 239
Dillon, Lord: II, 98
Dionigi, Signora Marianna: I, 69 & n, 88 n
Disraeli, Benjamin: II, 43 n, 62 n
Domenichino: I, 65
Donner, H. W.: in bibliographical note, I, 297
Dorme, Lady: II, 110
Douglas, Mrs. Sholto (*née* Isabel Robinson): I, 364 & n, 365, 370, 378 & n; II, 3 & n, 120 & n
Douglas, Sholto: I, 364
Dowden, Edward: I, *xxv, xxvi,* 3 n, 15 n, 21 n, 26 n, 28 n, 29 n, 30 n, 36 n, 43 n, 53 n, 66 n, 88 n, 112 n, 117 n, 139 n, 146 n, 147 n, 170 n, 182 n, 190 n; in bibliographical notes, I, 4, 5, 6, 9, 11, 13, 15, 17, 22, 26, 30, 32, 35, 37, 40, 42, 44, 45, 47, 54, 55, 57, 70, 72, 73, 74, 78, 80, 83, 87, 88, 90, 92, 94, 105, 110, 111, 114, 121, 125, 130, 133, 134, 136, 137, 138, 139, 142, 146, 147, 150, 154, 157, 158, 161, 165, 172, 186, 225, 340; II, 251
Dowling, Mrs.: I, 313
Dowton, William: I, 267
Drake, Mr.: II, 234
Dunbar, Mrs.: II, 213
Dunlap, W.: I, 335 n
Dunn, Henry: I, 57 & n, 83, 212, 215
Dunn, Waldo H.: I, *x, xxvi* n
Dunston, Emily: II, 304 & n, 305, 321
Dunston, Sarah E.: II, 304 & n, 305
Du Plantis, Louise: I, 92 & n
Du Plantis, Mme. Merveilleux: I, 89, 92 & n
Du Plantis, Zoide: I, 90, 92 & n
Dyer, George: I, 280, 302 n, 303
Dyer, Mrs. George: I, 302 n

E

Edgcumbe, Frederick: I, *x*
Edgcumbe, Richard: I, 6 n
Edinburgh Review, the: I, 217, 307; II, 204, 265

Edwin (a servant): II, 248

Eldon, Lord: I, 19 & n, 28 & n

Eliot, George: II, 125 n

Elise (the Shelleys' Swiss maid): *see* Foggi, Elise

Elizabeth (Mrs. Gisborne's attendant): II, 82, 105, 111, 112

Elliott, Frederic: II, 79

Elliott, Mrs. Frederic (*née* Jane Perry): II, 79

Ellis, Mr.: II, 237, 238, 239, 242, 246

Elliston, Robert William: I, 254, 312, 313 n, 325; II, 344

Ercilla, Alonzo de: II, 104 n

Esdaile, Charles: II, 165 n

Esdaile, Edward Jeffries: II, 165 n

Esdaile, Mrs. Edward Jeffries: *see* Shelley, Ianthe

Esdaile, William: II, 165 n

Euripides: I, 122, 123 n

Eustace, John Chetwoode: I, 57 & n

Evans, Mr.: I, 274

Examiner, the: I, 15 & n, 19, 21 & n, 24 & n, 30, 36 n, 41 & n, 42 n, 64, 76, 80 n, 84 & n, 97, 166, 217, 250 & n, 262 n, 270, 282, 283, 287 n, 304 n, 344 n; II, 143 & n, 149, 195, 203, 209 & n, 289 n, 303, 308 & n, 354; prosecution of, I, 121 & n

F

Falconet, M.: I, 60

Farrer, Annie: II, 152, 154, 177

Farrer, Mrs.: II, 151, 152, 154, 160, 177, 185

Fascolo, Ugo: II, 106 n

Fauntleroy, Henry: I, 311 & n

Felichi, Signora: I, 56, 150

Fellowes, H. W.: I, 207 n

Fergusson, Mr.: II, 253

Ficino, Marsiglio: II, 90 n

Field, Miss: I, 141

Fielding, Henry: II, 36

Fielding, Mrs.: I, 195

Filicaja, Vincenzo da: II, 106 n

Finch, Mr.: II, 263

Finch, Rev. Robert ("Col. Calicot Finch"): I, 68–69 & n, 101, 103, 105, 109, 117 n

Finden, Edward F.: II, 58 n

Finden, William: II, 58 & n, 62, 67, 76, 92

FitzRoy, Captain Robert: II, 306

FitzRoy, Sir Charles Augustus: II, 306

Fletcher (Byron's servant): I, 298

Florrista: I, 61

Fodor, Mme.: I, 294

Foggi, Elise: I, 26 & n, 32, 34, 49 & n, 52 n; marriage to Paolo, I, 53 n, 64, 95, 148; and the Hoppner scandal, I, 146 & n, 147 & n, 149

Foggi, Paolo: I, 53 & n, 60; and Elise, I, 53 n, 64, 148; spreads scandal about Shelley, I, 108 & n, 114 & n, 126 n, 141, 148, 160

Foggi, Signor: I, 86, 93

Foote, Maria, Countess of Harrington: I, 309 & n, 311 & n, 326

Ford, John: I, 269, 371 & n

Forman, H. B.: I, *xxvi;* in bibliographical notes, 47, 155, 186, 192, 204, 211, 215, 227, 230, 232, 279, 300, 316; II, 10, 14, 25, 37, 42, 47, 50, 51, 104, 143, 289, 290

Forman, M. B.: I, *x*

Forster, John: II, 290

Foster, Mr.: II, 309

Frederickson, C. W.: in bibliographical note, I, 4

Freeborn, Mr.: I, 190 n, 191, 214; II, 183

Freeman, Betsey: II, 118

Furnivall, Frederick J.: I, 31 n

Furnivall, Dr. George Frederick: I, 31 & n, 35, 39, 41

G

Galignani, William: I, 96 n; II, 10 & n

Galignani's Messenger: I, 96 & n, 104, 113, 119 & n, 120, 280, 317; II, 10 n, 158, 159, 163, 167

Galileo: II, 106 & n, 108

Galloni, M.: II, 80 n, 153 n, 155 n, 182, 186, 195, 198, 209 & n, 214, 244

Galloni, Mme.: *see* Mason, Laura

Gamba, Count Pietro: I, 155, 162 & n, 230, 231, 246 n, 304 & n, 307, 315, 319; II, 4 & n

Garcia, Manuel: I, 295

Garnett, Mme.: I, 374

Garnett, Richard: I, *xxv;* in bibliographical notes, 155, 166, 235, 244, 263, 282, 303, 305, 308

Gaskell, D.: II, 99 & n, 107 & n, 109, 153

Gaskell, Mrs. D.: II, 99 n, 107, 153

Gatteschi, Signor: I, *xxi, xxxii;* II, 152 n, 193 & n, 194, 195, 196 n, 197, 198, 203, 204, 205, 206, 207, 211, 215, 217, 224, 226, 245, 252, 254, 255, 256, 260, 270, 271, 272, 273; contributions to *Rambles,* II, 194 n, 199 & n, 202, 224, 226; blackmails Mary, II, 194 n, 251 n, 252–61 *passim*

Genest, John: I, 311 n

George IV, King of England: I, 116 & n

Georgine, Signor: I, 127

Germains, Lady M.: II, 259

Gibbon, Edward: I, 14 n, 21

Gibson, Thomas: II, 313 n

Gifford, William: I, 26 & n, 287 & n, 371 & n

Gilbert, Creighton: I, *x;* in bibliographical note, II, 94

Ginocchio, Signor Agostino: I, 240

Gipps, Sir George: II, 299, 306, 317

Gisborne, John: I, *vi,* 51 n, 52 n, 54, 57 & n, 62, 69 n, 70, 72, 73 n, 81 n, 92, 100, 102, 103, 104, 106 n, 107, 108, 109, 110, 112, 115, 120 & n, 121, 126, 134, 138 & n, 139, 145, 150 n, 151 n, 152, 159 & n, 163 n, 165, 166, 168, 171, 196, 198, 206 n, 224, 247, 249, 259, 278, 281; II, 63 n, 65, 71, 82, 85, 86, 87, 89, 92, 96, 105, 108, 110, 351; the Shelleys' opinion of, I, 77, 81; death, II, 111 & n

Gisborne, Maria (Mrs. John): I, *vi,* 51 & n, 52 n, 54 n, 72 n, 73 n, 77, 82 n, 89 n, 90 n, 91 n, 92 n, 103 n, 105, 106, 107, 120 & n, 166, 172 n, 182 n, 197, 203 n, 206 n, 207 n, 232, 247, 249, 259, 273 & n, 278, 281 & n; II, 63 & n, 351; introduction to Shelleys, I, 51 & n; history of Mary's relations with, I, 51 n; Godwin on, I, 55; the Shelleys' opinion of, I, 77, 81; defends *Political Justice,* I, 104; return to England, I, 106 & n; return to Italy, I, 114 n; breach with Shelleys, I, 114 n, 119 & n; final return to England, I, 143 & n, 144 & n, 150 n, 151 n

Giuseppi (the Gisbornes' servant): I, 91, 93, 101, 108, 109, 112 & n

Gladstone, William Ewart: II, 299

Gliddon, Alistatia (Mrs. Arthur): I, 268 & n, 271, 274, 276, 277, 293, 301, 304, 347

Gliddon, Anne: I, 347

Gliddon, Arthur: I, 268 & n, 271, 274, 276, 293, 304, 347

Gliddon, G.: I, 274

Gliddon, Kate: II, 90

Godwin, Emily (Mrs. William, Jr.): II, 223, 244

Godwin, Mary Jane (Mrs. William): I, 4, 14 n, 15 & n, 16, 23, 26 n, 32, 35, 39, 42, 46, 112, 146 & n, 165, 245, 248, 254, 255, 261, 273 & n, 280, 313, 324, 325, 326, 336, 338, 344, 377; II, 51, 52, 74, 80, 83, 86, 88, 100, 106,

108, 113, 114, 115, 116 n, 122; her death, II, 149 & n

Godwin, William: I, *xxx,* 3 n, 4, 5 & n, 6 n, 14 n, 15 n, 16, 17, 25 & n, 30, 31, 32, 33, 35, 36, 42, 43, 44, 45, 51 n, 55, 73 n, 79, 91, 92, 102, 108, 109, 110, 111, 134, 135 & n, 136, 144, 146 & n, 154, 164, 190, 193, 195, 196, 197, 199 n, 206 n, 207, 217, 219, 221, 229, 236, 247, 248, 254, 255, 258 & n, 259, 265, 273, 287 n, 294, 302, 306, 310, 313, 315, 334, 343, 344, 364 n, 370; II, 4, 27, 30, 32 & n, 51, 58 & n, 59, 72, 73, 74, 80, 86, 89, 90, 97, 98 & n, 99, 100, 106, 108, 110, 112, 128 n, 143, 152, 191, 344, 346, 350 n, 351; Shelley's financial relations with, I, 15 & n; *Mandeville,* I, 46; on Mrs. Gisborne, I, 55; lawsuit, I, 73 & n, 172; *Political Justice,* I, 104; Shelley's request to Gisbornes for a loan to, I, 112 & n; and *Valperga,* I, 150 n, 156, 159 & n, 171; insistence on etiquette, I, 243; bankruptcy, I, 317–18; government post, II, 83 & n, 90, 91, 93; Mary's attachment to, II, 88; death, II, 112, 113, 114; burial, II, 113 & n, 114 & n; Mary Hays' letters to, II, 114; his unpublished memoirs, II, 115, 116 & n, 119; body removed to Bournemouth, II, 340 n

Godwin, William, Jr.: I, 32, 135, 164 & n, 256, 258, 259, 270, 275, 276, 277, 335, 338, 344, 352 & n; II, 64 n, 223 & n, 244 n

Goethe, Johann Wolfgang von: I, 192 & n

Goldoni, Carlo: II, 106 n, 179

Goldsmith, Oliver, quoted, II, 63 & n

Gongora y Argote, Luis de: II, 104 n

Gordon, Mr.: I, 262

Gordon, Sir Alexander and Lady Duff: II, 134

Gordon, George S.: I, *x,* 7

Gore, Catherine Frances: II, 43 n, 78 n

Gore, Cecilia: II, 193

Goring, Augusta, Lady Vane (*née* Augusta Harvey, Trelawny's third wife): II, 152 & n, 167 & n, 203, 311 n

Gott, Joseph: I, 282

Grant, Mr.: I, 191

Grawler, Captain: II, 306

Gray, Duncan: I, *x*

Gregson, John: I, *vi, xxix;* II, 53 & n, 157, 219, 220, 223, 225, 226, 227, 230, 231, 232, 233, 235, 242, 243, 244, 245, 246, 282

Grey, Captain: II, 306

Grey, Lord: II, 83 n, 280

Grey, Lord (the younger, formerly Lord Howick): II, 280, 299, 317

Gribble, Francis H.: II, 347, 353

Grisi, Giulia: II, 84

Gryffydh, Jane: *see* Peacock, Mrs. Thomas Love

Grylls, R. Glynn: I, *x, xxvii,* 58 n, 378 n; II, 347; in bibliographical notes, I, 191, 208, 375; II, 29, 62, 66, 107, 246, 298, 315

Guarini, Giovanni Battista: II, 106 n

Guggert, Dr.: II, 292, 293, 294

Guicciardini, Francesco: II, 106 n

Guiccioli, Count: II, 95 n, 96

Guiccioli, Countess Teresa: I, 150 & n, 155 & n, 162, 163, 167, 168 n, 182, 183, 188, 189, 198, 210, 215, 219, 226, 231, 270, 291, 304 n, 310, 363; II, 4, 58 & n, 73, 99, 102, 148 & n, 230

Guido Reni: I, 65

Guitera, Signor: II, 192, 193 n, 213, 215, 216, 224, 226, 229, 245, 253

Guitera, Signora: II, 213, 245

Guppy, Henry: I, *x*

H

Hackett, E. Byrne: I, *x*

Händel, Georg Friedrich: I, 241, 271, 284

Hahn-Hahn, Countess Ida Maria: II, 243 & n, 247

Hale, Mrs.: II, 111

Halford, Mr.: II, 134

Hamilton, Lady: I, 273

Hammond, Marianna ("Hammy"): II, 153 & n, 154, 156, 160, 161, 162, 172, 177, 183, 185, 193, 198, 201 n, 204, 214, 215, 217, 230, 237, 241, 245, 261

Hampden, John: I, 19

Hanson, John: I, 199 n, 207 & n, 208 & n, 215, 297 n

Hanson, Mary Anne: *see* Countess of Portsmouth

Harbottle, Mrs.: I, 141

Hare, Mr.: II, 186, 207

Hare, Mrs.: II, 41 & n, 50 n, 52, 153, 154, 157, 170, 180, 201, 203, 204, 208, 209, 215, 221, 227, 232, 243, 245, 261, 294, 321, 338

Harley, Charlotte: I, 135

Harper, Henry H.: *see Letters of Mary W. Shelley*

Harry (servant at Marlow): I, 32 & n

Harvey, Col.: *see* Hervey

Harwood, Mrs.: I, 319

Havens, Raymond D.: I, *x*

Hay, Alexander: I, *vii, ix;* II, 135 n, 357 n

Hay, Captain: I, 162 & n, 165, 291

Haydn, Joseph: I, 268, 284

Haydon, Benjamin Robert: I, 52 & n; II, 173 n

Haynes, "Pea Green": I, 311 n

Hays, Mary: letters to Godwin, II, 114

Hayward, Abraham: I, *xxxii;* II, 129 n, 143 n, 214 n

Hayward, R.: I, 14 n, 15 & n

Hazlitt, Isabella Bridgwater (William Hazlitt's second wife): I, 255 n, 303

Hazlitt, Sarah Stoddart (William Hazlitt's first wife): I, 255 n, 257, 303

Hazlitt, William: I, 25 & n, 212 & n, 255 & n, 257, 260 & n, 262 n, 268 n, 269, 270, 302 n, 303, 307, 318 & n; II, 117, 351: reviews *Posthumous Poems,* I, 307 & n

Hazlitt, William, Jr.: II, 117 n

Healy, Dennis M.: I, 376 n, 378 n; in bibliographical notes, 374, 379

Heath, Mr.: II, 62

Henley, Captain: I, 291

Henneickstein, Mme.: I, 214

Herrera, Fernando: II, 104 n, 123 & n

Hervey, Mr.: II, 207

Hervey (*or* Harvey), Col.: II, 152 & n

Heslop, Mrs.: I, 244, 246

Hessey, J. A.: I, 292 n

Hetherington, Henry: II, 149 n

Hill, R. H.: I, *x, xxvii; see also Bodleian Quarterly Record* and *The Shelley Correspondence in the Bodleian Library*

Hill, Walter M.: I, *ix*

Himmel, Friedrich Heinrich: I, 271

Hinton, Lord: II, 193

Hitchener, Elizabeth: I, 206

Hobhouse, John Cam: I, 298 & n; II, 95 & n, 233

Hodges, Mr.: I, 314

Hodgetts, the: II, 248

Hogan, Frank J.: I, *x*

Hogg, John (brother of T. J. Hogg): II, 105

Hogg, Mrs. (mother of T. J. Hogg): II, 105

Hogg, Mrs. Thomas Jefferson: *see* Williams, Jane

Hogg, Prudentia (sister of T. J. Hogg): II, 105

Hogg, Prudentia Sarah (daughter of T. J. Hogg): II, 109 n, 237

Hogg, Sarah (sister of T. J. Hogg): II, 105

Hogg, Thomas Jefferson: I, *vi, xxx–xxxi,* 17, 24, 47 n, 64, 66 n, 69 n, 96, 109, 129, 160 &

n, 168, 172, 196, 206, 207 n, 212 & n, 261, 277, 278, 281, 305 n, 351, 352 & n, 368 n; II, 4 n, 39 n, 41, 64, 72, 80 & n, 84, 86 & n, 92, 98, 103, 105, 106, 109 & n, 112, 118, 131 n, 150 & n, 157 & n, 160, 173, 290, 295, 323, 345; love letters from Mary to, I, 7 & n; Mary's dislike of, I, 7 n, 24, 66, 304, 307; and Jane Williams, I, 281 & n, 356 & n, 357; treatment of Jane, II, 162, 178, 189; in bibliographical note, II, 126

Holcroft, Ellen: I, 273, 274, 313

Holcroft, Fanny: I, 273

Holcroft, Louisa: I, 254 & n, 257, 273 n, 338; II, 348

Holcroft, Thomas: I, 254 & n; II, 191

Holcroft, Thomas, Jr.: I, 313, 314 & n, 320 n; II, 264 n, 265 n, 294, 295, 348, 349

Holland, Lord: I, 221; II, 147, 182

Holmes, Edward: I, 268, 271, 274, 304 & n, 309 & n

Homer: I, 104, 110, 159, 277

Hook, Theodore: I, 255 & n

Hookham, Thomas: I, *vi, xxxi,* 3 n, 4, 16 n, 37, 41, 42, 43, 103 n; II, 21, 137, 152, 172, 195, 263 n, 264 n, 265 n, 285, 286, 311, 312, 327; publishes *History of a Six Weeks' Tour,* I, 35 n, 43 n; and G. Byron's Shelley letters, II, 263–70 & n, 294–96

Hooper, Mr.: I, 6

Hoppner, Belgrave: I, 58 & n, 67 & n, 79 n, 146 n, 147 & n

Hoppner, Isabelle May (Mrs. Belgrave): I, 58 & n, 67 & n, 79 n, 146 n, 147

Hopwood, Charles: II, 209 & n

Hopwood, William: II, 209 & n

Horace: I, 14 n

Houwald, Christoph Ernst: II, 14 & n

Hume, Dr. and Mrs.: I, 28 n

Hume, David: II, 15

Humphreys, Mr.: I, 348 & n

Hunt (the murderer, brother of Blanc Hunt): I, 280

Hunt, Blanc: I, 271, 280

Hunt, Henry (nephew of Leigh Hunt): I, 201 n, 206, 262, 267, 272, 283, 284; admiration of Shelley, I, 65–66 & n

Hunt, Henry Sylvan (son of Leigh Hunt): I, 84, 151 n, 231 & n, 232, 235, 240, 241, 242, 243, 250, 251, 253, 258, 279, 284, 302, 308, 318, 330; II, 89, 142, 145, 146, 157, 160 & n, 162, 168 & n, 170, 171, 175, 178, 193, 198, 206, 207, 215, 223, 241, 293, 325, 328

Hunt, Irving: I, 253, 308

Hunt, Isaac: name of father and grandfather of Leigh Hunt, I, 266 n

Hunt, John (brother of Leigh Hunt): I, 64 n, 66 n, 198 n, 199, 200, 201 n, 214 n, 245, 262, 267 n, 275, 277, 279 & n, 282, 285 n, 287 n, 295, 296, 306, 317; imprisoned, I, 121 n; dispute with Leigh Hunt over *Examiner,* I, 262, 264, 265–66 & n, 271–72, 282–84, 285, 291; trial for publishing *Vision of Judgement,* I, 286–87 & n, 301–302

Hunt, John (son of Leigh Hunt): I, 26, 76, 77, 81, 84, 151 n, 232, 233, 235, 241, 253, 258, 308

Hunt, Julia: II, 142

Hunt, Leigh: I, *vi, xxx, xxxi,* 15 & n, 16, 17, 18, 21 n, 22 n, 23 & n, 24 & n, 25, 26 n, 28 & n, 29, 30, 31, 33, 35 n, 36, 38, 39, 40, 41 & n, 42 & n, 43 n, 47 & n, 48, 50, 64, 65 n, 69 n, 74, 75, 76 & n, 77, 78 & n, 80 n, 83, 84, 85, 86 n, 97, 98, 110, 112, 121 n, 138, 141, 153, 158, 164, 181, 182, 183, 185, 188, 189, 190 n, 191 n, 192, 193, 194, 195, 198, 199, 201, 202, 203, 204, 205, 208, 209, 211, 214, 216 n, 217, 220, 221, 222, 224, 226, 229 & n, 230, 236, 242 n, 247, 248, 250 n, 256 n, 257, 260 n, 261 n, 262 n, 270 n, 282, 285 & n, 287 n, 291, 292, 300, 304 n, 305, 306, 307, 338, 356; II, 4, 24, 42, 51, 84, 131 n, 136 n, 138, 141 n, 142 n, 146, 147 & n, 150, 160 n, 162, 170, 173, 175, 181, 197, 198, 204, 222, 234 n, 235 n, 289 n, 300 n, 302 n, 303 n, 309, 351; Shelley's loans to, I, 15 & n; article on "Young Poets," I, 15 n; Shelley's invitation to, I, 64 & n, 65; quotations from letters, I, 64 n, 66 n, 78 n, 80 n, 81 n, 138 n; attacks *Quarterly* for review of *Revolt of Islam,* I, 84 & n; portrait of, by Wildman, I, 76 & n; plans to go to Italy, I, 151 & n; departure from England, I, 152, 154 & n, 159, 172; arrival in Leghorn, I, 172 n; on Shelley's heart, I, 187 n; inscriptions for graves of Shelley and Williams, I, 192 n; and Byron, I, 200–203 & n; estrangement from Mary, I, 208–209 & n, 236; on Shelley, I, 229 n; reconciliation with Mary, I, 230, 231, 236; moves to Florence, I, 245 & n; dispute with brother over *Examiner,* I, 263, 264, 265–66 & n, 271–72, 282–84, 285; biographical essay on Shelley, I, 264 & n, 272, 275, 278, 281, 285, 286, 294 & n; 316–17 & n, 339–40; birthday celebrated at Novello's, I, 274–75; return to England, I, 329 & n; Mary's first meeting with, I, 347; Mary's payment of Shelley's intended legacy to, I, 349 & n; II, 218, 223, 228; financial difficulties, II, 160, 168, 178, 293, 297; granted a pension, II, 303 & n

Hunt, Marianne (Mrs. Leigh): I, *vi, xxxi*, 16, 19, 20 n, 21, 22 n, 23 n, 24 & n, 25 n, 28 n, 30, 31, 34, 35, 38, 39, 41, 42, 44 & n, 47 n, 49, 50, 61, 76 n, 81, 107, 117, 125, 166, 172, 189, 195, 200, 204, 205, 208, 209, 210 & n, 212, 214 n, 215, 220, 221 & n, 224, 226, 228, 229, 231, 235, 236, 251 n, 263, 265 n, 267 & n, 276, 284, 291, 295 n, 300, 303, 318 n, 347; II, 4 & n, 24, 90, 121, 122, 127, 128, 140, 145, 146, 165, 197, 218, 228, 234, 291, 303, 310, 328, 351; and her silhouette of Shelley, I, 282, 284, 287, 302, 305, 307

Hunt, Mary Florimel Leigh: I, 22 & n, 26, 84, 151 n, 158, 232, 235, 241, 244, 253, 258, 308, 347; II, 4

Hunt, Mr. and Mrs.: I, 311

Hunt, Mrs. Blanc: I, 268, 271, 280, 301

Hunt, Percy: I, 28 n, 95, 151 n, 232, 235, 241, 258, 308

Hunt, Swinburne: I, 24 & n, 26, 65 & n, 95, 151 n, 232, 235, 241, 258, 279

Hunt, Thornton Leigh: I, 26 n, 27, 39, 76 n, 77, 81, 84, 151 n, 228, 232, 233, 235, 236, 239, 241, 249, 251, 253, 258, 268 & n, 269, 282, 284, 295 n, 302, 308, 330; II, 90, 289 n, 307, 308; *see also Correspondence of Leigh Hunt*

Hunt, Vincent: I, 229 n, 231 & n, 232, 234 n, 235, 239, 240, 242, 253, 258, 279, 284, 296 & n, 305, 308, 330, 347

Hunter, Nancy: I, 267, 295 & n, 296

Hunter, Mrs. Rowland (mother of Mrs. Leigh Hunt): I, 251, 261, 267 & n, 295, 296

Hunter, Rowland: I, 251 n, 260, 261, 267, 295 n; II, 90

I

Imlay, Fanny: I, 3 & n, 16; suicide, I, 16 n; compared to Allegra, I, 39

Imlay, Gilbert: I, 3 n

Indicator, the: I, 98, 112, 121 & n, 275

Ingpen, Roger: I, *xxv, xxvi, xxvii, xxix,* 43 n, 61 n, 139 n, 358 n, 372 n; in bibliographical notes, 359, 360, 362, 373, 378; II, 21, 111, 127; *see also Julian Edition*

Irby, Mr.: II, 154

Ireland, Fanny: II, 190, 191

Irving, Washington: I, *xxxii,* 313 & n, 319 n, 320 & n, 326 & n, 327, 328 n, 331 n, 332 & n, 333, 336 & n, 337, 338 n, 343 n; II, 21, 27 & n, 168, 347, 348, 349, 350 & n, 351

Ivanhoff, Alexy: II, 194, 197, 199, 204, 207, 209, 211, 213, 216

Ivanhoff, Mme.: II, 175, 194, 214, 215, 216, 220, 240

J

Jacquemont, Victor: I, 378 n

Jerrold, Douglas: I, *xxxii;* II, 85 n

Jewsbury, Geraldine: II, 33 & n

Jewsbury, Maria Jane: II, 33 n; opinion of Mary, II, 33 bib. n

Job, Book of: I, 306

John Bull: I, 255

Johnson, Mr. (husband of Jane Williams): I, 289 n

Johnson, R. B.: in bibliographical notes, I, 78, 231, 247

Johnson, Samuel: I, 228; II, 93

Joliffe, Hat: II, 144

Jones, Frederick L.: I, *xxvii,* 170–71 n; in bibliographical notes, 350; II, 59; *see also Bodleian Quarterly Record*

Jones, Miss (*or* Mrs., aunt of T. J. Hogg): II, 105

Jones, Mr.: II, 135

Jonson, Ben: II, 303 n

Josephine, Empress of France: II, 20

Julian Edition of Shelley's Works: I, *xxvii;* in bibliographical notes, I, 4, 5, 6, 11, 13, 27, 29, 46, 47, 50, 59, 61, 62, 67, 83, 107, 108, 136, 137, 139, 142, 144, 155

Juvenal: I, 241

K

Kaiseroff, Mme.: II, 41 & n, 51, 240, 244, 247, 248

Kaiseroff, Natalie: II, 41 n, 51, 201, 210, 240, 244, 247, 248, 250, 258

Kamenou, Tersitza (Trelawny's second wife): I, 344 n

Karge, Laura Lister: II, 339

Kean, Edmund: I, 25, 287 & n, 290, 294, 295, 315, 316, 324, 332, 334; II, 8, 98, 350 n

Keats, John: I, *xxix,* 15 n, 24 & n, 47 n, 69 n,

185, 198 & n, 211 & n, 214, 226, 260 n, 279, 284; II, 10 n, 166 n, 173 n, 344; illness and death, I, 138 & n, 139; Shelley's lines on, I, 226–27

Kelly, Frances Maria: I, 361 & n

Kelsall, Thomas Forbes: I, 264 n, 292, 297 n

Kemble, Charles: I, 296 & n; II, 81 n

Kemble, Fanny: I, 25 & n, 81 & n, 106, 118 & n, 121, 122 & n

Kendall, Rev. John: I, 28 n

Kennedy, Benjamin Hall: II, 60, 62, 67, 69, 70, 75, 77

Kenney, James: I, 254 & n, 255, 256, 257, 273, 274, 313 & n, 343; II, 12 n, 113 n, 347, 348, 350 n

Kenney, James, Jr.: I, 274

Kenney, Louisa Mercier (Mrs. James Kenney, formerly Mrs. Thomas Holcroft): I, 254 & n, 255, 257, 258, 273, 274, 312, 313, 319, 320 & n; II, 348, 350 n

Kenney, Therese: I, 274

Kent, Elizabeth ("Bessy," sister of Mrs. Leigh Hunt): I, 20 & n, 22, 23 & n, 24, 26 n, 27, 64, 67, 77, 81, 84, 95, 98, 107, 201 n, 205, 206, 209 n, 210 n, 232, 256 n, 258, 261, 267 n, 277, 278, 282, 284, 295, 301, 305, 318 & n; II, 127

Kent, Laura (Mrs. Tom): I, 295, 296, 301

Kent, Tom: I, 81 & n, 265 & n, 267 & n, 301; debut on stage, I, 295–96 & n

Kenyon, John: II, 129 n

Kinnaird, Douglas: I, 202, 302

Kirkup, Seymour: I, 190 n; II, 173 & n

Knatchbull-Hugessen, Sir Edward: I, 292 n

Knowles, T. Sheridan: I, 322 n, 324 n; II, 141 n

Knox, Alexander Andrew: I, *xxxii;* II, 151 & n, 152, 154, 156 & n, 157, 158, 160, 164, 166, 167, 168, 170, 173, 175, 176, 177, 180, 182, 183, 185, 186, 187, 189, 190, 191, 193, 206, 226, 231, 235, 244, 245, 248, 250, 251 n, 253, 254, 255, 256, 257, 258, 259, 261, 270, 271, 272, 273, 276, 277, 278, 279, 285, 292, 295, 300, 320, 322, 325, 326, 327, 328, 331, 332, 337, 340; goes abroad with Mary and Percy, II, 153; and the Gatteschi letters, II, 194 n, 251–61 *passim;* debts in Paris, II, 275–80

Knox, Dr. Vicesimus: I, 260 n

Knox, George: II, 151 n

Knox, Susan Armstrong (Mrs. Alexander Andrew): II, 152 n

Kock, Charles Paul de: II, 107 & n

L

Lackington, Mr.: I, 31 n

Ladies' Monthly Museum, the: I, 367 & n

Lake, Mr.: II, 348

Lamartine, M. de: II, 312

Lamb, Charles: I, *xxix,* 47 n, 239, 254 & n, 255, 259, 268 & n, 271, 273, 277, 280, 285, 286, 294 & n, 309, 312, 323, 325, 328, 340, 361 & n; II, 351; on Hunt's poetry, I, 260; defence of Hunt and Hazlitt, I, 268–70 & n; fable on a Peacock and a Hog, I, 276; superannuation, I, 318

Lamb, Mary: I, *xxxii,* 47 n, 239, 254 & n, 255, 257, 260, 271, 276, 280, 285, 286, 307, 309, 312, 328, 340

Lambert, Mr.: I, 6 & n

Lambert (J. H. Payne's "man Friday"): I, 338

Lambton, Mr.: I, 363

Landor, Walter Savage: I, *xxxii;* II, 12 n, 173 n, 290 & n, 291

Lane, Mr. Arthur: II, 190, 191

Laporte, Mr.: II, 44

Lardner, Dr. Dionysius: II, 83, 90 n, 104 & n, 122 & n

Larkins, Margaret: II, 171

Larkins, Mr.: II, 294

Larkins, Mrs.: II, 145, 245, 296, 305

La Scoto, Signor: I, 150

Lastri, Marco: I, 353 n

La Vega, Garcilaso de: I, 104 n, 123 & n, 124 & n

Lavers: I, 300

Lawrence, Dr. William: I, 85 & n

Lawrence, Mr.: II, 33, 85, 193

Lawrence, Sir Thomas: I, 85 & n

Leader, John Temple: II, 166 & n, 167, 215, 253, 254

Lega (Byron's servant): I, 213, 298

Leichhart, Dr.: II, 306

Leigh, Augusta: I, 200 n, 298, 302; II, 60

Leigh, Chandos, first Lord Leigh: II, 110, 111, 163, 168, 178

Leland, Thomas: II, 5 & n

Lennox, Lady Sussex: *see* Lady Sussex

Lennox, Lord William Pitt: II, 237 & n, 239, 241, 242, 243, 286

Leon, Luis de: II, 104 n

Leopold, R. W.: in bibliographical note, I, 367

Letters of Mary W. Shelley: I, *xxvi,* 21 n, 115 n; in bibliographical notes, 22, 25, 49, 52, 64, 75, 78, 82, 86, 98, 119, 125, 258, 263, 282,

288, 296, 305, 308, 319, 331, 348, 350; II, 90, 128, 136, 141, 218

Lewell, Mr.: II, 194, 196

Lewes, George Henry: II, 125 n

Lewis, Sir George Cornwall: II, 152 n

Liberal, The: I, 151 n, 183, 198 n, 199 & n, 202, 206, 212 & n, 214, 217, 221, 226, 228, 286 n; II, 61

Lind, Jenny: II, 309 & n, 322, 327, 331

Lindley, Robert: II, 84 & n

Lindsay, Robert: II, 15 & n

Linton, Mrs.: II, 348

Lisle, Lord de: II, 236

Lister, Mr.: II, 52

Liston, Mr.: I, 335

Literary Examiner, the: I, 262, 266, 275, 282, 285, 306

Livy: I, 14

Locke, John: I, 14 n

Lockhart, John Gibson: II, 40

London Magazine, the: I, 268 & n, 272 & n

Long, Mrs.: II, 215, 225, 227

Long, Percy W.: I, *x*

Long, Walter: II, 227

Longdill, P. W.: I, 17 n, 25 & n, 27 n, 28 & n, 30, 33, 34, 37, 43

Longley, Dr. C. T.: II, 56, 60, 62, 69, 70

Longman, Mr. (publisher): I, 196, 299

Lonsdale, Lord: I, 237, 242, 243, 246

Louis Philippe, King of France: II, 148, 312

Low, Mary: I, 226 & n

Lowry, Dr.: II, 337

Lowther, Lady: II, 80

Lucas, E. V.: I, *x;* in bibliographical note, 361

Lucas, Mrs.: I, 27

Lucian: I, 14 n

Lumley, Mr.: II, 242, 246, 278, 280, 286, 292, 312, 331

Lyndsay, David: I, 167 & n, 350–51 & nn, 378 n

Lytton, Earl of: in bibliographical note, II, 125

M

Maberley, Miss: II, 208

Macaulay, Thomas Babington: II, 265

Macchiavelli, Nicolo: I, 117; II, 83, 90 n

MacDonald, Mr.: II, 176, 177

McEliney, Miss: *see* Perry, Mrs. Erskine

MacIntosh, Sir James: II, 31

Mackay, Miss (aunt of A. A. Knox): II, 189, 190

Macready, William Charles: I, 322 n, 324 n; II,

124 n, 136 & n, 182

Madocks, Mr. (of Marlow): I, 33 & n, 35, 36, 206 n

Maistre, Mme. Joseph de: II, 159, 184, 186, 189, 216, 220

Maitland, General: I, 290 n

Malthus, Thomas Robert: I, 135

Manners-Sutton, Charles (Speaker of the House of Commons, later Lord Canterbury): II, 57 & n, 82, 89, 91, 93 & n

Manners-Sutton, Mrs. Charles (later Lady Canterbury): II, 89, 153, 236, 323

Mantell, Walter Baldock Durant: II, 138 & n

Manzoni, Alessandro: II, 5 n, 148

Maria (servant of Mary Shelley): I, 231; II, 84

Marianne (servant of Mary Shelley): II, 158, 201, 202, 211, 216, 245, 275, 286, 320, 321

Marini, Giambattista: II, 106 n

Marryat, Frederick: II, 66 & n

Marshall, Mr.: I, 371; II, 5, 35, 38

Marshall, Mrs. Julian: I, *xxv, xxvi,* 72 n, 146 n, 147 n, 150 n, 176 n, 216 n, 366 n, 368 n; II, 352; in bibliographical notes, I, 4, 5, 9, 11, 13, 15, 17, 22, 26, 30, 32, 35, 40, 44, 45, 47, 57, 58, 73, 74, 78, 80, 87, 110, 114, 125, 134, 146, 147, 150, 152, 157, 158, 161, 165, 172, 179, 186, 190, 192, 196, 200, 204, 211, 215, 216, 225, 227, 230, 232, 235, 237, 244, 263, 282, 285, 300, 305, 308, 311, 316, 319, 350, 356, 357, 371; II, 14, 25, 37, 42, 47, 50, 51, 73, 81, 85, 89, 92, 100, 104, 107, 119, 121, 218

Martineau, Harriet: II, 133

Martini, Signor: II, 193 n, 213, 215, 226, 253, 255, 259

Mary (servant of Mary Shelley): II, 291

Masi, Sergeant Major Stefano: I, 163, 164, 167; affray with, I, 162–69 & nn

Mason, Laura (Mme. Galloni): I, *xxxi,* 83 n; II, 80 & n, 84, 153 & n, 155 & n, 160 & n, 162, 165, 169, 170, 171 & n, 172, 174, 176, 177, 180, 182, 184, 186, 187, 198, 209 & n, 214, 234, 241, 244, 261

Mason, Mr. (George William Tighe): I, *xxx,* 83 n, 105 & n, 113 n; II, 153 n, 171

Mason, Mrs. (Mrs. Tighe, Lady Mountcashell): I, *xxx,* 82, 83 n, 101, 105, 113 n, 134, 140 n, 143 & n, 157, 183, 185, 189, 212, 237, 243, 270, 284, 289, 302; II, 84, 153 n, 171; and Claire, I, 83 n, 141; her dream of Shelley and Percy, I, 185; coldness to Mary, I, 188

Mason, Nerina (Signora Cini): I, *xxxi,* 83 n;

II, 80 & n, 84, 160 & n, 169, 170, 171 & n, 172, 173, 174, 175, 176, 180, 182, 209, 241, 261

Massinger, Philip: I, 269, 290 n

Massingham, H. J.: II, 347, 353

Mather, Mrs.: *see* Dyer, Mrs. George

Mathews, Charles: I, 343 & n; II, 235

Matthews, Anne: I, 291

Mavrocordato, Prince Alexander: I, 117 n, 125 & n, 133 & n, 134, 136, 137, 142 & n, 150 n, 151, 153, 161, 265, 304

Maxwell, Lady: II, 111

Mayer, Mr.: II, 209

Mazzi, Signor: II, 193 n, 194, 199

Meadows, Mrs.: I, 88 n

Medici, Lorenzo de: II, 90 n

Medwin, Mrs. Thomas (Anne, Baroness Hamilton of Sweden): I, 315 & n; II, 24 & n

Medwin, Thomas: I, *xxx, xxxi,* 118 n, 129 n, 133, 155 n, 165, 167 n, 229 n, 291, 300 & n, 315 n, 316; II, 4, 14, 24 & n, 41 & n; 290, 350 n; the Shelleys' opinion of, I, 129–30, 131; his *Conversations of Lord Byron,* I, 308 & n, 315 & n; marriage, I, 315 & n; memoir of Shelley, I, 315 & n; *Life of Shelley,* II, 287–90 & n, 307–308 & nn, 309–310

Memon, Mr.: II, 264 n, 295

Mendoza, Diego Hurtado de: II, 104 n, 123 & n, 124

Meredith, George: II, 130 n

Meredith, Mrs. George: *see* Peacock, Mary Ellen

Mérimée, Prosper: I, *xxxii,* 374 n, 376 & n, 377, 378, 379; II, 11 n

Metastasio, Pietro Trapassi: II, 106 n

Methuen, Lord and Lady: II, 249

Methuen, Mr.: II, 231, 249, 327

Methuen, Mrs.: *see* Sanford, Horatia

Metropolitan Magazine: II, 66 & n

Michael Angelo: I, 242

Milanie, Mlle.: I, 48 & n

Mildmay, Mr.: II, 79

Mill, Mr.: I, 281

Mills, Mr.: II, 139

Milly, *see* Shields, Amelia

Milman, Henry Hart: I, 198

Milner, H. M.: I, 259 n

Milnes, Richard Monckton: II, 166 & n, 167, 182

Milton, John: I, 252; quoted, 284, 287

Mitchell, Mr.: II, 242, 280, 285, 301, 312, 327

Mitchell, Sir T.: II, 306

Mitford, Mr.: II, 154

Molière: I, 22

Montagu, Basil: I, 307 n

Montagu, Mrs. Basil: I, 307

Montemayor, Jorge de: II, 104 n

Montgomery, James: I, 260

Montgomery, Mr.: II, 90, 92, 106, 108

Monti, Vincenzo: II, 93 n, 94, 106 n

Moore, Anastasia Mary: II, 12 & n

Moore, Helen: I, *xxv, xxvi;* in bibliographical notes, 232, 237, 249, 372

Moore, Thomas: I, 69 n, 154 n, 201, 298 & n, 313 n, 368 n, 376; II, 12 & n, 20, 25 & n, 26, 32, 40, 58 n, 59, 214 n, 348, 350 n, 351; *Life of Byron,* I, *xxx,,* 298–99, 313 & n, 371 n; II, 13 n, 24, 25, 28–29, 30, 31, 34, 35, 37, 60; in bibliographical note, I, 127; Shelley's opinion of, I, 130

Morgan, Lady Sydney: I, *xxxii,* 290 & n, 327; II, 129 n, 134, 135, 298 & n

Morning Chronicle, the: I, 14, 24, 265, 318 & n; II, 278

Morris, Mrs.: I, 313

Morrison, Mr. A. C. H.: II, 110, 111, 115

Mountcashell, Lady: *see* Mrs. Mason

Moxon, Edward: I, *vi, xxx;* II, 91 n, 127, 133 n, 136 n, 194, 202, 223, 263 n, 265 n; prosecution of, I, 132 n, 149 & n, 150

Mozart, Wolfgang Amadeus: I, 124, 241, 257, 268, 271, 294

Murillo: II, 148

Murray, John: I, *vi, xxx,* 25 n, 26 & n, 97, 144 n, 198 & n, 201 & n, 202, 298 n, 371 n; II, 40, 192 & n, 350 n; proposal concerning Shelley's works, I, 352–53

Murray, Lord C.: I, 244, 307

Murray, Sir John: I, *vi, xxvi,* 146 n, 147 n; in bibliographical notes, I, 18, 59, 150, 199, 202, 203, 207, 213, 218, 219, 222

N

Napoleon: II, 125 n

Nash, John: I, 135, 164 & n

Nathan, Mr.: I, 314

Neale, William Johnson: II, 52 n

Negri, Signor: II, 142

New Monthly Magazine: I, 256 & n, 306, 346, 378; II, 39 n, 43 & n, 52, 66, 150

Newby, Mr.: II, 308 & n, 310

Newton, A. Edward: I, *x*

Newton, Gilbert Stuart: I, 313 & n, 343 & n; II, 348

Nichols: II, 141

Nicoll, W. R.: I, *xxvi;* in bibliographical notes, I, 29, 47, 61

Nicolls, Lieut. Edward: II, 130 n, 216 & n

Nicolls, Mrs. Edward: *see* Peacock, Mary Ellen

Nitchie, Elizabeth: I, *ix,* 69 n, 156 n

Noel, Lady: I, 229 n

Norfolk, Duke of: II, 277, 278

Norman, Sylva: I, *x,* 289 n

Normanby, Lord: I, 346 n; II, 149

Norton, Mrs. Caroline: II, 39 n, 97, 104, 106, 118, 120 & n, 122 n, 148, 167

Norton, William: II, 167 & n

Nott, Dr.: I, 160 & n

Novello, Cecilia: I, 261 n, 330

Novello, Charles Arthur: I, 261 n, 309, 330

Novello, Clara Anastasia: I, 261 n, 294 & n, 306, 330; II, 4

Novello, Edward: I, 261 n, 330

Novello, Emma: I, 261 n, 330

Novello, Florence: I, 261 n, 330

Novello, Frank: I, 271, 274, 275, 295

Novello, Joseph Alfred: I, 261 n, 271, 330; II, 96, 159 n, 163

Novello, Mary Sabilla: I, 261 n, 271, 330

Novello, Mary Victoria: *see* Clarke, Mrs. Charles Cowden

Novello, Mrs. Vincent (*née* Mary Sabilla Hehl): I, 261 & n, 268, 271, 274, 275 n, 276, 277, 278, 279, 280, 284, 286, 293, 294, 301, 303, 304, 306, 318, 330

Novello, Sydney: I, 261 n

Novello, Vincent: I, *xxxii,* 47 n, 210 n, 261 & n, 266 & n, 268, 271, 272, 274, 275, 276, 277, 278, 279, 280, 283, 284, 285, 286, 293, 294, 301, 303, 304, 306, 309, 318, 330, 372 n; II, 243, 351

O

Odysseus: I, 288 n, 304, 314, 316, 319, 344 n

Ollier, Charles: I, *xxx,* 29 & n, 31 n, 35 n, 49 & n, 61, 78 n, 84, 86 n, 112, 125, 126 & n, 134, 136, 144 n, 150 & n, 151, 152, 153, 155, 158, 159, 195, 206 n, 279 n; II, 52 n, 103

Ollier, Mrs. Charles: I, 279; II, 79, 101

O'Neil, Miss: I, 78 n, 94

Ovid: I, 239

Owen, Hugh: II, 333 n

Owen, Robert: I, 366 n

Owen, Robert Dale: I, 366 n

Owen, William: I, 85 & n

Oxford, Lady: I, 346; II, 60

P

Pacchiani, Francesco: I, 117 & n, 118 n, 125 n, 127 & n, 130, 131, 134, 135 n, 144 n, 161; disgusts the Shelleys, I, 121 & n, 128–29; stories about him, I, 131–32, 133

Paganini, Nicolo: II, 44 & n, 84

Palma, Count Alerino: I, 348 & n

Palmerston, Lord: II, 280

Papantonio, Michael: I, *x*

Park (or Parke), John: I, *v,* 190 n

Parker, Mr.: I, 88 n

Parry, William: I, 348 & n

Parry-Jones, Miss Corbet: I, 88 & n

Parry-Jones, Sir Love: II, 88 n

Partington, Wilfred: in bibliographical note, II, 16

Partridge, Mrs.: I, 52 & n

Pasta, Giudetta: I, 304 & n, 313, 325 & n, 326, 328, 343

Paston, George: in bibliographical note, II, 144

Paton, Miss (*later* Lady Williams): I, 338, 339

Paul, Aubrey: I, *xxxii;* II, 248, 339, 340

Paul, C. Kegan: I, 51 n

Paul, Lady (Mrs. Paul or perhaps her mother-in-law): II, 67

Paul, Mr. (banker): II, 52, 294

Paul, Mrs. (*née* Georgina Beauclerc): II, 55, 69, 80, 151, 157, 203, 204, 206, 215, 241, 243, 255, 274, 277, 282, 305, 311 & n, 316, 334

Paul, Sir John: II, 74

Paulus, Heinrich Eberhard Gottlob: II, 288 n

Pavis, Mr.: II, 10

Payne, Mrs.: I, 270 & n, 276

Payne, John Howard: I, *vi, xxvi, xxxii,* 254 n, 319 n, 320 n, 331 n, 338 n, 352 n; II, 347, 348, 350 & n, 351, 352, 353; letters to Mary, I, 322 n, 328 n, 332 n, 333 n; performance of *Clari,* I, 323 & n; proposal to Mary and rejection, 332–33 & n; II, 347 ff

Peacock, Mary Ellen (Mrs. Edward Nicolls, Mrs. George Meredith): I, *xxxi,* 197 & n; II, 107, 130 n, 216 & n, 217, 222

Peacock, Mrs. Samuel (mother of Thomas Love Peacock): I, 15, 21 & n, 40; II, 92

Peacock, Mrs. Thomas Love (*née* Jane Gryf-fydh): I, 68 n, 110 & n, 197 & n, 281; II, 91, 92, 106

Peacock, Thomas Love: I, *xxx, xxxi,* 6, 13 n, 15 & n, 18, 21 & n, 22, 24, 30, 40, 46, 47 n.

49, 52, 56 n, 63, 64, 65, 66 n, 74, 78 n, 79,
84, 85, 87, 109, 110, 125, 126 n, 136, 152,
155, 179, 185, 187, 194, 195, 196, 197, 199
& n, 205, 206 & n, 207, 261, 264 n, 281,
300 n, 303, 307, 316 n, 339, 340, 341 n, 353,
358 & n, 360, 362; II, 32, 91–92, 103, 106,
130 n, 131 n, 132, 137, 216, 217, 219, 222,
225, 227, 230, 231, 232, 233, 234, 235, 265,
266, 267, 270, 295, 300, 313, 333 n; *Melin-court*, I, 24 & n; Mary's opinion of, I, 30; and
Marianne St. Croix, I, 67 n; marriage, I, 68 n,
110 & n, 197 n; appointment in East India
Company, I, 75 & n

Peake, Richard Brinsley: I, 259 n

Pearson, Henry Hugh (*later* Henry Hugo Pier-son): I, *xxxii;* II, 156 n, 158 n, 159, 166, 167,
170, 172, 173, 175, 203 & n; sets Shelley's
songs to music, II, 159 n, 163; travels with
Mary and Percy, II, 161

Pearson, Hugh Nicholas: II, 158 n

Pechell, Captain and Mrs.: II, 272, 278, 291 n

Peck, W. E.: I, *xxvii,* 190 n; in bibliographical
notes, I, 46, 172; II, 11, 28; *see also Julian
Edition*

Peel, Sir Robert: II, 90, 91, 93, 262, 278, 282,
299, 306

Pellicer, Signor: II, 122 & n

Pépé, General Guglielmo: II, 125 & n

Pèpi (servant): I, 120 & n, 121, 126, 134

Peronne, M.: II, 251, 271, 272

Perry, Catherine: II, 79

Perry, Erskine: II, 79

Perry, Henry: II, 209

Perry, Jane: *see* Elliott, Mrs. Frederic

Perry, Mrs. Erskine (*née* Miss McEliney): II, 79

Petrarch: I, 117, 295; II, 83, 90 n

Pforzheimer, Carl H.: I, *vii, x, xxvi* n; II, 346

Pierre (servant): II, 276

Pierson, Henry Hugo: *see* Pearson, Henry Hugh

Pilford, Captain: I, 43 & n, 45

Pinkerton, John: II, 15 & n

Planché, Gustave: I, 376 n

Platt, Mr.: I, 15 n

Platt, Mrs.: I, 15

Ploennium, Mme. de; II, 288 n

Polidori: Gætano: II, 94 n, 95 & n, 96

Polidori, John William: I, 14 n, 70 n

Politian: II, 90 n

Poole, John: I, 312, 313 n

Pope, Alexander: II, 34; quoted, I, 229 & n

Portsmouth, Countess of (*née* Mary Anne Han-son): I, 207 & n

Portsmouth, Lord: I, 207 n

Poynton, A. B.: I, *x*

Pozzo, Mme.: II, 174

Pringle, Colonel: II, 243, 322, 323, 324

Pringle, Mrs.: II, 293, 322, 323, 324, 327

Prinoth (Leghorn tradesman): I, 134, 135

Procter, Bryan Waller: I, *xxxii,* 255 & n, 265,
266, 271, 272, 278, 280, 294, 297 n, 307 &
n; II, 141 n, 351; subsidizes *Posthumous
Poems,* I, 264 & n, 280

Procter, Mrs. Bryan Waller: *see* Skepper, Anne

Prout, Dr.: II, 328, 329, 333

Pulci, Bernardo, Luca, and Luigi: II, 90 n

Purniance, Mr.: I, 113

Q

Quarterly Review: I, 97, 217, 268 & n; II, 35;
J. T. Coleridge's review of *Revolt of Islam,*
I, 66 & n, 84 & n, 90 & n; review of *Prome-theus Unbound,* I, 156 & n

Quevedo y Villegas, Francisco de: II, 104 n

Quin, Mr.: II, 129 n

R

Radcliffe, Mrs. Anne: I, 214

Radin, Herman T.: I, *x*

Raphael: I, 65; II, 148, 164 & n

Ratchford, Fannie E.: I, *x*

Rawlinson, Mr.: II, 152, 168, 175, 221, 225,
291, 292, 294

Redding, Cyrus: I, *xxxii;* II, 10 n

Redesdale, Lord: II, 154

Redi, Francesco: I, 285 n

Reeze, Mr.: I, 225

Requy, Ida: I, 144

Requy, Mme.: I, 144

Reveley, Henry: I, 51 n, 54 & n, 56, 57 & n,
58, 62, 72, 77 & n, 83, 86, 90, 92, 93, 100,
102, 103, 104, 105, 106 & n, 108, 109 & n,
110, 112, 115, 135, 136, 138, 139, 151, 152,
154, 156, 164, 165, 171, 224, 278; II, 82,
89, 111, 112; his steamboat, I, 82 n, 87 n,
114 n; wish to marry Claire, I, 83 n; buys
boat for Shelley, I, 138 n

Reynolds, Frederick: I, *xxx*

Reynolds, John Hamilton: I, 15 n

Ricci, Appolonia: I, 104 & n, 108, 109, 110, 112

Ricci, Carlotta: I, 104 & n, 108, 109, 112

Ricci, Mme.: II, 180

Rio, M.: II, 163 n, 182

Rio, Mme.: II, 182

Robecchi, Signor: II, 215, 285

Roberts, Carlo: II, 330 & n, 331, 337

Roberts, Captain Daniel: I, 155 n, 156, 171 &
n, 183, 186, 196 n, 197, 208 & n, 215, 223,
228, 291; II, 14

Robertson, Charles: I, 274, 309

Robinson, Ada: II, 242, 243, 246

Robinson, Charles: I, 378 n; II, 135, 136, 137
& n, 262, 296, 299, 306, 307, 314, 315, 318

Robinson, Eliza: II, 97, 120 & n, 125, 132, 161,
202, 209

Robinson, George: I, 378 n; II, 19, 167

Robinson, Henry Crabb: I, *xxxii,* 69 n, 254 n

Robinson, Isabel: *see* Douglas, Mrs. Sholto

Robinson, Joshua: I, *xxxii,* 376, 377, 378 n; II,
4, 12 n, 136, 167

Robinson, Julia: I, 373 n, 378 n; II, 77 n, 80, 82,
120 & n, 132, 161, 167, 202

Robinson, Julian: I, 378 n; II, 173, 190, 227,
234

Robinson, Mrs. Alfred: II, 167

Robinson, Rosa (Mrs. Aubrey William Beauclerc): I, 378 n; II, 97, 120 & n, 132, 137,
161, 202, 204 & n, 313, 334

Robinsons, the: I, 129

Roebuck, Mr.: II, 149

Rogers, Mrs.: II, 215

Rogers, Samuel: II, 10 n, 129 n, 147 & n, 148,
157, 163, 182, 200, 203, 244, 252, 284, 350 n,
351

Romance of Mary W. Shelley: I, *xxvi,* 320 n,
322 n, 327 n, 328 n; II, 347 & n, 353; in bibliographical notes, I, 311, 320, 321, 322, 323,
324, 325, 326, 327, 328, 329, 332, 333, 334,
335, 336, 337, 338, 339, 340, 357, 361, 363,
369; II, 38, 44

Romand, M. de: II, 244, 248

Romano, Carlo: II, 193 n, 255

Rosini, Professor: I, 124

Rossetti, Lucy M.: I, *xxv, xxvi;* in bibliographical notes, 4, 172, 300, 357; II, 50, 103, 113

Rossetti, William Michael: I, 70 n; in bibliographical note, II, 96

Rossini, Gioachino: I, 64, 76, 294

Rothwell, Richard: II, 33 & n, 141

Rouge, M.: II, 288 n

Rousseau, Mme.: II, 286

Rousseau, Jean Jacques: I, 12, 91

Rubio, Signor: II, 250

Russell, Lord John: II, 280, 299; in bibliographical notes, 130, 214

S

St. Aubyn, Elizabeth: II, 41

St. Croix, Marianne de: I, 67 & n, 84

St. John, Charles Robert: II, 313 n, 316, 318 & n

St. John, Ferdinand: II, 316, 337

St. John, Mrs. Charles Robert: *see* Shelley,
Lady Jane

Sainte-Beuve, Charles Augustin: II, 148 & n

Salisbury, Sir William: II, 81

Sanborn, F. B.: see *Romance of Mary W. Shelley*

Sand, George: II, 320 & n

Sanford, Horatia (Mrs. Methuen): II, 180, 215,
225, 226, 227, 231, 249, 255, 282, 327

Sanford, Mr.: I, *xxxii;* II, 152, 170, 175, 176,
180, 203, 204, 209, 215, 221, 226, 227, 237,
238, 239, 240, 242, 245, 246, 247, 249,
274, 282, 285, 286, 287, 291, 294, 323, 328

Sanford, Mrs.: II, 152, 170, 173, 175, 176, 177,
180, 192, 203, 204, 209, 215, 225, 226, 227,
238, 240, 245, 246, 249, 251 & n, 274, 280,
282, 285, 286, 287, 291, 321, 323, 327, 328

Sartoris, Edward John: II, 203

Saunders, Mr.: I, 217 & n, 228

Saunders, Mrs.: I, 217 n

Schiller, Friedrich von: II, 284 & n

Schinas, Dr.: I, 341

Schrevelius, Cornelius: I, 107 & n, 109

Scoles, Joseph John: I, 190 n

Scott, Sir Walter: I, *xxxii,* 82 & n, 90, 214, 260,
290 & n, 313 & n

Scribe, Eugène: I, 352 n

Sefton, Lord: II, 312

Severn, Joseph: I, *xxxii,* 69 n, 176 n, 221, 282;
II, 173 n; and Shelley's burial, I, 190 n, 211,
214, 252; portraits of Trelawny and Keats,
I, 284, 311 & n; portrait of Shelley, II, 229 n,
234, 235 & n

Severn, Mrs. Joseph: II, 212

Sgricci, Tommaso: I, 117 & n, 126, 127 & n,
129, 131, 132, 133, 144 n, 346 n; his performances, I, 122–24 & n, 127–28, 132–33

Shaftesbury, Lord: I, 318

Shakespeare, William: I, 133, 206, 222, 225,
309

Sharp, William: in bibliographical note, II,
212

Sharpe, Sutton: I, 376 n

Shelley, Charles Bysshe: I, 16 & n, 17, 19 n,
25 n, 195, 300 n; birth, I, 3 n; death, I, 3 n,
355 n

Shelley, Clara Everina: I, 30, 32, 34, 35, 37,

38, 39, 41, 42, 44, 45, 46, 57; birth, I, 27n, 31n; christening, I, 47n; last illness, I, 57n, 58; death, I, 57n, 63 & n, 74

Shelley, Elizabeth (Shelley's sister): II, 51, 55n

Shelley, Harriet Westbrooke: I, 3 & n, 5, 6, 9n, 17n, 33, 195n, 206, 207n, 316n, 317, 339, 355n; II, 131n, 267, 308; suicide, I, 15n, 16n

Shelley, Hellen (Shelley's sister): II, 151, 166, 204, 215, 222, 315, 326, 330, 332

Shelley, Ianthe (Mrs. E. J. Esdaile): I, 16 & n, 17, 19n, 25n, 195, 206n; II, 165 & n, 199, 204, 207, 208, 214, 288, 307, 308

Shelley, John (Shelley's brother): II, 217, 258

Shelley, Lady Elizabeth (Shelley's mother): I, 258 & n, 260n; II, 31, 54, 90, 112, 220, 221, 222, 225, 226, 231, 243, 246, 248n, 293, 300

Shelley, Lady Frances: I, 6n

Shelley, Lady Jane (wife of Sir Percy Florence Shelley, by first marriage Mrs. Charles Robert St. John): I, *xxv, xxxi,* 73n, 187n, 215n; II, 114n, 313 & n, 315, 316, 318, 320, 321, 322, 323, 325 & n, 326, 327, 328, 329, 330, 331, 333, 334, 335, 336n, 337, 338, 340 & n, 357n; *see also Shelley Memorials* and *Shelley and Mary*

Shelley, Margaret (Shelley's sister): II, 41, 326, 330, 332

Shelley, Mary Wollstonecraft: I, 5n, 13n, 14n, 15n, 19n, 21n, 22n, 25n, 26n, 27n, 28n, 29n, 30n, 31n, 39n, 47n, 48n, 49n, 51n, 52n, 56n, 57n, 59n, 65n, 67n, 68n, 76n, 82n, 86n, 102n, 110n, 114n, 120n, 121n, 126n, 140n, 142n, 144n, 156n, 168n, 172n, 186n, 190n, 199n, 203n, 229n, 256n, 261n, 264n, 320n, 327n, 352n; II, 63n, 67n, 77n, 159n, 348; as a letter writer, I, *xxix;* II, 281; literary work, I, *xxx;* friendships, I, *xxxii;* II, 351; correspondents, I, *xxxii;* II, 343–46, 363–65; elopement with Shelley, I, 3n, 8 & n, 234, 235, 299; poverty in London, I, 3–7, 3n; II, 109; love letters to Hogg, I, 7n; and Claire, I, 7n, 14, 45, 126n, 149; tour of Devon and residence at Bishopgate, I, 8n; journey to and residence in Switzerland, I, 9–13; and her mother's works, I, 14n; marriage, I, 16, 17n, 18 & n; house at Marlow, I, 18 & n, 19, 36, 45; thoughts of going to Italy, I, 31, 33, 36, 38, 40, 41, 43, 45; passage from letter quoted in *Examiner,* I, 37, 41; break with Isabel Booth, I, 46, 47; departure for Italy, I, 47 & n; settles at Baths of Lucca, I, 52–53 & nn; journey to Este, I, 57n, 58;

copies Byron's poems, I, 58–59, 197, 198, 199, 202, 213 & n, 216, 218; journey from Este to Rome and Naples, I, 59–60, 63n; excursions to environs of Naples, I, 62 & n; studies painting, I, 65; asks Claire to write about William's death, I, 72; grief over loss of Clara and William, I, 73–75, 81; in house near Leghorn, I, 73 & n, 76; on the difficulty of painting Shelley, I, 76; arrival in Florence, I, 82 & n; arrival in Pisa, I, 95 & n; offers to write for *Indicator,* I, 98; copies Shelley's translation of Spinoza, I, 103n; occupies Gisbornes' house, I, 108 & n; describes christening in Casa Ricci, I, 109; in house at San Giuliano, I, 113 & n; breach with Gisbornes, I, 114n, 119 & n; Italian letter to Hunt, I, 115–16n; meets Emilia Viviani, I, 118n; meets Mavrocordato, I, 125 & n; hears Sgricci at Lucca, I, 127–28; meets Edward and Jane Williams, I, 129n; studies Greek, I, 133, 134; advises Claire about Allegra, I, 139–42; refers to death of first child, I, 141 & n; desire to visit Rome, I, 143 & n; and the Hoppner scandal, I, 146–49 & nn; settles in Pisa, I, 150 & n; plans for summer of 1822, I, 154, 155 & n, 158, 160, 167; meets Trelawny, I, 155n; on the Masi affray, I, 162–69 & nn; removes to Casa Magni, I, 169 & n; on Shelley's boat and its name, I, 170–71 & n, 193n; on life at Casa Magni, I, 170, 171, 179, 180; and Miss Curran's portrait of Shelley, I, 175–77 & n, 178–79 & n, 199, 205, 281, 284, 297 & n, 302 & n, 305, 310 & n, 341; orders mosaics for locket, I, 175–77 & n; portraits of her, I, 175n; her miscarriage, I, 177 & n, 179; her narrative of Shelley's death and burial, I, 181–86; and Shelley's heart, I, 187 & n; II, 114n, 340n; desire to write Shelley's life, I, 187; II, 13, 18; Trelawny's kindness, I, 188, 203, 205, 211, 226, 230 & n, 236; plans to write and edit Shelley's MSS, I, 189, 193, 195; sends Shelley's ashes to Rome, I, 190–91; removes to Genoa, I, 191 & n; decides to remain in Italy, I, 193; shares house with Hunts, I, 193 & n, 194, 195, 208–209, 210; financial arrangements with Sir Timothy, I, 195, 199n, 208, 212, 213 & n, 216 & n, 217 & n, 220, 260 & n, 273, 289, 300 & n, 303, 310, 355 & n, 358–60, 361, 375–76; II, 6–9, 11, 20n, 47–48, 53 & n, 54–57 & n, 69–71, 218; on cause of the *Don Juan's* sinking, I, 196 & n, 197, 223; refers to self as "moonshine," I, 198 & n; writes for *Liberal,* I, 199, 212 & n, 214; nervousness, I, 200; mediates between Byron and Hunt, I, 200–203 & n; reminded of Shelley by Byron's voice, I, 204 & n; and Shelley's manuscripts, I, 205, 206 & n, 247; estrangement from Hunt, I, 208–209 & n, 236; Jane's account of her treatment of Shelley, I, 209–10 n; and Shelley's grave, I, 219–20, 222–23, 225; on her return to England, I, 220, 221, 224, 225–26, 231; reconciliation with Hunt, I, 230, 231, 236; journey from Genoa to Paris, I, 232–47; on Shelley and nature, I, 235, 242; arrival in Paris, I, 248 n, 249; on dramatization of *Frankenstein,* I, 251, 256, 259 & n, 260; arrival in London, I, 258; mediates between John and Leigh Hunt, I, 263, 265–66, 271–72, 282–84, 285; articles in *London Magazine,* I, 272 & n, 287, 292 & n; plans for writing, I, 272, 287, 294, 346, 353, 376; on Shelley's reputation, I, 286; desire to write a tragedy, I, 287 & n; II, 98; moves to Kentish Town, I, 296 & n; suppresses *Posthumous Poems,* I, 303, 316 n; and Medwin's book on Byron, I, 308 & n; and Moore's *Life of Byron,* I, *xxx,* 313 & n, 371 n, 376; II, 13 n, 20, 24, 25, 28–29; to play Desdemona in Pisa, I, 316; on Hunt's essay on Shelley, 316–17 & n; and Payne, 319 n, 332–33 & n; II, 347–53; and Irving, I, 319 n, 327, 328 n, 331–33 & nn, 336 & n, 338 n; II, 347 ff; sketch of Shelley in *Last Man,* I, 341; defence of Velluti, I, 344 & n; II, 354–56; and Trelawny's relations with Byron, I, 348 & n; trip to Dieppe, I, 364 & n, 365; break with Jane, I, 368 & n, 369–71; II, 3, 17; offers to write for Murray, I, 371 & n; II, 5 & n, 20, 31, 32, 33–35, 37; trip to Paris, I, 373 & n; and Mérimée, I, 374 & n, 376 & n, 377; has smallpox, I, 374, 375, 376, 377 & n; II, 4; and Galignani's edition of Shelley, II, 10–11 & n, 28; and Trelawny's *Adventures of a Younger Son,* II, 13, 36, 38, 39–41, 45–46, 49, 50, 52, 101–102, 103; and Trelawny's wish to write Shelley's life, II, 13 & n, 23–24; her portrait by Rothwell, II, 33 n; articles for *New Monthly,* II, 39 & n; Trelawny's proposal, 47 & n, 49; and the notes to Byron's poems, II, 57–58, 60–62, 67 & n; at Harrow, II, 70, 72, 75, 77, 82, 100; on writing for the annuals, II, 97; on her own poetry, II, 97–98; her grave, II, 114 n, 340 n, 359–60; plans to

edit Godwin's memoirs and correspondence, II, 115, 116 & n, 117, 119; her sense of loneliness, II, 119–20; on omissions in *Queen Mab,* II, 127, 129 n, 131 & n, 134 & n; travels in 1840, II, 146 & n; and letters to Gatteschi, II, 152 n, 194 n, 251–61 *passim;* travels abroad in 1842–43, II, 154, 156 n, 156–91 *passim;* financial problems after Sir Timothy's death, II, 221, 222, 226, 231, 232, 233, 243, 245, 262, 291, 297; and G. Byron's Shelley letters, II, 263–70 & n, 294–96; and Claire's fear of Gatteschi, II, 270–73; sale of Castle Goring, II, 274; purchase of 24 Chester Square, II, 274; and Knox's Parisian debts, II, 275–80, 281; and Medwin's *Life of Shelley,* II, 287–90 & n, 307–308 & nn, 309–10; at Field Place, II, 321; last illness and death, II, 340 n, 357–60; her character, II, 350–52; Lady Jane Shelley's love for, II, 359

——, reading of: Latin and Italian, I, 11; Livy, Lucian, Horace, Locke, I, 14 n; Gibbon, I, 21; Ariosto, I, 53, 54, 55; Tasso, I, 56; Latin, I, 77, 91; Dante, I, 77; Boccaccio, I, 77; Spanish, I, 90, 91, 120; Greek, I, 120, 209; II, 64; Sophocles, I, 129; Homer, I, 277; Virgil's *Georgics,* I, 318

——, observations of:

on her own moods: before Shelley's death, I, 21, 66–67; after Shelley's death, I, 186, 188, 192, 194, 204, 205, 209, 232, 259, 277, 278, 342; II, 82, 87–88, 108, 119–20, 121

on her own character: reputation for coldness, I, 216 & n; impatience, I, 233; II, 161; treatment of Shelley, I, 236; dread of publicity, I, 367; II, 13, 27; want of resolution, II, 98; tendency to brood, II, 108, 161; uncompanionableness, II, 250

on other persons: the French, I, 9, 243; the Swiss, I, 12–13; the English in Italy, I, 54; the Savoyards, I, 238–39, 240; the Italians, I, 238; the Germans, II, 162, 167, 277; Hogg, I, 7 n, 24, 66, 304, 307, 357; Peacock, I, 30; Cobbett, I, 37; Mrs. Gisborne, I, 51 n, 77, 81; Mr. Gisborne, I, 77, 81; Reveley, I, 77; Queen Caroline, I, 116; Pacchiani, I, 117, 121, 131–32; Sgricci, I, 117, 122–24 & n, 128, 129; Emilia Viviani, I, 118, 124; Medwin, I, 129, 130, 131; II, 24; Jane Williams, I, 130, 346–47; Edward Williams, I, 130–31; Byron, I, 140–41, 208, 265; II, 29; Trelawny, I, 155–56, 188, 231; II, 64; Shelley, I, 186, 341; Procter, I, 265, 278–79; 280–81; Novello,

I, 277; Velluti, I, 344–45; Percy Florence, II, 4, 83, 84–85, 88, 192; Bulwer-Lytton, II, 84, 109; Lord Brougham, II, 86; Mrs. Norton, II, 104, 120–21; Mr. and Mrs. Gaskell, II, 107; Knox, II, 166; Pearson, II, 166, 175–76; Laura Mason, II, 180, 182; Lady Jane Shelley, II, 316, 334, 339

on other writers: Ariosto, I, 54, 55; Spenser, I, 55, 91; Boccaccio, I, 77; Byron, I, 150, 153, 213, 219; II, 60–62; Scott, II, 15; Boswell, II, 93; Bulwer, II, 124; Miss Martineau, II, 133; Dante, II, 283; Keats, II, 283; Landor, II, 291

on the theater, ballet, and opera, I, 22, 48 51, 64, 77, 123, 156, 287, 294–95, 304

on art, I, 270, 295; II, 148, 164 & n

on music, I, 272, 284; II, 84

on political and social conditions: England, I, 96–98, 120, 125, 290; II, 25, 42, 262, 277, 278, 280, 282, 299; Spain, I, 104, 246; Tuscany, I, 113; Naples, I, 118, 120, 125; Italian marriage customs, I, 118; Greece, I, 125, 136–37, 137–38, 143–44, 151, 153, 164, 342, 355; America, II, 73, 327–28; peace and "republican principles," II, 73; France, II, 148, 313–14; Europe in 1848, II, 313–14, 317–18

on scenery and places: the Alps, I, 10, 12; Geneva, I, 10–11, 12; Italy, I, 47–48, 50; Pisa, I, 50, 96; Leghorn, I, 51; Baths of Lucca and environs, I, 53, 54–55; Rome, I, 60, 63, 65, 96, 99; Naples, I, 99; Gulf of Spezia, I, 181; Turin, I, 234; between Turin and Susa, I, 235; Mont Cenis, I, 237; Mont Blanc, I, 242

————, works of:

Lodore, I, xxx, 3 n; II, 72 & n, 75, 78 & n, 83 & n, 86, 89, 90 & n, 101, 102, 106, 108, 109, 144, 196, 344

History of a Six-Weeks' Tour, I, xxx, 11 bib. n, 13 bib. n, 35 & n, 42 n, 43 & n; II, 195 & n, 196

Frankenstein, I, xxx, 14 & n, 25 n, 26, 29 & n, 31 & n, 35, 39 n, 66, 70 n, 82, 213 n, 251, 256, 259, 260 & n, 291; 353; II, 144

"The English in Italy," I, 122–23 n, 346 & n; II, 35 & n

Valperga, I, xxx, 144 & n, 145–46 & n, 150 & n, 153 & n, 156 & n, 159 & n, 171 & n, 224 & n, 243, 245–46, 255, 270, 282; II, 144

Mathilda, I, 156 & n, 161, 164, 172, 182, 224

"On Ghosts," I, 272 n

"The Bride of Modern Italy," I, 273 n

"The Choice," I, 278 & n, 281

The Last Man, I, xxx, 341 & n; II, 22

Letters to *Examiner* on Velluti, I, 344 n; II, 354–56

Proserpine and *Midas,* I, 350 & n; II, 59 & n

Perkin Warbeck, I, xxx, 371 & n; II, 7 n, 11, 15, 20, 22–23, 26–27, 28, 29, 31

article on Mérimée, I, 376 & n; II, 11 & n

Rambles in Germany and Italy, I, xxx; II, 146 n, 156 n, 159 n, 164 n, 194 n, 195–96 & n, 202, 206 & n, 209, 214 n, 226 & n, 227, 314 & n

edition of *Posthumous Poems,* I, xxx, 264 & n, 278, 280, 281, 286, 291, 292 & n, 295, 301, 307, 308; II, 346

edition of Shelley's *Poetical Works,* I, xxx; II, 91 & n, 126 & n, 127, 129 & n, 130, 131 & n, 132–33, 134 & n, 150

edition of Shelley's *Essays and Letters,* I, xxviii; II, 91 & n, 133–34 & n, 136 & n, 137, 139–40, 141, 142, 143 & n, 144 & n

Falkner, I, xxx; II, 108, 110 & n, 120 & n

"Modern Italy," II, 11 & n, 16 & n, 17 & n

"Loves of the Poets," II, 19 & n

stories in *Keepsake,* II, 62, 63 n

biographies in Lardner's *Cyclopedia,* II, 83, 90 & n, 92, 93–96, 99, 103–104 & n, 106 & n, 108, 122 & n, 123–24, 200

poems in *Keepsake,* II, 98 & n, 99–100

"O Listen While I Sing to Thee," II, 159 n

Shelley, Mrs. John: II, 217, 258

Shelley, Percy Bysshe: I, vi, xxix, xxx, xxi, 3 n, 4 n, 5 n, 6 n, 8 n, 9 n, 13 n, 14 n, 15 n, 18, 20, 21 & n, 22, 23 & n, 25 & n, 26, 27, 30 n, 33 n, 37 n, 39 n, 40 n, 42 n, 44 n, 46, 47 & n, 48, 49 & n, 50, 51 n, 52 & n, 54, 55 & n, 56, 57 n, 58, 59, 60, 61, 63, 67 n, 69, 72, 73, 74, 77, 79, 80, 81, 82, 83, 84, 85 & n, 86 & n, 87, 88, 90, 98, 99, 100, 101, 102, 104, 106 & n, 109, 110, 111, 113 n, 114 & n, 118 n, 119, 120 n, 123, 128, 133, 134, 137, 138, 139, 140 & n, 143 & n, 144 & n, 145, 147, 148, 149, 150, 151, 152, 154, 155 & n, 162, 165, 168, 182, 188, 192 n, 193, 195 n, 197, 200, 201 & n, 205, 222, 224, 236, 239, 242, 243, 246, 248 & n, 249, 251 n, 255 n, 260 n, 278, 284, 288, 301, 302, 317, 339, 340, 350, 352, 353 & n, 355, 357, 358, 359; II, 33, 37, 41, 72 n, 76, 88, 98, 99, 109, 119, 124, 130, 138, 143, 150, 151, 166, 173 n, 191, 200, 213, 266, 267, 270, 274 n, 283,

288, 289 & n, 290, 291, 295, 296, 301, 309, 310, 311, 333 n, 344, 346, 348, 350 n, 351, 352; and the relations between Mary and Hogg, I, 7 n; Chancery case, I, 16–17 & n, 19 n, 25 n, 27 n, 28 & n, 37; health, I, 29 & n, 45, 49, 51, 53, 56, 62, 64, 66, 68, 71, 76, 89, 91, 93, 94, 95, 96, 105, 106, 108, 113, 120, 124, 126, 127, 130, 142, 144, 145, 153, 164, 166, 171, 177; arrested for debt, I, 43 & n, 45; his grave, I, 73 n, 190 n, 191, 219–20, 222–23, 225; financial difficulties in 1819, I, 87 & n, 89; translates Spinoza, I, 103 & n, 196; and Godwin, I, 112 & n; and his first boat, I, 138 & n; finishes Mary's letter to Claire, I, 141–42; invites Hunt to Italy, I, 151 n; the *Don Juan,* I, 155 n, 158, 170–71 & n, 192–93 & n, 196 & n, 197; and Ollier, I, 159 & n; and Allegra's death, I, 169–70 & n; goes to meet Hunt, I, 172 & n, 181; sails from Leghorn for Lerici, I, 172 n, 183; his death, I, 172 n, 178; II, 11; his delight in Lerici, I, 179; his visions, I, 180 & n; Jane's vision of, I, 180–81; his body discovered, I, 184 n, 185; cremation, I, 185 & n, 187; his heart, I, 187 & n; burial, I, 190–91 & n, 214 & n; Byron's attitude toward, I, 203 & n, 229, 230; admiration of Homer, I, 277; intended legacy to Hunt, I, 349 & n; II, 218; engraved portrait by Finden, II, 58 n, 67 & n; legacy to Claire, II, 218 & n, 219, 221, 223, 224, 234; portrait by Severn, II, 229 n, 234, 235 & n; Bulwer-Lytton on, II, 284 & n; *see also under* Shelley, Mary Wollstonecraft

————, works of:

Laon and Cythna or *Revolt of Islam,* I, 29 n, 31 & n, 35 & n, 39 n, 66 & n, 82, 90 n, *Rosalind and Helen,* I, 31 & n, 49 & n; *Witch of Atlas,* I, 55 n; translation of *Symposium,* I, 56; II, 19 n, 139–40; *Prometheus Unbound,* I, 65 & n, 91, 92, 112, 156 & n, 224, 239–40 & n; II, 10; *The Cenci,* I, 73 n, 78 & n, 79, 94, 111; *The Mask of Anarchy,* I, 80 & n, 81 & n, 84, 342 & n; *Peter Bell the Third,* I, 86 & n, 112; II, 143; *Alastor* I, 90 n, 279 & n; *Adonais,* 90 n, 185, 189; II, 10; *Ode to Liberty,* I, 104 n; *Letter to Maria Gisborne,* I, 111, 112, 196 & n; *Oedipus Tyrannus,* I, 116 n; *Epipsychidion,* I, 118 n, 199 n; *A Defence of Poetry,* I, 126 n, 199 & n, 200, 206, 212 & n; II, 138, 143 & n; *Hellas,* I, 126 n, 150 & n, 163–64 & n, 167; II, 10; *Queen Mab,* I, 262 & n; *Essay on Love,* II, 19 n;

Essay on Devils, II, 139 & n; *Essay on Christianity,* II, 288 n; *Triumph of Life,* II, 345; *Prince Athanase,* II, 345

Shelley, Sir John: I, 6 & n, 110, 200

Shelley, Sir Percy Florence: I, *xxx, xxxi,* 5 n, 83, 87 & n, 93, 104, 105, 108, 111, 112, 113, 130, 142, 143, 144, 145, 154, 164, 168, 169 & n, 171, 177, 181, 185, 187 n, 195, 197, 206, 216, 224, 225, 231, 232, 233, 235, 236, 239, 241, 243, 244, 245, 248, 249, 250, 251, 265, 279, 282, 284, 291, 293, 299, 300 n, 302, 306, 308, 309, 310, 313, 315, 318, 321, 330 & n, 341, 349 n, 355 & n, 359, 361, 362, 363, 365, 367, 375, 377, 378 n; II, 4, 6, 8, 9, 11, 14, 18, 20, 21, 30, 31, 32, 33 & n, 34, 35, 37, 38, 41, 42, 43, 44, 46, 47, 48 & n, 52, 53, 54, 55, 64, 66, 72, 74, 75, 80, 81, 82, 84, 86, 87, 91, 93, 97, 98, 99, 100, 102, 104, 105, 106, 110, 112, 113 & n, 114 & n, 120, 123, 125, 132, 136, 137, 140, 141, 142, 144, 146, 147, 151, 152 & n, 153, 154, 156 & n, 158, 159 n, 160, 162, 163, 164, 165, 166, 168, 169, 170, 171, 172, 173, 174, 175, 176, 178, 179, 180, 181, 182, 183, 184, 185, 186, 187, 188, 190, 193, 194 & n, 195, 197, 198, 199, 200, 201, 203, 204, 205, 206, 207, 208, 209, 213, 214, 215, 217, 218, 219, 220, 222, 223, 225, 226, 227, 228, 229, 230, 231, 232, 235, 237, 238, 239, 241, 243, 244, 245, 246, 247, 248, 250, 252, 253, 255, 257, 258, 260, 261, 262, 263, 271, 272, 273, 276, 279, 280, 281, 282, 287, 291, 292, 293, 294, 295, 298, 300, 301, 302, 303, 304, 305, 310, 311, 313, 319, 320, 321, 322, 323, 324, 325, 326, 327, 328, 329, 330, 331, 333, 334, 335, 337, 338, 344, 357 n, 359, 360; birth, I, 71 n, 74 n, 83 n, 84; middle name suggested by Miss Stacey, I, 88 n; has measles, I, 98, 101, 102; Mary's fears for him, I, 205, 210; education, I, 372, 373; II, 6, 44–45, 51, 56, 57, 60 & n, 62, 65, 66–67, 70, 73, 77, 78, 88, 92, 109, 110–11, 115, 119, 144 n, 148; Mary's descriptions of, II, 83, 84–85, 88, 89, 108, 117–18, 192; comes into inheritance, II, 219, 221; presented at Court, II, 236; plans to enter Parliament, II, 274, 277, 278, 281, 284, 297, 299, 305, 314, 315, 318; marriage, II, 313 n, 316, 318; and Field Place, II, 319 n, 321; his grave, II, 340 n

Shelley, Sir Bysshe: I, 3 n, 7 n, 109

Shelley, Sir Timothy: I, *vi, xxix,* 43 n, 67 n, 85 n, 88 n, 109, 119 & n, 193, 195, 200, 208,

212, 213 n, 229 n, 249, 258, 264 n, 307, 316 n, 317, 340, 349 & n, 355, 362, 367, 372, 373, 375; II, 20, 21, 30, 31, 34, 41, 42, 43, 44, 45, 48 & n, 51, 53 n, 60 n, 66, 72, 77, 80, 87, 90, 106, 110, 111, 112, 120, 126, 127, 144 n, 147 n, 151, 157, 166, 195, 204, 205, 209, 210, 214, 217, 218, 228, 231, 246, 274 n, 297, 353; and a maintenance for Mary and Percy Florence, I, 213 n, 215 & n, 216 & n, 217 & n, 220, 237, 247, 260 & n, 273, 280, 289, 295, 300 & n, 303, 310, 315, 341 n, 355 & n, 358–60, 375–76; II, 6–9, 11, 20 n, 47–48, 53 & n, 54–57 & n, 69–71; his death, II, 218 n, 219 & n, 262; his will, II, 219, 220, 222

Shelley, William: I, 14, 15, 16, 18, 20, 22, 23, 24, 25, 26, 28, 32, 33, 34, 35, 37, 39, 40, 42, 44, 46, 47, 49, 57, 60, 61, 64, 65, 177, 181, 239; birth, I, 14 n; christening, I, 47 n; illness at Rome, I, 71–73; death, I, 73 & n, 74, 75, 76 & n, 81 & n, 148; grave, I, 73 n, 74, 79 & n, 94 & n, 110–11, 113, 185 & n, 191; portrait by Miss Curran, I, 175 n, 310, 314, 338; II, 191

Shelley and Mary: I, *xxv, xxvi*, 14 n, 15 n, 68 n, 69 n, 72 n, 89 n, 91 n, 92 n, 103 n, 127 n, 129 n, 135 n, 146 n, 147 n, 156 n, 162 n, 175 n, 176 n, 190 n, 199 n, 207 n, 211 n, 260 n, 279 n, 300 n, 308 n, 368 n; II, 126 n, 287 n, 288 n, 352; in bibliographical notes, 4, 5, 6, 7, 9, 15, 17, 22, 26, 30, 32, 35, 37, 40, 42, 44, 45, 54, 55, 57, 58, 61, 63, 70, 72, 73, 74, 78, 80, 83, 87, 88, 90, 92, 93, 94, 101, 102, 103, 104, 105, 106, 107, 108, 110, 111, 112, 114, 115, 120, 121, 125, 134, 135, 136, 138, 139, 143, 144, 145, 146, 147, 150, 152, 154, 157, 158, 161, 165, 166, 172, 177, 179, 186, 190, 192, 196, 200, 207, 211, 216, 225, 230, 232, 235, 237, 244, 249, 258, 263, 272, 282, 285, 303, 305, 308, 311, 319, 350, 371; II, 73, 85, 89, 92, 100, 107

Shelley Correspondence in the Bodleian: I, *xxvii;* in bibliographical notes, 7, 17, 31, 37, 38, 40, 42, 191

Shelley Memorials: I, *xxv;* in bibliographical notes, 15, 54, 55, 61, 70, 87, 88, 90, 92, 103, 111, 114, 146, 147, 154, 157, 161, 177, 179, 190, 196, 207, 225; II, 100

Shelley Society, the: in bibliographical notes, I, 342

Shelley-Rolls, Sir John C. E.: I, *vi, vii, ix, x, xxvi* n

Shields, Amelia (Milly): I, 28 & n, 44 & n, 64, 91, 95

Signorelli, Vera: I, *x*

Simond, J.: II, 11 n

Sinclair, John: I, 156 & n

Sismondi, Jean de: I, 62

Skepper, Anne (Mrs. Bryan Waller Procter): I, 307 & n

Skipworth, Sir Guy: II, 111

Slater, Mr.: I, 372 & n, 373; II, 6, 35, 44, 54, 55, 56, 57, 65, 67 n

Smiles, Samuel: in bibliographical notes, I, 353, 371; II, 5, 26, 29, 93

Smith, Dr. Southwood: II, 136 n, 304, 309, 323, 324, 325, 331

Smith, Eliza: I, 254

Smith, Harry B.: in bibliographical note, I, 4

Smith, Horace: I, 23 & n, 40 n, 47 n, 55 n, 110 & n, 125, 240, 248, 251 & n, 253, 254 & n, 255, 256, 258, 306 & n, 319, 346; II, 39 & n, 50, 118 & n, 137, 138, 257 & n, 258, 347; and Trelawny's *Adventures,* II, 45–46

Smith, Horace, Jr.: I, 254, 319

Smith, L. Herman: I, *x*

Smith, Mr.: I, 282

Smith, Mrs.: II, 173, 181

Smith, Mrs. Spencer: II, 60

Smith, Mrs. Horace: I, 251, 254, 255, 256, 346; II, 118 & n, 257

Smith, Rosalind: I, 254 & n; II, 257 & n

Solis y Ribadeneyra, Antonio de: I, 90

Sontag, Henriette: II, 4

Sophocles: I, 129, 134, 136

Southey, Robert: I, 66 & n, 268 & n, 269; II, 130, 134 & n, 200 & n

Spagnoletti, P.: II, 84 & n

Spectator, The: I, 91; II, 143 & n

Spenser, Edmund: I, 55, 91

Spinoza, Baruch: I, 103 & n

Stacey, Flint: I, 88 n

Stacey, Sophia: I, 88 & n, 99 n

Staël, Mme. de: II, 20, 31, 32, 34, 354

Stanhope, Capt. Robert: II, 79

Stanhope, Charles, Fourth Earl of Harrington: I, 311 n, 348 n

Stanhope, Mrs. Leicester: II, 74, 79, 145, 216

Stanhope, Mrs. Robert: II, 79

Stanley, Lord: II, 299

Stanley, Edward, Bishop of Norwich: II, 309 n, 327

Stead, William Force: I, *x*

Stephanie (Claire's maid): II, 274, 275, 277, 286

Stewart, Miss: II, 213, 214

Stone, Julius: II, 48

Stone: Miss: II, 163

Strauss, David Friedrich: II, 288 n

Stuart, Isobel: in bibliographical note, I, 47

Stuart, Mrs.: II, 316

Stuart (*or* Stewart), Mrs. (one of Shelley's creditors): I, 3 n, 6 & n

Sumner, Charles: I, *xxxii;* II, 128; his account of Mary, 128 n

Sussex, Berkeley (son of Lady Sussex): II, 226, 230, 245, 247

Sussex, Charley, Consuelo, and Sussex (children of Lady Sussex): II, 230, 231, 280

Sussex, Lady: II, 175, 192, 193 n, 194 n, 221, 222, 225, 226, 229, 230, 231, 245, 247, 251, 253, 254, 255, 256, 257, 258, 259, 260, 261, 270, 271, 272, 273, 278, 280

Sussex, Lord: II, 175, 225, 271

Swann, Arthur: I, *x*

Sykes, Sir Charles: I, 190 n, 214

T

Taaffe, John: I, 117 n, 142, 144 n, 156, 161, 162, 163, 165, 166, 167, 168 & n, 310

Talfourd, Thomas Noon: II, 117 & n, 121, 149 & n, 150, 200 & n

Talleyrand: II, 253

Tantini, Mme.: I, 103

Targioni, Giovanni: I, 227 & n

Tasso, Torquato: I, 55, 56, 60, 91; II, 106 & n, 108

Tassoni, Alessandro: II, 106 n

Taylor, Sir Henry: II, 133 n

Taylor, William: II, 200 & n

Terazzi (tradesman): I, 134, 135

Thaw, Mrs. A.: II, 142

Theobald, Mr.: II, 129 n

Thierry, Jacques Nicholas Augustin: I, 353 & n

Thomas, Mr.: I, 227, 228

Thomas, Mrs.: I, 211 & n, 225, 246, 300; comment on Mary, I, 213 n

Thomas, Richard: I, 228

Thorold, Lady: II, 79

Thrale, Mrs. Hester: II, 93

Tighe, George William: *see* Mr. Mason

Tita (Byron's servant): I, 163 & n, 167, 169

Titian: II, 212

Titman, Captain: II, 337

Tonelli, Signora: I, 86 & n, 88, 90

Torlonia, Messrs. (bankers): I, 178 & n

Torrey, Norman L.: I, *ix*

Trelawny, Charlotte (sister of E. J. Trelawny): II, 102, 118, 120, 122

Trelawny, Col. Charles Brereton: I, 155 n, 348

Trelawny, Edward John: I, *vi, xxvi, xxx, xxxi, xxxii,* 19 n, 57 n, 155 & n, 156 n, 162, 169 n, 170, 171, 180, 181, 183, 184, 185, 186 n, 187 n, 189, 190 n, 192, 196 n, 197, 204, 208 & n, 210, 211 n, 214 n, 217, 225 & n, 228, 230, 246 & n, 248, 265, 282, 284, 285 & n, 287, 289 n, 294, 308, 315 n, 316; II, 4, 5, 49 n, 63 & n, 66 n, 76, 81 n, 106, 113 n, 120 n, 131 & n, 132 n, 152 n, 166 n, 173 n, 191, 203, 215, 251, 253, 254, 316, 317, 335, 340 n, 344, 347, 351, 352; Mary's first impressions of, I, 155–56; account of Shelley's death referred to, I, 172 n; plans to raise the *Don Juan,* I, 186 & n, 192–93 & nn; kindness to Mary, I, 188, 205, 211, 226, 230 & n, 236; his account of cremation for the *Liberal,* I, 187; and Shelley's grave, I, 190 n, 219–20 & nn, 222–23, 225; praise of Shelley, I, 203; on Mary's character, I, 216 n; and Rose, I, 221 & n; epitaph for Keats, I, 226–27 & n; sails with Byron for Greece, I, 231, 236, 250 & n; in Greece, I, 288 & n, 301, 304 & n, 314, 319; account of Byron's last days, I, 298 n, 299; Severn's portrait of, I, 311 & n; marriage to Tersitza Kamenou, I, 344 & n; and Byron, 348 & n; *Adventures of a Younger Son,* II, 12 n, 13, 19, 36, 38, 39 n, 39–41, 45–46 & nn, 49, 50, 52 & n, 101–102, 103; plan to write Shelley's life, II, 13 & n, 18, 23–24; attitude toward Mary, II, 18 & n, 24; proposal to Mary, II, 47 & n, 49; in America, II, 73, 84; returns from America, II, 100 & n; and Augusta Goring, II, 167 & n; and Mary's portrait, II, 336 & n, 339; *Recollections of Byron, Shelley and the Author* in bibliographical notes, I, 165, 178, 229; *Records of Byron, Shelley and the Author* in bibliographical note, 193

Trelawny, Eliza: I, 226 & n

Trelawny, Maria Julia: II, 63 & n, 80 & n

Trelawny, Mrs. Edward J.: *see* Goring, Augusta, and Kamenou, Tersitza

Trelawny, Mrs.: I, 291; II, 80, 118, 120

Trelawny, Zella: I, 344 n; II, 25 & n, 42, 51 & n, 52, 74 n, 80, 118

Turbati, Mrs.: I, 290

Turner, Cornelia (Mrs. Oswald, *née* Cornelia Boinville): I, 66 & n; II, 151 & n, 163 n, 176
Turner, Oswald: I, 66 & n; II, 163, 176, 250

U

Ulysses: see *Odysseus*
Uwins, Dr.: II, 113 n

V

Vaccà Berlinghieri, Andrea: I, 92 & n, 94, 95, 101, 102, 103, 120, 221 n, 346 n
Van Doren, Carl: I, 67 n
Vane, Lady: II, 255
Varley, John: I, 159 & n; on Shelley, 160 & n
Vega, Lope de: II, 104 n
Velluti, Giovanni-Battista: Mary's defence of, I, 344–45 & n; II, 354–56
Vestris, Mme.: II, 141 n
Victoria, Queen of England: II, 154, 206
Villegas, Vicente Espinel-Esteban de: II, 104 n
Vincent, E. R.: in bibliographical notes, II, 94, 96
Vincenzo (Byron's servant): I, 163 n
Virgil: I, 110, 159, 318
Vivian, Mrs.: II, 213, 215
Viviani, Emilia: I, 118 & n, 124, 127 & n, 129, 130, 132, 133, 140 n, 141, 142 & n, 144 n, 160 & n; introduction to Shelleys, I, 117 n, 118 n; marriage to Biondi, I, 160 & n; conclusion of friendship with, I, 161; Mary's fictional portraits of, I, 273 n
Voltaire: I, 91

W

Walker, Mr.: I, 367
Walker, Sarah: I, 255 & n, 257
Walker, W. S.: I, 156 n
Wallack, James William: I, 259
Walpole, Horace: II, 34
Walpole, Sir Hugh: I, *x*
Watson, Dr.; II, 153
Watts, Alaric A.: I, *xxx*, 350 n; II, 59 n
Watts, William: in bibliographical note, II, 127
Watts, Zillah (Mrs. Alaric A.): II, 59 & n
Weale: II, 106
Webb, Mr.: I, 90, 92 n, 150
Weber, Carl Maria von: I, 304
Webster, Lady Frances Wedderburn: II, 60
Wedd, A. F.: in bibliographical note, II, 114

Wedgwood, J. T.: II, 11 n, 28
Wellington, Duke of: II, 90, 93
Wenlock, Lord: II, 80
West, Mr.: I, 13, 14
West, William E.: I, 347
Westbrook, Eliza: I, 17 & n, 79 & n, 206 & n
Westbrook, Harriet: *see* Shelley, Harriet Westbrook
Westbrook, John: I, 16 & n, 17 & n, 28 n, 317
Westmacott, Richard: I, 190 n
Westminster Review, the: I, *xxx,* 300 n, 316 n, 346 n, 376 & n; II, 11 & n, 19 n, 27 n, 35 & n
White, Newman I.: I, *ix,* 90 n, 92 n, 156 n, 229 n; II, 149 n; in bibliographical note, 149
White, William: II, 263 n, 265 n
Whitehead, Miss: I, 289 & n
Whitton, William: I, *vi, xxix,* 43 n, 195, 199 n, 207, 208 & n, 213 n, 258, 260 & n, 280, 300 n, 303, 318, 341 n, 358 & n, 359; II, 53 n, 54, 65
Wieland, Christoph Martin: I, 4 & n
Wiffen, J. F.: II, 124 & n
Wiggins, Mr.: II, 337
Wilhaman, Mrs. G.: II, 242, 243
Willats, William: II, 236, 241, 243, 245, 274 & n, 291 n
William (servant): II, 292, 293
Williams, Dina (Mrs. Henry Sylvan Hunt): I, 248, 308 & n, 318; II, 51, 72, 83, 84, 86, 98, 105, 157, 160 & n, 162, 168 & n, 170, 171, 173, 175, 181, 183, 193, 197, 198, 206, 207, 212, 215, 216, 217, 237, 293, 304
Williams, Edward: I, 103 n, 129, 131, 133, 139, 144, 150 & n, 154, 155 & n, 160, 162 n, 164, 167 & n, 168 & n, 171, 177, 180, 182, 183, 186, 194 & n, 197, 204, 205, 223, 224, 227, 229 n, 256, 261, 288, 289 n, 299, 301, 315 & n, 316 & n, 317, 357; II, 17, 351; introduction to Shelleys, I, 129 n; Mary's first impression of, I, 130–31; upsets Shelley's boat, I, 138 n; Shelley's opinion of, I, 142; suggests title for *Hellas,* I, 150 n; moves into Casa Magni, I, 169–70 & n, 171; his death, I, 172 n; discovery of his body, I, 184 n, 185; cremation of, I, 185 & n, 187; his "mother-in-law," I, 315 & n, 317
Williams, Edward Medwin ("Med," son of Edward and Jane Williams): II, 83, 84, 85, 86, 98, 168, 190, 192, 193, 206, 222, 253
Williams, Jane (Mrs. Edward Williams, *later* Mrs. T. J. Hogg): I, *xxx, xxxi,* 129, 133, 144, 150 & n, 155 & n, 157, 158, 160, 165,

167 & n, 168, 177, 180, 181, 182, 184, 185, 187, 188, 191 & n, 192, 194 n, 195, 196, 197, 198, 199, 200, 203, 205, 210, 211, 212, 223, 224, 227, 249, 250, 253, 256, 259, 261, 268, 271, 273, 274, 275, 276, 278, 286, 288, 289, 291, 293, 295, 296 n, 299, 301, 302, 303, 304, 306, 308, 309, 310, 314, 315 & n, 316, 317, 319, 322, 324, 325, 327 n, 329, 330, 331, 334, 337, 338, 340, 343, 344, 346, 352; II, 17, 41, 49, 51, 52, 62, 64 & n, 67 n, 72, 73, 79, 80, 81, 82, 83 n, 84, 86, 89, 90, 92, 97, 98, 99, 100, 105, 106, 107, 108, 109, 112, 117, 118, 121, 128, 130, 147, 150, 152, 157 & n, 160, 162, 165, 168, 170, 171, 173, 175, 181, 183, 193, 197, 198, 204, 208, 212, 215, 216, 227, 241, 289, 290, 302, 308, 351; introduction to the Shelleys, I, 129 n; Mary's first impression of, I, 130; Shelley's opinion of, I, 142; moves into Casa Magni, I, 169–70 & n, 171; her vision of Shelley, I, 180–81; leaves for England, I, 191 n, 193, 194; arrives in England, I, 206, 207; on Mary's character and treatment of Shelley, I, 209–10 n, 216 n; on Hunt, I, 249; and Hogg, I, 281 & n, 356 & n, 357; II, 162, 178; events in life before meeting Shelleys, I, 289 n; breach with Mary, I, 368 n, 369–71; II, 3, 17

Williams, John: II, 333 n
Williams, Lady: *see* Miss Paton
Williams, Mrs. John: II, 333
Williams, Stanley T.: II, 347
Wilmot, Sir Eardly: II, 299
Wilson, John ("Christopher North"): II, 10 n; review of *Alastor*, I, 90 n
Wise, T. J.: I, *vi, x, xxvi, xxvii,* 139 n; in bibliographical notes, I, 29, 47, 61, 108, 130,

137, 142, 155, 186, 340, 342; II, 5, 150, 290, 308
Wolcot, John: I, 25 & n
Wollstonecraft, Charles: II, 313
Wollstonecraft, Edward (brother of Mary Wollstonecraft): II, 135 n
Wollstonecraft, Edward, Jr.: I, *xxxii;* II, 135 n, 299
Wollstonecraft, Elizabeth: *see* Berry, Mrs. Alexander
Wollstonecraft, Everina: I, 14 n; II, 86, 101, 102, 135, 136, 146, 157 & n, 181, 261, 262, 307
Wollstonecraft, Mary: I, 3 n, 5, 39, 83 n, 189, 258, 372; II, 98, 113, 191, 344, 351, 352; *Rights of Woman,* I, 14 n; *Posthumous Works,* I, 152 & n; Letters from Norway, I, 152 & n; her graves, II, 114 & n, 340 n
Wood, Mrs.: II, 38
Wordsworth, William: I, 255; II, 115, 130, 134, 157; quoted, I, 242 & n, 293 & n
Woulfe, Mrs.: II, 195, 203
Wright, Mr.: (one of Shelley's creditors): I, 44
Wright, Mr.: I, 210, 211 n, 300
Wright, Frances: I, 366 & n, 367; II, 37, 38
Wright, Mrs. Gabrielle: I, 210, 211 & n, 246, 300, 315 & n

X

Xenophon: I, 134

Y

Young, Owen D.: I, *x*
Young, Westmacote: II, 129 n
Ypsilanti, Prince Alexander: I, 126 n, 136, 137

The Letters of Mary W. Shelley

COLLECTED AND EDITED BY FREDERICK L. JONES

HAVE BEEN SET ON THE LINOTYPE

IN ELEVEN-POINT GRANJON

WITH ONE POINT OF LEADING

AND HAVE BEEN PRINTED IN TWO VOLUMES

ON WOVE ANTIQUE PAPER

UNIVERSITY OF OKLAHOMA PRESS

NORMAN